W9-AWI-970

Visual Basic® .NET Power Coding

Visual Basic®
.NET Power Coding

Paul Kimmel

♦▼Addison-Wesley

Boston • San Francisco • New York • Toronto • Montreal
London • Munich • Paris • Madrid
Capetown • Sydney • Tokyo • Singapore • Mexico City

The publisher offers discounts on this book when ordered in quantity for bulk purchases and special sales. For more information, please contact:

  U.S. Corporate and Government Sales
  (800) 382-3419
  corpsales@pearsontechgroup.com

For sales outside of the U.S., please contact:

  International Sales
  (317) 581-3793
  international@pearsontechgroup.com

Visit Addison-Wesley on the Web: www.awprofessional.com

Library of Congress Cataloging-in-Publication Data

Kimmel, Paul.
    Visual Basic .NET power coding / Paul Kimmel.
        p. cm.
    ISBN 0-672-32407-5 (pbk. : alk paper)
    1. Microsoft Visual BASIC.   2. BASIC (Computer program language)   3. Microsoft .NET.   I. Title.

  AQ76.73.B3K544 2003
  005.2"768—dc21   2003048166

ISBN: 0-672-32407-5
Text printed on recycled paper
1 2 3 4 5 6 7 8 9 10—CRS—0706050403
First printing, July 2003

This book is dedicated to my brother David Kimmel.
Dave lives a life somewhere between Mr. Smith Goes to Washington
and a Steven Seagal movie. He is humble and kind
and a most excellent friend. I love you, brother.

Pauly

Contents
at a Glance

Contents

Preface

A journey of a thousand miles begins with a single step.

—Confucius

Introduction

By the time you are reading this I will be well into my third year working with .NET. After looking at some of the books already written about .NET, I tried to figure out what you, the reader, would be interested in by the time you had some .NET under your belt. We planned a bit in conceiving and producing this book. Now that .NET has been out for a while, I feel many readers are ready for some chewy stuff on Visual Basic .NET (VB .NET).

Who Should Read This Book

I wrote this book for professionals who have gotten past the basics and are ready for some torque. This book assumes you have read an introductory book on VB .NET, progressed through a more advanced book like *Visual Basic .NET Unleashed* [Kimmel 2002b], and are now ready to turn on the hyperdrive.

There is just a modicum of introductory material inside these pages. If you need to know how to write loops, conditional statements, functions, or subroutines, then set this book on your shelf and try something written at the introductory level until you're comfortable with that material. Then come back to this book.

If you're the kind of code slinger who has trophy projects on your shelf, then this is the book for you. Read on.

What's in This Book

One chapter can be labeled a beginner's chapter, and that is Chapter 1. Chapters 2 through 18 contain advanced subject matter that will help you manage challenging problems whose solutions may be impossible to find in the help files and difficult to locate in other books.

Early chapters in this book cover subjects like inheritance and delegates because even seasoned Visual Basic 6 veterans might be a bit lost when it comes to these subjects. After all, neither inheritance nor delegates existed in Visual Basic 6, and delegates are unique to .NET.

Reflection

In Chapter 4 we will jump into the deep water with Reflection. If you have heard of Run Time Type Information (RTTI), think of Reflection as RTTI on anabolic steroids. All the things that can be done with Reflection haven't even been invented yet, but what has been invented and discovered is amazing.

For example, .NET code is converted to Intermediate Language (IL) code before it is just-in-time compiled (JITted) and run. .NET emulates the Java byte code model to a limited degree. VB .NET supports emitting new types at runtime directly into IL and then creating instances of those types on-the-fly. This book will show you how to emit IL using Reflection and provide you with a means of extending your code in the most fundamental ways after it is deployed.

Assemblies

"DLL hell" is vaporized in VB .NET by adding metadata to assemblies. For now think of an assembly as an application that carries extra information with it, eliminating the need to monkey around with the registry and Globally Unique Identifiers (GUIDs) so much.

Another cool technology is the ability to dynamically load assemblies over an HTTP wire. This means you can implement automatically deployable and updatable Windows applications emulating the thin client browser model.

Windows Forms–based applications provide a richer client experience than Web Forms–based applications, and thin client programming using assemblies may finally allow the convergence of Web and Windows development technologies.

This book will demonstrate how to use assembly metadata as well as how to implement thin client Windows applications that deploy over the Web and seamlessly update without user intervention.

Multithreading

There are times when you absolutely need multithreading capabilities. I will demonstrate how to use synchronous and asynchronous processes, thread pooling, and the thread class to safely incorporate multithreaded behavior and even how to do so with Windows Forms controls.

Multithreading in VB .NET is definitely a cruise missile you want in your arsenal. Learn how to use threads safely and professionally.

COM Interop

A huge body of code exists in the COM world. Microsoft hasn't pulled the plug on COM, so why should you? Even Visual Studio .NET (VS .NET) uses COM; look at the Add-Ins Manager.

COM Interop allows you to use COM components in .NET and .NET code in COM-based applications. In this book you will learn the ropes of COM Interop in VB .NET.

Remoting

Moving toward open standards, Microsoft has developed new ways to solve existing problems. Remoting supports the management of solutions in a distributed environment. Read Chapter 8 to learn how to serialize objects and implement remoting for your distributed projects.

Building Components

Historically, building advanced components for Visual Basic often required using ActiveX and a C++ compiler. VB .NET supports building professional components for VB .NET *with* VB .NET.

By working through Chapter 9 you will have an opportunity to build user controls, custom controls, and server controls. Several examples demonstrate the nuts and bolts of implementing and testing controls and adding those controls to VS .NET.

ADO.NET

A sweeping change in .NET is found in ADO.NET technology. .NET follows the disconnected data model necessary for Web applications. The disconnected nature of ADO.NET is supported by XML DataSets, which replace the Recordset.

DataSets are based on XML and require you to rethink the way you build database, client-server, and Web-enabled applications. This book demonstrates how to use DataSets and work with disconnected data, as well as how to use XML and XML schemas (XSD) to connect to any kind of data anywhere.

Web Services

One of the most exciting new technologies is Web Services. A Web Service represents code that can be called from anywhere in the world. Web Services use open standards protocols, like SOAP and XML, allowing any connected computer to request services from any other computer.

You will learn about XML, SOAP, Web Services, and UDDI as you read the pages of this book. I will provide many examples and describe these technologies (and acronyms, like UDDI).

ASP.NET, Debugging, and Security

The world of exciting new innovations includes ASP.NET. The ASP.NET model facilitates building Web applications very similar to how you build Windows-based applications.

While writing this book I was also working on an enterprise solution using ASP.NET. Through that experience, I learned the best practices for implementing, debugging, and securing Web applications and included them in the confines of this book.

You will have an opportunity to learn about Web Forms and server controls, as well as managing state using caching and XML serialization, connecting Web applications to data, and using the Policy Manager and new security attributes in .NET.

After reading this book you will agree that there is much to VB .NET.

Where to Get the Source Code

You can download all the source code from *http://www.softconcepts.com.* Like the cobbler who makes new shoes for his kids, I have time to update my own Web site, and occasionally things get moved around. Follow the Source Code link on the main page to find the source code for this book. If you have any questions or general feedback then send me some e-mail at *pkimmel@softconcepts.com*.

Looking Ahead

I wrote this book to be readable from cover to cover, beginning with Chapter 1. I was also mindful that many readers are busy and may not have the time to read hundreds of pages in one sitting.

The many code listings will help you find examples to support the theoretical material presented; the chapters are organized to require only a modest amount of interdependency. If you are looking for answers to specific questions, you may be able to find all the material in one location.

I stand behind what I write, and I strive to offer the most accurate and informative content available. If you have any specific questions, feel free to e-mail me at *pkimmel@softconcepts.com*. Any feedback is appreciated.

Happy reading.

Acknowledgments

I would like to thank Sondra Scott at Addison-Wesley. I appreciate her many years of commitment to me and the chance to continue writing for the readers. It takes many people to get a book from concept to publication. Many of the people at Addison-Wesley do so quietly, consistently, and professionally book after book, asking for no recognition. I appreciate their help and know it couldn't be done without them. I would especially like to thank John Cottrell and Lowell Mauer. John and Lowell have many years of combined wisdom and programming experience. Thanks, guys, for technical editing.

A shout out to Sharon Cox, now at Wiley. Thank you, Sharon, for patiently waiting for me to finish this book. Sorry about the scheduling confusion. Tell Chris I will finish the wireless book right away.

David Fugate is my agent at Waterside. David referees when things get hectic. Thank you, David, for keeping the flow going in both directions.

I would like to thank Dan O'Donnell at Intel, Matt Markley, Adena Wilder, and Lisa Cozzens at Microsoft. These folks work at the other end of technical support at Intel and Microsoft, and I believe they set the standard for technical customer assistance. Thank you for your professional and courteous help.

A special thank you to the JET team at Multnomah County for helping me make a home away from home these many months. Thanks to Steve Chennault, Peggy Duerscherl, Karin Britton, Yvette Yutze, Brooke Riddick, Geoff Caylor, Bill Arnold, Mark Davis, Kathy Erwin, Robert Phillips, Lewis Gouge, Frank Bubenick, Joe Shook, John Armitage, Eric Cotter, John Deal, Jeff Braunstein, and Lisa Yeo. We're in the stretch now.

Thanks to Sara Kelsay, Erin, Rhiannon, and Lorinda at Wynne's for food and adult beverages, and we say goodbye to Yonnie who has moved on to bigger and better things.

It is my family that makes all things possible. Thanks to my mom, Jacqueline Benavides, for babysitting when everyone is sick and for trips to the airport. Thanks to my brother Jim Kimmel for emergency appliance repairs while I am out of town. Thanks to my younger brother Nicholas—who started at Michigan State University in 2002—for house sitting. (It was nice to have Mom and Dad Bourbonais and Grandma Blumenthal over for the holidays, up from Tampa, Florida. Hope you enjoyed the first year of retirement.) And thanks to my extended family in Oregon—Mark Davis, who takes trips to Vegas with me, and Joe Shook, Geoff Caylor, and Eric Cotter for playing Warcraft III and Unreal to help pass the time. A special thanks to my good friend Rob Golieb for sending me books for Christmas. The perfect gift.

Last and most importantly, thank you Lori, Trevor, Doug, Alex, and Noah—my wife and kids—for being flexible, lovable, and the best part of my life. I love you dearly, Dad.

About the Author

Paul Kimmel is the founder of Software Conceptions, Inc. Paul has been developing object-oriented software for more than a decade. Paul has written many books on object-oriented programming and .NET, including *Advanced C# Programming* for McGraw-Hill/Osborne and Sams' *Visual Basic .NET Unleashed*. He is a monthly columnist for *Windows Developer Magazine*, a bimonthly contributor to codeguru.com's Visual Basic Today, and a regular contributor to InformIT.

While writing this book Paul was helping build an enterprise ASP.NET application in Portland, Oregon. He is available to help design and implement applications anywhere in North America and can be contacted at *pkimmel@softconcepts.com*.

Paul resides with his wife, Lori, and children—Trevor, Doug, Alex, and Noah—in Okemos, Michigan. Okemos is a sleepy little suburb full of mostly sensible people, near the beautiful Michigan State University campus.

About the Technical Reviewers

John P. Cottrell started programming in Basic in 1982 and since then has written applications in many different languages. He started programming in Visual Basic with version 4 in 1996 and has been coding in VB .NET since June 2000. John lives in Sugar Hill, Georgia, and in his spare time enjoys programming, coin collecting, and spending time with his wife, Adelle, and three-year-old daughter, Katy.

Lowell Mauer has been in data processing for over 23 years as a programmer, an instructor, and a consultant. He has taught programming at Brooklyn College in New York City and Montclair State College in New Jersey. He has developed and marketed several Visual Basic applications, including a SQL Server-based reservation system for a private golf course. Lowell currently is a senior consultant in New York City.

Power Language Essentials

Part I includes a brief introduction to fundamental language concepts and the cornerstones of .NET development.

Basic Language Constructs

Willst du immer weiter schweifen?
Sieh, das Güte liegt so nah.[1]

—Göethe

Introduction

As promised, this is your introductory chapter. If you are reading this, you are ready to see how Visual Basic .NET (VB .NET) handles at top speed. It will be helpful for you to first understand some important fundamentals; some things are unique to .NET, so you may not have encountered them even if you have programmed in languages other than Visual Basic 6 (VB6).

Everything in .NET is subclassed from the Object class. However, there are types that behave like native types with the benefit of features found in classes. Chapter 1 illustrates the difference between value types and reference types, reviews the essential fundamentals of the new object-oriented idiom (the class), talks about nondeterministic object cleanup and garbage collection, and shows you how to look at the Intermediate Language (IL) code generated by the VB .NET compiler.

Understanding these features of VB .NET will help you quickly progress to more advanced concepts. Without further ado, let's continue.

Declaring Variables

When you declare a variable in VB6 you use the `dim` statement. VB .NET supports the `dim` keyword. The difference is that you can and are encouraged

---

1. "Will you go wandering on and on? See, the Good lies so near."

to dim variables, create instances of them, and provide initial values all on the same line in VB .NET.

Declaring and creating an instance is referred to as *instantiation*. Here are several examples of declaring variables, followed by examples of instantiating objects.

```
Dim I As Integer = 5
Dim S As String = "Welcome to Valhalla Tower Material Defender!"
Dim ADate As DateTime = DateTime.Now
Dim Objects As New Object(){1, 2, DateTime.Now, "Some Text"}
Dim Log As EventLog = New EventLog()
```

The first statement declares an integer `I` initialized to 5. The second statement initializes a string variable and initializes it to "Welcome to Valhalla Tower Material Defender!" The third statement declares a `DateTime` structure and initializes it to the current date and time. The fourth statement is more complex; it declares an array of `Object` and initializes the array to heterogeneous values, demonstrating the initializer list idiom. The last statement declares and initializes an `EventLog` class and instantiates the `EventLog` object `Log`.

Several things may jump out at you when examining these examples. First, every statement has an initial value. We have been telling programmers to provide initial values for years. VB .NET is not COM-based VB6, and you are encouraged to provide initial values at the point of declaration. Second, you might notice there is no Hungarian prefix notation or any other notation. Admittedly, `I` and `S` are not great variable names; the point is that prefix notations are discouraged, even by Microsoft, because the reason they were used in the first place no longer exists. Prefix notations were employed for weakly typed languages like C, not strongly typed languages like VB .NET. In addition to avoiding prefixes, you should add the statements `Option Explicit On` and `Option Strict On` to the beginning of every module, or at the project level, to ensure that variables are declared and everything is bound early.

The last thing you need to know is that every single variable in the list of examples is an object. That means each variable actually may have one or more fields, properties, methods, or events. Collectively these are referred to as *members*. You can find out what the members are by (a) looking them up in the integrated help documentation or (b) typing the variable or type name followed by the dot operator (`.`), which will prompt Intellisense to provide you with a list of members. For example, typing "I." in the code editor will list the members of the `Integer` type.

NOTE: Intellisense is a technology that uses Reflection to provide a dynamic list of the members of classes in Visual Studio .NET. Intellisense is a great time-saver when it comes to learning about the .NET Framework.

In the Options dialog, on the Text Editor, All Languages, General item, you can uncheck the Hide advanced members option and Intellisense will provide you with an expanded list of members.

Some of the variables in the five statements listed earlier are referred to as *value types* and others are referred to as *reference types*. There is a distinction in the ways value types and reference types are created and managed; to work effectively in VB .NET you need to know this information, which is presented in the next section.

Value Types and Reference Types

Every type in .NET (including types like `Integer` as well as the `EventLog` class) is derived from the `Object` class. This means that every type has `Sub New`, `Equals`, `GetHashCode`, `GetType`, `ReferenceEquals`, `ToString`, `Finalize`, and `MemberwiseClone` methods. What isn't obvious are the differences between types like `Integer` and `EventLog`.

.NET has a Common Language Specification (CLS). The Visual Basic types you may be familiar with from VB6 don't exactly exist in .NET proper. Yes, there is an `Integer` type in VB .NET, but it is based in the `System.Int32` value type defined in the CLS. Of course, having made it this far, you already know that you can use most of the types you are accustomed to; the compiler will convert the VB types to CLS types.

Regardless, both `Integer` and the `EventLog` class have the same root, the `Object` class. But they behave differently. If simple types like `Integer` had to be instantiated like `EventLog` and carried around the baggage of `EventLog`, .NET would be cumbersome to use. The problem is how to have smart types even for simple things like integers without the overhead of heap allocation and the constructor calling convention. The solution was to branch the .NET framework very early into to main kinds of types: value types and reference types.

Value types are literally types subclassed from the `System.ValueType` class. *Reference types* do not follow this inheritance ascendancy. Types derived from `ValueType` are *structures*; types not derived from `ValueType` are *classes*. A noticeable difference is that `ValueType` children are usually not created by invoking the `Sub New` constructor and fall into simpler categories.

TIP: The structure construct replaces the type construct used in VB6.

More importantly, value types remain lightweight by not carrying Run Time Type Information (RTTI)—called just *type information* in .NET. Reference types do carry type information.

However, both value types and reference types can be queried for type information. When you need type information for a reference type like `EventLog`, you simply request it by invoking the `GetType` method. When you need type information for a value type, just like the reference type, you request the type information by invoking `GetType`.

What is the difference? The difference is that when you request type information on a value type, a process called *boxing* occurs. We'll return to boxing in a moment. For now, just keep in mind that value types provide the convenience and performance of native types—which don't really exist in .NET—with the power and flexibility of classes, all happening quietly behind the scenes.

Structures

Structures replace the types used in VB6. When you want something a little simpler than a class, you have the choice of defining a structure.

Structures are more powerful in VB .NET than types were in VB6. Unlike the type construct in VB6, which supported the ability to define only fields, the structure construct in VB .NET supports the ability to define constants, enumerations, fields, properties, methods, and events. For the most part structures are classes that don't have the overhead of type information (unless requested), do not require (but do support) using the `Sub New` constructor, and cannot be inherited from.

Subtler differences between structures and classes may be a little harder to detect. They are briefly listed here for reference.

- Structures are value types. Classes are reference types.
- Structures are allocated in stack memory. Classes are allocated in heap memory.

- Structure members are `Public` by default. Class fields and constants are `Private` by default; everything else in a class is `Public`.
- Only class members can be declared protected. The protected access modifier is not supported for structures. (See the Using Access Modifiers section later in this chapter for more information.)
- Methods in structures cannot handle events.
- Structure fields cannot specify initializers, that is, initial values.
- Structures implicitly inherit from the `System.ValueType` class.
- Structures cannot be subclassed.
- The garbage collector never calls the `Finalize` method for a structure.
- Nonshared constructors can be defined in structures but they must take parameters

For general purpose use, you declare a structure variable and interact with members of structures using the variable name and dot operator just as you would with a class.

Referring back to the `DateTime` statement earlier in the chapter, you can declare a `DateTime` variable and initialize it to the current date and time as follows:

```
Dim rightNow As DateTime = DateTime.Now
```

You could also invoke a similar operation on an `Integer` variable by requesting its string representation.

```
Dim anInt As Integer = 5
MsgBox(anInt.ToString())
```

You can also pass data to the parameterized version of a structure's constructor by using the `New` operator.

```
Dim d As DateTime = New DateTime(1966, 2, 12)
Console.WriteLine(d.ToLongDateString())
Console.ReadLine()
```

The variable `d` is instantiated with year 1966, month 2, and day 12. The second statement invokes an operation on the `DateTime` structure using the variable `d`.

Structures are significantly more advanced than VB6 types. Most of the time when you are defining new types you will want to define a class.

Structure Assignment

Structures are associated with the variable they are assigned to. When you assign one instance of a structure to a new variable, you are making a copy of that structure. All of the values of the first structure are copied to the second structure. Each structure occupies a separate space in memory.

When you assign a structure to `Nothing`, all of the field values in that structure are set to their null equivalent. For example, initializing the `Date-Time` variable `d` to `Nothing` would change the date value to Monday, January 1, 0001.

Structure Equality Testing

When you perform equality testing on structures, you will need to compare every field to ensure that the structures contain identical values. Comparing to structure variables—rather than the fields within—would always yield inequality.

We will look at the grammar for defining structures in the upcoming Defining Structures and Classes section.

Classes

Classes in VB6 were actually more closely related to COM interfaces. VB .NET supports classes and interfaces. Classes in VB .NET support implementation inheritance. Implementation inheritance is completely new in VB .NET (see Chapter 3). For now let's return to our comparison between structures and classes vis-à-vis value types and reference types.

Classes are reference types. This means instances of classes are created on the heap using the `Sub New` constructor. Classes carry their RTTI with them and support all of the things you would expect from a fully object-oriented programming language. (Refer to Chapter 4 for more details on type information.)

VB .NET classes support inheritance, polymorphism, encapsulation, information hiding, and associations. VB .NET classes do not support templates and multiple inheritance. The template and multiple inheritance idioms are supported in C++ but are perceived by many to introduce more problems than they solve. But these beliefs are subject to much conjecture.

To create instances of a class—referred to as *instantiating* a class—you declare a class variable just as you would a structure variable, but you introduce the `New` operator. The `New` operator allocates memory to the class variable and invokes the `Sub New` method, which plays the role of constructor in VB .NET. Here is an example of creating a new instance of an `EventLog` component.

```
Dim Log As EventLog = New EventLog()
```

After you have created an instance of a class, you invoke operations and access members by using the dot-operator syntax. For example, to set the `Source` property of the `Log` object you might write the following:

```
Log.Source = "MySource"
```

Classes and objects may become confusing when you use a class like an object. Let's take a moment to review the differences between classes and objects.

A class is a *description* of a type. An object is an *instance* of a type. For example, one blueprint (class) can be used to create many homes (objects). However, you can also use a class like an object. This happens when you invoke a shared member.

Shared members exist at the class level and are shared across all instances of an object. When we use a class like an object, we refer to that class as a *metaclass*. For example, there are several overloaded versions of the `EventLog.WriteEntry` method. (We'll discuss overloading in Chapter 2. For now think of overloading as methods that have the same name, in the same class, but with different arguments. The compiler figures out what method you mean by the arguments you pass to the method.) Regarding the `EventLog.WriteEntry` method, several overloaded versions can be called without creating an instance of the `EventLog` class. For example,

```
EventLog.WriteEntry("MySource", "Test!")
```

writes an entry to the event log using the class `EventLog` and the shared method `WriteEntry`. This is just mechanics, but it does seem to cause some confusion among some VB developers. What further exacerbates the confusion is that VB supports variables and classes with identical names. For example, you could declare and create an `EventLog` object as follows:

```
Dim EventLog As EventLog = New EventLog()
```

You may want to avoid defining variables that match class names. Fortunately, the compiler is smart enough to resolve these ambiguities, but the human reader may find the code confusing. Read the Defining Structures and Classes section for examples.

Value Types, Reference Types, and Memory

Value types and reference types behave differently in memory. It is important to have a mental image depicting the differences between value types and reference types. You are less likely to induce memory leaks in VB .NET if you understand these differences. However, you can still trip over instances where two reference types refer to the same object and one reference disposes of the object.

When you declare two value types and assign one to the other, VB .NET performs a copy. Then you have two distinct variables occupying different chunks of memory (Figure 1.1).

When you perform assignment of two reference types you are creating an alias; both names refer to the same chunk of memory. If you modify the properties of one reference type, the change is reflected in the other named reference type (Figure 1.2). If you want separate objects, occupying different chunks of memory, you must allocate memory to each reference type and perform a member-wise copy of each property.

If you are familiar with how C++ or Object Pascal deal with pointers, you understand how reference types work in Visual Basic .NET. In C++ vernacular, reference types perform a shallow copy and value types perform a deep copy.

Boxing and Unboxing

While you are coding you need to be familiar with the difference between value types and reference types, especially when you perform assignment. However, you don't need to worry about value types and reference types as they relate to acquiring type information. Reference types carry their type information with them; if you request type information for value types, the compiler will make it available behind the scenes.

When you request type information for a value type, like `DateTime`, .NET boxes the value type. There is literally a `box` instruction emitted to IL that creates a reference object, copies the value type to the new object, and returns the type information. When your code is finished with the task requiring a reference type, the IL `unbox` instruction is executed. Figure 1.3

```
Dim Date1 As DateTime = New DateTime(2002, 2, 12)
Dim Date2 As DateTime = Date1
```

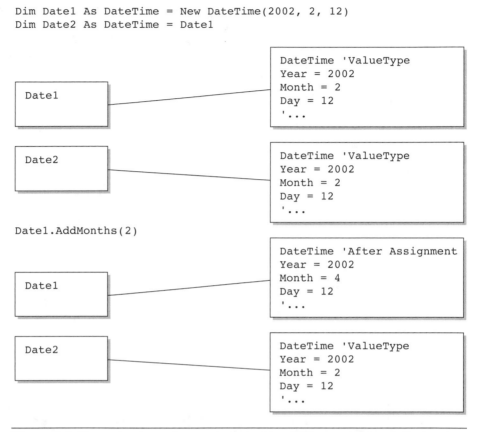

Figure 1.1 Two value types (`DateTime` structure) after assignment. Each value type structure refers to a separate chunk of memory, and the `'ValueType` variables reside at separate locations in memory. Value type assignment performs a deep copy. Modifying one value type has no effect on any other.

shows some IL code in the `ildasm.exe` utility (see the Intermediate Language section at the end of this chapter for an explanation) that boxes an `Integer` structure when the type information is requested.

```
Module Module1
  Sub Main()
    Dim I As Integer = 5
    Console.WriteLine(I.GetType().FullName)
  End Sub
End Module
```

```
Dim Log1 As EventLog = New EventLog()
Dim Log2 As EventLog = Log1
```

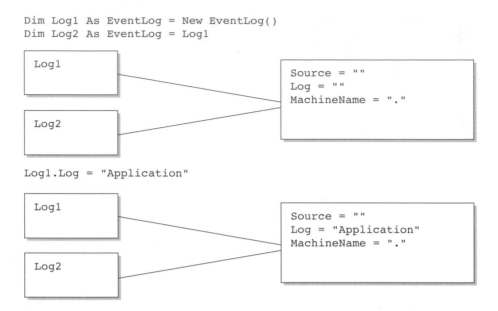

```
Log1.Log = "Application"
```

Figure 1.2 Two reference types (EventLog objects) after assignment. Each object refers to the same chunk of memory. Reference type assignment is analogous to someone having both a given name and a nickname—both names refer to the same person. In the figure, the names Log1 and Log2 refer to the same object.

```
 Module1::Main : void()                                               _ □ ×
.method public static void  Main() cil managed
{
  .entrypoint
  .custom instance void [mscorlib]System.STAThreadAttribute::.ctor() = ( 01 00 00
  // Code size       27 (0x1b)
  .maxstack  1
  .locals init ([0] int32 I)
  IL_0000:  nop
  IL_0001:  ldc.i4.5
  IL_0002:  stloc.0
  IL_0003:  ldloc.0
  IL_0004:  box         [mscorlib]System.Int32
  IL_0009:  callvirt    instance class [mscorlib]System.Type [mscorlib]System.Objec
  IL_000e:  callvirt    instance string [mscorlib]System.Type::get_FullName()
  IL_0013:  call        void [mscorlib]System.Console::WriteLine(string)
  IL_0018:  nop
  IL_0019:  nop
  IL_001a:  ret
} // end of method Module1::Main
```

Figure 1.3 The box instruction at IL_0004, which copies the Integer structure to a reference type to get the type information.

The preceding code fragment requests the type information, which implicitly instructs the compiler to box the `Integer` structure. The full name of the Visual Basic .NET `Integer` type is `System.Int32`. The Common Type Specification does not define an `Integer` type. `Integer` was maintained to promote familiarity with VB6.

You may also have noticed from the IL listing shown in Figure 1.3 that the `unbox` instruction is not called. While you need to know that types like `Integer` are really objects derived from the `Object` class, and you need to know that the `ValueType` classes make simple types behave like native types, you don't need to worry about when the compiler boxes and unboxes. The compiler has the responsibility of box and unboxing. All you and I need to know is that value types behave like native types but actually contain data and methods.

Defining Structures and Classes

We know that classes are reference types and structures are value types, literally derived from the `System.ValueType`. We also know that structures have replaced the type construct from VB6. What may not be so obvious is that both classes and structures support fields, properties, methods, constructors, and events. It also may not be immediately apparent that structures support only private or public members.

The structure is more like the C or C++ struct construct than it is like the VB6 type construct. However, because the VB6 type construct no longer exists, structure is the closest (and intended) replacement.

This section demonstrates how to declare each type of member that you can define in structures and classes. The examples in this section are brief since you will see dozens of examples throughout the rest of this book.

Adding Fields

Fields are the data members of structures and classes that maintain the type's state information. As a general rule, fields use the private access modifier, which means they are accessible only internally.

`StickMan.sln` contains a class and structure that are identical. Both the `StickMan` class and `StickMan` structure contain precisely the same elements. Each type draws a stick figure and is capable of making the Stick-Man perform some basic movements. The code can be identical because neither the class nor the structure uses things that aren't allowed in structures. (See the earlier Structures section to review the differences between classes and structures.)

The `StickMan` type defines four fields.

```
Private FOwner As Form
Private FX, FY As Integer
Private FPosition As Integer
```

NOTE: Visual Basic .NET is not case-sensitive. If it were, we could use camel-cased names for fields and Pascal-cased names for properties. (In camel-casing, the first initial of the first word is lower-cased and the first initial of each subsequent word in the name is upper-cased, for example, `anInteger`. In Pascal-casing, the first letter of all words in the name are upper-cased, for example, `MyFunction`.) However, since Visual Basic .NET is not case-sensitive and the Hungarian notation is discouraged for .NET, in this example I adopted an `F` prefix to denote a field and dropped the `F` for properties.

The first field is a form. Since the StickMan is not a control, we need a canvas to draw on; a form works fine. The next two fields are X and Y offsets. These values are used to position the StickMan. The `FPosition` field is used to make the legs move when the StickMan moves.

Making fields private is a wise strategy. The fundamental premise is that providing unfettered access to state variables (fields) makes it more difficult to prevent misuse. Of course, technically you can make data public, but this debate has been held and the outcome has been decided. Make fields private and provide limited access through properties.

Adding Properties

Properties are like fathers and fields are like daughters in old-fashioned farm tales. Fathers provide limited access to the daughters (showing the prospective suitor the double-barrel shotgun) until the daughters reach maturity and then continue to provide firm guidance.

Properties are members that are used like fields but behave like methods. About ten years ago the common thinking was that programmers would be wise to access data through functions; but functions are inconvenient to use to read and write fields, and some programmers simply ignored this advice. The property idiom was developed to provide the ease of use of fields and the benefit of methods. If fields are private and properties constrain access to fields, the only way the state of an object can be wrong is if the producer—referring to the person who writes the code—implemented the properties inappropriately.

There are two properties for the StickMan, an X property and a Y property. The X and Y properties are associated with the X and Y fields, respectively. (As you read the code below, keep in mind the convention adopted to use an F prefix for fields.)

```
Public ReadOnly Property X() As Integer
   Get
      Return FX
   End Get
End Property

Public ReadOnly Property Y() As Integer
   Get
      Return FY
   End Get
End Property
```

These two properties are defined as read-only. Applying the ReadOnly modifier means that the value of the property can only be read. Grammatically this means that you can implement only a Get block. If you want consumers (the persons using the code) to be able to use properties as left-hand-side values and right-hand-side values—shortened to l-value and r-value, respectively—you will need to implement both Get and Set blocks. (Get blocks are called getters and Set blocks are called setters.)

If you elect to allow consumers to move the StickMan by changing one positional value at a time, you could implement setters for the X and Y properties. The revised code would appear as follows.

```
Public Property X() As Integer
   Get
      Return FX
   End Get
   Set(ByVal Value As Integer)
      ' Validate Value before assigning
      FX = Value
   End Set
End Property
```

```
Public Property Y() As Integer
  Get
    Return FY
  End Get
  Set(ByVal Value As Integer)
    ' Validate Value before assigning
    FY = Value
  End Set
End Property
```

The setters are the gatekeepers. Theoretically, as long as the producer does not introduce any errors internally and the setters screen potential values, the state of a class can never be invalid. I refer to the validation code in setters as *sentries*; the role of the sentry is to keep bad data from getting into the underlying field.

Adding Methods

Methods are simply member procedures. Public methods are those that you want consumers to be able to call directly, and private methods are the ones that you as the producer will call to support the public behavior.

The StickMan implements several public methods that describe a kind of movement. The `StickMan.Run` method accepts a direction and a distance, moving the StickMan very quickly the number of times expressed by the `Distance` variable. Direction is implemented as an enumeration named `Direction`. The code for the `Enum` and `Run` methods follows.

```
Public Enum Direction
  Down
  DownLeft
  Left
  UpLeft
  Up
  UpRight
  Right
  DownRight
End Enum


Public Sub Run(ByVal Where As Common.Direction, _
  ByVal Distance As Integer)
```

```
Dim I As Integer = Distance
For I = 1 To Distance
  Walk(Where)
  Thread.Sleep(75)
Next

End Sub
```

TIP: You will need to set the `Option Strict On` statement to enforce strict type checking. This is a good practice.

The enumeration provides us with an opportunity to use strongly typed values that have semantic meaning rather than simple integers. The `Run` method takes a direction and uses the distance as a loop control to call `Walk` with a very short wait period.

As a general strategy, try to keep the number of public methods to no more than a handful. Use as many private methods as you need to support the public interface. Constraining the number of public methods will make your classes easier for consumers to use and less susceptible to instability if the classes do need to be changed.

Adding Constructors

Constructors are special methods invoked before an object is created. A constructor's job is to initialize an object. If you combine a constructor that initializes an object to a valid state and property methods that only allow valid states, your objects should remain in a valid state.

In VB6 we didn't have constructors; we did have the `Class_Initialize` method. The difference between `Class_Initialize` and a VB .NET constructor is that we can pass arguments to constructors. We can't do that with the `Class_Initialize` method.

NOTE: C++ implements constructors as methods with no return type that have the identical name as the class. C# follows C++ in this regard, and by convention Object Pascal uses the keyword `constructor` and the name `Create`.

Constructors are implemented as a `Sub New` method in VB .NET. When you instantiate an object with the new keyword, as in

```
Dim Log As EventLog = New EventLog()
```

you are really invoking the `New` method. If you use the F8 key (with the VB6 keyboard scheme), you can step into a statement that instantiates an object (assuming you have the source for that object's class) and see for yourself that you are stepping into a subroutine named `New`.

Implementing a Sub New Method

Every form has a default constructor that accepts no arguments. Every time you create a Windows Form, the form will contain a constructor that calls `InitializeComponent`. Here is the constructor from the `StickMan.sln` example program.

```
Public Sub New()
  MyBase.New()

  'This call is required by the Windows Form Designer.
  InitializeComponent()

  'Add any initialization after the InitializeComponent() call

End Sub
```

Calling an `Initialize` method is a good strategy for implementing constructors; as demonstrated in a Form's constructor, an `Initialize` method keeps the constructor simple. In the case of a Windows Form, `Initialize-Component` actually creates instances of the controls defined on your form.

In the listing above we can see that there is a statement, `MyBase.New`, and `InitializeComponent`. `MyBase` refers to the parent class of this class, and `MyBase.New` calls the parent constructor of the Form. Having to remember to call inherited methods is a wrinkle you will have to get used to in VB .NET. (Chapter 2 covers inheritance in greater detail.)

The other thing that is evident in the constructor in the listing is that there are no arguments. We can implement an overloaded constructor that contains arguments, also referred to as *parameters*.

Parameterized Constructors

A parameterized constructor is a `Sub New` method that accepts one or more arguments. Constructor parameters are defined the same way you would define any other method's parameters. First type the specifier, parameter name, type, and a default value if you want one. Applied to the StickMan, here is a parameterized constructor used for both the structure and class versions of StickMan.

```
Public Sub New(ByVal Owner As Form, _
   ByVal X As Integer, ByVal Y As Integer)

   FOwner = Owner
   FX = X
   FY = Y
   Draw()

End Sub
```

StickMan defines three required parameters: a form, an X value, and a Y value. The form is used as the drawing surface, and the X and Y values represent the horizontal and vertical positions, respectively. It is important to note that you may implement a parameterized constructor only for structures. The structure construct implements a default constructor that you may not override.

When you create an instance of a structure without parameters, you do not use the New keyword. If you invoke the parameterized constructor for a structure, you must use the New keyword. This difference between classes and structures is where we run into trouble.

The structure version of StickMan has a default constructor. This means that we can create a structure StickMan instance without calling the parameterized Sub New method. The implications are that we have a StickMan without a form to draw on. This leads to an improperly initialized StickMan and a NullReferenceException when the structure StickMan tries to draw itself. Alternatively, the class StickMan does not implement a nonparameterized Sub New method; as a consequence we must invoke the parameterized constructor for the class StickMan, which helps ensure that it is properly initialized.

As a general rule, reserve structures for very simple types and use classes for almost everything else. You have more control when you use a class, and control is the name of the game.

Adding *Finalize* and *Dispose* Methods

Visual Basic .NET uses nondeterministic memory management. *Deterministic* means you do it. *Nondeterministic* means that .NET does it. How does nondeterministic memory management work, and why do we have it? These are very insightful questions. As the resident code guru, you should know the answers.

Languages like C++ and Object Pascal use deterministic memory management. This means the producer creates an object and then releases the object when it is no longer needed. The problem deterministic memory management introduced is referred to as *memory leaks*, and one of the symptoms of memory leaks is referred to as the *slicing problem*. The slicing problem, and consequently a memory leak, occurs when two references refer to the same object in memory and one reference deletes the memory while the other reference attempts to use the memory. The memory has been sliced off. Another form of memory leak is when objects are created and the reference variable goes out of scope; that is, the pointer no longer exists but the memory does. Memory leaks are probably the biggest cause of serious defects for software developers.

To help us, the concept of *garbage collection* was invented. In garbage collection, the language keeps track of allocated memory and cleans up after programmers automatically. (Garbage collection is similar to the relationship most teenagers have with their mothers: Teenagers mess it up and moms clean it up. Perhaps only teenagers who are extremely fastidious should program in C++.) The idea is that computers are good at tedious tasks and people are not. If the garbage collector is implemented correctly, memory leaks will no longer exist, at least in theory.

NOTE: You can tell the garbage collector to run by invoking the `GC.Collect` method, but this is not a recommended practice. It's one thing to be sloppy and hope your mother cleans up after you; it's entirely another to order your mom to do it.

Visual Basic .NET uses nondeterministic memory management, which means that when you are finished with an object, the garbage collector decides when to destroy the memory. The implication of nondeterministic memory management in VB .NET is that you can implement a destructor, but you won't know when it will be called.

Implementing a `Finalize` Method

Destructors in VB .NET are implemented as a protected method named `Finalize`. The garbage collector will call your `Finalize` method if you implement one, but you won't know when that will be. The best thing to do is to try not to need deterministic memory management. This is not always possible, so the next subsection will demonstrate how to compensate for nondeterministic memory management. But first, let's finish talking about `Finalize`.

You may implement a `Finalize` method. If you do, note the following:

- `Finalize` cannot be public.
- You can't invoke `Finalize` directly.
- `Finalize` is never overloaded by convention but must be overridden if you are going to introduce new behavior. (We will talk more about overriding and overloading in Chapter 2.)
- `Finalize` never takes any arguments.

`Finalize` is always defined as follows:

```
Protected Sub Finalize()
  ' Cleanup code here
End Sub
```

Remember, you need to implement this method only if you have some specific cleanup you need to do. Managed .NET objects will be cleaned up automatically.

Implementing a *Dispose* Method

Another convention employed in VB .NET is to implement a public method `Dispose` that performs deterministic clean up for you. The `Dispose` method is implemented as a public subroutine that takes no arguments. `Dispose` can be implemented reliably as follows:

```
Private Disposed As Boolean = False
Public Sub Dispose()
  If(Disposed) Return
  Disposed = True
  GC.SuppressFinalize(Mc)
  ' Clean up here
End Sub
```

Consumers can call `Dispose` if there is something specific that must be cleaned up before the garbage collector gets around to it. By using a Boolean you can prevent the `Dispose` method from running a second time, and since you are cleaning up specifically you can tell the garbage collector that it will no longer need to run `Finalize` for the object. In the case of a form, the `Form` class (as well as many other controls) already implements a `Dispose` method. If you want to extend the behavior of a form's `Dispose` method, you will need to overload the `Dispose` method. Assuming the parent class already has a `Dispose` method, you can overload it and call the parent method as follows:

```
Private Disposed As Boolean = False
Public Overloads Sub Dispose()
  MyBase.Dispose()
  If(Disposed) Return
  Disposed = True
  GC.SuppressFinalize(Me)
  ' Clean up here
End Sub
```

The revision adds the `Overloads` keyword and invokes the `MyBase.Dispose` method. It is up to the parent class to prevent its `Dispose` behavior from running more than one time, so you just call `SuppressFinalize` in your `Dispose` method.

If you want consumers to know that your class implements a `Dispose` method, you can implement the `IDisposable` interface. `IDisposable` defines one method, `Dispose`. If the `IDisposable` interface is implemented by a parent class, you do not need to introduce the `Implements` statement a second time in the child class. (Chapter 2 will clarify the discussion on inheritance and implementing interfaces if it is new to you.)

The mechanics of implementing the `IDisposable` interface are demonstrated in the code fragment below.

```
Public Class MyDisposableClass
  Implements IDisposable
  Public Sub Dispose() Implements IDisposable.Dispose
  End Sub
End Class
```

The `Implements` statement indicates that we will be implementing the methods defined by the named interface, and the `Implements` clause after the `Dispose` method completes the contract between this class and the `IDisposable` interface.

Using Events

Whether you use the `WithEvents` statement or work with events using `AddHandler` and `RemoveHandler`, you are using delegates. Events are supported by a new class called `Delegate` in .NET. Delegates are completely new and introduce many powerful concepts. In this section I will briefly demonstrate how to add an event member to a class or structure. (Chapter 3 contains a complete discussion of the new `Delegate` idiom in VB .NET.)

To add an event member to a class or structure, use the `Event` keyword, followed by the name and the method signature that event handlers must have. (*Method signature* refers to the type, number, and order of arguments.) For example, suppose we wanted to track the location of StickMan. We could implement a `Moved` event that consumers could handle and receive notification of StickMan's location. Listing 1.1 demonstrates the conventional technique for adding events to classes and structures.

Listing 1.1 Convention for Implementing Events in Classes and Structures

```
1:  Public Class StickMan
2:
3:     ' Other code
4:
5:     Public Event Moved(ByVal X As Integer, ByVal Y As Integer)
6:
7:     Private Sub OnMoved(ByVal X As Integer, ByVal Y As Integer)
8:        RaiseEvent Moved(X, Y)
9:     End Sub
10:
11:    Private Sub Move(ByVal Y As Integer, ByVal X As Integer)
12:       ChangeRow(Y)
13:       ChangeColumn(X)
14:       OnMoved(X, Y)
15:       FOwner.Refresh()
16:    End Sub
17:
18: End Sub
```

Line 5 introduces the event named `Moved`. Its signature is a subroutine that takes two `Integer` arguments. By convention we raise events in a procedure with an `On` prefix and the same root as the event. Thus a `Moved` event would be raised from an `OnMoved` subroutine. Wherever we want to raise the `Moved` event we would invoke `OnMoved`, as demonstrated in line 14.

Now let's look at the way we would handle events. For now we will use the VB6 `WithEvents` statement. (In Chapter 3 we will explore the revised way of handling events.)

Assuming a consumer wanted to handle `Moved`, we would need to tell the consumer about the event. We do this by introducing the reference in a `WithEvents` statement. The `StickMan.sln` sample application tracks the location of StickMan by handling `Moved`. The additional code appears next.

```
WithEvents Man As ClassBasics.StickMan
Private Sub Man_Moved(ByVal X As Integer, _
  ByVal Y As Integer) Handles Man.Moved

  Text = String.Format("StickMan Demo - X: {0}, Y: {1}", X, Y)
End Sub
```

The `WithEvents` statement introduces the variable `Man` and adds the list of events associated with the `Man` reference to the `Method Name` combobox in the code editor. You can code the handler manually or use the code editor to automatically generate the handler. (Refer to Figure 1.4 for a visual guide.) To generate the `Moved` handler using the code editor, select the `Man` reference from the `Class Name` combobox (shown near the top left of Figure 1.4), and pick the event name from the `Method Name` combobox (shown near the top right of Figure 1.4).

TIP: Events are a good way to enforce loose coupling. As you can infer from the `StickMan.Moved` event, StickMan has no knowledge of the objects receiving the `Moved` event. Using events in this way allows you to build classes without foreknowledge of consumer classes.

Whenever `StickMan.OnMoved` is invoked, the event handler will be called, and in our implementation, the location of the StickMan will be displayed in the `Text` property.

Using Access Modifiers

Access modifiers (also referred to as *access specifiers*) are keywords that describe who has access to members of types. There are five access modifiers in VB .NET: `Public`, `Protected`, `Friend`, `Protected Friend`, and `Private`. Each modifier allows a specific level of access to the thing it modifies.

Public access is the least restrictive access. Like public restrooms, anybody has access. If you have ever visited most gas station restrooms, you know this is both a good thing and a bad thing. Public restrooms are good when you need to use one, but you certainly don't want a public restroom in

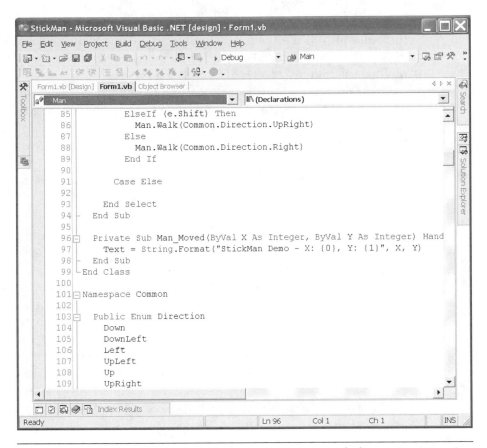

```
 85              ElseIf (e.Shift) Then
 86                  Man.Walk(Common.Direction.UpRight)
 87              Else
 88                  Man.Walk(Common.Direction.Right)
 89              End If
 90
 91          Case Else
 92
 93      End Select
 94    End Sub
 95
 96    Private Sub Man_Moved(ByVal X As Integer, ByVal Y As Integer) Hand
 97        Text = String.Format("StickMan Demo - X: {0}, Y: {1}", X, Y)
 98    End Sub
 99  End Class
100
101 Namespace Common
102
103    Public Enum Direction
104        Down
105        DownLeft
106        Left
107        UpLeft
108        Up
109        UpRight
```

Figure 1.4 Use the `Class Name` and `Method Name` comboboxes to generate event handlers in VB .NET.

your house. In the VB .NET context, public access means both consumers and producers can access the element adorned with the `Public` keyword.

Private access is the opposite of public access. Private access means only the producer can access elements adorned with the `Private` modifier. This means the author of a type is the only person who can access private elements in that type. Like first dates, most things are best kept private. Where types are concerned, making just a few public makes your types easier to use. Use too many public elements and your classes will seem schizophrenic.

The `Protected` modifier is used in inheritance relationships. Protected means private to consumers and public to generalizers. A *generalizer* is a consumer who subclasses, or creates child classes from, your class. Make members of types protected if you think a generalizer may want to extend the behavior of a member. Because we are talking about behaviors, the implication is that we are talking about methods. Generally this is true. Virtual methods should be protected. Keep fields private.

The `Friend` and `Protected Friend` modifiers are used less often. Elements modified by `Friend` are accessible only within the assembly in which they are defined. The `Protected Friend` modifier is a combination of `Friend` and `Protected`. Only generalizers within the same assembly can access `Protected Friend` elements.

Several general rules are inferred by specific modifiers. Here is an overview of some of the key implications.

- Classes are generally public. Nested classes are more often protected or private.
- Fields should almost always be private.
- Properties are almost always public, but sometimes they are protected.
- Methods are found using all modifiers. Keep the number of public methods to a minimum, perhaps less than a half-dozen per type.
- Events are most often public.
- The members of an interface are always public, and you cannot explicitly adorn method declarations in an interface with any modifier.
- Do not rely on default access. Always adorn every element of a type with the access you want it to have rather than relying on default access.

If you find yourself providing many public members of classes and structures, determine whether there is a natural subdivision; if so, split the type into more than one type. Otherwise it is best to be explicit and intentional about the access modifier you apply to every member.

Understanding Object-Oriented Concepts

In this section I want to review some basic object-oriented concepts to ensure that we are all on the same page. If you are sure you understand the difference between a metaclass, a class, and an object and you know what encapsulation and information hiding, association, aggregation, inheritance, and polymorphism are, skip to the last section in this chapter to read about the `ildasm.exe` utility. If you need to review these concepts, stay tuned.

Objects, Classes, and Metaclasses

Occasionally I hear things that are astounding. I was at a user's group in Charlotte, North Carolina, and heard a smart person say to a group of a hundred or so developers that there is "no difference between a class and an object." Not a single person challenged him. I hope this was out of politeness, but I have heard this often enough when talking to other VB programmers that I can understand if there is some confusion.

NOTE: Since there is a root class named `Object` in .NET (and one named `TObject` in Delphi), it is no wonder that the difference between classes and objects is confusing.

Just in case you are not sure, there is a world of difference between a class and an object. In the physical world a class is akin to the blueprint of a house, and an object is akin to a house built following that blueprint. The difference between classes and objects is similar to the fact that no one wants to live in a blueprint.

Classes describe things and *objects* are instances of those things. That is, for the most part, objects have memory and state and classes do not. This is where it can become confusing again, but only a little bit.

What about shared members? Shared members can record state, and shared members can be invoked. Precisely so. When a class is used in this manner, like an object, we refer to that as a *metaclass*. Metaclasses are classes used as if they represented an object. Usually, though, a class is a description of a thing and an object is an instance of that thing.

Information Hiding and Encapsulation

Encapsulation is when we make fields, properties, methods, and events become members of types. We say that the type encapsulates the member. Encapsulation deals with the concept of part and whole. Members are part of types, the whole.

Information hiding refers to when we employ access modifiers to logically conceal members from consumers. The more restrictive the access modifier, the more information we are hiding. Again, like first dates, the less we reveal about a class the better. Of course, if you don't reveal anything, there is no second date. (I'm not going to try to come up with an arranged marriage analogy.) When it comes to information hiding you want to reveal enough to secure a second date but never as much as you would reveal if married.

As a general rule, apply this test: Classes should introduce approximately a half-dozen public members. If you have significantly more than that, you should split up the class. If you have markedly fewer than a half-dozen members, you should consolidate the class. The number of nonpublic members should be whatever is sufficient to support the public members.

Association, Aggregation, and Inheritance

Association refers to a relationship where one object refers to an instance of another object but is not responsible for creating that other object. Unidirectional association means that only one class is aware of the other, and bidirectional association means that both objects in the relationship are mutually aware of, but not responsible for, each other.

Aggregation refers to containment. When one object contains a reference to another and is responsible for constructing that other object, this is called aggregation. (Sometimes this is referred to as *composition*.)

Inheritance refers to one class having members of another class. The class inherited from is referred to as the *parent* or *superclass*, and the class inheriting is referred to as the *child* or *subclass*.

Unlike VB6, VB .NET implements actual inheritance. VB6 implemented interface inheritance.

Polymorphism

Polymorphism has to do with inheritance. When a parent class is defined, the parent may introduce a method named `Foo`. A subclass may introduce an extended version of `Foo`. Which `Foo` is invoked depends on whether we have an instance of the parent or the child. A reasonable person might wonder why it would ever depend on whether we had the parent or the child. The answer is that sometimes we don't know or care whether we are dealing with a parent or a child. We want to write code in such a way that it doesn't matter.

Let's take an example. The `Object` class (sounds a bit ridiculous to say "`Object` class," doesn't it?) in VB .NET introduces a method called `GetType`. With it you can request type information for the `Object` class. Consequently every class has a `GetType` method. However, if we are dealing with `Button` we do not want `Object`'s type record; we want `Button`'s. We do not need to know the type of the class (all we need is an instance) for `GetType` to return the correct type record—that's polymorphism.

Polymorphism is based on doing the right thing without knowing the type of an object. The theoretical implication is that we can define methods that interact with the most general type but perform correctly when they are presented with a more specific type. The technical implication is that there exists—created by the compiler—an array of methods, referred to as a *virtual methods table*, and a mechanism that knows how to index the array of methods to find the right method. So, even if you have a variable reference whose type is `Object`, you can assign a subtype to that variable and methods in common will behave correctly based on the actual type rather than the declared type.

Intermediate Language

The Java language introduced the concept of byte code. The evolution of programming languages dictates that some things survive and some don't. Hopefully, the good ideas are propagated and the bad ones are not.

Intermediate Language, or IL, is similar to the idea of Java byte code. If the compiled form of a programming language is general enough, the compiled code can be separated from the platform on which it runs. The idea behind Java is that the compiler creates byte code, and some other tool converts the byte code to a platform-specific version of the code that runs on that specific platform. These other tools are often referred to as *JITters*, from the abbreviation for JIT compilers. (JIT is an acronym for just-in-time, as in just-in-time compilation.)

There is a good chance that someone, right now, is creating a JITter to convert VB .NET IL code to run on a Linux or UNIX platform.

One of the things we can do with IL is snoop around and look at what the VB compiler does with our source code. More than just being curious, it is possible to emit IL dynamically in VB .NET. This means we can define new types after our VB .NET source code is compiled, at runtime. (I wonder if the ability to emit IL and define new types dynamically will have applications in artificial intelligence, too.) Chapter 4 demonstrates how to emit IL at runtime.

A program that ships with .NET is the `ildasm.exe` utility, whose name derives from what the tool does: `ildasm` is an IL disassembler. This utility allows you to open an assembly—a compiled .NET application—and look at the IL code written by the compiler. Figure 1.3 (page 12) shows the `box` instruction automatically emitted by the compiler.

A good learning aid is to discover or explore what our precursors have done or are doing. You can find the `ildasm` utility in the `C:\Program Files\Microsoft Visual Studio .NET\FrameworkSDK\Bin\` folder of the Visual Studio .NET application.

Summary

Chapter 1 provided you with an object-oriented overview. By now you know that many things are familiar in .NET because they are similar to VB6, and you likely have discovered those things that trip you up.

The purpose of this book is to go beyond teaching you basic syntax, to demonstrating the most advanced features of the VB .NET. In that regard it is important to realize that everything about .NET is a class. When you have mastered object-oriented concepts, what is left is to discover the available classes and what problems they solve.

Because VB .NET diverges from VB6 regarding classes and interfaces, Chapter 2 explores this divergence. Understanding these vital differences is critical in optimizing your experience with VB .NET.

Inheritance and Interfaces

*If you cannot be strong and you cannot be weak
then you will be defeated.*

—The Art of War, *Sun Tzu*

Introduction

Inheritance, aggregation, and interfaces are three of your strongest allies in object-oriented programming. What has been missing from Visual Basic until now is inheritance. Visual Basic supported aggregation and interfaces; Visual Basic .NET supports inheritance, aggregation, and interfaces.

With the incorporation of inheritance into VB .NET some new capabilities are now available. Also, the way interfaces are used has changed. Chapter 2 demonstrates how to make the most of inheritance, aggregation, and interfaces.

Inheriting Classes

Inheritance is a big subject. VB .NET supports single inheritance. This means that a new class can inherit an existing class. This can happen over and over again, layering in new capabilities and functionality every time a new class is created from an existing class. In fact, the entire Common Language Runtime (CLR) inherits from at least one other class, the `Object` class.

We need to discuss several things so you can get the greatest benefit from inheritance. A good place to start is terminology. Several terms are associated with inheritance, and using them in discourse promotes concise communication. Unfortunately several terms are synonyms, which lends to confusion. Let's take a minute to review the terminology associated with inheritance relationships; then we'll proceed from there.

Inheritance Terminology

As mentioned above, talking about inheritance can be a little confusing because there are several synonyms. However, using appropriate synonyms adds richness to our discussion as long as we are not introducing unnecessary confusion.

When referring to a class relative to the class it inherits from, it is acceptable to use any of the following terms: *subclass*, *child class*, or *derived class*. When referring to a class inherited from, any of the following terms are acceptable: *superclass*, *parent class*, or *base class*. These terms are used in synonymous pairs. Generally we pair parent and child, superclass and subclass, and base class and derived class. Probably the easiest relationship to picture is that of parent and child. You are the child of your mother and father, either of whom is your parent. If you have children, relative to your child you are the parent.

I could stick to one pair of terms, perhaps parent and child, but this is an advanced book and it is unlikely that you will encounter only one set of terms in the great wide world. Thus I will use the terms that sound best in a particular context, just as you would expect anyone else you are communicating with to do.

Occasionally you will hear terms such as *grandparent* or *sibling* (seldom *uncle* or *second cousin*). The meanings of these terms are the same as their understood meanings when it comes to personal relationships. A grandparent is the parent of a class's parent. A sibling is a class that has the same parent as another class. *Grandparent* and *sibling* are used less frequently than *parent* and *child*, but you should understand their meanings.

Using a variety of terms adds richness and precision to communication. The terms mentioned here weren't introduced to add confusion; rather, they were added to eliminate confusion. Probably the first person who used *parent* and *child* did so because *superclass* and *subclass* did not seem clear to the audience. Reasonable synonyms were picked by the speaker. By reading this book you will learn to use inheritance terms by encountering them in context. If you are still confused about terminology, post a sticky note on your computer and where you will see it while reading until you finish the book. By then you will have mastered the verbiage.

The `Inherits` Statement

There are two kinds of inheritance in VB .NET: inheritance from classes and inheritance from interfaces. Whether you are inheriting a class or an interface, you apply the idiom the same way. Add a statement using the keyword `Inherits` followed by the name of the class or interface you want to inherit from.

In this section we focus on class inheritance and its related implications. Refer to the Inheriting Interfaces section later in this chapter for information on inheriting from interfaces.

Every time you add a Windows Form to a Windows application you are inheriting from the `System.Windows.Forms.Form` class. Look at the code behind a Windows Form. The `Inherits` statement in a Windows Form is identical to how you will indicate inheritance for any class. The only thing that will change is the name of the thing you are inheriting from. Here is an excerpt from a Windows Form indicating inheritance.

```
Public Class Form1
   Inherits System.Windows.Forms.Form
```

As shown, the inheritance statement immediately follows the class header (`Public Class Form1`). The class header begins a class definition and, in this case, indicates we are talking about a public class named `Form1`. (The keyword `Public` is an access modifier. Refer to the Access Modifiers section in this chapter for more information.) The `Inherits` statement in the excerpt above uses the fully qualified namespace path and the class. All you have to specify in the `Inherits` statement is the class. Assuming the `System.Windows.Forms` namespace is imported, the `Inherits` statement could be rewritten as follows:

```
Inherits Form
```

When a derived class is created, it inherits all the members of the base class. There is an exact one-to-one mapping between the members in a base class and those in a derived class until you add new members to the derived class. And that is precisely a reason for creating a derived class: to add new members to an existing class.

Other reasons for deriving a new class—remember, when I say *derive* think *inherit from*—are to extend or change the behavior of an existing base class. The basic idea is that you need a class to fulfill a need. If you are fortunate you will discover a class that is pretty close to what you want. You can then inherit from this class and add new members or modify existing members to make the new class precisely what you need. (In Chapter 1 we discussed how to add members to a class.)

Let's take a moment to go over the `NotInheritable` modifier; then we will explore how to extend existing members.

The `NotInheritable` Modifier

You can use the `NotInheritable` modifier to terminate the branch of an inheritance hierarchy. Modifiers like `NotInheritable` are used in the class header. Suppose we have a derived shape class for an ellipse and derived from that class a circle. If we want to terminate inheritance at the `Circle` class, we could define the class header with the `NotInheritable` modifier.

```
Public Class NotInheritable Circle
```

All classes are inheritable unless marked with the `NotInheritable` modifier.

Abstract Classes

The opposite of `NotInheritable` classes are classes that must be inherited from before they can be used. In the object-oriented vernacular, such classes are referred to as *abstract classes*.

Abstract classes are closely related to interfaces. Abstract classes have members that must be implemented just like interfaces. The biggest difference between abstract classes and interfaces is that you can inherit some implementation from abstract classes but interfaces contain no implementation. Use abstract classes when derivatives are part of the same family, such as the shape, ellipse, and circle example in the previous section. Use interfaces when the capabilities span disparate kinds of objects.

You indicate that a class is an abstract class by adding the `MustInherit` modifier. (Clearly `MustInherit` and `NotInheritable` are mutually exclusive.) Listing 2.1 shows the `Shape` class mentioned earlier implemented as an abstract class.

Listing 2.1 Defining an Abstract Class by Using the `MustInherit` Modifier

```
Public MustInherit Class Shape
  Private FRect As System.Drawing.Rectangle

  Public Sub New()

  End Sub

  Public Sub New(ByVal Rect As System.Drawing.Rectangle)
    FRect = Rect
```

```
End Sub

Public MustOverride Sub Draw(ByVal G As Graphics)

Protected Overridable Function GetRect() As System.Drawing.Rectangle
   Return FRect
End Function

End Class
```

The first line of text in the listing indicates that Shape is an abstract class. We can provide some implementation, but Visual Basic .NET does not allow us to create an instance of the Shape class. This is reasonable too. Consider the problem of implementing the Draw method; without knowing what kind of shape we are talking about, how would we render the shape?

NOTE: As an advanced developer you know that you could implement the Shape class and use an enumeration to determine what kind of shape to draw. For example, based on a ShapeType property you could write condition logic in the Draw method to render the correct kind of shape. Interestingly enough, this is precisely the kind of scenario in which you would want to use derivative classes and a polymorphic drawing behavior to eliminate the conditional code.

Using polymorphism is generally considered a best practice, but there is no enforcement agency. Our discussion illustrates what is so challenging about writing software; the decision-making process is highly subjective.

The MustOverride Modifier

Abstract classes (those defined with the MustInherit modifier) are expected to have at least one abstract member. Abstract members are those that must be overridden in a derived class.

Listing 2.1 defines the Draw method as an abstract method. This is clear by the presence of the MustOverride modifier in the subroutine header and the absence of a method body.

Every derivative class will have to provide an implementation of the Draw method or they themselves will be abstract. If a derivative class does not implement abstract methods, you must add the MustInherit modifier to the class header.

The *Overridable* Modifier

If you want to allow a consumer to extend the behavior of a method, you need to create a virtual method. Virtual methods in Visual Basic .NET are designated as such by adding the `Overridable` modifier to the procedure header.

The `GetRect` method in Listing 2.1 is a virtual method. Derivative classes can extend the behavior of `Shape.GetRect` by implementing a new version of `GetRect` and using the `Overrides` modifier. (See the Overriding Methods and Properties subsection for examples and more discussion.)

The *NotOverridable* Modifier

If you want to terminate a particular method so that derivative classes do not further extend the behavior of that method, add the `NotOverridable` modifier to the procedure header.

Assume we define a class derived from `Shape` in Listing 2.1. We could override the `GetRect` method and add the `NotOverridable` modifier to terminate further extension, as shown below.

```
Protected NotOverridable Overrides Function GetRect()
As System.Drawing.Rectangle
```

Children containing the preceding method would not be able to further customize the `GetRect` method.

Overriding Methods and Properties

As implied in the previous section, extending or replacing the behavior of methods and properties in a derived class is referred to as *overriding*. Use the `Overrides` modifier to indicate you are extending the behavior of a virtual member in a base class. Overridden members can invoke the method in the parent class to provide part of the solution or to completely replace the behavior in the parent class.

If the parent class member you are overriding is a virtual method—that is, it is declared with the `MustOverride` modifier—you cannot call the parent class's version of the method. If the parent method is declared with the `Overridable` modifier, in the derived version you can invoke the parent method or not, as you choose. Listing 2.2 demonstrates a `Rectangle` class derived from `Shape`.

Listing 2.2 Implementing a `Rectangle` Class Derived from the `Shape` Abstract Class

```
Public Class Rectangle
  Inherits Shape

  Public Sub New(ByVal Rect As System.Drawing.Rectangle)
    MyBase.New(Rect)
  End Sub

  Public Overrides Sub Draw(ByVal G As Graphics)
    G.DrawRectangle(Pens.Red, GetRect())
  End Sub
End Class
```

The `Draw` method in Listing 2.2 overrides the abstract method used in the `Shape` class. Since the `Draw` method in Listing 2.1 is purely abstract, we cannot call `Draw` in Listing 2.1.

Calling Base Class Methods

Sometimes you will want to invoke the behavior in a base class. For example, when you overload a `Sub New` constructor, you need to call the base class constructor before doing anything else in the derived class constructor.

The reserved keyword `MyBase` is used to refer to members in a base class. Listing 2.2 demonstrates calling the `Sub New` constructor in the `Shape` base class. The relevant portion is extracted below.

```
Public Sub New(ByVal Rect As System.Drawing.Rectangle)
  MyBase.New(Rect)
End Sub
```

TIP: The `MyBase` keyword cannot be used to get around encapsulation rules. For instance, `MyBase` will not allow you to interact with private members in a base class.

Any time you want to refer to an inherited member, prefix the reference with the `MyBase` keyword and the member-of operator. It goes without saying that this applies to all inherited base members.

Comparing the *Me* and *MyClass* Keywords

The keyword Me is an object that is an internal reference to self. (Me has the same function as this in C++ and C# and self in Delphi.) You can use the Me reference to self so that the Integrated Development Environment (IDE) will display the Intellisense list of members for an object, or you can use it to clarify intent. For example, if a method has an argument whose name is identical to that of a field, you can use Me to clarify which is the field and which is the argument.

Another keyword, MyClass, does not represent an object but is used internally to clarify intent. When you use MyClass with the member-of dot operator (.), you are indicating that you want to access the member of the containing class. MyClass keeps member access from working in a polymorphic way. MyClass causes method access to be treated as if that member were implemented with the NotOverridable modifier. Listing 2.3 helps illustrate the differences between Me and MyClass.

Listing 2.3 Using the Me and MyClass Keywords

```
1:   Imports System.Drawing.Drawing2D
2:
3:   Public Class Form1
4:       Inherits System.Windows.Forms.Form
5:
6:   [ Windows Form Designer generated code ]
7:
8:     Private Sub Button1_Click(ByVal sender As System.Object, _
9:       ByVal e As System.EventArgs) Handles Button1.Click
10:       Refresh()
11:       Dim P As Polygon = New Polygon()
12:       P.Draw(CreateGraphics)
13:     End Sub
14:
15:     Private Sub Button2_Click(ByVal sender As System.Object, _
16:       ByVal e As System.EventArgs) Handles Button2.Click
17:       Refresh()
18:       Dim P As ChildPolygon = New ChildPolygon()
19:       P.Draw(CreateGraphics)
20:     End Sub
21: End Class
22:
23: Public Class Polygon
24:
```

```
25:    Public Overridable Function GetPoints() As PointF()
26:
27:       Dim Path As New GraphicsPath()
28:       Path.AddString("Parent", New FontFamily("Arial"), _
29:          0, 20, New Point(10, 10), New StringFormat())
30:
31:       Return Path.PathPoints
32:
33:    End Function
34:
35:    Public Overridable Sub Draw(ByVal G As Graphics)
36:       G.DrawPolygon(Pens.Blue, GetPoints())
37:    End Sub
38:
39: End Class
40:
41: Public Class ChildPolygon
42:    Inherits Polygon
43:
44:    Public Overrides Function GetPoints() As PointF()
45:       Dim Path As New GraphicsPath()
46:       Path.AddString("Child", New FontFamily("Arial"), _
47:          0, 20, New Point(10, 10), New StringFormat())
48:
49:       Return Path.PathPoints
50:    End Function
51:
52: End Class
```

Listing 2.3 contains the code from the form in `MyClassDemo.sln`. The code contains three classes. The first class is the `Form` class; the remaining two classes are a parent and child class combination that draws a polygon based on a Bézier curve. The first 22 lines define the form and contain two button-click event handlers. `Button1` instantiates the `Polygon` class and invokes the `Draw` method. `Button2` instantiates the `ChildPolygon` class and invokes `Draw` too. In this discussion we will focus on lines 35 through 37 in the `Polygon` class, specifically line 36 and how it behaves if we use `MyClass` or `Me`.

TIP: Pierre Bézier invented Bézier curves for the automotive industry. Bézier curves are drawn by connecting points and can yield very complex curves.

NOTE: Listing 2.3 demonstrates some extra tidbits that will be helpful for you to know. Line 6 represents code that has been compressed by a `Region` directive. The `Region` directive supports custom code outlining, which is a good organization tool.

A second useful point is that modules no longer define the boundaries of types in VB .NET. As you can see in the listing, three classes are defined in the same module. The class header and `End Class` statement explicitly define the boundaries of a class.

Line 36 invokes the `Graphics.DrawPolygon` method. More importantly, it calls the `GetPoints` method. `GetPoints` is defined in the `Polygon` and `ChildPolygon` classes as a virtual method. Whenever we invoke a method internally, it is the same as if we prefixed that method with `Me`. For example, calling `GetPoints` on line 36 is exactly the same as calling `Me.GetPoints`.

When we invoke `Me.GetPoints`—implicitly, on line 36—we are instructing the method to be invoked polymorphically. That is, we are expecting `GetPoints` to be called based on the type of the object `Me`. When `Me` is a `Polygon` object, `Polygon.GetPoints` is called. When `Me` is a `ChildPolygon` object, `ChildPolygon.GetPoints` is called. As a result, `Button1` draws the Bézier curve defined by the string `"Parent"` and `Button2` draws the curve described by the string `"Child"`. Normally this is what you want: polymorphic behavior controlled by the actual type of the object.

Sometimes you will want to controvert polymorphic behavior. If in line 36 we prefix `GetPoints` with `MyClass`, then because the `MyClass` keyword resides in the `Polygon` class, we would always draw the curve described by the `GetPoints` method in the `Polygon` class. That is, changing `GetPoints` in line 36 to `MyClass.GetPoints` would mean that we would always display the curve described by the text `"Parent"` regardless of the type of the object invoking the `Draw` method.

Most of the time you will want the default polymorphic behavior described earlier. Occasionally you may want to supplant the default behavior and coerce a class to behave in a nonpolymorphic way; however, this is pretty rare.

Replacing Methods and Properties

Sometimes you will want to stifle polymorphic behavior or use a name in a base class a new way in a derived class. This is referred to as *shadowing* and is accomplished by using the `Shadows` modifier.

You can add the Shadows modifier to any member of a derived class to hide a member with the same name in a parent class. The member types of the parent and child do not have to be the same. Listing 2.4 demonstrates how to use the Shadows modifier and provides an example of an instance when you might employ Shadows.

Listing 2.4 Using the Shadows Keyword to Reintroduce a Name in a Parent Class

```
1:   Public Class Form1
2:       Inherits System.Windows.Forms.Form
3:
4:   [ Windows Form Designer generated code ]
5:
6:   Private Sub Button1_Click(ByVal sender As System.Object, _
7:     ByVal e As System.EventArgs) Handles Button1.Click
8:     Dim N As New NonShadowed()
9:     N.Number = Convert.ToInt32(TextBox1.Text)
10:  End Sub
11:
12:  Private Sub Button2_Click(ByVal sender As System.Object, _
13:    ByVal e As System.EventArgs) Handles Button2.Click
14:    Dim S As New Shadowed()
15:    S.Number = Convert.ToInt32(TextBox2.Text)
16:  End Sub
17: End Class
18:
19: Public Class NonShadowed
20:    Public Number As Integer
21: End Class
22:
23: Public Class Shadowed
24:    Inherits NonShadowed
25:
26:    Private Sub Check(ByVal Value As Integer)
27:      Const Mask = "{0} is not within the range 1 to 10"
28:
29:      If (Value < 1) Or (Value > 10) Then
30:        Throw (New Exception(String.Format(Mask, Value)))
31:      End If
32:    End Sub
33:
34:    Public Shadows Property Number() As Integer
35:    Get
```

```
36:      Return MyBase.Number
37:    End Get
38:
39:    Set(ByVal Value As Integer)
40:      Check(Value)
41:      MyBase.Number = Value
42:    End Set
43:    End Property
44:
45: End Class
```

Suppose you have a class that contains a public field. Further suppose you can't or don't want to change the existing class but want to add some sanity checking on the field; perhaps you want to constrain the possible values of the field. Listing 2.4 contrives such a scenario.

Listing 2.4 contains a form with two `TextBox` and two `Button` controls. The first `TextBox` and `Button` pair assigns an integer value to a public field `Number` in the `NonShadowed` class. The second `TextBox` and `Button` pair demonstrates a new class that shadows `Number` and reintroduces `Number` as a property. By making `Number` a property we can add range checking.

Lines 1 through 17 define the `Form` class with code generated by the Form Designer represented on line 4. Lines 19 through 21 represent a class with a public `Integer` field, and lines 23 through 45 represent a class derived from the `NonShadowed` class that shadows the `Number` member. Line 34 demonstrates the `Shadows` modifier and the new property introduces range checking. If the consumer assigns a number that is not between 1 and 10 (inclusive), an exception is thrown (lines 26 through 32).

Overloading the Sub New Constructor

`Sub New` is a Visual Basic .NET constructor. When you introduce additional constructors in the same class, overloading is implicit. When you introduce additional constructors in derived classes, overriding is implicit. Thus you cannot use the `Overloads`, `Overridable`, and `Overrides` modifiers on `Sub New`.

If you do not define a parameterless constructor for your classes, a default constructor is created for you at runtime. If you need to invoke a constructor on a base class, call `MyBase.New`, passing to the subclass's constructor any parameters it requires. Default parameterless constructors are invoked on subclasses automatically; thus you only need invoke an inherited constructor if you need to pass arguments to that subclass. Listing 2.2 (page 37) demonstrates an example of calling an inherited, parameter-ized constructor.

Access Modifiers

VB .NET uses an explicit grammar to describe relationships that can be inferred. For example, the `Overridable` and `Overrides` modifiers explicitly confer a virtual relationship. This is grammatical handicapping. Because it was anticipated that concepts like virtual methods might be confusing to VB developers, an explicit syntax was devised for VB .NET. Other languages like C++ and C# do not use an explicit syntax; instead, they rely on inference.

Thus far we have not fully discussed the most important modifiers, the ones that support information hiding. Information hiding is the notion of conceptually hiding information to alleviate the burden of class consumers by reducing the number of members a class consumer must become familiar with.

TIP: By keeping the number of public members of a class to just a few, your classes will be easier to use.

NOTE: Information hiding supports ease of use by allowing you to expose only the methods, properties, and events essential for using your classes. The idea that classes will expose only a few key behaviors suggests that you will have a larger number of classes than you would if your classes exposed dozens of public members. This is correct and for good reason.

Singular, short methods are easier to reuse. Classes with a few key public members are easier to use. And since classes are the entities we use to orchestrate new behaviors, it is better to have singular methods and classes with a small number of public members, even if that requires a greater number of classes.

Systems that have more complex members and few classes will likely be more fragile and less extensible than systems with singular methods and a greater number of classes with few public members. The physical analogy that supports this idea is the notion of a band versus an orchestra: It is easier to orchestrate very complex music with a large number of specialized instruments and musicians than it is with a few talented musicians and their instruments.

When you are producing a class, you must concern yourself with every aspect of the class. When you are consuming a class, you need concern yourself only with the public members and the protected members if you are deriving a new class. This is information hiding.

As mentioned in Chapter 1, five modifiers support information hiding. The following bulleted list briefly describes these modifiers.

- `Public` denotes members that are accessible by both consumers and producers, that is, everybody.
- `Protected` denotes members that are accessible by the producer and by consumers who are generalizing. Generalizing occurs when you are deriving or inheriting from an existing class. (You are likely to encounter the word *generalize* when you are talking about inheritance in general or when referring to Unified Modeling Language [UML] models.)
- `Friend` denotes members that are accessible within the same assembly.
- `Protected Friend` denotes a combination of the `Friend` and `Protected` modifiers.
- `Private` denotes members that are accessible to the producer only. Private members may be accessed only internally in the class in which they are defined.

The question becomes a subjective one. How do you determine which modifier to use? Of course, you could make everything public, but you would be missing out on one of the key tenets of object-oriented programming, information hiding. You could make everything private, but then no one would be able to use your classes. Clearly the answer lies somewhere in between.

All that anyone can tell you are some basic guidelines. This is one of the things that makes programming (especially object-oriented programming) tough. Object-oriented programming requires a lot of subjective good taste, and taste is, well, a matter of taste.

Below I share with you a few basic rules I apply.

- Keep public interfaces small, preferably to about a half-dozen public members.
- Favor many classes with simple interfaces to classes with monolithic, do-all methods.
- Use as many private methods as you want to support the public behavior; having many singular methods are significantly preferable to having a few monolithic methods. (This latter statement is critical, no matter what anyone else tells you.)

- If something feels wrong after you have learned more about the system's needs, change it.
- Use the `Protected` and `Overridable` modifiers if you think a consumer may want to extend the behavior. (I have read a few recommendations that suggest you should make all methods protected and virtual because you never know what generalizers will want to reuse, but this is probably overkill and will make your program's internal representation bigger and slower.)

Methods are the things we use to create new behaviors. The more methods we have, the more ways we can orchestrate those methods. Classes are the entities we use to describe a system. The more classes we have, the more flexibility we have in describing the system. If you are going to make a mistake, err on the side of a few short public methods with many protected and private methods and many classes. Monolithic methods and monolithic procedures are often signs of a system that will not be robust or extensible.

Inheritance versus Aggregation

When you derive a new class from an existing base class (that is, when you inherit), you get a copy of the members of the base class. We refer to this as an *is-a* relationship, as in "A Jeep is a car."

When a class contains another object, this is referred to as *containment* or *aggregation*. However, if you define members in the containing class that are implemented in terms of the contained class, you can make the containing class look a bit like and behave like the contained class. The aggregation relationship is referred to as a *has-a* relationship.

This promotion of members in a contained object is referred to in .NET vernacular as *surfacing constituent object members*. Technically, the aggregate can perform some of the same operations as a derived class but will not pass the *is-a* test. To perform type checking in Visual Basic .NET, use the `TypeOf` and `Is` operators. For example, if you want to determine the type of the `sender` argument passed to an event handler, you could write the following code.

```
If(TypeOf sender Is Button) Then
```

Choose inheritance when you want a derived type to be the same basic type as its parent and have the same members as the parent. Choose aggregation when you are defining a whole–part relationship; that is, the contained object is a part of the object that contains it. Also choose aggregation if you want to refine the interface of the contained object, for example, when a class has too many features or public members inappropriate for your needs. Wrap the existing class in a new class and surface only those constituent members that satisfy your new need.

The Adapter Pattern

Wrapping a class inside another class to change the contained class's interface is referred to as the *Adapter pattern* [Gamma et al. 1995]. Patterns reflect the names for problems, the solutions to those problems, and the consequences of applying the pattern. For example, when you need to change the interface of a class to get it to work with other classes in a system, this is the Adapter pattern too. Patterns are important because they solve challenging problems in a reliable way and prevent reinventing the wheel.

The study of patterns is beyond the scope of this book, but when I use a particular pattern to solve a problem I will indicate the name of the pattern. You can look up the pattern in a book on patterns, like the "Gang of Four" book referenced in the preceding paragraph, to explore the problem, solution, and consequences of that pattern.

The Adapter pattern generally uses multiple inheritance [Gamma et al. 1995]. Visual Basic .NET does not support multiple inheritance, but it does support single inheritance and aggregation; hence we can achieve the aims of using the Adapter pattern by combining inheritance and aggregation.

To demonstrate, let's take the shape classes defined earlier in this chapter and use an Adapter pattern, specifically a `UserControl` object, to make our shape classes work with a Windows Form.

Creating a `UserControl` Shape

A `UserControl` object is a container control derived from the `Control` class. `UserControl` objects are most often used to create business object controls; generally, `UserControl` objects contain many constituent controls to create a reusable piece of a solution.

For our purposes we are using a `UserControl` because it contains a drawing surface. (We need the drawing surface so we have something on which to render our shapes.) Listing 2.5 implements an enumeration and a `UserControl`. Based on the shape type represented by the enumeration, the `UserControl` will render a specific shape on the drawing surface. The complete solution is contained in `Adapter.sln`.

Listing 2.5 Creating a `UserControl` Object to Adapt Shape Classes to Work with a Windows Form

```
1:   Public Enum ShapeType
2:      Ellipse
3:      Rectangle
4:      Circle
5:      FilledCircle
6:   End Enum
7:
8:   Public Class ShapeControl
9:      Inherits System.Windows.Forms.UserControl
10:
11: #Region " Windows Form Designer generated code "
12:
13:     Public Sub New()
14:         MyBase.New()
15:
16:         'This call is required by the Windows Form Designer.
17:         InitializeComponent()
18:
19:         Me.SetStyle(ControlStyles.SupportsTransparentBackColor, True)
20:         BackColor = Color.Transparent
21:         ShapeType = ShapeType.Circle
22:
23:     End Sub
24:
25:     [Windows Form Designer generated code]
26:
27: #End Region
28:
29:    Private FShapeType As ShapeType
30:    Private FShape As Shape = Nothing
31:
32:    Public Property ShapeType() As ShapeType
33:    Get
34:      Return FShapeType
35:    End Get
36:    Set(ByVal Value As ShapeType)
37:      If (Value = FShapeType) Then Return
38:      FShapeType = Value
39:      Changed()
40:    End Set
41:    End Property
```

```
42:
43:    Private Function GetRect() As System.Drawing.Rectangle
44:      Return New System.Drawing.Rectangle(0, 0, Width - 1, Height - 1)
45:    End Function
46:
47:    Protected Sub Changed()
48:      FShape = New Shape() {New Ellipse(GetRect()), _
49:        New Rectangle(GetRect()), New Circle(GetRect()), _
50:        New FilledCircle(GetRect())}(FShapeType)
51:
52:      Invalidate()
53:    End Sub
54:
55:    Protected Overrides Sub OnPaint(ByVal e As PaintEventArgs)
56:      MyBase.OnPaint(e)
57:      If (FShape Is Nothing) Then Exit Sub
58:      FShape.Draw(e.Graphics)
59:    End Sub
60:
61:    Protected Overrides Sub OnResize(ByVal e As System.EventArgs)
62:      MyBase.OnResize(e)
63:      Changed()
64:    End Sub
65: End Class
```

The constructor on lines 13 to 23 sets the control style to support a transparent background; this will make the shape look like it is on the form rather than on the UserControl. The constructor also sets the default shape to be a circle and the background color to Color.Transparent. The enumeration on lines 1 to 6 support the various shape types.

Lines 32 to 41 define a ShapeType property. When a consumer changes the ShapeType property, the Shape object is created and the UserControl is invalidated, causing the shape to be updated. Lines 43 to 53 use an array and the enumerator to determine which shape object to create. The array is an array of shapes. Each element of the array is created dynamically and a specific shape is returned when the ShapeType property is used to index the array. (We could have used a Select Case statement to get the same result.)

The overridden OnPaint and OnResize methods ensure that the shape is painted when the UserControl is repainted or resized.

Defining Interfaces

Interfaces define what is referred to as a *contract*. Literally, an interface is a type that contains method, property, or event headers only, with no implementations. Interfaces can be inherited, which is a way of extending the contract, and interfaces can be implemented.

Interfaces themselves are never created, nor are they ever fleshed out and provided with an implementation. When a Visual Basic .NET class accepts an interface contract, the class must implement every member defined in the interface. This is the crux of the contractual obligation.

Basic Guidelines

Some basic guidelines for defining interfaces exist to support the expectations consumers will have when they use your interfaces. Some of these guidelines are enforced by the interface idiom, and consequently you have to follow them. Other guidelines are suggestions that consumers will expect you to adhere to.

- Interfaces define method, property, or event signatures only and contain no implementations.
- Interfaces can have any access—that is, they can use any access modifier. The members of an interface are always public and cannot have any access modifiers.
- Interfaces can be nested.
- Interfaces can be implemented as shared, abstract, or virtual members.
- No security attributes may be attached to interface members.
- Interfaces are understood to be invariant; once you release an interface for consumption, you should never change that interface. Always create a new interface to extend an existing interface.
- Like classes, it is better to define a few closely related members in an interface. A large number of members would make the interface unwieldy and difficult to use. This is referred to as *factoring* interfaces.
- Use an `I` prefix to distinguish an interface from a class, and use Pascal-casing for your interfaces. (In Pascal-casing, the first letter in each word in the name is capitalized, for example, `IMyInterface`.)
- You cannot create an instance of an interface.

By applying all of these guidelines, you can define interfaces and examine some existing interfaces. Interfaces are not that hard to define or understand in practice. (Refer to the Comparing Abstract Classes to Interfaces section near the end of this chapter for a comparative discussion on inheriting abstract classes versus implementing interfaces.)

Defining an Interface

Interfaces are defined in a block statement with a header. Inside the interface are the method, property, and event signatures you deem essential to your interface. You have to have at least one member in an interface, but you are not required to use all these elements. Here is an example that demonstrates the grammatical aspects of interfaces.

```
Public Interface IFoo
   Sub Foo()
End Interface
```

Suppose we want to know when a class supports GDI+ drawing. We could define an interface `IDrawable` that contains one method, `Draw`.

```
Public Interface IDrawable
   Sub Draw(ByVal G As Graphics)
End Interface
```

Any class that implements the `IDrawable` interface would have to provide an implementation of the `Draw` method. From the signature—it takes a `Graphics` object—we can assume that a class implementing `IDrawable` would be able to create a graphical representation on a drawing surface represented by the `Graphics` object.

NOTE: The `IEnumerator` and `IEnumerable` interfaces conspire to support the Iterator pattern [Gamma et al. 1995]. The Iterator pattern solves the problem of devising a common means of iterating over the elements in a group using a consistent interface.

`IEnumerator` defines the `MoveNext` and `Reset` methods and the `Current` property. Look up `IEnumerator` and `IEnumerable` in the Visual Studio .NET help documentation for more information.

Interfaces are used all over the Common Language Runtime. For example, arrays and collections implement `IEnumerable`, which defines one member, `GetEnumerator`. `GetEnumerator` returns an object that implements `IEnumerator`. In turn, `IEnumerator` defines a common way of iterating over items in a list, collection, or array.

Implementing Interfaces

The most common operation with interfaces that you will want to perform is implementation. You indicate that you want to implement an interface similar to the way you did so in VB6. The way to implement the members of an interface has changed. Let's take a look at implementing the `IDrawable` interface (see Listing 2.6). A synopsis follows the listing.

Listing 2.6 Implementing the `IDrawable` Interface

```
1:   Imports System.Drawing
2:
3:   Public Class Form1
4:       Inherits System.Windows.Forms.Form
5:
6:   [ Windows Form Designer generated code ]
7:
8:   Private Sub Draw(ByVal DrawableObject As IDrawable)
9:       DrawableObject.Draw(CreateGraphics)
10:  End Sub
11:
12:  Private Sub Button1_Click(ByVal sender As System.Object, _
13:    ByVal e As System.EventArgs) Handles Button1.Click
14:
15:  Dim S As New GraphicString()
16:  S.Text = "Visual Basic .NET Power Coding"
17:  S.Location = New PointF(10, 150)
18:  Draw(S)
19:
20:  Dim B As New GraphicButton()
21:  B.Location = New Point(10, 10)
22:  B.Size = New Size(75, 50)
23:  Draw(B)
```

```
24:
25:    End Sub
26: End Class
27:
28: Public Interface IDrawable
29:    Sub Draw(ByVal G As Graphics)
30: End Interface
31:
32: Public Class GraphicString
33:
34:    Implements IDrawable
35:    Private FText As String
36:    Private FLocation As PointF
37:
38:    Public Property Text() As String
39:      Get
40:        Return FText
41:      End Get
42:      Set(ByVal Value As String)
43:        FText = Value
44:      End Set
45:    End Property
46:
47:    Public Property Location() As PointF
48:    Get
49:      Return FLocation
50:    End Get
51:    Set(ByVal Value As PointF)
52:      FLocation = Value
53:    End Set
54:    End Property
55:
56:    Public Sub Draw(ByVal G As Graphics) _
57:      Implements IDrawable.Draw
58:
59:      G.DrawString(FText, New Font("Courier", 20), _
60:        Brushes.Blue, FLocation)
61:
62:    End Sub
63:
64: End Class
65:
66: Public Class GraphicButton
67:    Implements IDrawable
```

```
68:
69:    Private FLocation As Point
70:    Private FSize As Size
71:
72:    Public Property Location() As Point
73:    Get
74:       Return FLocation
75:    End Get
76:    Set(ByVal Value As Point)
77:       FLocation = Value
78:    End Set
79:    End Property
80:
81:    Public Property Size() As Size
82:    Get
83:       Return FSize
84:    End Get
85:    Set(ByVal Value As Size)
86:       FSize = Value
87:    End Set
88:    End Property
89:
90:    Public Sub Draw(ByVal G As Graphics) _
91:       Implements IDrawable.Draw
92:
93:      ControlPaint.DrawButton(G, New Rectangle(FLocation, FSize), _
94:        ButtonState.Normal)
95:
96:    End Sub
97: End Class
```

Lines 1 through 26 implement the Form1 class. When Button1 is clicked, one instance each of GraphicButton and GraphicString are created. Each of these objects implements IDrawable; as a result, they can be passed to a method that accepts any object that implements IDrawable (see lines 8 through 10).

Lines 28 through 30 define the IDrawable interface. The contract stipulates that any class implementing this interface must define one method, Draw, which is defined to take a single Graphics object.

Lines 32 through 64 define the GraphicString class, and lines 66 through 97 define the GraphicButton class. Both classes implement IDrawable.

`GraphicString` has `String` and `Point` properties, and `GraphicButton` has `Size` and `Point` properties. `GraphicString` implements `IDrawable.Draw` on lines 56 through 62, and `GraphicButton` implements `IDrawable.Draw` on lines 90 through 96.

The `Implements` statements at the beginning of the `GraphicString` and `GraphicButton` classes indicate that these two classes accept the `IDrawable` contract and will implement `Draw`. The `Implements` clauses in the `Draw` methods in the `GraphicString` and `GraphicButton` classes complete the requirements of the contract. (You indicate that a method is implementing an interface method by adding `Implements` *interface.membername* at the end of the method, where *interface* is the actual name of the interface and *membername* is the name of the member you are implementing. In our example, `Implements IDrawable.Draw` indicates that these methods are implementing the interface method.)

In Visual Basic .NET you can call the interface method directly or through a reference to the interface, as we did in line 9 of Listing 2.6.

Adding Properties to an Interface

You can add properties to interfaces by declaring the property header only. When you implement the interface, you define a property in the class implementing the interface and add an `Implements` clause to the end of the property header. If we want to extend `IDrawable` to include a `Point` property named `Location`, we can use the following code.

```
Public Interface IDrawable
  Sub Draw(ByVal G As Graphics)
  Property Location() As Point
End Interface
```

After we have extended the contract this way, consumers of this version of `IDrawable` would have to implement the `Location` property too. A suitable implementation (by itself; just copy the following code to a class) might appear as demonstrated next.

```
Public Property Location() As Point Implements IDrawable2.Location
  Get
    Return FLocation
  End Get
  Set(ByVal Value As Point)
    FLocation = Value
  End Set
End Property
```

In the revision the `Implements` clause is all we need to make this the implementation of the `Location` property, and `FLocation` is presumed to be a field in the containing class.

Adding Events to an Interface

Extending our theme, we could add an event to the `IDrawable` interface. Perhaps we might like to let a consumer know that the `Draw` method has been invoked. If we add an `OnDraw PaintEventHandler` event, consumers of our interface could raise this event when the `Draw` method is called. The code fragment that follows demonstrates the addition of the `PaintEventHandler` event.

```
Public Interface IDrawable

  Property Location() As Point
  Sub Draw(ByVal G As Graphics)
  Event OnDraw As PaintEventHandler

End Interface
```

The preceding interface adds the event to the interface. The following code could be copied and pasted into a class that implements the `IDrawable` interface. (I have included the revised `Draw` method to demonstrate how the event might be raised.)

```
Public Sub Draw(ByVal G As Graphics) _
  Implements IDrawable.Draw

  G.DrawEllipse(Pens.Red, GetRect())
  DoDraw(G)

End Sub

Public Event OnDraw As PaintEventHandler _
  Implements IDrawable.OnDraw

Private Function GetRect() As Rectangle
  Return New Rectangle(FLocation.X, FLocation.Y, _
    FSize.Width, FSize.Height)
End Function

Private Sub DoDraw(ByVal G As Graphics)
  RaiseEvent OnDraw(Me, New PaintEventArgs(G, GetRect()))
End Sub
```

The Draw method literally performs the Draw operation. (In the example we are drawing an ellipse using GDI+.) Before the Draw operation exits we invoke a DoDraw method. Following convention, DoDraw raises the event for us. The implementation of the OnDraw event follows the Draw method, and GetRect and DoDraw are added for convenience.

The only code we had to add to support the IDrawable contract was code for Draw, Location, and OnDraw. The rest of the code was added for convenience. For example, GetRect was reused to ensure that the boundaries for drawing and drawing from DoDraw are identical.

Inheriting Interfaces

Interfaces are considered invariant. This simply means that after you publish an interface you are not supposed to change it. Suppose we had published the IDrawable interface from the last section and then decided that we wanted to change the interface. The solution to this problem is to use interface inheritance.

To indicate that a new interface is derived from an existing interface, we must use the Inherits statement (similar to deriving a new class). Continuing our example, then, we could define a new interface, IDrawable2, and indicate that it is derived from IDrawable. The code for the new interface would begin as shown below.

```
Public Interface IDrawable2
   Inherits IDrawable
End Interface
```

So far IDrawable2 has the same member as our original IDrawable interface: one method member named Draw. We can now add to IDrawable2 new members identical to the ones we discussed in the latter part of the last section. Here is the completed IDrawable2 interface.

```
Public Interface IDrawable2
   Inherits IDrawable

   Property Size() As Size
   Property Location() As Point
   Event OnDraw As PaintEventHandler

End Interface
```

The contract now states that classes that implement IDrawable2 must provide an implementation for the Draw method, the Size and Location properties, and the OnDraw event. Combining all the elements, Listing 2.7 demonstrates a Shape class that implements the IDrawable2 interface.

Listing 2.7 Implementing the IDrawable2 Interface

```
Public Class Shape
  Implements IDrawable2

  Private FSize As Size
  Private FLocation As Point

  Public Property Size() As Size Implements IDrawable2.Size
  Get
    Return FSize
  End Get
  Set(ByVal Value As Size)
    FSize = Value
  End Set
  End Property

  Public Property Location() As Point Implements IDrawable2.Location
  Get
    Return FLocation
  End Get
  Set(ByVal Value As Point)
    FLocation = Value
  End Set
  End Property

  Public Sub Draw(ByVal G As Graphics) _
    Implements IDrawable2.Draw

    G.DrawEllipse(Pens.Red, GetRect())
    DoDraw(G)

  End Sub

  Public Event OnDraw As PaintEventHandler _
    Implements IDrawable2.OnDraw
```

```
Private Function GetRect() As Rectangle
  Return New Rectangle(FLocation.X, FLocation.Y, _
    FSize.Width, FSize.Height)
End Function

Private Sub DoDraw(ByVal G As Graphics)
  RaiseEvent OnDraw(Me, New PaintEventArgs(G, GetRect()))
End Sub

End Class
```

You have seen all these elements before. Listing 2.7 puts them together in a complete class. You can test the code in the `InterfaceDemo.sln` solution.

Multiple Interface Inheritance

Visual Basic .NET does not support multiple class inheritance, but it does support multiple interface inheritance. If a class inherits from multiple interfaces, the class must implement all the members defined by all the interfaces the class inherits from.

When a class will implement multiple interfaces, indicate each interface in a comma-delimited list in the `Implements` statement.

```
Implements IDrawable2, IFoo
```

If two interfaces declare members with identical signatures, you will need to resolve the implementation in the implementing class. For example, suppose `IDrawable2` and `IFoo` define identical `Draw` methods. You could indicate that a single `Draw` method provides the implementation for both interfaces.

```
Public Sub Draw(ByVal G As Graphics) Implements IDrawable2.Draw,
IFoo.Draw
  ' Code here
End Sub
```

If two or more interfaces inherit from a common base interface and a class implements both derived interfaces, the duplicate members inherited from the common base are treated as if they need to be implemented only one time. Here is a brief example demonstrating how to resolve the conflict.

```
Public Interface IA
   Sub Foo()
End Interface

Public Interface IB
   Inherits IA
End Interface

Public Interface IC
   Inherits IA
   Sub Foo2()
End Interface

Public Class AClass
   Implements IB, IC
   Public Sub Foo() Implements IA.Foo
   End Sub
   Public Sub Foo2() Implements IC.Foo2
   End Sub
End Class
```

Interfaces IB and IC inherit from interface IA. Interface IC introduces Foo2. If a class implements both IB and IC, the consumer would need to implement only IA.Foo and IC.Foo2. The consumer would not and cannot implement IB.Foo and IC.Foo. The conflict is resolved by implementing the conflicting method as it is defined in the base class.

Comparing Abstract Classes to Interfaces

Before interfaces existed, abstract classes were used to solve the same kinds of problems interfaces can now solve. How Microsoft elected to invent interfaces when many programmers already used abstract classes is a conversation I was not privy to.

Interestingly enough, abstract classes and interfaces solve similar but orthogonal problems. Abstract classes allow you to define an interface with or without a partial implementation; interfaces do not allow you to provide any implementation. The fact that abstract methods and interface methods have no implementation is where they are identical. Where interfaces and abstract methods are orthogonal is where you will find abstract methods and interface methods.

Abstract methods span a vertical inheritance tree, and interfaces span horizontally across different kinds of objects. Use abstract methods (that is, `MustOverride` methods) when you are defining behaviors that are shared across classes that have a common ancestry. Use interfaces when you are describing behaviors that span classes that do not share a common ancestry.

For example, a class `Automobile` may describe an abstract method `Start`, but there is no such car called just "automobile." A derived class, `Maserati`, is a kind of car and as such would need to provide an implementation of the method `Start`. `Automobile` is clearly an abstract class, and `Maserati` is a specific subclass. Hence we are referring to abstract methods and inheritance.

Consider an alternate example. The volume on a television can be attenuated by pressing a button on the television or by pressing a button on a remote control device. The television and the remote control do not share a common ancestry. We would not say a remote control is a television or vice versa. Thus the remote control and television share a common interface; perhaps we would refer to this interface as the `IControl` interface. Both the remote control and the television itself would provide a set of controls for attenuating the volume and related state values, like the channel.

Here are some basic guidelines to remember when comparing abstract classes and interfaces.

- Abstract classes may be partially implemented, but interfaces never are.
- Classes support single inheritance; interfaces support multiple inheritance.
- If you inherit from an abstract class, all children are updated when the parent is updated. Interfaces are invariant; once you release an interface you should never modify it.
- If the behavior spans different kinds of objects, use an interface. For similar kinds of objects, use abstract classes.
- Use interfaces to support a little additional functionality, and use abstract classes for large related functionality.

Summary

Visual Basic .NET now supports class inheritance. VB6 supported interface inheritance, and VB .NET still does. Inheritance and implementation of interfaces have changed in subtle, grammatically different ways. However, the biggest change is the new support for class inheritance. When Microsoft says that Visual Basic .NET is a first-class language, one of the things the company is clearly referring to is class inheritance. Inheritance is a very powerful tool that will help us build more powerful applications.

The general guidelines provided in this chapter will help you decide when to use class inheritance and when to implement interfaces, as well as how to choose between using abstract classes and interfaces. This chapter also demonstrated how to create derived classes and use access modifiers to specify abstract classes and methods and how to support encapsulation and information hiding.

Delegates

The time has come, the Walrus said, to talk of many things.
Of Shoes—of ships—of sealing wax—of cabbages and kings.

—Through the Looking Glass, *Lewis Carroll*

Introduction

There are few truly new innovations. Babbage and Turing were describing computers decades ago. Delegates are not completely new either. Delegates are an evolutionary revision to some pretty old concepts. ("Pretty old" is relative. In the computer industry, anything more than a few years old is pretty old.) When you have a good grasp on what is familiar about delegates, you will find it quite an easy task to learn what has evolved.

Very plainly, delegates are events wrapped up in classes. Objects in Windows (or any event-driven operating system) rely on three fundamental concepts: properties, methods, and events. Events support some powerful programming models. Hence it makes perfect sense that the event-handling model in VB .NET needed to evolve—and it has. Events exist and are associated with special classes referred to as delegates.

In this chapter we look at how to declare and raise events and how delegates provide a more robust implementation of the event-handling model.

Implementing Event Handlers

Windows is an event-based, or messaging, operating system. This means that Windows applications communicate by sending messages to controls that have Windows handles, and controls that have Windows handles can forward messages to constituent controls.

NOTE: Event-driven operating systems date back at least to the 1970s, when they were used at Xerox's Palo Alto Research Center (PARC). The evolution of messaging, events, and event handlers was adopted more recently in microcomputer programming languages. (On reflection, I recall using callback functions, an essential precursor to event handlers, in C++ and Turbo Pascal as early as 1992.)

A good book by Freiberger and Swaine [1984], *Fire in the Valley: The Making of the Personal Computer* (later made into the TNT movie *Pirates of Silicon Valley*, 1999), tells one version of the story describing how Windows and Macintosh computers were derived from innovations at Xerox PARC.

A few years ago programmers had to handle raw messages. Later, in an evolutionary step, raw messages were converted to method invocations. The messages are commonly referred to as *events*, and the methods that respond are dubbed *event handlers*.

An event handler is quite literally a method designated to respond to message events. One of the most common tasks you will perform is to associate event handlers with control events and then write code for those handlers. This is very similar to how to we created event handlers in VB6. We'll begin here to find some familiar ground and then proceed by exploring what has been revised.

Using the Form Designer

The easiest way to generate an event handler is to double-click on a control. The Form Designer will generate the event handler designated as the default event. For example, if you double-click on a form, the `Load` event handler will be generated, and focus will be switched to the Code Designer view.

So far this is exactly like VB6. However, there are differences. The signature of the `Load` event handler looks different, and the event handler is wired to the control differently. Listing 3.1 shows a VB .NET form that contains just the `Load` event handler.

Listing 3.1 Code for a VB .NET Form with the Generated `Load` Event Handler

```
1:  Public Class Form1
2:      Inherits System.Windows.Forms.Form
3:
4:  #Region " Windows Form Designer generated code "
5:
6:      Public Sub New()
```

```
 7:     MyBase.New()
 8:
 9:     'This call is required by the Windows Form Designer.
10:     InitializeComponent()
11:
12:     'Add any initialization after the InitializeComponent() call
13:
14:   End Sub
15:
16:   'Form overrides dispose to clean up the component list.
17:   Protected Overloads Overrides Sub Dispose(ByVal disposing As Boolean)
18:     If disposing Then
19:       If Not (components Is Nothing) Then
20:         components.Dispose()
21:       End If
22:     End If
23:     MyBase.Dispose(disposing)
24:   End Sub
25:
26:   'Required by the Windows Form Designer
27:   Private components As System.ComponentModel.IContainer
28:
29:   'NOTE: The following procedure is required by the Windows Form Designer
30:   'It can be modified using the Windows Form Designer.
31:   'Do not modify it using the code editor.
32:   <System.Diagnostics.DebuggerStepThrough()> _
33:   Private Sub InitializeComponent()
34:     '
35:     'Form1
36:     '
37:     Me.AutoScaleBaseSize = New System.Drawing.Size(6, 15)
38:     Me.ClientSize = New System.Drawing.Size(292, 260)
39:     Me.Name = "Form1"
40:     Me.Text = "Form1"
41:
42:   End Sub
43:
44: #End Region
45:
46:   Private Sub Form1_Load(ByVal sender As System.Object, _
47:     ByVal e As System.EventArgs) Handles MyBase.Load
48:
49:   End Sub
50: End Class
```

At first glance this seems like a lot of code. However, if you look at the code in a VB6 .frm file (see Listing 3.2), you'll see that the VB .NET code is not that much longer.

Listing 3.2 Code for a VB6 Form with the Generated Load Event Handler

```
1:  VERSION 5.00
2:  Begin VB.Form Form1
3:     Caption        =    "Form1"
4:     ClientHeight   =    2400
5:     ClientLeft     =    48
6:     ClientTop      =    432
7:     ClientWidth    =    3744
8:     LinkTopic      =    "Form1"
9:     ScaleHeight    =    2400
10:    ScaleWidth     =    3744
11:    StartUpPosition =   3   'Windows Default
12: End
13: Attribute VB_Name = "Form1"
14: Attribute VB_GlobalNameSpace = False
15: Attribute VB_Creatable = False
16: Attribute VB_PredeclaredId = True
17: Attribute VB_Exposed = False
18: Option Explicit
19:
20: Private Sub Form_Load()
21:
22: End Sub
```

NOTE: Here is a VB6 trick I can't help sharing because it illustrates the kind of mischief a curious person can get into. Open a .cls file in VB6 and change the attribute VB_PredeclaredId to True just as it is shown in line 16 in Listing 3.2. Save the .cls file.

The VB6 class represented by the .cls file will be an autocreated class just as forms are in VB6. The attribute VB_PredeclaredId makes this auto-created mechanism work. Attributes have changed significantly in VB .NET, but this technique demonstrates that the notion of attributes has existed for some time. Refer to Chapter 5 for more information on VB .NET attributes.

I digress. Back to the code in Listing 3.1, which explicitly defines a class by using the class header (line 1) and the `End Class` statement (line 50). A constructor appears in lines 6 through 14 and a destructor in lines 17 through 24, and lines 37 through 40 contain form initialization code. Note that all the code from lines 4 to 44 is managed by the Form Designer.

Notice the signature of the `Load` event handler in lines 46 and 47 of Listing 3.1. `Load` has two parameters and a `Handles` clause at the end of the procedure header. The `Handles` clause indicates that this method—`Handles MyBase.Load`—handles the base class's `Load` event. (Refer to the upcoming subsection on the `Handles` clause for more information on this keyword and to the subsection on `EventHandler` for more information on the arguments passed to the `Load` event.)

TIP: Avoid writing code directly in the event handler itself. Implement a well-named method that describes the action to be taken and invoke that event from the handler. This will make your code more readable.

Using the Form Designer is the easiest way to generate event handlers. You already know how to click on controls and add code; we won't elaborate on this point any longer.

Using the Code Editor

The next step familiar to VB6 developers is to generate events in the Code Editor (or Code Designer). The Code Editor has a list of class names at the top left of the editor and a list of method names at the top right. Select a class and a method, and .NET will generate any event handler available for you.

It is important to keep in mind that inheritance is an integral part of VB .NET. If you look at the list of method names for the `Form1` control (see Figure 3.1), you are likely to be disappointed—the list is very short.

There is a reason the list is short. We are looking at the events for `Form1`. `Form1` is derived from `Form`, in which all the events are defined. If you select `Base Class Events` in the list of class names under `Form1`, you will quickly see that the list of method names has increased substantially.

Select `Base Class Events` from the class name list and the `Click` method from the method name list to generate a `Click` event handler. You will quickly see that understanding the impact inheritance has on event name filtering is all you need to know to generate events in the Code Editor.

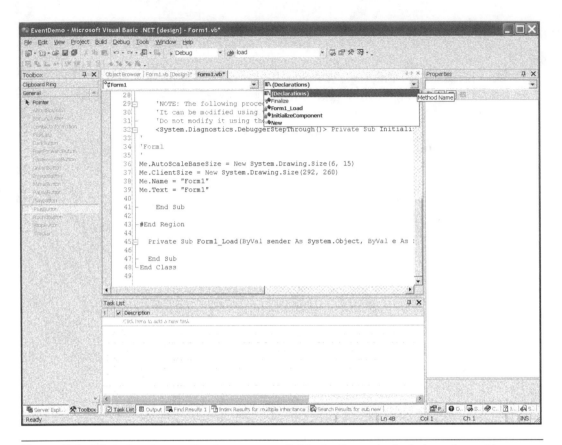

Figure 3.1 A list showing method names available for the selected class (`Form1`).

The Handles Clause

Visual Basic .NET no longer hides the mechanism that wires events to event handlers when those events are generated by the Form Designer or the Code Editor. The mechanism for this is the `Handles` clause.

Because the `Handles` clause is a prominent part of the code, it should be apparent that you can write the code manually to handle events at design time. For instance, if we want the `Form Load` and `Click` handlers to respond in the same way, we can simply add a `MyBase.Click` event to the comma-delimited list of events a particular method handles. Listing 3.3 shows the revision.

Listing 3.3 A Single Event Handler for Handling Multiple Events

```
Private Sub Form1_Load(ByVal sender As System.Object, _
  ByVal e As System.EventArgs) Handles MyBase.Load, MyBase.Click

  MsgBox("Called on Load and Click")
End Sub
```

The `Handles` clause is now understood to mean that `Form1_Load` will handle both the `Form.Load` and `Form.Click` events. This will work as long as the signatures of the events are identical. That is, one method can respond for any or all methods whose events have identical signatures. (I have not tested the limits of the number of events a single method can respond to or how long the `Handles` clause can be, but based on the implementation, it should be a very large number of events.)

The `EventHandler` Class

The signature of the `Load` and `Click` events (and many basic events in .NET) is a method that takes an object and a `System.EventArgs` argument. (This is actually the signature of a delegate class named `EventHandler`. We'll come back to the subject of delegates in the What Are Delegates? section later in this chapter.)

For now let's explore the arguments of the signature of this basic event handler.

The `sender` Argument

You have read by now that classes in Visual Basic .NET are derived from the `Object` class. Similarly, `sender` is defined as an object. This means that literally any type can be passed to satisfy the `sender` argument. What is usually passed is the originating object.

The result is that you can use runtime type checking to determine the class of the object that invoked a particular event. Of course, you could write code that depends on the specific object to which you assigned the event handler, but this is less robust, and if you change the name of the object, the code will be wrong. Referring to Listing 3.3, we could revise the code to refer to the object we know is associated with the `Form1_Load` handler.

```
Private Sub Form1_Load(ByVal sender As System.Object, _
   ByVal e As System.EventArgs) Handles MyBase.Load, MyBase.Click
      MsgBox(Me.Name & " called on Load and Click")
End Sub
```

The revised code relies on the reference to self, `Me`. Specifically, the code relies on the method being associated with the form.

How can we implement the code to be less dependent on the specific type of the object? Or how can we write the code to respond differently based on the actual invoker of the event? The answer is that we have to write the code to query the type of the `sender` object.

```
Private Sub Form1_Load(ByVal sender As System.Object, _
   ByVal e As System.EventArgs) Handles MyBase.Load, MyBase.Click

     If (TypeOf sender Is Form1) Then
        MsgBox(CType(sender, Form1).Name & " called on Load and
Click")
     End If

End Sub
```

The revised code is more robust. The `If` statement checks to see if the type of the `sender` object is an instance of `Form1`. If it is, `sender` is dynamically cast (cast at runtime) to its actual type. Casting the `sender` object supports accessing the members of that type. (For instance, object does not have a name property. However, if `sender` is an instance of `Form1` and we cast it to `Form1`, we can access the `Form.Name` property.)

By using dynamic type checking we take specific action based on the real type of the object that raised the event.

The `EventArgs` Argument

The `EventArgs` argument is a stub. In some instances events will want to pass additional information. For example, a mouse event may want to pass the position of the mouse. Keyboard events may want to pass the state of the keyboard. Paint events may want to pass the device context.

Other kinds of events actually use the `EventArgs` class, or derived classes, to pass additional information to the event handler. The `Paint` event handler passes a `PaintEventArgs` object that has a `Graphics` property representing the device context, or canvas, of the invoking object. You can use this `Graphics` object to perform custom painting, as we did in Chapter 2.

Handling Multiple Events with One Handler

You now know that you can manually associate similarly signatured events to a single event handler. You can accomplish this task by adding the name of the control and the name of the event in a `Handles` clause.

You may wonder why you would do this. The answer is that you have more than one metaphor that performs the same operation. (A control is a metaphor for invoking an operation.) For example, think of a form that has a menu that closes the form as well as a button that closes the form. Both the menu and the button are *metaphors* for closing the form. Thus, in addition to performing the same operation, both metaphors should share the same code. The short fragment that follows demonstrates this technique.

```
Private Sub ButtonClose_Click(ByVal sender As System.Object, _
   ByVal e As System.EventArgs) _
   Handles ButtonClose.Click, MenuItemExit.Click

   Close()
End Sub
```

The event handler was generated by double-clicking the button. From the `Handles` clause it is clear that this event handler handles the `Button-Close.Click` event. I manually typed `MenuItemExit.Click` to add code for the menu item. The implication is that the user can perform the same operation—closing the form—by clicking the button or selecting the menu item.

A reasonable person might argue that the savings are minimal. In this example, yes, but when coding we have the opportunity to build habits that work efficiently and effectively in all circumstances. By sharing events that perform identical operations, we converge the code to one function. By calling a well-named function, the code does not need a comment, and we have to change the code in only one place if revisions are needed. To reiterate, we get speed, extensibility, and reliability by building solid general habits and employing them dogmatically. The preceding fragment demonstrates the following habits:

- Sharing event handlers for metaphors that perform identical operations forces code to converge toward consistent, reliable behavior.
- Implementing the event handlers by invoking a well-named method mitigates the need for comments, resulting in saved time and speedier coding.
- Making the code converge means that we can add more behavior in a single locus, enhancing extensibility.
- Finally, using a method to implement the behavior means that some other code path can invoke (think *reuse*) the behavior.

Convergent, well-named code helps programmers code at a much faster pace and yields a high-quality result. The objective is to make this style of programming second nature by practicing good habits.

Implementing Multiple Respondents

You know that you can make one method respond to multiple events. You can also make multiple event handlers respond to a single event. When an event invokes more than one method, this is referred to as *multicasting*.

By implementing multiple event handlers it is possible to layer behavior. For example, a producer can implement a custom `Paint` event handler for a user control, and a consumer of that control can implement a custom event handler too without overwriting the event handler associated with the `Paint` event by the producer. (We will return to this subject and provide examples in an upcoming section, What Are Delegates?)

Using the `WithEvents` Statement

If you declare a variable using the `WithEvents` statement, the handlers for the events associated with the type of the variable can be generated by selecting the object in the class name list and the events in the method name list. Here's an example in case you're not familiar with the `WithEvents` statement.

```
Private WithEvents MyButton As Button
```

When the variable has been declared, the name will show up in the class name list. Based on the preceding code statement, `MyButton` will be in the method name list, and when you select `MyButton`, the method name list will include all the events associated with the `Button` type. By picking the `Click` event, for instance, the `Click` event handler will be generated.

You will still need to construct an instance of `MyButton`, but the `Click` handler will be associated with the control when `MyButton` is created. The following fragment demonstrates how to dynamically create the `Button` control.

```
MyButton = New Button()
MyButton.Text = "Click Me!"
Controls.Add(MyButton)
```

These three statements construct an instance of the `Button` class, set the `Text` value for the button, and add the button to the form's `Controls` collection. The last step is imperative; if you forget this step, messages won't get sent from the form to the button.

You can use the `WithEvents` statement and the `Handles` clause to define and associate event handlers at design time—when you are coding—or you can use `AddHandler` and `RemoveHandler` statements to manage event handlers dynamically at runtime.

TIP: Use a `WithEvents` statement and a `Handles` clause together, or use the `AddHandler` statement—but don't use both options at once.

Adding and Removing Event Handlers

Visual Basic .NET extends event handlers by supporting the dynamic association of events at runtime. This means you can write code in such a way as to create controls and tie them to other controls without knowing what those controls will be in advance. The result is that you can dynamically customize your application after it has been compiled and shipped.

You might recall that the `AddressOf` operator in VB6 supported passing the address of a procedure to a Windows API procedure. The passed address of the procedure is referred to as a *callback function*. Windows and other languages have supported callbacks for many years. VB6 allowed callback functions to support Windows API methods that needed them, but you could not use callbacks within your VB6 application.

Essentially, callback functions have now been extended to include internal use within a Visual Basic .NET application. The address of a procedure is at the heart of a delegate. Although a delegate is more than support for callback functions, this is the crux of what delegates are. (We'll return to delegates in a moment.)

Now that we have reviewed callbacks, we can talk about what callbacks have to do with events and event handlers. An event handler is a method whose address has been given to another function. When an event is raised, the method is invoked—called back—via the address of the procedure.

In a nutshell, events need callback functions, but VB6 provided limited support. Visual Basic .NET provides extended support for callback functions, which extends direct control over event handlers to you.

The AddHandler Statement

The `AddHandler` statement is used to associate an event handler with an event. The `AddHandler` statement has the following general syntax.

```
AddHandler object.event, AddressOf eventhandler
```

The first parameter is the object and event, and the second is the callback (also known as the event handler).

We could dynamically create a `Button` control and associate a handler with the `Click` event. The only requirement is that the event handler must have the same signature as the one expected by the event member.

```
Dim ADynamicButton As Button = New Button()
ADynamicButton.Text = "AddHandler"
AddHandler ADynamicButton.Click, AddressOf MyClick
Controls.Add(ADynamicButton)
```

The preceding control dynamically creates a button, and the third statement associates a method named `MyClick` with the button's `Click` event. Here is a reasonable implementation of `MyClick`.

```
Private Sub MyClick(ByVal sender As Object, ByVal e As System.EventArgs)
  MsgBox("Click!")
End Sub
```

What is not apparent from this code is that the `AddressOf MyClick` clause creates an instance of the `EventHandler` delegate. To demonstrate this you could rewrite the code to explicitly create the `EventHandler` delegate.

```
AddHandler ADynamicButton.Click, New EventHandler(AddressOf MyClick)
```

NOTE: I can't speak on behalf of Microsoft, but I can make a reasonable guess about why `AddressOf` and implicit creation of delegates are supported in Visual Basic .NET: familiarity and ease of use. Visual Basic has always been known as an approachable development environment. However, if we don't explore more advanced concepts, we can't take advantage of the more advanced features of Visual Basic .NET. Delegates are definitely something we want to exploit to the hilt.

Another thing that is not apparent is that you can associate more than one handler with a single event (refer to the What Are Delegates? section). Removing a handler effectively turns off the associated event response. Think of radio stations and radios: Several radio stations broadcast, and each radio can tune to the different stations. Each radio station can have many listeners, and each can tune in or out.

The `RemoveHandler` Statement

You can prevent a specific event handler from being invoked by disassociating the handler with the event. This is accomplished by using the `Remove-Handler` method. The following code would remove the handler we added in the previous section.

```
RemoveHandler ADynamicButton.Click, AddressOf MyClick
```

The syntax of `RemoveHandler` is identical to that of `AddHandler`; simply substitute `RemoveHandler` for `AddHandler`.

Assigning Event Handlers at Runtime

You know the mechanics of adding and removing event handlers at runtime. What you may not know is when or why you might actually use this capability.

The first obvious reason is that if you are going to add controls to your application at runtime, you will need event handlers to respond to those controls' events. Second, classes that are not controls but have events will need handlers to listen for those events. And there is at least one more thing you can do with the addresses of methods. (Keep in mind that event handlers are referred to as *event handlers* only because they are associated with events; more generally, event handlers are just the addresses of functions.) The third use of handlers is to dynamically change the behavior of a method by passing various callbacks to that method.

Using Callbacks to Implement Dynamic Sort Behavior

Suppose we elect to write a sort algorithm. The sort algorithm can be written to sort some elements of an array in ascending order, descending order, or in either order by passing a comparison callback to the sort method.

Let's keep the sort simple so we can focus on the dynamic callback behavior. Assume we want to pass an array of any kind of object to our sort method. This will work as long we implement a comparison function that knows how to compare the elements of the array. Passing a dynamic comparison function to our sort algorithm allows us to write a generic sort algorithm and use the comparison function to affect the sort order and resolve the type of the data. Listing 3.4 demonstrates such a solution.

Listing 3.4 Passing a Dynamic Comparison Function to a Sort Algorithm

```
1:  Public Class Form1
2:      Inherits System.Windows.Forms.Form
3:
4:  [ Windows Form Designer generated code ]
5:
6:    Private Delegate Function Compare(ByVal lhs As Object, _
7:      ByVal rhs As Object) As Boolean
8:
9:    Private Function Greater(ByVal lhs As Object, _
10:     ByVal rhs As Object) As Boolean
11:
12:     Return CType(lhs, String) > CType(rhs, String)
13:
14:   End Function
15:
16:   Private Function Less(ByVal lhs As Object, _
17:     ByVal rhs As Object) As Boolean
18:
19:     Return Not Greater(lhs, rhs)
```

```
20:
21:    End Function
22:
23:    Private Sub Sort(ByVal Items() As Object, ByVal CompareFunction As Compare)
24:
25:       Dim I, J As Integer
26:       For I = Items.GetLowerBound(0) To Items.GetUpperBound(0) - 1
27:          For J = I + 1 To Items.GetUpperBound(0)
28:             If (CompareFunction(Items(I), Items(J))) Then
29:
30:                Dim Temp As Object = Items(I)
31:                Items(I) = Items(J)
32:                Items(J) = Temp
33:
34:             End If
35:          Next
36:       Next
37:
38:    End Sub
39:
40:    Private Sub Button1_Click(ByVal sender As System.Object, _
41:       ByVal e As System.EventArgs) Handles Button1.Click
42:
43:       Dim Items(ListBox1.Items.Count - 1) As Object
44:       ListBox1.Items.CopyTo(Items, 0)
45:       Sort(Items, AddressOf Less)
46:       ListBox1.Items.Clear()
47:       ListBox1.Items.AddRange(Items)
48:
49:    End Sub
50: End Class
```

Lines 6 and 7 define the signature of our comparison function; it takes two objects and returns a Boolean. Notice that we are introducing the keyword `Delegate`. Don't worry about that right now; just keep in mind that the `Delegate` keyword is used to define delegates. For now simply think of the statement on lines 6 and 7 as a way to define the signature of a callback function.

Lines 9 through 14 and lines 16 through 21 define two functions that have the same signature as the delegate. (Compare them with lines 6 and 7.) Lines 23 through 38 define the `Sort` method. `Sort` takes an array of the most generic type, `Object`, and a `Compare` delegate. That is, the `Sort` method takes the address of a function that takes two object arguments and returns a Boolean.

Depending on which function we pass to Sort—Greater or Less—we will get a different result. If we pass Greater, we will get a sort in ascending order; if we pass Less, we will get a sort in descending order. If we create other functions that compare different data types, we can use the same Sort method to compare integers or any other array of data.

Using the *IComparer* Interface to Implement Dynamic Sort Behavior

Applying a dynamic comparator for a sort is a well-known solution. As a result, the Microsoft engineers have implemented a slightly different solution to dynamic sort behavior.

It would be reasonable for you to expect that ListBox controls can sort data, and you would be right. In addition, controls and classes that represent collections were implemented to support dynamic comparators. Microsoft used a slightly different approach for sort comparisons: an interface. (We covered interfaces in Chapter 2 and we'll discuss function pointers later in this chapter.) Listing 3.5 demonstrates how to implement the IComparer interface with the System.Array.Sort method to control the nature of the comparisons.

Listing 3.5 Implementing the IComparer Interface

```
1:   Public Class Form1
2:       Inherits System.Windows.Forms.Form
3:
4:   [ Windows Form Designer generated code ]
5:
6:     Private Class Comparer
7:       Implements IComparer
8:
9:       Private Function Compare(ByVal lhs As String, _
10:        ByVal rhs As String) As Integer
11:
12:        If (lhs > rhs) Then
13:          Return 1
14:        ElseIf (lhs < rhs) Then
15:          Return -1
16:        Else
17:          Return 0
18:        End If
```

```
19:
20:     End Function
21:
22:     Public Function Compare(ByVal x As Object, _
23:        ByVal y As Object) As Integer Implements IComparer.Compare
24:
25:        Return Compare(CType(x, String), CType(y, String))
26:     End Function
27:
28:  End Class
29:
30:  Private Sub Button1_Click(ByVal sender As System.Object, _
31:     ByVal e As System.EventArgs) Handles Button1.Click
32:
33:     Dim S(ListBox1.Items.Count - 1) As String
34:     ListBox1.Items.CopyTo(S, 0)
35:     Array.Sort(S, New Comparer())
36:     ListBox1.Items.Clear()
37:     ListBox1.Items.AddRange(S)
38:
39:     End Sub
40: End Class
```

Lines 6 through 28 define a private nested class that implements the IComparer interface. Since the comparer is used only by the form itself, it is an excellent candidate for nesting. (A *nested class* is defined inside another class. Try to do that with your father's VB.) The Comparer class implements the public Compare function (lines 22 through 26) to complete the contract represented by the IComparer interface. The overloaded private version of the Compare function (lines 9 through 20) enables us to separate the conversion to a string type from the actual comparisons. Passing arguments to an overloaded method is a strategy I employ to avoid temporary variables and to keep methods short.

The elements of the ListBox are copied to the array, and the Comparer and the array are passed to the Array.Sort method. The result is a sorted array. The Array.Sort method uses a very fast quick-sort algorithm; thus for most arrays of data, the Array.Sort method performs very well.

A final word here to be clear. This section and the preceding one were not added to demonstrate how to sort a ListBox. The ListBox was used to provide visual feedback. To sort a ListBox, set the ListBox.Sorted property to True. Use the IComparer or callback functions when you don't have the convenience of a `ListBox` and the `ListBox.Sorted` property. You certainly don't want to create `ListBox` control to sort nonvisual data.

Sorting is a common problem. If you are using a collection or a control that contains an array or a collection, examine that class's properties and methods. The class may already contain sorting capabilities, and you should probably use those before rolling your own sort.

Declaring Events in Classes, Structures, and Interfaces

We have examined a variety of ways to use events as consumers. Now we need to explore how to use events as producers. This section demonstrates how to declare event members for classes, structures, and interfaces. Keep in mind, though, that the event grammar is the same regardless of which type the event is defined in.

There are two basic signatures for events, as shown below.

```
Modifiers Event signature
Modifiers Event Name As delegate
```

TIP: Events cannot define a return type. That is, events must always have subroutine-style signatures.

The first example above defines an event by signature. An event includes the name of the event and the arguments for name, type, and number. The second example above defines an event as a delegate, and the delegate provides the signature of the event. Here is an example of an event that uses an existing delegate, `EventHandler`.

```
Public Class Event1
  Public Event Handle As EventHandler

  Public Sub Raise()
    RaiseEvent Handle(Me, System.EventArgs.Empty)
  End Sub
End Class
```

TIP: By convention we use a method to raise events rather than littering our types with `RaiseEvent` statements.

The fragment defines a class that has a public access modifier and is defined as an event handler. `EventHandler` is the delegate used for events like `Click`. The `Raise` method demonstrates how to use `RaiseEvent`. This code works correctly whether any event handler is defined or not. `Me` satisfies the `sender` argument, and the shared `System.EventArgs.Empty` object satisfies the `EventArgs` argument of `EventHandler`. (To review how to create instances of objects and how to associate event handlers with the events of those objects, refer to two earlier sections in this chapter: Using the `WithEvents` Statement and The `AddHandler` Statement.)

If you replace `Class` with `Interface` or `Structure` in the fragment containing the definition of the `Event1` type, the event handler definition will remain the same. But remember that declarations within an interface can't use access modifiers (so remove the keyword `Public` on the `Raise` method), and we can't implement any code (so remove `Raise`'s method body). The following two examples demonstrate the differences between implementing the interface and the structure.

```
Public Interface IEvent1
   Event Handle As EventHandler
   Sub Raise()
End Interface


Public Structure Event1
   Public Event Handle As EventHandler

   Public Sub Raise()
     RaiseEvent Handle(Me, System.EventArgs.Empty)
   End Sub

End Structure
```

To implement the same event using a method signature we need to replace the `As` clause with the method signature. The revision to the event definition follows.

```
Event Handle(ByVal sender As Object, ByVal e As System.EventArgs)
```

You must use methods whose signatures match the event signature whether that signature is expressed literally or as defined by a delegate.

More important than the syntax is the motivation for using events. If you reexamine the `Event1` class (or the interface or structure) you will notice that there is no indication of the objects that will be handling the `Handle` event. This is critical. Because we do not have a reference to a specific object and aren't invoking a specific method, any object that has a method with a matching signature can handle the event raised by `Event1`. This is the essence of loose coupling, and loosely coupled code is our goal.

What Are Delegates?

Now you know how to consume and produce events, and we'll see many examples of these throughout this book. But you may be asking yourself, "What is the big deal about delegates?"

For the most part, after reading the earlier sections in this chapter you know everything you need to know. However, there is an important chunk of information we still need to cover. Delegates are actually classes. For years we have had function pointers—also called *procedural types*—but these implementations were not classes. They were simple instances of single function pointers. The result was that every programmer had to write code to determine whether the function pointer was assigned to something, and if you wanted to stored multiple values for the function pointer, you had to track these multiple pointers with custom code too.

Delegates are classes that contain these capabilities, thus eliminating the need for developers to roll their own. Delegate classes can determine whether something is actually assigned to the delegate by keeping an internal list. The algorithm can be understood as follows: *For every callback function in the internal list, call the function.*

In addition to supporting callback functions, delegates can check to see whether any function pointers are associated with a particular delegate by maintaining an internal list, and delegates can use that list to multicast. *Multicasting* simply means calling all the function pointers in the invocation list. The result is that one delegate can actually invoke many functions.

As Paul Harvey would say, "That's the rest of the story."

Why Are Delegates So Important?

There is so much hubbub about delegates because they are central to the Windows operating system and .NET itself. Delegates are used to support the event-driven model in Windows. Delegates are used to support dynamic method behaviors (as demonstrated earlier in this chapter), and delegates are used to register worker functions with asynchronous and multithreaded behavior.

In a nutshell, if you don't understand delegates, then dynamic methods, asynchronous behavior, thread pooling, and multithreading will not be available to you.

Defining Delegates

Delegates are defined by preceding the signature of a method with the keyword `Delegate`. To define a delegate, type the access modifier, the keyword `Delegate`, and a procedure heading. The following excerpt from Listing 3.4 demonstrates the grammar.

```
6:  Private Delegate Function Compare(ByVal lhs As Object, _
7:     ByVal rhs As Object) As Boolean
```

By quick inspection you can determine that the only difference between a method heading and a delegate is the inclusion of the keyword `Delegate`. While events must be subroutines, delegates that are not used to handle events can be subroutines or functions.

You can use the constructor syntax to create a new instance of a delegate type, or you can create a delegate implicitly by taking the address of a method that has the signature of a particular delegate. For example, when a method expects an event handler and you take the address of a method that has the same signature as the event handler, you will be implicitly creating an instance of an event handler delegate. Here are two examples yielding the same result.

```
Sort(Items, AddressOf Less)
Sort(Items, New Compare(AddressOf Less))
```

The first line is taken from line 45 in Listing 3.4 and implicitly creates an instance of the `Compare` delegate. The second line is the more verbose example, which demonstrates constructing an instance of the `Compare` delegate and initializing the delegate with the address of a procedure that has the signature of the delegate. You can use the first form to create the delegate as long as the compiler can determine the delegate type by context. If you get an error related to a delegate and you are using the abbreviated code to construct the delegate, switch to the verbose syntax.

When you are performing visual programming tasks, you will likely be using existing delegates like the `EventHandler` delegate. For more advanced tasks you may need to define your own delegates or use other existing delegates, such as the `WaitCallback` delegate used with the `ThreadPool` class for multithreaded operations.

Exploring Existing Delegate Types

You will encounter several existing delegates as you continue learning more about VB .NET. It is important to keep in mind that these delegate types are constrained by the procedure signatures used to define them. Determine the signature and you will know the kind of data passed when the delegate is invoked. You can easily rely on the help system to provide you this information on a case-by-case basis.

Rather than try to provide you with a comprehensive list, I will mention two very common delegates here briefly. The first is `EventHandler`, and the second is `PaintEventHandler`.

Both `EventHandler` and `PaintEventHandler` have a first argument in common, `sender`, defined as an `Object` type. The `sender` argument is usually the control that invoked the delegate. The second argument for `EventHandler` is a `System.EventArgs` parameter, and for `PaintEventHandler` it is `System.Windows.Forms.PaintEventArgs`.

NOTE: Etymology is the study of languages. If you have worked with more than one programming language, you have implicitly studied languages. Computer languages, like spoken languages, evolve rather than spring up from nowhere. Visual Basic .NET is an evolution of Visual Basic with influences from Anders Hejlsberg. Hejlsberg mixed in aspects of Object Pascal (available under the product name Delphi). The ways event handling and delegates work have evolved from the Delphi support for procedural types; the `sender` argument is commonly found in Delphi event handlers.

`EventArgs` is really a placeholder in anticipation of event handler delegates that may need more information, like `Paint` events. `PaintEventArgs` contains an instance of the `Graphics` object that represents the painting surface of the control that raised the event. (Delphi programmers know the painting surface as the *Canvas*, and most Windows programmers know that the painting surface is referred to as a *Device Context*, or DC.)

By handling the `Paint` event you can get an instance of a control's `Graphics` object and perform custom painting when the control needs to be painted. The `Shape` classes demonstrate custom painting. Refer to Chapter 2 for examples that demonstrate the `Paint` event handler.

Delegates for Multithreading

A couple of delegates are defined to support invoking methods. These delegates are used with asynchronous processes and multithreaded classes. The `MethodInvoker` class is used to create delegates for procedures that return no data and take no arguments; `MethodInvoker` delegates are used with the `Invoke` method of controls. The `WaitCallback` delegate is defined with a signature that takes a single `Object` parameter. The `WaitCallback` delegate is used for multithreading with the `ThreadPool` class. The signature of both delegates follows.

```
Public Delegate Sub MethodInvoker()
Public Delegate Sub WaitCallback(ByVal state as Object)
```

For more information on asynchronous and multithreaded programming, read Chapter 6, which provides several examples demonstrating how to use the `Invoke` method and the `WaitCallback` delegate.

Summary

Chapter 3 demonstrated how events are supported in Visual Basic .NET. There is no question whether we need events, event handlers, and delegates—Windows is an event-based operating system. The question is whether or not the event model should be accessible to Visual Basic .NET programmers. The answers is a resounding yes.

Visual Basic .NET supports visually associating events and handlers at design time. It also supports associating events and handlers programmatically. VB6 did not support the underlying mechanism for the event model: function pointers (procedural types).

Visual Basic .NET has complete access to the event model and the underlying technology. In this chapter you learned how to associate event handlers with events visually at design time and programmatically at runtime, and how to use function pointers. Function pointers are concealed in classes called *delegates* in an internal list. As you learned in this chapter, delegates are an evolution of raw function pointers. Because delegates are classes, they have the ability to do more than just store the address of a function. Delegates support storing the addresses of multiple functions and invoking all those functions, as well as determining when no function is available.

Events, event handlers, and delegates are critical to basic Windows programming because they support how Windows fundamentally works. Additionally, delegates support some advanced idioms and are beneficial for new features like multithreading.

CHAPTER 4

Reflection

If you got the grits, serve 'em!

—Stanley Crouch

Introduction

Reflection is one of the most powerful concepts in Visual Basic .NET. It is definitely one of my favorite topics. Programmers at any level might reasonably ask, "What is Reflection?" Reflection is the ability to dynamically discover type information. More than that, Reflection helps programmers apply that information to use types dynamically. Generally, when we say *dynamically* we mean that we can do something at runtime that we didn't know about at design time.

Reflection technology supports things like late binding (which comes from COM), and it allows your code to interact with code that your code had no prior knowledge about. Reflection literally supports loading an assembly, dynamically discovering information about types and their members, and invoking operations on those types and members.

By themselves the cool capabilities I described above represent a logical evolution of static Run Time Type Information (RTTI). Reflection supports more advanced behavior, too. A programmer can use Reflection to dynamically create new types at runtime and then invoke operations on those types. (This sounds a bit like science fiction. Imagine, a smart application is learning and writing its own object-oriented code as it learns.)

Everything that can and will be done with Reflection hasn't been discovered yet, but there will be evocative applications for Reflection. Some great ones exist. The best ones are yet to be discovered. We'll explore Reflection in detail in this chapter.

Implicit Late Binding

Visual Basic .NET still supports late binding. Late binding is what happens when the type of an object is general and the instance of an object is specific. For example, if you declare a variable as an `Object` type and initialize a `Button` control, assigning the `Button` instance to the `Object` variable, you are using late binding. Late binding is supported through Reflection. Listing 4.1 offers an example.

Listing 4.1 An Example of Late Binding Using Reflection

```
Private Sub Button1_Click(ByVal sender As System.Object, _
  ByVal e As System.EventArgs) Handles Button1.Click
  Dim C As Object
  C = New Button()
  C.Text = "Test"
  C.Bounds = CType(sender, Control).Bounds
  C.Location = New Point(C.Location.X, C.Location.Y + C.Size.Height + 10)
  AddHandler CType(C, Control).Click, AddressOf Button1_Click
  Controls.Add(C)
End Sub
```

Listing 4.1 is an event handler for a control named `Button1`. The first line of code in the event handler declares a variable that is typed as an object. The object `C` is initialized as a button. The button's `Text` property is set. The bounding region of the button is defined. A `Click` event handler—this handler for convenience—is associated with the dynamic button, and the button is added to the form's `Controls` collection.

There are several problems with the code in Listing 4.1. The first one will be obvious if you type the code in Visual Studio .NET: Intellisense doesn't know the type of `C` and as a result cannot offer any assistance while we are programming. A second obvious problem is all the muddled code we have to write to access some of the members of the button. One example of muddled code is where we have to dynamically cast the `sender` argument reflecting the button we clicked as a `Control` to access the `Bounds` property. A second example of muddled code is the dynamic typecast to add the event handler (on the line with `AddHandler`). We can't even assign the event handler using late binding without a type conversion. (Type conversions are performed with `CType`.)

Late binding is supported but is an anachronistic behavior that should be left in the past. Late binding permits the use of variables without declaring them and without dynamically casting types, although this can lead to slower running code and runtime errors.

NOTE: I know that many programmers work carefully and have used late binding successfully for years, but I am not writing to reaffirm what may be popular. The responsibility I have is to relate best practices. Strongly typed, explicit code that does not rely on late binding is less error-prone, more concise, and generally better than the alternative.

Visual Basic programmers have been relying on late binding for quite some time, but it has always been a bad practice. Relying on weak type checking, late binding, and implicit code writing results in buggy, convoluted code.

TIP: Use `Option Strict On` and explicit code to get the benefit of Intellisense and to write code that is less error-prone.

At the top of every source code module, place the `Option Strict On` statement. This will prevent you from using weakly typed practices. If `Option Explicit` is `Off`, you can write code like this:

```
Dim MyCustomer = New Customer()
```

Unfortunately, the type of object is implicit and you will be using late binding. `Option Strict On` will force you to write the more explicit form of declaration and construction.

```
Dim MyCustomer As Customer = New Customer()
```

When you use `Option Strict On` the IDE will find unsupported, weakly typed code. You will have to declare the types of variables. Also, VB .NET will catch instances where your code is performing conversions that might lead to lost information, such as implicitly assigning the result of a function that returns a `Long` value to an `Integer` variable. Listing 4.2 demonstrates the slightly leaner, revised code for Listing 4.1.

Listing 4.2 A Revised Version of Listing 4.1 That Uses Strict Type Checking

```
Private Sub Button1_Click(ByVal sender As System.Object, _
   ByVal e As System.EventArgs) Handles Button1.Click

   Dim NewButton As Button = New Button()
   NewButton.Text = "Test"
   NewButton.Bounds = CType(sender, Control).Bounds
   NewButton.Location = New Point(NewButton.Location.X, _
      NewButton.Location.Y + NewButton.Size.Height + 10)
   AddHandler NewButton.Click, AddressOf Button1_Click
   Controls.Add(NewButton)

End Sub
```

The revised code is almost the same length as the original code. By using verbose code you will add extra lines to declare variables, but you will
avoid confusion, get the benefit of Intellisense, and not have to perform as
many type conversions.

Notice that we still have to cast the **sender** parameter to a control to access the **Bounds** property of the **sender** parameter. (Recall that the **sender**
parameter represents the object that invoked the event handler.) With
sender, the .NET developers made a judgment call: Using a generic type
for the event handler parameter meant they had to write many fewer event
handlers, resulting in a smaller framework. Had Microsoft defined event
handlers that took a specific kind of **Control** argument, they would have
had to define custom event handlers for all the controls that currently exist
and those yet to be created. Clearly doing so is untenable and would be impossible to manage.

Discovering Type Information at Runtime

There will be many instances when you need to discover type information
without writing weakly typed code. As shown in the last section, we can use
the **sender** argument of an event handler to obtain properties from the object that raised an event. Type information is literally defined by a class
named **Type**, defined in the **System** namespace.

To some extent, talking about Reflection and talking about the **Type**
class go hand in hand. There are too many members in the **Type** class to list

here, so I won't do it. I will tell you that all the information is available in the integrated help documentation, and you can discover just about anything you want to about a type by requesting an object's type information. The easiest way to request type information is to invoke `GetType`. For example, `Button1.GetType` returns the `Type` object for `Button1`.

In the preceding section we simply cast `sender` to a control with `CType(sender, Control)`. You will not want to do that in a robust application. The `sender` parameter can be anything. We could add a sentinel to Listing 4.2. If the type of the `sender` parameter is not the type we are interested in—a control—then we can exit the subroutine. The following statement demonstrates how to check the type of an object.

```
If Not (TypeOf sender Is Control) Then Return
```

TIP: Use a list of sentinels to avoid nested or complicated `If` conditional logic.

NOTE: Some people like to write positive `If` conditional statements that perform a positive condition test. For example, `If` *condition* `Then` *perform some code*. This was actually taught at the university I attended, Michigan State University. I prefer to write a sentinel. A *sentinel* is code that acts as a guard condition, like the challenge, "Halt! What is the password?" If you don't know the password, you are not admitted. A sentinel checks the negative condition and exits if the test fails. We can write the code as `If Not` *condition* `Then Return`.

The `TypeOf` keyword gets the type information of the first parameter and checks to see if its type is the same as the operand on the right-hand side of the `Is` keyword. Thus we understand the preceding code statement to mean, "If `sender`'s type is not a control, exit the subroutine." To paraphrase Francis Bacon, "Princes to keep due sentinel."

Loading Assemblies

One of the capabilities I have been referring to is the ability to load an assembly at runtime, then discover and invoke operations on that assembly. One of the compelling applications of this technology is the new thin client programming. *Thin client* is coming to mean automatic deployment of updates of

Windows applications over the Internet. (Refer to Chapter 10 for more information on this subject.)

Although you could load any assembly and randomly search for members, in practice you will probably have an idea of what you are looking for. Either way, the code for loading an assembly and invoking members is pretty much the same. You will need to load the assembly, create an instance of a type in that assembly, and bind and invoke a member. I will demonstrate each of these subjects in this section.

Loading an Assembly

The `Assembly` class is defined in `System.Reflection`. You can use the shared `Assembly.Load` and `Assembly.LoadFrom` methods to dynamically load an assembly. The `Assembly.Load` method requires an `AssemblyName` parameter, which is comprised of version, culture, and a strong name or public key. It is easier to use `Assembly.LoadFrom` and simply provide the assembly name.

The following statement demonstrates how to load an assembly. (Make sure you add an `Imports System.Reflection` statement in the module containing code referring to the `Assembly` class.)

```
Dim MyAssembly As [Assembly] = _
   [Assembly].LoadFrom(Application.ExecutablePath)
```

TIP: When you use keywords that are also variables or types, enclose that keyword variable in brackets, as demonstrated above by `[Assembly]`.

The `Assembly.LoadFrom` method might throw an `ArgumentNullException`, `FileNotFoundException`, `BadImageException`, `SecurityException`, or `FileLoadException`. (Refer to the Understanding Reflection and Security section later in this chapter for more information on security exceptions.) For example, you might want to catch a `FileNotFoundException` and allow the user to browse for the assembly. Here is an example of code that catches a `FileNotFoundException` and displays the contents of the exception's message.

```
Try

   Dim MyAssembly As [Assembly] = _
      [Assembly].LoadFrom(Application.ExecutablePath)

Catch X As System.IO.FileNotFoundException
```

```
            MsgBox(X.Message, MsgBoxStyle.Exclamation)
        End Try
```

The **Try** block attempts to perform the action. The **Catch** block performs the error handler behavior. In this instance we catch the specific exception object and display the exception message. (I use **X** by convention to represent the exception object. You can use anything you want, but exception-handling blocks are supposed to be short, and **X** is sufficient.)

After the assembly is loaded, you will want to retrieve some information from the assembly or perform some operation defined by one of the types in the assembly. Our example demonstrates an assembly that loads itself. In the next subsection we'll create a new Hello World assembly and invoke an operation in that assembly.

Invoking Reflected Methods

Having loaded an assembly, we want to interact with the types and the members of those types. I have contrived a simple **HelloWorld.dll** assembly that has a class with one shared method. Listing 4.3 demonstrates how to load that assembly and invoke a shared method.

Listing 4.3 Loading an Assembly and Invoking a Shared Method

```
1:   Const Path As String = _
2:      "C:\Books\Addison-Wesley\Visual Basic .NET Power Coding\" + _
3:      "SOURCE\CHAPTER 4\HelloWorld\bin\HelloWorld.dll"
4:
5:   Dim HelloWorld As [Assembly] = _
6:      [Assembly].LoadFrom(Path)
7:
8:   Dim ReflectedClass As Type = _
9:      HelloWorld.GetType("HelloWorld.ReflectedClass")
10:  ReflectedClass.InvokeMember("HelloWorld", _
11:     BindingFlags.InvokeMethod Or BindingFlags.Public _
12:     Or BindingFlags.Static, _
13:     Nothing, Nothing, Nothing)
```

Lines 1, 2, and 3 contain a really long file path. I left the long file path in place to introduce you to a convenient trick. You can drag a project from the Solution Explorer to the Code Editor to correctly and easily copy long file paths. (When you experiment with the code in Listing 4.3, instead of recreating the file path on lines 1 through 3, simply copy the sample code to a `C:\temp` directory or something short and similar.) Lines 5 and 6 load the assembly from the file path constant.

Lines 8 and 9 retrieve a type from the loaded assembly that we know exists because we wrote it. If you wanted to get all the types defined in the assembly, you could call `GetTypes` (note the plural) on line 9 and assign the result to an array of types.

Lines 10 through 13 might be hardest to follow. This code is simply calling the method `ReflectedClass.HelloWorld`. The first parameter is the name of the method we are invoking. The second argument refers to the binding flags that tell Reflection what to look for. According to the `Or'd` `BindingFlags` enumerated values, we are invoking a public, static method. (`Static` is a synonym for `Shared` in this context. The C# language uses `Static` instead of `Shared`; Microsoft had to choose one word, and `Static` apparently won.)

The last three arguments represent a binder, an instance to invoke the member on, and the arguments to pass. In this simple example, we don't need a binder (we'll return to the `Binder` class in a minute), and the `HelloWorld` method is static, which means we do not need an instance of the class to invoke the method on. Finally, `HelloWorld` as I defined it has no arguments, so passing `Nothing` for the array of arguments is satisfactory.

The end result is that the statement started on line 10 invokes the `ReflectedClass.HelloWorld` method. More commonly, we will be interacting with members that are not shared. It will be helpful to have an object, use a binder, and pass parameters. Next let's take a look at how we create and use an instance and pass parameters. After that, we'll review the `Binder` class.

Creating an Instance from a Type Object

Most applications will not conveniently have all static methods with no parameters. A more realistic situation is that we will need to invoke an instance member and pass arguments to methods. To accomplish this we need to create an instance of the dynamically Reflected objects. There are two ways we can accomplish this: (1) we can use the `Activator` class to create an instance, or (2) we can invoke a constructor method. Both examples are demonstrated next.

Creating an Instance with the `Activator` Class

The `Activator` class supports creating .NET assemblies and COM objects dynamically. The `Activator` class contains four shared methods—`Create-`

ComInstanceFrom, CreateInstance, CreateInstanceFrom, and GetObject—that will load COM objects or assemblies and create instances of the named typed. For example, GetObject allows you to create an instance of a remote object or an XML Web Service.

The code in Listing 4.4 demonstrates how to create an instance of ReflectedClass, which was introduced in Listing 4.3.

Listing 4.4 Using the Activator.CreateInstance Method to Dynamically Create a Reflected Type

```
Dim HelloWorld As [Assembly] = [Assembly].LoadFrom(Path)
  Dim ReflectedClass As Type = HelloWorld.GetType( _
    "HelloWorld.ReflectedClass")
Dim Instance As Object = Activator.CreateInstance(ReflectedClass)
```

The first statement uses Path as defined in Listing 4.3. (We are still working with the same HelloWorld assembly.) The second statement uses the GetType method to get a type from the dynamically loaded assembly. (We could have obtained the name of the type in a variety of ways, including listing all types with GetTypes and allowing the user to select a type.) The third statement uses the Activator.CreateInstance method, passing the type of the object, to create an instance of the Reflected type. After the third statement executes, the result is an instance of the ReflectedClass defined in the HelloWorld namespace.

If we set Option Strict Off, we could invoke a method on Instance. For example, we could write Instance.ShowMessage("Hello World!"), and late binding and implicit Reflection would take care of the invocation for us. A reasonable programmer might elect to do this and could argue that this is a good example of when you may not want to use Option Strict On.

We'll come back to binding a method with parameters in a minute. For now let's look at the second way to create an instance using Reflection.

Dynamically Invoking a Constructor

The System.Reflection namespace contains classes named *membertype*Info. For example, ConstructorInfo represents a constructor. There are classes representing constructors, methods, fields, properties, events, members (in general), and parameters. Following convention, these classes are named ConstructorInfo, MethodInfo, FieldInfo, PropertyInfo, EventInfo, MemberInfo, and ParameterInfo, respectively. Each of these classes is an object-oriented representation of the type information for an element. The admission pass is the `System.Type` class. If you request an instance of the type information for any type, you can obtain the type information for any element of that type. Of course, you are not guaranteed to be able to get any information about assemblies; security plays a role, too. (See the Understanding Reflection and Security section later in this chapter for more information.)

NOTE: Attribute information is handled a little bit differently. Use the `Get-CustomAttribute` and `GetCustomAttributes` methods of any `System.Type` object to request attribute information.

We can use this knowledge to obtain the type information for constructors. If you request a `ConstructorInfo` object from a type, you can use that constructor to create an instance of the class. Listing 4.5 demonstrates how to request a `ConstructorInfo` object and create an instance of `ReflectedClass`.

Listing 4.5 Obtaining a `ConstructorInfo` Object and Creating an Instance of a Reflected Type

```
Dim HelloWorld As [Assembly] = [Assembly].LoadFrom(Path)
Dim ReflectedClass As Type = HelloWorld.GetType("HelloWorld.ReflectedClass")
Dim Constructor As ConstructorInfo = _
  ReflectedClass.GetConstructor(New System.Type() {})

Dim Instance As Object = Constructor.Invoke(New Object() {})
Instance.ShowMessage("ConstructorInfo")
```

The first two statements you have already seen. The third statement uses the type object, `ReflectedClass`, and requests a single `ConstructorInfo` type record. The argument `New System.Type() {}` is used to tell the `GetConstructor` method which constructor to retrieve. The array of types is used to match parameters. For example, if the constructor you wanted to obtain required a string argument, you would pass the type information for a string (see the upcoming Passing Method Arguments section). The statement containing `Constructor.Invoke` (in Listing 4.5) passes an array of matching parameters to the actual constructor. Because we passed an empty array of `System.Type` objects, we need to invoke the constructor with an empty array of `Object` parameters.

Listing 4.5 invokes the ShowMessage method. From the listing it is apparent that we are using the Option Strict Off, late bound form of the method invocation.

NOTE: Hopefully these examples demonstrate some of the vast power inherent in object-oriented systems with a coherent framework. Without a common type—Object—and type objects, it would be very difficult or impossible to implement and support capabilities like Reflection.

Any type may have zero or more of any of the elements described. For instance, constructors can be overloaded; hence a class may have multiple constructors. To reflect reality, the System.Type class also has plural forms of the get methods. The plural form—for example, GetConstructors()—returns an array of the type information objects. You can use the plural form of the Get*membertype* method to retrieve all the elements of a specific kind. For example, all the properties can be obtained and displayed as demonstrated in Listing 4.6.

Listing 4.6 Iterating All the Properties of a Type

```
Dim FormType As Type = Me.GetType
Dim Properties As PropertyInfo() = FormType.GetProperties()
ListBox1.Items.Clear()

Dim [Property] As PropertyInfo
For Each [Property] In Properties
  ListBox1.Items.Add([Property])
Next
```

The first statement gets the type information for the containing object. (The example code is in LoadAssembly.sln, and Me represents a form.) The second statement gets all the PropertyInfo records. The third statement clears a ListBox; we'll use the ListBox to display the property information. The For Each loop employs an enumerator behind the scenes and adds every PropertyInfo representation to the ListBox.

A couple of implied things are going on in Listing 4.6. The variable [Property] uses brackets because Property is a reserved keyword. In the statement where we are adding items to the ListBox, the [Property] argument resolves to [Property].ToString(). We can add objects to a

ListBox, but a string representation of those objects is displayed in the ListBox. (This is an advanced book. We have to have a few enigmas for you to figure out.)

Passing Method Arguments

Realistically you are likely to invoke nonstatic methods. You are also likely to have to invoke methods that have parameters. Listing 4.5 demonstrated how to invoke a constructor with null arguments. If we have a constructor that has some arguments, all we need to do is modify the array of types to indicate which constructor to request and then invoke that constructor with matching argument types.

To demonstrate parameterized method invocation, we will make some adjustments to our example. A constructor with a string argument might appear as follows:

```
Public Sub New(ByVal Message As String)
```

The call to the GetConstructor method for the preceding constructor would be

```
GetConstructor(New System.Type(){GetType(String)})
```

We are indicating that GetConstructor should return the Sub New constructor that has a single string parameter. To invoke the constructor with a string argument, we need to pass a string to that constructor. Here is the invocation call.

```
Dim Instance As Object = Constructor.Invoke( _
    New Object() {"It's all about the crowbar love!"})
```

NOTE: In case you're curious, "crowbar love" is a reference to the Half-Life video game. Half-Life is a very graphic, multiplayer game, and one of the weapons is a crowbar. On my birthday, a good friend of mine, Eric Cotter, brought me a crowbar in the middle of a postwork game of Half-Life.

The same technique for passing arguments to constructors is used to pass arguments to methods.

Reviewing the Binder Class

The `Binder` class is an abstract class that you must inherit from to use. Binders are used to perform type conversions. The `InvokeMember` method of `Type` objects can accept a `Binder` object that describes how to perform type conversions between the types of arguments passed to `InvokeMember` and the actual types needed by the member being invoked.

To create a binder you will need to inherit from `System.Reflection.Binder` and override `BindToMethod`, `BindToField`, `SelectMethod`, `SelectProperty`, and `ChangeType`.

TIP: The `System.Type` class has a `DefaultBinder` property you can use if you need a binder but don't need special binding behavior.

In addition to being used to bind methods for dynamically invoking members, binders are used in other contexts. ASP.NET uses binding to bind the results of functions and properties to controls on a Web page. (Refer to the help documentation on the `Binder` class for a long example of a custom binder.)

Using the DefaultMemberAttribute

The `DefaultMemberAttribute` is applied to a type and takes a string argument indicating the name of the default member. The default member can be invoked by `InvokeMember` without passing the name of the member to invoke. For example, if we apply the `DefaultMemberAttribute` to `ReflectedClass`, naming the `HelloWorld` method as the default member, we can invoke `HelloWorld` without naming the method. Listing 4.7 shows the `ReflectedClass` class and a call to `InvokeMember` that relies on the `DefaultMemberAttribute`.

Listing 4.7 Applying and Invoking a Default Member

```
Imports System.Reflection

<DefaultMember("HelloWorld")> _
Public Class ReflectedClass
```

```
    Private FMessage As String
    Public Sub New(ByVal Message As String)
      FMessage = Message
    End Sub

    Public Sub New()
    End Sub

    Public Shared Sub HelloWorld()
      MsgBox("HelloWorld")
    End Sub

    Public Sub ShowMessage(ByVal Text As String)
      MsgBox(Text, MsgBoxStyle.Information, "Reflected Method")
    End Sub

End Class

'Excerpt from Form code
Private Sub InvokeDefaultMember()

  Dim HelloWorld As [Assembly] = [Assembly].LoadFrom(Path)
  Dim ReflectedClass As Type = HelloWorld.GetType("HelloWorld.Re-
flectedClass")
  ReflectedClass.InvokeMember("", _
    BindingFlags.Public Or _
    BindingFlags.Static Or BindingFlags.InvokeMethod, _
    Type.DefaultBinder, Nothing, Nothing)

End Sub
```

NOTE: Listing 4.7 is not a complete listing. To test the code in Listing 4.7, run the `LoadAssembly.sln` and call the `InvokeDefaultMember` method.

The `DefaultMemberAttribute` is applied to the class (as shown in the second line of the listing). The `InvokeDefaultMember` method at the end of Listing 4.7 demonstrates that we can invoke the default member implicitly by making the first argument to `InvokeMember` an empty string. The `BindingFlags` still have to reflect how the member was defined, as demonstrated in the listing.

Reflecting Members

Just as you are likely to reflect types and create instances, you will encounter scenarios where you want to explore other members of types. In this section I will demonstrate how to use Reflection to request other kinds of members.

Reflecting Methods

`Type` objects are used to interact with members of a type. You use `Type.InvokeMember` to invoke Reflected members whether those members are methods, properties, events, fields, or whatever. The key to invoking the member correctly is providing the correct information to the `InvokeMember` method, including the correct `BindingFlags` enumerated values. Listing 4.8 demonstrates how to invoke a protected method member.

Listing 4.8 Invoking a Protected Member Method by Using Reflection

```
Dim Instance As ReflectMembers = New ReflectMembers()
Dim T As Type = Instance.GetType()
T.InvokeMember("ProtectedMethod", _
  BindingFlags.InvokeMethod Or BindingFlags.NonPublic _
  Or BindingFlags.Instance, _
  Nothing, Instance, New Object() {})
```

The method we are invoking is defined in the `ReflectMembers` class in the `ReflectMembers.sln` example program. The first statement creates an instance of the `ReflectMembers` class. The second statement obtains a `Type` object for `ReflectMembers`. (The first two statements are identical for all the examples in the rest of this section; I won't repeat the descriptions again later.) Using the `Type` object we can call `InvokeMember`, invoking a method named `ProtectedMethod`.

The first argument of `InvokeMember` is the name of the member. (There are a couple of overloaded versions of `InvokeMember`. You can explore the variations in the help documentation.) The second parameter is the bitmasked `BindingFlags`. We use `BindingFlags.InvokeMethod`, `BindingFlags.NonPublic`, and `BindingFlags.Instance` strung together with `Or` to create the correct bitmask. `InvokeMethod` tells Reflection that we are looking for a method; `NonPublic` tells Reflection that we are looking for a nonpublic method; and `Instance` (as opposed to `Static`) tells Reflection that we are referring to a nonshared member.

The third argument of `InvokeMember` in Listing 4.8—represented by `Nothing`—is the `Binder` argument (refer to the Implementing a Simple Custom Binder subsection later in this section for an example of a binder). We aren't converting any data, so we don't need a binder.

The fourth argument is the object against which we want to invoke the member. Keep in mind that we can use late binding if `Option Strict Off` is set at the top of the module, and if we aren't loading the assembly using Reflection, we would invoke the member in the normal way. That is, we would simply create an object and call the method.

The final argument is the array of parameters we are passing to the method. `ProtectedMethod` has no arguments; thus we pass an empty array of objects to `InvokeMember`.

Reflecting Parameters

If you are reflecting types and methods because you don't know what is available in the assembly, you are likely not to know what a particular method's parameters are. You can use Reflection to obtain information about the order, type, and adornment of method parameters. The first step is to get the `MethodInfo` record for a particular method and then request the array of parameters. Listing 4.9 demonstrates how to obtain the parameters for a Reflected method.

Listing 4.9 Getting Parameter Information by Using Reflection

```
1:  Private Sub ReflectParameter()
2:    Dim Instance As ReflectMembers = New ReflectMembers()
3:    Dim T As Type = Instance.GetType()
4:    Dim Method As MethodInfo = T.GetMethod("PublicFunction")
5:
6:    Dim Parameters() As ParameterInfo = _
7:      Method.GetParameters()
8:
9:    Dim Parameter As ParameterInfo
10:   For Each Parameter In Parameters
11:     WriteParameter(Parameter)
12:   Next
13: End Sub
14:
```

```
15: Private Sub WriteParameter(ByVal P As ParameterInfo)
16:    Dim s As StringBuilder = New StringBuilder()
17:
18:    s.Append("Name=")
19:    s.Append(P.Name)
20:    s.Append(", Type=")
21:    s.Append(P.ParameterType().ToString())
22:    s.Append(", IsOptional=")
23:    s.Append(P.IsOptional().ToString)
24:    s.Append(", Position=")
25:    s.Append(P.Position.ToString())
26:    s.Append(", DefaultValue=")
27:    s.Append(P.DefaultValue.ToString())
28:    Console.WriteLine(s.ToString())
29: End Sub
```

TIP: Strings are immutable in .NET. If you are going to perform multiple string concatenations, using a `System.Text.StringBuilder` object will be much faster than using a `String` object.

Listing 4.9 demonstrates how to request the `MethodInfo` object for `PublicFunction` in line 4. From the `MethodInfo` object named `Method` (line 7) we can request all the parameters for that method. Lines 9 through 12 iterate through all the `ParameterInfo` objects returned by `GetParameters` and writes some of the details of each parameter to the console. Knowing the type, order, default values, and specifiers for a method's parameters will allow you to explore and invoke methods dynamically.

Reflecting Any Member

You can use the `Type.GetMember` and `Type.GetMembers` methods to request a `MemberInfo` object or an array of `MemberInfo` objects, respectively. A `MemberInfo` object is a general form of a specific type record. `GetMembers`, for example, will return all the members for a type, including methods, fields, properties, and events.

Reflecting Properties

When you reflect properties, you will need to keep in mind that there is a property setter and a property getter. The setter behaves like a subroutine and takes an argument to set the underlying field of the property, and the getter behaves like a function, returning a value. Listing 4.10 contains code that demonstrates how to set and get the value of a property using Reflection.

Listing 4.10 Setting and Getting Property Members by Using Reflection

```
Dim Instance As ReflectMembers = New ReflectMembers()

Dim T As Type = Instance.GetType()
T.InvokeMember("PublicProperty", _
  BindingFlags.SetProperty Or BindingFlags.Public _
  Or BindingFlags.Instance, _
  Nothing, Instance, New Object() {"Naughties"})

Dim Value As Object
Value = T.InvokeMember("PublicProperty", _
  BindingFlags.GetProperty Or BindingFlags.Public Or _
  BindingFlags.Instance, _
  Nothing, Instance, New Object() {})

Console.WriteLine("PublicProperty=" + Value.ToString())
```

In summary, Listing 4.10 requests a `Type` object. The `Type` object is used to call `InvokeMember` twice, setting and getting a property value. The first `InvokeMember` call sets the value of the property, working approximately like a method invocation. We use the enumerated value `Binding-Flags.SetProperty` to indicate that we want to invoke a property setter, and we pass the parameter based on the type of the property. (`PublicProperty` is defined as a string property.)

The second call to `InvokeMember` uses `BindingFlags.GetProperty` to request the getter. The second invocation behaves like a function, as illustrated by the assignment to the return `Value`. If we have specified `Option Strict On`, then `Value` must be an `Object` type because `InvokeMember` returns an object. If `Option Strict` is `Off`, then `Value` can be the type we know `InvokeMember` is returning; in Listing 4.10 it returns a string.

Reflecting Fields

As a general guideline fields are always private. In conjunction with that guideline, fields are usually exposed via public properties. This section contains some examples that demonstrate various kinds of field values. Like properties, field values can be used as right-hand-side and left-hand-side values. When you reflect a field, you need to indicate whether you want to get or set the field value.

Reflecting Public Fields

The code in Listing 4.11 demonstrates how to use `BindingFlags.Get-Field` to use the value of a Reflected field as a right-hand-side value and `BindingFlags.SetField` to use a field as a left-hand-side value. The code in Listing 4.11 assigns a public field the string value of the name of an intense action thriller, *Training Day*.

Listing 4.11 Reflecting a Public Field by Using `GetField` and `SetField`

```
Dim Instance As ReflectMembers = New ReflectMembers()

Dim T As Type = Instance.GetType()
T.InvokeMember("PublicField", _
  BindingFlags.SctFicld Or BindingFlags.Public _
  Or BindingFlags.Instance, _
  Nothing, Instance, New Object() {"Training Day"})

Dim Value As Object

Value = T.InvokeMember("PublicField", _
  BindingFlags.GetField Or BindingFlags.Public Or _
  BindingFlags.Instance, _
  Nothing, Instance, New Object() {})

Console.WriteLine("PublicField=" + Value.ToString())
```

If you compare Listings 4.10 and 4.11 you will quickly see that they are very similar. The biggest difference is that we are referring to a field in Listing 4.11; hence we use `BindingFlags.GetField` when we want to read the value of a field and `BindingFlags.SetField` when we want to write the value of a field.

Reflecting Nonpublic Fields

A more likely scenario is that you will want to obtain the value of fields that are not public. We'll add a twist. The Reflection code in Listing 4.12

incorporates a custom binder. The custom binder (defined in Listing 4.13 in the next subsection) supports assigning a string of digits to an integer field. That is, the binder performs a type conversion when it makes sense to do so, as it does when the value we are assigning to the field is the string representation of an integer.

There is one other issue suggested by this code: security. If any code could load an assembly and use Reflection to poke around in nonpublic areas of your types, the potential for abuse is serious. Fortunately Microsoft has an aggressive security model, and you can prevent code from reflecting nonpublic members and types (see the Understanding Reflection and Security section later in this chapter).

Here is Listing 4.12.

Listing 4.12 Reflecting a Private Field Value and Using a Custom Binder

```
1:  Private Sub ReflectPrivateField()
2:    Dim Instance As ReflectMembers = New ReflectMembers()
3:
4:    Dim T As Type = Instance.GetType()
5:    T.InvokeMember("PrivateField", _
6:      BindingFlags.SetField Or BindingFlags.NonPublic _
7:      Or BindingFlags.Instance, _
8:      New SimpleBinder(), Instance, New Object() {"13"})
9:
10:   Dim Value As Object
11:
12:   Value = T.InvokeMember("PrivateField", _
13:     BindingFlags.GetField Or BindingFlags.NonPublic Or _
14:     BindingFlags.Instance, _
15:     Nothing, Instance, New Object() {})
16:
17:   Console.WriteLine("PrivateField=" + Value.ToString())
18:
19: End Sub
```

Lines 5 through 8 represent using a private field as a left-hand-side value. `BindingFlags.SetField` means we will be providing a value for the field, and `BindingFlags.NonPublic` indicates that we are looking for a nonpublic field. Lines 12 through 15 represent using the field as a right-hand-side value.

You know that the field `PrivateField` is an integer because I am telling you that it is. However, notice that the array of arguments in line 8 is passing a string value "13" to the field. This works because I implemented a custom binder, which I am also passing to `InvokeMember`. `SimpleBinder` is defined in the next subsection in Listing 4.13.

Implementing a Simple Custom Binder

Binders are used with Reflection (as demonstrated in Listing 4.12) to convert values, and binders are also used to do things like bind fields to controls in ASP.NET Web pages.

The `System.Reflection.Binder` class is a `MustInherit` class. In the object-oriented vernacular, `MustInherit` classes are called *virtual abstract classes*. Technically speaking, a `MustInherit` class will have several members that must be overridden; that is, several members are adorned with the `MustOverride` modifier.

`SimpleBinder` in Listing 4.13 provides only the service of converting a string to an integer. As a result you will see that I provided an implementation for all the `MustOverride` methods for `SimpleBinder`, but all the methods except `ChangeType` are stubs.

Listing 4.13 Implementing a Custom Binder

```
1:   Public Class SimpleBinder
2:      Inherits System.Reflection.Binder
3:
4:      Public Overrides Function ChangeType( _
5:         ByVal value As Object, _
6:         ByVal type As Type, _
7:         ByVal culture As CultureInfo _
8:      ) As Object
9:
10:     Try
11:        If (value.GetType() Is GetType(String)) Then
12:           Return CInt(value)
13:        Else
14:           Return value
15:        End If
16:     Catch
17:        Return value
18:     End Try
19:
```

```
20:    End Function
21:
22:    Public Overrides Function SelectProperty( _
23:       ByVal bindingAttr As BindingFlags, _
24:       ByVal match() As PropertyInfo, _
25:       ByVal returnType As Type, _
26:       ByVal indexes() As Type, _
27:       ByVal modifiers() As ParameterModifier _
28:    ) As PropertyInfo
29:
30:    End Function
31:
32:    Public Overrides Function BindToMethod( _
33:       ByVal bindingAttr As BindingFlags, _
34:       ByVal match() As MethodBase, _
35:       ByRef args() As Object, _
36:       ByVal modifiers() As ParameterModifier, _
37:       ByVal culture As CultureInfo, _
38:       ByVal names() As String, _
39:       ByRef state As Object _
40:    ) As MethodBase
41:
42:    End Function
43:
44:    Public Overrides Function BindToField( _
45:       ByVal bindingAttr As BindingFlags, _
46:       ByVal match() As FieldInfo, _
47:       ByVal value As Object, _
48:       ByVal culture As CultureInfo _
49:    ) As FieldInfo
50:
51:    End Function
52:
53:
54:    Public Overrides Sub ReorderArgumentArray( _
55:       ByRef args() As Object, _
56:       ByVal state As Object _
57:    )
58:
59:    End Sub
60:
61:    Public Overrides Function SelectMethod( _
62:       ByVal bindingAttr As BindingFlags, _
63:       ByVal match() As MethodBase, _
64:       ByVal types() As Type, _
```

```
65:       ByVal modifiers() As ParameterModifier _
66:    ) As MethodBase
67:
68:    End Function
69:
70: End Class
```

To create a binder you must inherit from `System.Reflection.Binder` and provide an implementation for `ChangeType`, `SelectProperty`, `BindToMethod`, `BindToField`, `ReorderArgumentArray`, and `SelectMethod`. Listing 4.13 provides stubs that satisfy this requirement. The only method that does anything in the listing is `ChangeType`.

`ChangeType` is implemented in lines 4 through 20. The biggest part of the function is the long parameter list. For our purposes all we want to do is determine whether the `value` parameter can be converted to an integer and return the converted integer. In all other cases we return the `value` parameter; the conversion is 7 lines long, spanning lines 10 through 16.

Reflecting Events

Rounding out the implementation of members we can reflect are events, which are critically important to Windows-based programming (and all event-driven operating systems). Reflection supports discovering events and assigning event handlers to Reflected events, as demonstrated in Listing 4.14.

Listing 4.14 Assigning an Event Handler to a Reflected Event

```
1:   Private Sub ReflectEvent()
2:     Dim Instance As ReflectMembers = New ReflectMembers()
3:
4:     Dim T As Type = Instance.GetType()
5:     Dim [Event] As EventInfo
6:
7:     [Event] = T.GetEvent("PublicEvent", _
8:       BindingFlags.Public Or BindingFlags.Instance)
9:
10:    [Event].AddEventHandler(Instance, New _
11:      EventHandler(AddressOf Handler))
12:    Instance.DoEvent()
13:
14:    End Sub
```

Line 4 gets the `Type` object for `ReflectMembers` created on line 2. An `EventInfo` variable is declared on line 5. (Remember you can use keywords by putting them in brackets, but you may want to avoid doing so.) Line 7 gets the `EventInfo` object by calling `GetEvent` and naming the event. (I used instructional names for the members of `ReflectMembers`; that's why there is an event named `PublicEvent`.)

Line 10 uses the `EventInfo` object to call `AddEventHandler`. `AddEventHandler` needs an object to associate the handler with (`Instance`), and `System.Delegate` is constructed and initialized with the address of a method that matches the `EventHandler` signature. (Refer to Chapter 3 on delegates.) Finally, to test that everything is wired correctly, line 12 calls a method that raises the event.

Practical Applications of Reflection

A common and practical application—binding properties to controls—uses Reflection behind the scenes. This works in Windows Forms and Web pages.

`DataBinding.sln` contains an example of user-defined type `Customer` and a place to store customers as well as a `Contacts` class that can contain an `ArrayList` of contacts. The `ArrayList` implements an interface called `IList`, which supports enumeration that allows us to bind controls directly to our objects. The sample application is shown in Figure 4.1.

The `Customer` class contains two properties, `Name` and `WebSite` (as shown in the figure). The `Contacts` class contains an `ArrayList` field and a `ReadOnly ArrayList` property named `Items`. Here is the implementation of the `Contacts.Items` property.

```
Public ReadOnly Property Items() As ArrayList
  Get
    If (FItems Is Nothing) Then FItems = New ArrayList()
    Return FItems
  End Get
End Property
```

NOTE: The `Items` property employs a strategy known as *lazy instantiation*. Lazy instantiation allows us to defer object creation until we need it. The spin-up time for classes is reduced by the cost of the lazy object, and we are sure that the object is created only when it is absolutely requested. In the preceding fragment, the `ArrayList` is created on first request.

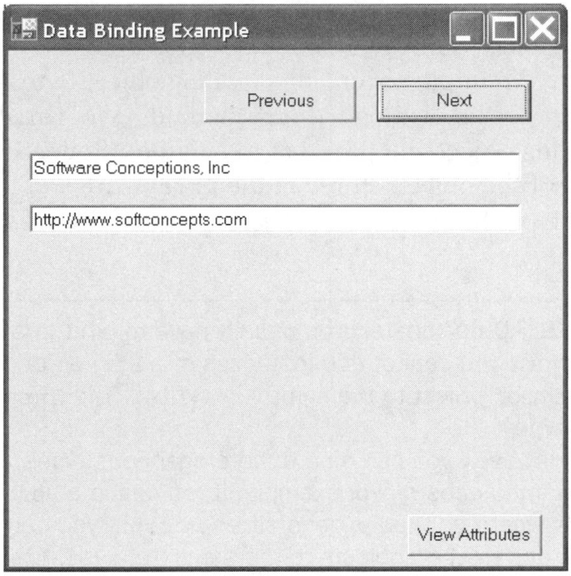

Figure 4.1 A simple form bound directly to the shown `TextBox` controls by using Reflection and `DataBindings`.

The property uses the `ReadOnly` modifier, which means we can and will implement only a property getter. We will bind to the `Contacts.Items` property.

To bind one of the `TextBox` controls to a specific property of our customer—aside from adding customers to a `Contacts` object—we need to determine which property of the `TextBox` we are binding to and which property of `Customer` we will get the data from. `TextBox.Text` is an appropriate property of the `TextBox` to bind to, and it is reasonable to bind the `Customer.Name` property to that. Here is the single line of code needed to accomplish this.

```
TextBox1.DataBindings.Add("Text", FContacts.Items, "Name")
```

Assuming we have an instance of `Contacts` named `FContacts`, we invoke the `TextBox1.DataBindings.Add` method. The first argument represents the `TextBox` property to bind to. The second argument is our data source; it's pretty cool that we can bind right to our `Contacts.Items` collection. The third property is the name of the field in the `Contacts.Items` data source that we want to get data from. Literally, now, `TextBox1` is a data-bound control; it is bound to a `Contacts` object.

It is interesting to note that `ArrayList` does not have a property named `Name`. `Name` is discovered by Reflection against a single object in the `Array-List`. We implicitly create a binding object by passing the necessary arguments to the overloaded `Add` method. (We can also manually construct a binding object and pass that to `Add` too.) Reflection is used to examine the type of the objects stored in the `ArrayList` and to bind to the elements of that type. In this instance the object is a `Customer` object.

NOTE: Unfortunately you usually have to bind to a homogeneous object. For example, you cannot add instances of a `Person` object and an instance of a `Customer` object to the same `ArrayList`. The `ArrayList` must contain all of one type.

However, you can bind to heterogeneous types as long as all types have the same ancestry. For example, if you define a `Person` class and a `Customer` class where `Customer` generalizes `Person`, you can add both `Customer` objects and `Person` objects to the same `ArrayList` and the binding will still work.

To make navigation automatic, implement an event handler for the buttons and change the position of the `BindingContext` associated with a particular control. For example, to implement forward navigation, increment the `Position` property of the `BindingManagerBase` object. In the following statement, `TextBox1.BindingContext.Item` returns a `BindingManagerBase` object.

```
TextBox1.BindingContext.Item(FContacts.Items).Position += 1
```

Incrementing the `Position` property of the `BindingManagerBase` will safely navigate to the next element in the collection. If all the controls on a form are bound to the same data source, you need to change the position of only one to update all. Decrement the position to move backward. The `BindingManagerBase` will not allow you to increment or decrement outside of the range of elements.

One of the benefits of an object-oriented framework is generalization and reuse. By generalizing how controls are bound, we have greater flexibility with what we bind to. Of course, we can bind to an ADO.NET `DataSet` object, or we can bind directly to collections of objects as demonstrated.

Reflecting Custom Attributes

In Chapter 5 you will learn about attributes: how to use some of the interesting existing attributes and how to create customer attributes. We'll leap ahead a bit for a moment and take a look at the mechanics of requesting attributes by using Reflection. At the heart of our technical demonstration is the `Attribute` class and the `GetCustomAttributes` method. Listing 4.15 demonstrates how to request attributes for a specific type. (In Chapter 5 you will learn that any element might have attributes applied; the same code demonstrated in Chapter 5 will return Reflected attributes for members as well as types.)

Listing 4.15 Reflecting Attributes

```
Dim Attributes() As Object
Attributes = GetType(Customer).GetCustomAttributes(True)

Dim A As Attribute

For Each A In Attributes
  If (TypeOf A Is DescriptionAttribute) Then
    Debug.WriteLine(CType(A, DescriptionAttribute).Description)
  End If
Next
```

The first step is to determine whether you want one or all of the attributes. In our example we want all of the attributes for a type; thus we declare an array of objects. (`GetCustomAttributes` returns an array of objects that are actually attributes.) The second statement requests all the attributes for the type of `Customer`. The argument `True` passed to `GetCustomAttributes` instructs Reflection to search ancestors for inherited attributes too. Pass `False` to `GetCustomAttributes` to ignore ancestral attributes.

TIP: The `DescriptionAttribute` is used specifically to provide a text description in the `Properties` window for components.

The remaining code simply iterates through the array of attributes returned. In Listing 4.15 we are specifically looking for the `DescriptionAttribute` object defined in the `System.ComponentModel`. If any of the attributes applied to the type are `DescriptionAttribute` objects, the `Description` property of the attribute is written to the `Output` window.

Understanding Reflection and Security

Suppose you downloaded some code from the Internet. If any of that code could poke around on your system, load any assembly, and perform any operation, then .NET would be problematic indeed. However, instead of opening security holes, Microsoft has advertised that security risks have been diminished by the security model introduced in .NET.

Chapter 18 goes into security at length, so I will refer you to that chapter for the complete picture. In general, code must be granted `Reflection-Permission` to obtain information about nonpublic members. Without `ReflectionPermission` code can obtain information about public types and members; enumerate types, modules, and assemblies; and invoke public members.

You might be concerned about code downloaded from the Internet performing some malicious activity, which might include accessing the file system or emitting code and modifying your .NET applications. The default security policy does not extend Reflection, environment, registry, DNS, or socket permissions to Internet code, and it has only limited permissions—like read-only access for file IO, printing, security, and Web permissions.

If security is an immediate risk to your project, read Chapter 5 on attributes and then skip ahead to Chapter 18. (You can also explore the help documentation links like `ms-help://MS.VSCC/MS.MSDNVS/cpguide/html/cpconadministeringsecuritypolicy.htm` in Visual Studio .NET.)

Emitting IL Code at Runtime

You have more than likely heard that Visual Basic .NET, and in fact all .NET code, is emitted to an Intermediate Language (IL) form when you compile an application. The IL code is actually just-in-time compiled (JITted) before it is actually executed. This follows the Java model of byte code. The foundation for doing this is probably similar to the reasons that Sun implemented Java that way: someone envisions porting .NET to non-Windows machines. It makes sense and is a good idea.

Imagine, some vendor will port VB .NET to the Mac, Linux, and UNIX. Now smart VB .NET programmers everywhere can work on software for any company, anywhere. If you want to see some IL code, run the `ildasm.exe` (IL disassembler) utility in the framework `bin` directory and explore one of the .NET assemblies created in this chapter (see Figure 4.2). If you are familiar with assembler, you will detect a similarity between IL and assembly code for Intel-based processors.

TIP: You can use Windows Explorer to search for `ildasm.exe` if you aren't sure where your .NET framework code is located.

.NET supports and actually facilitates emitting IL code at runtime. This capability is implemented in the `System.Reflection.Emit` namespace as a collaboration of classes ending with the suffix `Builder`. A builder is a class that emits IL code; examples include `AssemblyBuilder`, `Constructor-Builder`, `CustomAttributeBuilder`, `EnumBuilder`, `EventBuilder`, `Field-Builder`, `ILGenerator`, `LocalBuilder`, `MethodBuilder`, `ModuleBuilder`,

```
/ SimpleBinder::ChangeType : object(object,class [mscorlib]System.Type,cla...  _ □ X
.method public virtual instance object   ChangeType(object 'value',
                                                     class [mscorlib]S
                                                     class [mscorlib]S
{
  // Code size       69 (0x45)
  .maxstack  2
  .locals init ([0] object ChangeType)
  IL_0000:  nop
  IL_0001:  nop
  .try
  {
    IL_0002:  ldarg.1
    IL_0003:  callvirt    instance class [mscorlib]System.Type [mscor
    IL_0008:  ldtoken     [mscorlib]System.String
    IL_000d:  call        class [mscorlib]System.Type [mscorlib]Syste
    IL_0012:  bne.un.s    IL_0024
    IL_0014:  ldarg.1
    IL_0015:  call        int32 [Microsoft.VisualBasic]Microsoft.Visu
    IL_001a:  box         [mscorlib]System.Int32
    IL_001f:  stloc.0
    IL_0020:  leave.s     IL_0043
    IL_0022:  br.s        IL_0029
```

Figure 4.2 IL disassembler showing the fragment of the IL code for the `SimpleBinder` class created earlier in the chapter.

`ParameterBuilder`, `PropertyBuilder`, and `TypeBuilder`. As you can detect by the names, there is a builder for most of the major elements of code. There are also structures in `System.Reflection.Emit` representing tokens like events, fields, methods, parameters, properties, and the like.

The `Builder` classes, tokens, and `ILGenerator` are designed to facilitate emitting IL code at runtime. You might ask, "Why would I want to do this?" I can't tell you all the reasons you might want to emit IL; I don't think most of them have been invented yet. I can tell you that Microsoft has offered some likely scenarios for emitting IL, including creating dynamic modules, running script in a browser, running script in an ASP.NET Web page, and compiling regular expressions. (See the help information on the `System.Text.RegularExpressions` namespace in Visual Studio .NET for more information on regular expressions.)

Some of the tasks you can perform with the `Reflection.Emit` classes include defining and saving an assembly at runtime; defining and saving modules at runtime; defining, creating instances of, and invoking members of types at runtime; and defining symbolic debugging formation for debuggers and code profilers.

TIP: A good resource on regular expressions is the e-book *Regular Expressions in .NET* by Dan Appleman [2002]. This 75-page book is available in PDF format for download.

Emitting is easily a subject that will ultimately need its own book. Unfortunately we have a limited amount of space; instead of trying to describe all the types in `Reflection.Emit` I will pick one example. Regular expressions provide a language for finding and replacing text patterns. Compiled regular expressions can be converted to machine code instead of regular expression instructions, providing an optimization. Regular expressions are useful, and emitting compiled regular expressions sounds like fun (at—let me look—2:29 in the morning), so we'll create an example that emits compiled regular expressions at runtime.

A Quick Review of Regular Expressions

The `Regex` class is one of the mainstays of the `System.Text.RegularExpressions` namespace. `Regex` has shared and instance methods that escapes and unescapes special metacharacters; match an input string against a pattern string; split strings; and replace patterns found in an input string. (You can look up individual `Regex` class members in the Visual Studio .NET help documentation.)

A common use for a regular expression is to provide a pattern and an input string and let the `Regex` class indicate whether the input string matches the pattern. Regular expressions can be very simple or quite complex. For example, you can check whether a string of characters are all digits with a very simple regular expression.

```
^\d+$
```

An example of a more complex regular expression changes a date in the format *month/day/year* to the format *day-month-year*.

```
\b(?<month>\d{1,2})/(?<day>\d{1,2})/(?<year>\d{2,4})\b
```

The regular expression `^\d+$` is read, "Start at the beginning of the string and match one or more digits until the end of the string." This pattern will match contiguous digits. The second regular expression stores the first one or two digits in `<month>`, the second one or two digits in `<day>`, and the final two or four digits in `<year>`.

NOTE: Designate your company's toolsmith as the person who specializes in regular expressions. When someone needs to perform some parsing, instead of writing code, have the toolsmith put together a single regular expression.

Clearly regular expressions can be terse. (That's one reason a book like *Regular Expressions in .NET* by Dan Appleman is helpful.) But consider the cost in lines of code that would perform an equivalent parsing operation. The regular expression parser packs a powerful punch in a single line of terse characters.

Compiled Regular Expressions

If you use a regular expression one time, you can invoke one of the shared methods. For example, `Regex.IsMatch("12345", "^\d+$")` will return `True`, indicating that the input string `"12345"` is in fact a contiguous string of digits. If you are going to invoke an operation on the same regular expression many times, explicitly create an instance of the `Regex` class, and call the instance method.

```
Imports System.Text.RegularExpressions
Dim Expression As Regex = New Regex("^\d+$")
Regex.IsMatch("12345")
```

The `Imports` statement is placed at the top of the module. The `Regex` object is declared and created as a field in the class, and the `Regex.Is-Match` method is invoked multiple times, perhaps passing in the input string as a variable. (The code fragment shows a constant.)

NOTE: I performed a couple of simple tests evaluating a million random string digits and got about a 50 percent better performance result with compiled regular expressions, but this is not scientific. I would consider this an optimizing step. For example, if you have a search engine scanning millions of Web pages for HTML content, you might want to experiment with compiled regular expressions and perform your own analysis.

Another refinement you can make is to compile the regular expression. As defined in the preceding code fragment, the regular input string is parsed and compared using an interpreter. If you create an instance of the regular expression object with the `RegexOptions.Compiled` argument, the regular expression is converted to IL code and JITted, purportedly resulting in better performance. To compile the regular expression introduced in the prior fragment we need to make the following revision to the constructor invocation.

```
Dim Expression As Regex = New Regex("^\d+$", RegexOptions.Compiled)
```

Emitting a Type Dynamically

Emitting code dynamically is easier than it could be but is not for the weak of heart. Experimenting with emitted code, it took me about two minutes to create a simple type with a couple of fields, properties, a constructor, and validation methods for the properties. It took about ten hours to create approximately the same class and assembly emitting code with Reflection, representing about two orders of magnitude difference in time.

The benefit of emitting code is that you will be able to truly create dynamic, postdeployment behaviors. As good as the classes in the `Emit` namespace are, there is still a tremendous amount of work involved. In a nutshell, you have to write code to do all the things you would do manually in the Visual Studio .NET IDE. For example, you have to create an assembly; add modules to that assembly; define types; and add fields, properties, methods, events, constructors, and code to all those elements. And that will get you a basic type. The good news is that after you get the IL code right, your emitter should work every time.

To demonstrate some of what is involved I borrowed from the `ReflectionEmit` sample that ships with Visual Studio .NET. (You can usually find this code in the `FrameworkSDK\Samples\Technologies\Reflection\ ReflectionEmit\vb\EmitAssembly.vb` sample file. The best way to find this file is to search in Windows Explorer.) The `CreateCallee` method, taken from the `EmitAssembly.vb` sample code, is provided in Listing 4.16.

Listing 4.16 Emitting a Dynamic Type to Memory by Using Reflection

```
1:   ' Create the callee transient dynamic assembly.
2:   Private Shared Function CreateCallee(appDomain As AppDomain, _
3:     access As AssemblyBuilderAccess) As Type
4:
5:     ' Create a simple name for the callee assembly.
6:     Dim assemblyName As New AssemblyName()
7:     assemblyName.Name = "EmittedAssembly"
8:
9:     ' Create the callee dynamic assembly.
10:    Dim [assembly] As AssemblyBuilder = _
11:      appDomain.DefineDynamicAssembly(assemblyName, access)
12:
13:    ' Create a dynamic module named "CalleeModule" in the callee assembly.
14:    Dim [module] As ModuleBuilder
15:    If access = AssemblyBuilderAccess.Run Then
16:      [module] = [assembly].DefineDynamicModule("EmittedModule")
17:    Else
18:      [module] = [assembly].DefineDynamicModule("EmittedModule", _
19:      "EmittedModule.mod")
20:    End If
21:
22:    ' Define a public class named "HelloWorld" in the assembly.
23:    Dim helloWorldClass As TypeBuilder = [module].DefineType( _
24:      "HelloWorld", TypeAttributes.Public)
25:
26:    ' Define a private String field named "Greeting" in the type.
27:    Dim greetingField As FieldBuilder = helloWorldClass.DefineField( _
```

```
28:        "Greeting", GetType(String), FieldAttributes.Private)
29:
30:    ' Create the constructor.
31:    Dim constructorArgs As Type() = {GetType(String)}
32:    Dim constructor As ConstructorBuilder = _
33:      helloWorldClass.DefineConstructor( _
34:      MethodAttributes.Public, CallingConventions.Standard, _
35:      constructorArgs)
36:
37:    ' Generate IL for the method. The constructor calls its superclass
38:    ' constructor. The constructor stores its argument in the private field.
39:    Dim constructorIL As ILGenerator = constructor.GetILGenerator()
40:    constructorIL.Emit(OpCodes.Ldarg_0)
41:    Dim superConstructor As ConstructorInfo = _
42:      GetType(Object).GetConstructor(Type.EmptyTypes)
43:    constructorIL.Emit(OpCodes.Call, superConstructor)
44:    constructorIL.Emit(OpCodes.Ldarg_0)
45:    constructorIL.Emit(OpCodes.Ldarg_1)
46:    constructorIL.Emit(OpCodes.Stfld, greetingField)
47:    constructorIL.Emit(OpCodes.Ret)
48:
49:    ' Create the GetGreeting method.
50:    Dim getGreetingMethod As MethodBuilder = _
51:      helloWorldClass.DefineMethod("GetGreeting", _
52:      MethodAttributes.Public, GetType(String), Nothing)
53:
54:    ' Generate IL for GetGreeting.
55:    Dim methodIL As ILGenerator = _
56:      getGreetingMethod.GetILGenerator()
57:    methodIL.Emit(OpCodes.Ldarg_0)
58:    methodIL.Emit(OpCodes.Ldfld, greetingField)
59:    methodIL.Emit(OpCodes.Ret)
60:
61:    ' Bake the class HelloWorld.
62:    Return helloWorldClass.CreateType()
63: End Function 'CreateCallee
```

I certainly don't want to discourage anyone from experimenting with `Reflection.Emit` because it is really cool and some good things will come out of this technology. However, keep in mind that all the code above produces approximately the following code in an in-memory assembly and module.

```
Public Class HelloWorld
  Private Greeting As String
  Public Sub New(S As String)
    MyBase.New()
    Greeeting = S
  End Sub
  Public Function GetGreeting() As String
    Return Greeting
  End Function
End Class
```

As you can see, Listing 4.16 does not emit a lot of code. Fortunately there are bound to be tool builders that will extend `Reflection.Emit` and create tools that will emit more code with simpler constructs. Let's take a moment to understand how the code is emitted.

Lines 6 and 7 create an assembly name, which is used to create an assembly (think ".NET application") on lines 10 and 11. `DefineDynamicAssembly` creates an in-memory assembly. (This code emits an assembly to memory, not to disk.) Lines 15 through 20 are used to determine the kind of module to create. (Modules are units of code.) If `AssemblyBuilderAccess.Save` is used to create the dynamic assembly, the `AssemblyBuilder.Save` method can be used to write the assembly to a file. After line 20 executes, a module as been emitted. We can add code to modules.

Notice the rampant use of *name*`Builder` classes. These are the classes we spoke of earlier in the chapter, from the `System.Reflection.Emit` namespace. The `Builder` classes make our job quite a bit easier, although not easy. Lines 23 and 24 create a `TypeBuilder` object, which is used to emit classes and structures.

Lines 27 and 28 add the `Greeting` field to the type (using a `Field-Builder`) by providing a name, field type, and access specifier. (These are things you would actually do if you were writing this code from scratch.)

Lines 31 through 47 emit a constructor that calls the superclass constructor and assigns the `constructor` parameter to the `Greeting` field. `OpCodes` are defined in the help documentation. `OpCodes` are pure IL; they look like pseudo-assembly code when emitted to a file. (You can use `ildasm.exe` to view IL code in a compiled assembly.) For example, line 43 actually invokes the parent class constructor. Line 43 equates to `MyBase.New()`.

Lines 50 through 59 emit the `GetGreeting` function. `MethodBuilders` generate subroutines and functions. You specify a name, access specifier, return type, and argument types. `GetGreeting` is defined to return a string and take no arguments, as codified in line 52. Consistently throughout Listing 4.16, the `Builder` objects are used to request an `ILGenerator` object.

The `ILGenerator` class is actually emitting the code (see lines 57 through 59). Finally we call `TypeBuilder.CreateType` to create the `HelloWorld` class on line 62.

It takes quite a bit of work to rough-frame a dynamic assembly. You can use two tricks to help you get started: (1) think of the emitted code the same way you would if you were typing in the code, and (2) actually write a demo program and create the code manually. Use `ildasm.exe` to view the IL generated when you type the code and emulate that code. There are differences, and you will want to make some aspects of your emitter generic, allowing the emitted code to vary. If you want an emitter to emit the same code, you might as well write the code one time.

Let's get back to where we left off in the preceding section: emitting compiled regular expressions.

Emitting a Compiled Regular Expression Dynamically

Someone has already made at least one utility based on Reflection. (There will probably be dozens of good ones by the time you read this.) The `Regex` class has a `CompileToAssembly` method that will generate a dynamic assembly with very little effort.

From our previous discussion we can discern the value of a dynamically generated assembly containing compiled regular expressions. Recall that compiled regular expressions can offer performance benefits over uncompiled regular expressions. Suppose you have some useful regular expressions that your customers are using heavily in your deployed applications— or better, you create a tool that allows you to experiment with regular expressions and automatically bundle and ship them to customers when you get them right. You could allow the customer to dynamically compile the most heavily used expressions on demand. Listing 4.17 demonstrates how you can emit a compiled regular expression on demand. (The complete example program is defined in `ReflectionEmit.sln`.)

Listing 4.17 Emitting a Compiled Regular Expression into an Assembly at Runtime

```
1:  Imports System.Reflection
2:  Imports System.Text.RegularExpressions
3:
4:  Private Sub EmitRegularExpressionAssembly()
5:    Dim Expression As String = InputBox("Expression")
6:    Dim Title As String = InputBox("Expression Name")
```

```
7:
8:    Dim CompilationInfo() As RegexCompilationInfo = _
9:      {New RegexCompilationInfo(Expression, RegexOptions.Compiled, _
10:     Title, "CompiledRegularExpressions", True)}
11:
12:   Dim Name As AssemblyName = New AssemblyName()
13:   Name.Name = "Regex"
14:   Regex.CompileToAssembly(CompilationInfo, Name)
15: End Sub
```

This code emits a relatively complex assembly containing a class that inherits from the `RegexRunner`, `RegexRunnerFactory`, and `Regex` classes. (A lot of work someone did for us.) The code we have to write is relatively straightforward.

Lines 1 and 2 import the namespaces we need to emit the compiled regular expression assembly. Lines 5 and 6 ask the user for a regular expression and a name for that expression, representing a user interface. Lines 8, 9, and 10 are key. The statement beginning on line 8 and ending on line 10 creates an instance of an array of `RegexCompilationInfo` objects. We can add multiple expressions by defining multiple `RegexCompilationInfo` objects. Our array has only one. The regular expression is passed to `RegexCompilationInfo` first, followed by `RegexOptions`. `RegexOptions.Compiled` will cause our regular expression to be compiled when it is emitted. The third argument is the expression name, the fourth is the namespace, and the last argument indicates whether the access modifier is public for the regular expression class emitted.

Lines 12 and 13 create an assembly name for our regular expression assembly, and line 14 emits the assembly. When finished there is a DLL assembly named `regex.dll` that you can reference and invoke regular expressions on or that you can load dynamically using Reflection and use in the same application that emitted the regular expression assembly. (See `ReflectionEmit.sln` for a working demo program.)

Summary

Some chapters are pure fun, and some chapters are difficult. Chapter 4 was a little of both for me. There is a lot of material in this chapter. To summarize, we spoke of three different programming languages and technologies:

Reflection in Visual Basic .NET, regular expressions, and Intermediate Language. The uses of Reflection, regular expressions, and emitted IL code are likely new to many people.

The challenge for me was adding substantive material without writing 400 pages on this one subject. The challenge for you may have been that everything in this chapter was new to you, and learning about three languages is a tall order.

Regular expressions need a book of their own. Emitting code will need a whole book, too. When I wrote this chapter there were no whole books on Reflection in .NET and only an e-book on .NET regular expressions (a great one by Appleman [2002]). Look down. That is the precipice of the bleeding edge.

CHAPTER 5

Attributes

Never mistake a clear view for a short distance.

—Paul Saffo, Institute for the Future

Introduction

I started working on my first .NET book project in 1998 or 1999. Of course I thought Visual Studio 6 would simply become version 7 and that VB6 would become VB7; I hadn't heard of C# at that point, and I hadn't heard the term .NET in the late 1990s. I have been using and exploring the .NET Framework and Visual Basic .NET for some time now—a couple of years at least—and the more I use it, the more impressed, amazed, and intrigued I become.

It doesn't take very long to get past the changes in VB .NET grammar, but the framework is like the deep blue sea. In general it will take the average VB6 programmer a few months to tackle the grammatical changes in VB .NET. The framework will take more time to master. The .NET Framework, common to all .NET languages, is broad and deep. Several facets make it a compelling choice for businesses, managers, and developers alike. If I am successful, by the end of this book you will understand that you are at a distinct disadvantage if you are using older, pre-.NET technologies.

Attributes are an important part of .NET's compelling story. Attributes play a role in providing metadata for applications, supporting the code access declarative security model, emitting IL, and emitting code and assemblies using the CodeDOM. We'll explore these aspects of attributes in this chapter.

Applying Attributes

In .NET code is compiled to an assembly. The assembly contains IL code and metadata. IL is a state between source code and machine language. By

125

emitting IL the CLR has one more opportunity to examine code before it is just-in-time compiled (JITted) and to compare the security permissions requested against those granted. Also, the total number of compilers and JITters is dramatically reduced (see the note). In addition to IL, .NET assemblies contain metadata. Metadata allows assemblies to carry additional information around that uniquely identifies the assembly. Metadata is added to assemblies via attributes.

NOTE: A second reason to compile code to a byte code form (IL is analogous to Java byte code) is to reduce the number of compilers that must be written. If a compiler writes to a machine language, vendors will need to produce one compiler for every machine operating system and every language supported. By compiling to an intermediate form, vendors need to write only one compiler per language and one JITter per operating system.

The reasoning is pretty straightforward, as presented by John Gough [2002] in *Compiling for the .NET Common Language Runtime (CLR)*. If all byte code is created equal, there needs to be only one JITter per operating system that converts any byte code compiled from any language into machine language suitable for the target operating system. Instead of one compiler for each language for each operating system, compiling to an intermediate form results in one compiler per language and one JITter per operating system.

Suppose there were 10 languages supported on 10 operating systems. Without an intermediate form there would be 10×10 compilers. With an intermediate form there are only 10 compilers and 10 JITters, or 20 applications instead of 100.

The concept of metadata was implemented for .NET to help relieve "DLL hell." The role of attributes is to associate metadata, or extra information, with an assembly. Metadata mitigates the need to store information that uniquely identifies an application in a separate location, the registry. Attributes play a central role here.

Reviewing Attribute Conventions

Like everything else in .NET, attributes are just classes. The good news is that if you know how to use classes, you have won half the battle. (We'll cover conventions for custom attributes in the Creating Custom Attributes section later in the chapter.)

NOTE: Any class can be used as an attribute, but it will probably lead to a lot of confusion if you do so. However, it might be fun to experiment with classes applied as attributes even if your adventures aren't especially fruitful.

By convention attributes are classes with an `Attribute` suffix. When you apply an attribute, by convention you drop the `Attribute` suffix. For example, if you apply the `DefaultMemberAttribute` to a class, you drop the `Attribute` suffix and apply the attribute using attribute notation, as demonstrated below.

```
<DefaultMember("Item")> Public Class HasDefaultMember
...
```

NOTE: I'm not sure why dropping the `Attribute` suffix is supported or has become a convention. I can't think of a logical explanation, so I guess that dropping the `Attribute` suffix is supported for convenience.

The attribute is applied in the same line as the entity it is applied to in Visual Basic .NET. If you want to apply the attribute in the preceding line, you must use the line continuation character (_). Here is the `DefaultMemberAttribute` applied to `HasDefaultMember` using the line continuation character.

```
<DefaultMember("Item")> _
Public Class HasDefaultMember
...
```

It is important to recognize that you are invoking a constructor call with the attribute syntax. The parameters you are passing, called *positional arguments* or *named arguments* (not shown in the code fragment above), are parameters to the `Attribute` class constructor. Refer to the Creating Custom Attributes section for more information on positional and named arguments.

Applying Attributes to Entities

The most common use of attributes is to apply them to assemblies, classes, other types, or members. Since there are a lot of attributes (and we have the ability to create additional custom attributes), I won't make any effort to exhaustively list available attributes. Instead I will demonstrate several examples that show how to apply attributes and introduce a few interesting attributes, so you will know how to apply any attribute you encounter.

Using the `DefaultMemberAttribute`, `DefaultPropertyAttribute`, and `Default` Modifier

The `DefaultMemberAttribute` is applied to indicate that a member of a class is the default member that will be called when the `InvokeMember` method is invoked. For example, if you obtain a `Type` object for a specific type and use that object to call `InvokeMember`, you can leave blank the member name argument for `InvokeMember`. If a default member exists, it will be called by `InvokeMember`. Listing 5.1 offers an example.

NOTE: These three subjects were placed in this section together because they sound related. Doing so provided me with an opportunity to introduce two new attributes and clarify the distinction between `DefaultPropertyAttribute` and the `Default` modifier.

Listing 5.1 Implementing and Invoking Default Members Using Reflection

```
<DefaultMember("IsDefault")> _
Public Class HasDefaultMember

  Public Shared Sub IsDefault()
    Console.WriteLine("IsDefault DefaultMember invoked")
  End Sub

End Class

Public Sub TestDefaultMember()
  Dim t As Type = _
    Type.GetType("DefaultMemberDemo.HasDefaultMember")

  ' We don't need the default member's name
  t.InvokeMember("", BindingFlags.Static Or _
    BindingFlags.Public Or BindingFlags.InvokeMethod, _
    Nothing, Nothing, Nothing)
End Sub
```

HasDefaultMember in Listing 5.1 demonstrates how to apply the De-
faultMemberAttribute to the class, supplying the name of the member
that is the default member. The second method—TestDefaultMember—
demonstrates how to invoke the default member using Reflection. (Chapter
4 covered Reflection in depth.) Notice that we did not need to express the
member name—the first argument to InvokeMember—to invoke the default member. The DefaultPropertyAttribute is applied at the class
level too. (Technically it is limited to the class level because of the At-
tributeUsageAttribute used when the DefaultPropertyAttribute
was defined. Refer to the Creating Custom Attributes section later in this
chapter for more information.) The DefaultPropertyAttribute is defined in the System.ComponentModel namespace and is initialized with the
name of the component property that will be the default selected property
in the Properties window when the control is selected. The Default-
PropertyAttribute is applied identically to the DefaultMemberAt-
tribute. (Refer to Chapter 9 for more information.)

If you are trying to make a property behave as the default property, for
example, when you use an object in a context where a property is expected,
you want to use the Default modifier. The Default modifier indicates that
a property is the default property; however, this modifier can be applied
only to indexed properties in .NET. The reason for this is that VB6 used
Set, Get, and Let, which acted as cues to the compiler that you were referring to a property when no property was typed in the code. VB .NET does
not support Get, Set, and Let for properties, but a cue is still needed. Thus,
the array operators play the role of cues to the compiler. Listing 5.2 demonstrates how to define a class that uses the Default modifier and a client
method that interacts with the default property.

Listing 5.2 Using the Default Property Modifier on Indexed Properties

```
Public Class HasDefault
  Inherits ReadOnlyCollectionBase

  Public Shared Function CreateNew() As HasDefault
    Dim Instance As HasDefault = New HasDefault()
    Instance.InnerList.Add("Never ")
    Instance.InnerList.Add("mistake ")
    Instance.InnerList.Add("a ")
    Instance.InnerList.Add("clear ")
    Instance.InnerList.Add("view ")
    Instance.InnerList.Add("for ")
```

```vb
    Instance.InnerList.Add("a ")
    Instance.InnerList.Add("short ")
    Instance.InnerList.Add("distance")
    Instance.InnerList.Add("!")


    Return Instance
  End Function


  Default Public ReadOnly Property Item(ByVal Index As Integer) As
String
    Get
      Return CType(InnerList(Index), String)
    End Get
  End Property

End Class

Public Sub TestDefault()
  Dim HasDefault As HasDefault = HasDefault.CreateNew
  Dim I As Integer

  For I = 0 To HasDefault.Count - 1
    Console.Write(HasDefault(I))
  Next
  Console.WriteLine()
End Sub
```

The `Default` modifier is employed in the `ReadOnly` property `Item` defined in the `HasDefault` class that inherits from `ReadOnlyCollection-Base`. (`ReadOnlyCollectionBase` is defined in `System.Collections`; hence, you will have to use an `Imports` statement with the code as it is.) The `TestDefault` subroutine creates an instance of the `HasDefault` class (by using the factory method `CreateNew`) and uses a `For` loop to iterate over all the elements in the `HasDefault` object. Notice that I am not explicitly referring to the `Item` property in the line of code `Console.Write(Has-Default(I))`; however, if you place a breakpoint in the `Item` getter method, you will see that the `Default` property is being invoked. This is true even though the code looks as if we are referring to an array of `HasDefault` objects.

Using the `Obsolete` Member Attribute

The `ObsoleteAttribute` is used to mark elements of code that are being deprecated in future versions and will no longer be supported. The basic version of the `ObsoleteAttribute` requires no parameters and will display a message in the Task List indicating that the element is obsolete (see Figure 5.1). Listing 5.3 demonstrates an example of the `ObsoleteAttribute`.

Listing 5.3 Using the `ObsoleteAttribute`

```
<Obsolete()> _
Public Sub TestDefault()
  Dim HasDefault As HasDefault = HasDefault.CreateNew
  Dim I As Integer
  For I = 0 To HasDefault.Count - 1
    Console.Write(HasDefault(I))
  Next
  Console.WriteLine()
End Sub
```

You can pass a custom string message and a Boolean indicating whether the obsolete element is treated as an error by the compiler. The `Obsolete-Attribute` can be applied to all elements of code except parameters, return values, modules, and assemblies.

Applying Attributes

There are a large number of existing attributes, and because attributes are just classes you can expect that number to grow. The most important thing

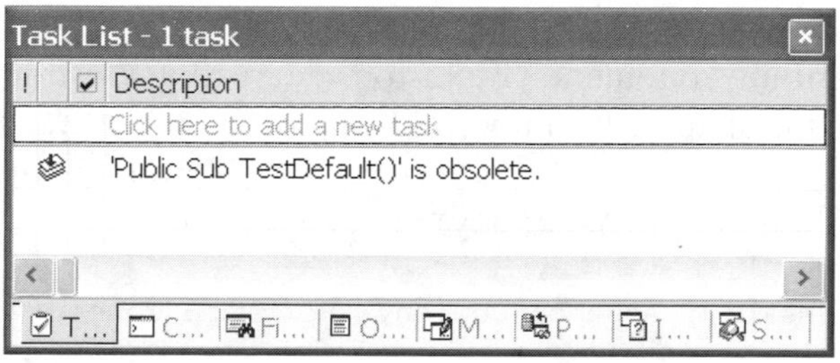

Figure 5.1 A message in the Task List indicating elements marked as obsolete.

is to realize how an attribute is applied and then to look for attributes just as you would look for preexisting code when you have a particular problem to solve. To recap, when you apply an attribute, you are essentially constructing an instance of that attribute's class, passing the positional and named arguments to initialize the class.

NOTE: If you want to find some specific examples of code, you can download the shared Common Language Infrastructure dubbed *Rotor*. By using a tool like grep you can search the source code in Rotor for a specific example of code, such as classes that define attributes applicable to parameters. Here is an example of such a command: `grep —i —d "AttributeTargets.Parameter" *.cs`. A compilable version of grep actually ships with the Rotor source code.

How attributes are used is dictated by the `AttributeUsageAttribute` and the `AttributeTargets` enumeration. Refer to the Specifying Attribute Usage section later in this chapter for more information.

Using Assembly Attributes

The word *assembly* is used in several contexts. There is the `Assembly` class that represents an instance of a compiled assembly. There is the notion of a compiled assembly that contains metadata and IL, and there is the `Assembly` keyword used to demark assembly-level attributes. You will most commonly find assembly-level attributes in a file named `AssemblyInfo.vb`, although you may find assembly-level attributes in any module.

Two things are required for assembly-level attributes. The first is that when the attribute is defined, it must have the `AttributeTargets.All` or `AttributeTargets.Assembly` enumerated value in the list of arguments used to initialize the `AttributeUsageAttribute`. The second requirement is that you must use the `Assembly` keyword followed by a colon (`:`) in the attribute statement. (Refer to the Creating Custom Attributes section later in this chapter for more information on the `AttributeUsageAttribute`.) The next fragment demonstrates a common assembly-level attribute you will find in the `AssemblyInfo.vb` file.

```
<Assembly: AssemblyCompany("Software Conceptions, Inc.")>
```

The preceding assembly-level attribute adds company information to aid in identifying the originator of the assembly. The value of attributes can be reflected or, as is the case with attributes used to identify code authors, you can use the `FileVersionInfo` class to retrieve information consistent with what you might expect to find in an About dialog.

NOTE: By convention assembly-level attributes have an `Assembly` prefix and an `Attribute` suffix. The suffix is used by convention when naming attribute classes but dropped when the attribute is applied (as in the code above).

The next section demonstrates an example of using assembly-level attributes to create a brief About dialog.

Creating an About Dialog with Assembly Attributes

About dialogs are pretty common. In this section I will demonstrate how to use Reflection to read assembly-level attributes (Listing 5.4), and then you can imagine how those capabilities might have been used to create the `FileVersionInfo` class. The `FileVersionInfo` class was used to create the About dialog in Figure 5.2, and the code is provided in Listing 5.5.

Listing 5.4 Obtaining Application Information by Using Reflection

```
1:  Option Explicit On
2:  Option Strict On
3:
4:  Imports System.Reflection
5:  Imports System.Text.RegularExpressions
6:  Imports System.Type
7:
8:  Public Interface IVersionInformation
9:
10:   ReadOnly Property ProductName() As String
11:   ReadOnly Property ProductVersion() As String
12:   ReadOnly Property FileDescription() As String
13:   ReadOnly Property LegalCopyright() As String
14:   ReadOnly Property Comment() As String
15:
16: End Interface
17:
18: Public Interface IReflectedAttributes
```

```
19:   ReadOnly Property Attributes() As Object()
20: End Interface
21:
22: Public Class ReflectedVersionInformation
23:
24:   Implements IVersionInformation, IReflectedAttributes
25:
26:   Private FAttributes As Object() = Nothing
27:
28:   ReadOnly Property Attributes() As Object() _
29:     Implements IReflectedAttributes.Attributes
30:   Get
31:     If (FAttributes Is Nothing) Then
32:       FAttributes = System.Reflection.Assembly.GetExecutingAssembly(). _
33:         GetCustomAttributes(True)
34:     End If
35:
36:     Return FAttributes
37:   End Get
38:   End Property
39:
40:   Private ReadOnly Property GetAttribute( _
41:     ByVal Name As String) As Attribute
42:   Get
43:     Dim A As Attribute
44:     For Each A In Attributes
45:       If (A.GetType().FullName = Name) Then
46:         Return A
47:       End If
48:     Next
49:
50:     Return Nothing
51:   End Get
52:   End Property
53:
54:   ReadOnly Property ProductName() As String _
55:     Implements IVersionInformation.ProductName
56:   Get
57:     Try
58:       Return CType(GetAttribute( _
59:         "System.Reflection.AssemblyProductAttribute"), _
60:           AssemblyProductAttribute).Product
61:     Catch
62:       Return String.Empty
```

```
63:     End Try
64:
65:   End Get
66:   End Property
67:
68:   ReadOnly Property ProductVersion() As String _
69:     Implements IVersionInformation.ProductVersion
70:   Get
71:
72:   End Get
73:   End Property
74:
75:   ReadOnly Property FileDescription() As String _
76:     Implements IVersionInformation.FileDescription
77:   Get
78:     Try
79:       Return CType(GetAttribute( _
80:         "System.Reflection.AssemblyTitleAttribute"), _
81:         AssemblyTitleAttribute).Title
82:     Catch
83:       Return String.Empty
84:     End Try
85:
86:   End Get
87:   End Property
88:
89:   ReadOnly Property LegalCopyright() As String _
90:     Implements IVersionInformation.LegalCopyright
91:   Get
92:     Try
93:       Return Regex.Unescape(CType(GetAttribute( _
94:         "System.Reflection.AssemblyCopyrightAttribute"), _
95:         AssemblyCopyrightAttribute).Copyright)
96:     Catch
97:       Return String.Empty
98:     End Try
99:
100:   End Get
101:   End Property
102:
103:   ReadOnly Property Comment() As String _
104:     Implements IVersionInformation.Comment
105:   Get
106:     Try
```

```
107:        Return CType(GetAttribute( _
108:          "System.Reflection.AssemblyDescriptionAttribute"), _
109:          AssemblyDescriptionAttribute).Description
110:
111:      Catch
112:        Return String.Empty
113:      End Try
114:    End Get
115:    End Property
116:
117: End Class
```

I combined a couple of techniques in this example. The `Reflected-VersionInformation` class created in lines 22 through 117 demonstrate how to obtain assembly-level information using Reflection. `ReflectedVersionInformation` shows you how to get the kind of information you might want to display in a dialog box. In addition to obtaining assembly-level infor-

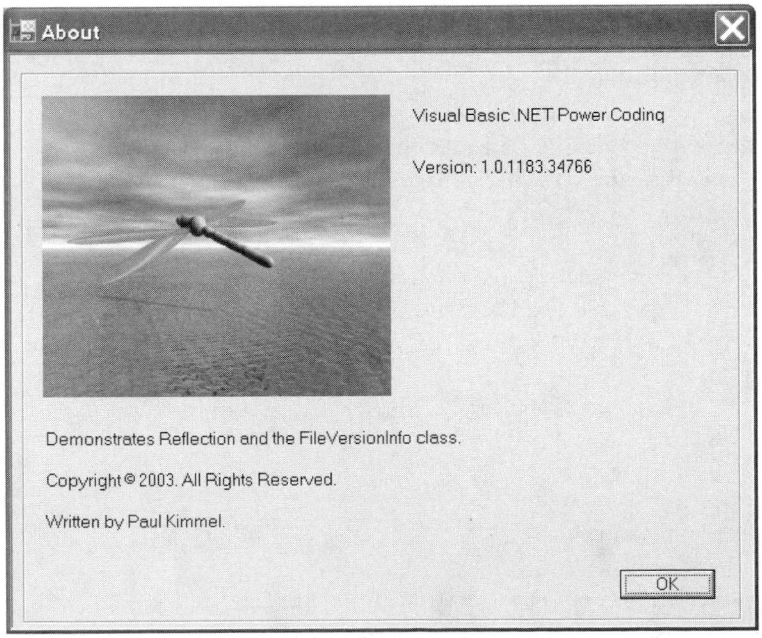

About

Visual Basic .NET Power Coding

Version: 1.0.1183.34766

Demonstrates Reflection and the FileVersionInfo class.

Copyright © 2003. All Rights Reserved.

Written by Paul Kimmel.

OK

Figure 5.2 The About dialog example. (The graphic image was created using Bryce 5.)

mation, the `ReflectedVersionInformation` class implements the `IVersionInformation` interface. Using this second technique I can implement my About dialog in terms of the `IVersionInformation` interface rather than a specific class, for example, instead of the `ReflectedVersionInformation` class.

NOTE: *Caution*: You cannot obtain the version information by reflecting the `AssemblyVersionAttribute`. The assembly version information is used to create an `AssemblyQualifiedName`, and the version number is embedded as part of that. As a result, the `ReflectedVersionInformation` class, as written, does not return the version number.

The second technique is referred to as *interface programming*. Using interfaces instead of classes makes it very easy to change an implementation simply by changing the instance of the class that implements a particular interface. Of course, Microsoft has already mitigated the need for reading file version information using Reflection attributes by implementing the `FileVersionInfo` class. Listing 5.5 defines the `VersionInformation` class and implements the `IVersionInformation` interface.

NOTE: I am not advocating using an interface to obtain file version information. If you want file version information, use the `FileVersionInfo` class. However, implementing interactions in terms of interfaces is a dynamic and flexible way to program as a general strategy. Refer to Listing 5.6 for an example of interface programming.

Listing 5.5 Creating an About Dialog by Using the `FileVersionInfo` Class

```
1:  Option Explicit On
2:  Option Strict On
3:
4:  Imports System.Reflection
5:  Imports System.Text.RegularExpressions
6:  Imports System.Type
7:
8:  Public Interface IVersionInformationObject
9:    ReadOnly Property FileVersionInfo() As FileVersionInfo
10: End Interface
11:
12: Public Interface IVersionInformation
```

```
13:
14:    ReadOnly Property ProductName() As String
15:    ReadOnly Property ProductVersion() As String
16:    ReadOnly Property FileDescription() As String
17:    ReadOnly Property LegalCopyright() As String
18:    ReadOnly Property Comment() As String
19:
20: End Interface
21:
22: Public Class VersionInformation
23:    Implements IVersionInformation, IVersionInformationObject
24:
25:    Private FFileVersionInfo As FileVersionInfo
26:
27:    Public Sub New()
28:      FFileVersionInfo = _
29:        FileVersionInfo.GetVersionInfo(Application.ExecutablePath)
30:    End Sub
31:
32:    ReadOnly Property FileVersionInfo() As FileVersionInfo _
33:      Implements IVersionInformationObject.FileVersionInfo
34:    Get
35:      Return FFileVersionInfo
36:    End Get
37:    End Property
38:
39:    ReadOnly Property ProductName() As String _
40:      Implements IVersionInformation.ProductName
41:    Get
42:      Return FFileVersionInfo.ProductName
43:    End Get
44:    End Property
45:
46:    ReadOnly Property ProductVersion() As String _
47:      Implements IVersionInformation.ProductVersion
48:    Get
49:      Return "Version: " + FFileVersionInfo.ProductVersion
50:    End Get
51:    End Property
52:
53:    ReadOnly Property FileDescription() As String _
54:      Implements IVersionInformation.FileDescription
55:    Get
```

```
56:      Return FFileVersionInfo.FileDescription
57:   End Get
58:   End Property
59:
60:   ReadOnly Property LegalCopyright() As String _
61:      Implements IVersionInformation.LegalCopyright
62:   Get
63:      ' If we don't unescape then we get the literal text in VB
64:      Return Regex.Unescape(FFileVersionInfo.LegalCopyright)
65:   End Get
66:   End Property
67:
68:   ReadOnly Property Comment() As String _
69:      Implements IVersionInformation.Comment
70:   Get
71:      Return FFileVersionInfo.Comments
72:   End Get
73:   End Property
74: End Class
```

Listing 5.5 is straightforward. The `VersionInformation` class implements the `IVersionInformation` interface and returns the version information from the `FileVersionInfo` object.

The `VersionInformation` class demonstrates the assembly attributes that contain specific kinds of version information. For example, the `FileVersionInfo.LegalCopyright` property (lines 60 through 66) is used to contain copyright information. I used the literal value `\xa9` to create the copyright symbol (©). We then have to unescape the literal to correctly display the copyright symbol. The `AssemblyCopyrightAttribute` I used to create the output appears below.

```
<Assembly: AssemblyCopyright("Copyright \xa9 2003. All Rights
Reserved.")>
```

Line 64 of Listing 5.5 shows how to unescape the literal string value to turn the literal text `\xa9` to ©. Basic tricks like the one just described give your applications a professional fit and finish.

As an example of interface programming, Listing 5.6 demonstrates how we can switch back and forth between the two versions of the class that returns file version information.

Listing 5.6 Interface Programming Using the `FormAbout` Class

```
1:  Imports System.Reflection
2:
3:  Public Class FormAbout
4:      Inherits System.Windows.Forms.Form
5:
6:  [ Windows Form Designer generated code ]
7:
8:    Public Shared Sub About()
9:      With New FormAbout()
10:        .ShowDialog()
11:      End With
12:
13:      Dim Form As FormAbout = New FormAbout()
14:      Form.Show()
15:
16:
17:    End Sub
18:
19:
20:    Private Sub FormAbout_Load( _
21:      ByVal sender As Object, _
22:      ByVal e As System.EventArgs) Handles MyBase.Load
23:
24:      Dim Info As IVersionInformation = New VersionInformation()
25:      'Dim Info As IVersionInformation = _
26:        'New ReflectedVersionInformation()
27:
28:      LabelProductName.Text = Info.ProductName
29:      LabelProductVersion.Text = Info.ProductVersion
30:      LabelFileDescription.Text = Info.FileDescription
31:      LabelLegalCopyright.Text = Info.LegalCopyright
32:      LabelComments.Text = Info.Comment
33:
34:    End Sub
35:
36: End Class
```

Instead of a specific class, we declare an `IVersionInformation` variable in line 24, and then we create an instance of a specific class that implements that interface. Comment line 24 and uncomment lines 25 and 26 to switch to the `ReflectedVersionInformation` type. The balance of the code remains the same because we are requesting data from the interface variable.

Creating Custom Attributes

Attributes are simply classes derived from the `System.Attribute` class. Attributes convey metadata—extra information—about entities in .NET. For this reason they are an essential part of .NET. Attributes can be subclassed just like any other class, thus permitting you to create custom attributes.

To create a custom attribute you need to create a new class that inherits from `System.Attribute`, apply the `AttributeUsageAttribute` to that class, and define named and positional arguments. I will demonstrate each of these techniques in the subsections that follow. (The sample solution for this section is the `CustomAttributeDemo.sln` file.)

The custom attribute constructed in this example facilitates the creation of a user interface generator tool. The basic idea is that a user interface generator (`UserInterfaceGenerator.csproj`) reads the properties of a type and generates controls at runtime for that type. The `ControlHintAttribute` class defined below allows a programmer to provide a hint indicating what kind of control the generator should create.

Specifying Attribute Usage

Listing 5.7 shows the complete custom attribute listing to provide a control hint to a user interface generator. I will refer to that code throughout the remainder of this section. The example in Listing 5.7 is provided in the `CustomAttribute.vbproj` example project.

Listing 5.7 Creating a Complete Custom Attribute

```
1:  <AttributeUsage(AttributeTargets.Field Or AttributeTargets.Property, _
2:    AllowMultiple:=False)> _
3:  Public Class ControlHintAttribute
4:    Inherits System.Attribute
5:
6:    Private FControlType As Type
7:    Private FForce As Boolean
8:    Private FDescription As String
```

```
 9:
10:    Public Sub New(ByVal ControlType As Type)
11:       FControlType = ControlType
12:    End Sub
13:
14:    Public ReadOnly Property ControlType() As Type
15:    Get
16:       Return FControlType
17:    End Get
18:    End Property
19:
20:    Public Property Force() As Boolean
21:    Get
22:       Return FForce
23:    End Get
24:    Set(ByVal Value As Boolean)
25:       FForce = Value
26:    End Set
27:    End Property
28:
29:    Public Property Description() As String
30:    Get
31:       Return FDescription
32:    End Get
33:    Set(ByVal Value As String)
34:       FDescription = Value
35:    End Set
36:    End Property
37:
38: End Class
```

The first piece of the custom attribute puzzle is contained in lines 1 and 2 of Listing 5.7. We need to apply the `AttributeUsageAttribute` to the custom attribute. The `AttributeUsageAttribute` is used to provide additional information about our custom attribute. The first argument, `AttributeTargets`, is a named argument that indicates the kind of entities this particular attribute is valid on. Line 1 indicates that our custom attribute will be valid on—that is, we can apply it to—fields and properties only. (Several other possible values can be referenced; look up the `AttributeTargets` enumerated type in the .NET help documentation.) This positional argument to the constructor represents the `ValidOn` property of the `AttributeUsageAttribute` class.

We also can specify the named arguments `AllowMultiple` and `Inherited`. `AllowMultiple` is `False` by default (it is redundant to list the named argument if setting the default value) and `Inherited` is `True` by default. The `AllowMultiple` named argument indicates whether or not we can apply the custom attribute to the same entity more than one time. The `Inherited` named argument indicates whether or not our attribute is inherited by derived classes or overridden members. Based on the application of the `AttributeUsageAttribute` in Listing 5.7, our attribute can be applied only one time to any particular entity and will be inherited.

Inheriting from the Attribute Class

The second piece of creating a custom attribute is to inherit from the `System.Attribute` class. This step, shown in line 4 of Listing 5.7, speaks for itself. There are no members of `System.Attribute` that we must override in our custom attribute. Simply add the inheritance statement as demonstrated.

Defining Positional Arguments

An argument is positional when it is initialized as a parameter to the constructor. You will provide values for positional arguments first and in the order that they appear. Generally the value of a positional argument is implemented as a `ReadOnly` property in the custom attribute class. You can see this reflected in the `Sub New` constructor in Listing 5.7. Line 10 defines a positional argument named `ControlType`, which is in turn available as a `ReadOnly` property in lines 14 through 18.

Defining Named Arguments

Named arguments are passed to the constructor by indicating the property name followed by the `:=` operator and a suitable value for the named argument. Listing 5.7 defines two possible named arguments: `Force` and `Description`. The idea in this instance is that `Force` is used to indicate that `ControlType` is the type of control that should be created, and `Description` allows the consumer to provide some descriptive text. You are not required to provide a value for the named arguments, but you must provide values for positional arguments.

The balance of the code is very straightforward. By examining the code in Listing 5.7 it is apparent that we are basically setting class properties in `ControlHintAttribute`. The next section demonstrates how we can use Reflection in our applications to explore this information.

Reflecting Attributes

Attributes are read using Reflection. The `CustomAttributeDemo.sln` file contains several example projects that use `ControlHintAttribute`. Several classes in the `UserInterfaceGenerator.vbproj` project are capable of generating custom user interfaces. (There are two flavors: `WindowsInterfaceGenerator` creates a Windows Forms user interface, and `WebInterfaceGenerator` creates a Web Forms user interface.) Listing 5.8 contains the implementation of `ExWindowsUserInterface`, taking into account the possibility that the control has the `ControlHintAttribute` applied. `ExWindowsUserInterfaceGenerator` inherits from `WindowsUserInterfaceGenerator`, which in turn implements the `IUserInterfaceGenerator` interface.

Listing 5.8 Creating a Custom User Interface

```
1:   Option Strict On
2:   Option Explicit On
3:
4:   Imports System.Reflection
5:   Imports System.Drawing
6:   Imports CustomAttributeDemo
7:
8:   Public Interface IUserInterfaceGenerator
9:
10:    ReadOnly Property Parent() As Object
11:    ReadOnly Property List() As IList
12:    Sub ClearControls()
13:    Sub CreateUserInterface(ByVal Type As Type)
14:    Sub AddControl(ByVal PropertyInfo As PropertyInfo, _
15:      ByVal Index As Integer)
16:
17: End Interface
18:
19: Public MustInherit Class UserInterfaceGenerator
20:    Implements IUserInterfaceGenerator
21:
22:    Private FParent As Object
23:    Private FList As IList
24:
25:    Public Sub New(ByVal Parent As Object, _
26:      Optional ByVal List As IList = Nothing)
```

```
27:      FParent = Parent
28:      FList = List
29:    End Sub
30:
31:    ReadOnly Property Parent() As Object _
32:      Implements IUserInterfaceGenerator.Parent
33:    Get
34:      Return FParent
35:    End Get
36:    End Property
37:
38:    ReadOnly Property List() As IList _
39:      Implements IUserInterfaceGenerator.List
40:    Get
41:      Return FList
42:    End Get
43:    End Property
44:
45:    MustOverride Sub ClearControls() _
46:      Implements IUserInterfaceGenerator.ClearControls
47:
48:    Sub CreateUserInterface(ByVal Type As Type) _
49:      Implements IUserInterfaceGenerator.CreateUserInterface
50:
51:      Dim properties() As PropertyInfo = Type.GetProperties()
52:
53:      Dim I As Integer
54:      For I = 0 To properties.Length - 1
55:        AddControl(properties(I), I)
56:      Next
57:    End Sub
58:
59:    MustOverride Sub AddControl(ByVal PropertyInfo As PropertyInfo, _
60:      ByVal Index As Integer) _
61:      Implements IUserInterfaceGenerator.AddControl
62:
63: End Class
64:
65: Public Class WindowsInterfaceGenerator
66:    Inherits UserInterfaceGenerator
67:
68:    Public Sub New(ByVal Parent As Object, _
69:      Optional ByVal List As IList = Nothing)
70:      MyBase.New(Parent, List)
71:    End Sub
```

```
72:
73:    Public Overrides Sub AddControl( _
74:      ByVal PropertyInfo As PropertyInfo, ByVal Index As Integer)
75:
76:      Dim Label As System.Windows.Forms.Label = _
77:        New System.Windows.Forms.Label()
78:      Label.AutoSize = True
79:      Label.Text = PropertyInfo.Name
80:      Label.Location = New Point(10, (Index + 1) * 25)
81:      Control.Controls.Add(Label)
82:
83:      Dim TextBox As System.Windows.Forms.TextBox = _
84:        New System.Windows.Forms.TextBox()
85:      TextBox.Name = PropertyInfo.Name
86:      TextBox.Location = New Point(100, (Index + 1) * 25)
87:      TextBox.Width = 250
88:      TextBox.DataBindings.Add("Text", List, PropertyInfo.Name)
89:      Control.Controls.Add(TextBox)
90:
91:    End Sub
92:
93:    Overrides Sub ClearControls()
94:      Control.Controls.Clear()
95:    End Sub
96:
97:    Protected ReadOnly Property Control() As _
98:      System.Windows.Forms.Control
99:    Get
100:     Return CType(Parent, System.Windows.Forms.Control)
101:   End Get
102:   End Property
103:
104: End Class
105:
106:
107: Public Class ExWindowsInterfaceGenerator
108:    Inherits WindowsInterfaceGenerator
109:
110:   Public Sub New(ByVal Parent As Object, _
111:     Optional ByVal List As IList = Nothing)
112:     MyBase.New(Parent, List)
113:    End Sub
114:
115:   Public Overrides Sub AddControl( _
116:     ByVal PropertyInfo As PropertyInfo, ByVal Index As Integer)
```

```
117:
118:    Dim Label As System.Windows.Forms.Label = _
119:       New System.Windows.Forms.Label()
120:    Label.AutoSize = True
121:    Label.Text = PropertyInfo.Name
122:    Label.Location = New Point(10, (Index + 1) * 25)
123:    Control.Controls.Add(Label)
124:
125:    Dim Instance As System.Windows.Forms.Control = _
126:       CreateControl(PropertyInfo)
127:
128:    Instance.Name = PropertyInfo.Name
129:    Instance.Location = New Point(100, (Index + 1) * 25)
130:    Instance.Width = 250
131:    Instance.DataBindings.Add("Text", List, PropertyInfo.Name)
132:
133:    Control.Controls.Add(Instance)
134: End Sub
135:
136: Protected Function CreateControl( _
137:    ByVal PropertyInfo As PropertyInfo) _
138:       As System.Windows.Forms.Control
139:
140:    Dim Attributes() As Object = _
141:       PropertyInfo.GetCustomAttributes( _
142:       GetType(ControlHintAttribute), False)
143:
144:
145:    If Attributes.Length = 0 Then
146:       Return New System.Windows.Forms.TextBox()
147:    End If
148:
149:    Dim ControlHintAttribute As ControlHintAttribute = _
150:       CType(Attributes(0), ControlHintAttribute)
151:
152:    Dim Instance As Object = _
153:       Activator.CreateInstance(ControlHintAttribute.ControlType)
154:
155:    Return CType(Instance, System.Windows.Forms.Control)
156:
157:  End Function
158:
159: End Class
```

Listing 5.8 is a bit on the long side. It shows the interface programming technique again, this time with one interface and three classes. The `IUser-InterfaceGenerator` interface defines what an user interface generator should have. The `UserInterfaceGenerator` class realizes all of `IUser-InterfaceGenerator` and implements all the code that might be found to be common between all user interface generators (as defined by me).

Lines 19 through 63 implement the `UserInterfaceGenerator` class, which is an abstract class (as inferred from the `MustInherit` modifier on line 19). When you see the `MustInherit` modifier, you should expect to find `MustOverride` methods. (`MustOverride` is the VB .NET modifier that indicates a method is purely abstract.) By combining an interface with an abstract class we can implement all the code that all user interface generators might need. The `UserInterfaceGenerator` class provides a reasonable implementation for everything except `IUserInterfaceGenerator.ClearControls` and `IUserInterfaceGenerator.AddControls`. Because Windows Forms and Web Forms need instances of different controls, we will need to implement a specific version of each of these methods. (See the `CustomAttributeDemo.sln` file for an example of a user interface generator that creates a dynamic Web page.)

Lines 107 through 159 in Listing 5.8 implement the `ExWindowsInterfaceGenerator` class. All we have to do is implement the `AddControl` method. `AddControl` calls the `CreateControl` method. `CreateControl`—in lines 136 through 157—requests the custom attributes for the current `PropertyInfo` object. Lines 140 through 142 request all attributes that are `ControlHintAttribute` objects. Because we applied the `Attribute-UsageAttribute` with `AllowMultiple` equal to `False` (Listing 5.7) there will be at most only one `ControlHintAttribute`. In lines 145 through 147 of Listing 5.8, we return an instance of the `System.Windows.Forms.Text-Box` control if a `ControlHintAttribute` was not found.

We pick up on line 149 when there is a `ControlHintAttribute`. Lines 149 and 150 convert the `Attribute` object to its specific type. Lines 152 and 153 use the `Activator.CreateInstance` shared method to create an instance of the control type associated with the attribute, and line 155 casts the generic object type returned by the `Activator.CreateInstance` method to a `System.Windows.Forms.Control` object as expected. Listing 5.9 shows a Windows Forms application using the `ExWindowsInterfaceGenerator` class.

Listing 5.9 Using `ExWindowsInterfaceGenerator` in a Windows Forms Application

```
1:  Private Sub Form1_Load(ByVal sender As System.Object, _
2:    ByVal e As System.EventArgs) Handles MyBase.Load
3:
4:    Dim TestTypes() As TestType = _
5:      New TestType() {New TestType("Paul", "Kimmel")}
6:
7:    Dim Generator As IUserInterfaceGenerator = _
8:      New ExWindowsInterfaceGenerator(Me, TestTypes)
9:
10:   Generator.CreateUserInterface(GetType(TestType))
11: End Sub
```

Lines 4 and 5 create an array of objects called `TestType`. `System.Array` (arrays) implement the `IList` interface, so we can pass the array of objects to the `ExWindowsInterfaceGenerator` constructor and bind the array to the dynamic controls as they are created. Line 10 creates the user interface. If we apply the `ControlHintAttribute` to any of the properties in `TestType` (see Listing 5.10), that kind of control will be created.

Listing 5.10 Applying the `ControlHintAttribute`

```
<ControlHint(GetType(Label))> _
Public Property FirstName() As String
Get
  Return FFirstName
End Get
Set(ByVal Value As String)
  FFirstName = Value
End Set
End Property
```

A `Label` control will be created for the `FirstName` property.

Clearly you can extend the user interface generators in several useful ways. You could write code that inserts spaces between Pascal-cased property names. You could insert some clever code to manage spacing between labels and controls, and you could use the data bindings to implement navigation. None of these things represent real difficulties. The real difficulty is how to add code to dynamically generated controls and forms. I think this is the real reason we don't see a lot of general-purpose form generators. However, you can quickly create some very advanced dynamic user interfaces.

Emitting Attributes to IL

You can use Reflection to emit IL directly. (Refer to Chapter 4 for more information on Reflection in general.) IL is an intermediate form similar to Java byte code that is created between the compile and link processes. By emitting IL the CLR has one more opportunity to perform security checks, and the number of compilers that have to be created is dramatically reduced. For example, if Borland implements a .NET compiler for Delphi, Borland has to implement only one compiler to emit IL. Then any existing linker can be used to write the emitted IL to a particular platform. Without IL, vendors would have to write a compiler for each language and operating system. With IL, each vendor needs to compile only to IL, and then one specific operating system vendor's linker can be used to convert the IL to machine language for that operating system, regardless of the originating language.

When you write emitters, you need to emit as IL all the entities you would write in Visual Basic .NET. This includes attributes. Listing 5.11 implements an emitter that emits the equivalent of a Hello, World! application, demonstrating how to emit attributes and other entities. (The emitted IL is shown in Figure 5.3.)

```
Class1::Main : void(string[])

.method private hidebysig static void  Main(string[] A_0) cil managed
{
  .entrypoint
  .custom instance void [mscorlib]System.STAThreadAttribute::.ctor() = ( 01 00 00 00 )
  // Code size       11 (0xb)
  .maxstack  1
  IL_0000:  ldstr      "Hello, World!"
  IL_0005:  call       void [mscorlib]System.Console::WriteLine(string)
  IL_000a:  ret
} // end of method Class1::Main
```

Figure 5.3 The emitted IL created by the code in Listing 5.11, which can be viewed using the `ildasm.exe` utility.

Listing 5.11 Defining an Emitter That Creates a Console Application

```
1:   Imports System
2:   Imports System.Reflection
3:   Imports System.Reflection.Emit
4:
5:   Public Class EmitAttributeDemo
6:
7:     Public Shared Sub Main(ByVal Args() As String)
8:       Emitter.Run()
9:     End Sub
10:
11: End Class
12:
13: Public Class Emitter
14:
15:    Public Shared Sub Run()
16:      Dim E As Emitter = New Emitter()
17:      E.Emit()
18:    End Sub
19:
20:    Private AssemblyName As AssemblyName
21:    Private AssemblyBuilder As AssemblyBuilder
22:    Private ModuleBuilder As ModuleBuilder
23:    Private TypeBuilder As TypeBuilder
24:    Private MethodBuilder As MethodBuilder
25:
26:    Public Sub Emit()
27:      Const Name As String = "Hello.exe"
28:      AssemblyName = New AssemblyName()
29:      AssemblyName.Name = "Hello"
30:
31:      AssemblyBuilder = AppDomain.CurrentDomain. _
32:        DefineDynamicAssembly(AssemblyName, _
33:        AssemblyBuilderAccess.Save)
34:
35:      ModuleBuilder = AssemblyBuilder.DefineDynamicModule( _
36:        "Class1.mod", Name, False)
37:
38:      TypeBuilder = ModuleBuilder.DefineType("Class1")
39:
40:      MethodBuilder = TypeBuilder.DefineMethod("Main", _
41:        MethodAttributes.Private Or MethodAttributes.Static _
42:        Or MethodAttributes.HideBySig, _
43:        CallingConventions.Standard, Nothing, _
```

```
44:         New Type() {GetType(System.String())})
45:
46:      Dim CustomAttributeBuilder As CustomAttributeBuilder = _
47:        New CustomAttributeBuilder( _
48:        GetType(System.STAThreadAttribute).GetConstructor( _
49:        New Type() {}), New Object() {})
50:
51:      MethodBuilder.SetCustomAttribute(CustomAttributeBuilder)
52:
53:      AssemblyBuilder.SetEntryPoint(MethodBuilder)
54:
55:      Dim Generator As ILGenerator = MethodBuilder.GetILGenerator()
56:      Generator.Emit(OpCodes.Ldstr, "Hello, World!")
57:
58:      Dim MethodInfo As MethodInfo = GetType(System.Console).GetMethod( _
59:        "WriteLine", BindingFlags.Public Or BindingFlags.Static, _
60:        Nothing, New Type() {GetType(String)}, Nothing)
61:
62:      Generator.Emit(OpCodes.Call, MethodInfo)
63:      Generator.Emit(OpCodes.Ret)
64:
65:      TypeBuilder.CreateType()
66:      AssemblyBuilder.Save(Name)
67:
68:    End Sub
69:
70: End Class
```

When you program, you create a solution and a project and define types that have members. When you write an emitter, you have to write code that emits analogous elements. For example, you need to emit an assembly and that assembly will have modules. Each module will have types, and those types will have members. The ability to emit these elements is captured in builder classes defined in the `System.Reflection.Emit` namespace. For example, if you want to emit an assembly, you need an `AssemblyBuilder`, and types are emitted with `TypeBuilder` objects.

Each of these builders are hierarchically dependent. For example, assemblies exist in `AppDomains` and are therefore requested from `AppDomains`. Lines 31 through 33 in Listing 5.11 demonstrate how to request a dynamic assembly. From the assembly we request a module in the form of a `ModuleBuilder`, shown on lines 35 and 36. Emitters progress this way until we get to individual lines of code.

Lines 46 through 51 demonstrate how to create and emit an attribute. The first thing we need to do is get the `Type` object for the attribute we want to emit. Then from the `Type` object we can request its constructor. Both of these steps are defined in lines 48 and 49. From the `ConstructorInfo` object requested we can create an instance of the `System.Reflection.Emit.CustomAttributeBuilder` object. To apply the attribute we invoke the `SetCustomAttribute` method on the builder that represents the entity we want to apply the attribute to. Line 51 applies the attribute represented by the `MethodBuilder`. Also, the `STAThreadAttribute` is applied to the `Main` method for the console application.

Here is a recap of the steps necessary to emit an attribute.

1. Obtain a `Type` object for the type of the attribute you want to emit.
2. Request a `ConstructorInfo` object for that attribute's type, invoking `Type.GetConstructor`.
3. Create a new instance of the `CustomAttributeBuilder`, passing the `ConstructorInfo` object to the constructor for the `CustomAttributeBuilder`.
4. Invoke *Entity*`Builder.SetCustomAttribute`, passing the `CustomAttributeBuilder` to the `SetCustomAttribute` method. (*Entity* represents an instance of a `Builder` class, such as `Method` in `MethodBuilder`.)

Emitting Attributes by Using the CodeDom Classes

Emitting IL is a low-level way to use Reflection to emit assemblies. You can emit a .NET language—instead of IL—by using the classes in the `System.CodeDom` namespace. CodeDOM can be used to emit and compile code (`System.CodeDom.Compiler`); applications that write .NET code using CodeDOM are referred to as *code generators*.

Listing 5.12 demonstrates how to create a code generator that generates VB .NET code and compiles that code to an executable assembly. The example uses CodeDOM to generate Visual Basic .NET code that produces an assembly equivalent to the emitted IL assembly from Listing 5.11.

Listing 5.12 Creating a Code Generator

```
1:  Option Strict On
2:  Option Explicit On
3:
```

```vb
4:  Imports System.CodeDom
5:  Imports System.CodeDom.Compiler
6:  Imports System.Reflection
7:  Imports System.IO
8:  Imports System.Text.RegularExpressions
9:
10: Module CodeDOMAttributeDemo
11:
12:   Sub Main()
13:     Generator.Run()
14:   End Sub
15:
16: End Module
17:
18: Public Class Generator
19:
20:   Private CommentString As String = _
21:     " Hello.vb - This code was generated by the CodeDOM.\r\n" + _
22:     " Copyright (c) 2002. All Rights Reserved.\r\n" + _
23:     " Written by Paul Kimmel. pkimmel@softconcepts.com\r\n"
24:
25:   Public Shared Sub Run()
26:     Dim G As Generator = New Generator()
27:     G.Generate()
28:   End Sub
29:
30:   Public Sub Generate()
31:     Dim CodeGenerator As ICodeGenerator = _
32:       New VBCodeProvider().CreateGenerator
33:     Dim FileName As String = "Hello.vb"
34:
35:     Dim Stream As StreamWriter = New StreamWriter( _
36:       New FileStream(FileName, FileMode.Create))
37:     Try
38:       Dim Comment As CodeCommentStatement = _
39:         New CodeCommentStatement(Regex.Unescape(CommentString))
40:
41:       CodeGenerator.GenerateCodeFromStatement( _
42:         Comment, Stream, Nothing)
43:
44:       Dim CompileUnit As CodeCompileUnit = _
45:         New CodeCompileUnit()
46:
47:       CompileUnit.AssemblyCustomAttributes.Add( _
48:         New CodeAttributeDeclaration("AssemblyDescriptionAttribute", _
```

```
49:              New CodeAttributeArgument( _
50:                New CodePrimitiveExpression("Code generated by CodeDOM"))))
51:
52:          Dim [Namespace] As CodeNamespace = _
53:            New CodeNamespace("HelloWorld")
54:
55:          [Namespace].Imports.Add( _
56:            New CodeNamespaceImport("System"))
57:
58:          CompileUnit.Namespaces.Add([Namespace])
59:
60:          Dim TypeDeclaration As CodeTypeDeclaration = _
61:            New CodeTypeDeclaration("Hello")
62:
63:          TypeDeclaration.IsClass = True
64:
65:          [Namespace].Types.Add(TypeDeclaration)
66:
67:          TypeDeclaration.TypeAttributes = TypeAttributes.Public
68:
69:          Dim MemberMethod As CodeEntryPointMethod = _
70:            New CodeEntryPointMethod()
71:
72:          MemberMethod.Name = "Main"
73:          MemberMethod.ReturnType = Nothing
74:
75:          MemberMethod.Attributes = _
76:            MemberAttributes.Public Or MemberAttributes.Static
77:
78:          MemberMethod.Statements.Add( _
79:            New CodeMethodInvokeExpression( _
80:              Nothing, "Console.WriteLine", _
81:              New CodeArgumentReferenceExpression() _
82:              {New CodeArgumentReferenceExpression( _
83:                Chr(34) + "Hello, World!" + Chr(34))}))
84:
85:          TypeDeclaration.Members.Add(MemberMethod)
86:
87:          CodeGenerator.GenerateCodeFromCompileUnit( _
88:            CompileUnit, Stream, Nothing)
89:
90:        Finally
91:          Stream.Close()
92:        End Try
93:
```

```
94:        Dim Compiler As ICodeCompiler = _
95:          New VBCodeProvider().CreateCompiler
96:
97:        Dim CompilerParameters As CompilerParameters = _
98:          New CompilerParameters()
99:
100:       CompilerParameters.GenerateExecutable = True
101:       CompilerParameters.MainClass = "HelloWorld.Hello"
102:       CompilerParameters.OutputAssembly = "Hello.exe"
103:
104:       Dim CompilerResults As CompilerResults = _
105:         Compiler.CompileAssemblyFromFile( _
106:         CompilerParameters, "Hello.vb")
107:
108:     End Sub
109: End Class
```

The code generator defined in Listing 5.12 implements a simple Hello, World! application named `Hello.exe`. Like emitting IL, the code generator creates an executable assembly. (You can create DLLs or generate the code only.)

When you implement a code generator, you need to write code to create all the elements you would add if you were writing the code directly. The difference is that you must do this in the context of the classes in the `System.CodeDom` namespace. If you follow the code in lines 30 through 108—the `Generate` method—you can discern the elements we are generating by class name.

Lines 31 and 32 demonstrate how to declare `CodeGenerator` as an interface and request a specific generator. In line 32 we create a new `VBCodeProvider` and use that class to create the code generator. If we swapped `CSharpCodeProvider` for `VBCodeProvider` and left all the other code the same, the code generator would generate C# code.

We want to generate code and save it to a file; we can use `StreamWriter` and `FileStream` as demonstrated in lines 35 and 36. The code is written to a file named `Hello.vb` in lines 87 and 88. Lines 38 through 42 demonstrate how to create an object that represents a comment and writes that comment to the stream containing the generated code.

Lines 47 through 50 demonstrate how to add attributes to the method. We add the `AssemblyDescriptionAttribute`, representing an assembly-level attribute that describes the assembly.

If you follow the rest of the code, you can see the elements you would expect in a VB .NET application. `CodeCompileUnit` in line 44 represents a unit. `CodeNamespace` in line 52 represents a namespace, to which we can add `Imports` statements, as demonstrated in lines 55 and 56. Line 58 demonstrates how to add a type to the namespace, including adding the `Public` access modifier in line 67. Lines 69 through 85 demonstrate adding a method to the new type. Generally we would add a `CodeMemberMethod`, but our console application needs an entry point. We use the `CodeEntry-PointMethod` to indicate that `Main` will be our entry point for the console application.

Generating lines of code yields the most monolithic part of the generator. A call to `Console.WriteLine("Hello, World!")` requires all the code on lines 78 through 83. Basically, every element of the code statement has a constituent class in the `CodeDom` namespace. For example, the `Code-ArgumentReferenceExpression` class is used to create an expression that is passed to `CodeMethodInvokeExpression`.

Lines 87 and 88 write the code to the `Hello.vb` file. Line 91 closes the file stream, and lines 94 through 106 create an instance of the VB .NET compiler and compile the `Hello.vb` module to `Hello.exe`.

Attributes and Declarative Security

Attributes are used to support Microsoft's new Code Access Security model. There are two ways you can apply Code Access Security in .NET: imperative security and declarative security. Both support the same basic kinds of security. The only difference is that declarative security is employed using attributes, and imperative security is employed in code.

Generally, you can use Code Access Security classes either imperatively or declaratively. However, assembly-level security must be applied declaratively; that is, by using attributes. Read Chapter 18, Code Access Security, for more information on the Code Access Security model in .NET.

Summary

.NET solves "DLL hell" by creating a new kind of thing, referred to as an *assembly*. The big difference between an assembly and previous kinds of applications is that assemblies combine metadata with the portable executable.

Metadata contains extra information that conveys meaning about the assembly, including things like strong names and version information. As a result .NET does not have to go to the registry to discern one .NET assembly from another, even if both assemblies have the same name.

Chapter 5 demonstrated how attributes can be applied to add metadata to an assembly and how to create custom attributes. Attributes are read using a new technology referred to as *Reflection*. In this chapter you also got a taste of an advanced use of Reflection by exploring examples of emitter and code generator programs. Attributes and Reflection are just two powerful reasons (among a list of many) to switch to .NET.

Multithreading

. . . and there were many things ahead calculated to arouse the
Machiavelli latent in him, could he but insert a wedge.

—*F. Scott Fitzgerald*, This Side of Paradise

Introduction

Multithreading is the double-edged sword in Visual Basic .NET. Multithreading is one of those things that programmers get excited about, but if used excessively or incorrectly, multithreading can do more harm than good.

Visual Basic .NET has the good old Timer control, as well as direct support for asynchronous processing and multithreading using the `ThreadPool` and `Thread` classes. Chapter 6 shows how to employ asynchronous behavior and multithreading in your VB .NET applications.

Familiar Slight of Hand with the Timer Control

Visual Basic 6 programmers learned how to get a lot of mileage out of the Timer control. VB .NET has a Timer too, and to help provide you with a familiar footing we will start with using the Timer in VB .NET.

Using the Timer control is not multithreaded programming. The Timer control relies on the event model. The Timer control hooks into the operating system's timer—the same clock that drives your CPU—and keeps track of ticks. The ticks are used to measure the passage of time, and the `Timer.Interval` property is compared to how much time has passed. When the interval has elapsed, the Timer control raises the `Tick` event. If you write an event handler for the `Tick` event, you can perform background tasks at regular intervals.

TIP: Double-click on any control to generate the default event handler.

To use the Timer control, select the Timer from the toolbox in a Windows Forms application, and place the Timer control into the component tray in the designer. (All controls that are not visible at runtime are placed in the component tray.) Double-click on the Timer to generate an event handler for the `Tick` event.

Keep in mind that the `Timer.Tick` event occurs on the same thread as the rest of the code in a Windows Forms application. That means that other code is waiting while the `Tick` event handler code is running. For this reason, if you put too much code in the `Timer.Tick` event handler, your application's performance will deteriorate. That's why the Timer is really good only for lightweight background tasks. A simple example is to use a Timer to display the date and time in a status bar. (Refer to the `TimerDemo.sln` file available with this book.)

Create a time-keeping status bar by adding a `StatusBar` control to a Windows Form and a Timer control to the component tray for that form. Double-click on the Timer control to generate the `Tick` event handler and add code to set the date and time. Listing 6.1 shows the `Tick` event handler from the `TimerDemo.sln` main form.

Listing 6.1 Appropriately Demonstrative Code for a `Timer.Tick` Event

---

```
Private Sub Timer1_Tick(ByVal sender As System.Object, _
    ByVal e As System.EventArgs) Handles Timer1.Tick

  StatusBar1.Text = DateTime.Now

End Sub
```

You can satisfy yourself that the Timer is not using a separate thread—that is, it is not multithreaded—by adding a breakpoint on the `StatusBar1.Text = DateTime.Now` statement. When the application breaks, select Debug|Windows|Threads, and you will see that only one thread is running (Figure 6.1). You can also call the `Control.InvokeRequired` method. Controls inherit `InvokeRequired`; this method returns `True` if the thread it is called from is different from the thread the control is on. You will need to know about `InvokeRequired` for asynchronous and multithreaded processing.

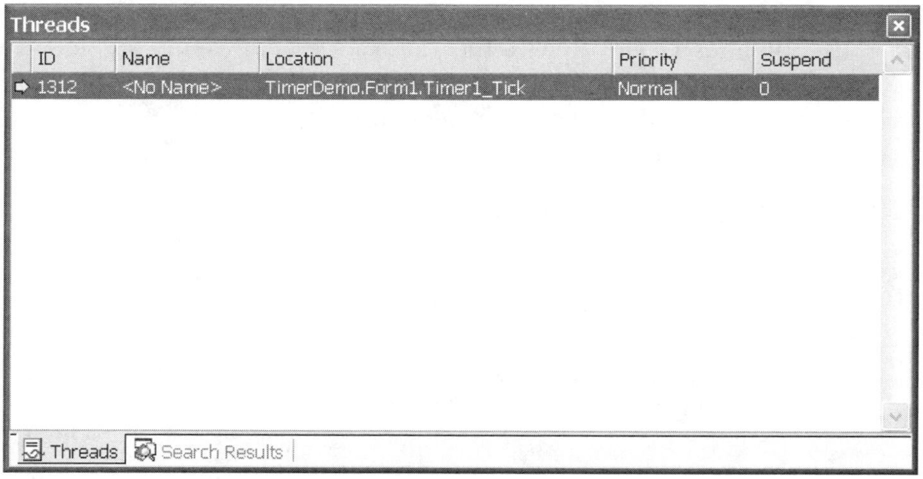

ID	Name	Location	Priority	Suspend
➡ 1312	<No Name>	TimerDemo.Form1.Timer1_Tick	Normal	0

Figure 6.1 The `Threads` window shows the running threads.

Comparing Synchronous and Asynchronous Behavior

Synchronous code executes in the order in which it occurs in the compiled program. Asynchronous code executes out of order. When an asynchronous call occurs, the call is made to the asynchronous invoke method and immediately returns. The flow of execution resumes while the asynchronous process finishes separately. You can write code to block until the asynchronous process finishes, or you can pass a callback method to the asynchronous process so it will notify you by invoking the callback when the data is ready.

The `GcdDemo.sln` file demonstrates code that determines the greatest common divisor of two numbers. The sample application calculates the greatest common divisor using recursion, demonstrating both synchronous and asynchronous calls to the `Calculate` method. If you step through the asynchronous calls, you will see that the code does not appear to go to the asynchronously invoked method at the point at which it is called. By placing a breakpoint in the asynchronous worker method, you can see the worker thread that is spun up to process the asynchronous code. Open the `Threads` window when the asynchronous method's breakpoint is reached.

Programming Synchronous Behavior

Listing 6.2 demonstrates a synchronous call to the `Calculate` method on lines 4 through 13. The `Calculate` method employs recursion to calculate the greatest common divisor. When we invoke `Calculate` synchronously on lines 19 and 20 with the `Invoke` method, we use a delegate to manage the invocation. The signature of the delegate simply needs to match the signature of the method we want to invoke.

Listing 6.2 A Synchronous Call to a Recursive Method

```
 1: Private Delegate Function MyDelegate(ByVal Numerator As Long, _
 2:   ByVal Denominator As Long) As Long
 3:
 4: Private Function Calculate(ByVal Numerator As Long, _
 5:   ByVal Denominator As Long) As Long
 6:
 7:   If (Numerator Mod Denominator = 0) Then
 8:     Return Denominator
 9:   Else
10:     Return Calculate(Denominator, Numerator Mod Denominator)
11:   End If
12:
13: End Function
14:
15: Private Sub MenuItem5_Click(ByVal sender As System.Object, _
16:   ByVal e As System.EventArgs) Handles MenuItem5.Click
17:
18:   SetResult(Numerator, Denominator, _
19:     Invoke(New MyDelegate(AddressOf Calculate), _
20:     New Object() {Numerator, Denominator}))
21:
22: End Sub
23:
24: Private Sub SetResult(ByVal Numerator As Long, _
25:   ByVal Denominator As Long, ByVal Gcd As Long)
26:
27:   Const mask As String = _
28:     "{0}. The greatest common divisor of {1} and {2} is {3}"
29:
30:   Static I As Integer
31:   I += 1
32:
33:   ListBox1.Items.Insert(0, _
34:     String.Format(mask, I, Numerator, Denominator, Gcd))
35: End Sub
```

When we call the `Invoke` method (lines 19 and 20) we pass the address of the method as a delegate and the parameters to that method as an array of objects; this happens on line 20. `Invoke` returns the value of the `Calculate` method, which is the greatest common divisor `Gcd`. `Numerator`, `Denominator`, and `Gcd` are passed to `SetResult` to write formatted output.

Technically you do not have to call `Invoke` to call the `Calculate` method in this example. In this instance there is no reason to use `Invoke` to call `Calculate` other than to demonstrate the `Invoke` method. However, you will need to use the Invoke method if the calling thread is different than the thread of the Windows control with which you want to interact. For example, suppose you wanted to calculate the greatest common divisor on a separate thread and display the value in a Windows Forms control. Then you could use `Invoke` to interact with the Windows Forms control. As described, `Invoke` would marshal the data from the `Gcd` thread onto the same thread as the one containing the Windows control. Using `Invoke` to marshal data onto a control's thread is a safe way to use multithreading in Windows Forms applications.

Programming Asynchronous Behavior

The asynchronous method `BeginInvoke` is employed syntactically the same as the `Invoke` method. You pass the method to call using a delegate and the arguments to the method using an array of type `Object`. The delegate plays the role of work to perform, and `BeginInvoke` creates a separate worker thread to complete the task represented by the delegate. Listing 6.3 demonstrates the `BeginInvoke` method.

Listing 6.3 An Asynchronous Method Invocation

```
1:  Private Sub SetResult(ByVal Numerator As Long, _
2:     ByVal Denominator As Long, ByVal Gcd As Long)
3:
4:     Const mask As String = _
5:        "{0}. The greatest common divisor of {1} and {2} is {3}"
6:
7:     Static I As Integer
8:     I += 1
9:
10:    ListBox1.Items.Insert(0, _
11:       String.Format(mask, I, Numerator, Denominator, Gcd))
12: End Sub
```

```
13:
14: Private Delegate Sub AsynchDelegate(ByVal Numerator As Long, _
15:   ByVal Denominator As Long)
16:
17: Private Sub AsynchCalculate(ByVal Numerator As Long, _
18:   ByVal Denominator As Long)
19:
20:   SetResult(Numerator, Denominator, _
21:     Calculate(Numerator, Denominator))
22:
23: End Sub
24:
25: Private Sub MenuItem6_Click(ByVal sender As System.Object, _
26:   ByVal e As System.EventArgs) Handles MenuItem6.Click
27:
28:   BeginInvoke(New AsynchDelegate(AddressOf AsynchCalculate), _
29:     New Object() {Numerator, Denominator})
30:
31: End Sub
```

The biggest difference between Listings 6.2 and 6.3 is that we call `BeginInvoke` in line 28 of Listing 6.3. I defined a slightly new delegate that represents the work to complete asynchronously. `AsynchCalculate` calls `SetResult`, passing `Numerator`, `Denominator`, and the result of the `Calculate` method. The calculated greatest common divisor is the same; the difference is that we can keep interacting with the graphical user interface during calculation.

TIP: The `Invoke`, `BeginInvoke`, `EndInvoke`, and `CreateGraphics` control methods are safe to call from any thread.

Completing Asynchronous Calls

Our example in Listing 6.3 calls a subroutine, `AsynchCalculate`. Because we are not expecting any data back from `AsynchCalculate`, we can let the asynchronous method finish without further attention. However, if you are expecting information back from an asynchronous call, you will want to handle the completion of the asynchronous process.

There are four ways to complete an asynchronous call. You can poll the `IAsyncResult.IsCompleted` property, block with `EndInvoke`, use a `Wait-`

`Handle`, or employ a delegate. The first three ways are discussed here; Chapter 3 covers delegates.

The `BeginInvoke` method returns an object that implements the `IAsyncResult` interface. You can poll `IsCompleted` or request a `WaitHandle` from the `IAsyncResult` object. If you pass a delegate to `BeginInvoke`, you can complete the call there, as we did in Listing 6.3. Finally, you can call `EndInvoke` to request the data after the asynchronous call has finished, or call `EndInvoke` immediately. `EndInvoke` will block until the asynchronous call finishes.

Polling `IAsyncResult.IsCompleted`

IAsyncResult.IsCompleted returns a Boolean, and you use it like any other Boolean value. Listing 6.4 demonstrates how to call the `Calculate` method from `GcdDemo.sln`, wait until `IsCompleted` is `True`, and then obtain the value with `EndInvoke`.

Listing 6.4 Polling `IAsyncResult.IsCompleted`

```
Dim Result As IAsyncResult = BeginInvoke( _
  New MyDelegate(AddressOf Calculate), New Object() {532, 16})

While (Not Result.IsCompleted)
  Application.DoEvents()
End While

SetResult(532, 26, EndInvoke(Result))
```

The `While` loop uses `IsCompleted` to poll. We can add work in between the `While` and `End While` statements or just wait until `IsCompleted` is `True`. In our example, we call `Application.DoEvents` to allow the Windows message queue to clear out; otherwise the delegate containing the `Calculate` method won't have time to process. Finally, when the loop terminates, we can call `EndInvoke` to obtain the result, as shown.

Blocking with `EndInvoke`

In Listing 6.4 we could take out the `While` loop and achieve approximately the same effect. The statement containing `EndInvoke` would block until the asynchronous result is ready. Of course, if we cut out the `While` loop, there would be no opportunity to do additional work. Alternatively, we could insert lines of code between `BeginInvoke` and `EndInvoke` to get some work done asynchronously and then block. This is simulated in Listing 6.5; the comment is where we would place our lines of code.

Listing 6.5 Blocking with `EndInvoke`

```
Dim Result As IAsyncResult = BeginInvoke( _
  New MyDelegate(AddressOf Calculate), New Object() {532, 16})

' Insert some code to perform some work here

SetResult(532, 26, EndInvoke(Result))
```

Using `WaitHandle` Objects

Thus far we have completed asynchronous calls using delegates, polling with `IAsyncResult.IsCompleted`, and blocking with `EndInvoke`. The last way I'll demonstrate here is to block using a `WaitHandle`.

The `IAsyncResult.AsyncWaitHandle` property permits you to specifically define the wait conditions for the block. You can call `WaitHandle.WaitOne`, `WaitHandle.WaitAll`, or `WaitHandle.WaitAny` to block, passing `IAsyncResult.AsyncWaitHandle` to these methods.

Use the `WaitHandle` class for things like processing several asynchronous requests and then waiting until they all finish, waiting for any of several requests to finish, or waiting a specific amount of time and setting a timeout if the request hasn't finished. Listing 6.6 demonstrates how we can send several pairs of integers to the greatest common divisor calculator and then wait until the calculations for all the pairs are finished.

Listing 6.6 Blocking by Using a `WaitHandle`

```
Dim Result As IAsyncResult = _
  BeginInvoke(New MyDelegate(AddressOf Calculate), _
  New Object() {652, 18})

Result.AsyncWaitHandle.WaitOne(5000, False)
SetResult(652, 18, EndInvoke(Result))
```

Listing 6.6 blocks for up to five seconds (represented by the 5,000 milliseconds passed to `WaitOne`) waiting for the asynchronous call to `Calculate` to return.

You can explore more about the `WaitHandle` class in the `System.Threading` namespace help documentation.

Processing Asynchronously in the .NET Framework

Many important aspects of the .NET framework support asynchronous programming. You can interact asynchronously with File IO, HTTP, TCP, XML Web Services, ASP.NET Web Forms, and message queues with MSMQ Microsoft's Message Queue. The asynchronous invocation works the same whether you are using File IO, XML Web Services, or whatever.

Two examples in the subsections that follow demonstrate how to asynchronously invoke an XML Web Service and use File IO streams.

Invoking XML Web Services Asynchronously

Chapter 13, Creating Web Services, and Chapter 14, Advanced Web Services, thoroughly cover Web Services. I don't want to repeat all that information here, so for now I'll just give you the broad strokes of asynchronous Web Services.

A Web Service is a DLL that allows you to invoke methods across the Internet. The data requested is returned as text in a special format referred to as *XML*. (Remember, we are just broadly covering the basics here.)

When you find a Web Service you want to use, you will need to rely on Web Services Description Language (WSDL, pronounced *whiz-dal*). In short, the `wsdl.exe` utility application uses the CodeDOM to generate a proxy class on your client machine. The proxy class creates proxy types for types exported by the Web Service and adds proxy methods to simplify invoking the Web Service methods. One form of the proxy methods is a synchronous method and the other form represents asynchronous proxy methods.

Assume you have a Web Service that exports the `Calculate` method. The `wsdl.exe` utility application would generate a proxy class that implements a `Calculate` method and a pair of methods, `BeginCalculate` and `EndCalculate`. Call `BeginCalculate` to invoke the Web Service method asynchronously and `EndCalculate` when the data is ready. The Web Service proxy class inherits from `SoapHttpClientProtocol`. The proxy methods call the `SoapHttpClientProtocol.BeginInvoke` and `SoapHttpClient-Protocol.EndInvoke` methods inherited in the proxy class.

Now that we have this information under our belts, all we have to do is apply the information we already know about invoking methods asynchronously. The code in Listing 6.7 assumes that we have created a Windows client application and added a Web Reference to a Web Service containing the `Calculate` method exported by the Web Service.

Listing 6.7 Creating an Instance of a Proxy Class and Invoking a Method Asynchronously

```
1:   Public Class Form1
2:      Inherits System.Windows.Forms.Form
3:
4:      [ Windows Form Designer generated code ]
5:
6:
7:      Private Service As localhost.Service1 = New localhost.Service1()
8:
9:      Private Sub Calculate(ByVal Numerator As Long, _
10:        ByVal Denominator As Long)
11:
12:        Service.BeginCalculate(Numerator, Denominator, _
13:          AddressOf Callback, Nothing)
14:
15:    End Sub
16:
17:    Private Sub Callback(ByVal Result As IAsyncResult)
18:
19:        Dim Value As Long = Service.EndCalculate(Result)
20:        MsgBox("Result=" & Value)
21:
22:    End Sub
23:
24:    Private Sub Button1_Click(ByVal sender As System.Object, _
25:        ByVal e As System.EventArgs) Handles Button1.Click
26:
27:        Calculate(Convert.ToInt64(TextBox1.Text), _
28:          Convert.ToInt64(TextBox2.Text))
29:
30:      End Sub
31:  End Class
```

Line 7 demonstrates how to create an instance of the Web Service proxy class. The name `localhost` represents the namespace of the proxy class, which reflects the host name of the computer owning the Web Service. The example Web Service resides on my laptop, hence `localhost`. Line 7 is no different than the code needed to create any object.

Lines 12 and 13 demonstrate how to invoke the Web Service asynchronously. The first two arguments are those needed by the `Calculate` method, and the third argument is the callback method. When the data is ready, the Web Service invokes the callback method. In Listing 6.7 the callback method is named `Callback`.

The basic idea is still the same. Call the asynchronous `Begin` method and use one of the polling completion techniques described in the Completing Asynchronous Calls subsection earlier in this chapter.

Invoking File Operations Asynchronously

The `System.IO.Stream` class is the base class for several IO classes. Defined in the `Stream` base class are methods for invoking IO operations asynchronously. The convention used for asynchronous methods is to prefix asynchronous methods with `Begin` and `End`. For example, the `Stream` classes implement the methods `Read` and `Write` for synchronous IO operations and `BeginRead` and `EndRead` and `BeginWrite` and `EndWrite` for asynchronous operations. Listing 6.8 demonstrates an asynchronous file read.

Listing 6.8 An Asynchronous Read Using the `FileStream` Class

```
1:   Imports System.IO
2:
3:   Public Class Form1
4:       Inherits System.Windows.Forms.Form
5:
6:   [ Windows Form Designer generated code ]
7:
8:     Private Stream As FileStream = Nothing
9:     Private Data() As Byte
10:
11:    Private Sub Button1_Click(ByVal sender As System.Object, _
12:      ByVal e As System.EventArgs) Handles Button1.Click
13:
14:      If Not (Stream Is Nothing) Then Return
15:      Stream = New FileStream("..\AsyncFileIO.sln", FileMode.Open)
```

```
16:
17:     ReDim Data(Stream.Length)
18:     Stream.BeginRead(Data, 0, Stream.Length, _
19:       AddressOf Finished, Nothing)
20:   End Sub
21:
22:   Private Sub Finished(ByVal Result As IAsyncResult)
23:
24:     Dim BytesRead = Stream.EndRead(Result)
25:     TextBox1.Text = System.Text.ASCIIEncoding.ASCII.GetString(Data)
26:     Stream.Close()
27:     Stream = Nothing
28:   End Sub
29:
30: End Class
```

TIP: The `System.Text.ASCIIEncoding` namespace contains classes and code for managing character encoding. For example, we can convert an array of bytes to string by calling the `ASCII.GetString` method as demonstrated in Listing 6.8, line 25.

Again, as we have seen throughout this section, we start the asynchronous operation with a `Begin` method and obtain the actual data in the callback method with the `End` method. `BeginRead` is shown in line 18 and `EndRead` in line 24.

We need to be careful with files as we cannot open an unlimited number of files without closing files, and other users will not be able to use a file that we are using. Listing 6.8 demonstrates how we close `FileStream` (line 26) after we have finished with the data. The only minor difficulty we have here is that we might not get all the data in one shot. If the number of bytes read doesn't equal the total number of bytes requested, we need to go back to the well and request more bytes. You have to solve this problem whether you read the file synchronously or asynchronously.

As an exercise, modify the code comparing the bytes actually read to those requested and call `BeginRead` until all the bytes have been read. Experiment with large files to test your solution. (Hint: Use a loop that totals the bytes read and calls `BeginInvoke` from the callback until the total bytes equals the number of bytes in the file.)

Use the Timer control for very lightweight background tasks. Use the `Timer` class in the `System.Threading` namespace when you need lightweight background processing in non-Windows Forms applications. Employ the asynchronous model when you need out-of-order processing, that is, when you need an extra worker thread. You also have two more options. You can use multithreading in the `ThreadPool` class or spin up your own `Thread` object. We'll continue our discussion by exploring multithreading.

Programming with Threads

Asynchronous programming provides you with access to lightweight multithreading. The `ThreadPool` and `Thread` classes provide you with heavyweight multithreading. The `ThreadPool` class manages a collection of worker-thread objects waiting for work. Because `ThreadPool` has threads waiting around, this class may be more efficient to use. Alternatively, you can use the `Thread` class directly, but while this gives you a little more control, the `Thread` class also requires more responsibility.

As a general practice there is no reason why you cannot use the `Thread-Pool` class for all your threading needs. The `ThreadPool` class is a bit easier to use, and you will get the same multithreaded performance results with a bit less work than if you create instances of the `Thread` class directly.

The remainder of this chapter demonstrates how to use multithreading in Visual Basic .NET using threads from the `ThreadPool` class as well as the `Thread` class. Finally, I will show you how to tie it all together to use multithreading in Windows Forms applications.

Multithreading with the `ThreadPool` Class

You get almost the same benefit from using the `ThreadPool` class as you do from using the `Thread` class. Both provide a means of multithreading in VB .NET and both incur almost the same liability. The liability is that threads can be significantly more challenging to debug than single-threaded applications because of very subtle bugs that are hard to find.

I will demonstrate how to use the `ThreadPool` class in this subsection and the `Thread` class later in this chapter. Although I encourage you to use threading in VB .NET, I recommend that you use multithreading sparingly and be prepared to expend extra effort in code reviews and testing the threaded parts of your applications.

The `ThreadPool` class manages the creation and destruction of threads on your behalf; all you have to do is provide the `ThreadPool` class with some work to do. The work is indicated using a delegate (again illustrating the importance of delegates in VB .NET). Listing 6.9 demonstrates the mechanics of using the `ThreadPool` class in multithreading.

Listing 6.9 Basic Multithreading with the `ThreadPool` Class and Delegates

```
1:   ' Caution: This console application has a bug in it.
2:   ' It was written expressly to demonstrate
3:   ' the mechanics of the ThreadPool class and problems
4:   ' with shared data accessed from multiple threads.
5:
6:   Imports System.Threading
7:
8:   Module Module1
9:
10:    Private Value As Integer = 0
11:    Private Reset As ManualResetEvent = New ManualResetEvent(False)
12:
13:    Sub Main()
14:      ThreadPool.QueueUserWorkItem(New WaitCallback(AddressOf Increment))
15:      Increment2()
16:      Reset.WaitOne()
17:      Console.WriteLine(Value)
18:      Console.ReadLine()
19:    End Sub
20:
21:    Public Sub Increment(ByVal State As Object)
22:      Dim I As Integer
23:      For I = 1 To 100
24:        Value += 1
25:      Next
26:
27:      Reset.Set()
28:    End Sub
29:
30:    Public Sub Increment2()
31:      Dim I As Integer
32:      For I = 1 To 100
33:        Value += 1
34:      Next
35:    End Sub
36:
37: End Module
```

The example application in Listing 6.9 is a console application defined in `ThreadPoolDemo.sln`. The `Main` subroutine in lines 13 through 19 represents the main thread and line 14 represents the second thread created using `ThreadPool`.

To create a thread using `ThreadPool` we pass an instance of a `WaitCallback` delegate to the shared method, `ThreadPool.QueueUserWorkItem`. A `WaitCallback` delegate is a subroutine that has a single argument, an `Object`.

The subroutines `Increment` and `Increment2` run on separate threads and increment the variable `Value` by 1 up to 100. The value of `Value` after both threads run should be 200. (And it probably will be every time.)

The code works as follows. Line 14 queues a work item into `ThreadPool`, which will grab an available thread or create a new one. We don't care; that's the job of the `ThreadPool` class. Line 15 invokes `Increment2`. Because both methods are short, `Increment2` will probably finish before `Increment` because it takes a smidgen of time longer to start up the thread in the queue. However, each method runs on a separate thread, which you can verify by opening the `Thread` window in Visual Studio .NET.

Line 16 uses `ManualResetEvent`, which inherits from `WaitHandle`, to block until `Increment` signals `ManualResetEvent` in line 27. Without `ManualResetEvent` this application would finish before the increment on the second thread would have a chance to finish. When the second thread is finished, `Value` is written to the console, and the `Console.ReadLine` method waits for the user to press enter before closing the console window.

To summarize, here are the basic steps for multithreading with the `ThreadPool` class.

- Create a `ManualResetEvent` or `AutoResetEvent` object that is not signaled, that is, invoke the constructor with `False`.
- Define a method that has the same signature as a `WaitCallback` delegate.
- Invoke `ThreadPool.QueueUserWorkItem`, passing a `WaitCallback` delegate initialized with the address of your procedure representing work.
- Block until all threads have had a chance to finish.

Exploring Thread Safety

What about thread safety? We are accessing `Value` from two separate threads and `Reset` from a different thread than the one it was created on. Is this safe? Let's closely examine what is going on here.

First, it is important to realize that the module concept was carried over from Visual Basic 6, but a module really equates to a class in which every member is shared. This means that all members of a console application can be accessed from any thread. Listing 6.10 illustrates the module and class relationship.

Listing 6.10 Illustrating the Relationship between Modules and Classes

```
1:  Imports System.Threading
2:
3:
4:  Public Class Class1
5:
6:    Private Shared Value As Integer = 0
7:    Private Shared Reset As ManualResetEvent = _
8:      New ManualResetEvent(False)
9:    Public Shared Sub Main()
10:
11:     Dim C As Class1 = New Class1()
12:     ThreadPool.QueueUserWorkItem( _
13:       New WaitCallback(AddressOf C.Increment))
14:     C.Increment2()
15:     Reset.WaitOne()
16:     Console.WriteLine(Value)
17:     Console.ReadLine()
18:   End Sub
19:
20:   Public Sub Increment(ByVal State As Object)
21:     Dim I As Integer
22:     For I = 1 To 100
23:       Value += 1
24:     Next
25:     Reset.Set()
26:   End Sub
27:
28:   Public Sub Increment2()
29:     Dim I As Integer
30:     For I = 1 To 100
31:       Value += 1
32:     Next
33:   End Sub
34:
35: End Class
```

Notice that Listing 6.10 defines a class, `Class1`, with a shared `Main` subroutine. `Class1.Main` can be used as a startup routine just as `Module1.Main` was. For instance, C# does not have the module idiom, and as a result you have to create console applications in C# by using a class with a static (shared) `Main` method.

Thus, we now know that module members are really shared class members and that we must treat them as such. Back to our question: Is it safe to modify `Value` and `Reset` from different threads? The answer is no.

When you run the code in Listing 6.9 (or 6.10) you will get the right result for very large numbers, even in this simple application. Correct results might lead you to believe that the program is working correctly; but it is not.

Lines of code yield several lines of assembly code, and a multithreaded application can interrupt another thread down to the individual lines of assembly code. This means that the intermediate modifications to `Value` could be trounced by another thread. As defined, the methods `Increment` and `Increment2` execute so quickly you are unlikely to detect this problem. However, if you change the upper limit of each loop from 100 to 10,000,000—so that these methods take a few milliseconds to run—you will then sporadically get incorrect results. Our example is a very simple application; imagine how subtle the threaded bugs might be in a production application. For this reason it is important to scrutinize multithreaded code very carefully, especially if it runs critical systems that may adversely impact human life. In a moment, we will talk about making the application thread-safe.

What about the `ManualResetEvent` object in line 11 of Listing 6.9—are we using `ManualResetEvent` safely there? The answer is yes. Why? We are modifying `ManualResetEvent` from only a single thread, so there is no chance that a second thread will goof it up for us. If only one thread accesses shared data, there are no worries.

Employing Multithreading Safely

Unfortunately, there is no way to write guidelines for every situation, but we can examine how to make Listing 6.9 (or 6.10) interact with the shared integer correctly. We can also derive some basic guidelines for multithreading in general.

The shared variable `Value` in Listing 6.9—implicit as a member of a module—and in Listing 6.10 needs to block when it is being modified. We can use the `SyncLock` statement to make sure that `Value` is incremented without interruption by another thread (Listing 6.11).

Listing 6.11 Using SyncLock to Enhance Thread Safety

```
1:  Imports System.Threading
2:
3:  Module Module1
4:
5:    Private Value As Integer = 0
6:    Private Reset As ManualResetEvent = New ManualResetEvent(False)
7:
8:    Sub Main()
9:      ThreadPool.QueueUserWorkItem( _
10:       New WaitCallback(AddressOf Increment))
11:      Increment2()
12:      Reset.WaitOne()
13:      Console.WriteLine(Value)
14:      Console.ReadLine()
15:    End Sub
16:
17:    Public Sub Increment(ByVal State As Object)
18:      Dim I As Integer
19:      For I = 1 To 10000000
20:        AddOne()
21:      Next
22:      Reset.Set()
23:    End Sub
24:
25:    Public Sub Increment2()
26:      Dim I As Integer
27:      For I = 1 To 10000000
28:        AddOne()
29:      Next
30:    End Sub
31:
32:    Public Sub AddOne()
33:      SyncLock GetType(Module1)
34:        Value += 1
35:      End SyncLock
36:    End Sub
37:
38: End Module
```

Listing 6.11 contains code almost identical to Listing 6.9. The only difference is that in this new listing we actually modify **Value** in a method named AddOne. Wrapped around the statement—line 34—that modifies the shared (or, effectively, global) variable Value is what is referred to as a *mutex*. SyncLock accepts an expression that yields a unique value. The Type object for a type is commonly used as demonstrated in line 33. Until the End SyncLock statement (line 35) executes, all other threads will be blocked at line 33.

Using SyncLock works well. However, a problem can occur if what is referred to as a *deadlock* occurs. A deadlock exists when there are two or more interdependent threads, for example, Thread A is waiting on thread B while B is waiting on A. Deadlock can be difficult to debug. The more complex and diverse the interactions between threads, the more difficult bugs caused by multithreading can be to resolve. The following general practices can help diminish the number of defects caused by multithreading.

- Avoid using global or shared variables between threads.
- If you use a global or shared variable, permit only one thread to modify it.
- If multiple threads must interact with a global or shared variable, use SyncLock to synchronize their interaction, and be mindful of deadlocks.
- Use multithreading sparingly.
- Use asynchronous processing for lightweight tasks.
- Use the ThreadPool class for heavyweight tasks.

Following the guidelines above will help you eliminate common multithreading problems. Be prepared to spend a disproportionately large amount of time testing, reviewing, and debugging the multithreaded parts of your applications, making sure that the payoff for using threads is large enough to make the extra development time worth the effort.

Multithreading with the Thread Class

The same problems that you may encounter with the ThreadPool class exist for the Thread class as well. As a result, the same guidelines apply too. (Refer to the previous subsection, Multithreading with the ThreadPool Class, for a general discussion of threading problems and resolutions.) I encourage you to use the ThreadPool class for the specific reason that it is easier to do so. With that in mind, this section demonstrates how to use the Thread class since you are likely to encounter it in someone else's code and may occasionally elect to use the Thread class directly yourself.

The `Thread` class works very similarly to the `ThreadPool` class. Whereas the `ThreadPool` class contains and manages worker threads, when you create an instance of the `Thread` class, you have a single thread, and you have to manage every aspect of that thread yourself. Thus, you have more control, but with control comes responsibility.

The basic process for multithreading with the `Thread` class is outlined below.

1. Define a method that matches the signature of the `ThreadStart` delegate. The signature for `ThreadStart` matches a subroutine with no parameters.
2. Declare and instantiate an instance of the `Thread` class, passing the address of your worker method to the `Thread` class's constructor.
3. Invoke the `Thread.Start` method to start the thread.

Optionally, you can set the `Thread.IsBackground` property to `True`. This will cause the background thread to terminate when the main thread terminates. You can set `Thread.Priority` to `ThreadPriority.BelowNormal` or `ThreadPriority.Lowest` to let the graphical user interface have a higher priority. Finally, you can invoke `Sleep`, `Interrupt`, `Suspend`, `Join`, `Resume`, or `Abort` to exert control over individual threads. As is true with threads in the `ThreadPool` class, use `ManualResetEvent` or `AutoResetEvent` as a means of blocking while waiting on a thread. For familiarity, Listing 6.12 reimplements the code in Listing 6.10, using the `Thread` class.

Listing 6.12 Multithreading with the `Thread` Class

```
1:  Imports System.Threading
2:
3:  Module Module1
4:
5:     Private Value As Integer
6:
7:     Sub Main()
8:
9:        Dim Thread1 As Thread = New Thread(AddressOf Increment)
10:       Increment2()
11:       Thread1.Start()
12:       Thread1.Join()
13:
14:       Console.WriteLine(Value)
```

```
15:      Console.ReadLine()
16:    End Sub
17:
18:    Public Sub Increment()
19:      Dim I As Integer
20:      For I = 1 To 10000000
21:        AddOne()
22:      Next
23:    End Sub
24:
25:    Public Sub Increment2()
26:      Dim I As Integer
27:      For I = 1 To 10000000
28:        AddOne()
29:      Next
30:    End Sub
31:
32:    Private Sub AddOne()
33:      SyncLock GetType(Int32)
34:        Value += 1
35:      End SyncLock
36:    End Sub
37: End Module
```

The difference between Listing 6.9 and Listing 6.12 occurs in the `Main` subroutine in lines 7 through 16 (Listing 6.12) and the absence of the `ManualResetEvent` object. Line 9 declares a new `Thread` object and initializes it to `Increment`, representing the work for the thread to complete. In this case I simply passed the address of `Increment` to the `Thread` constructor, which is treated as an implicit instance of the `ThreadStart` delegate. The thread is explicitly started in line 11, after `Increment2` is called, and we use `Thread1.Join` in line 12 to block until `Thread1` terminates. In Listing 6.12, `Thread1.Join` plays the role that `ManualResetEvent` plays in Listing 6.9.

Multithreading in Windows Forms

Much of the .NET framework is not considered thread-safe. This means that it isn't safe to invoke operations directly from one thread to a method in a .NET framework class. This is especially true of Windows Forms controls.

However, this doesn't mean you can't use multithreading in Windows Forms applications; it just means you have to be careful when you do. When interacting with the .NET framework, you need to use the synchronous `Invoke` or asynchronous `BeginInvoke` and `EndInvoke` methods to interact with Windows Forms controls. (You can call `Invoke`, `BeginInvoke`, `EndInvoke`, and `CreateGraphics` across threads safely.)

Listing 6.13 demonstrates how to interact with Windows Forms. The code simulates an animated graphic. By using a thread and a `GraphicsPath` object, the code draws the yin yang symbol (☯) repeatedly while the graphical user interface is allowed to run.

Listing 6.13 Safely Combining Multithreading with GDI+ in a Windows Forms Application

```
1:  Imports System.Threading
2:  Imports System.Drawing
3:  Imports System.Drawing.Drawing2D
4:  Imports System.Text.RegularExpressions
5:
6:  Public Class Form1
7:      Inherits System.Windows.Forms.Form
8:
9:  [ Windows Form Designer generated code ]
10:
11:   Private Sub Form1_Load(ByVal sender As System.Object, _
12:     ByVal e As System.EventArgs) Handles MyBase.Load
13:
14:     Start()
15:
16:   End Sub
17:
18:   Private Thread As Thread
19:   Private Sub Start()
20:     Thread = New Thread(AddressOf ThreadStart)
21:     Thread.IsBackground = True
22:     Thread.Start()
23:   End Sub
24:
25:   Private Sub ThreadStart()
26:     While (Thread.CurrentThread.IsAlive)
27:       Try
28:         Invoke(New MyDelegate(AddressOf Draw))
29:       Catch
```

```
30:        End Try
31:
32:        Thread.CurrentThread.Sleep(50)
33:      End While
34:   End Sub
35:
36:    Private Delegate Sub MyDelegate()
37:
38:    Private Sub Draw()
39:      Dim Path As GraphicsPath = New GraphicsPath()
40:      Path.AddString(Chr(91), New FontFamily("Wingdings"), _
41:        0, 44, New Point(10, 10), New StringFormat())
42:
43:      Dim Graphics As Graphics = CreateGraphics()
44:      Graphics.SmoothingMode = SmoothingMode.AntiAlias
45:
46:      Static I As Integer = 0
47:      I = (I + 1) Mod (Path.PointCount - 1)
48:      Graphics.DrawLine(Pens.Black, Path.PathPoints(I), _
49:        Path.PathPoints(I + 1))
50:      If (I = Path.PointCount - 2) Then Invalidate()
51:
52:    End Sub
53:
54: End Class
```

Line 9 emulates code outlining in Visual Studio .NET. The designer-generated code remained unmodified, so there was no point in showing it. The `Form1_Load` event starts the multithreaded drawing process in line 14. `Start` creates an instance of the `Thread` class, passes the address of the `ThreadStart` procedure, sets `Thread.IsBackground` to `True`, and starts the thread in line 22.

The drawing thread runs in the background until the application is closed. The actual drawing is pushed onto the same thread synchronously using the form's thread-safe `Invoke` method in line 28. In line 32 the thread sleeps for 50 milliseconds, adding to the animated effect. I used a `Try . . . Catch` block in lines 27 through 30 because it is possible for the main form to be in the process of being disposed between the time the `While` check occurs in line 26 and the `Invoke` method occurs in line 28. Without the exception handler you may intermittently get an `ObjectDisposedException` when you close the form.

Admittedly, code of the quality and complexity demonstrated in Listing 6.13 is best left for the `Tick` event of the Timer control. However, it is succinct enough to fit tidily in this chapter and demonstrate the use of the `Thread` class. Reserve the `Thread` class in actual applications for when you need maximum control and are willing to take maximum responsibility.

Multithreading with the `Timer` Class

The basic behavior of a timer is that you provide an interval of time and an event handler representing work; when the interval has elapsed, the event handler is called. Suppose that you are not building a Windows Forms application but want this basic behavior, or that you are in Windows and want a multithreaded version of your basic Timer behavior. You can use the `System.Threading.Timer` class.

The `System.Threading.Timer` class is a multithreaded timer. When the wait interval elapses, the delegate is invoked on its own thread, unlike the `Timer.Tick` event, which occurs on the same thread as the one the Windows Form is on. Besides the fact that the `System.Threading.Timer` class is not a control, everything else about the threaded Timer is familiar.

To use the `System.Threading.Timer` class, create an instance of the `Timer` class, passing an instance of the `TimerCallback` delegate. Additionally, pass any additional information you need to the state argument, a due time, and a period. The due time and period are expressed in milliseconds. Due time indicates how long to wait before the Timer wakes up, and the period expresses the interval. Listing 6.14 demonstrates how to use the `System.Threading.Timer` class.

Listing 6.14 Using the Multithreaded `Timer` Class, Distinct from the Timer Control

```
1:  Imports System.Threading
2:
3:  Module Module1
4:
5:    Private Finished As Boolean
6:
7:    Sub Main()
8:      Dim Timer As Timer = _
9:        New Timer(AddressOf TimerCallback, Nothing, 5000, 5000)
10:     While (Not Finished)
11:       Thread.Sleep(100)
12:     End While
```

```
13:    End Sub
14:
15:    Public Sub TimerCallback(ByVal State As Object)
16:      Static I As Integer = 0
17:      I += 5
18:      If (I > 30) Then Finished = True
19:
20:      Console.WriteLine(I & " seconds have elapsed")
21:
22:    End Sub
23: End Module
```

The example uses an implicit instance of a delegate (line 9). `AddressOf TimerCallback` is implicitly converted to a `System.Threading.TimerCallback` delegate. As expressed by the second argument, `Nothing`, we aren't passing additional information. The Timer in Listing 6.14 will wait five seconds, invoke the delegate, and then invoke the delegate every additional five seconds.

Summary

Multithreading in Visual Basic .NET is one of .NET's many powerful features. Unfortunately, this one aspect has a huge potential for misuse. I encourage you to use multithreading in your VB .NET applications when the perceived or real payoff exceeds the potential for headaches. Use multithreading sparingly.

As you learned in this chapter, you have many choices when its comes to synchronous, asynchronous, and multithreaded programming in VB .NET. Consider using the Timer control for short, lightweight synchronous tasks. Use asynchronous calls for lightweight processing, and use the `ThreadPool` class when you need threading. Of course, you can also use the `Thread` class. If you do, remember that you can reduce the number of problems with multithreading by keeping the number of interactions between threads to a minimum and using synchronization when you must modify variables across threads.

Solution Building

Part II demonstrates advanced technologies in VB .NET that form the building blocks for enterprise software development.

COM Interop

Forget the past; let it lie down and stretch out in its grave.

—*from* Black House *by Stephen King and Peter Straub*

Introduction

Microsoft has a responsibility to not abandon existing clients when shifting technologies. Supporting the new and the old often requires Microsoft to ship a huge volume of binaries with operating systems and tools like Windows and Visual Studio .NET. New competitors often aren't saddled with the need to support old clients, and these new competitors are quick to point out how much of a computer's resources Microsoft's tools seem to take. It is ironic that Microsoft's continued support of old and new technologies is used against the corporation in the media.

Recently my company switched ISPs. The new vendor didn't know how to adequately configure the Netopia router it provides for "free" with the service to work with my configuration, which included an Internet Security and Acceleration (ISA) server playing the role of firewall. I called Microsoft support to ensure that I had ISA configured correctly for Exchange, Internet Information Services, and the new router. (I understand that Netopia's router has a built-in firewall and Dynamic Host Configuration Protocol, or DHCP, server, to which I may switch at a later date.) Microsoft worked with me to double-check my ISA and Exchange configuration as well as troubleshoot problems with the Netopia router configuration. It turned out that I had missed a few settings on ISA and the router was configured incorrectly. Acting as advocate, Microsoft contacted the ISP and Netopia until we were able to find someone who really knew the Netopia router. The problem was eventually resolved; Microsoft hung in there for the duration when others gave up. The total cost of the service call was $241, which is slightly less than I paid the ISP to set up the router incorrectly. This kind of commitment to customer service makes Microsoft head and shoulders above many companies in many industries. (I work with a lot of vendors—phone companies, cable providers, shippers, retailers, and many more—and I find Microsoft's service to be second to none.)

Why did I take a paragraph to tell you all this? Because I want you to know that Microsoft's commitment to its customers includes that level of commitment to us, its *developer* customers.

Microsoft understands that there is a tremendous amount of money, time, and effort already invested in the Common Object Model (COM) technologies and that we need some continued support. The wheel has turned and a better overall solution has been engineered, but Microsoft hasn't forced us to abandon all our efforts. With COM Interop, .NET supports incorporating older COM code into newer .NET applications and even retrofitting new .NET code into COM-based applications. This means you can use your VB6 COM libraries in .NET, and if you want, you can incorporate .NET into VB6.

In this chapter I demonstrate how COM Interop supports using COM-based technologies with .NET and vice versa. From among the many issues related to this topic, I have selected to show you how to use COM in .NET and use .NET with COM, to explain how error handling is managed, and to talk about debugging and deploying mixed-mode applications.

Calling COM from .NET Code

Most likely a programmer will want to use old COM-based code in new .NET applications (rather than the other way around), for the simple reason that there is probably much more COM code out there than .NET code. (Eventually the momentum will shift and COM will likely be left by the roadside somewhere, but that day is still a long way off.) Let's start with how the mechanism for using COM in .NET works in general, and then we'll continue with an example.

When you want to use an old VB6 COM object (or some other language-based COM object) in .NET, .NET wraps a *runtime callable wrapper* (RCW) around the COM binary. This RCW manifests itself as an assembly named `Interop.<assemblyname>.dll`, where `<assemblyname>` is the name of the binary containing your COM code. For example, if I have a VB6/COM DLL named `ConvertApp.dll`, when I add a reference to this library Visual Studio .NET will read the type library of that binary and generate `Interop.ConverterApp.dll`. A few housekeeping items have to be managed for calls between .NET and COM to take place successfully.

.NET code runs in managed memory. By *managed* we mean that .NET objects can be moved in memory at any time: the Common Language Runtime manages allocating and reclaiming memory and performing type checking. COM code runs in unmanaged memory. If you move a COM DLL, your application will break. The RCW also needs to marshal .NET types to and from COM types. For example, if a COM type needs a BSTR (pronounced *beaster*), which is the COM equivalent of a string, use a .NET string. .NET uses a value typed class, `String`, to represent strings. The RCW must marshal the .NET value type `String` to a BSTR to successfully call a COM method that needs a string.

Where does the support from Microsoft come in? The support provided for us is that the RCW—or Interop assembly—is automatically generated for us. Thus we can write .NET code and call the COM object as if we were calling a .NET object because, from the .NET side of the fence, the RCW makes it look like we are using .NET objects. The marshaling to COM types is done for us. A lot of excellent graphic representations of the relationships between .NET code, the RCW, and COM are available on the Web and in the Visual Studio .NET help documentation, so I won't repeat those here. However, in a moment I will review some practical tools that will help you see the actual output from COM libraries and RCW assemblies.

Let's start by walking through all the steps in which you may be involved. These will likely include some degree of authorship of a COM binary and the consuming .NET application.

Creating a Test COM Object

To ensure that you have some COM code to work with I will provide some here. The output of an ActiveX DLL project in VB6 is a COM binary. Listing 7.1 contains a VB6 project group that contains an ActiveX DLL project and a Standard EXE application that tests the library. This is consistent with a VB6 project you may have lying around. Perhaps you want to reuse the ActiveX library but update the client application to ASP.NET or a Web Service. (Additionally, the Standard EXE project can be used to experiment if you still have VB6. I do, although it is getting dusty.)

Listing 7.1 A VB6 ActiveX DLL Project That Converts Temperature Units

```
Option Explicit

Public Function ToFahrenheit( _
  ByVal Temp As Double) As Double
```

```
    ToFahrenheit = Temp * 9 / 5 + 32
End Function

Public Function ToCelsius( _
   ByVal Temp As Double) As Double

   ToCelsius = (Temp - 32) * 5 / 9
End Function
```

I created a new ActiveX DLL project in VB6 and added the code shown in Listing 7.1 to the `.cls` file. If you were writing a math library or an aviation or weather program, the formula for temperature conversion used in this code might be useful.

That's really all there is to it. If I compile a project containing the code in Listing 7.1, the result is a COM binary. Depending on style, a simple VB6 user interface to test this library might consist of a form with a label, a text box, and two command buttons, supported by the code in Listing 7.2.

Listing 7.2 A VB6 Test Program for the ActiveX DLL Project

```
Option Explicit

Private Sub CommandCelsius_Click()
   Dim Converter As ConverterApp.Converter
   Set Converter = New ConverterApp.Converter

   On Error GoTo Handler
   Text1.Text = Converter.ToCelsius(CDbl(Text1.Text))

   Exit Sub

Handler:
   MsgBox Err.Description
End Sub

Private Sub CommandFahrenheit_Click()

   Dim Converter As ConverterApp.Converter
   Set Converter = New ConverterApp.Converter

   On Error GoTo Handler
```

```
Text1.Text = Converter.ToFahrenheit(CDbl(Text1.Text))


Exit Sub

Handler:
  MsgBox Err.Description
End Sub
```

Your style might not match mine because I started programming in C++ before VB1 and, since C++ has strong type checking, I never picked up the habit of the popular VB naming conventions. Nonetheless I think you can follow the code easily.

NOTE: If you have a COM binary but have lost track of the specifications or want to verify what it contains, you can use the `OleView.exe` utility. Run this utility from the command prompt, select File|View TypeLib, and pick the COM binary whose type library you want to view. `TemperatureConverter.dll` is shown in Figure 7.1. If you can read Interface Definition Language (IDL), which looks awful, you are in luck. The members are shown in the library section of the view.

You also have the option of using the Object Browser in Visual Studio .NET. After you have added a primary Interop assembly to a Visual Studio .NET solution, select View|Other Windows|Object Browser or press F2 to show the Object Browser. The Object Browser will show you all the assemblies and members in one centralized location. Click on any element in the Object Browser to view more information about that element or to navigate to the associated code (for your source code).

Add a reference to the ActiveX DLL project. Compile and run the Standard EXE, then try some well-known numbers. For example, passing 32 to `ToCelsius` should yield 0, and passing 100 to `ToFahrenheit` should yield 212.

Importing a COM Binary into .NET

The preceding section is consistent with steps every VB6 programmer might have performed before .NET was released. Notice there is no dependency on .NET because we are talking about technology that preceded .NET.

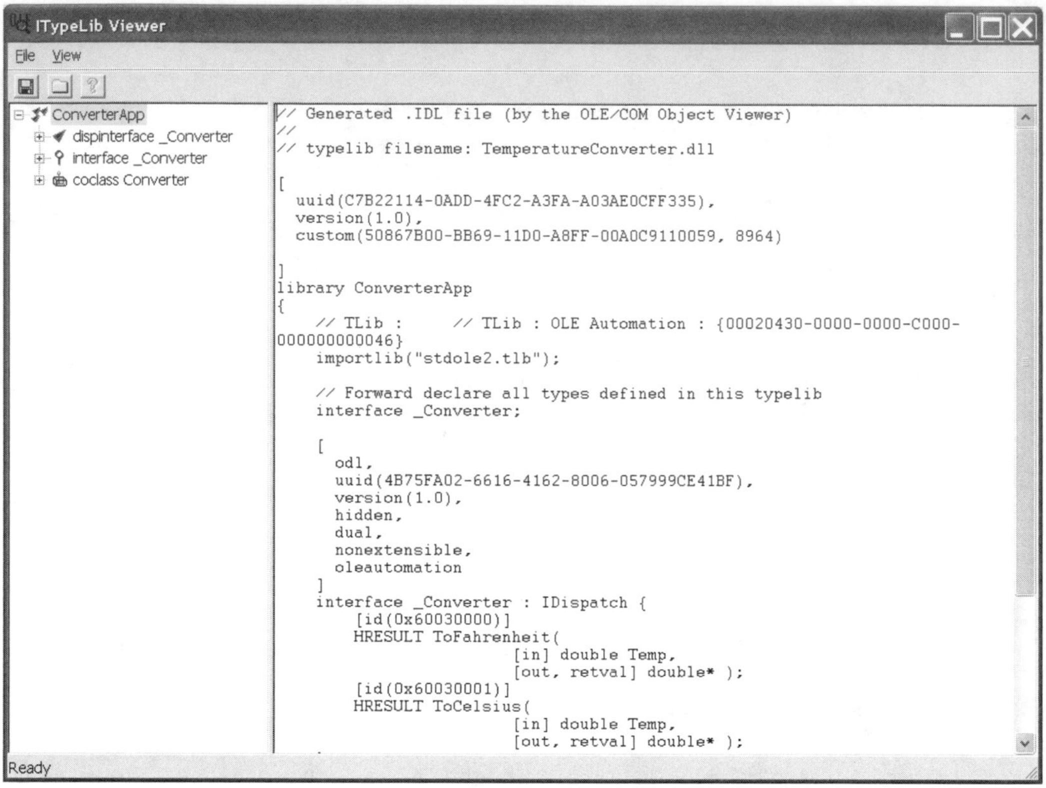

Figure 7.1 Using the `OleView.exe` utility to view the type library for `Temperature-Converter.dll`.

Now we have to tell .NET about our COM binary. There are two ways to do this. You can run the `tlbimp.exe` utility that runs with .NET and figure out the necessary switches (which you might want to do if you are a notepad and command-line commando), or you can add a reference to the COM binary and let .NET run `tlbimp.exe` on your behalf. The easiest way to use the command-line tool is to type `tlbimp.exe` followed by the name of the COM binary, for example, `tlbimp TemperatureConverter.dll`. This is a bit like sticking your head in the sand because a dozen or so related issues deal with namespaces, assembly versions, strong names, and how arrays are treated. However, the Visual Studio .NET IDE will handle these issues on our behalf, so we'll rely on that method.

TIP: Type `tlbimp /?` at the command prompt to see the list of command-line switches for the type library importer tool.

To import a COM binary into a .NET project, follow these steps.

1. Select the project in the Solution Explorer.
2. Select Project|Add Reference from the main menu.
3. In the Add Reference dialog, select the COM tab.
4. Find the COM binary you want to import by component name or path in the dialog or use the Browse button to search for it.
5. In the Add Reference dialog, click the Select button.
6. Click OK.

The preceding steps will add a reference to the COM binary and generate the RCW as `Interop.<assemblyname>.dll`. In our example code you will see the `ConverterApp` reference and the RCW `Interop.Converter-App.dll` added to the Solution Explorer. You need to click the Show All Files button at the top of the Solution Explorer to adjust the view to show hidden files, for example, a generated Interop assembly (Figure 7.2). If you are curious about the code generated by the COM Interop technology, you can open the RCW assembly with the `ildasm.exe` utility. The command-line

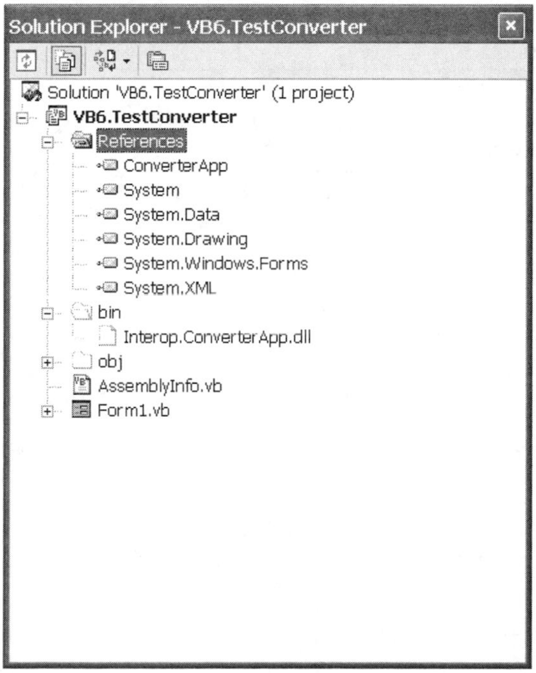

Figure 7.2 The Interop assembly for the COM binary `ConverterApp.dll`.

statement `Ildasm Interop.ConverterApp.dll` will open the Interop assembly in the IL disassembler (Figure 7.3).

Now the capabilities of the COM binary are ready to use just as if you had imported a .NET assembly. In a way you actually did import a .NET assembly; you imported the CodeDOM-generated `Interop.Converter-App.dll`.

Using Early Bound COM Objects

The most direct and easiest way to use the new COM/.NET code is to employ early binding. Just import the namespace and declare an instance of the class, then you are ready to go. By default the generated namespace is the name of the COM binary you imported. There are actually two types you can declare plus an interface. The interface will represent the interface implicitly declared by your VB6 class, the `Converter` interface. This is named `_Converter` in IL. Next there is a thin wrapper class named `Converter` that represents the bare-bones implementation of the `Converter` implementation in VB6. (VB6 combines interface declaration and implementation in one

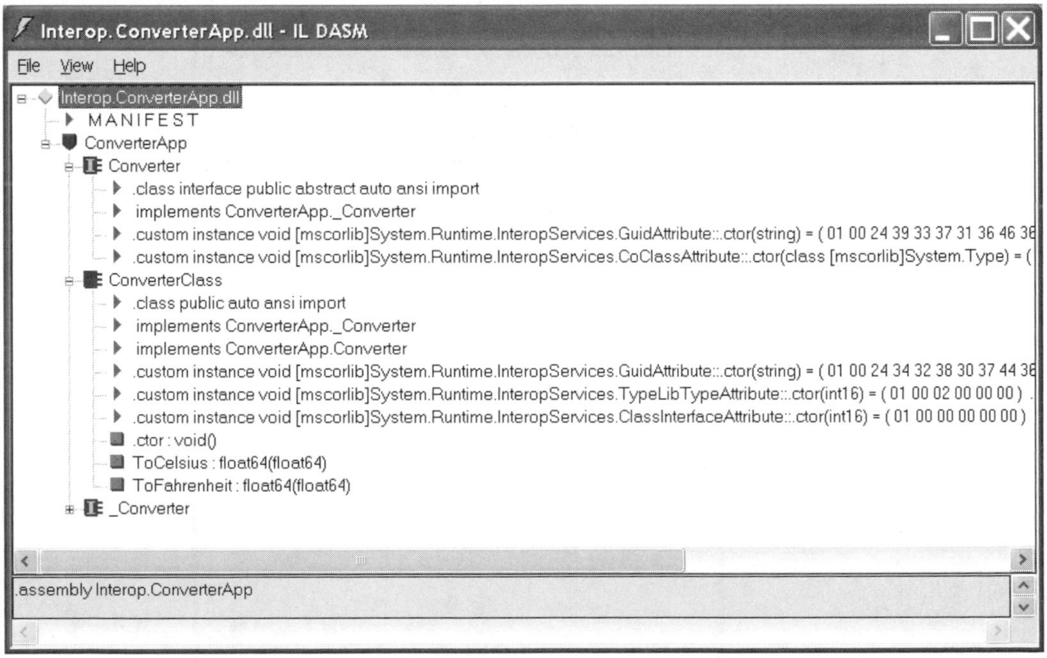

Figure 7.3 An `ildasm` view of the generated Interop assembly.

.cls file.) Finally we have a `ConverterClass` that was generated for us. `ConverterClass` mixes in the basic methods of all .NET classes (for example, `Equals`, `GetHashCode`, `GetType`, `ReferenceEquals`, and `ToString`), making `ConverterClass` the most complete .NET implementation. If you want to implement the `Converter` interface and provide new implements, use `Implements Converter`. If you want to declare an instance of the `Converter` class, use `ConverterClass`, although `Converter` will work too.

NOTE: It is interesting that COM Interop provides so many pieces, but keep in mind that COM is comprised of interfaces and implementations. It is VB6, not COM, that often combines both into one .cls file. (Although in VB6 you can have an interface as well as a second class implement that interface too.) COM Interop provides us with the interface, the VB6 (or imported implementation of that interface), and a .NET version of an implementation of that interface, which mixes in the imported code and .NET basic functions inherited from `System.Object`.

If you examine the IL, you will see that `ConverterClass` inherits from `System.Object` and implements the `Converter` interface. Of course the implementation of the imported `Converter` interface is delegated to the imported implementation of `Converter` too. This is quite an elegant solution, one that may be difficult for programmers to invent on their own without a lot of experience and knowledge of inheritance, interface implementations, and delegation. These are all difficult skills to come by when VB6 has done much of this work for us in the past.

Listing 7.3 contains a .NET application that is similar to the VB6 test application (Listing 7.2). This application provides an input text box and two buttons for bidirectional conversion.

Listing 7.3 A .NET Windows Forms Test Application for the Imported `ConverterApp` COM DLL

```
1:  Public Class Form1
2:      Inherits System.Windows.Forms.Form
3:
4:
5:  [ Windows Form Designer generated code ]
6:
7:    Public Property Temperature() As Double
8:    Get
9:      Return Convert.ToDouble(TextBox1.Text)
```

```
10:    End Get
11:    Set(ByVal Value As Double)
12:      TextBox1.Text = Value.ToString()
13:    End Set
14:    End Property
15:
16:    Private Sub ButtonFahrenheit_Click( _
17:      ByVal sender As System.Object, _
18:      ByVal e As System.EventArgs) _
19:      Handles ButtonFahrenheit.Click
20:
21:      Try
22:        Temperature = (New ConverterApp.ConverterClass()). _
23:          ToFahrenheit(Temperature)
24:
25:      Catch X As Exception
26:        MessageBox.Show(X.Message)
27:      End Try
28:
29:    End Sub
30:
31:    Private Sub ButtonCelsius_Click( _
32:      ByVal sender As System.Object, _
33:      ByVal e As System.EventArgs) _
34:      Handles ButtonCelsius.Click
35:
36:      Try
37:        Temperature = (New ConverterApp.ConverterClass()). _
38:          ToCelsius(Temperature)
39:      Catch X As Exception
40:        MessageBox.Show(X.Message)
41:      End Try
42:
43:    End Sub
44: End Class
```

I didn't use an `Imports` statement for the `ConverterApp` even though I certainly could have. (`Imports ConverterApp` would cover it.) Instead I used a verbose form of object instantiation inline (lines 22 and 37) to show that COM Interop can be treated on an equal footing with other .NET code. Clearly, if you want to, you could provide an `Imports` statement, declare an instance of the `ConverterClass`, instantiate the `ConverterClass`, and then invoke the method—but these are just extra lines of code.

What about Garbage Collection?

How does garbage collection fit into the COM model of incrementing and decrementing counters? This is a pretty good question, and the answer has been provided on our behalf.

From an assemblies perspective, the COM object is a .NET object represented by the class in the RCW. As a result the wrapper class—in our example, `ConverterClass`—is collected by .NET's garbage collector. `System.Runtime.InteropServices` takes care of managing calls to `IUnknown_AddRef` and `Release` for us. (If you are curious, after a cursory glance this behavior is defined in the Rotor source in `\sscli\clr\src\bcl\system\runtime\interopservices\gchandle.cs`.)

For our purposes, if the COM binary behaves well, the garbage collector should be able to tell it when .NET is done with it; then COM object management behavior should take over.

Using Late Bound COM Objects

Although early binding is convenient because you get string type checking and help from Intellisense when using the objects, sometimes you just want or need to defer object creation and employ late binding.

NOTE: If you have set `Option Strict On`, late binding is not allowed in VB .NET.

Late binding directly to COM objects is accomplished by using Reflection and the `ProgId` (name) or `CLSID` (Globally Unique Identifier, GUID) of the COM object. Get the `Type` information for the COM object by using the `ProgId` or `CLSID`, and use an activator to create an instance of the type. Listing 7.4 is code from `VB6.ComLateBinding.sln`, a console application that demonstrates a basic late binding example.

Listing 7.4 Late Binding Directly to a COM Object

```
Imports System.Reflection

Module Module1

  Sub Main()
```

```
Dim T As Type = Type.GetTypeFromProgID("ConverterApp.Converter")
Dim Instance As Object = Activator.CreateInstance(T)

Console.WriteLine(Instance.ToCelsius(212).ToString())
Console.ReadLine()

End Sub

End Module
```

In Listing 7.4 I used `ProgId` because the name is easier to remember and access than the GUID.

I should share a couple words of caution at this juncture. Late binding exists to make it easier to get started with VB programming, but it can be an expensive proposition. Late binding is inefficient in terms of executing speed, is often difficult to debug, and is unavailable in VB .NET when `Option Strict` semantics are on. A big part of the problem is that there is no way for the compiler to perform string type checking on late bound objects. I encourage you to avoid late binding as much as possible.

Consuming COM Events in .NET

The .NET event model is based on delegates. When you import a COM binary, .NET (`tlbimp.exe`) generates the necessary delegates to synchronize COM events with .NET delegates. The COM binary is referred to as the *source* and the .NET client is referred to as the *sink*. If you look in the Interop assembly for the COM binary, you will see the generated delegates that follow the _*sinkeventinterface*_*eventhandler*`EventHandler` naming convention. For example, if we define an `Address` class in VB6 with an event `OnAddressChanged`, the .NET type library importer will generate a sink event delegate class named `__Address_OnAddressChangedEventHandler`. However, by the time the type library importer has finished, all of this complexity will be bottled up in the RCW class and the event will look a managed code event named `OnAddressChanged`, which you can consume just like a .NET delegate. Listing 7.5 provides a partial business class in VB6 representing an `Address` class with an `OnAddressChanged` event. Listing 7.6 shows how easily that same event is consumed in a .NET client.

Listing 7.5 A Partially Complete `Address` Class in VB6 with a Public Event

```
1:  Option Explicit
2:
3:  Private FAddressLine1 As String
4:  Private FCity As String
5:  Private FState As String
6:  Private FZipCode As String
7:
8:  Public Event OnAddressChanged(ByVal Address As Address)
9:
10: Public Property Get AddressLine1() As String
11:    AddressLine1 = FAddressLine1
12: End Property
13:
14: Public Property Let AddressLine1(ByVal Value As String)
15:    FAddressLine1 = Value
16:    AddressChanged
17: End Property
18:
19: Public Property Get City() As String
20:    City = FCity
21: End Property
22:
23: Public Property Let City(ByVal Value As String)
24:    FCity = Value
25:    AddressChanged
26: End Property
27:
28: Private Sub AddressChanged()
29:    RaiseEvent OnAddressChanged(Me)
30: End Sub
```

Line 8 declares the public event `OnAddressChanged`. The event is raised in a single private method, `AddressChanged`, which is called in the `Property Let` statements for each of the `Address` properties defined. As you would expect, when any of the `Address` properties are used on the left side of an assignment, the `Let` method is called and then the `Address-Changed` method is called, raising the event. If you compare the IL for the imported `Address` class without the event and with the event (Figure 7.4),

Figure 7.4 `__Address`, `__Address_Event`, `__Address_EventProvider`, `__Address_OnAddressChangedEventHandler`, and `__Address_SinkHelper` were all added to create a .NET delegate representing the COM event `OnAddressChanged`.

you will see a significant increase in the amount of code generated to encapsulate the public event in Listing 7.5 to wrap the code into a multicast delegate. The end result is that the COM event looks and works like any other delegate in .NET (see Listing 7.6). Thus COM Interop creates a multicast delegate in the RCW that makes COM events easy to consume in .NET.

Listing 7.6 Using COM Interop to Create a Multicast Delegate in the RCW

```
 1:  Imports AddressProject
 2:
 3:  Public Class Form1
 4:      Inherits System.Windows.Forms.Form
 5:
 6:  [ Windows Form Designer generated code ]
 7:
 8:    Dim Address As AddressClass
 9:    Private Sub Form1_Load(ByVal sender As System.Object, _
10:      ByVal e As System.EventArgs) Handles MyBase.Load
11:
12:      Address = New AddressClass()
13:      AddHandler Address.OnAddressChanged, _
14:        AddressOf OnAddressChanged
15:
16:    End Sub
17:
18:    Private Sub OnAddressChanged( _
19:      ByVal Sender As AddressProject.Address)
20:
21:      TextBoxAddress.Text = Sender.AddressLine1
22:      TextBoxCity.Text = Sender.City
23:
24:    End Sub
25:
26:    Private Sub Button1_Click(ByVal sender As System.Object, _
27:      ByVal e As System.EventArgs) Handles Button1.Click
28:
29:      Address.AddressLine1 = "1313 Mockingbird Ln."
30:      Address.City = "Lansing"
31:
32:    End Sub
33: End Class
```

In our .NET client (in Listing 7.6) there is no evidence of COM. COM Interop permits us to treat the imported event as if it were any .NET multicast delegate. In effect, the runtime callable wrapper has generated one for us. All we have to do to consume the event is declare and create the object (lines 8 and 12, respectively) and add the event handler (shown in lines 13 and 14). The event handler is defined in lines 18 through 24. There is nothing to indicate the presence of COM. Microsoft programmers have done the heavy lifting for us.

Calling .NET Code from COM

It is likely that companies and programmers will eventually have enough code that COM-based clients will be calling .NET servers. I can imagine scenarios where individual programmers sneak in .NET parts as a bridge to the future for companies slow to switch to .NET or so they can use highly prized third-party solutions available only in .NET. Calling .NET from COM is supported by COM Interop. In this section, to be thorough, I included an example of .NET to COM Interop relationship, including the preparatory steps necessary to make the mechanics work.

Recall that metadata was incorporated in .NET assemblies to mitigate "DLL hell." This metadata consists of an assembly manifest that provides information about types and member names, playing the same role as COM type libraries. Using the assembly manifest information, .NET can generate a *COM callable wrapper* (CCW) that marshals calls from COM to .NET, quietly converting COM types to .NET types. The steps involved are roughly analogous to the steps of consuming a COM binary in .NET, but in reverse. To perform the reverse operation we use the `tlbexp.exe` tool to create the CCW and `regasm.exe` to make appropriate entries in the registry, allowing the COM clients to find the .NET servers.

The mechanics are the most important part of our example, so I will use the temperature conversion code—this time implemented in .NET—to allow us to focus on the process rather than the code. (Note: If you want to export some .NET code to COM as quickly as possible, skip to the Exporting to COM Made Easy subsection.)

Creating a Test .NET Class Library

We can implement `TemperatureConverter.sln` as a class library in .NET. We are purposefully creating an assembly that contains a class that can be consumed by a COM client application. This is not the most thorough way to create the class library for this purpose; later we will add polish with some adornments.

COM doesn't know anything about parameterized constructors. Thus, we can have any constructors we like, but we must have a default constructor. Additionally, any properties, methods, fields, or events that we want exposed to COM must be public. By default, public members will be exposed to COM. Listing 7.7 offers a .NET implementation of the temperature converter containing the public constructor and the two conversion methods.

Listing 7.7 A .NET Implementation of the `Converter` Class for Use in a COM Client

```
1:  Public Class Converter
2:
3:     Public Sub New()
4:
5:     End Sub
6:
7:     Public Function ToFahrenheit( _
8:        ByVal Temperature As Double) As Double
9:
10:     Return Temperature * (9 / 5) + 32
11:
12:    End Function
13:
14:    Public Function ToCelsius( _
15:       ByVal Temperature As Double) As Double
16:
17:     Return (Temperature - 32) * 5 / 9
18:
19:    End Function
20:
21: End Class
```

This class is simple enough to not require any explanation except that the empty default constructor is not explicitly required. Recall that VB .NET will create an empty default constructor for us if we fail to define one. The next thing we need to do is tell COM about our .NET assembly.

Exposing .NET Types to COM

The manifest information in a .NET assembly needs to be converted into IDL in a type library. The generated `.tlb` file plays the role of CCW. In addition, we have to tell the registry where to find the type library and .NET assembly. (Remember, we are going backward into DLL hell.) This is all accomplished with the command-line tools `tlbexp.exe` and `regasm.exe`, which both ship with .NET.

The `tlbexp.exe` utility reads the assembly manifest information of an assembly and generates the IDL. The `regasm.exe` tool adds entries in the registry for the assembly and the type library. You can automate these steps together in a batch file or `.cmd` file by running the `tlbexp.exe` utility first, following by `regasm.exe`. The following steps will make things easier.

1. Select Start|Program Files|Visual Studio .NET|Visual Studio .NET Tools|Visual Studio .NET Command Prompt. This step will open a command prompt with the right environment variables, including path information to `tlbexp.exe` (`C:\Program Files\Microsoft Visual Studio .NET\FrameworkSDK\Bin`) and `regasm.exe` (`C:\WINNT\Microsoft.NET\Framework\v1.0.3705`).

2. Change directories to the `bin` folder containing your .NET assembly. (In our example, this is the folder containing `TemperatureConverter.dll`.)

3. Type `tlbexp` *assemblyname* and press Enter. (For our example, the command is `tlbexp TemperatureConverter.dll`.) This will create a file with the same name and a `.tlb` extension. (The `.tlb` file contains the IDL, which you can explore with `OleView.exe`.) Note that you can skip the `tlbexp.exe` command (this step) if you use the `/tlb` switch with `regasm.exe`.

4. Next run `regasm` *assemblyname* `/tlb /codebase`. (For our example, the command is `regasm TemperatureConverter.dll /tlb /codebase`.)

NOTE: When you export a type library and register that library for COM Interop, you will get the following warning:

RegAsm warning: Registering an unsigned assembly with /codebase can cause your assembly to interfere with other applications that may be installed on the same computer. The /codebase switch is intended to be used with signed assemblies. Please give your assembly a strong name and re-register it.

The `/codebase` switch tells `regasm.exe` to store path information that helps locate your registered assemblies. However, in this case you can ignore the error. Strong names are for registering public assemblies in the Global Assembly Cache (GAC). You should put assemblies in the GAC only if you want everyone to be able to use them. This is not necessarily the case with COM Interop assemblies; more likely you want only your application to use them, so don't put them in the GAC.

However, if you do want to make your assembly public and register it in the GAC, use the `sn.exe` utility to make a strong name key file. Associate that key with your assembly in the `assemblyinfo.vb` file using an assembly attribute (the attribute is already there) and use `gacutil.exe` to place the assembly into the GAC. Again, do this only if you want everyone to know about and share the assembly.

Thus for our example we can run `regasm TemperatureConverter.dll /tlb /codebase` to create the type library and register the assembly in one step. The `/tlb` switch generates the type library, and the `/codebase` switch tells the registry about the physical file location of the .NET assembly. If we don't use the `/codebase` switch, COM won't be able to find our assembly. By default the COM client will look in the GAC, and we haven't taken any steps to put the assembly there. (That is, `TemperatureConverter.dll` isn't in the GAC, so we need to use the `/codebase` switch.)

NOTE: If any open clients are using the type library and assembly, you may need to close them before unregistering, deleting, or modifying the assembly and type library. Remember, this is COM now. As a result we will need to unregister the assembly if we plan to make modifications to it in the same location from which it was registered. To unregister the assembly, type `regasm TemperatureConverter.dll /unregister` at the command prompt. Our assembly will now show up in developer tools like Visual Studio 6. For example, `TemperatureConverter.tlb` will be listed in the VB6 References dialog as `TemperatureConverter`.

Consuming .NET Assemblies in VB6

Consuming `TemperatureConverter` in VB6 is accomplished by adding a reference to `TemperatureConverter.tlb` in the References dialog (Figure 7.5) and writing code to instantiate instances of the `Converter` class. Keep in mind that the CCW makes the assembly look like a COM object; thus we use `TemperatureConverter` as if it were a COM object. Listing 7.8 contains some simple client code that consumes the .NET `Converter` class.

Listing 7.8 Using the .NET Server in VB6

```
Private Converter As TemperatureConverter.Converter

Private Sub CommandToCelsius_Click()
```

```
    On Error GoTo Handler
       Text1.Text = Converter.ToCelsius(CDbl(Text1.Text))
    Exit Sub
Handler:
  MsgBox Err.Description

End Sub

Private Sub CommandToFahrenheit_Click()
  On Error GoTo Handler
     Text1.Text = Converter.ToFahrenheit(CDbl(Text1.Text))
  Exit Sub

Handler:
  MsgBox Err.Description

End Sub

Private Sub Form_Load()
  Set Converter = New TemperatureConverter.Converter
End Sub
```

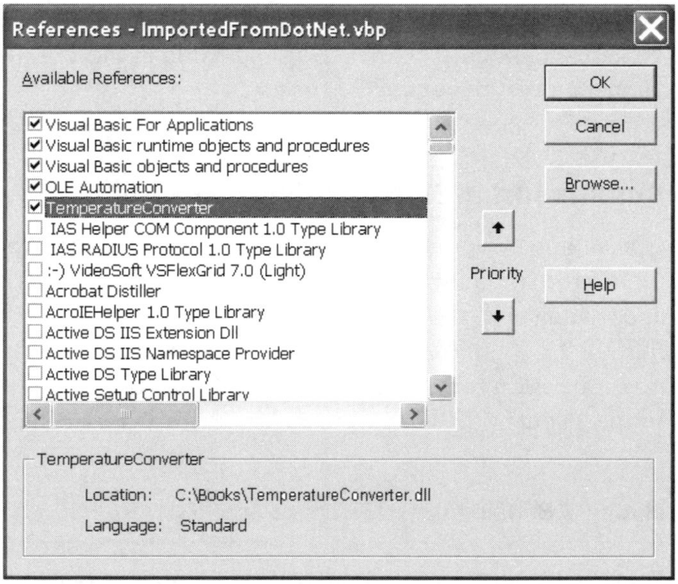

Figure 7.5 The type library for our .NET assembly in the VB6 References dialog.

From the listing you can see that the `TemperatureConverter.Con-verter` class is declared and used in the usual way.

Exposing .NET Delegates to COM

Visual Basic 6 takes care of a lot of housekeeping for us. We generally don't worry about IDL, type libraries, or interfaces like `IDispatch`, `IUnknown`, `ISinkEvents`, and `IConnectionPoints`. Visual Basic 6 takes care of these low-level elements of COM on our behalf. However, when we want to raise events in .NET sources and handle those events in COM sinks, we have to convert .NET delegates (events in .NET) to COM connection points (events in COM). This is managed by specifically declaring an interface that maps method signatures in an interface to event members in a class. We combine the code with attributes that tell `tlbexp.exe` what kind of IDL to generate.

Listing 7.9 provides an example of a .NET source that exposes delegates to COM by simulating connection points in .NET. After a description of this code, Listing 7.10 provides an example of a VB6 client consuming the .NET source.

Listing 7.9 Exposing .NET Events to COM by Simulating Connection Points

```
1:  Imports System.Runtime.InteropServices
2:
3:  Public Delegate Sub ConvertDelegate( _
4:     ByVal Temperature As Double)
5:
6:
7:  <InterfaceType( _
8:     ComInterfaceType.InterfaceIsIDispatch)> _
9:  Public Interface TemperatureEvents
10:    Sub ConvertToFahrenheit(ByVal Temperature As Double)
11:    Sub ConvertToCelsius(ByVal Temperature As Double)
12: End Interface
13:
14:
15: <ComSourceInterfaces( _
16:    "TemperatureConverter.TemperatureEvents")> _
17: Public Class Converter
18:
19:    Public Event ConvertToCelsius As ConvertDelegate
20:    Public Event ConvertToFahrenheit As ConvertDelegate
```

```
21:
22:    Public Function ToFahrenheit( _
23:      ByVal Temperature As Double) As Double
24:
25:      OnConvertToFahrenheit(Temperature)
26:      Return Temperature * (9 / 5) + 32
27:
28:    End Function
29:
30:    Public Function ToCelsius( _
31:      ByVal Temperature As Double) As Double
32:
33:      OnConvertToCelsius(Temperature)
34:      Return (Temperature - 32) * 5 / 9
35:
36:    End Function
37:
38:    Private Sub OnConvertToFahrenheit( _
39:      ByVal Temperature As Double)
40:      RaiseEvent ConvertToFahrenheit(Temperature)
41:    End Sub
42:
43:    Private Sub OnConvertToCelsius( _
44:      ByVal Temperature As Double)
45:      RaiseEvent ConvertToCelsius(Temperature)
46:    End Sub
47:
48: End Class
```

Line 1 imports `System.Runtime.InteropServices`, which introduces Interop classes like the attributes we'll be using in the listing. Lines 3 and 4 declare a new delegate, `ConvertDelegate`, which accepts a `Temperature` value. We want to expose to VB6 clients those events that match the signature of `ConvertDelegate`; thus we need to expose the events in a dispinterface that simulates COM connection points in IDL. This is accomplished by defining an interface in .NET, adding method signatures that match the events, and adorning the interface with the `InterfaceTypeAttribute`. The interface containing the two method signatures that become our event connection points is defined in lines 7 through 12. The `InterfaceTypeAttribute` is applied in lines 7 and 8; `ComInterfaceType.InterfaceIsDispatch` indicates that the COM interface needs to be exposed as a dispinterface.

Lines 15 through 48 implement the `Converter` class with the new events. We have two events: `ConvertToCelsius` and `ConvertToFahrenheit`. When `ToCelsius` is called, the `ConvertToCelsius` event is raised. `Convert-ToFahrenheit` is raised when `ToFahrenheit` is called. The actual events are raised in the associated private methods (following a .NET convention).

The `ComSourceInterfacesAttribute` (lines 15 and 16) associates the event source interface `TemperatureEvents` in line 9 with the `Converter` class and the events in lines 19 and 20.

When we are ready to implement the COM client, the CCW takes care of mapping the .NET delegates (`ConvertToFahrenheit` and `Convert-ToCelsius`) to the COM connection points on our behalf. Consequently the VB6 code is written as if we were using an event source that originated from COM. Listing 7.10 contains code that consumes the .NET event source by using the `WithEvents` statement as you'd expect.

Listing 7.10 A COM Client Consuming .NET Events

```
1:  Private WithEvents Converter As TemperatureConverter.Converter
2:
3:  Private Sub CommandToCelsius_Click()
4:     On Error GoTo Handler
5:       Text1.Text = Converter.ToCelsius(CDbl(Text1.Text))
6:     Exit Sub
7:  Handler:
8:     MsgBox Err.Description
9:
10: End Sub
11:
12: Private Sub CommandToFahrenheit_Click()
13:    On Error GoTo Handler
14:      Text1.Text = Converter.ToFahrenheit(CDbl(Text1.Text))
15:    Exit Sub
16:
17: Handler:
18:    MsgBox Err.Description
19:
20: End Sub
21:
22: Private Sub Converter_ConvertToCelsius( _
23:    ByVal Temperature As Double)
24:
25:    MsgBox "Converting " & Temperature & " to Celsius"
```

```
26:
27: End Sub
28:
29: Private Sub Converter_ConvertToFahrenheit( _
30:    ByVal Temperature As Double)
31:
32:    MsgBox "Converting " & Temperature & " to Fahrenheit"
33:
34: End Sub
35:
36: Private Sub Form_Load()
37:    Set Converter = New TemperatureConverter.Converter
38: End Sub
```

Recall that in VB6 we use a `WithEvents` statement when declaring a COM object to have the IDE expose the events in the Code Editor. If we pick the object from the Object drop-down list, the Code Editor will update the Procedure drop-down list to contain the event methods for us. If we select an event method, the Code Editor will stub out the event handler. The two event handlers are shown in Listing 7.10 in lines 22 through 34. The remaining code you have seen before.

If we were using a language like C++, we'd have to do more of the infrastructure work, but VB6 manages things like the connection points for us, and the CCW handles marshaling the data back and forth.

Applying Interop Attributes

You can employ several Interop attributes to manage how COM Interop behaves. I have included a few of them here to whet your appetite. Check the Visual Studio .NET help documentation for an exhaustive list.

The `ComRegisterFunctionAttribute` and `ComUnregisterFunction-Attribute` can be applied to a pair of shared methods that run code during the registration and unregistration processes. If you define one or the other method, you must also provide the symmetric operation. These two methods work in pairs, and `regasm.exe` will honk at you—failing to register—if you define a register function but no unregister function.

The `ComVisibilityAttribute` provides a way for you to conceal things from COM. By default public members are visible to COM. Initialize the `ComVisibilityAttribute` with `False` to make a public member invisible to COM. For example, lines 3 and 4 of Listing 7.9 define a delegate. .NET clients can use delegates directly, but the COM client won't be able to do anything with it. Thus we could apply the `<ComVisible(False)>` attribute to the delegate declaration to make it invisible to COM.

Finally there is the `ClassInterfaceAttribute`, which will generate an interface for your .NET classes based on the public managed types you define and the inherited types. `<ClassInterface(ClassInterface-Type.AutoDual)>` is good for testing since it saves you the time of explicitly declaring an interface for your class, but it can lead to versioning problems. When `ClassInterfaceType.AutoDual` is used, the `tlbexp.exe` utility generates an interface and an interface identifier (IID) for the interface. This permits clients to bind to a specific layout that will change as the class changes. Managed code won't be affected by the change because managed clients are talking directly to the class; unmanaged clients are talking to the class through the interface. If the underlying layout changes, the wrong behaviors may be invoked inadvertently. It is better to avoid using the `Class-InterfaceAttribute` and instead define a literal interface and implement that interface in the class you are exposing to COM.

Exporting to COM Made Easy

If you read the preceding subsections, you now know a lot about the manual process of COM-to-.NET Interop. If you skipped ahead because you are in a hurry, you have come to the right place. Earlier in the chapter I said that you could use `tlbimp.exe` to import a COM source or you could let the .NET IDE do it for you. The same is true for exporting a .NET source for use by COM. If you create a class library project, select File|Add New Item, and pick COM Class from the list of templates, .NET will create a class that uses the `ComClassAttribute`. The .NET IDE will manage exporting the type library and registering the .NET source for use with COM when you compile your class library. All you have to do is focus on writing the code.

To try this shortcut follow these steps.

1. Create a new .NET class library project.
2. Delete the default `Class1.vb` file.
3. Select File|Add New Item.
4. In the templates list, select the COM Class template item (Figure 7.6).
5. Add a simple method that returns a string, or type in the `ToFahrenheit` function used earlier in this chapter.
6. Build the code (shown in Listing 7.11).

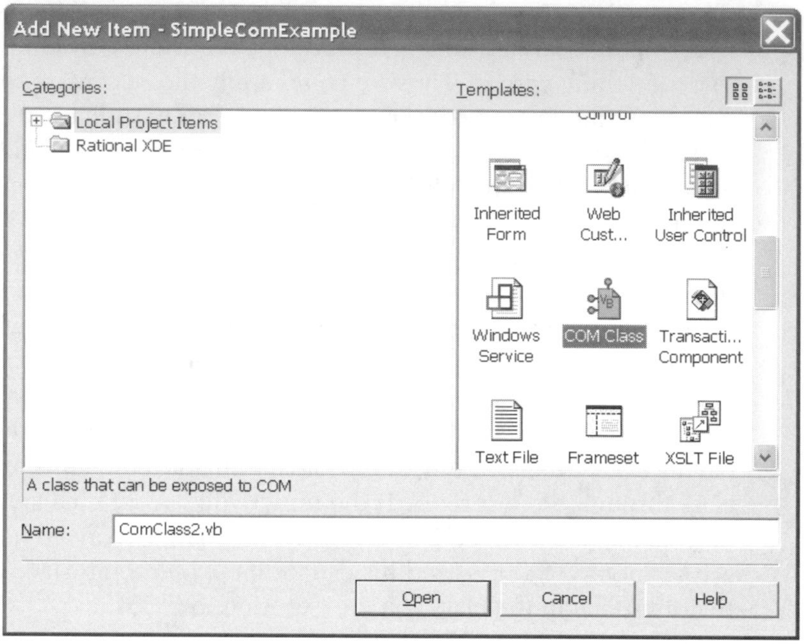

Figure 7.6 The COM Class template makes it easy to export a .NET source to COM.

7. Open VB6. Add a reference to the type library with the same name as the .NET assembly. (In my example the solution was named `Simple-ComExample.sln` and the assembly was named `SimpleComExample.dll`; thus the type library is named `SimpleComExample.tlb`.)

8. Declare an instance of the class using the `library.class` name syntax.

9. You will see and be able to invoke the method defined in the COM Class template.

Listing 7.11 Using the COM Class Template to Expose a .NET Source to COM

```
1:  <ComClass(ComClass1.ClassId, _
2:    ComClass1.InterfaceId, ComClass1.EventsId)> _
3:  Public Class ComClass1
4:
5:  #Region "COM GUIDs"
6:      ' These  GUIDs provide the COM identity for this class
7:      ' and its COM interfaces. If you change them, existing
```

```
 8:      ' clients will no longer be able to access the class.
 9:      Public Const ClassId As String = _
10.        "BD0327C9-6680-423C-9503-F6C90C97C301"
11:      Public Const InterfaceId As String = _
12:        "DD916514-BE48-40C9-8E5E-486EB6522C47"
13:      Public Const EventsId As String = _
14:        "3C7B3C24-3986-4C92-9A64-699D96067106"
15: #End Region
16:      ' A creatable COM class must have a Public Sub New()
17:      ' with no parameters, otherwise, the class will not be
18:      ' registered in the COM registry and cannot be created
19:      ' via CreateObject.
20:      Public Sub New()
21:         MyBase.New()
22:      End Sub
23:
24:      Public Function ToFahrenheit( _
25:        ByVal Temperature As Double) As Double
26:
27:         Return Temperature * 9 / 5 + 32
28:      End Function
29:
30: End Class
```

The only code I added was the function `ToFahrenheit` in lines 24 through 28. After building the class library containing this code, the `.tlb` file was generated and the necessary registry entries were created to make `ComClass1` available to VB6. Pretty easy.

While a big application is likely to need a lot of manual tweaking, you can try to get as much mileage out of automated approaches as possible. I would use the COM Class template unless something specific prevented me from doing so.

Understanding Error Handling in COM Interop

COM Interop supports error handling from .NET to COM and from COM to .NET. Each `HResult` in COM is mapped to a .NET exception. Hence, if an exception is thrown in a .NET source, the CCW maps the exception to an `HResult` using the `ISupportErrorInfo` interface, which results in an `Err` object being created in VB6. If a VB6 COM source raises an error, the

RCW converts the VB6 COM `HResult` into a .NET exception, and the mapped exception is thrown in .NET. Check out the VS .NET help topic `ms-help://MS.VSCC/MS.MSDNVS/cpguide/html/cpconhresultsexceptions.htm` for a complete mapping between `HResult` values and .NET exception classes.

Importing ActiveX Controls into .NET

You can use your favorite ActiveX controls in .NET. The `aximp.exe` tool creates a wrapper around an ActiveX control that exposes the types of the ActiveX controls as members of a control that inherits from `System.Windows.Forms.Control`. The wrapper manages interactions between the client application and the wrapped ActiveX control. You can add an ActiveX control (`.ocx`) to the Toolbox from the Tools|Custom Toolbox menu. In the Custom Toolbox dialog, select the COM Components tab (which is selected by default), and check the ActiveX controls you want to import. The `aximp.exe` utility will run, creating a wrapper for the control and adding a reference to the wrapper control in the References section.

`UsesActiveXControl.sln` adds the Microsoft Web Browser control (`SHDocVw.dll`) and incorporates this control into a Windows Form. Figure 7.7 shows the Customize Toolbox with the ActiveX control selected. Figure 7.8 shows the control in the Toolbox, and Figure 7.9 shows a reference to the wrapper class in the References section of the Solution Explorer. (By convention the original ActiveX file name has an `Ax` prefix added; thus `SHDocVw.dll` is managed by the wrapper `AxSHDocVw.dll`.)

Debugging Interoperable Components

There does not appear to be a direct way to simultaneously debug both COM and .NET source code at the same time. However, you can debug .NET-to-COM and COM-to-.NET Interop relationships by debugging the library and using the client as the hosting application. For example, if you want to debug a COM library that is being consumed by a .NET client, you can debug the COM client by using the .NET client as the hosting application. Similarly, you can debug a .NET library by using the COM client as the hosting application.

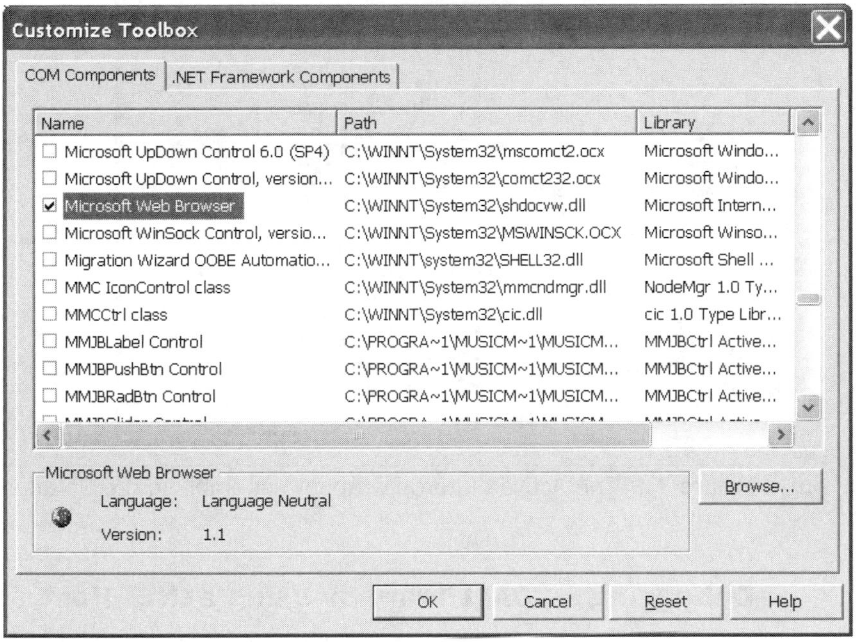

Figure 7.7 A selected ActiveX control in the Customize Toolbox.

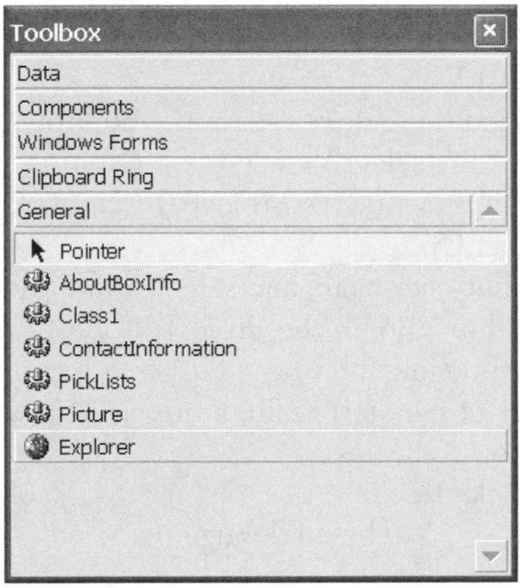

Figure 7.8 The imported ActiveX control in the .NET Toolbox.

Figure 7.9 The ActiveX Interop wrapper assembly in the Solution Explorer.

Debugging a COM Library by Using a .NET Host

For example, suppose we want to debug the `Address.cls` class defined in `AddressProject.vbp` (VB6). This is a class library. We can't run the class library unless we do so in the context of a hosting application. Let's say we just happen to have the `VB6.ConsumeEvent.exe`, a .NET client that consumes instances of `AddressProject.Address` objects. To debug the `Address` class in VB6 using the .NET host, we would follow these steps.

1. Start VB6.
2. Open the `AddressGroup.vbg` project group in VB6.
3. In VB6, select View|Project Explorer.
4. Click on AddressProject. Right-click the project and select Set as Start Up.
5. Right-click again and select AddressProject Properties.
6. Still in VB6, in the Project Properties dialog (Figure 7.10), click the Debugging tab.
7. Select the Start radio button and browse to the `VB6.ConsumeEvent.exe`.
8. Click OK.
9. Press F5 to begin debugging.

If you follow the steps above to begin debugging the VB6 COM library, you will see the host application start up. Set breakpoints in the COM li-

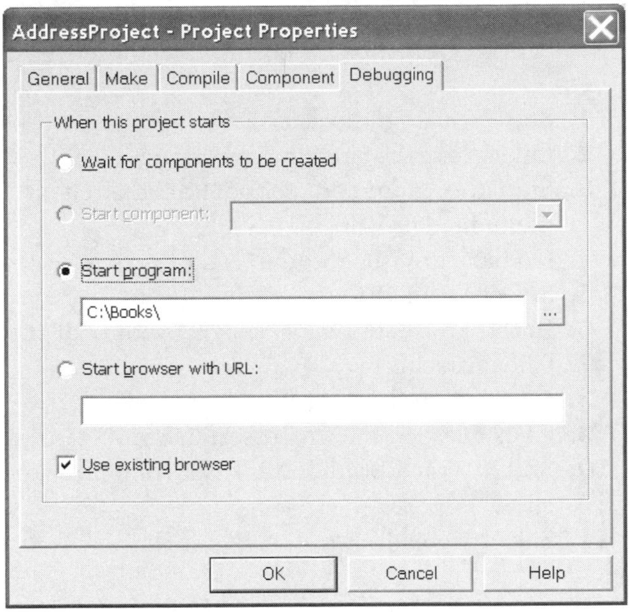

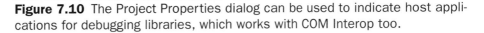

Figure 7.10 The Project Properties dialog can be used to indicate host applications for debugging libraries, which works with COM Interop too.

brary code (`Address.cls`) so that when the host application calls into the COM source, the VB6 debugger will stop on those breakpoints. Unfortunately, you can see only one side of the COM Interop relationship at a time, but you can successfully debug both client and server in this manner.

To debug both the COM component and the .NET assembly at the same time, specify the VS .NET IDE (`devenv.exe`) as the startup host program and the solution file (`.sln`) as the parameter. For example, in VB6 set the start program to `C:\Program Files\Microsoft Visual Studio .NET\Common7\IDE\devenv /run c:\`*solution*`.sln`. When you start the VB6 project, the VS .NET IDE will start, loading and running the .NET solution too, resulting in debug control over both the VB6 COM code and the VS .NET code.

Debugging a .NET Library by Using a COM-Based Host

Suppose now that we have a .NET library with types exposed to COM. We could test the .NET library with a COM host by opening the .NET library and attaching the debugger to the COM-based client host. To try debugging a .NET library from a COM host, follow these steps.

1. Start Visual Studio .NET.
2. Open `TemperatureConverter.sln`.
3. Start the `ImportedFromDotNet.exe` client application that we implemented in VB6.
4. Go back to Visual Studio .NET.
5. Select Debug|Processes.
6. In the Processes dialog, select `ImportedFromDotNet.exe`.
7. Click Attach.
8. Click OK in the Attach to Process dialog.
9. Click Close in the Processes dialog.
10. Still in Visual Studio .NET, set some breakpoints in the `Converter` class.
11. Select Debug|Start.

When you interact with the COM host and request something from the .NET server that hits one of your breakpoints, the .NET IDE will pause execution at that breakpoint. You can inspect and evaluate your .NET library as if it were any other running code. Again, you are not debugging COM-based and .NET code simultaneously, but this will get the job done.

I experimented with trying to get the debuggers to bounce back and forth. Perhaps this is possible or will be made to work in the future. For now it appears as if we will have to debug the pieces separately when using COM Interop. The good news is that ideally you are using only well-tested and debugged COM code and not writing any new COM code. If so, the debugging chore should be relegated to debugging the new .NET code only.

Additional Topics

You may want to explore some additional topics relative to COM Interop, including implementing custom marshaling by using the `ICustomMarshaler` interface, using custom exceptions, and multithreading in COM Interop. Check out *COM and .NET Interoperability* by Andrew Troelsen [2002] and *.NET and COM: The Complete Interoperability Guide* by Adam Nathan [2002]. Combined these provide about 1,500 pages that focus solely on issues related to COM Interop.

Summary

Writers have the mixed blessing of getting to look at (and struggle with) new products pretty early in their life cycles. I have been working with .NET for several years now and am still thrilled at its number of facets.

As you have seen in this chapter, the support for COM Interop is tremendous. What amazes me is that a couple of other authors wrote 700+-page books on COM Interop alone. Clearly the tools are getting better all the time, but the demand for what software must do is growing at an equally impressive pace. This suggests that we are going to need more specialists to understand the intricacies of our complex business.

Chapter 7 showed that you do not have to abandon good-quality COM-based code. You can bring all your COM code into .NET and even take some new .NET code to the old world for use in COM-based clients. If you are creating a new solution, I encourage you to use all .NET code, but .NET doesn't require that you do so.

CHAPTER 8

Remoting

The power of the passions, the force of the will,
the creative energy of the imagination, these make life.

—*The Princess of Tivoli (Disraeli)*
in Paul Smith, Disraeli: A Brief Life

Introduction

One of the splendid miseries of writing computer books is that you have to go out and get some practical experience about the subject. Many times this is possible, but occasionally it is not. Remoting is one of the few areas in this book where my experience is limited to nonproduction code, that is, sample applications. As I am writing this my colleagues and I are deliberating whether or not to use Web Services or .NET Remoting on a current project. Because we will unlikely be able to deploy clients or servers on the other end of the problem, Web Services will probably win. This brings us to the subject at hand. What is .NET Remoting and why should you care?

Remoting is the technology used to get two applications to interchange data. It is in the same category of problem and solution as CORBA and DCOM. Clearly Microsoft thinks that .NET Remoting is a best-of-category solution—otherwise, why would we need something other than DCOM?

To help you understand .NET Remoting in a general sense, I will share a story with you that perhaps will help you understand the concept behind .NET Remoting and its technology. Afterward I will include several examples that deal with the nuts and bolts of remoting.

Understanding .NET Remoting

Around the year my youngest son was born—about 1996—I was working on a big project in Chicago. The problem was to manage information related to tracking labor in North America, which included Canada and Mexico. If you recall, around that time we had whopping speeds of 9,600 baud on dial-up connections. Our applications had to process huge amounts of data through tiny connections over wide areas.

The application was to be implemented in Delphi, C, and DB2. At that time C was used for stored procedures, IBM's Universal database was still called DB2, and there were no ODBC drivers for DB2. We had to write everything: stored procedures in C, client software for Windows, server software, and connections to DB2 servers using a Software Development Kit (SDK) from IBM. In essence we had to figure out how to write a rough supplement for an absent connectivity layer to solve the business problem, and we had to write a distributed application for Windows.

My smart friend Andrew Wozniewicz came up with a nice solution that people had difficulty understanding but that worked in practice. The solution was to define abstract classes (remember that this was pretty early in COM's history, and I don't recall that DCOM was a choice) and then share those abstract classes on client and server. Implementations would exist only on the server. The client would declare variables using the abstract classes, and a factory method would return an actual object to the abstract variable definition. Hence, we implemented thin clients containing only abstract classes and fatter servers containing implementations for those classes. From the server to the database server we used what Andrew referred to as "amorphous blobs of data." These amorphous blobs represented data that we created in a predetermined format to which the server application and server applications on the database server had agreed. This is pretty good multitier architecture considering the state of technology at the time. I am familiar with all of this because I implemented the proof-of-concept vertical slice from Andrew's description.

When we were finished we had a client with abstract classes, a middle-tier business layer with abstract classes, and completely implemented child classes in the middle tier, which sent amorphous blobs of binary data to the database server. On the database server the blobs were unpacked and the DB2 SDK was used to invoke stored procedures.

To Andrew's credit he figured some of this out by gleaning how Delphi's very advanced IDE—at the time—worked with the Visual Control Library (VCL) at design time to get controls from the designer onto a form. As I mentioned in Chapter 3, Anders Hejlsberg was instrumental to implementing Borland's Delphi and Microsoft's .NET. History provides perspective, and it is very likely that some ideas in .NET evolved from Anders' dozen or so years at Borland.

The problem Andrew and I and many others had still exists. How do we get applications to share data on a LAN or WAN? Worse, the problem is exacerbated now because the network includes the highly distributed, heterogeneous Internet. In addition to having to send data between client and server on a LAN and WAN, now programmers are expected to send data between multiple clients and multiple servers, potentially running different operating systems and different language-based implementations, across every kind of network. .NET Remoting is a solution to the problem of implementing highly distributed applications.

Sadly, Andrew's amorphous blobs aren't completely sufficient as a public standard. What Microsoft has done is to allow us to define interfaces or abstract classes on the client and implement classes on the server, and instead of amorphous blobs we get XML and SOAP. As open standards, XML and SOAP can be deciphered by any platform. In addition, Microsoft's .NET Remoting technology takes care of packaging the XML and SOAP blob back and forth—called *marshaling*—for us. For the most part we only have to worry about writing the business solution; .NET takes care of the infrastructure.

Of course, as is true with any subject, if you dig deep enough you can start customizing and extending the provided behavior. However, the ultimate end result is that .NET Remoting was defined to support a highly distributed world of TCP and HTTP networks by building on open standards and hiding the most difficult aspects of managing connections, marshaling data, and reading and writing XML and SOAP. As a result, if you can understand inheritance, declare and implement an interface, and use attributes, you are ready to begin using .NET Remoting.

Marshaling Objects by Reference

Remoting handles data between client and server in two ways: (1) marshaling the data by reference and (2) marshaling the data by value. Marshaling by reference is analogous to having a pointer, and marshaling by value is analogous to having a copy. If we change a reference object, the original is changed, and changes to a copy have no effect on the original. To get your feet wet let's start with a quick marshal-by-reference example. (The Marshaling Objects by Value section later in this chapter talks about the other way data is moved back and forth.)

NOTE: Occasionally I will be accused of writing or saying something conde-
scending. That is never my intent. That said, depending on your level of com-
fort with technical jargon, words like *marshal* may sound ominous. This is an
advanced book, but if you are not comfortable with COM and DCOM, the word
marshal may trouble you. An easier term might be *shepherd*, as in herding
sheep. Because remoting moves data across a network, the data must be
packaged and unpackaged in an agreed-upon format and shepherded between
the application that has the data (the server) and the application that wants
the data (the client).

Several graphics on the Web depict this relationship—marshaling between
client and server—but I am not sure if they aid understanding or add to confusion. Rather than repeat those images, I encourage you to think of the code
that does the shepherding as the responsibility of .NET. These codified shep-
herds are referred to as *proxies*. The Remoting namespace contains the proxy
code.

Hello, Remote World!

Rather than torture you with another Hello, World! application, I will use a
sample application with a little more meat (not much but a bit more).

Suppose you work in the information technology department of a large
insurance company. This company owns several broker dealers that sell
mutual funds. As a result you are tasked with tracking all customer purchases of mutual funds, life and health products, and annuities. You can
cobble together a solution that requires the remote broker dealer offices to
run batch programs at night that upload data and combine the mutual fund
trades with Universal Life payments, mixing and matching the client PC's
database programs with your UDB, SQL Server, or Oracle databases.
When you are finished you have VB6 applications on the client workstations running ObjectRexx dial-up scripts to FTP servers late at night. Or,
you can use remoting and .NET to get everybody working together. Throw
out the Perl, .cmd, .bat, and .ftp scripts; toss the various and sundry import and export utilities written in C, VB6, and Modula; and get everything
working in real time.

Okay. We won't have enough time to tackle all of that in this section, but
we can create a client application that requests a customer and a server application that simulates servicing that request. Because the code would take
up a lot of space, we will simulate the client reading from the database. How-

ever, after you read Chapters 11, 12, and 16 on ADO.NET, you will be able
to incorporate the code to read from the database too. Figure 8.1 shows a
UML model of the design we will be using here. (I used Rational XDE, integrated into .NET, to create the UML class diagram.)

The class diagram accurately depicts the code that resides in the client
and server. An assembly named `Interface` contains the two interfaces: `IF-
actory` and `ITrade`. The assembly named `Server` implements (*realizes* in
the vernacular of the UML) `IFactory` and `ITrade` in `Factory` and `Trade`,
respectively, and the assembly named `Client` is dependent on the two interfaces. Note that there is no dependency on the actual implementations of
`IFactory` and `ITrade` in `Client`. If all the code on the server were on the
client, then arguably the server would not be needed. (This isn't precisely
true but logically makes sense.) Listings 8.1 and 8.2 contain the code for the
`Interface` and `Server` assemblies, in that order.

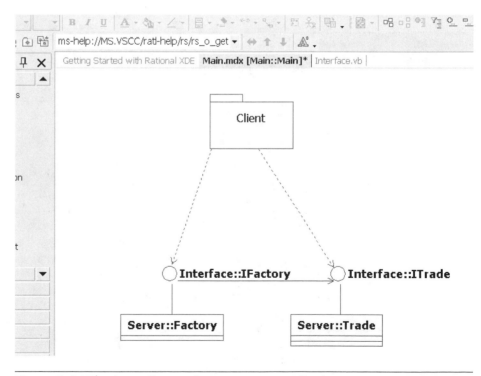

Figure 8.1 The class diagram for our server application.

Listing 8.1 The `Interface.vb` File Containing the `IFactory` and `ITrade` Interfaces

```
Public Interface IFactory

  Function GetTrade(ByVal customerId As Integer) As ITrade

End Interface

Public Interface ITrade

  Property NumberOfShares() As Double
  Property EquityName() As String
  Property EquityPrice() As Double
  ReadOnly Property Cost() As Double
  Property Commission() As Double
  Property RepId() As String

End Interface
```

Listing 8.2 The `ServerCode.vb` File Containing the Implementation of `ITrade` and `IFactory`

```
Imports System
Imports [Interface]
Imports System.Reflection

Public Class Factory
  Inherits MarshalByRefObject
  Implements IFactory

  Public Function GetTrade( _
    ByVal customerId As Integer) As ITrade _
    Implements IFactory.GetTrade
    Console.WriteLine("Factory.GetTrade called")

    Dim trade As Trade = New Trade()
    trade.Commission = 25
    trade.EquityName = "DYN"
    trade.EquityPrice = 2.22
    trade.NumberOfShares = 1000
    trade.RepId = "999"
```

```vbnet
      Return trade
    End Function

End Class

Public Class Trade
    Inherits MarshalByRefObject
    Implements ITrade

    Private FCustomerId As Integer
    Private FNumberOfShares As Double
    Private FEquityName As String
    Private FEquityPrice As Double
    Private FCommission As Double
    Private FRepId As String

    Public Property NumberOfShares() As Double _
      Implements ITrade.NumberOfShares
    Get
      Return FNumberOfShares
    End Get
    Set(ByVal Value As Double)
      FNumberOfShares = Value
    End Set
    End Property

    Public Property EquityName() As String _
      Implements ITrade.EquityName
    Get
      Return FEquityName
    End Get
    Set(ByVal Value As String)
      Console.WriteLine("EquityName was {0}", FEquityName)
      FEquityName = Value
      Console.WriteLine("EquityName is {0}", FEquityName)
      Console.WriteLine([Assembly].GetExecutingAssembly().FullName)

    End Set
    End Property

    Public Property EquityPrice() As Double _
      Implements ITrade.EquityPrice
    Get
      Return FEquityPrice
```

```
End Get
Set(ByVal Value As Double)
  FEquityPrice = Value
End Set
End Property

ReadOnly Property Cost() As Double _
   Implements ITrade.Cost
Get
  Return FEquityPrice * _
    FNumberOfShares + FCommission
End Get
End Property

Property Commission() As Double _
   Implements ITrade.Commission
Get
  Return FCommission
End Get
Set(ByVal Value As Double)
  FCommission = Value
End Set
End Property

Property RepId() As String _
   Implements ITrade.RepId
Get
  Return FRepId
End Get
Set(ByVal Value As String)
  FRepId = Value
End Set
End Property

End Class
```

The code in both listings is pretty straightforward. Listing 8.1 defines the two interfaces **IFactory** and **ITrade**. Listing 8.2 provides an implementation for each of these interfaces.

After scanning the code you might assume that all we need to do is add a reference in the client to each of the two assemblies containing the code in Listings 8.1 and 8.2 and we're finished. And you'd be right if we were building a single application. However, we are building two applications: client and server.

Suppose for a moment that we did add a reference to the `Interface` and `Server` assemblies. .NET would load all three assemblies—client, interface, and server—into the same application domain (`AppDomain`), and the client could create `Trade` and `Factory` objects directly or by using the interfaces. This is a valid model of programming, but it is not distributed. It works because .NET uses `AppDomain` for application isolation. All referenced assemblies run in the same `AppDomain`. However, when we run a client application and a separate server, we have two applications, each running in its own `AppDomain`. .NET Remoting helps us get data across application domains.

In our distributed example, `Client.exe` is an executable with a reference to `Interface.dll`. Both of these assemblies run in the `AppDomain` for `Client.exe`. `Server.exe` also has a reference to `Interface.dll`, and `Server.exe` and `Interface.dll` run in the `AppDomain` for `Server.exe`. The code we have yet to add is the code that creates the object on the client by making a remote request to the server.

Getting Client and Server Talking

Thus far we have written vanilla interface and class code. To get the client and server talking we have to use some code in the `System.Runtime.Remoting` namespace. The first step is to inherit from `MarshalByRefObject`. Listing 8.2 shows that both `Factory` and `Trade` inherit from `MarshalByRefObject`, which enables the classes to talk across application boundaries. The second piece of the puzzle is to tell the server to start listening, permitting the client to start making requests.

Listing 8.3 contains the code that instructs the server to start listening, and Listing 8.4 contains the code to get the client to start making requests. Both client and server are implemented as console applications (`.exe`) for simplicity. You can use .NET Remoting with a variety of hosting styles. (Refer to the Choosing a Host for Your Server subsection near the end of this chapter for more information.)

Listing 8.3 Telling the Server Application to Begin Listening for Requests

```
1:  Imports System.Runtime.Remoting
2:  Imports System.Runtime.Remoting.Channels
3:  Imports System.Runtime.Remoting.Channels.Http
4:
5:  Public Class Main
```

```
6:
7:    Public Shared Sub Main(ByVal args() As String)
8:
9:      Dim channel As HttpChannel = New HttpChannel(9999)
10:      ChannelServices.RegisterChannel(channel)
11:      RemotingConfiguration.RegisterWellKnownServiceType( _
12:        GetType(Factory), "Factory.soap", _
13:        WellKnownObjectMode.Singleton)
14:
15:      RemotingConfiguration.RegisterWellKnownServiceType( _
16:        GetType(Trade), "Trade.soap", _
17:        WellKnownObjectMode.Singleton)
18:
19:      Console.WriteLine("Server is running...")
20:      Console.ReadLine()
21:      Console.WriteLine("Server is shutting down...")
22:    End Sub
23:
24: End Class
```

From the code and the shared `Main` method you can tell that Listing 8.3 comes from a .NET console application. Lines 1 through 3 import namespaces relevant to remoting.

The first thing we need to do is declare a channel. I elected to use the HTTP protocol, and the `HttpChannel` constructor takes a port number. This is the port number on which the server will listen. If you want the server to automatically choose an available port, send 0 to the `HttpChannel` constructor. There are about 65,500 ports. If you want to specify a port number, just avoid obvious ports that are already in use like 80 (Web server), 23 (Telnet), 20 and 21 (FTP), and 25 (mail). Picking a port that is being used by another application will yield undesirable results. After we have elected a channel we need to call the shared method `RegisterChannel` (line 10).

Next we register the server as a well-known service type. (Inside the CLR there is a check to make sure that the service inherits from `MarshalByRefObject`.) We pass the `Type` object of the type to register, the Uniform Resource Identifier (URI) for the service, and the way we want the service instantiated. When you read *URI*, think *URL*. The URI identifies the service; by convention we use the class name and `.soap` or `.rem` for the URI. You can use any convention, but Internet Information Services (IIS) maps the `.soap` and `.rem` extensions to .NET Remoting. This is important when hosting remote servers in IIS. (Refer to the Choosing a Host for Your Server subsection near the end of this chapter.) You can pass the `WellKnownObjectMode.Singleton` or `WellKnownObjectMode.SingleCall` enumerated values to the registration method. `Singleton` is used to ensure that one object is used to service requests, and `SingleCall` will cause a new object to be created to service each request. (`SingleCall` causes a remoted server to respond like a Web application. The server has no knowledge of previous calls.)

The `Factory` type is registered in lines 11 through 13 and the `Trade` type in lines 15 through 17. After the server types are registered we use `Console.ReadLine` to prevent the server from exiting. To quit the server application, set the focus on the console running the server and hit the carriage return; the server will respond until then. Listing 8.4 contains the code that prepares the client to send requests to the server.

Listing 8.4 Preparing the Client Application to Begin Making Requests

```
1:  Private Sub Form1_Load(ByVal sender As System.Object, _
2:      ByVal e As System.EventArgs) Handles MyBase.Load
3:
4:      Dim channel As HttpChannel = New HttpChannel()
5:      ChannelServices.RegisterChannel(channel)
6:
7:      Dim instance As Object = _
8:        Activator.GetObject(GetType(IFactory), _
9:          "http://localhost:9999/Factory.soap")
10:
11:     Dim factory As IFactory = _
12:        CType(instance, IFactory)
13:
14:     Dim trade As ITrade = _
15:        factory.GetTrade(1234)
16:
17: End Sub
```

The client declares, creates, and registers a channel in lines 4 and 5. We don't need the port here when we register the channel; we will indicate the port when we request an instance of the object from the server. Lines 7 through 9 use the shared `Activator.GetObject` class to request an instance of the `Factory` class defined in the server. The URL (line 9) indicates the domain and port of the server and the name we registered the server with. Lines 11 and 12 convert the instance type returned by `Activa-tor` to the interface type we know it to be, and lines 14 and 15 use the `fac-tory` instance to request a `Trade` object.

To see that the value of the `trade` object (line 14) is actually a proxy, place a breakpoint in line 17 and use QuickWatch to examine the value of the `trade` variable (Figure 8.2).

Using Server-Activated Objects

In the example above we created what is known as a *server-activated object* (SAO). When you construct an SAO—for example, with `Activator.Get-Object`—only a proxy of the object is created on the client. The actual object on the server isn't created until you invoke an operation on that type via the proxy. (The proxy is transparent; thus the invocation occurs in the background when you call a method or access a property.) The lifetime of an SAO is controlled by the server, and only default constructors are called.

In a production application it is more than likely that you will want to permit the operator to manage the configuration of the server without having to recompile the server application. This can be handled in an application configuration file. `Example3\Client.sln` defines an application configuration

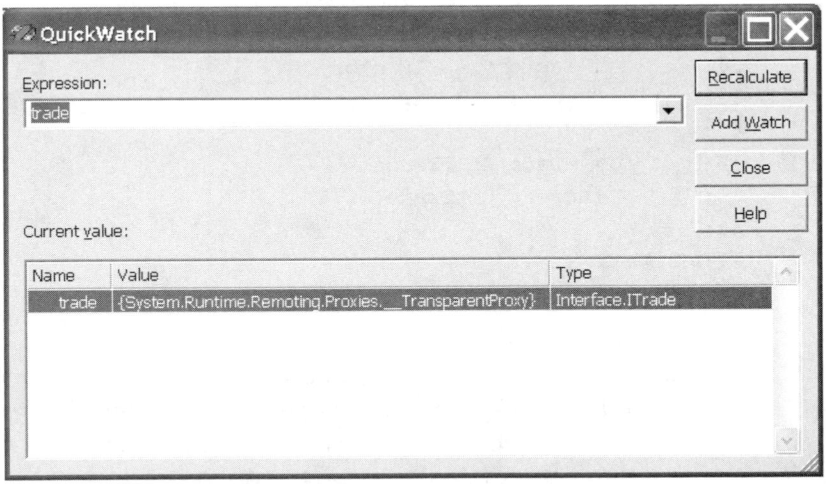

Figure 8.2 The local variable `trade` is an instance of the `TransparentProxy` class, indicating the unusual remoted relationship between client and server.

file for `server.vbproj`. You can add an application configuration file by accessing the File|Add New Item menu in Visual Studio .NET and selecting the Application Configuration File template from the Add New Item dialog. Listing 8.5 contains the externalized XML settings used to register the server. The revision to the `Main` class in Listing 8.3, which accommodates the application configuration file, is provided in Listing 8.6.

Listing 8.5 An Application Configuration That Externalizes Server Registration Settings

```xml
<?xml version="1.0" encoding="utf-8" ?>
<configuration>
  <system.runtime.remoting>
    <application>
      <channels>
        <channel ref="http" port="8080" />
      </channels>
      <service>
        <wellknown mode="Singleton"
          type="Server.Factory, Server"
          objectUri="Factory.soap" />
      </service>
    </application>
  </system.runtime.remoting>
</configuration>
```

The first statement describes the XML version and the text encoding (8-bit Unicode in the example). The `configuration` element indicates this is a configuration file. Typically, XML elements have an opening tag—for example, `<configuration>`—and a matching closing tag with a whack (`/`) inside the tag. Sometimes this is abbreviated to `/>`, as demonstrated with the `wellknown` element in Listing 8.5.

The third element indicates the relevant namespace, `system.runtime.remoting`. The `channel` element indicates the channel type and port. The `wellknown` element indicates the `WellKnownObjectMode` (`Singleton` in the example), the type information for the type we are registering (`Server.Factory`, in Listing 8.6), and the URI (`Factory.soap`). This is precisely the same information we provided in Listing 8.3, programmatically. Now, however, if we find that port 8080 is in use by a proxy server or another HTTP server, we can reconfigure the channel without recompiling.

Having modified the server application to store the server registration information in the `.config` file, we can modify Listing 8.3 to simplify the registration of `WellKnownServiceType`. Listing 8.6 shows the shorter, revised code.

Listing 8.6 Revised Code after Moving Registration Settings to `Server.exe.config`

```
Imports System.Runtime.Remoting
Imports System.Runtime.Remoting.Channels
Imports System.Runtime.Remoting.Channels.Http

Public Class Main

  Public Shared Sub Main(ByVal args() As String)

    RemotingConfiguration.Configure("Server.exe.config")

    Console.WriteLine("Server is running...")
    Console.ReadLine()
    Console.WriteLine("Server is shutting down...")
  End Sub

End Class
```

In the example we have removed the `channel` construction and calls to the shared method `RemotingConfiguration.RegisterWellKnownServiceType` that appeared in Listing 8.3. All we need to do now is pass the name of our `.config` file to the `RemotingConfiguration.Configure` method in Listing 8.6.

Keep in mind that when you add the Application Configuration File template to your project you will see an `App.config` file in the Solution Explorer with the rest of your source. When you compile your application, the `applicationname.exe.config` file is written to the directory containing the executable. While in the debug configuration mode, for example, you will see the `Server.exe.config` file written to the `.\bin` directory.

Using Client-Activated Objects

Client-activated objects (CAOs) are registered and work a bit differently than server-activated objects. A CAO is created on the server as soon as you create an instance of the CAO, which you can do by using `Activator.Cre-ateInstance` or the `New` constructor. The biggest difference between SAOs and CAOs is that CAOs do not use shared interfaces; rather, a copy of the shared code must exist on both the client and the server. Deploying code to client and server will mean more binaries on the clients, a more challenging deployment, and possible versioning problems.

To preclude re-reading all the code, I have reused the same `Factory` and `Trade` classes for our CAO example. However, I have gotten rid of the interfaces, placed the `Factory` class in the client (since we don't really need two server-side classes to demonstrate CAO), and shared the `Trade` class between client and server. Instead of literally sharing the `Trade` class in a third DLL assembly, I defined the `Trade` class in the `Server` assembly and used `soapsuds.exe` (a utility that ships with VS .NET) to generate the shared DLL. We'll go through each of these steps in the remaining parts of this section. (The code for this section can be found in the `Example2\Client.sln` solution.)

Implementing the Server for the CAO Example

The `Server.vbproj` file contains the same `Trade` class shown in Listing 8.3, so I won't relist that code here. The `Factory` class has been moved to the client (see the Implementing the Client subsection below). What's different about the server is how we register it. The revision to the `Main` class is shown in Listing 8.7.

Listing 8.7 Registering a Server for Client Activation

```
1:  Imports System.Runtime.Remoting
2:  Imports System.Runtime.Remoting.Channels
3:  Imports System.Runtime.Remoting.Channels.Http
4:
5:  Public Class Main
6:
7:    Public Shared Sub Main(ByVal args() As String)
8:
9:      Dim channel As HttpChannel = New HttpChannel(9999)
10:     ChannelServices.RegisterChannel(channel)
11:
12:     ' Code needed for client activation
13:     RemotingConfiguration.ApplicationName = "Server"
14:     RemotingConfiguration. _
15:       RegisterActivatedServiceType(GetType(Trade))
```

```
16:
17:     Console.WriteLine("Server is running...")
18:     Console.ReadLine()
19:     Console.WriteLine("Server is shutting down...")
20:   End Sub
21:
22: End Class
```

Registration for client activation is much simpler. We provide a name for the application and register the type we will be remoting. The application name is provided in line 13 and the `Trade` class is registered in lines 14 and 15 using the shared method `RemotingConfiguration.RegisterActivatedServiceType`, passing the type of the class to register. Recall that we actually have the implementation of the type—`Trade`—defined on the server.

That's all we need to do to the server's `Main` class—change the registration code.

Exporting the Server Metadata for the `Trade` Class

To construct an instance of a class in the client using the new operator, we need a class. Calling `New` on an interface—as in `Dim T As ITrade = New ITrade()`—won't work because interfaces don't have code. You can create a third assembly and share that code in both the client and server, or you can use the `soapsuds.exe` utility to generate a C# source code or a DLL that can be referenced in your client application. I implemented a batch file `mysoapsuds.bat` in the `Example2\Server\bin` directory that will create a DLL named `server_metadata.dll`. Here is the single command in that batch file.

```
soapsuds -ia:server -nowp -oa:server_metadata.dll
```

In this code, `soapsuds` is the name of the executable. The –`ia` switch is the name of the input assembly. (Note that the assembly extension—`.exe` for this example—is left off.). The –`nowp` switch causes `soapsuds` to stub out the implementations, permitting a dynamic transparent proxy to handle the method calls. The –`oa` switch indicates the output assembly name. In the example an assembly named `server_metadata.dll` will be generated. Next we will add a reference to this assembly in our client application.

Implementing the Client

The client application needs a definition of the interface and the type for client activation. We can actually share the code between client and server and use parameterized constructors for client activation; or, in our example, we use **soapsuds.exe** to generate a metadata DLL and give up parameterized constructors for remoted objects.

On the user's PC we need some kind of application as well as remoting registration code, and we can use a factory on the client to simulate constructor parameterization (if we are using **soapsuds**-generated metadata.) As a general rule it is preferable to use **soapsuds** to generate metadata and a factory for convenience, as opposed to shipping the server executable to every client. Listing 8.8 shows a Windows Forms implementation of the CAO client and a factory for the **Trade** class.

Listing 8.8 Implementing a Client-Activated Object and a Factory

```
1:  Imports System
2:  Imports System.Runtime.Remoting
3:  Imports System.Runtime.Remoting.Channels
4:  Imports System.Runtime.Remoting.Channels.Http
5:  Imports System.Runtime.Remoting.Activation
6:  Imports System.Reflection
7:  Imports Server
8:
9:  Public Class Form1
10:     Inherits System.Windows.Forms.Form
11:
12: [ Windows Form Designer generated code ]
13:
14:   Private Generator As Generator
15:
16:   Private Sub Form1_Load(ByVal sender As System.Object, _
17:     ByVal e As System.EventArgs) Handles MyBase.Load
18:
19:     Dim channel As HttpChannel = New HttpChannel()
20:     ChannelServices.RegisterChannel(channel)
21:
22:     ' Client-activated object code
23:     RemotingConfiguration.RegisterActivatedClientType( _
24:       GetType(Trade), _
25:       "http://localhost:9999/Server")
26:
```

```
27:        Dim Factory As Factory = New Factory()
28:        Dim Trade As Trade = Factory.GetTrade(5555)
29:        Trade.Commission = 25
30:        Trade.EquityName = "CSCO"
31:        Trade.EquityPrice = 11.0
32:        Trade.NumberOfShares = 2000
33:        Trade.RepId = 999
34:
35:        Generator = New Generator(Me, _
36:          GetType(Trade), Trade)
37:        Generator.AddControls()
38:
39:    End Sub
40:
41: End Class
42:
43: Public Class Factory
44:
45:    Public Function GetTrade( _
46:      ByVal customerId As Integer) As Trade
47:        Console.WriteLine("Factory.GetTrade called")
48:
49:        Dim trade As Trade = New Trade()
50:        trade.CustomerId = 555
51:        trade.Commission = 25
52:        trade.EquityName = "DYN"
53:        trade.EquityPrice = 2.22
54:        trade.NumberOfShares = 1000
55:        trade.RepId = "999"
56:
57:        Return trade
58:    End Function
59:
60: End Class
```

Listing 8.8 contains two classes: the Windows Forms class `Form1` and the `Factory` class. The `Form1` class creates and registers a channel in lines 19 and 20. Instead of using the `Activator` class to create the remote object, we call the shared method `RemotingConfiguration.RegisterActivatedClientType`, passing the type to register and the URI of the server-registered type (lines 23 through 25).

After the type that can be activated on the server is registered, we use the `Factory` class to create an instance of that type (lines 27 and 28). To provide you with additional calls to the server, I changed the values set by the `Factory` class. There is no requirement here, just extra code.

The `Generator` class used on lines 35 through 37 is extra code I added to create a Windows user interface. This code is included with the downloadable remoting example and creates a simple user interface comprised of text boxes and labels, created by reflecting the remote type.

Marshaling Objects by Value

Marshal-by-value objects are not remote objects. By-value objects are marked with the `SerializableAttribute` or implement the `ISerializable` interface. When a serializable object is requested from a remote server, the object is serialized into an XML or binary format and transmitted to the requester. Only data is shipped. Thus, if the serialized object has methods that need to be invoked, the code must exist on the recipient device. This is similar to how Web Services work. A Web Service returns an XML representation of an object that is comprised of data only. If you want to invoke operations on the data, you need the assembly that contains the methods. (This approach is used to return serialized data sets from an XML Web Service.)

In this section I offer another example using the `Factory` and `Trade` classes. The `Factory` class is a `MarshalByRefObject` that returns a by-value object, an instance of the serialized `Trade` class. In this example I need to share the implementation of the `Trade` class between client and server. The server will serialize a representation of the `Trade` class, and the client will deserialize the representation. Implicitly the deserialized data will be mapped to the shared implementation of the `Trade` class. The end result is that we get the data from the server—passing just the data—and reconstitute the actual object on the client.

On top of the basic example, I will provide an example of a customer version of the `Trade` class that implements `ISerializable`.

Employing By-Value Classes

In our revised example the `Factory` class is a marshal-by-reference class. (Recall this means that it inherits from `MarshalByRefObject`.) Further, I have converted the implementation of the `Trade` class to be a marshal-by-value class. Both classes inherit from their respective interfaces: `Trade` implements `ITrade`, and `Factory` implements `IFactory`. `Interface.dll`, containing the interfaces `ITrade` and `IFactory`, is shared by both client and server. On the server we configure and register the `Factory` class as remotable by using a `.config` file (as demonstrated in Listing 8.6) to manage registration of the server-activated class. As a result, only the `Trade` class contains modification. Listing 8.9 shows the complete, revised listing of the `Trade` class as defined on the server. The absence of `MarshalByRefObject` inheritance and the `SerializableAttribute` indicates that the `Trade` class is a by-value object in this listing.

Listing 8.9 Implementing the `Trade` Class as a By-Value Object

```
1:   <Serializable()>_
2:   Public Class Trade
3:
4:      Private FCustomerId As Integer
5:      Private FNumberOfShares As Double
6:      Private FEquityName As String
7:      Private FEquityPrice As Double
8:      Private FCommission As Double
9:      Private FRepId As String
10:
11:     Public Property CustomerId() As Integer
12:     Get
13:        Return FCustomerId
14:     End Get
15:     Set(ByVal Value As Integer)
16:        FCustomerId = Value
17:     End Set
18:     End Property
19:
20:     Public Property NumberOfShares() As Double
21:     Get
22:        Return FNumberOfShares
23:     End Get
24:     Set(ByVal Value As Double)
25:        FNumberOfShares = Value
26:     End Set
27:     End Property
28:
```

```
29:    Public Property EquityName() As String
30:    Get
31:      Return FEquityName
32:    End Get
33:    Set(ByVal Value As String)
34:      Console.WriteLine("EquityName was {0}", FEquityName)
35:      FEquityName = Value
36:      Console.WriteLine("EquityName is {0}", FEquityName)
37:      Console.WriteLine([Assembly].GetExecutingAssembly().FullName)
38:
39:    End Set
40:    End Property
41:
42:    Public Property EquityPrice() As Double
43:    Get
44:      Return FEquityPrice
45:    End Get
46:    Set(ByVal Value As Double)
47:      FEquityPrice = Value
48:    End Set
49:    End Property
50:
51:    ReadOnly Property Cost() As Double
52:    Get
53:      Return FEquityPrice * _
54:        FNumberOfShares + FCommission
55:    End Get
56:    End Property
57:
58:    Property Commission() As Double
59:    Get
60:      Return FCommission
61:    End Get
62:    Set(ByVal Value As Double)
63:      FCommission = Value
64:    End Set
65:    End Property
66:
67:    Property RepId() As String
68:    Get
69:      Return FRepId
70:    End Get
71:    Set(ByVal Value As String)
72:      FRepId = Value
```

```
73:    End Set
74:    End Property
75:
76: End Class
```

After a quick observation you will see that only the first couple of lines have changed and all the interface implementation code has been removed. Line 1 shows the use of the `SerializableAttribute` (defined in the `System` namespace), and I removed the statement `Inherits MarshalByRefObject`. This is all you need to do to indicate that an object can be sent back and forth in a serialized form, such as an XML document.

Additionally, the `IFactory` interface (not shown here, see Listing 8.1) has been modified to return a `Trade` value rather than the `ITrade` interface, and the `ITrade` interface—no longer required—has been removed from the `Interface.vb` source file.

Revising the Client to Use the By-Value Object

The client has to change very little to accommodate the marshal-by-value object. `Factory` is the remote object and it returns the `Trade` type, which we have referenced in both the client and the server. Because we are using a server-activated object—`Factory`—we only need to get an instance of the factory and invoke the `GetTrade` method. .NET automatically serializes the `Trade` object, and our locally declared `Trade` variable can handle the deserialized instance. We do not have to manage serialization on the server or deserialization on the client; this is automatic. Listing 8.10 contains the client code for the marshal-by-value `Trade` object.

Listing 8.10 Client Code for the By-Value `Trade` Object

```
1:    Imports System
2:    Imports System.Runtime.Remoting
3:    Imports System.Runtime.Remoting.Channels
4:    Imports System.Runtime.Remoting.Channels.Http
5:    Imports System.Reflection
6:    Imports [Interface]
7:
8:    Public Class Form1
9:        Inherits System.Windows.Forms.Form
10:
```

```
11: [ Windows Form Designer generated code ]
12:
13:    Private Generator As Generator
14:    Private trade As Trade
15:
16:    Private Sub Form1_Load(ByVal sender As System.Object, _
17:      ByVal e As System.EventArgs) Handles MyBase.Load
18:
19:      Dim channel As HttpChannel = New HttpChannel()
20:      ChannelServices.RegisterChannel(channel)
21:
22:      Dim Instance As Object = _
23:        Activator.GetObject(GetType(IFactory), _
24:        "http://localhost:8080/Factory.soap")
25:
26:      Dim Factory As IFactory = CType(Instance, IFactory)
27:      trade = Factory.GetTrade(1234)
28:
29:      trade.EquityName = "MSFT"
30:      Debug.WriteLine(trade.Cost.ToString())
31:      Generator = New Generator(Me, _
32:        GetType(Trade), trade)
33:      Generator.AddControls()
34:
35:    End Sub
36:
37: End Class
```

Note that in the example the `trade` variable (line 14) is declared as a `Trade` type. We are actually getting a serialized form of the `Trade` object from the server, and the client is automatically deserializing the object returned by the `Factory` method and reconstituting it as a `Trade` object. Because we have an implementation of the `Trade` class shared between client and server, this works nicely.

The balance of the code registers the server-activated `Factory` and uses the `Generator` class I defined to create a user interface. You can download `Example4\Client.sln` to experiment with this code.

Implementing `ISerializable`

The default behavior of the `SerializableAttribute` is to serialize all public properties. In a serialized form they are transmitted as public fields.

However, because we have the binary code on both the client and the server, the deserialized object can be reconstituted as a complete object. Completeness, here, means that we have properties, fields, methods, attributes, and events.

Generally this default behavior is sufficient. However, it may be insufficient if you want to serialize additional data that may not be part of the public properties but is beneficial to the class or intensive to calculate. Whenever you need extra data serialized you can get it by implementing the `System.Runtime.Serialization.ISerializable` interface. The help documentation tells you that you need to implement `GetObjectData`, which is the serialization method. What is implied is that you need the symmetric deserialization behavior. Deserialization is contrived in the form of a constructor that initializes an object based on serialized data.

In order to demonstrate custom serialization in the `Example4\Client.sln` file I added a contrived value to the `Trade` class used for debugging purposes. This contrived field, `DateTime`, holds the date and time when the object was serialized. When a `Trade` object is serialized, I include the current `DateTime` value. When the object is deserialized, the `DateTime` value is written to the Debug window. To affect the custom serialization I needed to change only the shared class we have been using all along. The complete listing of the `Trade` class is shown in Listing 8.11 with the revisions (compared with Listing 8.9) in bold font. (The actual source is contained in `Example4\Interface\Interface.vb`.)

Listing 8.11 Implementing Custom Serialization for .NET Remoting

```
1:  <Serializable()>_
2:  Public Class Trade
3:      Implements ISerializable
4:
5:      Private FCustomerId As Integer
6:      Private FNumberOfShares As Double
7:      Private FEquityName As String
8:      Private FEquityPrice As Double
9:      Private FCommission As Double
10:     Private FRepId As String
11:
12:     Public Sub New()
13:     End Sub
14:
15:     Public Sub New(ByVal info As SerializationInfo, _
```

```
16:      ByVal context As StreamingContext)
17:
18:      Debug.WriteLine("Started deserializing Trade")
19:      FCustomerId = CType(info.GetValue("CustomerId", _
20:        GetType(Integer)), Integer)
21:      FNumberOfShares = CType(info.GetValue("NumberOfShares", _
22:        GetType(Double)), Double)
23:
24:      FEquityName = CType(info.GetValue("EquityName", _
25:        GetType(String)), String)
26:
27:      FEquityPrice = CType(info.GetValue("EquityPrice", _
28:        GetType(Double)), Double)
29:
30:      FCommission = CType(info.GetValue("Commission", _
31:        GetType(Double)), Double)
32:
33:      FRepId = CType(info.GetValue("RepId", _
34:        GetType(String)), String)
35:
36:      Dim SerializedAt As DateTime _
37:        = CType(info.GetValue("SerializedAt", _
38:        GetType(DateTime)), DateTime)
39:
40:      Debug.WriteLine(String.Format( _
41:        "{0} was serialized at {1}", _
42:        Me.GetType.Name(), SerializedAt))
43:
44:      Debug.WriteLine("Finished deserializing Trade")
45:    End Sub
46:
47:    Protected Sub GetObjectData( _
48:      ByVal info As SerializationInfo, _
49:      ByVal context As StreamingContext _
50:      ) Implements ISerializable.GetObjectData
51:
52:      Console.WriteLine("Started serializing Trade")
53:
54:      info.AddValue("CustomerId", FCustomerId)
55:      info.AddValue("NumberOfShares", FNumberOfShares)
56:      info.AddValue("EquityName", FEquityName)
57:      info.AddValue("EquityPrice", FEquityPrice)
58:      info.AddValue("Commission", FCommission)
59:      info.AddValue("RepId", FRepId)
```

```
60:      info.AddValue("SerializedAt", DateTime.Now)
61:
62:      Console.WriteLine("Finished serializing Trade")
63:   End Sub
64:
65:
66:   Public Property CustomerId() As Integer
67:   Get
68:      Return FCustomerId
69:   End Get
70:   Set(ByVal Value As Integer)
71:      FCustomerId = Value
72:   End Set
73:   End Property
74:
75:   Public Property NumberOfShares() As Double
76:   Get
77:      Return FNumberOfShares
78:   End Get
79:   Set(ByVal Value As Double)
80:      FNumberOfShares = Value
81:   End Set
82:   End Property
83:
84:   Public Property EquityName() As String
85:   Get
86:      Return FEquityName
87:   End Get
88:   Set(ByVal Value As String)
89:      Console.WriteLine("EquityName was {0}", FEquityName)
90:      FEquityName = Value
91:      Console.WriteLine("EquityName is {0}", FEquityName)
92:      Console.WriteLine([Assembly].GetExecutingAssembly().FullName)
93:   End Set
94:   End Property
95:
96:   Public Property EquityPrice() As Double
97:   Get
98:      Return FEquityPrice
99:   End Get
100: Set(ByVal Value As Double)
101:    FEquityPrice = Value
102: End Set
103: End Property
```

```
104:
105:  ReadOnly Property Cost() As Double
106:  Get
107:    Return FEquityPrice * _
108:      FNumberOfShares + FCommission
109:  End Get
110:  End Property
111:
112:  Property Commission() As Double
113:  Get
114:    Return FCommission
115:  End Get
116:  Set(ByVal Value As Double)
117:    FCommission = Value
118:  End Set
119:  End Property
120:
121:  Property RepId() As String
122:  Get
123:    Return FRepId
124:  End Get
125:  Set(ByVal Value As String)
126:    FRepId = Value
127:  End Set
128:  End Property
129:
130: End Class
```

TIP: You need to include the `SerializableAttribute` even when you are implementing the `ISerializable` interface. Remember to add an `Imports` statement for `System.Runtime.Serialization`, or use the completely qualified name for the `ISerializable` interface when performing custom serialization.

Serialization and deserialization in Listing 8.11 are constrained to lines 15 through 63. The recurring pattern is a constructor and a method named `Get-ObjectData`. Both the constructor and `GetObjectData` take `Serialiation-tionInfo` and `StreamingContext` arguments. The constructor reads the streamed field values, and the serialization method, `GetObjectData`, writes the fields to be streamed. Since you will be writing both the serializer and deserializer you will know the order and type of the arguments streamed.

To serialize an object, write the fields using the `SerializationInfo` object in the `GetObjectData` method. Call `SerializationInfo.SetValue`, passing a name for the value and the value itself. For example, line 59 passes the literal `"RepId"` and the value of the field `FRepId`. When you deserialize the object in the constructor, use the `SerializationInfo` argument and call `GetValue`. Pass the name used to serialize the object and the type information for that value. It is a good practice to perform an explicit type conversion on the return value since `GetValue` returns an `Object` type. For example, lines 33 and 34 of Listing 8.11 call `GetValue`, passing the literal `"RepId"` and the `Type` object for the `String` class, and perform the cast to `String`.

Line 60 demonstrates how we can serialize an arbitrary value, `SerializedAt`. Lines 36 through 38 demonstrate how we can deserialize that same value, perform the type conversion, and assign the value to a local variable (or a field). In lines 40 through 42 I use the value `SerializedAt` to indicate when the client was serialized. Perhaps such a value could be used as a rough measure of latency. If you compared the `SerializedAt` time with the current time, you would know how long the serialization and deserialization behavior took in a single instance.

Comparing By-Reference to By-Value Objects

There are two ways to pass objects around: by value and by reference. By-reference objects are remoted objects that inherit from `MarshalByRefObject`. This means that they actually exist on the remote server. By-value objects are copied to the client and use the `SerializableAttribute`. It's important to decide when to use either technique.

Pass objects by reference to prevent a large object from clogging network bandwidth. You will also have to pass objects by reference when the object refers to resources that exist in the server domain. For example, `C:\winnt\system32` on the client is a completely different folder than `C:\winnt\system32` on the server.

Consider passing objects by value when the data on the client does not need to be maintained on the server. For example, if we are simply reporting on trade information, we don't necessarily need a reference to a `Trade` object on the server. Using a by-value `Trade` object will reduce round-trips to the server since the code resides on the client.

Think of by-value objects as similar to the data returned by a Web application: It is disconnected. Think of by-reference objects as the connected model of programming.

Writing to the Event Log

Thus far I have been using console applications to simplify the examples. However, you are more likely to use .NET Remoting for WinForms, WebForms, or NT Service applications. For debugging and tracing information for these applications you can use the event log. Chapter 17 gives more information on using the `EventLog` class for logging application events, but I'll mention it here briefly.

The easiest way to log application events is to invoke the shared method `EventLog.WriteEntry`, passing the event source and message to write. The event source is a unique name across all event logs, and the message is whatever text you want to appear in the log entry. By default, information will be written to the Application log. (Refer to Chapter 17 to read about creating custom logs and writing log entries to remote machines.)

Handling Remote Events

Microsoft included an example of using events in .NET Remoting in the help documentation at `ms-help://MS.VSCC/MS.MSDNVS/cpguide/html/cpconremotingexampledelegatesevents.htm`. (You can open this help topic by browsing to the referenced link in Internet Explorer or the URL control of the Web toolbar in the VS .NET IDE.) The example is a simple console-based, chat example that permits clients to communicate through a `Singleton` object. Rather than repeat that code here (and because I thought the example was fun), I include a WinForms-based version that is slightly more advanced and a lot of fun to play with. Here is the basic idea.

Recall that we talked about `Singleton` remoted objects. When we create a `Singleton MarshalByRefObject`, every client will get a transparent proxy—think "super pointer"—to the exact same object on the server. By exposing an event each client can add an event handler to the event. Now mix in delegates. Delegates are multicast in .NET. This means that the event is sent to all handlers. Thus, if one client raises an event, every client that has a handler in that object's invocation list will receive an event message. Combined with a `Singleton` Remote object reference, each client will be adding a handler to one object's multicast delegate invocation list. Voilà! A simplified chat application.

Understanding Remote Event Behavior

We have thought of remoting so far as clients having transparent proxy reference to an object on the server. However, when we need to raise an event on the server, the server is actually calling back to the client; the client handler becomes a server, and the server becomes the client. Consequently the client has a reference to the server, and when the roles are reversed, the server needs a reference to the client. We can solve this predicament by sharing code between client and server.

Invoking Remote Events

The example is comprised of three projects all contained in the \Chapter 8\Events\Chat\Chat.sln file. The solution includes the Chat.vbproj client, ChatServer.vbproj, and the shared class library General. The ChatServer.exe is a console application that has a reference to General.dll and configures ChatServer.ChatMessage as a well-known Singleton object using an application configuration file. The Chat.exe server is a Windows Forms application (see Figure 8.3) that has a reference to General.dll. Each instance of Chat.exe requests a reference to

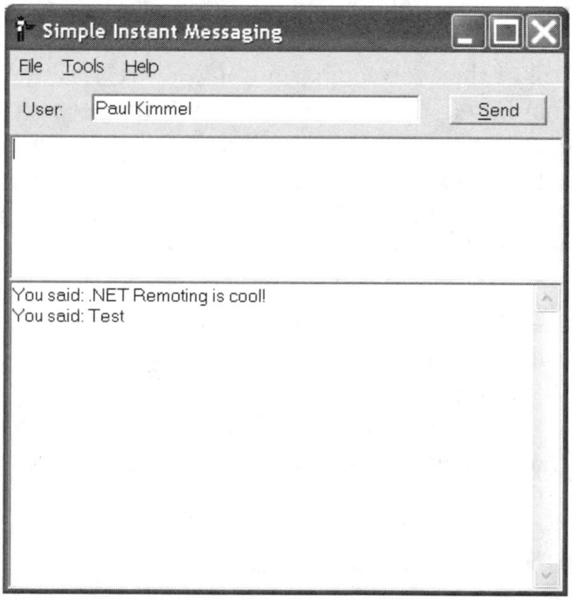

Figure 8.3 The simple instant messaging example.

the `ChatMessage` object created on the remote server. The server returns the same instance to every client that requests a `ChatMessage` object on the same channel from the same server. After the client gets the `ChatMessage` wrapper back, it assigns one of its event handlers to an event defined by the wrapper class. When any particular client sends a message to the server, a `ChatMessage` object raises an event and all clients get the event. As a result we can selectively echo the original message (or not) to the sender and notify each client of a message.

The server class simply uses a configuration file to register a `Singleton` instance of a `ChatMessage` wrapper object. You can see the code for the server in `\Chapter 8\Events\Server\Server.vb`. The shared `General.dll` assembly (which contains the wrapper) and the client that sends and handles events provide the most interesting functionality. We will go over most of that code next.

Implementing the Shared Event Wrapper

The code containing the shared event wrapper class is defined in `\Chapter 8\Events\General\Class1.vb`. `Class1.vb` defines three classes and a delegate. Listing 8.12 contains all the code for `Class1.vb`; a synopsis of the code follows the listing.

Listing 8.12 The Shared Classes That Manage Events between Client and Server

```
1:   Option Strict On
2:   Option Explicit On
3:
4:   Imports System
5:   Imports System.Runtime.Remoting
6:   Imports System.Runtime.Remoting.Channels
7:   Imports System.Runtime.Remoting.Channels.Http
8:   Imports System.Runtime.Remoting.Messaging
9:
10:  Imports System.Collections
11:
12:  <Serializable()>_
13:  Public Class ChatEventArgs
14:    Inherits System.EventArgs
15:
16:    Private FSender As String
17:    Private FMessage As String
18:
```

```
19:    Public Sub New()
20:      MyBase.New()
21:    End Sub
22:
23:    Public Sub New(ByVal sender As String, _
24:      ByVal message As String)
25:      MyClass.New()
26:      FSender = sender
27:      FMessage = message
28:    End Sub
29:
30:    Public ReadOnly Property Sender() As String
31:    Get
32:      Return FSender
33:    End Get
34:    End Property
35:
36:    Public ReadOnly Property Message() As String
37:    Get
38:      Return FMessage
39:    End Get
40:    End Property
41:  End Class
42:
43:  Public Delegate Sub MessageEventHandler(ByVal Sender As Object, _
44:    ByVal e As ChatEventArgs)
45:
46:  Public Class ChatMessage
47:    Inherits MarshalByRefObject
48:
49:    Public Event MessageEvent As MessageEventHandler
50:
51:    Public Overrides Function InitializeLifetimeService() As Object
52:      Return Nothing
53:    End Function
54:
55:    <OneWay()> _
56:    Public Sub Send(ByVal sender As String, _
57:      ByVal message As String)
58:
59:      Console.WriteLine(New String("-"c, 80))
60:      Console.WriteLine("{0} said: {1}", sender, message)
61:      Console.WriteLine(New String("-"c, 80))
62:
```

```
63:       RaiseEvent MessageEvent(Me, _
64:          New ChatEventArgs(sender, message))
65:    End Sub
66:
67:  End Class
68:
69:
70:  Public Class Client
71:     Inherits MarshalByRefObject
72:
73:     Private FChat As ChatMessage = Nothing
74:
75:     Public Overrides Function InitializeLifetimeService() As Object
76:        Return Nothing
77:     End Function
78:
79:     Public Sub New()
80:        RemotingConfiguration.Configure("Chat.exe.config")
81:
82:        FChat = New ChatMessage()
83:
84:        AddHandler FChat.MessageEvent, _
85:           AddressOf Handler
86:     End Sub
87:
88:     Public Event MessageEvent As MessageEventHandler
89:
90:     Public Sub Handler(ByVal sender As Object, _
91:        ByVal e As ChatEventArgs)
92:        RaiseEvent MessageEvent(sender, e)
93:     End Sub
94:
95:     Public Sub Send(ByVal Sender As String, _
96:        ByVal Message As String)
97:        FChat.Send(Sender, Message)
98:     End Sub
99:
100:    Public ReadOnly Property Chat() As ChatMessage
101:    Get
102:       Return FChat
103:    End Get
104:    End Property
105:
106: End Class
```

Lines 12 through 41 define a new type of event argument, `ChatEvent-Args`. `ChatEventArgs` inherits from `System.EventArgs` and introduces two new members: `Message` and `Sender`. `Message` is the content of the message sent by a client, and `Sender` is a user name. `ChatEventArgs` is an example of an object that the client needs for information purposes only; hence it was designated as a by-value object.

Lines 43 and 44 define a new delegate named `MessageEventHandler`. Its signature accepts the new event argument `ChatEventArgs`.

Lines 46 through 67 define the by-reference object `ChatMessage` that is the `Singleton` object shared by all clients. Every client on the same channel and originating from the same server will be referring to the same instance of this class. The class itself is easy enough, but it demonstrates some old concepts and introduces some new ones. Line 47 indicates that `ChatMessage` is a by-reference type. Line 49 exposes a public event; this is how all clients attach their event handlers to the `ChatMessage Singleton`. Lines 51 through 53 override the `MarshalByRefObject.InitializeLifetimeService` method. `InitializeLifetimeService` can be overridden to change the lifetime of a Remote object. `Return Nothing` sets the lifetime to infinity. (Refer to the Managing a Remoted Object's Lifetime subsection later in this chapter for more information.) Lines 55 through 65 define the `Send` message. Clients use `Send` to broadcast messages. All `Send` does is raise `Message-Event`. Note that `Send` is adorned with the `OneWayAttribute`, which causes the server to treat `Send` as a "fire and forget" method. `Send` doesn't care whether the recipients receive the message or not. This handles the case of a client dropping off without disconnecting its handler. (`Send` also displays trace information on the server application; see Figure 8.4.) That's all the `ChatMessage` class is: a class shared between client and server that wraps the message invocation.

Finally, we come to the `Client` class in lines 70 through 106. The `Client` class plays the role of the executable code that is remotable and shared between client and server. If you examine it closely you will see that it mirrors the `ChatMessage` class except that `Client` is responsible for allowing the server to call back into the client application. The `Client` class in `General.dll` plays the role of client-application-on-the-server when the roles between client and server are reversed. If we didn't have a remotable class shared between client and server, we would need to copy the client application into the directory of the server application. Remember that for clients to run code defined on a server, we need an interface or shared code in order to have something to assign the shared object to. When the roles between client and server are reversed—client becomes server during the callback—the server would need an interface or shared code to the client to

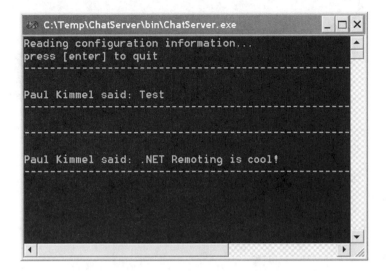

Figure 8.4 Trace information being written to the server console.

talk back to it. Thus for the same reason that we share code between client and server, we also share code between server and client.

TIP: For a comprehensive discussion of event sinks and .NET Remoting, Ingo Rammer [2002] has written a whole book, *Advanced .NET Remoting.*

Listing 8.13 contains the `Chat.exe.config` file that describes the configuration information to the well-known object registered on the server and the back channel to the client used when the client calls the server back.

Listing 8.13 The Configuration File for the Client Application

```
1:  <?xml version="1.0" encoding="utf-8" ?>
2:  <configuration>
3:    <system.runtime.remoting>
4:      <application>
5:        <channels>
6:          <channel
7:            ref="http"
8:            port="0"
```

```
 9:              />
10:          </channels>
11:          <client>
12:            <wellknown
13:               type="ChatServer.ChatMessage, General"
14:               url="http://localhost:6007/ChatMessage.soap"
15:            />
16:          </client>
17:        </application>
18:    </system.runtime.remoting>
19:
20:    <appSettings>
21:        <add key="user" value="Your Name Here!" />
22:        <add key="echo" value="true" />
23:    </appSettings>
24: </configuration>
```

The `<channels>` element describes the back channel used by server to client. By initializing the `port` attribute with `0` we allow the port to be dynamically selected. The `<client>` element registers the reference to the well-known `ChatMessage` class on the client. This allows us to create an instance of the `ChatMessage` class on the client using the `New` operator, getting a transparent proxy instance rather than the literal `ChatMessage` class also defined in the client. Without the `<client>` element we would need to use the Activator or we'd end up with a local instance of `ChatMessage` rather than the remote instance.

Finally, the `<appSettings>` element is used by the `ConfigurationSettings.AppSettings` shared property to externalize general, nonremoting configuration information.

Implementing the Client Application

The client application creates an instance of the `Client` class. `Client` represents the assembly shared by both client and server, allowing server to talk back to client. The client application (shown in Figure 8.3) actually registers its events with the `Client` class. Listing 8.14 provides the relevant code for the client application that responds to events raised by the remote `ChatMessage` object. (The `Client.vb` source contains about 400 lines of Windows Forms code not specifically related to remoting. Listing 8.14 contains only that code related to interaction with the remote object. For the complete listing, download `\Chapter 8\Events\Client\Client.vb`.)

Listing 8.14 An Excerpt from the Client Application Related to Remoting

```
1:  Option Strict On
2:  Option Explicit On
3:
4:  Imports System
5:  Imports System.Runtime.Remoting
6:  Imports System.Runtime.Remoting.Channels
7:  Imports System.Runtime.Remoting.Channels.Http
8:  Imports Microsoft.VisualBasic
9:  Imports System.Configuration
10:
11: Public Class Form1
12:     Inherits System.Windows.Forms.Form
13:     . . .
284:
285:    Public Sub Handler(ByVal sender As Object, _
286:      ByVal e As ChatEventArgs)
287:
288:      If (e.Sender <> User) Then
289:        Received = GetSenderMessage(e.Sender, e.Message) + Received
290:      ElseIf (Echo) Then
291:        Received = GetSendeeMessage(e.Message) + Received
292:      End If
293:
294:    End Sub
295:
296:    Private ChatClient As Client
297:
298:    Private Sub Form1_Load(ByVal sender As Object, _
299:      ByVal e As System.EventArgs) Handles MyBase.Load
300:
301:      Init()
302:
303:      ChatClient = New Client()
304:
305:      AddHandler ChatClient.MessageEvent, _
306:        AddressOf Handler
307:    End Sub
308:
309:    Private Sub Send()
310:      If (ChatClient Is Nothing = False) Then
311:        ChatClient.Send(User, Sent)
312:        Sent = ""
```

```
313:       End If
314:    End Sub
315:
316:    Private Sub Button1_Click(ByVal sender As System.Object, _
317:       ByVal e As System.EventArgs) Handles ButtonSend.Click, _
318:       MenuItemSend.Click
319:
320:       Send()
321:
322:    End Sub
323:
324:    Private Sub Form1_Closed(ByVal sender As Object, _
325:       ByVal e As System.EventArgs) Handles MyBase.Closed
326:
327:       If (ChatClient Is Nothing) Then Return
328:       RemoveHandler ChatClient.MessageEvent, _
329:          AddressOf Handler
330:    End Sub
331:    . . .
344:
345:    Private Sub Init()
346:       User = ConfigurationSettings.AppSettings("user")
347:       Echo = (ConfigurationSettings.AppSettings("echo") = "true")
348:    End Sub
349:    . . .
396: End Class
```

Listing 8.14 contains snippets from `Client.vb`. Parts that are basic to Windows Forms or programming in general were removed to shorten the listing. Lines 285 through 294 define an event handler named `Handler`. As you can see from the listing, this handler looks like any other event handler. Note that there are no special considerations made for remoting (although there should be; more on this in a moment).

Line 296 declares the shared instance of the `Client` object. `Client` is the remotable object that the server treats like a server when it needs to communicate back with us.

Lines 298 through 307 define the form's `Load` event handler. `Load` initializes the application settings (line 301), creates a new instance of the `Client` class, and associates the form's event handler with the `Client` class's event handler. `Client` is the actual object called back by `ChatMessage`.

`Button1_Click` in lines 316 through 322 calls a local `Send` method that invokes `Client.Send`. `Form1_Closed` (lines 324 through 330) removes the event handler. If for some reason this code isn't called, the server will try to call this instance of the client application for as long as the server is running. If we hadn't used the `OneWayAttribute`, removing the client application without removing the event would cause exceptions. Using the `OneWayAttribute` avoids the exceptions but could potentially send out tons of calls to dead clients. (An alternative is to skip using the `OneWayAttribute` on the server and remove delegates that cause an exception on the server.) The `Init` method (lines 345 through 348) demonstrates how to read configuration settings from an application `.config` file.

Remoting and Threads

.NET Remoting is easier than DCOM and other technologies, but writing distributed applications is still not a trivial exercise. Recall that reference to something missing from the event handler in Listing 8.14 in lines 285 through 294? What's missing is a discussion of threads.

When the event handler is called, it actually comes back on a different thread than the one that Windows Forms controls are in. Recall that in Chapter 6, Multithreading, I said that Windows Forms is not thread-safe. This means that it is not safe to interact with Windows Forms controls across threads. To resolve this predicament we need to perform a synchronous invocation to marshal the call to the event handler—a thread used by remoting—to the same thread the Windows Forms controls are on. In short, we need to add a delegate and call `Form.Invoke` to move the data out of the event handler onto the same thread that the form and its controls are on.

Other Remoting Subjects

Writing distributed applications well is one of those things that rests at the upper echelon of advanced topics. This chapter will get you started. However, if you are going to deploy a distributed application that employs remoting, you should explore in detail such other subjects as management of a remoted object's lifetime, asynchronous behavior and remoting, security issues related to remoting, and implementation of Remote behavior for a variety of host applications. This material will ultimately reside in several books. Ingo Rammer [2002] wrote one of the more comprehensive books currently available on remoting. I have included below a quick overview of these subjects to help guide further exploration.

Managing a Remoted Object's Lifetime

DCOM managed object lifetime by pinging the client to see if the client was still hanging out. This causes a lot of extra network traffic. .NET Remoting uses an approach similar to Java by supplying an object a lease. The basic idea is that an object has a default amount of five minutes of time to live (TTL). After five minutes the object is destroyed. If a remote object is accessed, the TTL is reset to the lease time (in the case of the default setting, five minutes). As long as the object is accessed within the TTL, it stays alive.

You can adjust the lifetime by adding a `<lifetime>` element to the `.config` file or implementing a sponsor. The sponsor answers the question, "My lease time is up; should I go away?" Whereas the lifetime is a static value, the sponsor can be dynamic, based on some programmatic logic. You implement a sponsor as a remotable object by implementing the `System.Runtime.Remoting.Lifetime.ISponsor` interface, by programmatically returning an `ILease` object from an overridden `InitializeLifetimeService` method, or by codifying the lifetime in a `.config` file. Listing 8.15 offers an example lease.

Listing 8.15 Changing the Default Lifetime by Using the Configuration File

```
<lifetime
  leaseTime="2M"
  sponsorshipTimeout="2M"
  renewOnCallTime="2M"
  leaseManagerPollTime="5S"
/>
```

This example sets the lease time, sponsor time-out, and renew time to two minutes. The polling interval is set to five seconds. (The units of measure are D for days, H for hours, M for minutes, S for seconds, and MS for milliseconds.) You cannot combine intervals. For example, you cannot define a lease time of `"2M5S"`.

In Listing 8.15, `leaseTime` represents the object's lease on life; `sponsorshipTimeout` represents the time-out period of a sponsor; and `renewOnCallTime` represents the extended amount of lease time on an object (this value is not accumulative). Finally, `leaseManagerPollTime` specifies how long the lease manager waits between polling intervals.

Asynchronous Remoting

.NET Remoting supports both synchronous and asynchronous method invocation. Use the `BeginInvoke` and `EndInvoke` methods combined with delegates to invoke remote operations asynchronously. Read Chapter 6 for more information on asynchronous processing.

Remoting Security Issues

You can employ authentication and encryption with .NET Remoting and use secure HTTP (HTTPS) to make distributed applications more secure. For secure HTTP you need a certificate. You can acquire a certificate from VeriSign (*http://www.netsol.com*) for free. For more information on remoting and security, read information on HTTPS, certificates, encryption, and authentication.

Choosing a Host for Your Server

The examples in this chapter host all the server applications as console applications, but you are not limited to console applications. You can also use .NET Remoting in Windows Forms, Web (hosting the remote server in IIS), and Service (Windows NT Service) applications. To create a remote server using any of these host types, use the project template to create the project for the particular type. Each style of host will have individuated requirements.

Summary

.NET Remoting is probably one of the most advanced subjects. In addition to replacing DCOM and being relevant to distributed application development (which you may not do every day) remoting involves threading, `Singletons`, security, networking, Reflection, `AppDomains`, the differences between marshaling by reference and by value, SOAP, XML, serialization, interfaces, and more.

Chapter 8 introduced .NET Remoting fundamentals. We discussed the difference between marshaling objects by value and by reference, server-activated objects and client-activated objects, `Singleton` and `SingleCall` remote objects, configuration files, custom serialization, and how to raise events from remote objects. These are the key elements of all .NET Remoting and will aid you in experimenting with distributed applications and further exploration.

CHAPTER 9

Building Custom Components

What would you attempt to accomplish if you knew you would not fail?

—A quote on a classroom wall in
Gilkey International Middle School in Portland, Oregon

Introduction

"What would you attempt to accomplish if you knew you would not fail?"

I liked that quote and thought it was fitting for this chapter. I wonder if Brian Walker, the "Rocket Guy" from Bend, Oregon, attended Gilkey International Middle School? Walker is building a rocket that he plans to launch into space; perhaps by the time you are reading this he will have succeeded.

While creating custom components is not nearly as challenging as launching a homemade rocket into space, the concept of "the sky is the limit" is an excellent metaphor for building custom components. You can create whatever components you want or need—you are limited only by your imagination. Microsoft's Visual Studio .NET offers tremendous support for building custom controls and components for Windows and the Web.

In this chapter you will learn just about everything you need to know about building components, including the basics of component building as well as how to professionally package and integrate those components into Visual Studio .NET for consumption by other programmers. The only thing I left out was your imagination—you have to supply that. I hope that while reading this chapter you are inspired by the words the Gilkey kids see every day.

Implementing a Custom Component

Creating custom components in Visual Basic 6 was too complicated. The single greatest deterrent to building great components in VB6 was that VB6 did not support inheritance. As a result you could not inherit from a VB6 `TextBox` control and extend it to do something new. Fortunately, Visual Basic .NET *does* support true inheritance, and this is all you need to create great components.

The distinction generally made between a component and a control—even though the terms are often used interchangeably—is that controls have a visual aspect at runtime and components do not. Examples of components include the `Timer`, `FileSystemWatcher`, and `EventLog` components. Examples of controls include the `TextBox`, `Label`, and `Button` controls. The visual aspect of a control is governed by a Windows handle. The Windows handle is used to send messages like `WM_PAINT` to a control. In this section I am referring specifically to a custom class that is a nonvisual component.

There are two general approaches you can take when building custom controls. The first approach is to inherit from the `System.Component-Model.Component` class and build your component from scratch. The second approach is to find a close existing component and inherit from that close match, extending it to incorporate the new behavior. For our first custom component we will begin with the second, easier, approach.

NOTE: On a project recently, a newer Windows programmer discovered the `EventLog` component. Rather than reinvent the wheel, the programmer began using `EventLog` for `Debug` and `Trace` messages. (The `EventLog` component can be registered as a `TraceListener`, which means it will receive `Trace` and `Debug` messages.) The problem was that every `Debug` and `Trace` message was going to the Application log by default, resulting in the Application log repeatedly filling up and throwing up—a euphemism for an exception.

Using `EventLog` for this purpose is intended. However, if you try it, send `Debug` and `Trace` messages to a custom log and be circumspect about the information you send to the Application log.

A good strategy for logging debug events while you are building and unit testing your application is to use a custom event log. The existing `EventLog` component supports doing this with some additional configuration steps. Suppose you want to ensure that everyone is using the same log file. You could generalize the existing `EventLog` class and add this custom class to your project, ensuring that everyone is sending debug information to a custom log rather than filling up the Application log. Listing 9.1 defines a custom `EventLog` component that inherits from `EventLog` and ensures that this instance writes to a custom log.

Listing 9.1 Implementing a Custom `EventLog` Component

```
 1:  Imports System.Reflection
 2:
 3:  Public Class DebugEventLog
 4:     Inherits System.Diagnostics.EventLog
 5:
 6:     Private Const LogName As String = "Debug"
 7:
 8:     Public Sub New()
 9:       MyBase.New()
10:       Log = LogName
11:       CheckSource()
12:     End Sub
13:
14:     Private ReadOnly Property SourceName() As String
15:     Get
16:       Return [Assembly].GetExecutingAssembly().FullName
17:     End Get
18:     End Property
19:
20:     Private Sub CheckSource()
21:
22:       ' Source does not exist anywhere
23:       If (Not SourceExists(SourceName)) Then
24:         CreateEventSource(SourceName, LogName)
25:         Source = SourceName
26:       Else
27:         ' Source exists in the right log
28:         If (LogNameFromSourceName(SourceName, _
29:           MachineName) = LogName) Then
30:           Source = SourceName
31:         Else
32:           MessageBox.Show(Message, "Event Log", _
33:             MessageBoxButtons.OK, MessageBoxIcon.Information)
34:         End If
35:       End If
36:
```

```
37:    End Sub
38:
39:    Private ReadOnly Property Message() As String
40:    Get
41:      Dim Mask As String = _
42:        "Source {0} already exists in log {1}." + _
43:        Environment.NewLine + _
44:        "Provide an alternate source name."
45:
46:      Return String.Format(Mask, SourceName, _
47:        LogNameFromSourceName(SourceName, MachineName))
48:    End Get
49:    End Property
50:
51: End Class
```

The basic behavior of an Event Log is that log names must be unique on a machine and an event source must be unique across all logs. Hence you may have only one event source with a particular name irregardless of the log that source is associated with. If you are creating `EventLog` components programmatically and assigning source names, you will need code to ensure the source name is unique. In Listing 9.1, lines 14 through 18 return the assembly name of the assembly containing a particular instance of `De-bugEventLog`. In addition to this name being irregular and unique to an assembly, the `CheckSource` method in lines 20 through 37 verify that the source name is unique on a particular machine and that our custom `Debug` log contains that source name.

When you want to ensure that debug code is written to a custom log, you can share a component like `DebugEventLog` with developers on your team.

The key lesson here is that components do not have to be complex or incorporate large changes to be useful. As a general principle, small, incremental changes are preferable to huge, monolithic changes. The benefit with `DebugEventLog` is that everyone's code behaves in a consistent way without each programmer needing to implement a copy of the code. Creating components for consistency and convergence is an excellent job for a person designated as a toolsmith.

For now you can test the `DebugEventLog` control by declaring an instance of it and invoking the `WriteEntry` method (Listing 9.2). You can find the code for Listings 9.1 and 9.2 in the sample solution file `Debug-EventLog.sln`.

Listing 9.2 Creating and Using the DebugEventLog Control

```
1:  Public Class Form1
2:      Inherits System.Windows.Forms.Form
3:
4:  [ Windows Form Designer generated code ]
5:
6:    Private Log As DebugEventLog
7:
8:    Private Sub Form1_Load(ByVal sender As System.Object, _
9:      ByVal e As System.EventArgs) Handles MyBase.Load
10:
11:     Log = New DebugEventLog()
12:
13:   End Sub
14:
15:   Private Sub Button1_Click(ByVal sender As System.Object, _
16:     ByVal e As System.EventArgs) Handles Button1.Click
17:     Log.WriteEntry(DateTime.Now.ToString())
18:   End Sub
19: End Class
```

You are not required to register components with the Toolbox or even involve the Toolbox when using components. After all, components are just classes, and you can do everything programmatically. The Toolbox is a convenience mechanism. We will look at how you can place components and controls in the Toolbox in the upcoming section Adding a Control to the Toolbox.

Implementing a Custom Windows Control

As mentioned earlier, components do not have a visual aspect at runtime; controls do. You can create a custom control by defining a new control that inherits from System.Windows.Forms.Control or an existing control, like the TextBox control. If you want to create a brand new control, inherit from the Control class. Intuitively it will be easier to create a control if you inherit from one that already has much of the functionality you need.

Defining a Regular Expression `TextBox` Control

You may use a `Validating` event to write code to validate the value of a `TextBox` control. Using an event handler is convenient for general purpose validation; however, if you find yourself using a specific kind of validation repeatedly, you can save time by incorporating that validation into a custom `TextBox` control.

Regular expressions represent a powerful means of performing pattern matching of a complex nature. The `RegexTextBox` control incorporates the power of regular expressions with `TextBox` validation.

Listing 9.3 defines a custom `TextBox` control that has a `Pattern` property. The `Pattern` property represents a regular expression. Assigning a regular expression string to `RegexTextBox` will validate the input against the regular expression. This control is a great building block for specifically typed `TextBox` controls. (The source code for `RegexTextBox` is contained in `RegexTextBox.sln`.)

By convention in .NET, methods raise events, and those methods have an `On` prefix. For example, a `Validating` event is raised by an `OnValidating` method. Thus, if you generalize a control with the `Validating` event and you want to extend the validation behavior, you will override the `OnValidating` event. Listing 9.3 demonstrates how to add a new property to a custom control and override a behavioral method.

Listing 9.3 Implementing the `RegexTextBox` Control

```
1:   Imports System.ComponentModel
2:   Imports System.Text.RegularExpressions
3:
4:   Public Class RegexTextBox
5:      Inherits TextBox
6:
7:      Private FPattern As String
8:
9:      Public Property Pattern() As String
10:     Get
11:        Return FPattern
12:     End Get
13:     Set(ByVal Value As String)
14:        FPattern = Value
15:     End Set
16:     End Property
17:
```

```
18:    Protected Overrides Sub OnValidating( _
19:      ByVal e As CancelEventArgs)
20:      If (Regex.IsMatch(Text, FPattern) Or _
21:        FPattern = String.Empty) Then
22:        e.Cancel = False
23:        MyBase.OnValidating(e)
24:      Else
25:        DoValidatingError(e)
26:      End If
27:    End Sub
28:
29:    Private Sub DoValidatingError(ByVal e As CancelEventArgs)
30:      Const Message As String = _
31:        "Text does not match pattern expression {0}"
32:
33:      If (MessageBox.Show(String.Format(Message, FPattern), _
34:        "Properties Window", MessageBoxButtons.OKCancel, _
35:        MessageBoxIcon.Exclamation) = DialogResult.OK) Then
36:        e.Cancel = False
37:        MyBase.OnValidating(e)
38:      Else
39:        e.Cancel = True
40:        MyBase.ResetText()
41:      End If
42:
43:    End Sub
44:
45: End Class
```

The private field `FPattern` holds the regular expression, and the public property `Pattern` is used to get and set the value of the underlying field. The `OnValidating` method overrides the inherited `OnValidating` method (see lines 18 through 27). Recall that we are overriding the behavior of a method that raises an event. To make sure that the original behavior happens we need to invoke the inherited method. I elected to invoke the inherited method only on the condition that my custom validation occurs. As a general rule, always invoke the base behavior. However, you can reserve the right to break from conventional wisdom as long as you are aware of possible adverse consequences (see Note below).

Finally, lines 29 through 43 enact some simple gyrations to let the `RegexTextBox` user decide whether to continue with an invalid value in the

`TextBox` control if the input value does not match the regular expression pattern.

NOTE: As a rule, programmers using a class should concern themselves not with how a class is implemented but with how a class works. After all, this is the reason we have access modifiers like `Public`, `Private`, and `Protected`. Users should worry about only public details. Alternatively, generalizers—that is, people who inherit from and extend existing classes—must concern themselves with the implementation details of public and protected members. Thus, Microsoft should release the source code to the base class libraries (BCLs), including the source code for ADO.NET and controls like `TextBox`. Releasing Rotor is a good first step, but Microsoft should follow Borland's lead and provide us with the source code for controls too. Clearly Borland suffered no deleterious effects for releasing its Visual Control Library (VCL); in fact, Borland reaped the benefit of a cottage industry of component builders. Borland's problems have never been related to its technology.

Having said all that, it is possible that conditionally calling the inherited `OnValidating` method may result in adverse side effects. Without the source code to `TextBox` it may be impossible to know for sure. If you experience problems with the conditional behavior of `RegexTextBox`, let me know at *pkimmel@softconcepts.com*.

Testing the Custom Component

Testing custom controls before inserting them into the Toolbox is as easy as declaring and creating an instance of the control. Listing 9.4 demonstrates how we might test the `RegexTextBox` control before incorporation into the Toolbox and general dissemination. Because the `TextBox` control has a Windows handle—`hWnd`—and needs to receive messages like `WM_PAINT`, it is essential that we add the programmatically created `RegexTextBox` to the form's `Controls` collection.

Listing 9.4 Declaring and Creating an Instance of `RegexTextBox` for Testing

```
1:  Public Class Form1
2:      Inherits System.Windows.Forms.Form
3:
4:  [ Windows Form Designer generated code ]
5:
6:    Private RegexTextBox1 As RegexTextBox
7:
```

```
8:    Private Sub Form1_Load(ByVal sender As System.Object, _
9:      ByVal e As System.EventArgs) Handles MyBase.Load
10:
11:      RegexTextBox1 = New RegexTextBox()
12:      RegexTextBox1.Pattern = "^\d+$"
13:      Controls.Add(RegexTextBox1)
14:
15:    End Sub
16: End Class
```

Line 13 demonstrates the step of adding the `RegexTextBox1` instance to the form's `Controls` collection. Line 12 shows a regular expression that matches a string containing one or more digits. The caret (`^`) and dollar sign (`$`) indicate expression boundaries. The result is that the text must be a contiguous string of digits with no preceding white space. If the string does not match, a message box appears to alert the user (Figure 9.1).

Regular expressions represent an entire language themselves. The regular expression language in .NET is designed to be compatible with Perl 5. *Regular Expressions with .NET* by Dan Appleman [2002] is an excellent 75 page e-book on .NET regular expressions.

Adding a Control to the Toolbox

If you define your control in a separate class library project, you can use the Tools|Customize Toolbox menu item to add the controls in that class library to the Toolbox. (You can also create a merge module project that will automate the process for you and ease sharing your control among other developers. We'll look at the manual process for now.)

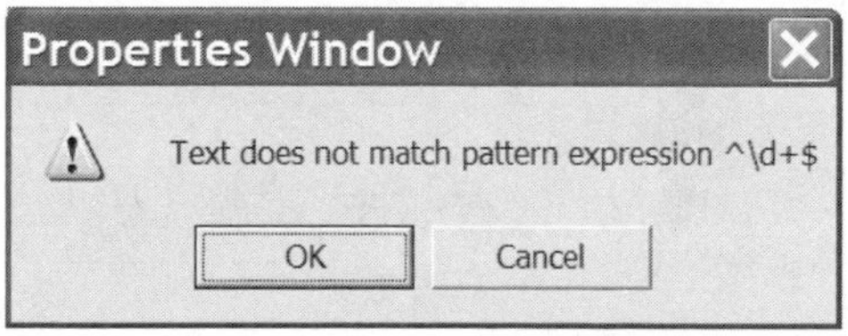

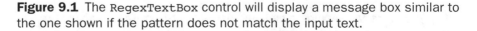

Figure 9.1 The `RegexTextBox` control will display a message box similar to the one shown if the pattern does not match the input text.

Continuing with our `RegexTextBox` control, we have tested the control and found it to work to our satisfaction. We can add a class library project (select File|Add Project|New Project) from the Add New Project dialog. Let's name the class library project `CustomControls` as shown in Figure 9.2. To complete the process of building the class library, we delete the basic `class1.vb` file added by the template; drag and drop the `RegexText-Box.vb` source file from the Windows Forms demo program to the `Cus-tomControls.vbproj` file (using the Solution Explorer); and build the class library project. When following along with this example, you may need to make some adjustments to the class library project and control source code. For example, I needed to add the `System.Windows.Forms.dll` assembly to the `CustomControls.vbproj` references list and the complete namespace `System.Windows.Forms` to the `Inherits` statement in the `RegexTextBox` source code file (see Listing 9.3).

To add the `RegexTextBox` control to the Toolbox, add a tab named My Controls by selecting Add Tab from the Toolbox's context menu. With the My Controls tab selected, select Customize Toolbox from the context menu, pick the .NET Framework Components tab of the Customize Toolbox menu, and click the Browse button. Browse to the `CustomControls.dll` assembly and

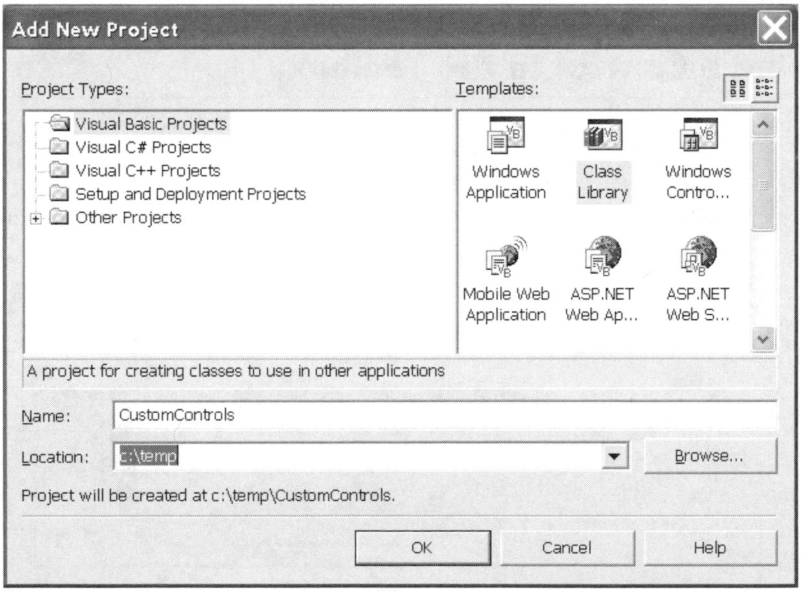

Figure 9.2 Adding a class library project from the Add New Project dialog.

click Open. You will see the name `RegexTextBox` appear in the name column of the Customize Toolbox dialog. Click OK to complete the operation. The new custom control is shown in the Toolbox in Figure 9.3.

You can now drag and drop the control from the Toolbox onto a form as you would any other control. The Form Designer will add a reference to the `CustomControls.dll` assembly and add the control to the form. You can test the control again to make sure it is working correctly with no undesirable side effects. For example, you can add a regular expression to the `Pattern` property (shown in Figure 9.4) and make sure the pattern validation works as planned.

Associating a Bitmap with Your Control

Borland's VCL source code and the high quality of that framework helped to enhance a cottage industry of component makers. Perhaps one of the best-known component creators is Ray Knopka. Ray implemented Raize Tools and perhaps helped set an expected standard for components in the industry. In addition to the components solving the purported problem, Ray created clever design tools, and the components integrated in such a way as to appear to belong to the VCL. Visual Studio .NET offers tremendous support for third parties to build integrated, professional, custom components and controls. An expected level of support is the ability to use a custom bitmap with your control. I describe here this first taste of custom control fit and finish.

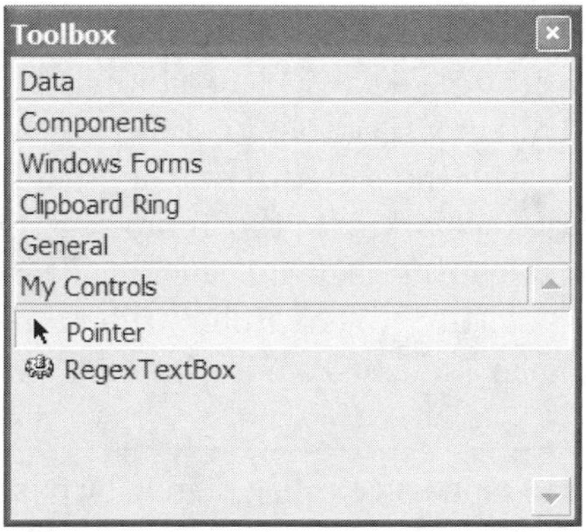

Figure 9.3 The `RegexTextBox` control shown on the My Controls tab of the Toolbox.

Figure 9.4 The `RegexTextBox` `Pattern` property shown in the Properties window.

NOTE: I use *component* and *control* interchangeably in this section. After all, in the .NET Framework all controls do inherit from `Component` at some level, and in that regard a control is a component.

It makes sense to think of a component's bitmap as extra information or metadata. For this reason you use attributes—specifically, the `Toolbox-BitmapAttribute`—to associate a bitmap with a custom component. If you apply the `ToolboxBitmapAttribute` to the component class, initializing the attribute with the path to a bitmap, that bitmap will be displayed in conjunction with the control in the Toolbox. A nice feature of .NET (if you are artistically inclined) is that you can actually draw the bitmap in the IDE and make it part of your project. Follow the numbered steps on the next page to create a bitmap and associate it with your custom control.

TIP: You can reuse an existing bitmap by passing the `Type` of the component that has the bitmap you want to reuse. For example, pass `GetType(System.Windows.Forms.TextBox)` to the `ToolboxBitmapAttribute` to use the `TextBox`'s bitmap with our custom `RegexTextBox`.

---

1. Select the custom control project from the Solution Explorer.
2. Click File|Add New Item.
3. In the Add New Item dialog, pick the Bitmap File template, provide a good name for the bitmap, and click OK.
4. Open the bitmap file in the IDE by double-clicking on it (if it is not already open), and open the Properties window. Change the Height and Width values to 16 each.
5. Draw your bitmap.
6. Use the bright green color as your transparency color (see Figure 9.5).
7. You have a couple of options for associating the bitmap with the control.
   a. Name the bitmap file identically to the class name except for the extension, and change the bitmap's Build Action to Embedded Resource (see Figure 9.6).
   b. Name the `.bmp` file anything you want, and then pass the filename to the `ToolboxBitmapAttribute`. (You can drag and drop the bitmap file from the Solution Explorer into the Code Editor, adding quotes after you drop the file.)

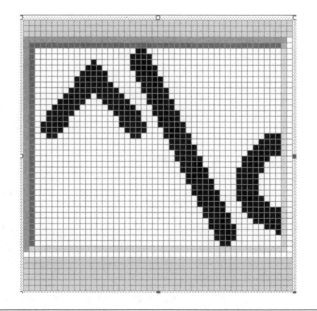

Figure 9.5 Use the bright green color (shown here as the medium gray bands near the top and bottom edges of the figure) as your transparency color.

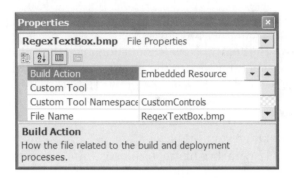

Figure 9.6 Change the bitmap file's Build Action to an Embedded Resource.

8. (If you chose option 7a, skip ahead to step 11.) If you chose option 7b, add a reference to `System.Drawing.dll` in the custom control's References list. (The `System.Drawing.dll` namespace contains the `ToolboxBitmapAttribute`.)

9. Add an `Imports System.Drawing` statement to the control's source file.

10. Apply the `ToolboxBitmapAttribute`, passing the complete path to the external file.

11. Build the control class library and select Customize Toolbox from the Toolbox's context menu, browse to the DLL containing the custom control, and click Open.

When you are finished you should see the custom control with the associated bitmap next to it. If you see the default cog symbol, something went wrong. Double-check to make sure you correctly followed the steps in the numbered list and try again.

There are several articles on associating a bitmap with a custom control. I tend to experiment to see what is true and what I can get away with. I was able to change the bitmap to 48 × 48 pixels and 256 colors even though the recommended specifications are 16 × 16 pixels and 16 colors. Using more pixels and colors provided me with a finer degree of control over creating the bitmap image, but creating cool icon-sized bitmaps requires more artistic talent than I have. If you do choose to deviate from the recommended specifications for Toolbox bitmaps—or any general recommendations—keep in mind that you may be causing a subtle bug in your programs. Document what you did carefully, permitting someone else to fall back to recommended practices.

Adding Documentation to the Toolbox

The Properties window displays a description at the bottom of the window for each property. You can provide a description of your custom control's properties with the `DescriptionAttribute`. Defined in the `System.ComponentModel namespace`, this attribute can be applied as demonstrated in Listing 9.5. (The result of the `DescriptionAttribute` from Listing 9.5 is shown in Figure 9.7.)

Listing 9.5 An Excerpt from `RegexTextBox` Demonstrating Use of `DescriptionAttribute`

```
<Description( _
"A regular expression used to validate the input text.")> _
  Public Property Pattern() As String
  Get
    Return FPattern
  End Get
  Set(ByVal Value As String)
    FPattern = Value
  End Set
End Property
```

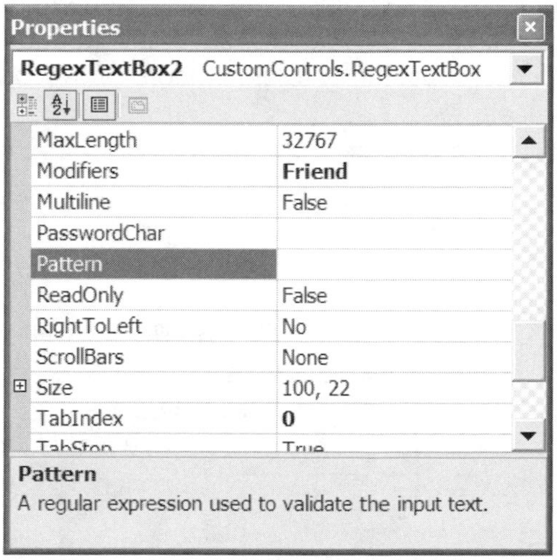

Figure 9.7 The `DescriptionAttribute` affects the display of a description of the `Pattern` property in the Properties window.

All the examples in this section can be found in `RegexTextBox.sln`, which contains `CustomControls.vbproj` and `RegexTextBox.vbproj`. We'll come back to more enhanced custom control capabilities after a brief detour. Let's look at creating custom user controls.

Implementing a Custom Windows User Control

A useful control on which to build is the user control. The user control can be designed, like a Windows form, which makes it an ideal candidate for designing business controls comprised of several constituent controls. The key is to flatten the properties of the constituent control, making the user control seem like a single control with several properties rather than a composite control.

The control I defined as the example for this section is a custom user control named `AddressUserControl`, which contains several constituent controls common to U.S. addresses (see Figure 9.8). I defined `AddressUserControl` as part of a class library and added the control to the Toolbox (see the earlier section Adding a Control to the Toolbox).

NOTE: An interesting addition to our `AddressUserControl` would be an address validation Web Service. Such a service would probably require its own separate care and feeding as well as a huge database. A vendor like Stamps.com could provide access to such a database for a small subscription fee or for the opportunity to bring users' attention to the vendor's products and services.

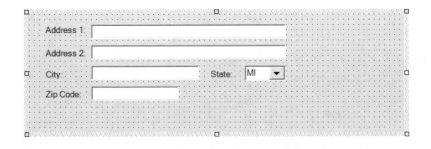

Figure 9.8 A custom user control containing typical address information.

Surfacing Constituent Properties

Figure 9.8 indicates that `AddressUserControl` contains labels, text boxes, and one combobox. What if we elected to allow a consumer to modify these values at design time? Intuitively you might think we could do so by making the `TextBox` controls public. However, this intuitive solution is not currently supported. Instead we have to add public properties that return the underlying `Text` property of these controls. This is referred to as *surfacing constituent controls*. The basic technique involves adding properties that get and set the values of properties belonging to the aggregate constituent controls. Listing 9.6 demonstrates the technique by listing the code for `AddressUserControl`.

Listing 9.6 Surfacing Properties of Constituent Controls on a User Control

```
1:   Imports System.Text.RegularExpressions
2:   Imports System.Windows.Forms
3:
4:   Public Class AddressUserControl
5:       Inherits System.Windows.Forms.UserControl
6:
7:   [ Windows Form Designer generated code ]
8:
9:   Public Property Address1() As String
10:  Get
11:     Return TextBoxAddress1.Text
12:  End Get
13:  Set(ByVal Value As String)
14:     TextBoxAddress1.Text = Value
15:  End Set
16:  End Property
17:
18:  Public Property Address2() As String
19:  Get
20:     Return TextBoxAddress2.Text
21:  End Get
22:  Set(ByVal Value As String)
23:     TextBoxAddress2.Text = Value
24:  End Set
25:  End Property
26:
27:  Public Property City() As String
28:  Get
```

```
29:      Return TextBoxCity.Text
30:    End Get
31:    Set(ByVal Value As String)
32:      TextBoxCity.Text = Value
33:    End Set
34:    End Property
35:
36:    Public Property State() As String
37:    Get
38:      Return ComboBoxState.Text
39:    End Get
40:    Set(ByVal Value As String)
41:      ComboBoxState.Text = Value
42:    End Set
43:    End Property
44:
45:    Public Property ZipCode() As String
46:    Get
47:      Return TextBoxZipCode.Text
48:    End Get
49:    Set(ByVal Value As String)
50:      TextBoxZipCode.Text = Value
51:    End Set
52:    End Property
53:
54:    Private Sub TextBoxZipCode_Validating(ByVal sender As Object, _
55:      ByVal e As System.ComponentModel.CancelEventArgs) _
56:      Handles TextBoxZipCode.Validating
57:
58:      If (Not Regex.IsMatch(ZipCode, "^\d{5}(-\d{4})?$")) Then
59:        e.Cancel = Not AcceptInvalidZipCode()
60:      End If
61:    End Sub
62:
63:    Private Function AcceptInvalidZipCode() As Boolean
64:      Const Mask As String = _
65:        "Zip code {0} is invalid"
66:
67:      Return MessageBox.Show(String.Format(Mask, ZipCode), "Error", _
68:        MessageBoxButtons.OKCancel, _
69:          MessageBoxIcon.Error) = DialogResult.OK
70:    End Function
71:
72: End Class
```

For each control I defined a public property that promoted the property that will become part of the `AddressUserControl`'s public interface and will be modifiable in the Properties window at design time and runtime.

Lines 54 through 70 demonstrate how we might incorporate validation into our user control. The event handler compares the value of the `ZipCode` property to the regular expression `"^\d{5}(-\d{4})?$"`. If `ZipCode` does not match the regular expression, a message dialog is displayed, allowing the user to override a failed match pattern. (The message dialog is displayed in the function `AcceptInvalidZipCode`.)

The regular expression on line 58 can be understood to mean a succession of five digits followed by a hyphen and an optional four more digits. The question mark after the group `(-\d{4})` makes the four trailing digits optional.

An excellent example of combining and layering code would be to incorporate our `RegexTextBox` from earlier in the chapter, replacing the plain-vanilla text box and event handler in the listing. Try this as an exercise.

Binding Data to a Custom User Control

.NET supports many powerful concepts that would be difficult to discover by trial and error. One such concept relates to data binding. We can actually bind the constituent controls in our `AddressUserControl` to the properties of a valid `DataSource` property. A valid `DataSource` property implements the `IList` interface and includes typed collections, `ArrayList` objects, and `DataSet` objects.

In order to demonstrate data binding I defined a new `AddressList` XML schema and used that schema to generate a strongly typed data set. (Read Chapter 12, Advanced ADO.NET, for more information on XML schemas and typed data sets.) Subsequent to defining the data set, an instance of the strongly typed Addresses table was created and data was added to the data table. With test data available it is easy to see the results of the `Data-Binding` statements. Listing 9.7 provides you with the source code (available for download as part of the `UserControlLibrary.sln` file).

Listing 9.7 Data Binding Examples with a Custom User Control and a Typed Data Set

```
1:  Imports System.Data
2:
3:  Public Class Form1
4:      Inherits System.Windows.Forms.Form
5:
```

```
 6:  [ Windows Form Designer generated code ]
 7:    Private Addresses As AddressList.AddressesDataTable
 8:
 9:    Private Sub Form1_Load(ByVal sender As System.Object, _
10:      ByVal e As System.EventArgs) Handles MyBase.Load
11:
12:      Addresses = New AddressList.AddressesDataTable()
13:      Addresses.AddAddressesRow( _
14:        "11546 Beaumont St", "", "Okemos", "MI", "48864")
15:
16:      Addresses.AddAddressesRow( _
17:        "1313 Mockingbird Ln.", "Apt 4", "Okemos", _
18:        "MI", "48864")
19:
20:      AddressUserControl1.DataBindings.Add( _
21:        New Binding("Address1", Addresses, "AddressLine1"))
22:
23:      AddressUserControl1.DataBindings.Add( _
24:        New Binding("Address2", Addresses, "AddressLine2"))
25:
26:      AddressUserControl1.DataBindings.Add( _
27:        New Binding("City", Addresses, "City"))
28:
29:      AddressUserControl1.DataBindings.Add( _
30:        New Binding("State", Addresses, "State"))
31:
32:      AddressUserControl1.DataBindings.Add( _
33:        New Binding("ZipCode", Addresses, "ZipCode"))
34:
35:    End Sub
36:
37:    Private Sub Button1_Click(ByVal sender As System.Object, _
38:      ByVal e As System.EventArgs) Handles Button1.Click
39:
40:      CType(AddressUserControl1.BindingContext(Addresses), _
41:        CurrencyManager).Position -= 1
42:    End Sub
43:
44:    Private Sub Button2_Click(ByVal sender As System.Object, _
45:      ByVal e As System.EventArgs) Handles Button2.Click
46:      CType(AddressUserControl1.BindingContext(Addresses), _
47:        CurrencyManager).Position += 1
48:    End Sub
49:
50: End Class
```

Lines 7 demonstrates how we can declare an instance of the nested, strongly typed `AddressesDataTable` (see Chapter 12). The `Form1_Load` event creates an instance of the data table, and lines 13 through 18 add rows to the table, providing us with something to look at as we navigate through the data.

For each public property defined in `AddressUserControl`, a `Binding` object was created and added to `AddressUserControl`'s `DataBindings` collection. For example, line 21 creates a new `Binding` object inline that binds the `AddressUserControl.Address1` property to the typed data table's `AddressLine1` field (the first and third arguments, respectively). The middle, or second argument, to the `Binding` object's constructor is the data source. This process is repeated for every constituent control's publicly promoted property (lines 20 through 33).

To support navigation I added buttons to the test form and implemented `Click` events for the buttons. In each `Click` event, `AddressUserControl`'s `BindingContext` for the `Addresses` table is obtained and cast to `CurrencyManager`. `CurrencyManager` inherits from `BindingBaseManager` and can be used to safely set the index position of the data source. The `Position` property is modified by using the decrement and increment operators in lines 41 and 47, respectively. `BindingContext` will not permit you to position the internal index to an invalid position.

As you can see from the listing (and by downloading and running the example), it is a relatively straightforward process to support binding typed data and implementing navigation with the support of the framework.

Examining Control Attributes

When you are creating custom controls, you want to be sure that your controls behave well and don't interfere with the proper behavior of the Visual Studio .NET IDE. Remember, it is your code running in the Form Designer when users are using your custom controls.

If you have public properties that raise an exception, for instance, when invalid data is assigned, you may want to prevent consumers from modifying a property of a control at design time. A couple of attributes control the accessibility of a property in the Properties window. The `EditorBrowsableAttribute` determines whether a property or method is visible in a designer. For example, Intellisense uses the `EditorBrowsableAttribute` to determine which members show up in the Intellisense list. The `DesignerSerializationVisibilityAttribute` is used to determine how a property is serialized by a designer. For example, if a required property throws an exception on an invalid value, then when the designer deserializes that null property the designer would fail on the exception. An exception at design time would prevent the IDE from opening your user control. The `BrowsableAttribute` is used to control whether a property shows up in the Properties window at design time. Combining these three properties can help you manage how your custom control behaves in the IDE at design time.

TIP: The attributes that affect the components discussed here are defined in the `System.ComponentModel` namespace.

Applying the `EditorBrowsableAttribute`

Suppose you elected to inhibit general access to the identity column from a typed data set for novice or intermediate programmers but allow advanced programmers to see it. You might choose to do this because an identity column is read-only and automatically generated. You could apply the `Editor-BrowsableAttribute` to the typed properties in the generated, strongly typed data set. Listing 9.8, using an excerpt taken from the `AddressList` typed data set and applied to the `AddressIDColumn` property, shows how to apply the `EditorBrowsableAttribute` to permit only advanced programmers to see an attribute in the IDE using Intellisense.

Listing 9.8 Applying the `EditorBrowsableAttribute`

```
<System.ComponentModel.EditorBrowsable( _
ComponentModel.EditorBrowsableState.Advanced)> _
Friend ReadOnly Property AddressIDColumn() As DataColumn
Get
  Return Me.columnAddressID
End Get
End Property
```

The attribute does not affect the property's actual availability. If programmers already know that the property exists, they can certainly use it in their code. With the application of the attribute as shown, it just won't normally show up in Intellisense and will be reported as an error in the Task List. Such an application of the attribute might discourage rampant abuse by novices. With the `EditorBrowsableState.Advanced` enumeration a member will not show up in Intellisense (Figure 9.9) unless the Hide advanced members option is unchecked in the Tools|Options dialog under the Text Editor, Basic folder (Figure 9.10).

Applying the `DesignerSerializationVisibility-Attribute`

Visual Studio .NET uses XML to serialize the resource files of things like forms and user controls. An unmanaged error during the serialization or deserialization process will make the IDE burp and likely fail to properly save or load your form or user control. It is certainly permissible to raise an unhandled exception in a control or form if you are going to require a consumer to handle the exception; however, the IDE cannot know about such requirements after the fact. Thus if you elect to implement a behavioral contract—the consumer must handle an exception—it is often prudent to prevent that method or property from being invoked during the serialization process.

You can apply the `DesignerSerializationVisibilityAttribute` with one of three `DesignerSerializationVisibility` enumerated values: `Content`, `Hidden`, or `Visible`. `Content` indicates that code will be serialized for the object, `Hidden` indicates that the member will not be serialized, and `Visible` causes the designer to serialize the member. By supplying the

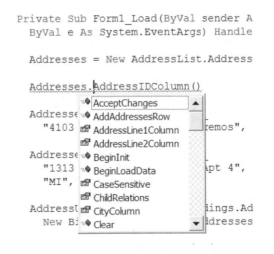

Figure 9.9 By default Intellisense will hide members marked with the `Editor-BrowsableState.Advanced` enumerated value.

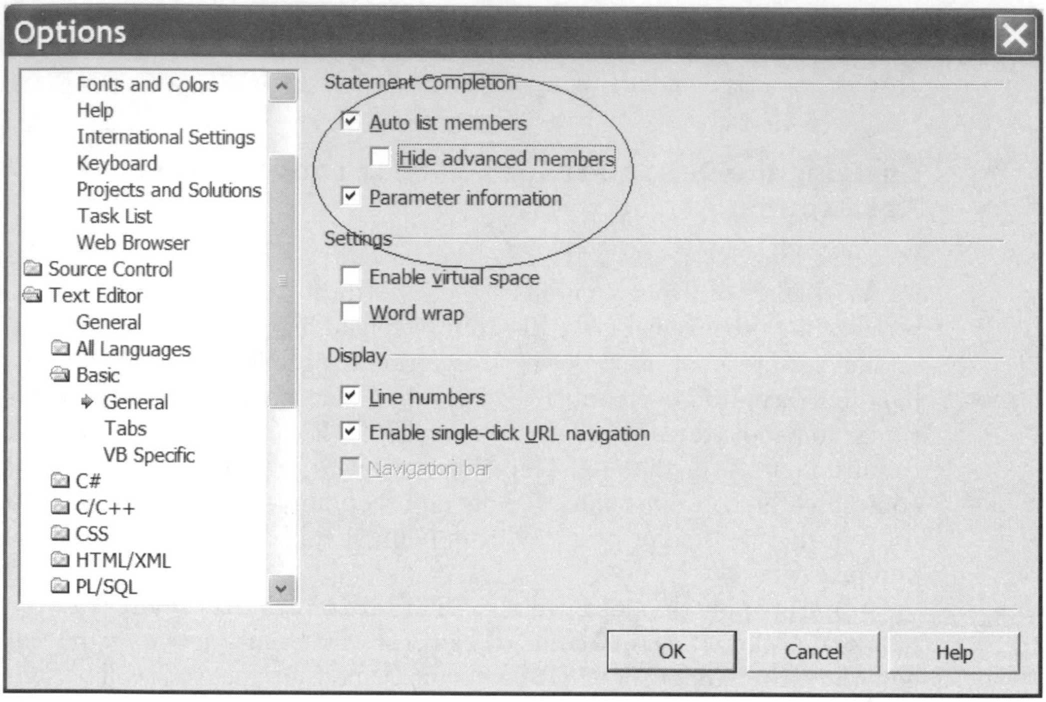

Figure 9.10 Advanced users will know to uncheck the Hide advanced members box in the Options dialog in the IDE to make all members visible in Intellisense.

DesignerSerializationVisibility.Hidden enumerated value to the DesignerSerializationVisibilityAttribute you can prevent a contract property, for example, from blowing up on serialization. Listing 9.9 shows how the DesignerSerializationVisibilityAttribute was used (in conjunction with the BrowsableAttribute, discussed next) in our generated typed data set to manage XML serialization during saving and restoring by the designer.

Listing 9.9 Applying the DesignerSerializationVisibilityAttribute

```
<System.ComponentModel.Browsable(false), _
System.ComponentModel.DesignerSerializationVisibility ( _
System.ComponentModel.DesignerSerializationVisibility.Content)> _
Public ReadOnly Property Addresses As AddressesDataTable
```

```
Get
  Return Me.tableAddresses
End Get
End Property
```

It is important to keep in mind that any code in a property's getter will be run when an object is serialized, and the setter's code will be run when an object is deserialized. It has been my experience that most code exists in setters, and for this reason it is deserialization—or opening a resource file—that is likely to cause most problems. The origination of a deserialization error can be difficult to resolve, especially when you are inheriting from user controls, unless you are specifically aware of the `DesignerSerializationVisibilityAttribute`.

Applying the `BrowsableAttribute`

The `BrowsableAttribute` determines whether a property shows up in the Properties window. Often you will discover this attribute employed with the `DesignerSerializationVisibilityAttribute`. Our sample application uses the `BrowsableAttribute` in a couple of places, including in the `Count` property. A consumer can't change the number of rows in a data set, and a reasonable value is unlikely to exist until the data set is populated. For this reason, the XML Designer applies the `Browsable(false)` attribute to the public and derived property `Count`, as shown in Listing 9.10.

Listing 9.10 Applying the `BrowsableAttribute`

```
<System.ComponentModel.Browsable(false)> _
Public ReadOnly Property Count As Integer
Get
  Return Me.Rows.Count
End Get
End Property
```

If you want to prevent a property from showing up in the Properties window, initialize a `BrowsableAttribute` with the literal `False`. I have found this attribute especially useful with Web user controls. Working on a big project in Oregon, I defined a base user control for a big Web application. The user control obtained its data from the business object. The data was set to a public property during user navigation. It doesn't make sense to permit this value to be set at design time because the data represents an object derived from a database read. Hence, I applied the `DesignerSerializationVisibility(DesignerSerializationVisibility.Hidden)` and `Browsable(False)` attributes to this property to ensure its availability during runtime yet prevent misuse or serialization errors at design time.

Using the `UITypeEditor` Class

If you have started wondering how to display list boxes, `NumericUpDown` controls, little boxes that contain colors, or dialog boxes for editing properties in the IDE, you have come to the right place. By creating a custom `UITypeEditor` instance you can add enhanced property editing to your custom control. To demonstrate I will show you how to display a list of states to choose from—a custom type editor—and how to associate that type editor and provide a default value for the `State` combobox in the `AddressUserControl`.

To implement a drop-down list of states in the `AddressUserControl`'s `State` combobox, we need to define a custom type editor and provide an overridden implementation for the methods `EditValue` and `GetEditStyle`. `EditValue` is invoked when the consumer attempts to modify the property in the IDE at design time, and `GetEditStyle` returns an enumerated `UIEditorEditStyle` value. Listing 9.11 contains the code for the custom type editor, dubbed `StateEditor`, followed by a synopsis.

Listing 9.11 A Custom Type Editor for Editing State Abbreviations in the Properties Window

```
1:  Imports System.Drawing.Design
2:  Imports System.Windows.Forms
3:  Imports System.Windows.Forms.Design
4:  Imports System.ComponentModel
5:
6:  Public Class StateEditor
7:     Inherits UITypeEditor
8:
```

```
 9:     Private editorService As _
10:       IWindowsFormsEditorService = Nothing
11:
12:     Private States() As String = _
13:       New String() {"AL", "AR", "AK", "AZ", "CA", _
14:         "DE", "FL", "GA", "HI", "IN", "MI", "OR", "PA"}
15:
16:     Private Function IsValidContext( _
17:       ByVal context As ITypeDescriptorContext) As Boolean
18:
19:       Return (context Is Nothing = False) _
20:         And (context.Instance Is Nothing) = False
21:
22:     End Function
23:
24:     Private Function IsValidProvider( _
25:       ByVal provider As IServiceProvider) As Boolean
26:
27:       Return provider Is Nothing = False
28:     End Function
29:
30:     Private Function GetService( _
31:       ByVal provider As IServiceProvider) _
32:       As IWindowsFormsEditorService
33:
34:       Return CType(provider.GetService( _
35:         GetType(IWindowsFormsEditorService)), _
36:         IWindowsFormsEditorService)
37:
38:     End Function
39:
40:     Public Overloads Overrides Function EditValue( _
41:       ByVal context As ITypeDescriptorContext, _
42:       ByVal provider As IServiceProvider, _
43:       ByVal value As Object) As Object
44:
45:       If (IsValidContext(context) = False Or _
46:         IsValidProvider(provider)) = False Then
47:         Return value
48:       End If
49:
50:
51:       editorService = GetService(provider)
52:       If (editorService Is Nothing) Then Return value
```

```
53:
54:    Dim control As ListBox = New ListBox()
55:    control.Items.AddRange(States)
56:    AddHandler control.SelectedValueChanged, _
57:      AddressOf SelectedValueChanged
58:
59:    editorService.DropDownControl(control)
60:    If Not (control.Text = String.Empty) Then
61:      Return control.Text
62:    Else
63:      Dim Attribute As Attribute = _
64:        context.PropertyDescriptor.Attributes( _
65:          GetType(DefaultValueAttribute))
66:
67:      If (Attribute Is Nothing = False) Then
68:        Return CType(Attribute, DefaultValueAttribute).Value
69:      Else
70:        Return value
71:      End If
72:    End If
73:  End Function
74:
75:  Public Overloads Overrides Function GetEditStyle( _
76:    ByVal context As ITypeDescriptorContext) _
77:      As UITypeEditorEditStyle
78:
79:    If (IsValidContext(context)) Then
80:      Return UITypeEditorEditStyle.DropDown
81:    Else
82:      Return MyBase.GetEditStyle(context)
83:    End If
84:
85:  End Function
86:
87:  Private Sub SelectedValueChanged(ByVal sender As Object, _
88:    ByVal e As EventArgs)
89:
90:    If (editorService Is Nothing) Then Return
91:    editorService.CloseDropDown()
92:  End Sub
93:
94: End Class
```

Lines 1 through 4 contain the namespaces used by the custom type editor. `System.Drawing.Design` contains the base class `UITypeEditor`. `System.Windows.Forms` contains the definition for the list box used as the control for the type editor beginning on line 54. `System.Windows.Forms.Design` contains the definition for the `IWindowsFormsEditorService` interface declared in lines 9 and 10. `System.ComponentModel` contains the definition for the `DefaultValueAttribute` and the `ITypeDescriptorContext` interface.

Line 7 is understood to mean that `StateEditor` *is-a* `UITypeEditor`, expressed as an inheritance relationship using the `Inherits` keyword in Visual Basic .NET.

The private methods are "worker bee" methods. `IsValidContext`, `IsValidProvider`, and `GetService` are all used to help simplify the `EditValue` and `GetEditStyle` methods. For example, `IsValidContext` is used to make sure that the context—that is, the component whose properties we are editing—is valid. The `ITypeDescriptorContext` interface refers to the component and the property we will be modifying. `IsValidProvider` is used to test whether `IServiceProvider` is valid. Our service provider is `IWindowsFormsEditorService`, which provides an interface for displaying `DropDownList` or dialog controls. We are using the `DropDownList` support provided by classes that implement `IWindowsFormsEditorService`. Finally, `GetService` is used to cast the generic `IServiceProvider` to an `IWindowsFormsServiceProvider`, which is the actual interface we know `IServiceProvider` to be returning in the context of `UITypeEditor`.

Lines 9 and 10 declare a local field that we use to store a reference to `IServiceProvider`, rather than continually requesting and typecasting it.

Lines 12 through 14 contain a partial list of U.S. state abbreviations. (Note that we can always go back and verify the data after we get the code working correctly.)

Lines 75 through 85 simply indicate the kind of `UITypeEditorEditStyle` this type editor will be displaying. If we have a valid context, we want to return a `UITypeEditorEditStyle.DropDown`; otherwise we defer to the inherited method (line 82).

The most challenging method to implement correctly is the `EditValue` method (see lines 40 through 73). The purpose of `EditValue` is to display the control used to edit the property value and retrieve the edited value. We are using a `ListBox` control, so we need to be able to both display and close it. Lines 45 through 48 ensure that the context is correct. If not, the passed-in value is returned. Lines 51 and 52 make sure that `IServiceProvider` exists; again, if not, the passed-in value is returned. Assuming we have a valid context (the component) and a valid provider (the IDE), we can proceed. Lines 54 through 57 declare and initialize a `ListBox` control. In line 55 we add the list of states to the `ListBox` control. In lines 56 and 57 we assign an event handler to the `SelectedValueChanged` event. Defined in lines 87 through 92, `SelectedValueChanged` is used to close the `ListBox` control after the user selects a value. `IServiceProvider` is used to display the control used to edit the property. If the control—the `ListBox` in our example—contains a value for its `Text` property in lines 60 and 61, the selected value is returned to the Properties window and consequently the related `States` combobox. If the user escaped the program or failed to select a state, Reflection is used to get the default value (indicated by a `DefaultValueAttribute` that we will supply) from the property itself.

Lines 63 through 65 request the `DefaultValueAttribute` from the context's property descriptor. If a `DefaultAttribute` is applied to the property—in this case the `State` property—that default value is returned (see lines 67 and 68).

The work left to do is to associate our type editor with the member we want to edit in the IDE.

Associating a Type Editor with a Control

We defined `StateEditor` as a `UITypeEditor` instance for editing the value of our `AddressUserControl`'s `State` property. We associate `StateEditor` with the `State` property by using the `EditorAttribute`. Listing 9.12 demonstrates an application of the `EditorAttribute` in conjunction with the `DefaultValueAttribute` and `CategoryAttribute`, which I describe in the remaining two subsections.

Listing 9.12 Associating a Type Editor with the Member to Edit

```
1:    <Editor(GetType(StateEditor), GetType(UITypeEditor)), _
2:    DefaultValue("CA"), _
3:    Category("Address Fields"), _
4:    Description("Partial list of U.S. state abbreviations.")> _
5:    Public Property State() As String
6:    Get
7:      Return ComboBoxState.Text
8:    End Get
9:    Set(ByVal Value As String)
10:      ComboBoxState.Text = Value
```

```
11:    End Set
12:    End Property
```

The `EditorAttribute` needs the type of our custom editor and the type of the base editor. We satisfy this requirement in line 1 by passing the type object of `StateEditor` (our custom type editor) and the base editor (the `UITypeEditor` instance itself) as arguments to the `EditorAttribute`. (We talked about the `DescriptionAttribute` earlier in this chapter, so we'll skip that attribute in this discussion.)

Supplying a Default Value

The `DefaultValueAttribute` can be used to associate a default value with a property. In our case we know that `StateEditor` is used with a specific field—the `State` field—but we have no way to know what future consumers may do with `StateEditor`. As a result it is safe to dynamically determine the default value by using the `ITypeDescriptorContext` interface's `PropertyDescriptor` and Reflection rather than supposing that there is some predetermined default value. (Keep in mind that in real life the producer of `StateEditor` may not be the same or only consumer.) Line 2 of Listing 9.12 above demonstrates how to use the `DefaultValueAttribute`.

Categorizing Control Properties

Properties in the Properties window can be ordered alphabetically or categorically. Suppose a consumer elects to modify all the properties we added representing parts of the address. By providing a `CategoryAttribute` (see line 3 of Listing 9.12 above) we can provide a means by which consumers can quickly access the properties they are most interested in. Figure 9.11 shows the result of using the `CategoryAttribute` in the Properties window.

Clearly there are other kinds of editors you may want to use in the Properties window. However, if we are ever to finish this chapter I have to leave some things for you to explore on your own. For example, if you want to display an icon or some other custom-painted graphic in the Properties window, you will need to define a `UITypeEditor` instance that overrides `GetPaintValueSupport` and `PaintValue`. `PaintValue` receives a `Graphics` object that represents the region of the editor in the Properties window. You can use this `Graphics` object to paint boxes with colors, gradient effects, or whatever you can squeeze into the small space provided. If you

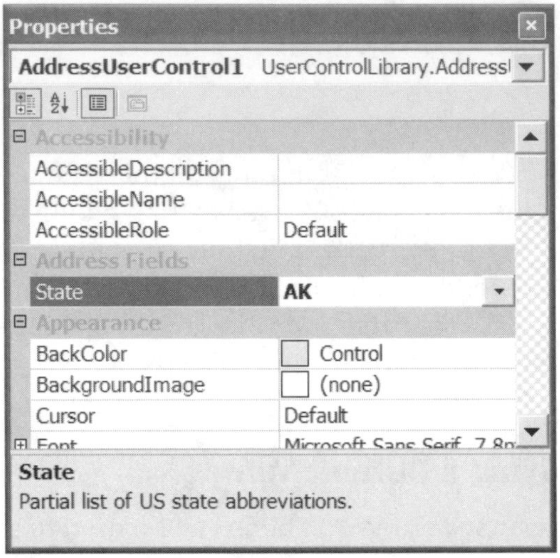

Figure 9.11 Categorical organization of properties in a custom control.

need to display a complex editor, such as one that requires a dialog form, you can use code similar to that found in Listing 9.11. The difference is that `UITypeEditorEditStyle` will become `UITypeEditorStyle.Modal`, and you will need to call the `IWindowsFormsEditorService.ShowDialog` method, converting the results in the dialog form into a value that is suitable for the property being edited. (My book *Advanced C# Programming* [2002] has an example of a dialog `UITypeEditor` in C#. You can download the source code for the dialog `UITypeEditor` from *http://www.softcon-cepts.com* for free or, better yet, pick up a copy of the book.)

Implementing Type Conversion

It is important for a visual framework to support type conversion. For example, controls have graphical properties, but it is often difficult or impossible to show an image in the small space provided in the Properties window. For the Properties window the path to the image might be fine, but the GUI needs to display the actual image. This duality constitutes a type conversion of an image between a file path and the actual image. Other kinds of data need other kinds of conversion; for instance, a color may be rendered as text when serialized to a resource file, but the actual color is rendered in the

GUI. Because various kinds of data conversions are needed to support the IDE and runtime applications, a general conversion mechanism is needed. .NET supplies two general conversion mechanisms.

If you define a new type, you can implement the `IConvertible` interface, which supports one-way, runtime conversion between a new type and an existing type. The mechanism for conversion—using the `IConvertible` interface—includes the shared methods in the `System.Convert` class. The process implements `IConvertible`, calls `System.Convert`, and uses members that make up the `IConvertible` interface to perform the conversion. For instance, `System.Convert.ToBoolean` tests an object to see if it implements `IConvertible` and then invokes the `IConvertible.ToBoolean` method. You aren't required to perform the conversion; simply provide the `ToBoolean` method. If it doesn't make sense to convert your object to a Boolean, raise an exception.

If you want to implement design time and runtime type conversion, you will want to implement a `TypeConverter` subclass. `TypeConverter` objects exist to support design time conversion, such as converting the file path of an image between the path and the image, depending on the context.

To demonstrate `IConvertible` and `TypeConverter`, I defined a new class, `Circle`, which supports what may be reasonable conversions for both runtime and design time type conversion. For instance, if we elect to use `Circle` as a property in a component, we may prefer to show the center point and radius values rather than try to render the circle in the Properties window. The subsections that follow contain the implementations of `Circle`, the conversion code, and some test code. (You can run and test the example code by downloading `ConversionDemo.sln`.)

Implementing the `IConvertible` Interface

Like all interfaces, `IConvertible` has specific members that we must implement. These methods are `GetTypeCode`, `ToBoolean`, `ToByte`, `ToChar`, `ToDateTime`, `ToDecimal`, `ToDouble`, `ToInt16`, `ToInt32`, `ToByte`, `ToString`, `ToType`, `ToUInt16`, `ToUInt32`, and `TUInt64`. You might recognize these as members of the `System.Convert` class.

In general, implement `IConvertible` under the following conditions:

- When you need to perform conversions to general, system types using `System.Convert`
- When you need to perform the conversion only at runtime
- When you need to convert only from a new type to an existing type but not back again

Listing 9.13 contains a reasonable implementation of the `Circle` structure. Because we need a class in which to hold the interface members, the `Circle` structure itself implements the `IConvertible` interface.

Listing 9.13 Implementing the `Circle` Structure and the `IConvertible` Interface

```
1:   Imports System.ComponentModel
2:
3:   <TypeConverter(GetType(CircleConverter))> _
4:   Public Structure Circle
5:     Implements IConvertible
6:
7:     Private FCenter As Point
8:     Private FRadius As Single
9:
10:    Public Sub New(ByVal X As Integer, _
11:      ByVal Y As Integer, ByVal Radius As Single)
12:      FCenter = New Point(X, Y)
13:      FRadius = Radius
14:    End Sub
15:
16:    Public Sub New(ByVal Center As Point, _
17:      ByVal Radius As Single)
18:      FCenter = Center
19:      FRadius = Radius
20:    End Sub
21:
22:    Public Property Center() As Point
23:    Get
24:      Return FCenter
25:    End Get
26:    Set(ByVal Value As Point)
27:      FCenter = Value
28:    End Set
29:    End Property
30:
31:    Public ReadOnly Property Left() As Integer
32:    Get
33:      Return FCenter.X - FRadius \ 2
34:    End Get
35:    End Property
36:
37:    Public ReadOnly Property Top() As Integer
```

```
38:   Get
39:     Return FCenter.Y - FRadius \ 2
40:   End Get
41:   End Property
42:
43:   Public ReadOnly Property Radius() As Single
44:   Get
45:      Return FRadius
46:   End Get
47:   End Property
48:
49:   Public ReadOnly Property Height() As Integer
50:   Get
51:     Return Convert.ToInt32(FRadius)
52:   End Get
53:   End Property
54:
55:   Public ReadOnly Property Width() As Integer
56:   Get
57:     Return Convert.ToInt32(FRadius)
58:   End Get
59:   End Property
60:
61:   Public ReadOnly Property ToBoundingRectangle() _
62:     As Rectangle
63:   Get
64:     Return New Rectangle(Left, Top, Width, Height)
65:   End Get
66:   End Property
67:
68:   Public ReadOnly Property ToBoundingRectangleF() _
69:     As RectangleF
70:   Get
71:     Return New RectangleF(Left, Top, Width, Height)
72:   End Get
73:   End Property
74:
75:   Public ReadOnly Property Area() As Single
76:   Get
77:     Return Math.PI * Math.Pow(FRadius, 2)
78:   End Get
79:   End Property
80:
81:   Public ReadOnly Property Circumference() As Single
```

```
82:    Get
83:      Return 2 * Math.PI * FRadius
84:    End Get
85:    End Property
86:
87:    Public ReadOnly Property Diameter() As Single
88:    Get
89:      Return 2 * FRadius
90:    End Get
91:    End Property
92:
93:    Private Function GetTypeCode() As TypeCode _
94:       Implements IConvertible.GetTypeCode
95:       Return TypeCode.Object
96:    End Function
97:
98:    Private Function ToBoolean( _
99:      ByVal provider As IFormatProvider) As Boolean _
100:     Implements IConvertible.ToBoolean
101:
102:     ThrowException("conversion to Boolean not supported")
103:     Return False
104:   End Function
105:
106:   Private Function ToByte( _
107:     ByVal provider As IFormatProvider) As Byte _
108:     Implements IConvertible.ToByte
109:
110:     ThrowException("conversion to Byte not supported")
111:     Return 0
112:   End Function
113:
114:   Private Function ToChar( _
115:     ByVal provider As IFormatProvider) As Char _
116:     Implements IConvertible.ToChar
117:
118:     ThrowException("conversion to Char not supported")
119:     Return Chr(0)
120:   End Function
121:
122:   Private Function ToDateTime( _
123:     ByVal provider As IFormatProvider) As DateTime _
124:     Implements IConvertible.ToDateTime
125:
```

```
126:     ThrowException("conversion to DateTime not supported")
127:     Return DateTime.Now
128: End Function
129:
130: Private Function ToDecimal( _
131:    ByVal provider As IFormatProvider) As Decimal _
132:    Implements IConvertible.ToDecimal
133:
134:    ThrowException("conversion to Decimal not supported")
135:    Return Decimal.Zero
136: End Function
137:
138: Private Function ToDouble( _
139:    ByVal provider As IFormatProvider) As Double _
140:    Implements IConvertible.ToDouble
141:
142:    ThrowException("conversion to Double not supported")
143:    Return Double.MinValue
144: End Function
145:
146: Private Function ToInt16( _
147:    ByVal provider As IFormatProvider) As Int16 _
148:    Implements IConvertible.ToInt16
149:
150:    ThrowException("conversion to Int16 not supported")
151:    Return Int16.MinValue
152: End Function
153:
154: Private Function ToInt32( _
155:    ByVal provider As IFormatProvider) As Int32 _
156:    Implements IConvertible.ToInt32
157:
158:    ThrowException("conversion to Int32 not supported")
159:    Return Int32.MinValue
160: End Function
161:
162: Private Function ToInt64( _
163:    ByVal provider As IFormatProvider) As Int64 _
164:    Implements IConvertible.ToInt64
165:
166:    ThrowException("conversion to Int64 not supported")
167:    Return Int64.MinValue
168: End Function
169:
```

```
170:  Private Function ToSingle( _
171:    ByVal provider As IFormatProvider) As Single _
172:    Implements IConvertible.ToSingle
173:
174:    ThrowException("conversion to Single not supported")
175:    Return Single.MinValue
176:
177:  End Function
178:
179:  Private Function ToUInt16( _
180:    ByVal provider As IFormatProvider) As UInt16 _
181:    Implements IConvertible.ToUInt16
182:
183:    ThrowException("conversion to UInt16 not supported")
184:    Return UInt16.Parse("0")
185:  End Function
186:
187:  Private Function ToUInt32( _
188:    ByVal provider As IFormatProvider) As UInt32 _
189:    Implements IConvertible.ToUInt32
190:
191:    ThrowException("conversion to UInt32 not supported")
192:    Return UInt32.Parse("0")
193:  End Function
194:
195:  Private Function ToUInt64( _
196:    ByVal provider As IFormatProvider) As UInt64 _
197:    Implements IConvertible.ToUInt64
198:
199:    ThrowException("conversion to UInt64 not supported")
200:    Return UInt64.Parse("0")
201:  End Function
202:
203:  Private Function ToSByte( _
204:    ByVal provider As IFormatProvider) As SByte _
205:    Implements IConvertible.ToSByte
206:
207:    ThrowException("conversion to SByte not supported")
208:    Return SByte.Parse("0")
209:  End Function
210:
211:  Private Overloads Function ToString( _
212:    ByVal provider As IFormatProvider) As String _
213:    Implements IConvertible.ToString
```

```
214:
215:    Return String.Format("{0},{1},{2}", _
216:       FCenter.X, FCenter.Y, FRadius.ToString())
217:
218: End Function
219:
220: Public Function ToType( _
221:    ByVal conversionType As Type, _
222:    ByVal provider As IFormatProvider) As Object _
223:    Implements IConvertible.ToType
224:
225:    If (conversionType Is GetType(String)) Then
226:       Return Me.GetType
227:    Else
228:       ThrowException(String.Format( _
229:          "conversion to {0} not 229: supported", _
230:          conversionType.ToString))
231:    End If
232:
233: End Function
234:
235:
236: Private Sub ThrowException(ByVal message As String)
237:    Throw New InvalidCastException(message)
238: End Sub
239:
240: End Structure
```

The listing is quite long for a book but is included in its entirety for completeness. A circle is defined by a center point and radius. I included methods to calculate the area and diameter and included the `Implements IConvertible` statement (line 5) to indicate that `Circle` implements, or realizes, the `IConvertible` interface.

All the methods in Listing 9.13 are self-explanatory. It is important to note that only conversions that made sense were actually implemented to perform a conversion. Conversions that don't make sense—like `ToDate-Time`—simply throw an exception. For the `Circle` structure it only made sense to implement `GetTypeCode`, `ToType`, and `ToString`. You will find practical implementations for these three methods; every other `IConvert-ible` method throws an exception. It is up to the consumer to trap exceptions when attempting a type conversion.

GetTypeCode (lines 93 through 96) returns the enumerated TypeCode value that defines the common type system type. ToType (lines 220 through 233) returns the Type object for supported conversion types. The Circle structure can be converted to a string representation, so the Type object for String is returned (lines 225 and 226) or an exception is thrown (lines 228 to 230) based on the conversionType argument. Finally, ToString (lines 211 through 218) actually performs the conversion to suitable, comma-delimited string representation of a circle.

Implementing a Type Converter

TypeConverter is a class that supports both design time and runtime type conversion. This class is especially useful with classes that need to be represented at design time in places like the Properties window. For our example, assuming a control had a circle property, it would be impractical to render the circle in the small field in the Properties window. However, the center point and radius numbers could easily be displayed. To support this practical conversion behavior, Listing 9.14 demonstrates a type converter for our Circle structure.

Listing 9.14 Implementing a Custom Type Converter for the Circle Structure

```
1:   Imports System.ComponentModel
2:   Imports System.Text.RegularExpressions
3:   Imports System.Globalization
4:
5:   Public Class CircleConverter
6:      Inherits TypeConverter
7:
8:      Private Const Pattern As String = _
9:         "^\d+,\d+,((\d+)|(\d+.\d+))$"
10:
11:     Public Overloads Overrides Function CanConvertFrom( _
12:        ByVal context As ITypeDescriptorContext, _
13:        ByVal sourceType As Type) As Boolean
14:
15:        Return sourceType Is GetType(Rectangle) Or _
16:           sourceType Is GetType(RectangleF) Or _
17:           sourceType Is GetType(String) Or _
18:           MyBase.CanConvertFrom(context, sourceType)
19:
```

```
20:    End Function
21:
22:    Private Function IsValidString( _
23:      ByVal Value As Object) As Boolean
24:
25:      Return Value.GetType Is GetType(String) _
26:        AndAlso Regex.IsMatch(CType(Value, String), _
27:          Pattern)
28:
29:    End Function
30:
31:    Public Overloads Overrides Function ConvertFrom( _
32:      ByVal context As ITypeDescriptorContext, _
33:      ByVal info As CultureInfo, _
34:      ByVal Value As Object) As Object
35:
36:      If (CanConvertFrom(Value.GetType)) Then
37:
38:        If (IsValidString(Value)) Then
39:
40:          Dim s() As String = _
41:            CType(Value, String).Split(New Char() {","})
42:
43:          Return New Circle(Convert.ToInt32(s(0)), _
44:            Convert.ToInt32(s(1)), Convert.ToSingle(s(1)))
45:
46:        ElseIf (Value.GetType Is GetType(Rectangle)) Then
47:
48:          Dim R As Rectangle = CType(Value, Rectangle)
49:          Return New Circle(R.X + R.Width \ 2, _
50:            R.Y + R.Height \ 2, R.Width \ 2 + R.Height \ 2)
51:
52:        ElseIf (Value.GetType Is GetType(RectangleF)) Then
53:
54:          Dim R As RectangleF = CType(Value, RectangleF)
55:          Return New Circle(R.X + R.Width \ 2, _
56:            R.Y + R.Height \ 2, R.Width \ 2 + R.Height \ 2)
57:        Else
58:          Return MyBase.ConvertFrom(context, info, Value)
59:        End If
60:
61:      End If
62:
63:      Return MyBase.ConvertFrom(context, info, Value)
```

```
64:    End Function
65:
66:
67:    Public Overloads Overrides Function CanConvertTo( _
68:      ByVal context As ITypeDescriptorContext, _
69:      ByVal destinationType As Type) As Boolean
70:
71:      Return destinationType Is GetType(Rectangle) Or _
72:        destinationType Is GetType(RectangleF) Or _
73:        destinationType Is GetType(String) Or _
74:        MyBase.CanConvertTo(context, destinationType)
75:
76:    End Function
77:
78:    Public Overridable Overloads Function ConvertTo( _
79:      ByVal context As ITypeDescriptorContext, _
80:      ByVal culture As CultureInfo, _
81:      ByVal value As Object, _
82:      ByVal destinationType As Type _
83:      ) As Object
84:
85:      If (CanConvertTo(destinationType)) Then
86:        If (destinationType Is GetType(Rectangle)) Then
87:          Return CType(value, Circle).ToBoundingRectangle
88:        ElseIf (destinationType Is GetType(RectangleF)) Then
89:          Return CType(value, Circle).ToBoundingRectangleF
90:        ElseIf (destinationType Is GetType(String)) Then
91:          Return CType(value, Circle).ToString()
92:        End If
93:      Else
94:        Return MyBase.ConvertTo(context, culture, _
95:          value, destinationType)
96:      End If
97:
98:    End Function
99:
100: End Class
```

To implement the `TypeConverter` class we need to inherit from `System.ComponentModel.TypeConverter` and override the behavior of four inherited methods: `CanConvertFrom`, `ConvertFrom`, `CanConvertTo`, and `ConvertTo`. The names of these methods imply the forward and backward nature of a type converter. CanConvertFrom answers the question, "Which types can I convert to my type?" ConvertFrom performs the conversion from some other type to my type. CanConvertTo answers the question, "Which types can my type convert to?" ConvertTo actually performs the conversion to the request type.

As you might imagine, this involves a significant amount of type checking. We must examine the type to convert to or from and answer the question of suitability. For example, lines 11 through 20 in Listing 9.14 indicate that CircleConverter can create a Circle (that is, convert from any of the test types to a Circle) from a Rectangle, RectangleF, String, or any type the base class can convert from. The Rectangle integer can be used as a bounding rectangle, and the approximate dimensions of a circle can be derived from a bounding rectangle. The RectangleF structure is a rectangle with floating-point corners and can be used to approximate a circle in the same way that a Rectangle integer can be used. Finally, a String type that contains three numbers representing the center and radius could be used to derive a circle. The ITypeDescriptorContext interface can be used to determine the context (think "containing thing") in which the conversion is being requested. You can include a condition in which a conversion is not supported for a particular context.

The ConvertFrom method (lines 31 through 64) is probably the most challenging method to implement. We have to write code that will convert from any particular type that we support to values sufficient to create an instance of our type. Because we support rectangles and strings, we need to write code that converts a rectangle or string to arguments suitable for a circle. For example, lines 36 through 44 determine whether the Value argument is an instance of a type we want to convert from. Line 38 checks to see whether Value is a string in the correct format. We defined the format, so we know it and can test for it in advance, using a regular expression to test the format and the String.Split method to actually subdivide the string. There are two points of interest here. First, we could have performed both the pattern check and the split with a regular expression. Second, we might want to add some error code rather than assuming there are three strings in the array and that those strings can be converted to the indicated type (lines 43 and 44). The two ElseIf conditions convert Rectangle types to Circle types, and the final Else condition invokes the base class behavior.

CanConvertTo and ConvertTo perform the analogous inverse conversion operations and are a bit simpler in our case. For example, converting from a Circle type to a Rectangle type is relatively easy because this behavior is supported in the Circle structure itself.

NOTE: Before you create a new converter, check the .NET Framework to determine whether a converter already exists. Check the TypeConverter Hierarchy help topic for a comprehensive list of converters. There are about three dozen listed in the Visual Studio .NET help documentation.

Associating a Type Converter with a Convertible Type

Next we need to tell the `Circle` structure and everybody else about the `CircleConverter` class. As you might have guessed, we use attributes to form the association between `TypeConverter` and `Circle`.

Use the `TypeConverterAttribute` to associate a custom type converter with the class that supports type conversion. Pass the Type `object` or the fully qualified name of the custom type converter to the `TypeConverterAttribute`. Line 3 of Listing 9.13 shows the `TypeConverterAttribute` applied with the `Type` object (returned by `GetType`) of the custom type converter, `CircleConverter`.

Using the `IConvertible` Behavior

You can download the `ConversionDemo.sln` program to test the implementation of `IConvertible` and `CircleConverter`. To invoke `IConvertible` methods, call `System.Convert`, passing an instance of a `Circle` object to the `Convert` class's shared methods. Listing 9.15 shows three event handlers that indirectly invoke methods in the `Circle` structure and attempt type conversions using the `IConvertible` interface.

Listing 9.15 Performing Runtime Type Conversion

```
Private Sub Button1_Click(ByVal sender As System.Object, _
  ByVal e As System.EventArgs) Handles Button1.Click
  TextBox1.Text = Convert.ToString(Circle)
End Sub

Private Sub Button2_Click(ByVal sender As System.Object, _
  ByVal e As System.EventArgs) Handles Button2.Click
  TextBox2.Text = Convert.GetTypeCode(Circle).ToString()
End Sub

Private Sub Button3_Click(ByVal sender As System.Object, _
  ByVal e As System.EventArgs) Handles Button3.Click
```

```
    TextBox3.Text = Convert.ToDecimal(Circle)
End Sub
```

Each conversion is a single line of code that invokes a shared member of the `System.Convert` class. Double-checking with Rotor we can verify (assuming you can read C# code) that the shared conversion methods attempt to convert the target object to an `IConvertible` instance and invoke the implementation of the like method on the object itself. For example, our `Circle` object will be typecast to an `IConvertible` instance, and `Convert.ToString` will invoke the equivalent of `CType(Circle, IConvertible).ToBoolean(Nothing)`, where `Nothing` is a null `IFormatProvider`. The shared `Convert` methods are overloaded. If you pass an `IFormatProvider` to `ToBoolean`, the provider will be passed on to the interface method instead of the literal `Nothing`. (The .NET Framework is implemented in C#; thus `null` is actually passed and the methods are declared `static`. `Null` and `static` are equivalent to VB's `Nothing` and `Shared`, respectively.)

`IFormatProviders` are objects that provide formatting instructions for conversions. Existing `IFormatProviders` include `CultureInfo`, `DateTimeFormatInfo`, and `NumberFormatInfo`. You can create a custom `IFormatProvider` for your types too. For example, we could implement `CircleFormatInfo` to describe relevant string representations of a circle. (Try this as an exercise.)

Using the Type Conversion Behavior

Type conversion can occur at design time or runtime. At design time it may be invoked by the IDE when an object needs to be displayed in the Properties window, for example, and we can perform explicit type conversion at runtime. Listing 9.16 demonstrates how to use the `TypeDescriptor` class to request the type converter for an object; subsequently, that type converter is used to perform the testing and conversion.

Listing 9.16 Performing Type Conversion Programmatically with a Type Descriptor

```
1:  Imports System.ComponentModel
2:
3:  Public Class Form1
4:      Inherits System.Windows.Forms.Form
```

```
5:
6:  [ Windows Form Designer generated code ]
7:
8:    Private Sub Button1_Click(ByVal sender As System.Object, _
9:      ByVal e As System.EventArgs) Handles Button1.Click
10:     TextBox1.Text = Convert.ToString(Circle)
11:   End Sub
12:
13:   Private Circle As Circle
14:
15:   Private Sub Form1_Paint(ByVal sender As Object, _
16:     ByVal e As System.Windows.Forms.PaintEventArgs) _
17:     Handles MyBase.Paint
18:
19:     e.Graphics.DrawEllipse(Pens.Red, _
20:       Circle.ToBoundingRectangle)
21:   End Sub
22:
23:   Private Sub Button2_Click(ByVal sender As System.Object, _
24:     ByVal e As System.EventArgs) Handles Button2.Click
25:     TextBox2.Text = Convert.GetTypeCode(Circle).ToString()
26:   End Sub
27:
28:   Private Sub Button3_Click(ByVal sender As System.Object, _
29:     ByVal e As System.EventArgs) Handles Button3.Click
30:     TextBox3.Text = Convert.ToDecimal(Circle)
31:   End Sub
32:
33:   Private Sub Form1_Load(ByVal sender As System.Object, _
34:     ByVal e As System.EventArgs) Handles MyBase.Load
35:
36:     Circle = New Circle(New Point(Me.Width \ 2, _
37:       Me.Height \ 2), Height \ 3)
38:   End Sub
39:
40:   Private Sub MenuItem4_Click(ByVal sender As System.Object, _
41:     ByVal e As System.EventArgs) Handles MenuItem4.Click
42:
43:     Dim About As String = _
44:       "IConvertible and TypeConverter Demo" & vbCrLf & _
45:      "Copyright " & Chr(169) & " 2002. All Rights Reserved." & _
46:       vbCrLf & _
47:       "By Paul Kimmel. pkimmel@softconcepts.com"
48:
```

```
49:      MessageBox.Show(About, "About", MessageBoxButtons.OK, _
50:         MessageBoxIcon.Information)
51:   End Sub
52:
53:   Private Sub MenuItem2_Click(ByVal sender As System.Object, _
54:     ByVal e As System.EventArgs) Handles MenuItem2.Click
55:
56:     Close()
57:
58:   End Sub
59:
60:   Private Sub MenuItem6_Click(ByVal sender As System.Object, _
61:     ByVal e As System.EventArgs) Handles MenuItem6.Click
62:
63:     Dim R = New Rectangle(100, 200, 75, 75)
64:     If (TypeDescriptor.GetConverter(GetType(Circle)). _
65:       CanConvertFrom(GetType(Rectangle))) Then
66:
67:       Circle = TypeDescriptor.GetConverter(GetType(Circle)). _
68:         ConvertFrom(R)
69:     End If
70:     Invalidate()
71:   End Sub
72:
73:   Private Sub MenuItem8_Click(ByVal sender As System.Object, _
74:     ByVal e As System.EventArgs) Handles MenuItem8.Click
75:
76:     Dim R = New RectangleF(150.5, 190.8, 33.7, 75.1)
77:     If (TypeDescriptor.GetConverter(GetType(Circle)). _
78:       CanConvertFrom(GetType(RectangleF))) Then
79:
80:       Circle = TypeDescriptor.GetConverter(GetType(Circle)). _
81:         ConvertFrom(R)
82:     End If
83:     Invalidate()
84:   End Sub
85:
86:   Private Sub MenuItem7_Click(ByVal sender As System.Object, _
87:     ByVal e As System.EventArgs) Handles MenuItem7.Click
88:
89:     Dim C As String = "200,200,160"
90:     If (TypeDescriptor.GetConverter(GetType(Circle)). _
91:       CanConvertFrom(GetType(String))) Then
92:
```

```
93:            Circle = TypeDescriptor.GetConverter(GetType(Circle)). _
94:              ConvertFrom(C)
95:         End If
96:         Invalidate()
97:
98:     End Sub
99: End Class
```

Listing 9.16 contains the code for the main form in `Conversion-Demo.sln`. (You can see the repeated code from Listing 9.15, too.) Three menu items are similar in nature in lines 60 through 98. The code declares some type—for example, a string in line 89—that is an alternate representation of a circle. Following the representative type we use the `TypeDescriptor.GetConverter` shared method and Reflection implicitly to get the type converter for a type (lines 93 and 94) and invoke one of the test operations. In lines 90 and 91 we get the type converter for the `Circle` structure and ask whether a circle can be created from a given string. If the test succeeds, the related conversion method is invoked, again using the type converter. Lines 93 and 94 get the `CircleConverter` and convert the string `C` to an instance of the private field `Circle`.

Finally, the `Invalidate` method causes the form to be repainted, and the paint event handler (lines 15 through 21) draws the circle on the test form.

TIP: If you use the `Option Strict On` directive, you will need to perform explicit type casts using `CType` to convert the generic return type of `ConvertFrom` and `ConvertTo` to the converted type. (No explicit type casting is shown in Listings 9.15 and 9.16.)

Use almost identical code to determine whether a circle can be converted to an alternate type, invoking the `CanConvertTo` and `ConvertTo` methods and retrieving the converted type from the `ConvertTo` method.

Implementing an Extender Provider

`IExtenderProvider` interfaces provide and extend the behaviors of existing classes. For example, you are probably familiar with the `ToolTip` control. You need to place only one `ToolTip` control on a Windows Form to extend every control on that form (including the form itself) to include a `ToolTip` property. This coordination is created by implementing a class that implements `IExtenderProvider` and applying the `ProvidePropertyAttribute` to that class.

While thinking about a good, practical example for an extender provider, I was searching the Web and was surprised to encounter Phillip Davis's "Extended Interfaces for Toolbars" at *http://www.codeproject.com/ cs/menu/extendedtoolbar.asp*. Davis reminded me that buttons on the Windows Forms toolbar aren't individuated to the extent that each button has its own click event. As a result, programmers have to use some kind of conditional logic in the `ButtonClick` event to determine which button was actually clicked. Clearly this situation should be rectified in future versions of .NET, but for now it is a suitable candidate for using an extender provider.

Borrowing and modifying Davis's solution, the objective is to implement an `IExtenderProvider` interface that permits us to track individual toolbar button `Click` events. Literally we are providing `Click` events to toolbar buttons without inheriting from `ToolBar` and `ToolBarButton`, but rather by extending the controls as they exist. Listing 9.17 demonstrates an implementation of an `IExtenderProvider` interface that allows you to associate a menu item with a toolbar button, borrowing the menu item's `Click` event.

Listing 9.17 Implementing an `IExtenderProvider` Interface

```
1:  Imports System.ComponentModel
2:  Imports System.Drawing
3:  Imports System.Windows.Forms
4:
5:  <ProvideProperty("MenuItem", GetType(ToolBarButton)), _
6:  ToolboxBitmap("..\Chapter 9\ClickProvider\Event1.bmp"), _
7:  Description("Provides a Click event for a ToolBarButton."), _
8:  Category("Events")> _
9:  Public Class ClickEventProvider
10:    Inherits Component
11:    Implements IExtenderProvider
12:
13:    Private hashtable As hashtable = New hashtable()
14:    Private ToolBar As ToolBar = Nothing
15:
16:    Public Function CanExtend( _
17:      ByVal extendee As Object) As Boolean _
18:      Implements IExtenderProvider.CanExtend
19:
```

```
20:      Return TypeOf extendee Is ToolBarButton
21:   End Function
22:
23:   Public Function GetMenuItem( _
24:     ByVal button As ToolBarButton) _
25:     As MenuItem
26:
27:     If (hashtable.Contains(button)) Then
28:        Return CType(hashtable(button), _
29:          MenuItem)
30:     End If
31:
32:     Return Nothing
33:   End Function
34:
35:   Public Sub SetMenuItem( _
36:     ByVal button As ToolBarButton, _
37:     ByVal item As MenuItem)
38:
39:     If (ToolBar Is Nothing) Then
40:        ToolBar = button.Parent
41:        AddHandler button.Parent.ButtonClick, _
42:          AddressOf ToolbarHandler
43:     End If
44:
45:     If (hashtable.Contains(button)) Then
46:        hashtable(button) = item
47:     Else
48:        hashtable.Add(button, item)
49:     End If
50:   End Sub
51:
52:   Private Sub ToolbarHandler(ByVal sender As Object, _
53:     ByVal e As ToolBarButtonClickEventArgs)
54:
55:     If (hashtable.Contains(e.Button)) Then
56:
57:        CType(hashtable(e.Button), _
58:          MenuItem).PerformClick()
59:
60:     End If
61:   End Sub
62:
63: End Class
```

If we want the extender to be accessible from the Toolbox, we can inherit from the `Component` class as demonstrated in line 10. Line 11 shows the `Implements` statement for the `IExtenderProvider` interface.

`IExtenderProvider` requires that you implement `CanExtend`, which answers the question, "Can this `IExtenderProvider` extend a specific type?" The `ClickEventProvider` class returns a Boolean for `CanExtend` by testing the type of the extendee against the `ToolBarButton` type. (If you wanted to implement a general extender like the `ToolTip` provider, you might test the extendee against a more general type like the `Control` class.)

We are extending a class by defining properties in the `IExtenderProvider` interface that will be associated with whatever class we associate this extender with. The `ProvidePropertyAttribute` in line 5 indicates the name of the property to add to the extendee; the second argument indicates that kind of objects that will be extended. Rather than actually implementing a property, we need to implement `Get`*name* and `Set`*name* methods, where *name* is the name we passed as the first argument to the `ProvidePropertyAttribute`. Thus, since we passed `MenuItem` (line 5), we need to implement `GetMenuItem` and `SetMenuItem`; the extendee will be provided with a `MenuItem` by this extender.

`SetMenuItem` (lines 35 through 50) is defined to associate our local `ToolbarHandler` with this extender. `ToolBar` raises a single `Click` event regardless of the button clicked. That `Click` event will occur here. (Keep in mind that events in .NET are multicast, so we can have the `ToolbarHandler` here and other consumers can add their event handlers too.) The second half of `SetMenuItem` uses the specific `ToolBarButton` instance as a key into a local hashtable and assigns the specific `MenuItem` instance to the hashtable index referred to by the button key. The indexing takes into account that the button may have been added once already (see line 45).

`GetMenuItem` (lines 23 through 33) checks whether the internal collection contains the argument `ToolBarButton`. If it does, `MenuItem` is returned. If not, `Nothing` is returned. By using the hashtable and button instances as keys we can associate a distinct `MenuItem` with each `ToolBarButton`.

Finally, `ToolbarHandler` (lines 52 through 61) plays the role of event handler for the toolbar itself. Because the clicked button is passed to `ToolbarHandler`, we normally would use the case or conditional statement in such a handler. In this instance we index the internal hashtable with the clicked button (line 55) and use the returned instance of `MenuItem` to invoke the `PerformClick` method (lines 57 and 58).

Unfortunately this solution to the `ToolBarButton` `Click` event problem is not wholly satisfactory, although Davis's conception is clever. The problem is twofold. First, the `ToolBarButton` should expose events relevant to a button, and second, the implementation in Listing 9.17 requires that there be a `MenuItem` for every `ToolBarButton`. However, we know from experience that there is seldom a one-to-one mapping between `ToolBarButton` instances and `MenuItem` instances.

Let's set aside the obvious chicanery of creating menu items that are invisible and disabled to support our implementation. We want and deserve tools that mitigate the need for such machinations, and the limited number and completeness of controls is something that needs to be addressed. There is at least one alternate solution. We could implement the extender provider to implement an actual `Click` event. Instead of tracking menu item and button associations, we could track toolbar buttons and event handlers. Intuitively this makes more sense. The difficulty here is that we cannot perform event handler assignments in the Properties window for Visual Basic .NET (although we can in C#). If we elected to implement the `IExtenderProvider` using event handlers, we would need to call the `Set`*name* and `Get`*name* methods directly, as shown below.

```
ClickEventProvider1.SetClick(ToolBarButton1, _
    AddressOf MenuItem2_Click)
```

This too clearly highlights the presence of `IExtenderProvider` and is less intuitive and convenient than simply modifying a property. An alternate `ClickEventProvider` can be found in the `ExtenderProviderDemo.sln` file. Both the menu item and the event handler implementations are available for download.

Creating a Windows Control Designer

When you modify control properties for visual controls, the control is generally updated immediately and you have an idea of the effect of your changes. However, what do you do if you want to experiment with several potentially complex changes or your changes will be evident only when code runs? You create a designer—that's what you do.

The .NET Framework introduces the `IDesigner` interface. From this interface a generic `ComponentDesigner` class was defined, and from the `ComponentDesigner` class a `ControlDesigner` class was defined. Basically, a designer is a class that allows you to associate a verb and behavior with a component or control. A verb (an action that will be displayed as a context menu item) is represented as text associated with an event handler you define. The Visual Studio .NET IDE knows how to read verbs from the `IDesigner` interface, display the verbs, and invoke the related event handler when the verb (context menu item) is clicked. Of course, once you hit the event handler, you are running code and the sky is the limit.

To demonstrate, I added a `RegexDesigner` to `CustomControls.vbproj`. The `RegexDesigner` provides us with a facility for testing a regular expression in the IDE, using the designer, without needing to compile and run the code using the `RegexTextBox`. The IDE tests the regular expression first, saving a compile and test cycle. In a big application a designer like the `RegexDesigner` can save a lot of time. Listing 9.18 provides the source code for the `RegexDesigner`.

Listing 9.18 Implementing a `ControlDesigner` Class with Two Verbs

```
1:  Imports System.Windows.Forms
2:  Imports System.Windows.Forms.Design
3:  Imports System.ComponentModel.Design
4:
5:  Public Class RegexDesigner
6:     Inherits ControlDesigner
7:
8:     Public Overrides ReadOnly Property Verbs() _
9:       As DesignerVerbCollection
10:    Get
11:      Return New DesignerVerbCollection( _
12:        New DesignerVerb() { _
13:          New DesignerVerb("About", _
14:            AddressOf AboutHandler), _
15:          New DesignerVerb("Test Expression", _
16:            AddressOf TestExpressionHandler)})
17:    End Get
18:    End Property
19:
20:    Private Sub AboutHandler(ByVal sender As Object, _
21:      ByVal e As System.EventArgs)
22:
23:      Dim About As String = _
24:        "Regex ControlDesigner" & vbCrLf & _
25:        "Copyright " & Chr(169) & " 2002. " & _
26:        "All Rights Reserved." & vbCrLf & _
27:        "By Paul Kimmel. pkimmel@softconcepts.com"
```

```
28:
29:       MessageBox.Show(About, "About", _
30:         MessageBoxButtons.OK, MessageBoxIcon.Information)
31:
32:    End Sub
33:
34:    Private ReadOnly Property TextBox() As RegexTextBox
35:    Get
36:      Return CType(Me.Control, RegexTextBox)
37:    End Get
38:    End Property
39:
40:    Private Property Pattern() As String
41:    Get
42:      Return TextBox.Pattern
43:    End Get
44:    Set(ByVal Value As String)
45:      TextBox.Pattern = Value
46:    End Set
47:    End Property
48:
49:    Private Property InputString() As String
50:    Get
51:      Return TextBox.Text
52:    End Get
53:    Set(ByVal Value As String)
54:      TextBox.Text = Value
55:    End Set
56:    End Property
57:
58:    Private Sub TestExpressionHandler( _
59:      ByVal sender As Object, _
60:      ByVal e As System.EventArgs)
61:
62:      Dim APattern As String = Pattern
63:
64:      If (FormRegexTester.ShowDialog( _
65:        APattern, InputString)) Then
66:        Pattern = APattern
67:      End If
68:
69:    End Sub
70:
71: End Class
```

Because the `ControlDesigner` class does a lot of the leg work of implementing the basic behaviors of `IDesigner`, we need to implement only the read-only `Verbs` property. `Verbs` returns a `DesignerVerbCollection`, which contains a `DesignerVerb` for each context menu item you want to support (lines 8 through 18). The `Verbs` property in Listing 9.18 defines two verbs: `About` and `Test Expression`. When the About context menu item is clicked, the `AboutHandler` is invoked by the IDE; when the Test Expression context menu item is clicked, the `TestExpressionHandler` is called. Thus when About is clicked in the IDE—we'll talk about associating the designer in a moment—a simple About dialog (as defined by lines 20 through 32) is displayed, and when Test Expression is clicked, the code in lines 58 through 69 is run.

`TestExpressionHandler` displays a custom dialog that facilitates testing the `Pattern` property of the `RegexTextBox` at design time. `FormRegexTester` is a custom dialog form I created with two input fields. One input field (`APattern`) represents the regular expressions and the second (`InputString`) represents a test input string (Figure 9.12). Enter values into each field and click the Test button. If the input string matches the regular expression pattern, the text in the status bar is updated to reflect a valid pattern-input string pair. Click OK to store the changes back into the component, or click Cancel to dump the changes.

Applying the Designer to the Control

The `ControlDesigner` and `ComponentDesigner` classes provide you with an easy-to-implement advanced way to visually design a control or component. In our example we implemented a regular expression tester. To associate this tester with a specific control, add the `DesignerAttribute` to the control class. The application of the `DesignerAttribute` is shown in Listing 9.19, a modification of an excerpt from Listing 9.3.

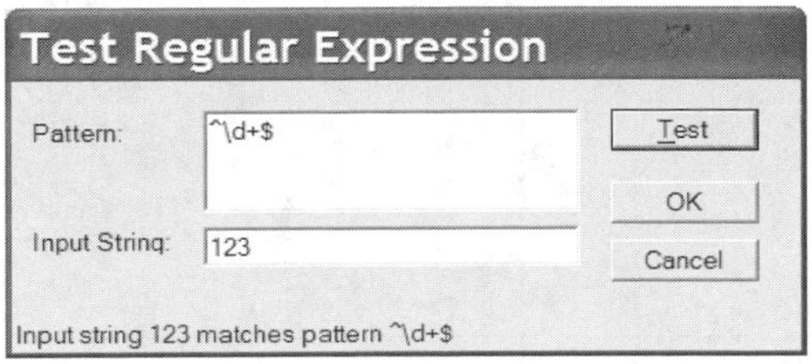

Figure 9.12 The regular expression test form for the `RegexDesigner`.

Listing 9.19 Using the `DesignerAttribute` to Associate a Control Designer with a Control

```
Imports System.ComponentModel
Imports System.Text.RegularExpressions
Imports System.Windows.Forms
Imports System.Drawing

<Designer(GetType(RegexDesigner))> _
Public Class RegexTextBox
  Inherits TextBox

  Private FPattern As String
. . .
```

After we compile and add our control along with the designer to the Toolbox, we should see the new verbs displayed in every instance of the control's context menu.

Testing the Control Designer

In order to test a control designer we need to associate it with the control and add the bunch to the Toolbox. Drag and drop an instance of the control to a form and right-click on the control. If everything is working correctly, you will see the verbs reflected as context menu items (Figure 9.13). Click

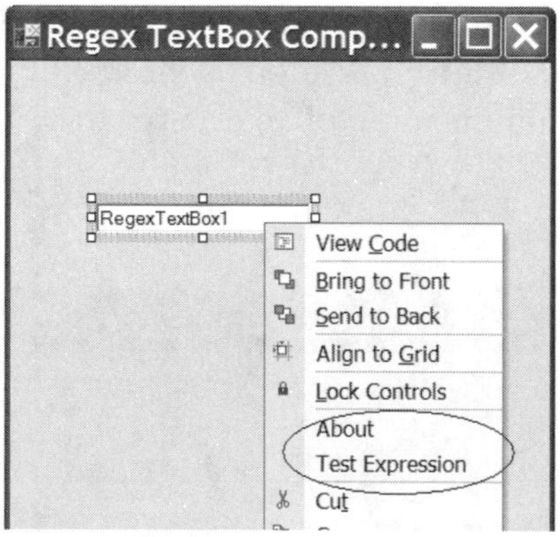

Figure 9.13 The `About` and `Test Expression` verbs reflected in an instance of the RegexTextBox's control designer, `RegexDesigner`.

any verb to invoke that operation. For example, to display the regular expression test dialog shown in Figure 9.12, click the Test Expression context menu item shown in Figure 9.13.

You have the option of implementing an `IDesigner` interface from scratch. However, it is easier to inherit from the ComponentDesigner or ControlDesigner classes as a way to save yourself some labor. It is worth noting that the `ControlDesigner` classes for Windows Forms and Web Pages are a bit different, branching at `HtmlControlDesigner` for Web Pages. With a bit of experimentation you shouldn't find it too difficult to make a `ControlDesigner` class for Web Controls.

Using Default Properties

Visual Basic 6 supported a wide variety of properties as default properties. This worked because we were required to use `Let`, `Get`, and `Set` when performing read and write operations against an object in VB6. However, `Let`, `Get`, and `Set` are not required or supported for VB .NET, so the compiler no longer has that codified cue. As a result a new cue was needed to differentiate a default property from an object assignment. The decision was made to support default properties only for properties that defined an indexer. The indexer is not require to be an integer, but the property must have an argument for us to use the `Default` keyword.

An example of a class with a default property is a class that has an `Item` property. `Item` properties are often indexed by integer values; hence it is the very presence of the indexer—as in `Foo(i)`—that differentiates an assignment to or from `Foo` and access of some indexed property of `Foo`. Listing 9.20 demonstrates two default properties for a strongly typed collection of `Customer` objects.

Listing 9.20 Two Default Properties of a Strongly Typed Collection

```
Default Public Property Item( _
  ByVal index As Integer) As Customer
Get
  Return CType(List(index), Customer)
End Get
Set(ByVal Value As Customer)
  List(index) = Value
End Set
```

```
End Property

Default Public Property Item( _
  ByVal Key As String) As Customer
Get
  Return List(IndexOf(Key))
End Get
Set(ByVal Value As Customer)
  List(IndexOf(Key)) = Value
End Set
End Property
```

The two default properties are part of a typed collection that inherits from `System.Collections.CollectionBase`. These two properties permit indexing of elements of the collection by an integer or string. You can download and explore `DefaultDemo.sln` for the complete listing.

There is a second context for default properties: the `DefaultPropertyAttribute`. This attribute indicates which property is the focus in the Properties window by default. Simply associate the `DefaultPropertyAttribute`, passing the name of the property as a string to the `DefaultPropertyAttribute`, with the control for which you want to define a default (or initial) property.

Because the literal verbiage is almost identical, it is important to establish whether you are conferring about an indexer—`Default Property`—or the initial property to edit—`DefaultPropertyAttribute`—when talking about default properties.

Implementing Custom Web Controls and Custom Web User Controls

Sadly, all chapters must draw to an end, even though this one seems to be interminable. I have enjoyed writing it and think I could write a whole book on component building—but there is much to do yet beyond component building. The question is how to bow out from this topic gracefully?

You are reading a book that suggests as a prerequisite a thorough understanding of object-oriented (OO) principles. Even if you haven't mastered

OO principles prior to reading this book, you should have a good understanding of them after reading Chapter 9. I will try to offer some concise, sage wisdom on Web controls in the short space of a few paragraphs.

If you need a composite control, you want to implement a Web user control. A good resource for Web user controls is the IBUYSPY portal source code available from Microsoft for free. As a second resort you may elect to inherit from an existing Web control. Finally, your last resort should be to inherit from `System.Web.UI.Control` and build a custom Web control from scratch.

Probably the most important method when defining a custom Web control is the `Render` method, which receives an `HtmlTextWriter` object. You need to literally send HTML to the rendering page to define the custom control. Fortunately `HtmlTextWriter` contains several shared public fields and instance methods that facilitate rendering HTML using words rather than coarse HTML literal values. This helps significantly.

From my own experience and from conversations with Susan Warren at Microsoft I can tell you that it is a good idea to build composite controls with user controls because it is the easiest choice. If you do need to build a control from scratch, you will need to have a considerable understanding of HTML, caching, and the event model for ASP.NET Web pages. Sadly, again, this exceeds the charter of this book. If that is an area of great interest to you, I encourage you to pick up a copy of *Developing Custom Controls for ASP.NET* by Donny Mack and Doug Seven [2003].

Summary

I thoroughly enjoy writing about and building components because these satisfying packages offer a big payoff with almost immediate results. Several authors—including Ray Konopka, Danny Thorpe, and Ray Lischner—seem to have specialized in writing books specifically about components. Unfortunately, these excellent books have focused on building components only for Delphi, as far as I can tell.

Chapter 9, although one of the longest chapters in this book, serves as just an introduction to topics related to creating custom components and controls for Windows and the Web. Much more could be written about designers, extenders, control data binding, component and control attributes, Toolbox presentation, component serialization, type editors, converters, format providers, and type descriptors. If you are interested in learning more about authoring components in VB .NET, I encourage you to write to my editor, Sondra Scott, at Addison-Wesley. Authors want readers for their books and will generally write about what their audiences want to read. Sending me an e-mail at *pkimmel@softconcepts.com* will help me learn about your interests, but the publishers and editors ultimately decide which books get published—so let them know what you want.

CHAPTER 10

Auto-Updating Smart Clients in .NET

Pretty is its own currency.

—*Jackson Wayfare*

Introduction

In "Death of the Browser?" published in *MSDN Magazine* online, Billy Hollis writes tongue-in-cheek about the imminent demise of HTML, script, and ASP browser-based applications. Hollis talks candidly about beleaguered browsers being overtaxed in an effort to create rich client applications.

We know that Windows has been a capable platform for creating rich client experiences since early versions of Visual Basic. We also know that deploying a Windows application is not nearly as easy as point-and-click browsing to Web applications. Historically, if you needed rich clients, you wrote Windows applications, and if you needed almost zero deployment and broader distribution, you implemented Web applications. With .NET the chasm between these approaches is narrowing.

.NET supports copy-and-paste deployment for Windows applications. Copy-and-paste deployment works because the extra information needed to run .NET applications (called *assemblies*) is carried around as metadata with the assembly. In conjunction with turbo-charged Run Time Type Information (Reflection) you can download assemblies over a network seamlessly in the background.

In this process a client starts with a very tiny application loader. The application loader refers to one or more assemblies using a URL. If the assembly does not exist on the client machine, it is downloaded. If the assembly exists on the client machine, the file date and time of the assembly on the client is compared to the file date and time of the assembly stored on the server. If the assembly on the server is newer, it is downloaded automatically. If the cached version is up-to-date, the cached version is used. This all occurs seamlessly without user intervention, prompts, verification dialog boxes, or anything; it just works. The result is automatic updating of applications with the ease of deployment of the Internet and a rich client experience.

There aren't enough of these thin, or smart, client applications for general expertise or wide acceptance, but some examples work beautifully. A fun example is the peer-to-peer application Terrarium, which uses an application updater to ensure that all peer clients are running the same version. The application updater works quite well in Terrarium, and my initial forays into thin client, auto-updating applications are encouraging.

NOTE: Terrarium is a peer-to-peer networked game. Programmers write plants and animals—including herbivores and carnivores—that compete for resources. If there are too many carnivores, they eat all the herbivores and die off; too many herbivores, they eat all the plants and die off. The goal is to create a competitive critter that outlasts all the others or to define a harmonious ecosystem that reaches a degree of homeostasis. The game offers several benefits: It is an engaging way to learn .NET programming, it demonstrates some of the cool features and capabilities of .NET, and it is a lot of fun to play.

In this chapter I tell you much of what is known to date about thin client, automatically updating Windows applications. Perhaps some of you will know a bit more, and I encourage you to contribute those experiences on your favorite forum. It is very likely that we will see a convergence of technologies so that programming for the Web and for Windows will be the same, resulting in rich clients as well as easy and broad deployment for all applications.

To begin we will take a look at a basic thin client application that deploys over the Web, and then we will tackle obstacles you are likely to encounter, including security management and deployment of COM components.

Implementing a Hello, World! Thin Client

A good first start for any application is the easiest to implement. They don't get any easier than the Hello, World! sample application tradition started by Brian Kernighan and Dennis Ritchie of C fame. Our sample application starts with a simple form with a single button. Clicking the button downloads a class library and executes the code. This all occurs with no intercession on the part of the user (apart from the button click).

NOTE: To try a .NET application downloaded from the Internet, navigate to *http://www.sellsbrothers.com/wahoo/wahoo.exe*. Wahoo! is very similar to the game Tetris. If you liked Tetris, you'll like Wahoo! More importantly, it is an engaging way to introduce smart client applications to nontechnical managers who may be skeptical.

To get started with as few obstacles as possible, let's assume that both the initial client and the downloaded extension will be run on the same workstation. However, the workstation is running Internet Information Services (IIS) and the class library is being served by that instance of IIS. The biggest obstacle for thin client updates is .NET security permissions. We'll cover those later in the chapter.

Building our thin client application requires a Windows Forms application and a second DLL in a Web shared directory. The ingredients we'll use have been introduced in several places throughout the book. To summarize, these include Reflection, an activator, an assembly, an object's type information, the .NET Framework, and a class library. Listing 10.1 contains the code for the thin client Windows Forms application.

Listing 10.1 The Thin Client Windows Forms Application

```
1:   Imports System.Reflection
2:
3:   Public Class Form1
4:       Inherits System.Windows.Forms.Form
5:
6:   [ Windows Form Designer generated code ]
7:
8:     Private Sub Button1_Click( _
9:       ByVal sender As System.Object, _
10:      ByVal e As System.EventArgs) Handles Button1.Click
11:
12:      Dim AnAssembly As [Assembly] = _
13:        [Assembly].LoadFrom( _
14:        "http://localhost/AutoUpdated/bin/AutomaticallyUpdated.dll")
15:
16:      Dim MyType As Type = _
```

```
17:      AnAssembly.GetType("AutomaticallyUpdated.AutoUpdated")
18:    Dim Instance As Object = Activator.CreateInstance(MyType)
19:
20:  End Sub
21: End Class
```

This straightforward code is consistent with code you are likely to find in even advanced thin client, smart updating Windows Forms applications. We need to import the `System.Reflection` namespace for its capabilities that support dynamic type discovery.

Lines 12 through 14 represent the smart update behavior. First we declare and initialize an `Assembly` object. `Assembly` is the name of a class and a reserved word. The reserved word doesn't do anything yet, but we need to indicate we mean the class rather than the reserved word by adding the brackets around the word `Assembly`. (Place any reserved words used in code as variables in brackets.) Lines 13 and 14 download a copy of the assembly we referred to by the URL if the assembly is not already in the browser's application cache. If the assembly is already in the cache, the file date and time, not the assembly version, is used by the browser to determine whether an updated assembly is needed. If the file date and time of the assembly on the server has a more recent date, the newer assembly is downloaded; otherwise the assembly from the cache is used.

From the assembly we can use Reflection to obtain the type information for a named object. This happens in line 17. Notice that the namespace and the class name is used in the `GetType` method. With the type information we can use several techniques to create an instance of the type. The example uses `Activator.CreateInstance` (line 18). `CreateInstance` is roughly analogous to the Application Programmer's Interface (API) method `CreateObject` used to create COM objects in pre-.NET applications.

The code in Listing 10.1 loads an assembly, gets the type information for a class, and constructs an instance of the class. That's enough for now. Listing 10.2 contains the code for the downloaded assembly.

Listing 10.2 A Simple Class Library for an Automatically Updating Smart Client

```
Imports System.Windows.Forms

Public Class AutoUpdated

  Public Sub New()
```

```
    MessageBox.Show("Hello Thin Client World!")
  End Sub

End Class
```

When an instance of `AutoUpdated` is created, a message box is shown. This is why we need to create only the instance in Listing 10.1 to see the dialog box. When we build industrial-strength smart client applications, we need to access all the members of the clients updated over a network. We will come back to this feature in a moment.

In order to update the client using the `http://` moniker we can create a Web shared directory. The easiest way to create a virtual directory is to use Windows Explorer options. Follow the numbered steps to create a virtual Web directory.

1. Browse to the project folder containing the `AutomaticallyUpdated. dll` project.
2. Right-click on the `AutomaticallyUpdated` folder and select Sharing and Security. Navigate to the Web Sharing tab (Figure 10.1).
3. On the Web Sharing tab, click the Share this folder bullet, then click the Add button. This brings up the Edit Alias dialog (Figure 10.2).
4. Change the Alias input field to `AutoUpdated` (using Figure 10.2 as a guide), set the Access permissions to Read, and set the Application permissions to Scripts.
5. Click OK to save the changes.

After you compile both assemblies in `HelloThinClientWorld.sln`, you will be able to run `HelloThinClientWorld.vbproj`, clicking the button to download and execute the code in the `AutomaticallyUpdated` folder. This simple example works without much configuration because both the executable and the DLL reside on the same workstation. .NET security permissions are not going to trip us up when the URL is part of the local Intranet. The basic idea is that your own code should be trustworthy.

Smart clients are an excellent choice for private business applications running on an internal network because they offer a rich client experience and you can easily provide smart updating. All you really need is to have the .NET Framework on all your clients. There should be no intellectual argument against this single precursor since having the .NET Framework is no different than having Java classes, other DLLs like the Windows API, and applications and their runtime libraries. (Most applications have supporting DLLs, which is precisely what the framework is.)

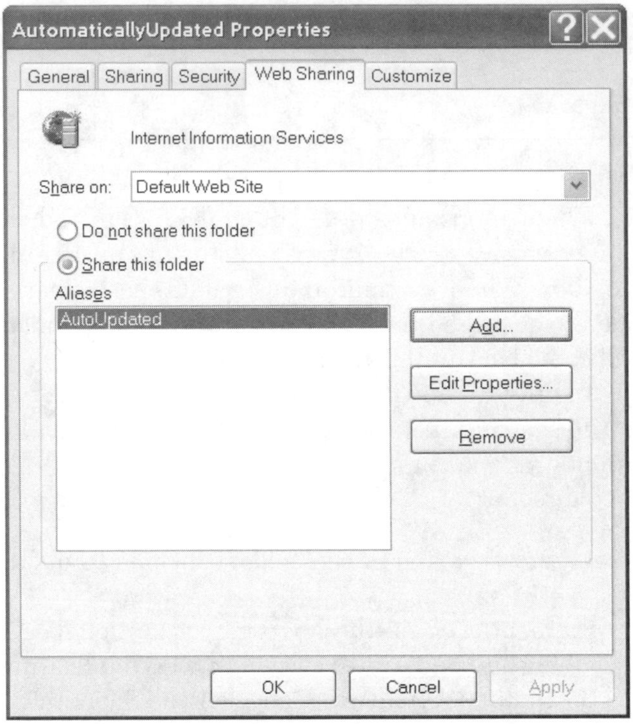

Figure 10.1 The Web Sharing tab.

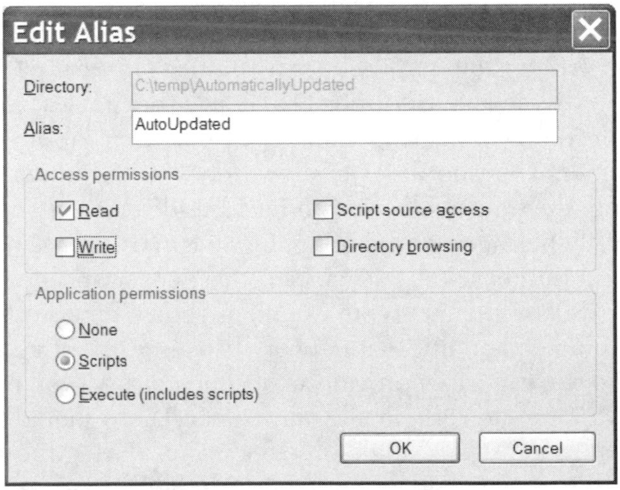

Figure 10.2 The Edit Alias dialog.

Smart clients are also a good choice for commercial applications. The only difference between the implementation of commercial applications and private ones is that you will need to perform some extra configuration if customers will be updating your applications over the Internet. Client workstations may not have the .NET Framework, and default security permissions are much more rigorous for applications downloaded from the Internet. We will cover client and server precursors for smart client applications next.

Configuring Smart Client and Server Precursors

If clients will be allowing smart updates from an external Internet site, those clients will need to be configured correctly to support downloading executable .NET assemblies. This section describes a manual process for configuring those clients. (Because manually configuring a large number of clients may not be practicable—and customers may not want to bother themselves—we will talk about automating the security policy information in the Creating a Microsoft Installer File to Manage Security Policies section later in this chapter.

As an overview, here are the summarized precursors for client workstations to support smart updates. Clients will need:

- A connection to the Internet
- The .NET Framework installed
- Your site added to the browser's list of trusted sites
- The security policy adjusted to trust your application's assemblies

Let's take a moment to look at the implications of each of these precursors and review the steps necessary to support smart updates on the client.

Connecting to the Internet

Connecting to the Internet sounds simple, but there are some specific implications relative to smart client updates. The first fact you should know is that .NET assemblies tend to be quite small because a lot of the functionality exists in the framework. This means quite complex applications will have relatively small, binary assemblies. The benefit is that even relatively slow dial-up connections should be able to download new clients. On the other hand, if the client workstation is not connected, a direct `Assembly.Load-From` method will fail even if the assembly has already been cached. You will get a `FileNotFoundException` on the client because either the file can't be found on the server or the file on the client cannot be compared to the file on the server—both because there is no Internet connection. To work in offline mode you will need to devise some strategy that uses a fail-over scheme if the online assembly can't be found.

Installing the .NET Framework

It has been amazing to hear about the resistance some people and companies have to installing the .NET Framework. PCs that run something as small as a Java applet have Java on them. PCs that run applications written in Delphi have some Borland runtimes on them. Visual Basic 6 applications drag along the VB runtime, and every Windows user has tons of disk space taken up in API DLLs and probably Microsoft Office DLLs too. Runtimes, frameworks, and APIs exist to factor out commonality so you are not paying storage costs for the same code over and over. Microsoft's .NET Framework is not significantly different in size than Java's Java Runtime Environment (JRE) or Borland's Visual Control Library. The 20 cents it costs for the 20MB in storage space for the .NET Framework isn't worth mentioning. The benefits you will get from this world-class framework are priceless.

You can download and install the framework from the Microsoft software or obtain a redistributable copy from your Visual Studio .NET distribution disks. I suspect that your next Windows upgrade will include the .NET Framework for obvious reasons, including the likelihood that many Microsoft applications will have been ported to .NET.

Adding to the Trusted Sites List

Having an Internet connection and the .NET Framework are obvious enough. However, if you want customers to be able to download your smart clients, including the application launcher, from the Internet, customers will need to make some adjustments to their browsers.

I run my computer footloose because I would rather restore an image on the very rare occasion I might download something nasty than have restrictions on what I can do while surfing. To ensure your customers can download executables, like your application launcher's assembly, have customers add your Web site to the workstation's list of trusted sites. Clearly customers will have to trust your company and want your product to be motivated to add your company to their trusted sites list. To adjust the browser security, follow these steps.

1. In Internet Explorer, select Tools|Options.
2. In the Tools|Options dialog, select the Security tab and click the Trusted sites icon (Figure 10.3).
3. Click the Sites button and type the URL of the trusted site in the dialog.
4. Click OK when you have added all the sites to which you want to extend trust.

Fun applications to experiment with are the Wahoo! game, available for download at *http://www.sellsbrothers.com/Wahoo/Wahoo.exe*, and the Football game (Figure 10.4), available at *http://www.softconcepts.com/Football/Football.exe*. (The latter is based on the popular Mattel football game from the 1970s. Apparently the game is making a comeback along with all the other retro 1970s memorabilia, and I got one for Christmas. I thought it would be

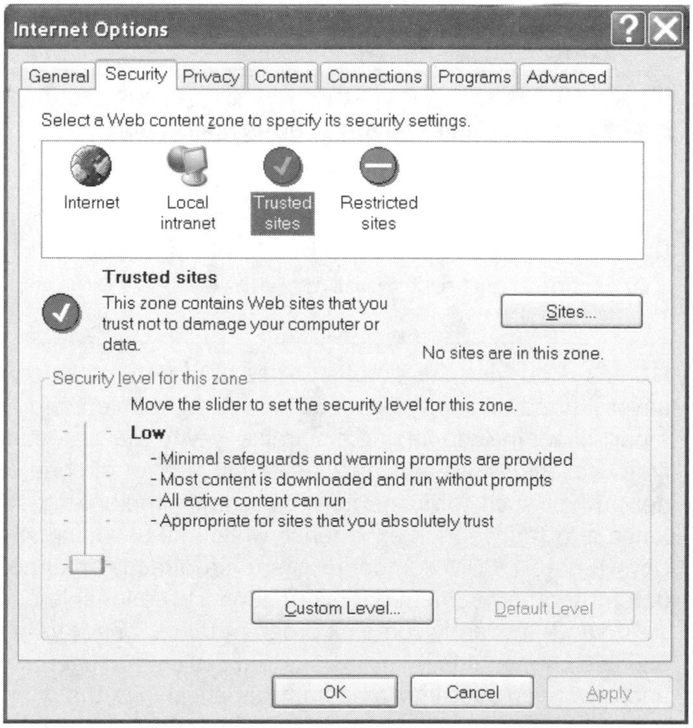

Figure 10.3 Changing the security settings for trusted sites.

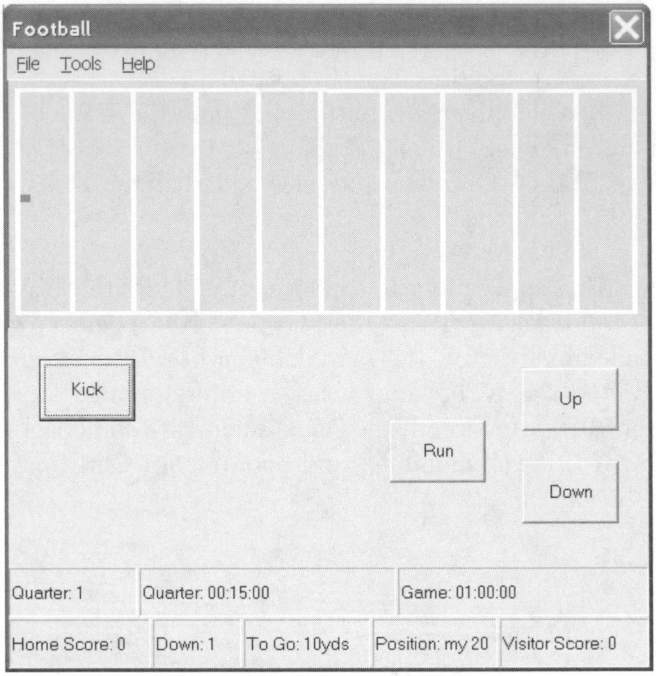

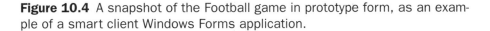

Figure 10.4 A snapshot of the Football game in prototype form, as an example of a smart client Windows Forms application.

fun to write a version for my PC, thus improving my chances of beating the sharper mind and reflexes of my wife, Lori.)

NOTE: Codifying the simplest rules of the American game of football takes several hundred lines of code. Challenging problems for this application as a smart client include finding a suitable way to manage audio. Even simple `.wav` files—for things like touchdowns—require a lot of code or an existing component. Most such components are currently implemented in COM. The challenge is offering a rich experience while still providing smart client updates. Unfortunately, COM components are not directly amenable to smart client updates. Another problem is how to support reasonable user inputs.

Even a modestly complex program takes longer to implement than writing a single chapter does. Writing custom device managers, audio and video tools, and advanced user interface controls are things that you and I may have to do—or at least provide—in commercial applications that will represent real hurdles to deploying smart client applications like video games. However, the average business application generally is comprised of rules and database reads and writes; joysticks and multimedia components are generally not needed. For this reason smart clients will likely be more useful for business applications first, and perhaps you will pardon me if the Football game audio is found wanting.

Adjusting Security Policy for Application Assemblies

Chapter 18 covers the management of security policies in more depth. For now we need a convenient and reliable way to manually allow clients to run our smart client assemblies downloaded from the Internet. The easiest way to do this is to run the Microsoft .NET Framework wizard, Trust an Assembly. To indicate that an individual assembly downloaded from the Internet can be trusted and allowed to run, follow these steps.

1. Click the Start|Control Panel|Administrative Tools|Microsoft .NET Framework Wizards applet.
2. Click the Trust an Assembly icon (Figure 10.5).
3. Complete the wizard by selecting options on each screen as directed.
4. For the first screen with the question, "What would you like to modify?" select the Make changes to this computer option. Click Next.
5. Type in the path or URL of the assembly to trust, or use the Browse button to navigate to that assembly. As an exercise, type in *http://www.softconcepts.com/Football/Football.exe*. Click Next.
6. Using the slider in Windows XP to give the executable Full Trust. Click Next.
7. Click Finish to complete the process.

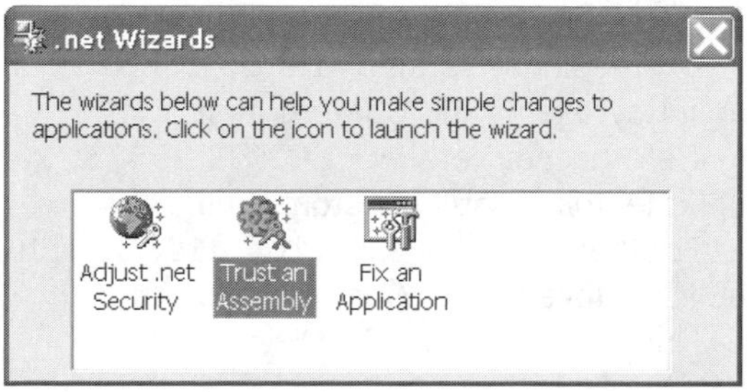

Figure 10.5 The Trust an Assembly wizard makes modifying security policies a bit easier.

At this point you can point your browser to *http://www.softconcepts.com/ Football/Football.exe* and the executable will download and start running automatically. (You should see the latest update of the game, similar to the game shown in Figure 10.4.)

You may want to experiment with varying degrees of trust for each assembly you want to download and execute from any specific provider. As an application implementer you want your customers to give you as much trust as possible; while as an application consumer you want to yield only as little trust as is necessary. Unfortunately there are few blanket rules for security, especially when it comes to the World Wide Web. As mentioned, we will talk more about security in Chapter 18.

NOTE: Downloaded assemblies exist in two places: the Internet cache managed by the browser and the .NET download cache. On my laptop the Internet cache is physically located at `C:\Documents and Settings\Pkimmel.SOFT-CONCEPTS\Local Settings\Temporary Internet Files`, which is the value set in the browser's Internet Options|Settings dialog. The .NET download assembly cache is physically located in `C:\WINNT\Assembly\Download`, which is the download part of the Global Assembly Cache (GAC).

You can view the contents of downloaded files in the GAC by running the `gacutil.exe` utility with the `/ldl` switch, as in `gacutil.exe /ldl`. After I downloaded the `Football.exe` file from the Web site, my .NET download cache contained the following contents:

Microsoft (R) .NET Global Assembly Cache Utility. Version 1.0.3705.0
Copyright (C) Microsoft Corporation 1998–2001. All rights reserved.

The cache of downloaded files contains the following entries:

    Football, Version=1.0.1104.41183, Culture=neutral,
PublicKeyToken=null, Custom=null
    expressions, Version=1.0.831.35692, Culture=neutral,
PublicKeyToken=null, Custom=null
    expressions, Version=1.0.831.36370, Culture=neutral,
PublicKeyToken=null, Custom=null
    Referenced, Version=1.0.683.25472, Culture=neutral,
PublicKeyToken=null, Custom=null
    Football, Version=1.0.1104.41183, Culture=neutral,
PublicKeyToken=null, Custom=null
    Number of items = 5

The contents of your .NET download cache will vary. However, if you download the `Football.exe` file from *http://www.softconcepts.com*, you should see an entry similar to the one shown above.

Configuring Server Precursors for Smart Client Assemblies

When you are configuring a Web site, you want to limit permissions to only those absolutely needed by your legitimate customers. There are enough people in the world trying to hack Web sites for fun and profit, and you and I don't need to encourage them. To permit customers to download your smart client assemblies from an intranet or the Internet, set access permissions to Read and application permissions to Scripts, as shown in Figure 10.6.

You can create any executable assembly and set Web sharing by right-clicking on the folder containing the executable, selecting the Sharing and Security context menu item, and navigating to the Web Sharing tab. The Web Sharing tab can be used to create a virtual directory and set permissions for that virtual directory. This shortcut yields the same results as establishing a virtual directory from the management console for IIS. Figure 10.7 shows the virtual Football directory in the management console on my laptop.

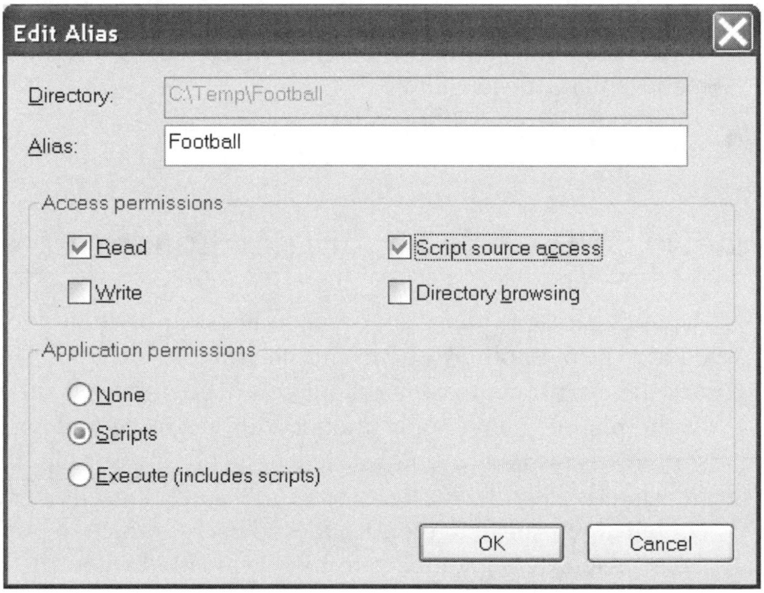

Figure 10.6 Set access permissions to Read and application permissions to Scripts for shared Web directories that contain smart client assemblies.

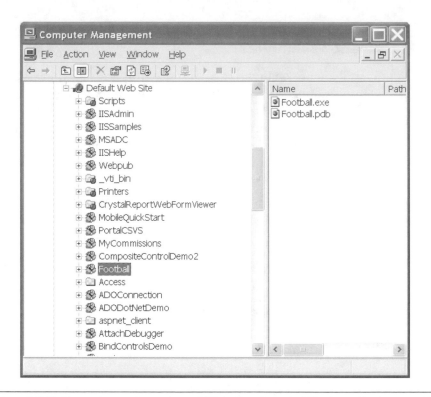

Figure 10.7 You can create a shared Web directory in Windows Explorer or the management console for IIS.

Considering a Generic Application Loader

An application loader is an executable assembly that contains just enough code to request other code from some remote location. The remote location may be an intranet server at your company or a Web site on the other side of the planet. All an application loader has to do is download one root assembly. If this root assembly refers to all other assemblies that your application needs, then when those assemblies are actually needed the root will contain a reference to their location. This reference to other assemblies will cause associated assemblies to be downloaded when the root assembly refers to them. As a result you can permit clients to download a very small application loader (an executable) from a network site, and that loader can play the role of root or request a root assembly. All associated assemblies will be backtracked to the original site and downloaded as needed. You do not need to execute an `Assembly.LoadFrom` statement for every assembly; just the root will do.

The drawback to this approach is that the application will not run if you are disconnected from the network. As mentioned earlier, a disconnected state will not permit a comparison between cached assemblies and assemblies at the networked location. However, what if it is permissible for the application to run even when the client PC is disconnected, obtaining any updates at a later time when the PC is connected? Under these circumstances you need an application updater that is smarter than the behavior you get from simply executing an `Assembly.LoadFrom` call. This scenario describes the behavior of the Terrarium game. Terrarium attempts to update assemblies when the application runs but falls back to current assemblies in the event that the PC is disconnected.

There is probably no specific definition of a single application loader. The general idea is that updates downloaded from the Internet are managed invisibly and conveniently to prevent a disconnected state from halting an application. The Terrarium game, for example, is downloaded and installed like a traditional application with all its assemblies in place. Then these assemblies arc downloaded and updated at the convenience of the connection state of the individual PC. This reflects a hybrid of traditional download and install behavior and smart client updates. It seems highly feasible that a root assembly could be downloaded and all assemblies copied at that point in time, followed by smart updates based on the connected state of the PC. Perhaps a generic commercial application updater will be made and sold just as installation utilities were made and sold in the last ten years. Such a generic application updater will need to consider disconnected states, version rollbacks, and evolving security policies to support the greatest number of consumer applications. Until a general, commercial product exists, each vendor will have to solve this predicament on a case-by-case basis.

Creating a Microsoft Installer File to Manage Security Policies

Downloading and running a .NET assembly from the Internet is not an automatic given. Security settings (see Chapter 18) are likely to change from customer to customer, and the default settings will evolve over time as more is understood about customers' basic security needs. If you are providing executable assemblies for download from the Internet, you may need to provide a reliable means for your customers to be able to run those assemblies. You could count on the customers knowing how to manage the security settings for .NET themselves; but if some actually don't know them, good customers may walk away from your application as a viable solution. As an alternative you could provide written instructions that describe how to manage security settings, or (the best alternative) you could automate the security modifications on the customers' behalf.

In this section we take a look at how to manually and programmatically manage permissions for smart client applications. There is enough information in this section for you to successfully perform the tasks described, but you will need to read Chapter 18 for more general background information on .NET security.

Defining a New Code Group

There are several ways to manage security. You can use the `caspol.exe` utility to manage code access security policy from the command line or a batch file, or you can use the .NET Framework Configuration utility console snap-in to manage security with a graphical user interface. We will use the .NET Framework Configuration snap-in because it is more convenient.

Suppose that a customer clicks on a link to your executable assembly and instead of the application starting up, the user sees an error message or, worse yet, nothing happens. Most users—including me—have a very short fuse when it comes to waiting for content from the Web. If the application doesn't start up and there is no apparent easy remedy, the user is likely to go to the next cool thing on the Web.

As techies we can manage security permissions on our machines, and we should be able to explain them to someone else if the need arises or we need to programmatically modify permissions for our applications. Back to our scenario.

For demonstration purposes, let's say you had problems running the Football game we talked about earlier in the chapter. You click on `Football.exe` and it doesn't run. You can give it permission to run by following the steps below.

1. Start the .NET Framework Configuration tool by opening a command prompt, changing the current directory to `C:\WINNT\Microsoft.NET\Framework\<version>\` (where *version* is the version of the .NET Framework whose policy you want to modify), and typing `mmc mscorcfg.msc`. These steps will open the .NET Framework Configuration snap-in (Figure 10.8). Alternatively, you can open the console by selecting Start|Control Panel|Administrative Tools|.NET Framework Configuration.

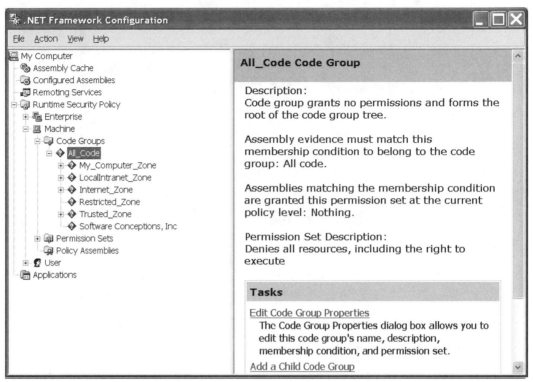

Figure 10.8 Use the .NET Framework Configuration console to set security permissions for .NET.

2. Expand the Runtime Security Policy folder and the Machine node. (This will allow you to set permissions for the workstation.)

3. Expand the Code Groups node and select New from the All_Code group's context menu. (This option is also available from the Action menu.) This step starts the Code Group wizard (Figure 10.9).

4. Provide a name and description for the code group, using Figure 10.9 as a visual guide. (Because `Football.exe` comes from Software Conceptions, for the figure I chose a name and description suitable to describe code from Software Conceptions.) Click Next.

5. Choose a condition type (Figure 10.10). In this example, let's use a specific URL, `http://www.softconcepts.com/Football/Football.exe`. Select the URL condition and type the precise URL. Be sure to include the moniker (`http://` or `ftp://`) since this is used as part of the membership condition. Although a URL is not the most secure way of identifying the source of code, it suits our purposes for now. Click Next.

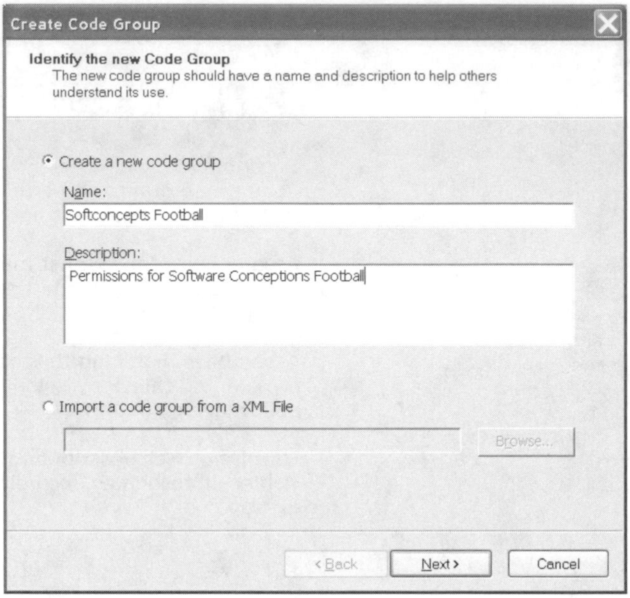

Figure 10.9 The Code Group wizard permits you to identify a new code group with which to associate permissions.

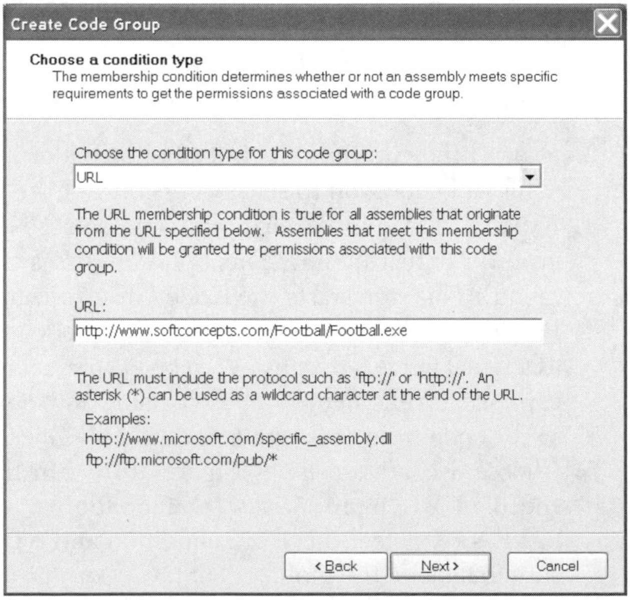

Figure 10.10 Choose the condition that determines membership in the code group, for example, a specific URL.

6. Assign a permission set to the code group (Figure 10.11). (On my particular workstation, the Internet group has execute permissions but limits many other permissions. Hence, for the figure I selected Use existing permission set and picked the Internet permission set.) Click Next.
7. Click Finish.

When you are done, you should see the Softconcepts Football child group in the All_Code code group.

Manually setting permissions isn't too difficult to do on an occasional basis; however, many Internet users may not be comfortable setting security permissions or may themselves not have sufficient privileges on their machines to do so. In addition, if you had to manage permissions for a wide variety of applications, it would become tedious to do so manually. We have the option of writing code to manage permissions for us; this approach—once the code has been perfected—is less prone to error and is much faster.

Managing Code Groups and Permissions Programmatically

Support for managing code groups and permissions can be found in the `System.Security` namespace. The classes in this namespace support performing

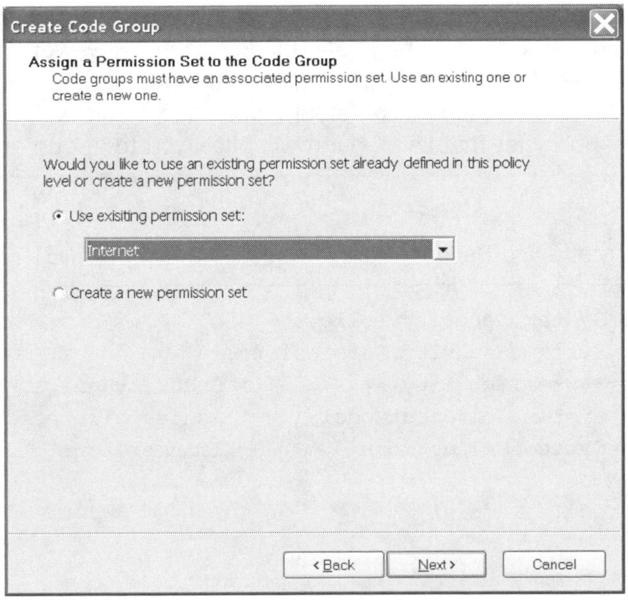

Figure 10.11 Assign a permission set to your code group.

operations analogous to those we performed in the .NET Framework Configuration tool. All we have to do is convert the operations to method signatures. To summarize, we need to complete the following tasks.

- Pick a security policy level.
- Pick a permission set.
- Create a policy statement, assigning the permissions set to it.
- Pick the conditions required for membership in that set.
- Create the code group, adding the membership conditions and policy information to that group.
- Provide a name and description for that code group.
- Save everything.

Listing 10.3 contains an example console application that adds a custom code group to the machine policy. The code group is approximately identical to the policy changes we made manually in the preceding section. You can find this console application, `SecuritySetupTest.vbproj`, as part of `Football.sln`.

NOTE: When you modify security settings using `caspol.exe` or the .NET Framework Configuration snap-in, you are modifying text in an XML file. For example, the machine policy is stored in `C:\WINNT\Microsoft.NET\Framework\<version>\CONFIG\security.config`. If you are feeling brave, you can modify these files directly. It is a good idea to make a backup copy if you modify the policy configuration files directly. However, if you make a mistake, you can delete the security policy files, and the next .NET application to run will write new versions with default information. This will in effect reset your security policy for that level, but it will allow you to get up and going again.

Listing 10.3 Managing Security Policy Programmatically in .NET

```
1:   Imports System.Security.Policy
2:   Imports System.Security.Permissions
3:   Imports System.Security            ' SecurityManager
4:   Imports System.ComponentModel      ' RunInstallerAttribute
5:   Imports System.Collections         ' IEnumerator
6:
7:   Public Module Module1
8:
9:     Public Sub Main()
10:      Dim machinePolicy As PolicyLevel = GetMachinePolicyLevel()
11:      If (Not (machinePolicy Is Nothing)) Then
```

```
12:
13:        Dim permissions As PermissionSet = _
14:          New NamedPermissionSet("Internet")
15:
16:        Dim policy As PolicyStatement = _
17:          New PolicyStatement(permissions)
18:
19:        Dim membership As IMembershipCondition = _
20:          New UrlMembershipCondition( _
21:          "http://www.softconcepts.com/Football/Football.exe")
22:
23:        Dim group As CodeGroup = _
24:          New UnionCodeGroup(membership, policy)
25:
26:        group.Description = "Permissions for Softconcepts Football"
27:        group.Name = "Software Conceptions, Inc."
28:        machinePolicy.RootCodeGroup.AddChild(group)
29:        SecurityManager.SavePolicy()
30:
31:      Else
32:        Debug.WriteLine("Failed to find user policy.")
33:      End If
34:
35:    End Sub
36:
37:
38:    Private Function GetMachinePolicyLevel() As PolicyLevel
39:      Dim policies As IEnumerator = _
40:        SecurityManager.PolicyHierarchy
41:
42:      While (policies.MoveNext())
43:
44:        If (CType(policies.Current, _
45:          PolicyLevel).Label = "Machine") Then
46:
47:          Return CType(policies.Current, PolicyLevel)
48:        End If
49:      End While
50:
51:      Return Nothing
52:
53:    End Function
54:
55: End Module
```

Lines 38 through 53 use an enumerator to find the machine policy. There should be an indexer and enumerator on `PolicyHierarchy` to simplify access. There may not be one to more readily support future policy levels.

The `Main` subroutine in lines 9 through 35 actually performs the steps to add the code group to the machine policy. Line 10 searches `PolicyHierarchy` to obtain the correct `PolicyLevel` object. If the `machinePolicy` object is found (line 11), we create an instance of the Internet permission set in lines 13 and 14. The permission set is used to create an instance of a `PolicyStatement` object (lines 16 and 17). Lines 19 through 21 set a membership condition. (The assembly must come from *http://www.softconcepts.com/Football/Football.exe*.)

Finally, the new code group is created, adding the membership condition and policy to the group, and a name and description are provided. The last step is to save the policy (line 29). When the code has finished running, you should be able to search the `security.config` file and find the entry for Software Conceptions, Inc.

Writing code to programmatically change policy settings is reliable once the code works correctly. However, this approach won't work for customers who can't run the assembly from the Internet because the policy modification application won't run for the same reason the original assembly didn't run. We have a solution to this problem too.

Managing Permissions by Using an Installer

Microsoft Installer (`.msi`) files are permitted to run from the Internet because they require user interaction—the user acknowledges operations as the installer runs. For this reason we can add security permissions to a `.msi` file, and a customer can run this `.msi` file to update the security policy. The actual code for modifying the security policy is almost the same, but we do need to create the `.msi` project and write the policy modification code as part of an `Installer` class. I will walk you through the steps of defining the setup project and show the complete listing for the installer. (You can download the complete solution as part of `Football.sln`, which includes the installer and the setup project.)

Implementing an Installer Library

The `System.Configuration.Install.Installer` class is the base class for custom installers. We can define a class in a class library project and add the project to a `.msi` project. The Microsoft Windows Installer will load and run the code in the custom installer. For this mechanism to work we have to inherit from `System.Configuration.Install.Installer` and apply the `RunInstallerAttribute` to the custom `Installer` class. Armed with this information, the Windows Installer will run our custom installer. We can program the custom installer to perform any installation task we might need, including modifying the security policy. Because `.msi` files are permitted to run from the Internet, this is an ideal way to update a customer's security policy.

Listing 10.4 contains the source code for our custom installer. Note the similarities between the installer and the console application discussed in the preceding subsection (Listing 10.3).

Listing 10.4 Implementing a Custom Installer

```
1:   Imports System.Security.Policy
2:   Imports System.Configuration.Install
3:   Imports System.Security.Permissions
4:   Imports System.Security              ' SecurityManager
5:   Imports System.ComponentModel        ' RunInstallerAttribute
6:   Imports System.Collections           ' IEnumerator
7:
8:   <RunInstaller(True)> _
9:   Public Class Installer1
10:    Inherits System.Configuration.Install.Installer
11:
12:    Public Sub New()
13:
14:      Dim machinePolicy As PolicyLevel = GetMachinePolicyLevel()
15:      If (Not (machinePolicy Is Nothing)) Then
16:
17:        Dim permissions As PermissionSet = _
18:          New NamedPermissionSet("Internet")
19:
20:        Dim policy As PolicyStatement = _
21:          New PolicyStatement(permissions)
22:
23:        Dim membership As IMembershipCondition = _
24:          New UrlMembershipCondition( _
25:          "http://www.softconcepts.com/Football/Football.exe")
26:
27:        Dim group As CodeGroup = _
28:          New UnionCodeGroup(membership, policy)
```

```
29:
30:        group.Description = "Permissions for Softconcepts Football"
31:        group.Name = "Software Conceptions, Inc."
32:        machinePolicy.RootCodeGroup.AddChild(group)
33:        SecurityManager.SavePolicy()
34:
35:     Else
36:        Debug.WriteLine("Failed to find the machine policy.")
37:     End If
38:
39:   End Sub
40:
41:
42:   Private Function GetMachinePolicyLevel() As PolicyLevel
43:      Dim policies As IEnumerator = _
44:        SecurityManager.PolicyHierarchy
45:
46:      While (policies.MoveNext())
47:
48:        If (CType(policies.Current, _
49:          PolicyLevel).Label = "Machine") Then
50:
51:          Return CType(policies.Current, PolicyLevel)
52:        End If
53:      End While
54:
55:      Return Nothing
56:
57:   End Function
58:
59: End Class
```

There is little need to repeat the elaboration of the code in Listing 10.4; it is almost identical to the code in Listing 10.3. The notable differences are that in Listing 10.4 we define public class `Installer1` as inheriting from `System.Configuration.Install.Installer` (line 10), indicating that `Installer1` is a custom installer. The `RunInstallerAttribute` indicates that an installer application should be run during the installation of the assembly containing this custom installer.

Now all we have to do is add `SecuritySetup.vbproj`, which contains the custom installer, to a setup project and tell the setup project what to do with the library.

Defining the Setup Project

Setup Project templates ship with Visual Studio .NET. (Check your version of Visual Studio .NET to determine whether the Setup Project template ships with your specific version.) We can add a Windows Installer setup project to `Football.sln`, which also contains `SecuritySetup.vbproj`, and use this project to manage the security policy modifications on our behalf.

Defining the setup project is a straightforward process. Follow these steps.

1. With `Football.sln` open (or your custom solution), select File|Add Project|New Project. This opens the Add New Project dialog.
2. In the Add New Project dialog, select the Setup and Deployment folder from the Project Types list, and pick the Setup Project template from the list of templates.
3. Name the template something suitable. (For `Football.sln` I named the template SetupFootballPermissions.)
4. Delete the User's Desktop and User's Programs menu folders from File System on Target Machine, leaving just the Application folder. We will install `SecuritySetup.dll` to the Program Files directory.
5. Right-click on the Application folder and select Add|Project Output. Select the SecuritySetup project as shown in Figure 10.12 (or the project containing your custom installer) and click OK. The resultant setup configuration should look like Figure 10.13.
6. Next we need to tell the Windows Installer how to treat the `SecuritySetup.dll` assembly. With the setup project selected in the Solution Explorer, click the View|Editor|Custom Actions menu item. Select the Install folder and pick Add Custom Action from the context menu. The custom action we want to perform is to install the `SecuritySetup.dll` assembly (see Figure 10.14). (Recall that installing a custom installer will run the installer code.)

TIP: You can run the Windows Installer from the Solution Explorer by right-clicking on the setup project and selecting Install from the context menu.

At this point we are all set. We can build our entire solution, which includes the `SecuritySetup.dll` assembly and the `SetupFootballPermissions` setup project. After we have built the project we can test the installation right from Visual Studio .NET. VS .NET will roll back previous installations and run the Windows Installer. If the custom installer makes

Figure 10.12 The SecuritySetup project containing our custom installer.

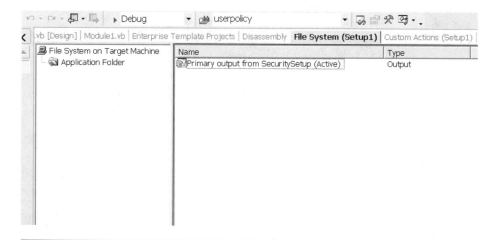

Figure 10.13 The setup configuration after we add the `SecuritySetup.dll` assembly.

Figure 10.14 The custom install action installs the `SecuritySetup.dll` assembly, which will run the customer installer code.

the correct modifications to the security policy, we are ready to deploy the `.msi` file. Placing this file conveniently on your Web site will give your customers an easy remedy in the event they cannot run your executable assembly from the Web.

Handling COM Components

Alas, poor ActiveX and COM components. Or, to paraphrase Stephen King and Peter Straub (from the excellent novel *Black House*), perhaps it is time to let this technology stretch out in its grave. What's that you say? You can't? I understand.

If you must insist on carrying COM and ActiveX controls into the future with you—out of necessity, of course—your application may not be ideal for smart client behavior. All is not lost though. The Terrarium game offers a hybrid solution that may work for you. Provide your customers with a traditional installation. This can be accomplished by mailing a CD-ROM or DVD or providing download access from the Web. Then, managed parts of your solution can be updated using smart client techniques. It may be difficult or impossible to update COM or ActiveX portions of your application without qualified user intercession, but you should be able to update the managed .NET assemblies without it.

Of course, if you are using bleeding-edge techniques like smart clients, I encourage you to reimplement the COM pieces in .NET. You are up to the challenge.

Other Ideas

Some other options might also prove useful with smart client applications. For example, you can employ HTTPS, which requires additional authentication, and you might be interested in exploring the Windows XP Intelligent Background Transfer Service.

It is too early to ascertain how smart client technology will shape the future of networking applications, but it is a good strategy to work toward melding Internet technologies with Windows technologies. The Internet clearly offers superlative performance when it comes to distribution and accessibility, and Windows offers a rich client experience. If Microsoft can merge Web development and Windows development technologies, consumers will have the best of both worlds. If Microsoft is feeling especially generous, it could combine these technologies in such a way as to allow them to be ported to other platforms.

Summary

Smart client application development is evolutionary. Clearly, we understand the richness of a windowing environment and the ubiquity of the Web. Developers and businesspeople can equally appreciate the benefits of both environments. The difficulty has been in reconciling these two worlds. With .NET we are seeing a window on a future world. This future world seamlessly integrates Windows and Web technologies where developers implement a single solution and end users benefit from increased productivity. Whether these applications are connected or not is a technological predicament that users shouldn't have to care about.

In this chapter I hope you have gotten a glimpse into a possible future, where no assumption is made about the connected state of any single user; where applications just run reliably and correctly; and where updates happen and technology disseminates naturally, like shared ideas around the campfire, as long as we all make money.

CHAPTER 11

ADO.NET Database Programming

I'm in it to win it like Yzerman.

—*"Wasting Time,"* Kid Rock

Introduction

ADO.NET is one of the jewels of the .NET framework. ADO.NET is a revision to ADO that emphasizes disconnected database programming. The reason for this is straightforward and the argument is valid. In the connected database model, a programmer obtains a handle to a database and holds it while performing operations against the database. This causes a problem related to the finite number of connections and the maintenance of those connections in a disconnected space, specifically the World Wide Web. The Web itself is disconnected in the sense that it uses a request-and-response model in which requests are made, the Web server responds, and in between there is a very loose relationship between the client (your browser) and the server (for example, IIS or Apache).

The number of simultaneous connections on the Web can be huge because the servers don't have to track the client connections and the browsers aren't holding onto something that the servers necessarily have to actively manage. Think of ordering lunch at the drive-through window of a fast food restaurant: you drive up, order and collect your food, and drive away—and the restaurateur's job is done. (Like browsing some Web sites, occasionally the service is a bit unsettling.) We know that this request-and-response model supports servicing a tremendous number of requests.

Because we are moving into a future where the number of users of an application—especially a Web application—may be huge, we need real tools that address this reality. With the revision to ADO Microsoft has disconnected the data from the database connection. With ADO.NET you make a request to the database. The database services the request, and the connection is dropped until the next request is made. There are a couple of practical concerns, but the educational literature and my own experience mitigate them.

The biggest concern is that if the data is disconnected, how can a record lock prevent someone else from changing the record? The answer is that technically records cannot be locked and some other user could change your data. The way you manage this problem is by writing WHERE predicates that ensure that your data has not been changed by some other user. For instance, using pseudo-code, you might write "Update my row with new values where some unique value equals a known value." Commonly the known value is some kind of auditing information, perhaps a date and time stamp. Record locks introduced difficulties of their own too.

ADO.NET facilitates massive application scalability because more users can be serviced if information about the user does not have to be maintained in the form of a connection and record locks.

You can read about design goals for ADO.NET in the .NET Framework Developer's Guide (the Visual Studio .NET help documentation). In general, other goals included leveraging current ADO technology, supporting the N-Tier programming model, and incorporating XML. You will find many similarities and parallels between ADO and ADO.NET, and what you know about writing SQL still applies. N-Tier programming is more clearly supported; you can even generalize ADO.NET classes to make typed ADO.NET data objects. Finally, XML is integral to ADO.NET. The result is that the meaning of what a database is will continue to evolve to include persistence entities that include and extend beyond just traditional databases.

This chapter discusses how to employ ADO.NET in a manner consistent with the most general use, which is to read and manage data from a traditional database. (Chapter 12 covers some advanced topics, including the use of stored procedures, transaction processing, and some additional benefits of XML in ADO.NET.)

Fundamentals of ADO.NET

Microsoft split ADO.NET into two camps: the SqlClient camp and the OleDb camp. The SqlClient camp represents Microsoft SQL Server 7.0 and higher, and the OleDb camp handles everything else, including Microsoft ACCESS, Microsoft SQL Server 6.5, Oracle, UDB, Sybase, Informix, and others. The notion of a camp refers to database providers. In addition to the two-camp model, Microsoft's .NET Framework supports extending ADO.NET by allowing vendors to implement their own provider classes. The result is that any database supplier could create its own custom provider classes for ADO.NET.

ADO.NET in general is made up of the `System.Data` and `System.Xml` namespaces. Classes that are general to ADO.NET are typically found in the `System.Data` namespace. For example, `DataSet`, a general class shared between providers, is defined in `System.Data`. Classes that are specific to a provider camp can be found in `System.Data.OleDb` or `System.Data.Sql-Client`. For classes in either camp to work with the general `DataSet` class, each camp must support the same basic capabilities. For example, to get data into a `DataSet` class you need a connection. There is a connection class in the `OleDb` namespace as well as one in the `SqlClient` namespace. These namespace-specific classes employ a prefix naming convention: OleDb classes are prefixed with `OleDb`, and SqlClient classes are prefixed with `Sql`. Thus the OleDb connection class is suitably named `OleDbConnection`; the SqlClient connection class, `SqlConnection`. For the most part both the OleDb and SqlClient connection classes implement the same members and operations. As a result of the similarities in OleDb and SqlClient classes, if you learn to use one or the other, you can easily use its alternative provider counterpart.

Two other important namespaces related to `System.Data` are `System.Data.Common` and `System.Data.SqlTypes`. The `Common` namespace defines classes for permissions, table column mappings, and some event argument types. The `SqlTypes` namespace defines native types for SQL Server.

As a general rule, you will most often use the `System.Data` and `System.Xml` namespaces and one or the other of the provider namespaces, `OleDb` or `SqlClient`. I will be using the `OleDb` providers in this chapter because I can reasonably gamble on your having a copy (or being able to get one) of the Northwind database. For informational purposes, it is worth noting that most of the code in this chapter could easily be substituted for classes in the `SqlClient` namespace, if you are using a newer version of Microsoft SQL Server. However, the `OleDb` classes represent the classes you will use for the greatest diversity of database providers.

Defining a Database Connection

As a general practice, I employ a style of programming that relies heavily on a technique referred to as *scaffolding* and commonly understood to mean a way of unit testing. This technique simply means that a little code is written that performs a complete job, and some test code is written to ensure the code works. As the body of code grows, existing code is regressively tested as each new chunk is added and tested. The promoted means of testing code is to use NUnit. The result of using NUnit or scaffolding is approximately the same except that using NUnit will result in your being able to use existing testing tools that will run your test suite automatically, accumulating and reporting on results.

NOTE: NUnit (see *http://www.nunit.org* for details) is modeled after JUnit, both of which are testing frameworks. The basic principle is that you implement a predetermined interface. Your test code implements this predetermined interface, and a test application can exercise your code by tapping into this interface. The test application uses the interface to test your code, accumulate results, and report on these results. The NUnit tools are getting better and becoming more popular all the time. It is worth doing some independent investigation on NUnit.

In accordance with the idea of building software that conceptually looks like an onion, where layers of test code are wrapped around successively growing complexity, I typically start with a connection to my database. (I start with the connection when building the database layer and start with other kinds of entities when building a graphical user interface or business object layer.) A connection is comprised of the `OleDbConnection` (or `SqlConnection`) class, a connection string, and a database. The connection can be dragged from the Toolbox or Server Explorer or created programmatically with code. The Server Explorer version is easiest because it manages the connection string automatically; however, below we will create the connection programmatically because this provides us with the greatest flexibility.

Defining a Connection String

Connection strings have the distinct honor of being difficult to remember. The basic syntax is to provide a provider name, a data source, a password, and a user name. Provider names tend to be cryptic and relatively easy to forget. The data source name is often a physical file path or a reference to an OleDb alias. The password and user name are self-explanatory.

Due in part to the cryptic provider names, we can borrow a foolproof means of defining a connection string. The technique involves using the Data Link Properties applet to create the connection string on our behalf. To define a connection string to the Northwind sample database, follow these steps.

1. In Windows Explorer, create a new text file form the File|New|Text Document menu. The default name will be `New Text Document.txt`. Rename this file to have a meaningful name and a `.udl` extension, for example, `connection.udl`.

2. The `.udl` extension is associated with a Microsoft Data Link file. Double-click this file to open the Data Link Properties applet (Figure 11.1).

3. Select the provider you want to use (in our example, we'll use the Microsoft Jet 4.0 OLE DB Provider) and click the Next button (Figure 11.1). The Data Link Properties dialog behaves like a wizard.

4. On the Connection tab, browse to the database location using the Browse button with the ellipsis. Enter a user name and password and

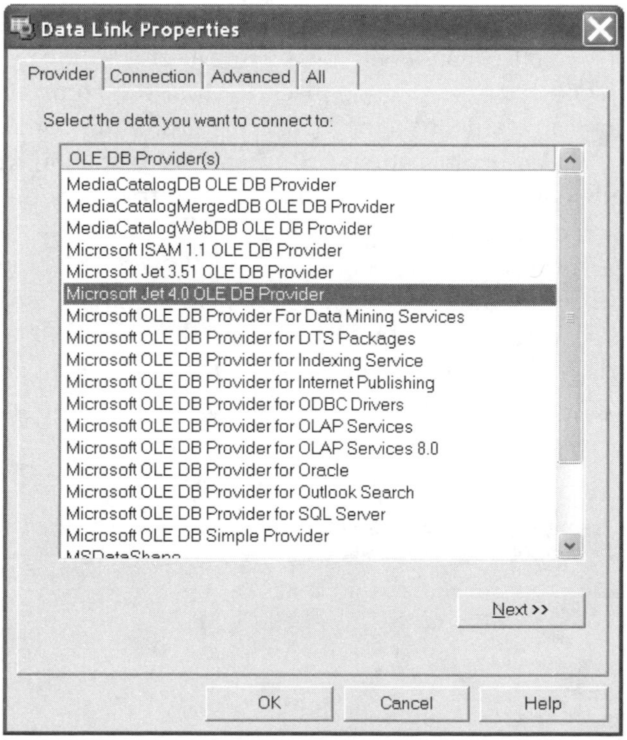

Figure 11.1 Using the Data Link Properties applet to manage connections.

click Allow saving password. Click Test Connection to ensure that your settings will work. (A default user name for the `Northwind.mdb` sample database is Admin; no password is required.)

5. You can modify values on the Advanced and All tabs, but we don't need to do that for our example. (You will benefit from exploring these independently; keep in mind that the specific values are provider dependent)

6. Assuming the test connection succeeded, click the OK button. This step will write the values you indicated as a connection string to the `.udl` file

The `.udl` file is just text. We can open it directly in VS .NET and extricate the connection string from the file. This technique has worked reliably regardless of the OLE DB provider used, so I keep it on hand.

Storing a Connection String

To store a connection string, you can copy the last line of text in the `.udl` file following the comment "Everything after this line is an OLE DB initstring." A `.config` file is a good place to store the connection string information. (You can store the connection string in an `App.config` file or a `Web.config` file for Web applications.) Storing the connection string information externally ensures that every chunk of code that uses the connection string will use it consistently.

Information like connection strings can be stored as key and value pairs in the `<appSettings>` section of a `.config` file. For simplicity you can use the key `"ConnectionString"`, and the value will be the literal connection string. Listing 11.1 shows an excerpt of the `Web.config` file for `ADODOT-NETDemo.sln`, with the `<appSettings>` element defined properly.

Listing 11.1 Using `<appSettings>` to Define a `ConnectionString` Key and Value

```
<?xml version="1.0" encoding="utf-8" ?>
<configuration>

  <appSettings>
    <add key="ConnectionString"
```

```
        value="Provider=Microsoft.Jet.OLEDB.4.0;Password="";Data
Source=C:\Program Files\Microsoft Visual Studio\VB98\NWIND.MDB;Persist
Security Info=True" />
  </appSettings>


<system.web>

  <!--  DYNAMIC DEBUG COMPILATION
```

The `<appSettings>` values are incorporated with the `<add>` tag, and the value must be on a single line of text. (It is shown wrapped in Listing 11.1—see the bold text—due to the limitations of the printed page.) The remainder of the `Web.config` file (at least for our example) contains default information created when the Web application solution was created by Visual Studio .NET. You can open a `Web.config` file and explore this information.

NOTE: Ensure that you remove embedded strings in the connection string. For example, the Data Link Properties applet uses double quotes ("") to indicate an empty password; simply remove the double quotes to indicate the password is blank. You will get an error indicating that the debugger couldn't start on the Web server and asking whether or not you want to disable debugging. Answer No to this prompt.

If you accidentally enter Yes in response to the error caused by the invalid `Web.config` file, you can reenable ASP.NET debugging on the Debugging page of the project's Property Pages (Figure 11.2).

Reading a Connection String

Values added to the `<appSettings>` element can be read using the shared, indexable property `System.Configuration.ConfigurationSettings.AppSettings` by key. For example, we could read `ConnectionString` with the statement `System.Configuration.ConfigurationSettings.AppSettings("ConnectionString")`. Rather than litter our application with this statement, we could opt to create a `Connection` class with a `ConnectionString` property that concealed the `AppSettings` statement, making the code simpler for everyone to use. Defining our own `Connection` class also provides us with a convenient location to write our test code.

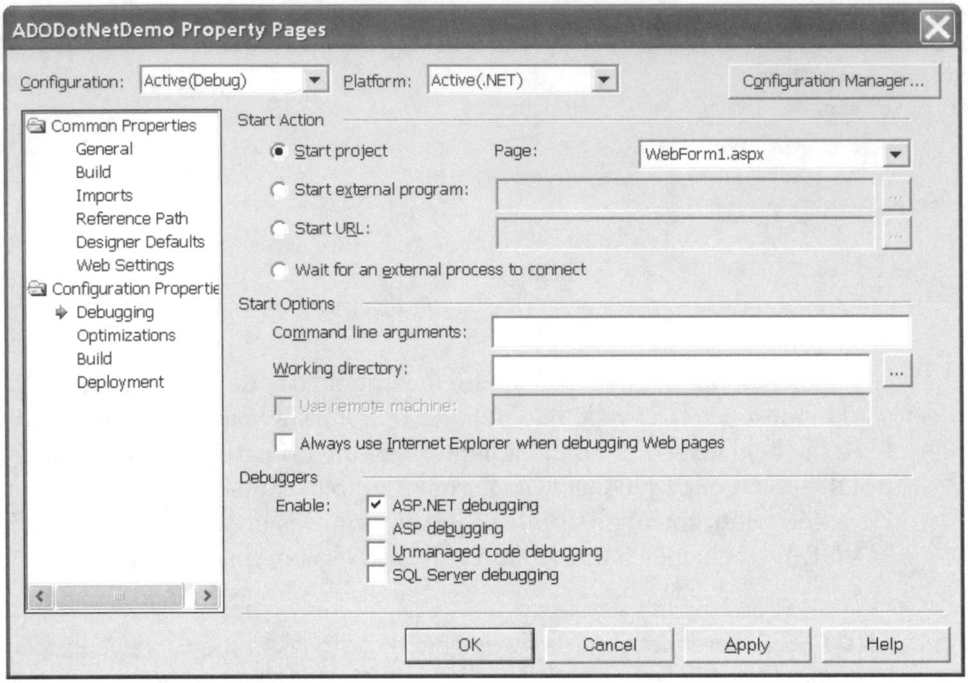

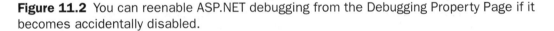

Figure 11.2 You can reenable ASP.NET debugging from the Debugging Property Page if it becomes accidentally disabled.

Testing the Connection

A convenient way to encapsulate solutions is to define your own classes. You can build on existing abstractions to create a contextual abstraction unique to your solution. This contextual abstraction will provide you with a convenient location to layer in things you need like connection strings and test code. Such a class to test our connection string might be implemented as demonstrated in Listing 11.2.

Listing 11.2 Creating a Contextual Wrapper for a Connection String

```
Imports System.Configuration
Imports System.Data.OleDb
Imports System.Diagnostics

Public Class Database
```

```
Private Shared Function GetConnectionString() As String
   Return ConfigurationSettings.AppSettings("ConnectionString")
End Function

Public Shared ReadOnly Property ConnectionString() As String
Get
   Return GetConnectionString()
End Get
End Property

Public Shared Sub Test()
   Dim C As OleDbConnection = New OleDbConnection(ConnectionString)

   Try
     C.Open()
     Debug.WriteLine(C.State)
   Catch
     Debug.WriteLine("Connection failed to open")
   Finally
     C.Close()
   End Try
End Sub

End Class
```

The `Database` class provides a wrapper for the connection string and a
convenient place for some test code.

Note that the code in Listing 11.2 represents my personal convention.
It is entirely up to you whether you employ this strategy or not; however,
Listing 11.2 does demonstrate the basic operations necessary for using an
`OleDbConnection` object. You must have a connection string and an `Ole-
DbConnection` object initialized with this string, and it is helpful to test
each of these elements separately as you begin building the database part
of your solution.

Finally, it is worth noting that with the notion of connection pooling,
.NET optimizes the number of physical connections created. When we are
using `OleDbConnection` objects, pooling is managed automatically; `Sql-
Connection` objects handle connection pooling implicitly. A key aspect of
how connections are pooled is the connection string. An identical connection
string is central to determining whether a connection in the pool can satisfy

the request for a new connection. For this reason using a strategy for ensuring that connection strings don't unnecessarily diverge works advantageously.

Filling a `DataSet` Object with an Adapter

The disconnected nature of ADO.NET translates to literal code behavior. The `DataSet` object in ADO.NET replaces the `Recordset` object in ADO as the central object for managing data. The literal difference vis-à-vis disconnectedness is that the `DataSet` object uses a connection (and an adapter) to get data but can work independently of the connection and adapter in your application. The only time the `DataSet` object needs the connection and adapter is when you are actually reading from or writing to the database. The rest of the time the `DataSet` object acts independently; think of a `DataSet` as a small subset of your database copied to the client.

`DataSet` objects are repositories for holding and managing data; however, they do not perform any of the tasks managed by a connection, nor do they perform the action of getting the data out of a `DataSet` and into the database through the connection. Moving the data out of a `DataSet` through the connection and into the database is the job of an adapter.

It is reasonable to wonder why we need all these classes. Quite simply, `DataSet` objects, adapters, and connections represent a separation of responsibilities. For example, by separating the `DataSet` behavior from adapter and connection behavior, programmers can create their own provider classes. If the job of the adapter were in the `DataSet` class, we would need both `OleDbDataSet` and `SqlDataSet` objects, and as a result, all the code shared between each version of the `DataSet` object would be repeated. By generalizing and finding useful subdivisions of labor, it is possible to reduce or eliminate redundant code. For this reason we have only one version each of `DataSet`, `DataTable`, `DataView`, and `DataRelation`, yet we have two versions each of adapters, connections, commands, command builders, and readers. This is really what object-oriented design and frameworks are about: converging general code and reducing the amount of specialized code. Listing 11.3 demonstrates how to use a connection and adapter to fill a `DataSet`. (Keep in mind that we are using an OleDb provider, Microsoft Access, but the code in the example will work with other databases simply by swapping the provider-specific classes. For example, swap an `OleDbConnection` class with a `SqlConnection` class to connect to Microsoft SQL Server 2000.)

Listing 11.3 Reading Data into a **DataSet** Object by Using an Adapter

```
Private Sub Page_Load(ByVal sender As System.Object, _
  ByVal e As System.EventArgs) Handles MyBase.Load

  Dim Connection As OleDbConnection = New _
    OleDbConnection(Database.ConnectionString)
  Dim Adapter As OleDbDataAdapter = _
    New OleDbDataAdapter("SELECT * FROM CUSTOMERS", Connection)

  Dim DataSet As DataSet = New DataSet("Customers")
  Adapter.Fill(DataSet)

  DataGrid1.DataSource = DataSet.Tables(0)
  DataGrid1.DataBind()

End Sub
```

The code demonstrates how to create a connection and an adapter. The adapter uses the **Connection** object to open (and close) a connection, filling the **DataSet** object. The example reads all of the Northwind sample database's **CUSTOMERS** table into the **DataSet**. The last two statements assign the **DataSet.Tables(0)** property to the **DataGrid1.DataSource** property of a Web control and calls the grid's **DataBind** method. This is a straightforward way to get data onto a Web form.

There are a couple of points of interest here. One is that we are using **Database.ConnectionString** from Listing 11.2. Another is that **OleDb-DataAdapter** is managing the state of the connection. A final point of interest is that a **DataSet** can contain many things, including more than one **DataTable**. When you read data into a **DataSet** object, the data returned by the queries are represented as **DataTable** objects, accessible through the **DataSet.Tables** property (as shown in Listing 11.3). You can also bind directly to the **DataSet**; however, if you do, you will end up with links in the **DataGrid** that allow you to navigate to every table in the **DataSet**.

The fundamental premise behind the **DataSet** class is that you read the entire row from the various tables into a **DataSet**. This may be one or many tables; for example, you'd use many tables for master–detail relationships. In coordination with many tables you can also add one or more **DataRelation** objects to the **DataSet** to express relationships between the tables in the **DataSet**. The result is that the **DataSet** is analogous to a subset database all by itself. With ADO technologies you can read and update single tables with a `Recordset` object and only read heterogeneous tables. Because the ADO.NET `DataSet` contains separate tables and relationships, you can read and update tables even if you are doing so with what appears to be a heterogeneous single table. (Refer to the Updating a `DataSet` section later in this chapter for more information.)

Using the `DataReader` Class

The `DataSet` class is a central figure in ADO.NET. However, you have other options for reading data. Suppose, for example, you only want to iterate through a set of data, perhaps browsing. You don't need to scroll back and forth, and you don't need to update the data. You have the option of using a `DataReader` object for read-only and forward-only data. The `DataReader` class yields better performance heuristics than the `DataSet` class for forward-only browsing. The technique for using a `DataReader` is similar to that for initializing a `DataSet`.

The `DataReader` is requested from a command object. We still need a connection, but we don't need an adapter or a `DataSet`. Listing 11.4 demonstrates how to initialize a command and `DataReader` object, using the reader to iterate over every row represented by the SQL SELECT statement.

Listing 11.4 Using a Connection and Command to Initialize a `DataReader` Object

```
Private Sub InitializeDropDownList()
  Dim Connection As OleDbConnection = _
    New OleDbConnection(Database.ConnectionString)

  Dim Command As OleDbCommand = _
    New OleDbCommand( _
    "SELECT CompanyName FROM CUSTOMERS", Connection)

  Dim Reader As OleDbDataReader
  Connection.Open()
  Try
    Reader = Command.ExecuteReader()
    While (Reader.Read())
      DropDownList1.Items.Add(Reader.GetString(0))
    End While
```

```
Finally
  Reader.Close
  Connection.Close()
End Try

End Sub
```

There are a couple of variations on Listing 11.4. For example, you can pass a `CommandBehavior` argument to `Command.ExecuteReader`, like `CommandBehavior.CloseConnection`, which instructs the reader to close the connection after the reader is obtained. In our example we used a verbose version that requires that we close the reader and then the connection explicitly. Readers and connections represent resources; hence it is helpful to use a `Try . . . Finally` block (referred to as a *resource protection block*) to ensure that the `Close` methods are called.

The basic behavior of the reader after it is obtained is to read all rows in a loop and process each row with a getter. To demonstrate, our example uses a `While` loop and the `GetString` method. The argument passed to `GetString` represents the ordinal column index. Because I requested only `CompanyName`, I knew that column `0` would contain the company name.

Using the `DataTable` and `DataView` Classes

The `DataTable` class in ADO.NET represents a single database table. The `DataView` class represents a navigable view of data. It is still possible to send a heterogeneous query to a database and display the results in one table or view, but it is preferable to request tables individually in ADO.NET and express the interrelationships as a `DataRelation` object. As mentioned earlier, the latter technique yields a `DataSet` object that can be updated by writing changes to each independent table but displayed as if it contained a single set of heterogeneous data. Having complex master–detail relationships that are updatable is the best of both worlds.

We can use code similar to that in Listing 11.3 to demonstrate how to fill a `DataTable`. When we have a `DataTable`, we can request a `DataView` directly. We also have the option of populating the `DataView` directly. Listing 11.5 demonstrates how to populate a `DataTable`, and the next subsection demonstrates how to express master–detail relationships in a `DataSet`.

Listing 11.5 Populating a `DataTable`

```
Private Sub InitializeGridWithTable()

  Dim Connection As OleDbConnection = _
    New OleDbConnection(Database.ConnectionString)
  Dim Adapter As OleDbDataAdapter = _
    New OleDbDataAdapter("SELECT * FROM CUSTOMERS", Connection)

  Dim Customers As DataTable = New DataTable("Customers")
  Adapter.Fill(Customers)

  DataGrid1.DataSource = Customers
  DataGrid1.DataBind()

End Sub
```

To initialize the `DataTable` I copied and pasted the code from Listing 11.3 to create Listing 11.5, substituting a `DataSet` everywhere with a `DataTable`. When you have a `DataTable` you can request a `DataView`. The `Data-Table.DefaultView` property will return the default `DataView` that represents the `DataTable`.

You also have the option of creating objects like `DataSet`, `DataTable`, and `DataView` programmatically, designing everything, and populating those ADO.NET elements from some source other than a database. In addition to ADO.NET working at a fundamental level with XML, ADO.NET uses data from providers, and a provider does not have to be a traditional database.

Defining Database Relationships

From a developer's perspective, .NET is a framework. There are marketing aspects to .NET too (which have led to a bit of confusion), but as developers we care about what the framework means and does for us. The .NET Framework is an object-oriented framework that ultimately conceals the underlying operating system from us. (There is even rampant speculation about porting .NET to some other operating system, like Linux.)

One of the many things that have been captured as classes is the notion of a relationship between data entities. This class is the `DataRelation` class, defined in `System.Data`. The `DataRelation` class is provider-agnostic; you use the same `DataRelation` class for SQL Server 7.0 that you use for IBM's UDB. The basic idea is that you read tables of data into a `DataSet` object and create instances of `DataRelation` objects that express the relationships between the entities. In this way you have both homogeneous tables in the `DataSet` and the ability to display these homogeneous tables in new heterogeneous ways.

Again, due to the general familiarity with the Northwind database, I have elected to use it for demonstration purposes. (Refer to the Tip below for several other excellent example databases that include .NET applications for you to experiment with and learn from.) Listing 11.6 demonstrates how to read two `DataTable` objects, express a `DataRelation`, and display this information in a `DataGrid` using a view.

Listing 11.6 Defining a Master–Detail Relationship by Using a `DataRelation` Object

```
Private Sub InitializeGridWithView()
  Const Customers As String = "Customers"
  Const Orders As String = "Orders"

  Dim Connection As OleDbConnection = _
    New OleDbConnection(Database.ConnectionString)

  Dim Adapter As OleDbDataAdapter = _
    New OleDbDataAdapter("SELECT * FROM CUSTOMERS", Connection)

  Dim DataSet As DataSet = New DataSet("CustomerOrders")
  Adapter.Fill(DataSet, Customers)

  Dim Adapter2 As OleDbDataAdapter = _
    New OleDbDataAdapter("SELECT * FROM ORDERS", Connection)

  Adapter2.Fill(DataSet, Orders)

  Dim Relation As DataRelation = _
    New DataRelation("CustomerOrders", _
    DataSet.Tables(Customers).Columns("CustomerID"), _
    DataSet.Tables(Orders).Columns("CustomerID"))
  DataSet.Relations.Add(Relation)
```

```
' DataGrid Web Control shows the first table
' DataGrid for Windows shows all tables
DataGrid1.DataSource = DataSet
DataGrid1.DataBind()


End Sub
```

The example code repeats the connection, adapter, and `DataSet` usage, placing the `Orders` and `Customers` tables into the `DataSet`. The code in bold font in Listing 11.6 demonstrates how to create a `DataRelation` object explicitly from two columns, one from each table. The relationship is that "customers have orders," which is expressed through the primary key `Customers.CustomerID` and the foreign key `Orders.CustomerID`. The last step is to add the `DataRelation` to the `DataSet Relations` collection.

You can express multiple relationships for each table in the `DataSet`. In the example the Web control `DataGrid1` shows the first table. If the grid in the listing were a Windows control, the code in Listing 11.6 would display links allowing a user to navigate through the rows, taking advantage of the expressed `DataRelation`.

TIP: You have several good options for sample Web and database applications for .NET. You can install the Fitch & Mather Stocks, Duwamish Books, or the IBuySpy portal applications. Fitch & Mather and Duwamish ship with Visual Studio .NET Enterprise Architect, and IBuySpy is available for download from Microsoft.

Using Command Objects

The `OleDbCommand` and `SqlCommand` classes represent the objectification of stored procedures and SQL. You need a way to send SQL text, stored procedures, and their incumbent parameters to data providers, and in .NET, you use the command object for this purpose. Listing 11.7 provides an example showing how to use a command object. Chapter 12 includes an example using a stored procedure.

Listing 11.7 Filling a DataSet by Using SQL and an OleDbCommand Object

```
Private Sub InitializeGridWithCommand()

  Dim Connection As OleDbConnection = _
    New OleDbConnection(Database.ConnectionString)

  Dim Command As OleDbCommand = _
    New OleDbCommand("SELECT * FROM CUSTOMERS", Connection)

  Dim Adapter As OleDbDataAdapter = _
    New OleDbDataAdapter(Command)

  Dim Customers As DataTable = New DataTable("Customers")
  Adapter.Fill(Customers)

  DataGrid1.DataSource = Customers
  DataGrid1.DataBind()
End Sub
```

Notice that Listing 11.7 is almost identical to Listing 11.5. The obvious difference is that I substituted literal SQL text to initialize the adapter with a command object.

Generating SQL with a Command Builder

An excellent benefit of object-oriented systems is that you have tidy compartments in which to place additional functionality, the classes themselves. The OleDbCommandBuilder and SqlCommandBuilder classes can use the command—whether literal text or command object—used to initialize an adapter and generate additional command objects. For example, when you write a SELECT statement, the schema (the columns and data types) can be inferred or read, and knowing the schema, substitution can be employed to replace SELECT with UPDATE, INSERT, or DELETE. A benefit of .NET is that the CommandBuilder class already exists and will do the work for us. Listing 11.8 demonstrates how to generate SQL for inserting, updating, and deleting from a selection statement.

Listing 11.8 Generating SQL with an `OleDbCommandBuilder` Object

```
Private Sub GenerateSQL(ByVal SQL As String)
  Dim Connection As OleDbConnection = _
    New OleDbConnection(Database.ConnectionString)

  Dim Adapter As OleDbDataAdapter = _
    New OleDbDataAdapter(SQL, Connection)

  Dim Builder As OleDbCommandBuilder = _
    New OleDbCommandBuilder(Adapter)

  TextBox2.Text = Builder.GetDeleteCommand().CommandText
  TextBox3.Text += Builder.GetInsertCommand().CommandText
  TextBox4.Text += Builder.GetUpdateCommand().CommandText

End Sub
```

The `OleDbCommandBuilder` object is initialized with an instance of an adapter. The `Builder Get` methods—like `GetDeleteCommand`—open a connection to read the schema. This can be an expensive operation, but in the course of normal programming you will probably have opened the connection anyway. Listing 11.9 provides an example of the generated SQL.

Listing 11.9 An `INSERT` SQL Statement Generated by `OleDbCommandBuilder`

```
INSERT INTO products( ProductName , SupplierID , CategoryID ,
QuantityPerUnit , UnitPrice , UnitsInStock , UnitsOnOrder ,
ReorderLevel , Discontinued ) VALUES ( ? , ? , ? , ? , ? , ? , ? ,
? , ? )
```

The parameterized values can be filled in by an adapter during the course of an adapter operation. For example, we can use a command builder to generate SQL and call an adapter's `Update` method. The update method will fill in the missing information.

Updating a DataSet

You are welcome to write SQL from scratch (or use stored procedures), or you can use a command builder, introduced in the preceding section, to write SQL for you. We will use generated SQL to perform an update.

NOTE: All providers are not created equal. I have experienced some difficulty getting the command builder to generate SQL for IBM's UDB database, and there are articles on the Web about other data providers. In one particular case the problem is probably related to the data itself. The database is a legacy database that isn't keyed properly, and the absence of primary keys seems to be the culprit. You always have the option of writing SQL from scratch or using stored procedures.

In the disconnected ADO.NET model, the DataSet keeps track of changes to the data. When we are ready to post changes back to the provider, we use a connection, an adapter, and a command builder. The command builder will generate SQL for us, and the adapter will fill in the parameterized arguments for the changed data. Listing 11.10 demonstrates updating a DataSet with an OleDbCommandBuilder object.

Listing 11.10 Updating a DataSet with SQL Generated by OleDbCommandBuilder

```
1:   Imports System.Data
2:   Imports System.Data.OleDb
3:
4:   Public Class Form1
5:       Inherits System.Windows.Forms.Form
6:
7:   [ Windows Form Designer generated code ]
8:
9:     Private Connection As OleDbConnection
10:    Private Adapter As OleDbDataAdapter
11:    Private Builder As OleDbCommandBuilder
12:    Private Customers As DataSet
13:
```

```
14:     Private Sub Form1_Load(ByVal sender As System.Object, _
15:       ByVal e As System.EventArgs) Handles MyBase.Load
16:
17:       Connection = New OleDbConnection(Database.ConnectionString)
18:       Adapter = New OleDbDataAdapter("SELECT * FROM CUSTOMERS", _
19:         Connection)
20:
21:       Customers = New DataSet("Customers")
22:       Adapter.Fill(Customers)
23:
24:       Builder = New OleDbCommandBuilder(Adapter)
25:       TextBox1.Text = Builder.GetUpdateCommand().CommandText
26:
27:       DataGrid1.DataSource = Customers.Tables(0)
28:
29:     End Sub
30:
31:     Private Sub ButtonUpdate_Click(ByVal sender As System.Object, _
32:       ByVal e As System.EventArgs) Handles ButtonUpdate.Click
33:
34:       Adapter.Update(Customers)
35:       Customers.AcceptChanges()
36:     End Sub
37:
38:     Private Sub ButtonCancel_Click(ByVal sender As System.Object, _
39:       ByVal e As System.EventArgs) Handles ButtonCancel.Click
40:
41:       Customers.RejectChanges()
42:
43:     End Sub
44: End Class
```

The Windows Forms sample application, `CustomBuilderDemo.sln`, contains a `DataGrid` object, two buttons, and a `TextBox` control. The `TextBox` is used to show the generated update command. (You can download the code and experiment with the sample.)

NOTE: Notice that `Database.ConnectionString` was used from earlier examples. To use the `Data.vb` module, add it to your project. You will also need to add an `App.config` file to your project. To do so, you can use the Application Configuration applet in the File|Add New Item dialog. If you use the Application Configuration template, the `.config` file will be generated for your assembly correctly, and you can copy and paste the `<appSettings>` configuration information from Listing 11.1.

Four private fields in lines 9 through 12 are used to support the form's behavior. We have used these four players before: `OleDbConnection`, `OleDbDataAdapter`, `OleDbCommandBuilder`, and `DataSet`. The basic behavior is that the four fields are initialized and the `DataSet` field is used to get data into `DataGrid1`. This happens in the `Form1_Load` event in lines 14 through 29. The use of `OleDbCommandBuilder` in line 24 generates the UP-DATE SQL statement, as well as INSERT and DELETE statements.

The first button is the update button, and the second button is a cancel button. The update button is associated with the event handler in lines 31 through 36, and the cancel button is associated with the event handler in lines 38 through 43. Because we generated the UPDATE SQL, actually updating the database is a relatively simple process.

Keep in mind that the `DataSet` is disconnected. This means that changes you made in the `DataGrid` are reflected in the `DataSet` but not the database. We need to invoke the `OleDbDataAdapter.Update` command on the `DataSet` to write the changes back to the database. The database update occurs in line 34. If the `Update` command does not raise an exception, `Customers.AcceptChanges()` in line 35 will run. `AcceptChanges` indicates that we want to keep the changes made to the `DataSet` too. This might seem backward, but it prevents you from needing to rehit the database if the database update fails. All you need to do on an exception is roll back the changes in the disconnected database. This is done by calling `DataSet.RejectChanges`. Calling `RejectChanges` is exactly how we implemented the cancel behavior (line 41).

It is worth mentioning that invoking Update on a `DataSet` saves all changes to the `DataSet`. Calling `AcceptChanges` or `RejectChanges` on the `DataSet` invokes the respective method on each `DataTable` in the `DataSet`. If you want to write changes only to a single table or row, pass that `DataTable` or `DataRow` (as the case may be) to the `OleDbDataAdapter.Update` command.

Adding Data to a `DataSet`

If you use controls like the Windows Forms `DataGrid`, adding rows to a table is as easy as navigating to the last position in the `DataGrid`. The `DataGrid` will insert the row automatically. Unfortunately this approach doesn't work for Web applications; you will need to know the mechanics for inserting new rows. That capability involves creating a blank row with the same schema as the table it will reside in and adding the row to the `DataTable`, as demonstrated in Listing 11.11.

Listing 11.11 Adding a New Row Programmatically

```
Private Sub ButtonAdd_Click(ByVal sender As System.Object, _
  ByVal e As System.EventArgs) Handles ButtonAdd.Click

  Dim Row As DataRow = Customers.Tables(0).NewRow()
  Row("CustomerID") = "HELLO"
  Row("CompanyName") = "Hello Fudge Company"
  Row("ContactName") = "Robert Golieb"
  Row("ContactTitle") = "Fudge Master"
  Row("Address") = "41 Hershey Street"
  Row("City") = "Hershey"
  Row("Region") = "Pennsylvania"
  Row("Country") = "US"
  Row("PostalCode") = "06123"
  Row("Phone") = "606-555-1212"
  Row("Fax") = "606-555-1213"
  Customers.Tables(0).Rows.Add(Row)
  DataGrid1.DataSource = Customers.Tables(0)

End Sub
```

The code in this listing first requests a new blank row. The `NewRow` method will return a blank row with the same schema as the table it was invoked against. We know the schema of the row, allowing us to use the column indexer to assign values to each column in the row. When finished we need to insert the row into the table's `Rows` collection. Finally, we need to cause the `DataGrid` to update. You can reassign the `DataSource` property as shown in the listing or simply invoke `DataGrid.Invalidate`.

NOTE: You can use a typed `DataSet` to make your database code more object-oriented. Instead of writing `Row("CustomerID")`, typed `DataSet` objects allow you to refer to a named object and column as if they were simply objects and properties. Chapter 12 provides more information about typed `DataSet` objects.

In our example the same row would be added repeatedly. To create a dynamic insert behavior you need to insert the row and then provide an interface for adding the data. In the case of a `DataGrid` the grid itself is a suitable control for adding data.

Windows applications are easier than Web applications to build and manage because the graphical user interface is connected to the code in Windows applications. With Web applications the user interface is a rendered Web page; you have to post back to the server to render a new page with the inserted row. However, the basic code for adding rows to a `DataSet` is the same for both kinds of applications.

Sorting and Filtering a `DataSet`

If you know how to write SQL, you know that you can sort and filter data with `ORDER BY` and `WHERE` clauses. However, this approach requires that you requery the database each time the view changes. Such requerying is an expensive and impractical operation, especially when you have thousands of simultaneous users and the data has already been queried.

With ADO.NET you have better alternatives. You can read data into a `DataSet` and change the view and order of the data without requerying the database. You can change the order and rows with the `DataView.RowFilter` and `Sort` properties or with the `DataTable.Select` method. The subsections that follow contain examples of each of these.

Filtering and Sorting a `DataView`

The `DataView` class has `RowFilter` and `Sort` properties. `RowFilter` and `Sort` are both string properties. You indicate the rows you want displayed in a `DataView` by modifying the `RowFilter` property with expressions that are similar to `WHERE` predicates in SQL, and you specify order by assigning string expressions that are similar to `ORDER BY` predicates in SQL. Here are three filter expressions followed by two sort expressions.

```
Address like '*Obere*'
City = 'Portland'
Region is null

CustomerID ASC
ContactName DESC
```

The first statement checks for `Address` fields containing the letters "Obere," as in "Obere Str." (an abbreviation for *Strasse*, the German word for *street*). The second expression performs a simple equality test, and the third example demonstrates how to find null fields. The fourth statement orders the `DataView` by `CustomerID` in ascending order, and the fifth statement orders the `DataView` by `ContactName` from Z to A.

Changing the `DataView` with `RowFilter` and `Sort` expressions does not alter the actual data nor does it require a connection to the database. As you might imagine, this reduces the traffic back and forth between the client and server, which can dramatically improve performance over a network or on the Internet. Listing 11.12 (from `CommandBuilderDemo.sln`) shows how we could use `TextBox` and `CheckBox` controls to facilitate dynamic ordering and sorting. The user can add expressions as desired and use the checkboxes to turn filtering and ordering on or off.

Listing 11.12 Ordering and Filtering Dynamically

```
1:   Private Sub CheckBox1_CheckedChanged( _
2:     ByVal sender As System.Object, _
3:     ByVal e As System.EventArgs) Handles CheckBox1.CheckedChanged
4:
5:     If (Customers Is Nothing) Then Return
6:     Try
7:       SetFilter(TextBoxFilter.Text, CheckBox1.Checked)
8:     Catch x As Exception
9:       MessageBox.Show(x.Message)
10:    End Try
11:
12:  End Sub
13:
14:  Private Sub SetFilter(ByVal Filter As String, _
15:    ByVal ApplyFilter As Boolean)
16:
17:    If (ApplyFilter) Then
18:
19:      Customers.Tables(0).DefaultView().RowFilter = _
20:        Filter
21:      DataGrid1.Invalidate()
22:
23:    Else
24:      Customers.Tables(0).DefaultView().RowFilter = ""
25:      DataGrid1.Invalidate()
```

```
26:
27:     End If
28: End Sub
29:
30: Private Sub CheckBox2_CheckedChanged( _
31:   ByVal sender As System.Object, _
32:   ByVal e As System.EventArgs) Handles CheckBox2.CheckedChanged
33:
34:     If (Customers Is Nothing) Then Return
35:     Try
36:       SetSort(TextBoxSort.Text, CheckBox2.Checked)
37:     Catch x As Exception
38:       MessageBox.Show(x.Message)
39:     End Try
40:
41: End Sub
42:
43: Private Sub SetSort(ByVal Expression As String, _
44:   ByVal ApplyFilter As Boolean)
45:
46:     If (ApplyFilter) Then
47:
48:       Customers.Tables(0).DefaultView().Sort = _
49:         Expression
50:       DataGrid1.Invalidate()
51:
52:     Else
53:       Customers.Tables(0).DefaultView().Sort = ""
54:       DataGrid1.Invalidate()
55:
56:     End If
57: End Sub
```

The code listing builds on the code in Listing 11.10. We assume that Customers is a DataSet containing at least one table. In Listing 11.12, the two CheckBox Changed event handlers make sure that Customers is not null (lines 5 and 34) before proceeding. If Customers is initialized, the values of the related TextBox and CheckBox controls are passed to appropriately named methods, SetSort and SetFilter.

Both SetSort and SetFilter work in similar ways. If the CheckBox control was cleared, the expressions are set to empty strings and DataGrid1 is invalidated (lines 24, 25, 53, and 54). If the Boolean argument `ApplyFil-ter` is `True`, the expression is assigned to the `DefaultView` property and the grid is invalidated. (Invalidating the grid will cause it to reflect the changes. You also have the option of reassigning the `DataGrid.Data-Source` property.)

In our example we request the `DefaultView` of a table, which returns a reference to the `DataView` representing the `DataTable`. With the `Data-View` we can set the `Sort` expression (lines 48 and 49) to change the order of the data and the `DataView.RowFilter` expression (lines 19 and 20) to change the rows that displayed in the view.

You are welcome to download `CommandBuilderDemo.sln` to experiment with `RowFilter` and `Sort` expressions. Refer to the Visual Studio .NET help documentation for specific information about the grammar, including more examples.

Filtering and Sorting Rows with a `DataTable`

A `DataTable` can be filtered and sorted by invoking the `Select` method. `Select` is overloaded to accept up to two string arguments. The first string argument represents the filtering expression, and the second string argument represents the sorting expression. When you invoke `DataTable.Se-lect` with a filter, a sort, or both, you get an array of `DataRow` objects representing the rows that matched the filter in the order specified by the `Sort` expression. Each `DataRow` is a reference to a row in the `DataTable`, so changes to values in the rows will be reflected back in the `DataTable`. One drawback is that you cannot bind a `DataRow` to controls like a `Data-Grid`. As a result, using the `DataTable.Select` statement is not a convenient way to change the appearance of data in a `DataGrid`. Continuing with the content of our earlier examples, the following code fragment demonstrates how to retrieve filtered and sorted rows from a `DataTable`.

```
Dim Rows() As DataRow = Customers.Tables(0).Select("City
                       = 'Portland'")
```

This single statement assumes that the `DataSet Customers` contains at least one table with a schema that describes a `City` column. This statement retrieves all rows whose fields in the `City` column contain the value `'Port-land'` (as in Portland, Oregon, or Portland, Maine).

If you want to specify a sort order too, pass the `Sort` expression as the second argument to the `DataTable.Select` method.

Summary

The initiative behind ADO.NET was to reimplement ADO using XML as a flexible and extensible format that is easily transmitted across networks like the Internet. We will talk more about XML and ADO.NET in Chapter 12.

The simple yet powerful revision to ADO in .NET is that the `DataSet` is disconnected. The benefit is that the client retrieves the data and can perform relevant operations without holding a connection to the database, returning to the database only when changes need to be posted. As you learned in this chapter, you can filter and sort data without requerying the database. You also learned that you have a variety of options, including using `DataReader` objects for faster forward and read-only data access, using the `CommandBuilder` class to generate SQL, building connection strings with the Data Link Properties wizard, and using application configuration files for storing and retrieving information like connection strings.

In the next chapter we will build on this information by looking at typed, object-oriented `DataSet` objects; XML serialization; stored procedures; database transactions; and a powerful programming technique that uses interfaces. Programming with ADO.NET interfaces will allow you to switch data providers—databases—without modifying your code.

CHAPTER 12

Advanced ADO.NET

By nature, men are nearly alike; by practice, they get to be wide apart.

—Confucius

Introduction

Often the smallest attention to details or the extra bit of wisdom makes all the difference in the world. In programming, knowing that a well-understood pattern applies to the problem you need to solve can turn several days of tedious effort spent hacking out a new (and possibly inferior) solution into just a couple hours of programming. And often it is the simplest evolutionary revisions that make all the difference in the utility of a technology. This latter concept applies to ADO.NET.

From Chapter 11 you know that ADO.NET revised ADO to address real problems of scalability and reliability when it comes to Internet programming. In this chapter I show you how ADO.NET has all the old reliable behaviors, like stored procedure and transaction support, that programmers demand plus new capabilities that give the *.NET* part of the name meaning. In addition to the old reliable behaviors, the new capabilities discussed here include how to create typed `DataSet` objects, how to use XML with `DataSet` objects to support serialization and ultimately transmittal of data over the Internet, and how to use data interfaces to implement a solution that supports easily switching between data providers.

TIP: If you switch data providers, remember to change your connection string. The `StoredProcedureDemo.sln` `App.config` file contains two `app-Settings`, one for each provider demonstrated.

The ability to use typed `DataSet` objects is one of my favorite features. The basic idea behind a typed `DataSet` object is that because everything is a class in .NET, you can inherit from and extend classes, including those that are key to ADO.NET, like the `DataSet`, `DataTable`, and `DataRow` classes. The result is more expressive and powerful database code that looks like objects and members rather than an SQL nightmare. We'll get to typed `DataSet` objects later in this chapter.

Updating a `DataView`

Typically when people hear the word *view*, they think of a read-only set of data derived from multiple tables. As we discussed in Chapter 11, the `DataView` represents a database view in .NET. Whereas you more than likely cannot update a view defined in your database, you are able to update a view in .NET by using the `DataView` class.

In case you have skipped around in this book, I'll take a moment to review. A `DataSet` is roughly akin to a subset of a database—although it is important to remember that data does not have to come from a database in ADO.NET. Within a `DataSet` you can have one or more `DataTables` and zero or more `DataRelations`. Each `DataTable` has what is referred to as its *default data view*. The default data view is usually analogous to the table if you were to display it in a grid. This default data view is actually represented by a `DataView` object.

If one or more of a `DataView` object's `AllowNew`, `AllowEdit`, or `AllowDelete` properties is set to `True`, you can modify a table by performing insert, edit, and delete operations on a `DataView` object. One version of the help documentation suggests that `DataView` objects are read only by default; however, the `AllowNew`, `AllowEdit`, and `AllowDelete` properties are set to `True` by default, suggesting that `DataView` objects are editable by default.

I implemented a moderately sized—257 lines for a book listing seems long—sample application that demonstrates simple inheritance for `DataTable` and `DataSet` objects. The sample `EditDataViewDemo.sln` contains code that will let you experiment with updating `DataView` objects. The basic idea is that you set `AllowNew`, `AllowEdit`, or `AllowDelete` to `True` for each kind of operation you want a specific `DataView` object to support. When you invoke `AddNew` on the `DataView` object, a `DataRowView` object is returned. You can modify the `DataRowView` object and send the changes back to the data provider.

When you invoke `AddNew`, a `DataRowView` object is created. The row is not added to the underlying table until `EndEdit` is called. If you call `AddNew` a second time, `EndEdit` is implicitly called on the first row because you may edit only one row at a time. When you are finished editing a new row, call `EndEdit` on the `DataRowView` object returned by `AddNew` or call `CancelEdit` to discard your changes. Listing 12.1 shows how to edit a `DataView` object. The `DataView` code is surprisingly easy, so I introduced some additional code that hints at inheritance from the `DataSet` and `DataTable` classes.

Listing 12.1 Updating a `DataView` Object

```
1:   Imports System.Data.OleDb
2:   Imports System.Configuration
3:
4:   Public Class Form1
5:       Inherits System.Windows.Forms.Form
6:
7:   [ Windows Form Designer generated code ]
8:
9:     Private OrderDetails As OrderDetails
10:    Private OrderDetailsView As DataView
11:    Private Row As DataRowView = Nothing
12:
13:    Private Sub Form1_Load(ByVal sender As System.Object, _
14:      ByVal e As System.EventArgs) Handles MyBase.Load
15:
16:      OrderDetails = New OrderDetails()
17:      OrderDetailsView = OrderDetails.Orders.DefaultView
18:      DataGrid1.DataSource = OrderDetailsView
19:
20:    End Sub
21:
22:    Private Sub ButtonInsert_Click(ByVal sender As System.Object, _
23:      ByVal e As System.EventArgs) Handles ButtonInsert.Click
24:
25:      Row = OrderDetailsView.AddNew()
26:
27:    End Sub
28:
29:    Private Sub ButtonUpdate_Click(ByVal sender As System.Object, _
30:      ByVal e As System.EventArgs) Handles ButtonUpdate.Click
```

```
31:
32:     Row.EndEdit()
33:     OrderDetails.Update()
34:     Row = Nothing
35:
36:   End Sub
37:
38:   Private Sub ButtonCancel_Click(ByVal sender As System.Object, _
39:     ByVal e As System.EventArgs) Handles ButtonCancel.Click
40:
41:     If (Row Is Nothing) Then Return
42:     Row.CancelEdit()
43:     Row = Nothing
44:
45:   End Sub
46:
47:   Private Sub ButtonDelete_Click(ByVal sender As System.Object, _
48:     ByVal e As System.EventArgs) Handles ButtonDelete.Click
49:
50:     If (Row Is Nothing) Then Return
51:     Row.Delete()
52:     Row = Nothing
53:
54:   End Sub
55: End Class
56:
57: Public Class Database
58:   Private Shared FConnection As OleDbConnection
59:
60:   Private Shared ReadOnly Property ConnectionString()
61:   Get
62:     Return ConfigurationSettings.AppSettings("ConnectionString")
63:   End Get
64:   End Property
65:
66:   Public Shared ReadOnly Property Connection() _
67:     As OleDbConnection
68:   Get
69:     If (FConnection Is Nothing) Then
70:       FConnection = New OleDbConnection(ConnectionString)
71:     End If
72:     Return FConnection
73:   End Get
74:   End Property
```

```
75:
76:   Public Shared Function GetAdapter( _
77:     ByVal SQL As String) As OleDbDataAdapter
78:
79:     Return New OleDbDataAdapter(SQL, Connection)
80:   End Function
81: End Class
82:
83: Public Class Details
84:   Inherits DataTable
85:
86:   Private FAdapter As OleDbDataAdapter
87:   Private FBuilder As OleDbCommandBuilder
88:
89:   Public Sub New()
90:     MyBase.New("Details")
91:     FAdapter = Database.GetAdapter( _
92:       "SELECT * FROM [Order Details]")
93:     FAdapter.Fill(Me)
94:
95:     FBuilder = New OleDbCommandBuilder(FAdapter)
96:   End Sub
97:
98:   Public ReadOnly Property Key() As DataColumn
99:   Get
100:     Return Columns("OrderID")
101:   End Get
102:   End Property
103:
104:   Public Sub Update()
105:     FAdapter.Update(Me)
106:     AcceptChanges()
107:   End Sub
108:
109: End Class
110:
111: Public Class Orders
112:   Inherits DataTable
113:
114:   Private FAdapter As OleDbDataAdapter
115:   Private FBuilder As OleDbCommandBuilder
116:
117:   Public Sub New()
118:     MyBase.New("Orders")
```

```
119:      FAdapter = Database.GetAdapter( _
120:        "SELECT * FROM [Orders]")
121:
122:      FAdapter.Fill(Me)
123:      FBuilder = New OleDbCommandBuilder(FAdapter)
124:    End Sub
125:
126:    Public ReadOnly Property Key() As DataColumn
127:    Get
128:      Return Columns("OrderID")
129:    End Get
130:    End Property
131:
132:    Public Sub Update()
133:      FAdapter.Update(Me)
134:      AcceptChanges()
135:    End Sub
136:
137: End Class
138:
139: Public Class OrderDetails
140:    Inherits DataSet
141:
142:    Public Sub New()
143:      MyBase.New("OrderDetails")
144:      Tables.Add(New Orders())
145:      Tables.Add(New Details())
146:      Relations.Add("Order Details", Orders.Key, Details.Key)
147:    End Sub
148:
149:    Public ReadOnly Property Orders() As Orders
150:    Get
151:      Return Tables("Orders")
152:    End Get
153:    End Property
154:
155:    Public ReadOnly Property Details() As Details
156:    Get
157:      Return Tables("Details")
158:    End Get
159:    End Property
160:
161:    Public Sub Update()
162:      Orders.Update()
```

```
163:        Details.Update()
164:    End Sub
165:
166: End Class
```

I created a `Database` class in lines 57 through 81 that makes it convenient to get a connection to the database. I used an `App.config` file and the `appSettings` element to externalize the connection string, as introduced in Chapter 11.

NOTE: You can drag and drop code onto the Toolbox for later use. I tend to forget the exact syntax of an `appSettings` element. By creating a tab in the Toolbox—I called mine "shortcuts"—I can drag the `appSettings` code onto the Toolbox and drop it into any project for later use. You can add code to the Toolbox just as you would any component. This is a great time-saver.

Lines 83 through 166 demonstrate that we can inherit from the basic ADO.NET `DataTable` and `DataSet` classes and extend them. I created a custom `Details` class (lines 83 through 109) and a custom `Orders` class (lines 111 through 137) by generalizing `DataTable` and a custom `OrderDetails` class (lines 139 through 166) by generalizing `DataSet`. As a result, extra information can be added to the classes. In the example, the custom classes are used to perform initialization and define DataRelations. A benefit of this strategy is that we can reuse these classes instead of writing initialization code all over the place. Actually Visual Studio .NET will create advanced, generalized ADO.NET classes for you. I created the examples here to introduce the notion of inheriting from ADO.NET classes. Refer to the Creating a Typed `DataSet` section later in this chapter for more information on defining XML Schemas and inheriting the `DataSet` and `DataTable` classes.

The code for updating the `DataView` object is very simple, as revealed by the relatively few lines required (see lines 1 through 55). Lines 9 through 11 define an instance of the typed `DataSet` class mentioned above, a `DataView` object, and a `DataRowView` object. The first class is my Frankenstein; the latter two classes are part of ADO.NET.

In the `Form1_Load` event (lines 13 through 20) I initialized the `DataSet` object, requested the `Orders` object's default `DataView` object (line 17), and associated `DataGrid1`'s `DataSource` property with the default `DataView` object. Normally we have been conditioned to think that a browse view has been created. With ADO.NET we can actually perform CRUD (create, read, update, and delete) operations. For now you can ignore the custom classes; simply focus on the fact that we have a `DataView` object.

NOTE: It is worth noting that you do not have to manually manage the `DataRowView` object if you are using a Windows Forms `DataGrid` object. `DataGrid` will perform CRUD operations automatically as you move the cursor in the grid or use keystrokes (such as pressing the Delete key). As an example, if you press Delete on a row, the `DataGrid` object's `Delete` method is called. The `DataGrid` object is used to conveniently allow you to see the results of the `DataRowView` methods.

The event handler in lines 22 through 27 demonstrates how to create a new row by calling the `DataView.AddNew` method. The return value for `AddNew` is assigned to the `DataRowView` field introduced in line 11. With the row we can perform other operations, including deleting, canceling, and updating. Lines 29 through 36 demonstrate how to update `OrderDetails`. I called `DataRowView.EndEdit` and updated the `DataSet` object. Chapter 11 showed that this can be accomplished by generating UPDATE SQL and calling the `OleDbDataAdapter.Update` method and the `DataTable` or `DataSet` objects' `AcceptChanges` methods. My custom `Update` method (invoked in line 33) conceals these steps, but they are performed. (You will have to download or visually trace the code to see them.) To cancel changes, call `DataRowView.CancelEdit` (line 42), and `DataRowView.Delete` will delete an added `DataRowView` object (line 51).

As you can see, the operations for managing a `DataView` object are easy to use. This is another benefit of ADO.NET. As the database subframework developers understand more about how programmers need to work with database code, the developers can converge and consolidate steps into higher, abstract steps. More happens with less effort.

NOTE: Talking about how programming is getting "easier" always feels like something that should be guarded. On many occasions managers have assumed this meant that the software would be easy to create. The reality is that programmer tools are increasing in power and capability (as they must), but the needs of users are still far outstripping the capability of the tools. At least for the foreseeable future, programmers will be playing catch-up to get software to do some of the things users want to be able to do.

If you wanted to write a simple text editor, you could put one together in a few minutes with VB .NET. However, no one wants a simple text editor because everyone has them. Modern, commercial-quality software applications like

Adobe Photoshop, Microsoft Word, and Bryce 5 have hundreds, perhaps thousands, of features and tens of thousands or millions of lines of code.

If asked, I would unequivocally state that .NET will help you build applications better, faster, and cheaper than ever before. Unfortunately, users will want more features, resulting in projects taking weeks, months, or years. A project I am working on has so many business rules that it will comprise more than a million lines of code by the time we're finished.

Programming with Stored Procedures

No programming language or tool would be considered complete without support for stored procedures, and of course you will find excellent support for stored procedures in the .NET Framework. As you probably know, your database provider will need to support stored procedures, and you will need to know how to write them (or know someone who does). All we have to do is transfer the knowledge from the old way to the new way.

Since stored procedures are generally an advanced topic for many developers, I will review the basic idea here. A stored procedure is analogous to a function. The difference between .NET stored procedures and functions is that stored procedures are written in a version of SQL and stored in the database and .NET functions are written in VB .NET and stored in a module. A general benefit of stored procedures is that you can treat one or more SQL operations as a single, homogeneous operation. An additional benefit is that the stored procedure is on the database, and in production systems this is generally some of your big iron. (By "big iron" I mean more computing power.) Real performance differences will vary, but using stored procedures does allow you to centralize SQL. Using stored procedures also provides for a nice division of labor, allowing database people to focus on writing SQL and VB .NET people to focus on writing Visual Basic code.

SQL Server, Oracle, and UDB all seem to have flavors of stored procedure languages. Microsoft calls its SQL Server stored procedure language T-SQL; Oracle calls its stored procedure language PL-SQL. I am not sure if UDB has a name for its stored procedure language, but until recently it was the C programming language.

Writing stored procedures varies by database provider, but from the VB .NET perspective the process is roughly the same. We need a procedure, a connection, an adapter, and a command object. Command objects serve double-duty, permitting you to pass raw SQL or the name of a stored procedure and parameters. Let's take a look at how we invoke a stored procedure with input and output parameters, as well as how to receive an open cursor (a result set).

Invoking a Stored Procedure

The direct way to invoke a stored procedure is to create a connection and a command and then initialize an adapter with the command. The adapter is used to fill a **DataSet**, and the command object contains the information that helps invoke the stored procedure. These basic steps are the same for OleDb or SqlClient providers; you will need to create and add parameters only if your stored procedure needs them.

TIP: Use Shift+Alt+Enter to toggle full-screen mode. The first time you press these keys, all the peripheral windows will be closed except for the menu and the Code Editor screen, providing you with the maximum amount of space for writing code.

The example code in **StoredProcedureDemo.sln** contains these basic steps with a twist. I wrote the code as one monolithic procedure so you could see a single linear progression of steps, but I used interfaces. ADO.NET is supported by common interfaces that the various provider classes must implement. For example, instead of declaring an **OleDbCommand** instance I can declare an **IDbCommand** instance. With this approach I can easily switch between **OleDbCommand** and **SqlCommand**, depending on the environment. Interface programming in general is a powerful strategy, and in this case, it supports switching between working disconnected on my laptop and back to the network development environment without changing my basic code base. (I will talk more about this in the Programming with ADO.NET Interfaces section later in this chapter.) Listing 12.2 contains a simple stored procedure call written using interface declarations.

Listing 12.2 Invoking a Stored Procedure without Parameters

```
1:  Imports System.Data.SqlClient
2:  Imports System.Data.OleDb
3:  Imports System.Configuration
4:
5:  Public Class Form1
6:      Inherits System.Windows.Forms.Form
7:
```

```
 8:   [ Windows Form Designer generated code ]
 9:     Private Sub Form1_Load(ByVal sender As Object, _
10:      ByVal e As System.EventArgs) Handles MyBase.Load
11:
12:        Dim ConnectionString As String = _
13:          ConfigurationSettings.AppSettings("ConnectionString1")
14:
15:        Dim Connection As IDbConnection = _
16:          New OleDbConnection(ConnectionString)
17:
18:        Dim Command As IDbCommand = _
19:          New OleDbCommand()
20:
21:        Command.CommandType = CommandType.StoredProcedure
22:        Command.Connection = Connection
23:        Command.CommandText = "[Catalog]"
24:
25:        Dim Adapter As IDataAdapter = _
26:          New OleDbDataAdapter(Command)
27:
28:        Dim DataSet As DataSet = New DataSet(Command.CommandText)
29:        Adapter.Fill(DataSet)
30:
31:        DataGrid1.DataSource = DataSet
32:     End Sub
33: End Class
```

Line 15 declares an `IDbConnection` object, and line 16 creates an instance of `OleDbConnection`. By implication `OleDbConnection` must implement the `IDbConnection` interface. (`SqlConnection` does too.)

Line 18 declares an `IDbCommand` object and line 19 creates an instance of `OleDbCommand`. The command is central to stored procedure invocation. The `CommandType` property is `CommandType.Text` by default. When calling a stored procedure, change the `CommandType` property to `Command-Type.StoredProcedure` (line 21). The command is assigned a reference to the connection object, and the stored procedure name is set as the value of `CommandText`. (The provider used in the example is Microsoft Access, which seems to prefer the square brackets, as in `[Catalog]`. Microsoft Access began supporting stored procedures in ADO 2.5 or 2.6.)

To wrap up we initialize the adapter with the command object and use the adapter to fill a `DataSet` object.

If a particular stored procedure does not return a cursor (think "result set"), you can call a command object's `ExecuteNonQuery` method. If you need only the first column of the first row—as you might need for an insert where a key is generated in the database—you can invoke `ExecuteScalar`.

You will want to perform several other tasks as well. During the course of a project you will likely need to pass parameters to a stored procedure, for example, when you insert a row. You may also need to get individual columns of data back from the stored procedure (in addition to getting a cursor). The next subsections demonstrate how to define SQL Server connection strings and how to use input and output parameters. (The examples use both the Microsoft Access and Microsoft SQL Server versions of the Northwind database.)

Defining an SQL Server Connection String

Because I am introducing a Microsoft SQL Server provider at this point, I have included this brief interlude to show you an example of an SQL Server connection string. I have used the same technique to store the SQL Server connection string in the `App.config` file. (The connection string shown in Listing 12.3 appears in the `App.config` file for `StoredProcedureDemo.sln`.)

Listing 12.3 contains a sample connection string for an SQL Server instance. You can copy these values from the Properties window (Figure 12.1). Select the database instance from the Server Explorer in Visual Studio .NET and press F4 to open the Properties window for that database instance.

Listing 12.3 A Sample SQL Server Connection String

```
<add key="ConnectionString"
    value="data source=SCI\EREWHON;initial catalog=Northwind;in-
tegrated security=SSPI;persist security info=True;workstation
id=PTK800;packet size=4096" />
```

TIP: When defining the connection string as a value in a `.config` file, remember that the actual connection string is one contiguous string of information. It is wrapped in Listing 12.3 due to the limitations of the printed page.

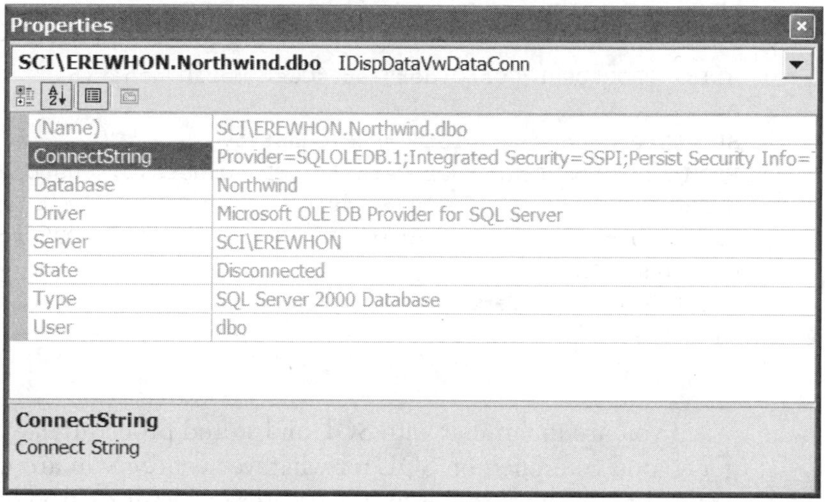

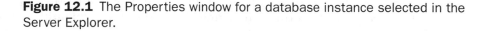

Figure 12.1 The Properties window for a database instance selected in the Server Explorer.

If you define the connection string from scratch, you will need to substitute information like `workstation id` with your workstation's name (instead of mine, used in Listing 12.3). As previously mentioned, it is easiest to add a connection to the Server Explorer and copy the connection string from the Properties window.

Using Input Parameters

When you perform most practical queries, you will be selectively returning a subset of data, performing filters, or ordering data. To get the parameters to the stored procedure, use the `Parameters` collection of a command object.

Parameters are provider-specific. For OleDb providers create instances of the `OleDbParameter` class, and for SqlClient providers create instances of the `SqlParameter` class. You also have the option of declaring parameters as `IDataParameter` types and instantiating either OleDb or SqlClient parameters. Listing 12.4 contains the `CustOrderHist` stored procedure, and Listing 12.5 shows the SqlClient code that invokes this stored procedure. `CustomerID` is a required input parameter.

Listing 12.4 A Stored Procedure Written in T-SQL

```
ALTER PROCEDURE CustOrderHist @CustomerID nchar(5)
AS
SELECT ProductName, Total=SUM(Quantity)
FROM Products P, [Order Details] OD, Orders O, Customers C
WHERE C.CustomerID = @CustomerID
AND C.CustomerID = O.CustomerID AND O.OrderID = OD.OrderID AND
OD.ProductID = P.ProductID
GROUP BY ProductName
```

If you are unfamiliar with SQL and stored procedures, you will need to get a good reference on SQL for whatever vendor you are using. (The flavors vary a bit but are based to a greater or lesser degree on ANSI SQL.) The procedure is a function that accepts a five-character string representing `CustomerID` and returns the names of products and quantities purchased by the customer. The detail information is assembled from the `Customers`, `Products`, and `Orders Details` tables. Here is Listing 12.5, demonstrating how to invoke the stored procedure defined in Listing 12.4.

Listing 12.5 Passing an Input Parameter to a Stored Procedure

```
1:   Private Sub InputParameterProcedure()
2:     Dim ConnectionString As String = _
3:       ConfigurationSettings.AppSettings("ConnectionString")
4:
5:     Dim Connection As IDbConnection = _
6:       New SqlConnection(ConnectionString)
7:
8:     Dim Command As IDbCommand = _
9:       New SqlCommand()
10:
11:    Command.CommandType = CommandType.StoredProcedure
12:    Command.Connection = Connection
13:    Command.CommandText = "CustOrderHist"
14:
15:    Dim Parameter As IDataParameter = _
16:      New SqlParameter()
17:      'New SqlParameter("@CustomerID", SqlDbType.NChar, 5)
18:
```

```
19:    Parameter.Direction = ParameterDirection.Input
20:    Parameter.ParameterName = "@CustomerID"
21:    Parameter.DbType = DbType.String
22:    Parameter.Value = "ALFKI"
23:    Command.Parameters.Add(Parameter)
24:
25:    Dim Adapter As IDataAdapter = _
26:       New SqlDataAdapter(Command)
27:
28:    Dim DataSet As DataSet = New DataSet(Command.CommandText)
29:    Adapter.Fill(DataSet)
30:
31:    DataGrid2.DataSource = DataSet
32: End Sub
```

Listing 12.5 is an excerpt from `StoredProcedureDemo.sln`. The example invokes a stored procedure against the SQL Server instance of the Northwind database. Much of the code is similar to that in Listing 12.2. Let's focus on the parameter aspect of this code.

The `CustOrderHist` stored procedure requires a single parameter, `CustomerID`. This parameter is a five-character string used to join the `Customers`, `Orders`, and `Products` tables and return the order history for that customer (as depicted in Listing 12.4). The single parameter is defined in lines 15 through 23 in Listing 12.5. Lines 15 through 17 demonstrate that the constructor is overloaded for the `SqlParameter` class. You can call the default constructor and initialize the parameter values as properties or call one of the overloaded constructors and pass in all the parameters when you construct the `SqlParameter` instance.

The constructor that takes three arguments is commented out (line 17). I used the default constructor and assigned `Direction` (line 19), `ParameterName` (line 20), `DbType` (line 21), and `Value` (line 22). The parameter is added to the command's `Parameters` collection in line 23. If more than one parameter is required, you simply repeat this process.

There are a couple of further points of interest here. Using the @ prefix, as in `@CustomerID`, is a required convention in SQL Server (and UDB); unfortunately, the @ prefix is a required factoid with ambiguous origins. A second piece of information is the use of the `DbType` property. Different database providers use different type enumerations. If you are using the `IDataParameter` interface, you need to find a type that closely matches one of the `DbType` enumerated values. SqlClient providers use `SqlType` enumerated values, and OleDb providers use `OleDbType` enumerated values. To a degree they are interchangeable. Check the help documentation for specific data types supported by the enumerations.

Based on the code written in Listing 12.4, when the code in Listing 12.5 runs, the order history for customer ALFKI (Alfreds Futterkiste) will be returned by the store procedure.

Using Output Parameters

Output parameters are initialized pretty much the same way that input parameters are (see Listing 12.5). The biggest difference for output parameters is that you have to express `ParameterDirection` as an output parameter and retrieve the value after the stored procedure has run.

An output parameter is commonly needed when a column value is generated at the time a row is inserted. For example, if `CustomerID` were a generated field, its value would not be known until a row was inserted into the database. If you need to hold onto an inserted record, you will need to get the identifier back after the insert. You can use output parameters to get the necessary data.

To demonstrate I borrowed a table from the Web database implemented with SQL Server at *http://www.softconcepts.com*. For earlier examples I used sample databases I thought you might have or could access. For this example I used a table you could easily recreate. Toward this end I included script to generate the table, the custom stored procedure, and the VB .NET code to insert a row and return an output parameter.

Defining a Table in SQL Server

There are several database vendors to choose from. I have worked on projects with Oracle, SQL Server, UDB, Informix, and a host of other enterprise servers and desktop databases. I chose SQL Server for this example because it was handy when writing this chapter. SQL Server integrates nicely with Visual Studio .NET, and it shouldn't be too difficult for you to get a copy of Microsoft Data Engine (MSDE). (There should be a copy of MSDE on your Visual Studio .NET discs, if you purchased the enterprise edition, and a copy is included in an MSDN subscription.)

You can create a new database in the Server Explorer if you have a registered SQL Server instance. When you create the new database, you can right-click on the Tables node for that database, select New Table, and define a new table right in the Visual Studio .NET IDE.

As an alternative, you can open an instance of the SQL Query Analyzer—which installs with SQL Server—and run the script in Listing 12.6 to create the table. To create the table, follow these steps.

1. Open the SQL Query Analyzer and log into the server instance that will house your table.
2. From the SQL Query Analyzer menu, select the Query|Change Database menu item and pick the database against which you want to run the script.
3. In the script window (Figure 12.2), type the script shown in Listing 12.6.
4. From the main menu, Select Query|Execute menu item to run the script.

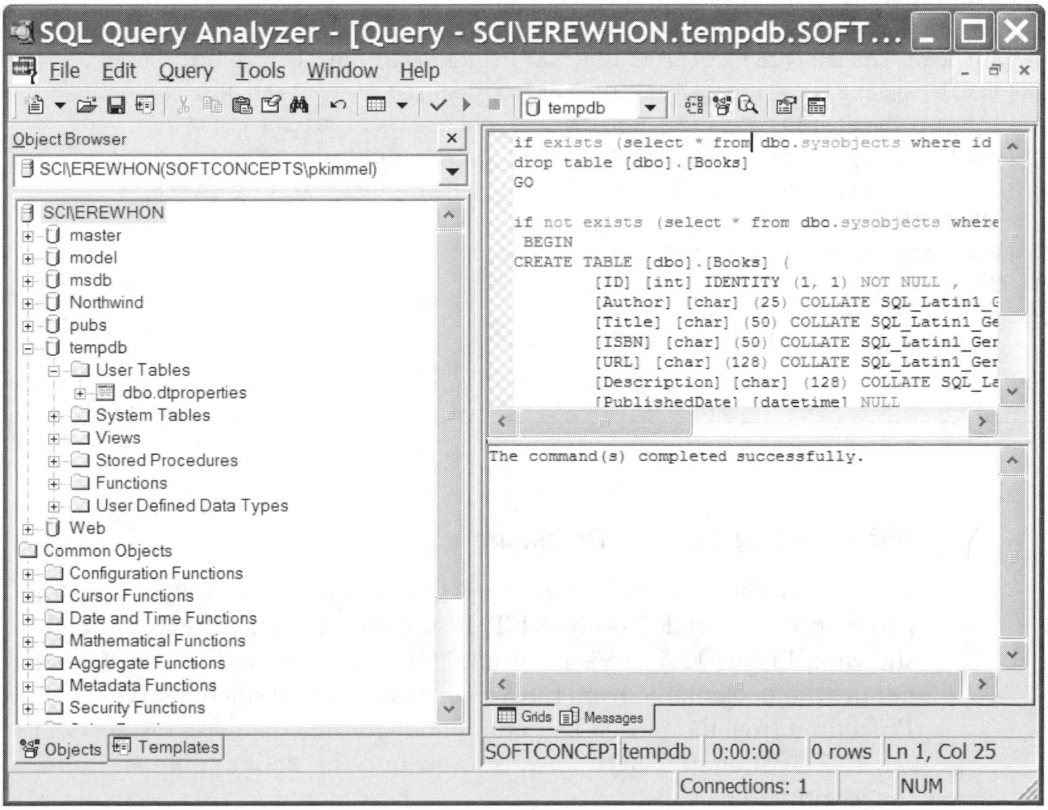

Figure 12.2 The SQL Query Analyzer, an invaluable tool for managing SQL databases.

When you perform the last step, the Books table will be created in the selected database. You can use the same database and the Books table to experiment with the exercises in the remaining two subsections.

Listing 12.6 The Script for Generating the Books Table

```
if exists (select * from dbo.sysobjects where id =
object_id(N'[dbo].[Books]') and OBJECTPROPERTY(id, N'IsUserTable') = 1)
drop table [dbo].[Books]
GO

if not exists (select * from dbo.sysobjects where id =
object_id(N'[dbo].[Books]') and OBJECTPROPERTY(id, N'IsUserTable') = 1)
BEGIN
CREATE TABLE [dbo].[Books] (
  [ID] [int] IDENTITY (1, 1) NOT NULL ,
  [Author] [char] (25) COLLATE SQL_Latin1_General_CP1_CI_AS NOT NULL ,
  [Title] [char] (50) COLLATE SQL_Latin1_General_CP1_CI_AS NOT NULL ,
  [ISBN] [char] (50) COLLATE SQL_Latin1_General_CP1_CI_AS NULL ,
  [URL] [char] (128) COLLATE SQL_Latin1_General_CP1_CI_AS NULL ,
  [Description] [char] (128) COLLATE SQL_Latin1_General_CP1_CI_AS
    NOT NULL ,
  [PublishedDate] [datetime] NULL
) ON [PRIMARY]
END

GO
```

Implementing a Stored Procedure

You can continue to work in the SQL Query Analyzer or create the stored procedure in Visual Studio .NET. I implemented the stored procedure shown in Listing 12.7 in Visual Studio .NET by selecting the database containing the Books table from the Server Explorer and selecting New Stored Procedure from the Stored Procedure node for that database instance. Listing 12.7, written in T-SQL, inserts a row into the Books table and returns the identity value.

Listing 12.7 A Stored Procedure for Inserting a Row into the Books Table

```
ALTER PROCEDURE AddBook
(
  @Author          char(25),
  @Title           char(50),
  @ISBN            char(50),
  @URL             char(128),
  @Description     char(128),
  @PublishedDate   DateTime,
  @ID              int OUTPUT
)
AS

INSERT INTO Books
(
  Author,
  Title,
  ISBN,
  URL,
  Description,
  PublishedDate
)

VALUES
(
  @Author,
  @Title,
  @ISBN,
  @URL,
  @Description,
  @PublishedDate
)

SELECT
  @ID = @@IDENTITY
```

In Listing 12.7 the ALTER PROCEDURE statement creates the stored procedure. The procedure accepts seven parameters. Six parameters are input parameters; the seventh is an output parameter. From the script in Listing 12.6 we can determine that the ID column is an identity column. (This is an autogenerated column in SQL Server.) When we insert the row, the identity column is generated, and the client will need that information for future operations. (In our example, we simply display the ID column value to the user.)

The INSERT INTO statement inserts all our input parameter columns. Because the ID column is generated, we don't need to insert this value. Finally we invoke a SELECT @ID = @@IDENTITY command to read the identity for the row we just inserted into the ID parameter. The client application can read this value from the object representing the ID parameter.

In Listing 12.7, the first statement set in bold font demonstrates how to declare an output parameter, and the second bold statement demonstrates how to select the generated identity for this row into the output parameter.

Obtaining an Output Parameter from a Stored Procedure

You can experiment with output parameters with any stored procedure that defines an output parameter. We'll continue with the Books table and the AddBook stored procedure defined in the preceding subsections. I included the code to run the stored procedure in a simple input form (Figure 12.3) to

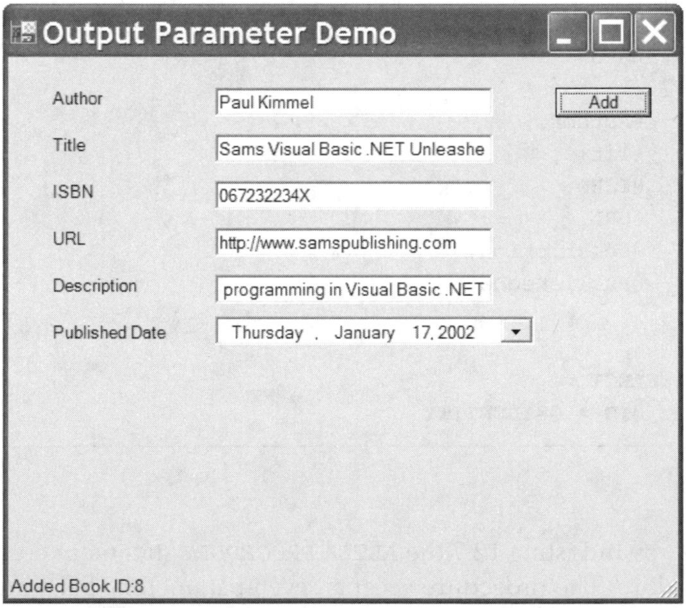

Figure 12.3 A simple input Windows Form application that culminates in running the AddBook stored procedure.

demonstrate one way to tie all the elements of a database application together. Listing 12.8 (available in `OutputPutParameterDemo.sln`) accepts input values and runs the `AddBook` stored procedure. The only change we might make in a production application is to separate the database code into a separate class, so it isn't so closely tied to a single form.

Listing 12.8 A Windows Form Application for Running the `AddBook` Procedure

```
1:  Imports System.Data.SqlClient
2:  Imports System.Configuration
3:
4:  Public Class Form1
5:      Inherits System.Windows.Forms.Form
6:
7:  [ Windows Form Designer generated code ]
8:
9:    Private ReadOnly Property Author() As String
10:   Get
11:     Return TextBoxAuthor.Text
12:   End Get
13:   End Property
14:
15:   Private ReadOnly Property Title() As String
16:   Get
17:     Return TextBoxTitle.Text
18:   End Get
19:   End Property
20:
21:   Private ReadOnly Property ISBN() As String
22:   Get
23:     Return TextBoxISBN.Text
24:   End Get
25:   End Property
26:
27:   Private ReadOnly Property URL() As String
28:   Get
29:     Return TextBoxURL.Text
30:   End Get
31:   End Property
32:
33:   Private ReadOnly Property Description() As String
34:   Get
35:     Return TextBoxDescription.Text
```

```
36:    End Get
37:    End Property
38:
39:    Private ReadOnly Property PublishedDate() As DateTime
40:    Get
41:      Return DateTimePickerPublishedDate.Value
42:    End Get
43:    End Property
44:
45:    Private Sub Button1_Click(ByVal sender As System.Object, _
46:      ByVal e As System.EventArgs) Handles Button1.Click
47:
48:      AddBook(Author, Title, ISBN, URL, _
49:        Description, PublishedDate)
50:
51:    End Sub
52:
53:    Private ReadOnly Property ConnectionString() As String
54:    Get
55:      Return ConfigurationSettings.AppSettings( _
56:        "ConnectionString")
57:    End Get
58:    End Property
59:
60:
61:    Private Sub AddBook(ByVal Author As String, _
62:      ByVal Title As String, ByVal ISBN As String, _
63:      ByVal URL As String, ByVal Description As String, _
64:      ByVal PublishedDate As DateTime)
65:
66:      Dim Connection As SqlConnection = _
67:        New SqlConnection(ConnectionString)
68:
69:      Dim Command As SqlCommand = _
70:        New SqlCommand()
71:
72:      Command.Connection = Connection
73:      Command.CommandType = CommandType.StoredProcedure
74:      Command.CommandText = "AddBook"
75:
76:
77:      Dim parameter As SqlParameter = _
78:        New SqlParameter("@Author", SqlDbType.Char, 25)
79:      parameter.Direction = ParameterDirection.Input
```

```
80:     parameter.Value = Author
81:     Command.Parameters.Add(parameter)
82:
83:     parameter = New SqlParameter("@Title", SqlDbType.Char, 50)
84:     parameter.Direction = ParameterDirection.Input
85:     parameter.Value = Title
86:     Command.Parameters.Add(parameter)
87:
88:     parameter = _
89:       New SqlParameter("@ISBN", SqlDbType.Char, 50)
90:     parameter.Direction = ParameterDirection.Input
91:     parameter.Value = ISBN
92:     Command.Parameters.Add(parameter)
93:
94:     parameter = _
95:       New SqlParameter("@URL", SqlDbType.Char, 128)
96:     parameter.Direction = ParameterDirection.Input
97:     parameter.Value = URL
98:     Command.Parameters.Add(parameter)
99:
100:    parameter = _
101:      New SqlParameter("@Description", SqlDbType.Char, 128)
102:    parameter.Direction = ParameterDirection.Input
103:    parameter.Value = Description
104:    Command.Parameters.Add(parameter)
105:
106:    parameter = _
107:      New SqlParameter("@PublishedDate", SqlDbType.DateTime, 8)
108:    parameter.Direction = ParameterDirection.Input
109:    parameter.Value = PublishedDate
110:    Command.Parameters.Add(parameter)
111:
112:    parameter = _
113:      New SqlParameter("@ID", SqlDbType.Int, 4)
114:    parameter.Direction = ParameterDirection.Output
115:    Command.Parameters.Add(parameter)
116:
117:    Connection.Open()
118:    Try
119:      Command.ExecuteNonQuery()
120:      UpdateStatusBar("Added Book ID:" + _
121:        parameter.Value.ToString())
122:    Catch e As Exception
123:      MessageBox.Show(e.Message, "Failed Insert", _
```

```
124:          MessageBoxButtons.OK, MessageBoxIcon.Error)
125:    Finally
126:       Connection.Close()
127:    End Try
128:
129:
130:  End Sub
131:
132:  Private Sub UpdateStatusBar(ByVal Message As String)
133:     StatusBar1.Text = Message
134:  End Sub
135:
136: End Class
```

The first 58 lines include property statements to read values for the form's controls. I prefer this approach since it permits me to change the underlying control, add validation, and use named properties disrupting the rest of the form's code. For example, if the `PublishedDate` property starts as a `Text-Box` control and then validates input and returns a `DateTime` value, I need to write this code only in the property getter (lines 39 through 43). Then, if I elect to reimplement the date and time using a `DateTimePicker` control, I can do so without disrupting any code that is dependent on the value since that code will be relying on the property and not the literal control.

Lines 61 through 130 demonstrate code that invokes the `AddBook` stored procedure. This code is very similar to the code in Listing 12.5; there are just many more parameters in Listing 12.8. The significant difference is that Listing 12.8 has to manage the output parameter. There are a couple of ways to do this. One way is to declare the output parameter as a separate parameter instance and read the value out of that instance. I simulated this approach in line 121. Although I reused the `parameter` variable for every parameter, creating a new parameter and assigning it to this variable, I assigned the output parameter last. In line 121 I simply read the value of the `parameter` object. A second alternative is to read the value from the `Com-mand.Parameters` collection. In our code this could be accomplished with the statement `Command.Parameters("@ID").Value`.

Finally, because the `INSERT INTO` statement does not return a cursor, the stored procedure is invoked with the `ExecuteNonQuery` method in line 119. The stored procedure is run between the statements that open and close the connection, which are protected by a `Try . . . Finally` block (lines 118 through 127). `Try . . . Finally` blocks march to this rhythm: create resource, try, use resource, and finally clean up the resource. Because opening the connection may fail, I want the connection variable to be defined outside of the `Try` block that ensures an open connection is closed. If I had resolved what to do in the event that the connection could not open, I could wrap that part of the code in an outer `Try . . . Catch` block. In the example, if the connection cannot be opened, the default behavior of raising the error is satisfactory.

One great benefit of stored procedures is that multiple operations can be treated as a single, homogeneous operation, reducing network traffic and taking advantage of powerful database servers. This homogeneity is demonstrated in Listing 12.7: Both the `INSERT INTO` and `SELECT IDENTITY` queries are run as one transaction to the database.

Debugging Stored Procedures in Visual Studio .NET

Visual Studio .NET was designed to support integrated debugging for SQL Server. Unfortunately, there are so many limitations on what a developer should and shouldn't do and the process for configuring debugging is convoluted enough that it is difficult to decipher how well this technology works. At this juncture I can tell you the benefit you are supposed to be able to derive, and I can also tell you I have not reliably and consistently been able to get integrated SQL debugging to work.

Visual Studio .NET was designed to allow you to debug SQL Server stored procedures in the Visual Studio .NET IDE using the same debugger you use to debug VB .NET code. The benefit here is powerful, and in Chapter 17 we will talk about integrated debugging tools, breakpoints, watches, and other benefits of integrated debugging. However, there are a lot of caveats, and the process for debugging is not clearly documented.

The first and perhaps most obvious caveat is that you should not debug a production database. The recommended approach is to have the SQL Server database start up with a user account rather than a system account. Additionally, debugging may lock rows and tables, making it impossible for other users to use the database while you are debugging it. This clearly suggests that SQL Server integrated debugging should be done on a duplicate, nonproduction database. The second stumbling block is that there are too many configuration steps and prerequirements, making it very difficult to configure stored procedure debugging. The writers of the help documentation need to refine the instructions and make the process much simpler.

A recommended process is to debug stored procedures with a local copy of the database running in MSDE on your workstation. This seems likely to be the least disruptive approach to other developers and users, but even the preconditions for configuring MSDE stored procedure debugging seem a bit unclear. In the next two subsections, I provide an overview of the steps to configure debugging for MSDE and SQL Server, but as I mentioned, this process needs refinement.

Configuring the Microsoft Data Engine for Stored Procedure Debugging

The steps for debugging MSDE described in this section are based on the Visual Studio .NET help topic "Enabling SQL Debugging on SQL 2000 Desktop Engines." You can view this material by inserting the following link in the URL address bar in Visual Studio .NET: `ms-help://MS.VSCC/MS.MSDNVS/vsdebug/html/vxlrfsettingupsqldebuggingenablingsqldebuggingonsql2000desktop.htm`.

1. Copy `MSSDI98.DLL` to the SQL Server `\binn` directory.
2. If Visual Studio .NET is not installed on the same workstation containing MSDE, complete steps 3, 4, and 5.
3. Copy `SQLDBG.DLL` to `\program files\common files\microsoft shared\sql debugging`. If Visual Studio .Net has been installed then `SQLDBG.DLL` should already be there.
4. Register the `SQLDBG.DLL` with `regsvr32 SQLDBG.DLL`.
5. Grant execute permission on the extended stored procedure `sp_sdidebug` to the debug user. The grant statement is `GRANT EXECUTE ON sp_sdidebug to username`.

These steps sound relatively easy to perform, but you will need to know some additional information and have additional skills to perform them. They worked for me the first time, but I was unable to reproduce them on more than one PC.

The best way to complete steps 1 through 4 is to install Visual Studio .NET on the same PC running MSDE. Otherwise you will have to locate copies of these files from other sources. Step 5 requires an available copy of Enterprise Manager or Query Analyzer. You can find the `sp_sdidebug` stored procedure in the Extended Stored Procedures in the master database. You may use Enterprise Manager to grant execute permissions or run the `GRANT` statement in step 5 in Query Analyzer.

The preceding five steps are moderately easy to perform; however, when I completed the steps and tried to run a stored procedure on one PC, I received the error message shown in Figure 12.4. The error suggests that the `sqldbreg.exe` and `sqldbg.dll` applications were inaccessible. Looking up this error in MSDE resulted in some additional sets of instructions. Part of the instructions suggested that the SQL debugger user must have read and executed NT File System (NTFS) permissions on `\WINNT\System32` and `\Program Files\Common Files\Microsoft Shared\SQL Debugging`. Where were these instructions in the help link for MSDE SQL debugging? Following up on the NTFS permissions issue, I came across instructions for configuring DCOM. The DCOM instructions should be for debugging across devices (remote debugging, where the Visual Studio .NET is on one workstation and the SQL Server instance is on another). Setting the permissions on my workstation and following the DCOM instructions, I figured I would ultimately kill two birds with one stone. Neither resolution seemed to solve the problem.

I consider myself a tenacious problem solver, so I began searching the Web for a resolution. I discovered several articles describing almost precisely what is in the help documentation, but nothing concrete that helped me resolve the particular error shown in Figure 12.4. After several hours I began to wonder how beneficial SQL stored procedure debugging is if it is limited to SQL Server and the process is not straightforward. Do I really want to debug stored procedures by stepping through them, or can I continue to live with debugging stored procedures by inspection and evaluation of the results? I fear that many people will come up with the following answer: If it is too difficult to do, skip it.

The concept of integrated stored procedure debugging is a great one. Configuration needs to be made easier, and the capability should be extended to all database providers.

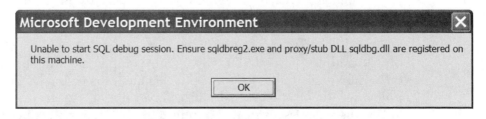

Figure 12.4 One of the errors you may get while trying to step into a stored procedure.

Configuring SQL Server for Stored Procedure Debugging

During all my efforts I had no particular difficulty in creating, editing, or running stored procedures in the Visual Studio .NET IDE. This is a nice feature; however, getting stored procedure debugging to work for the enterprise version of SQL Server seems to be more difficult than getting the desktop engine to work. Unfortunately, again, the documentation seems insufficient. Below I provide an overview of the precursors for debugging stored procedures in Visual Studio .NET.

1. You need a SQL Server 6.5 Service Pack 3 or greater instance running on a server. (The standard edition probably will not work here, and the help documentation recommends SQL Server 2000.)
2. You need Windows NT 4.0 or greater on the server; again, Windows 2000 is recommended.
3. You need Windows 98, ME, NT, or greater on the workstation, but 2000 is recommended. (If you are using Windows 98 or Windows ME, you will need to download, install, and configure DCOM on the workstation.)
4. You need to configure Remote Debugging components, which includes several files and service applications.
5. You need to configure SQL Server to run under a user account instead of running under the system account.
6. You need to run and configure DCOM, which is accomplished by running `dcomcnfg.exe`. The steps are different for Windows 2000 and XP, but they work toward the same end. Basically, you need to add the SQL Server user account to the Default Access Permissions for DCOM. (Some of the documentation suggests that this should be the SQLDebugger user, but to a limited extent the documentation suggests this should be the user account under which SQL Server is running. In reality this information is not clearly documented.)

In addition to the preceding precursors, here are a couple of other concerns to address. Several SQL Debugging components will be installed if you install Visual Studio .NET on both client and server, but having a development environment on your database server presents problems of its own. Finally, there are issues related to reinstalling SQL Server, which is something you are likely to do in a test environment, further complicating productive SQL debugging.

If you are anything like me, you might feel that this is too much to ask. Conceptually, debugging stored procedures is a good idea, especially since we can't seem to get away from them altogether. In practice these configuration issues and limitations suggest that this feature needs some work. (If you find a simple and reliable way to configure stored procedure debugging, please let me know at *pkimmel@softconcepts.com*.)

Using Transactions

The nature of a relational database is that the database designer tries to reconcile a reduction in redundancy and waste with an increase in complexity. This reconciliation is referred to in database jargon as *normalization*. The trade-off of normalization is the complexity introduced and the hoops we have to jump through to reassemble disparate tables into usable chunks. For example, from a programmer's perspective, orders and order details are related, but a reasonable database design would separate these pieces of information to avoid repeating order information for every detail item in the order. Then when the user wants to see a complete order, the order and detail information must be reassembled. Additionally, when operations need to be performed on an order, the programmer must ensure that an entire operation, which may span several tables, completes successfully. For instance it is usually considered unacceptable to bill a customer for an order but not deliver the ordered items. When we have operations that must be treated as a whole, we can protect them with transactions.

A transaction is the notion of treating a group of database interactions as one interaction. For example, when a customer orders some product, it is considered vital that all aspects of the order (including the items ordered, billing information, shipping, and any subsequent promises) be delivered. Such a promise may technically translate to adding data to the repository for the order, billing, and inventory information.

Listing 12.9 contains an excerpt from `TransactionDemo.sln`. The example demonstrates how complex database behavior can be as well as how to use a transaction object. The specific example in a production database would be better served if constraints between the tables managed the deletion of child tables, or at least if the code were converted to a stored procedure. Technically, however, the solution in Listing 12.9 functions well enough.

Listing 12.9 Executing Multiple Queries as Part of a Single Transaction

```
1:  Private Sub DeleteCustomer(ByVal CustomerID As String)
2:    If (Warning()) Then Exit Sub
3:
4:    Const DeleteCustomers As String = _
5:      "DELETE * FROM CUSTOMERS WHERE CustomerID = '{0}'"
6:    Const DeleteOrders As String = _
7:      "DELETE * FROM ORDERS WHERE CustomerID = '{0}'"
8:    Const DeleteOrderDetails As String = _
9:      "DELETE * FROM [Order Details] WHERE OrderID = '{0}'"
10:   Const SelectOrders As String = _
11:     "SELECT OrderID FROM Orders WHERE CustomerID = '{0}'"
12:
13:   Dim Transaction As OleDbTransaction
14:   Dim Command As OleDbCommand
15:   Connection.Open()
16:   Try
17:     Transaction = Connection.BeginTransaction()
18:
19:     Command = New OleDbCommand( _
20:       String.Format(SelectOrders, CustomerID), _
21:       Connection, Transaction)
22:
23:     Dim Reader As OleDbDataReader = Command.ExecuteReader()
24:     While (Reader.Read())
25:       Command = New OleDbCommand( _
26:         String.Format(DeleteOrderDetails, _
27:         CType(Reader("OrderID"), String)), _
28:         Connection, Transaction)
29:     End While
30:
31:     Reader.Close()
32:
33:     Command = New OleDbCommand( _
34:       String.Format(DeleteOrders, CustomerID), _
35:       Connection, Transaction)
36:
37:     Command.ExecuteNonQuery()
38:
39:     'Throw New Exception("Intentionally cause rollback")
40:
41:     Command = New OleDbCommand( _
42:       String.Format(DeleteCustomers, CustomerID), _
```

```
43:       Connection, Transaction)
44:     Command.ExecuteNonQuery()
45:
46:     Transaction.Commit()
47:   Catch
48:     Transaction.Rollback()
49:     Throw
50:   Finally
51:     Connection.Close()
52:   End Try
53:
54: End Sub
```

Listing 12.9 assumes that we are provided with a valid CustomerID. Line 2 is just a warning in the sample program reminding you to back up the database (NWIND.mdb) if you want to be able to restore it to its original condition after experimenting with this code. Lines 4 through 11 define some constant, parameterized SQL text that is used to complete the entire transaction. The first through third statements in that block delete the Customers, Orders, and Order Details rows, respectively. The fourth statement is used to get all the OrderID values.

The OleDbTransaction and OleDbCommand objects are declared in lines 13 and 14. These have to be declared outside of the Try . . . Catch . . . Finally . . . End Try block because each part of the block is a distinct scope. For example, if we defined the OleDbTransaction object in the Try part, it would not be accessible in the Finally or Catch parts of the exception handler.

The connection is opened in line 15. The DeleteCustomers method relies on the connection already being created and initialized. The Try part of the exception handler begins in line 16. The basic flow of the code in the Try part is to start the transaction (line 17), get all the OrderID values, and use those to delete the Order Details rows for this customer. Following the deletion of Order Details rows, rows for the Orders and Customers tables are deleted based on CustomerID.

Lines 23 through 29 show how to use OleDbDataReader to read all the OrderID values from the Orders table, using those identifiers to delete the Order Details rows. Remember to close the reader when finished with it (line 31).

Finally, if we execute all the commands and reach line 46, the transaction (that is, all changes following the time we began the transaction to this point) is committed to the database. If an error has occurred, the transaction (all changes) is rolled back, or undone. In line 49 we call `Throw` to rethrow the exception to the caller. The `Finally` block of code is always run, which is precisely what we want—we always want the connection to close at the end.

This code works correctly. However, I added the commented out `Throw` statement in line 39 to facilitate experimentation with the rollback behavior.

This listing presents some techniques I hope you can use in your own code. The first is in line 39. Line 39 demonstrates how to raise an exception. This is the preferred way of indicating an error in code that you write, and it mirrors what the framework does when it encounters an error. You can create and throw an instance of any exception, including custom exceptions. Another technique is using a `DataReader` object for forward-only data access. I also wanted to show you the rhythm of a `Try . . . Catch . . . Finally . . . End Try` block. It is harder to make mistakes in VB .NET than in some other languages, but mistakes will happen. You can use exception handlers to make sure things like database connections get cleaned up, and you can rethrow exceptions (line 49), allowing the database code to handle the database problem and some other chunk of code to handle error processing.

A final note: If you find yourself writing complex database interactions like the one shown in Listing 12.9, think "stored procedure." Complex transactions spanning multiple entities in a database are ideally suited for stored procedures.

Creating a Typed `DataSet`

ADO.NET is comprised of classes. As you know, classes can be generalized—inherited from—to extend existing behaviors and add new behaviors. One such set of generalizations is to create typed `DataSet`, `DataTable`, and `DataRow` objects. (We'll speak in terms of *typed `DataSet` objects*, but keep in mind the same basic principle applies to other ADO.NET classes by way of supporting inheritance.)

In general, when you use a `DataSet`, you can access a `DataTable` in that `DataSet` through the `DataSet.Tables` collection property. The same is true of `DataRow` objects: you can access rows through the `DataTable.Rows` collection. The end result is complicated-looking object strings and indexed collections, for example, `DataSet.Tables(0).Rows(1)`. This kind of code is a bit unsightly and considered weakly typed because we are dealing with ADO.NET types and generic objects returned from these types. Ultimately you get down to a row and have to typecast that field to work with a specific type of data.

The object-oriented paradigm promotes strongly typed objects, and there is every reason a good practical approach—using strong types—should be carried over into database applications. ADO.NET and Visual Studio .NET actually promote strongly typed `DataSet` objects using XML Schemas. I say that ADO.NET supports strongly typed objects because you can inherit from and extend ADO.NET types, and Visual Studio .NET facilitates this by providing an XML Schema designer. In fact, Visual Studio .NET goes one step further: It will generate the strongly typed ADO.NET classes for you.

In this section I'll show you how to add and create an XML Schema, generate strongly typed `DataSet` objects, and use those generalized types. To finish we'll compare similar weakly typed `DataSet` objects with strongly typed `DataSet` objects.

Defining an XML Schema

Visual Studio .NET uses templates to create projects and project items. A template at its essence is parameterized source code. For example, when you add a new class to a project, there is a `parameter.cs` file containing generic source code for a class. A wizard uses the automation model for Visual Studio .NET to replace the class name and incorporate the class file into your project. There are dozens of templates, including a template for an XML Schema. (XML Schema files have the `.xsd` extension and fall under the auspices of XSD.)

TIP: There are dozens of templates for Visual Basic .NET. To see examples of project templates, explore `\Program Files\Microsoft Visual Studio .NET\Vb7\VBWizards`. `VBProjects` and `VBProjectItems` in the same VB7 folder contain additional templates.

XSD refers to another technology in .NET that solves a practical problem. XSD, or XML Schemas and Data, allow you to convert weakly typed database code into strongly typed database code. Your code becomes more comprehensible, and it is possible to implement the code in the vernacular of the solution domain. We will begin by adding an XSD item to a project. (You can start a new Windows Forms or Web Forms application for this purpose. The sample application `TypedDataSetDemo.sln` contains my example code.) To add an XML Schema to a project, follow these steps.

1. With a project open in Visual Studio .NET, select File|Add New Item from the menu.
2. From the Add New Item dialog, select the XML Schema applet from the templates list.
3. In the Add New Item dialog, change the `.xsd` filename to `CustomerOrders.xsd` and click OK.

The preceding three steps will add a file named `CustomerOrders.xsd` to your project solution. The XSD file has its own designer, and the designer will generate a `.xsx` (resource) file and ultimately a `.vb` source file containing the generated typed `DataSet` objects.

With the XSD file selected and open in Visual Studio .NET, you will notice some changes in the IDE. The Toolbox will have an XML Schema tab, and a Schema menu will appear in Visual Studio .NET's main menu bar. These features exist to help you manually design the XML Schema, and you are welcome to use them if you want to define the schema from scratch. Fortunately we can also define the schema by inference by dragging and dropping tables from the Server Explorer.

Adding Multiple Tables to a `DataSet`

Let's suppose we have elected to create a strongly typed `DataSet` for the Northwind database. (I am assuming you have a data connection already in the Server Explorer.) We can drag tables from the Server Explorer onto the XML Schema designer, and the designer will generate the XML Schema code for us (Figure 12.5).

Figure 12.5 shows three tables in the XML Schema designer. Dragging the `Customers` table created the topmost element and the `Customers` element. I renamed the topmost element `CustomerOrders` by modifying the name property for this element in the Properties window. To insert additional tables in the schema I dragged and dropped them into the `CustomerOrders` element. The result is the visually defined schema shown in Figure 12.5. The figure looks a bit like an entity-relationship diagram, and that is a plausible way to think of it.

Behind the scenes, the schema designer is writing XML for us. You can view the XML by switching from the Schema view (shown in Figure 12.5) to the XML view by clicking the XML tab or by selecting XML Source from

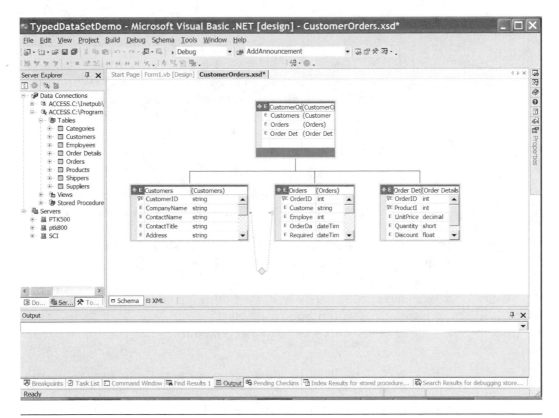

Figure 12.5 Defining an XML Schema by dragging tables from the Server Explorer in Visual Studio .NET.

the View menu. Just as the schema designer can read the schema and write XML for us, it can also write .NET source code, using the CodeDOM.

NOTE: The CodeDOM is a document object model for source code. .NET can be written capably to generate IL (byte code) and source code. Well-established patterns can be codified to automatically generate source code and compile executable assemblies.

At this point we have enough information to generate code. (In fact, one table is enough information with which to generate a typed `DataSet`.) However, we haven't expressed relationships that exist in the database, so we'll do that before generating the typed `DataSet` objects.

Defining a Master-Detail Relationship in the Schema

We know from earlier experiences that customers have orders and orders have order details. These relationships are expressed as primary keys between the `Customers.CustomerID` and `Orders.CustomerID` columns and the `Orders.OrderID` and `Order Details.OrderID` columns. We can express these relationships in the schema, and the designer will use them to generate additional XML and source code that takes advantage of them.

To add a relationship to the XML Schema, follow these instructions.

1. Select the `Customers` element in the schema designer. Right-click over `CustomerID` and select Add|New Relation from the context menu.
2. In the Edit Relation dialog (Figure 12.6), set the parent element to `Customers` and the child element to `Orders`.
3. The key fields should both be `CustomerID`.
4. You can create foreign key constraints at the bottom of the dialog. (Experiment with this as an exercise.)
5. Click OK to complete adding the relation.

After you close the Edit Relation dialog, a `keyref` element will be displayed in the Schema view attaching the `Customers` table to the `Orders` table. (At this point the Schema view really begins to look like an entity-relationship diagram.) Repeat the steps above to define a relationship between the `Orders` and `Order Details` tables. `Orders` and `Order Details` are joined by the `OrderID` field.

At this juncture we have a completely defined schema, including a `DataSet`, `DataTables`, relationships, and `DataRows`.

Generating a Typed `DataSet`

When tools start to get as good as the XML Schema designer, there is a brief period when managers talk about programmers being obsolete. This is hooey. I live in Michigan, and for a while we heard a lot about how robots were going to put car factory employees out of work. In reality, tools simply help tradespeople focus on more interesting problems. Writing XML and typed `DataSet` objects seems like a perfect job for a tool.

We have the option of previewing the `DataSet` from the Schema|Preview DataSet menu. However, if we need to make changes, we can do so at

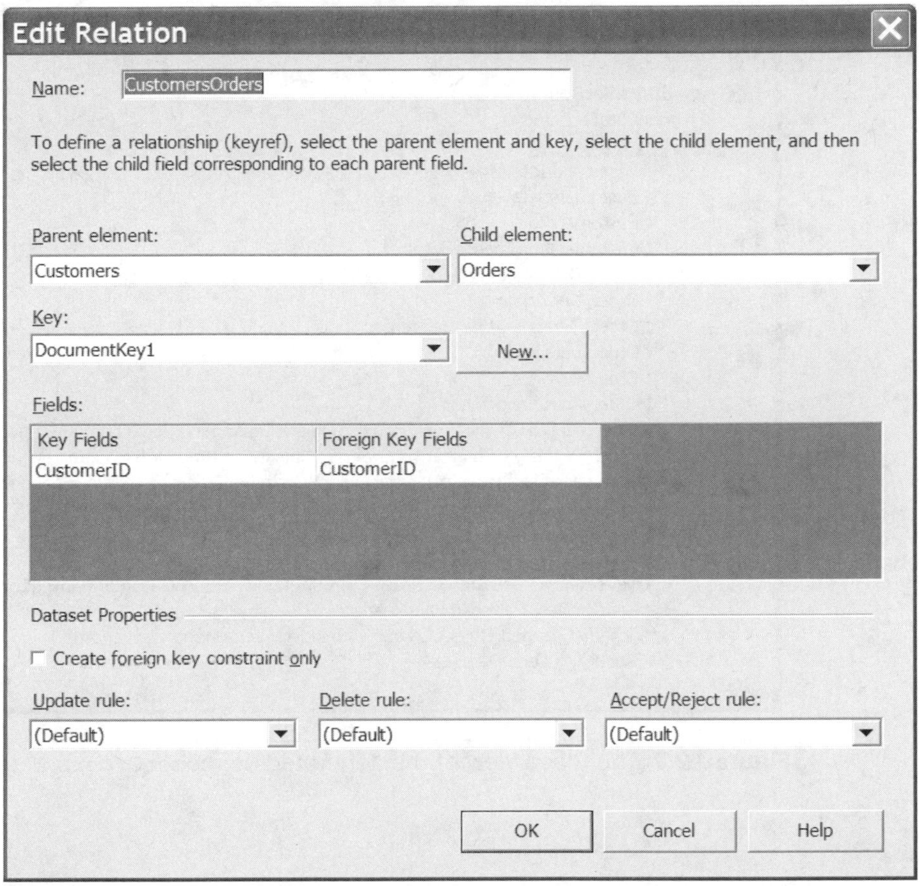

Figure 12.6 The Edit Relation dialog used to define a relationship between tables in a schema.

any time by modifying the schema visually and regenerating the DataSet. Let's go ahead and select Schema|Generate DataSet.

If you click the Show All Files button on the Toolbar at the top of the Solution Explorer, you will see that the CustomerOrders.xsd file has two down-line files, the .xsx resource file and a CustomerOrders.vb source code file (as long as we have generated the DataSet).

Our selections caused approximately 1,600 lines of code to be generated. To get a bird's-eye view of the generated code, you can open the Class view. Select View|Class View from the main menu to display the Class view (expanded in Figure 12.7 to show the typed DataSet).

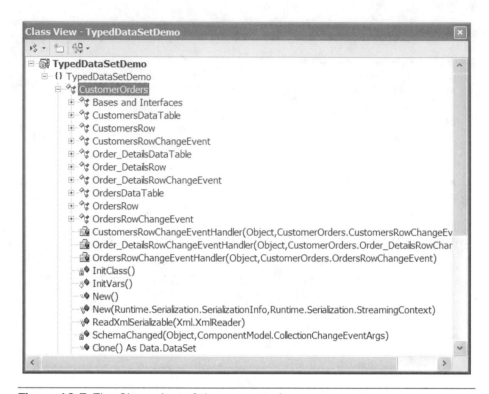

Figure 12.7 The Class view of the generated `CustomerOrders` `DataSet`.

Notice that all the elements in the Class view are subordinate to the `CustomerOrders` class. This means that these elements are nested. I won't provide the code listing here (see `CustomerOrders.vb` in `TypedDataSet-Demo.sln`), but I can tell you about the generated code. The `Customer-Orders` class inherits from the `DataSet` class. Within the `CustomerOrders` class are three `DataTable` objects: `CustomersDataTable`, `OrdersData-Table`, and `Order_DetailsDataTable`. These represent strongly typed objects inherited from the `DataTable` class. The `CustomerOrders` class also contains nested `CustomersRow`, `OrdersRow`, and `Order_DetailsRow` classes that inherit from the `DataRow` class. At this level of granularity the code becomes very OOPY. Instead of referring to `DataSet`, `DataTable`, and `DataRow` classes, we can refer to `Customers`, `Orders`, `Order_Details`, and properties within these classes. Writing code in the vernacular of the problem domain—in our example, customers and orders—makes code that is more comprehensible and useful in the particular domain.

The maintained benefit is that because we are using inheritance here, we are also still talking about DataSet, DataTable, and DataRow objects. The combined result is that we can use the ADO.NET skills we have worked hard to acquire yet write code that is domain-specific—that is, code that speaks to customers and orders.

Finally, it is worth mentioning that VB6 did not support nested classes but VB .NET does, and it makes sense to use nested classes in the present context. If you imagine that our typed DataSet has specific typed DataTable and DataRow objects, all used to coordinate relationships, it doesn't make sense to define these classes independently of the containing typed DataSet. For example, it wouldn't make sense to initialize a single DataRow without its containing DataTable. Nested classes take some getting used to, but they support some powerful idioms previously supported only in languages like C++ and Delphi.

Programming with Typed DataSet Objects

To work with typed DataSet objects you still need connections, commands, and adapters to initialize and manage the data. However, as I mentioned, the code begins to read as domain-specific code. Additionally, because the XML Schema designer has generated extended classes for us, things like the DataRelations can be built in the new, derived classes automatically. The code in Listing 12.10 demonstrates how to initialize the CustomerOrders DataSet and provides examples showing how the code maps the problem domain more closely.

Listing 12.10 Initializing the Typed CustomerOrders DataSet

```
1:  Imports System.Data
2:  Imports System.Data.OleDb
3:  Imports System.Configuration
4:
5:  Public Class Form1
6:      Inherits System.Windows.Forms.Form
7:
8:  [ Windows Form Designer generated code ]
9:
10:    Private CustomerOrders As CustomerOrders
11:    Private Connection As OleDbConnection
12:    Private AdapterCustomers As OleDbDataAdapter
13:    Private AdapterOrders As OleDbDataAdapter
```

```
14:    Private AdapterOrderDetails As OleDbDataAdapter
15:
16:
17:    Private Sub Form1_Load(ByVal sender As System.Object, _
18:      ByVal e As System.EventArgs) Handles MyBase.Load
19:
20:      Connection = New OleDbConnection( _
21:        ConfigurationSettings.AppSettings("ConnectionString"))
22:      AdapterCustomers = New OleDbDataAdapter( _
23:        "SELECT * FROM Customers", Connection)
24:
25:      AdapterOrders = New OleDbDataAdapter( _
26:        "SELECT * FROM Orders", Connection)
27:
28:      AdapterOrderDetails = New OleDbDataAdapter( _
29:        "SELECT * FROM [Order Details]", Connection)
30:
31:      CustomerOrders = New CustomerOrders()
32:
33:      AdapterCustomers.Fill(CustomerOrders, "Customers")
34:      AdapterOrders.Fill(CustomerOrders, "Orders")
35:      AdapterOrderDetails.Fill(CustomerOrders, "Order Details")
36:
37:      DataGrid1.DataSource = CustomerOrders.Customers
38:
39:    End Sub
40: End Class
```

As promised and as you can plainly see here, the initialization code hasn't changed much. I declare connections, a `DataSet`, and adapters to fill the `DataSet`. A few differences hint at future benefits. First of all, I declared a `CustomerOrders` type in line 10, and I assigned `DataGrid1.DataSource` to `CustomerOrders.Customers` (line 37) rather than `DataSet.Tables(0)`. Another benefit I am already getting is that the relationship exists between the `Customers`, `Orders`, and `Order Details` tables, but as you can see, there is no sign of this code in Listing 12.10. The relationships are created automatically in the initialization code for the `CustomerOrders DataSet`.

Keep in mind that only a small part of your ADO.NET code will be initialization code. The bulk of the code will be interactions with the data itself. When you begin using the `DataSet`, `DataTable`, and `DataRow` objects defined in the typed `DataSet`, you will get the greatest benefit of typed `DataSet` objects.

Assume I have a single instance of a row in a `Customers` table. I can interact with the data fields as typed properties of an individual customer. Here is a brief example.

```
Dim Customer As CustomerOrders.CustomersRow _
  = CustomerOrders.Customers.Rows(0)
Customer.Address = "1313 Mockingbird Ln."
```

The code is clearly referring to a `Customer.Address` field, and the type of the address is known to be a string, a typed value, rather than simply a field in a `DataSet`. In fact, if the `DataSet` object and `Rows` collection were not shown too, a discerning reader would not know that we are even referring to instances of ADO.NET objects. The statement `Customer.Address` is typed code in the language of the solution domain, customers and orders.

Typed `DataSet` objects are easy to use. If you are going to implement a database-centric solution, using typed `DataSets` will result in code that makes more sense in the solution domain than weakly typed ADO.NET classes. Additionally, if you are creating UML models as part of your design process, typed `DataSet` objects tie in nicely with a UML model that maps the problem domain rather than simply having an entity-relationship diagram of the database.

Serializing a `DataSet`

ADO.NET is captured internally as XML. The reason for this has to do with XML being (1) self-describing, (2) an open standard, and (3) captured as text, which is easily transportable over networks like the Internet.

Because ADO.NET is stored as XML it becomes easy to send `DataSets`—ADO.NET objects—over the Internet, persist them in an external file, or serialize them for purposes like caching. For example, since a `DataSet` is serializable, it can be stored in the session cache in ASP.NET Web applications. In fact, a `DataSet` can be cached using either of the in-process caching mechanisms or the two out-of-process caching mechanisms. (The out-of-process session caching mechanisms are `aspnet_state.exe` and SQL Server.)

Serialization for session caching and returning `DataSets` from XML Web Services happens automatically, but to facilitate your understanding of what is occurring, I have included a short example that demonstrates how to serialize a `DataSet` to a memory stream. Listing 12.11 serializes the `DataSet` to a stream and displays the serialized version of the `DataSet` in a `TextBox` control.

Listing 12.11 Serializing a `DataSet` to XML

```
1:  Imports System.Data
2:  Imports System.Data.OleDb
3:  Imports System.Configuration
4:  Imports System.IO
5:  Imports System.Text.ASCIIEncoding
6:
7:  Public Class Form1
8:      Inherits System.Windows.Forms.Form
9:
10: [ Windows Form Designer generated code ]
11:
12:    Private Products As DataSet
13:    Private Sub Form1_Load(ByVal sender As Object, _
14:      ByVal e As System.EventArgs) Handles MyBase.Load
15:
16:      LoadDataSet()
17:      DataGrid1.DataSource = Products.Tables(0)
18:      SerializeDataSet(Products)
19:
20:    End Sub
21:
22:    Private Sub LoadDataSet()
23:      Dim Connection As OleDbConnection = _
24:        New OleDbConnection(ConfigurationSettings. _
25:          AppSettings("ConnectionString"))
26:
27:      Dim Adapter As OleDbDataAdapter = _
28:        New OleDbDataAdapter("SELECT * FROM PRODUCTS", _
29:          Connection)
30:
31:      Products = New DataSet("Products")
32:
33:      Adapter.Fill(Products)
34:    End Sub
35:
36:    Private Sub SerializeDataSet(ByVal Data As DataSet)
```

```
37:
38:     Dim Stream As MemoryStream = New MemoryStream()
39:     Products.WriteXml(Stream)
40:     Stream.Position = 0
41:     TextBox1.Text = System.Text.ASCIIEncoding. _
42:       ASCII.GetString(Stream.GetBuffer())
43:
44:   End Sub
45:
46: End Class
```

The first half of the listing initializes a `DataSet` with the data from the `Products` table. Lines 36 through 44 serialize the `DataSet` and data as XML into a `MemoryStream` object, which in turn is used to convert the XML to a string. `MemoryStream` objects return an array of bytes, so I employed the shared method `System.Text.ASCIIEncoding.ASCII.GetString` to convert the array of bytes to a string.

You can write the XML form of the `DataSet` back to a `DataSet` object by using `DataSet.ReadXml`. You also have the option of using the more verbose `XmlSerializer` method to serialize and deserialize serializable objects, but the member methods `ReadXml` and `WriteXml` work best for `DataSet` objects.

Programming with ADO.NET Interfaces

.NET supports two flavors of polymorphism: (1) the polymorphism introduced through inheritance, virtual methods, and the virtual methods table, and (2) the polymorphism introduced with COM and interfaces. The first form, called *inheritance polymorphism*, means that all instances have a common classification. (For example, bears and goats can both be classified as mammals.) The second form of polymorphism, called *interface polymorphism*, means that all instances have a common capability but are not required to have a common classification. (For example, radios, televisions, hearing aids, telephones, and bullhorns all have the ability to attenuate volume, but they don't necessarily share a common classification.)

ADO.NET (and all of .NET, really) supports both forms of polymorphism. Interestingly, ADO.NET directly supports interface polymorphism by having classes in both kinds of providers—OleDb and SqlClient—implement interfaces. For example, both the `OleDbCommand` and `SqlCommand` providers implement the `IDbCommand` interface. As a result, both `OleDbCommand` and `SqlCommand` can have different implementations and classifications but can be manipulated by the same control; that is, they can be managed by the same code if the code is written to work with the `IDbCommand` interface rather than with one provider or the other.

You are not required to write your code to use interfaces; you simply have this option. However, it is important to note that interfaces provide an optimal kind of flexibility. Returning to the `IDbCommand` interface, if we write code to use `IDbCommand` to manage SQL or stored procedures, any class that implements `IDbCommand` will do. The implication then is that any provider will do. Let's draw a logical conclusion here. If you were writing a commercial application and you did not want to force a customer to use a specific database vendor, interfaces would let you write one body of code that allowed the customer to pick the database vendor. As long as that vendor offered database provider classes, or one of the existing providers worked, then customers would be free to pick and choose database vendors. They would not be locked into a particular choice based on your code.

The notion of using interfaces is so powerful that it is one of the patterns (a standard approach for a category of problem) promoted in *Design Patterns* by Erich Gamma and colleagues [1995]. It is probably no accident that interfaces were used with ADO.NET.

Because the ADO.NET interfaces already exist, all you have to do is use them. Instead of declaring a specific provider class like `OleDbConnection`, use the interface that a particular class implements. Declare your variables as interface types and create instances of the specific provider type based on some conditional criteria. You will find it amazingly simple to switch database providers if the need arises. A good architect should be able to help you design a database application that supports switching providers without changing or recompiling your code at all.

For a complete list of ADO.NET interfaces, refer to the Interfaces section of the System.Data Namespace help topic in Gamma et al. [1995].

Summary

Many of the features you have come to expect from database tools—and more—exist in ADO.NET. ADO.NET was designed to scale to meet the needs of a huge number of simultaneous Internet users and still support PC applications and connected enterprise database applications. Central to

ADO.NET is the disconnected nature supported by XML and the `DataSet`. Using XML as the underlying infrastructure means that complex data structures can easily be transported over the Internet as XML text, if you so desire. The serializable nature of XML means that mobile and briefcase applications will be easier to develop.

In this chapter, you learned how to update data by using a `DataView`; generate SQL with a command builder; program with stored procedures, transactions, and ADO.NET interfaces; define XML Schemas as a way to implement strongly typed `DataSet` objects; and serialize XML `DataSet` objects. You will find these skills invaluable for custom business, Web, and retail applications.

Web Programming

Part III will aid you in building professional applications for the Web, including a comprehensive discussion of XML Web Services and ASP.NET practical guidelines.

Creating Web Services

To paraphrase Thomas Jefferson: Break up teams into small autonomous groups so that they will get practice and improve.

—Paul Kimmel

Introduction

Web Services have been receiving a lot of publicity. While the whole .NET Framework represents a compelling reason to switch to .NET, XML Web Services is certainly a gem in the .NET crown.

XML Web Services are based on open technologies and will help you offer simple services to customers, support application integration between systems, and provide workflow solutions for your enterprise. Of course, before you can appreciate Web Services it is necessary to understand XML Web Services and the open standards technologies that form the underpinnings.

Chapter 13 provides you with a solid foundation in consuming and building XML Web Services. After reading this chapter, you will have a better understanding of how to use Web Services, and more importantly, you will be armed to convince your peers, managers, and customers of the technical advantages of XML Web Services.

Finding Web Services

Think of XML Web Services as code that runs across a network, the Internet being the best example of a network. Several technologies make XML Web

427

Services work. As you might imagine, you will need to find Web Services produced by others. You will need to determine what capabilities and information those Web Services provide, and you will need to incorporate those Web Services into your applications so that you can use the capabilities offered. Several acronyms surrounding Web Services may create some initial confusion, but these acronyms do represent technologies that play valuable roles.

Assuming you want to find Web Services offered by third parties, you will need the technology called *Universal Description, Discovery, and Integration* (UDDI). Think of UDDI as the yellow pages for Web Services. Just as there are several yellow pages providers for telephone numbers in various regions, there are "yellow pages" providers for Web Services. Generally, when you are looking for Web Services, you will be looking for host computers that have UDDI servers. For example, Microsoft has a UDDI server at *http://uddi.microsoft.com*.

A direct way to use UDDI is to select Project|Add Web Reference from the Visual Studio .NET toolbar. This will open the Add Web Reference dialog shown in Figure 13.1. When you enter a host URL in the Address combobox, the dialog will explore the Web site for files ending in `.disco`. These discovery (DISCO) files—another acronym associated with Web Services—contain XML-formatted information that points to a contract reference file. In short, the `.disco` file points to a `.asmx` file that represents the Web Service.

When you add a reference to an existing Web Service, the next technology, Web Services Description Language (WSDL, pronounced *whiz-dal*), kicks in. The next section demonstrates how WSDL is used to help consume Web Services.

Consuming Existing Web Services

Keep in mind that code in an XML Web Service is object-oriented code. You don't actually write the code behind the Web Service on the machine consuming the Web Service, but you do need code that represents the Web Service code. Generating this code is the role of WSDL.

WSDL figures out the methods and types exposed by the Web Service and creates a proxy class for the Web Service. This proxy class permits Web Service consumers—you and me—to refer to the methods and types exposed by the Web Service as if that code actually resided on our workstations.

When you add a reference to a Web Service, the WSDL technology adds a Web References folder to your project and a `Reference.vb` file to that folder. The `Reference.vb` file contains a class that inherits from `System.Web.`

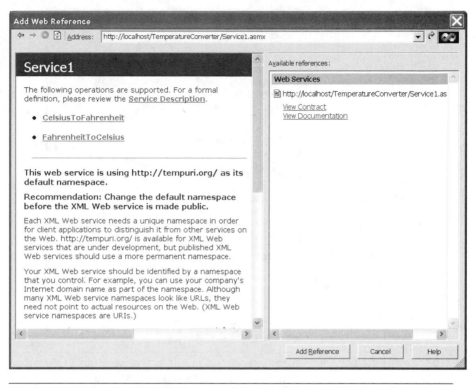

Figure 13.1 The Add Web Reference dialog, which uses UDDI technology to look for `.disco` files that point to Web Services.

`Services.Protocols.SoapHttpClientProtocol`. This class contains proxy methods for invoking the Web methods defined by the Web Service. In addition, any types that are returned by the Web Service's methods are represented by wrapper classes. These wrapper classes are the client's view of the types returned by the Web Service.

Additionally, when you add a Web reference, a folder named Web References shows up in the Solution Explorer in Visual Studio .NET (Figure 13.2). This folder includes a namespace name that is the same as the Web Service host name. For example, when you implement a Web Service on your workstation and refer to that service, the namespace name is `localhost`. Files that show up in the Web References folder include `.wsdl`, `.map`, and `.disco` files. The `.wsdl` file describes the Web Service methods, types defined in the Web Service, and invocation information. The `.map` file contains the URL statements that return the `.wsdl` and `.disco` information, and the `.disco` file contains information used by UDDI to discover the Web Service.

Figure 13.2 The Web References folder in the Solution Explorer, with the `localhost` namespace name and Web Services mapping files.

Adding a Web Reference to Your Project

For our first example, I created a Web Service that returns a type named `Commission`. The `Commission` type is a very simple type that stores a trade amount and a commission rate and then calculates the commission as the product of the trade amount and the commission rate. The Web Service is defined in `Commissions.sln`, and the ConsumeWebService Windows application consumes the Web Service.

To add a Web reference to a project, perform the following steps.

1. Open the Solution Explorer and select the project to which you want to add the Web Service.
2. From the right-click context menu, select the Add Web Reference menu item. This will open the Add Web Reference dialog.
3. Enter the host URL of the computer containing the Web Service. (In our example, the Web Service is on the same workstation; as a re-

sult, the URL to the Commissions Web Service is *http://localhost/Commissions/Service1.asmx.)*

4. When you select the Web Service, the Add Reference button will become enabled (see Figure 13.1). Click Add Reference.

Now you are ready to create an instance of the Web Service, invoke operations on the methods defined in the Web Service, and use the types exported by the Web Service.

Declaring an Instance of the Web Service Class

When you have added a reference to a Web Service, the WSDL technology and the generated proxy class allow you to add an `Imports` statement to the Web Service and declare instances of the Web Service class, invoke operations on the Web methods, and use the types exported by the Web Service. You already know how to perform these basic operations, but I will repeat them here because the new context may be disorienting.

Listing 13.1 demonstrates a simple Windows application that shows you how to add an `Imports` statement and consume the Commissions Web Service.

Listing 13.1 A Windows Application That Consumes the Commissions Web Service

```
1:  Imports ConsumeWebService.localhost
2:
3:  Public Class Form1
4:      Inherits System.Windows.Forms.Form
5:
6:  [ Windows Form Designer generated code ]
7:
8:    Private Service As Service1 = New Service1()
9:
10:   Private Sub Button1_Click(ByVal sender As System.Object, _
11:     ByVal e As System.EventArgs) Handles Button1.Click
12:
13:     TextBox1.Text = Service.GetCommission(555).Rate.ToString
14:
15:   End Sub
16: End Class
```

Line 1 shows how to add an `Imports` statement that refers to the host namespace added by the WSDL utility. Line 8 shows how to create an instance of the Web Service class. Note that this is precisely the same syntax you would use to create any instance of a class. Line 13 demonstrates an inline call to the Web method `GetCommission`. We could have declared a temporary variable of type `Commission`, assigned the result of `GetCommission` to that variable, and then assigned the rate value to the `TextBox.Text` property, but the behavior is the same.

Invoking Web Methods

Adding a reference to a Web Service permits you to declare types defined and exported by the Web Service and invoke methods in that service. Visual Studio .NET is an excellent tool, providing you with the same Intellisense information about Web Services, Web methods, and Web Service types that you get with classes defined in the .NET Framework.

The key to invoking a Web method is to determine the name of the method, prepare the method arguments, and respond to the return arguments. Of course, you can search the list of information provided by Intellisense to figure out the method signatures, or you can look at the XML in the WSDL file or the `Reference.vb` file. The XML in the WSDL file may be difficult to decipher, but the `Reference.vb` file is straightforward. Listing 13.2 shows the `GetCommission` Web method as it was generated by the WSDL utility.

Listing 13.2 The `GetCommission` Web Method Generated by the WSDL Utility

```
Public Function GetCommission(ByVal ID As Long) As Commission
  Dim results() As Object = _
    Me.Invoke("GetCommission", New Object() {ID})
  Return CType(results(0),Commission)
End Function
```

From the `Reference.vb` file it is clear that `GetCommission` accepts a `Long` integer and returns a `Commission` object. (Refer to the Creating a Web Service Application section later in this chapter for the code that implements the Commissions Web Service.)

Exploring the Web Service Proxy Class

We can consume Web Services without ever creating one, although as developers we will definitely want to create Web Services. The next section begins the discussion of creating Web Services. But first, indulge me for a moment longer while we complete our discussion of consuming Web Services.

There is more to explore about the Web Service proxy class. In Chapter 14 you will discover that the multithreading model in Visual Basic .NET supports calling Web methods asynchronously. Consequently the proxy class contains information for asynchronous calls to Web Services. Additionally, the proxy file contains classes that represent types exported by Web Services. Listing 13.3 (available in `Commissions.sln`) shows these pieces of the `Reference.vb` proxy file.

Listing 13.3 The Proxy Code for the Commissions Web Service

```
1:  '----------------------------------------------------------------
2:  ' <autogenerated>
3:  '     This code was generated by a tool.
4:  '     Runtime Version: 1.0.3705.0
5:  '
6:  '     Changes to this file may cause incorrect behavior and will be
7:  '     lost if the code is regenerated.
8:  ' </autogenerated>
9:  '----------------------------------------------------------------
10:
11: Option Strict Off
12: Option Explicit On
13:
14: Imports System
15: Imports System.ComponentModel
16: Imports System.Diagnostics
17: Imports System.Web.Services
18: Imports System.Web.Services.Protocols
19: Imports System.Xml.Serialization
20:
21: '
22: 'This source code was auto-generated by Microsoft.VSDesigner,
23: 'Version 1.0.3705.0.
24: '
25: Namespace localhost
26:
```

```
27:   '<remarks/>
28:   <System.Diagnostics.DebuggerStepThroughAttribute(), _
29:   System.ComponentModel.DesignerCategoryAttribute("code"), _
30:   System.Web.Services.WebServiceBindingAttribute( _
31:   Name:="Service1Soap", [Namespace]:="http://tempuri.org/")> _
32:   Public Class Service1
33:     Inherits System.Web.Services.Protocols.SoapHttpClientProtocol
34:
35:     '<remarks/>
36:     Public Sub New()
37:       MyBase.New()
38:       Me.Url = "http://localhost/Commissions/Service1.asmx"
39:     End Sub
40:
41:     '<remarks/>
42:     <System.Web.Services.Protocols.SoapDocumentMethodAttribute( _
43:     "http://tempuri.org/GetCommission", _
44:     RequestNamespace:="http://tempuri.org/", _
45:     ResponseNamespace:="http://tempuri.org/", _
46:     Use:=System.Web.Services.Description.SoapBindingUse.Literal, _
47:     ParameterStyle:= _
48:     System.Web.Services.Protocols.SoapParameterStyle.Wrapped)> _
49:     Public Function GetCommission(ByVal ID As Long) As Commission
50:       Dim results() As Object = Me.Invoke("GetCommission", _
51:         New Object() {ID})
52:       Return CType(results(0), Commission)
53:     End Function
54:
55:     '<remarks/>
56:     Public Function BeginGetCommission(ByVal ID As Long, _
57:       ByVal callback As System.AsyncCallback, _
58:       ByVal asyncState As Object) As System.IAsyncResult
59:         Return Me.BeginInvoke("GetCommission", New Object() {ID}, _
60:           callback, asyncState)
61:     End Function
62:
63:     '<remarks/>
64:     Public Function EndGetCommission( _
65:       ByVal asyncResult As System.IAsyncResult) As Commission
66:       Dim results() As Object = Me.EndInvoke(asyncResult)
67:         Return CType(results(0), Commission)
68:     End Function
69:   End Class
```

```
70:
71:     '<remarks/>
72:     <System.Xml.Serialization.XmlTypeAttribute( _
73:     [Namespace]:="http://tempuri.org/")> _
74:     Public Class Commission
75:
76:        '<remarks/>
77:        Public TradeAmount As Double
78:
79:        '<remarks/>
80:        Public Rate As Double
81:     End Class
82: End Namespace
```

The Web Service proxy class for `Service1` is defined in lines 28 to 69. The proxy class for the `Commission` type is defined in lines 72 through 81. The `Service1` proxy class looks complicated but really contains only proxies for invoking methods in the Web Service marked with the `WebMethodAttribute`. We defined only one Web method. Then why so much code? Well, you have to remember that we are invoking operations across the Web, so we need extra information to marshal calls across a network.

In addition, there are actually three methods for each Web method. One method is used to make synchronous calls to our Web method, and the remaining pair of methods is used for the asynchronous invocation of our Web method. Thus, given a Web method named `GetCommission`, we can expect three methods in the proxy class: `GetCommission`, `BeginGetCommission`, and `EndGetCommission`. `GetCommission` is the synchronous proxy call and `BeginGetCommission` and `EndGetCommission` are used to make an asynchronous call. Hence, if you sift through the noise in Listing 13.3, you will quickly realize that the proxy class contains code to hide the additional information needed to marshal calls across a network, making Web Services easier to use.

The second part of the `Reference.vb` file contains proxy classes for types that we are exporting. These proxy classes are generated by the WSDL utility using the CodeDOM. In our example (Listing 13.3) we export a `GetCommission` method, which returns a custom type `Commission`. The `Commission` proxy class represents a fields-only version of our custom type. In Chapter 14 I will show you how to return a fat version of objects returned by Web methods. The skinny, fields-only proxy class will suffice for now.

Creating a Web Service Application

Many of the technologies that support XML Web Services, like XML, are not new. What is new is the ease with which you can consume and implement Web Services. So far you know that Visual Studio .NET seamlessly employs UDDI, DISCO, and WSDL to incorporate XML Web Services into client applications. Creating Web Services is even easier. In a nutshell, you create an XML Web Service project by selecting the ASP.NET Web Service applet from the New Project dialog (Figure 13.3). After you have created the project, all you have to do is define methods and types and apply the `WebMethod` attribute to public methods you want to export. Listing 13.4 shows the complete (albeit short) listing for the Web Service containing the `GetCommission` Web method.

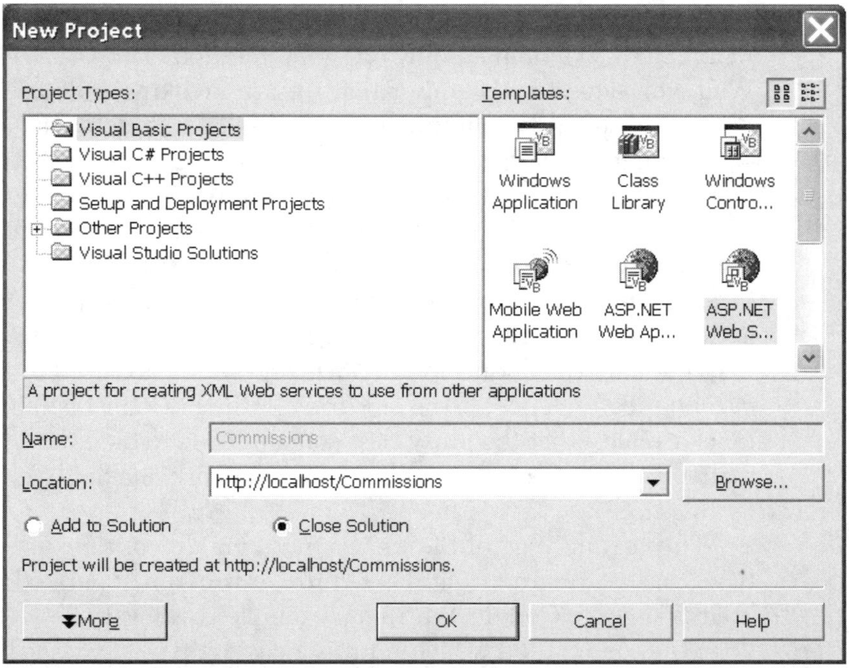

Figure 13.3 The New Project dialog creates a new ASP.NET Web application from a project template.

Listing 13.4 A Complete Web Service Using the `GetCommission` Web Method

```
1:  Imports System.Web.Services
2:
3:  <WebService(Namespace := "http://tempuri.org/")> _
4:  Public Class Service1
5:      Inherits System.Web.Services.WebService
6:
7:  [ Web Services Designer generated code ]
8:
9:      <WebMethod()> _
10:     Public Function GetCommission(ByVal ID As Long) As Commission
11:       Return New Commission(1000, 0.075)
12:     End Function
13:
14: End Class
```

The `WebService` attribute and `Inherits System.Web.Services.Web-Service` statements indicate that `Service1` is a Web Service. You can add all the supporting code you want, but only public methods tagged with the `WebMethod` attribute (line 9) will be represented by proxy methods when you import the Web Service. Everything else about the Web Service class is consistent with any class.

Applying the `WebService` Attribute

The `WebService` attribute is applied to a Web Service class automatically by the project template. The default `Namespace` named argument is `tempuri.org`. Before you deploy the Web Service you should modify the `Namespace` value to point to your company's URL. For example, I would modify my Web Services as follows: `<WebService(Namespace := "http://www.softconcepts.com/")>`. This uniquely identifies your Web Services even if other vendors define Web Services with similar types and methods. You can also specify `Name` and `Description` named arguments for the `Web-Service` attribute. These values will show up in the description page, for example, when someone browses to the Web Service in the Add Web Reference dialog.

Writing a Web Method

To implement a Web method, define a public method and apply the `Web-Method` attribute. There are few limitations to the kind of information you can pass to and return from a Web method. You can pass and return simple data types to XML Web Services. You can also return complex types from Web methods, such as the `Commission` type demonstrated in `Commissions.sln`. And because XML is an integral part of ADO.NET and the ADO.NET `DataSet` is serializable, you can return an ADO.NET `DataSet` from a Web method. For more examples of returning complex data types and `DataSet` objects from Web Services, refer to Chapter 14.

Debugging and Testing Web Services

There are a few convenient ways to test a Web Service. You can test a Web Service with the integrated debugger or without the integrated debugger, or you can use the Build and Browse menu. Each method is described in the subsections that follow.

Testing Web Services with the Integrated Debugger

You can set breakpoints and run your XML Web Service as an application. This approach will create a test Web Page, from which you can invoke the Web methods. When the executing test page reaches a breakpoint, control will switch to the Visual Studio .NET integrated debugger, and you can step through and evaluate your Web Service code as you would any other application.

Figure 13.4 shows an example of a test page returned by the `.asmx` file. Every method tagged with the `WebMethod` attribute (for example, `GetCommission`, shown in Figure 13.4) is listed near the top of the service description test page. You can click on the link for a particular method, which will render a test page for that method (Figure 13.5). Enter data values in the text box for each parameter and click the Invoke button. The results are returned as a page containing XML (Figure 13.6).

It is worth noting that when you invoke a Web method in your code, all you need to worry about is the value of the response. The XML text is used to move the data across the network, but the actual XML is managed by the technology. From our perspective all we are worried about is the result value, not the XML. Interestingly, the test page's XML response does pro-

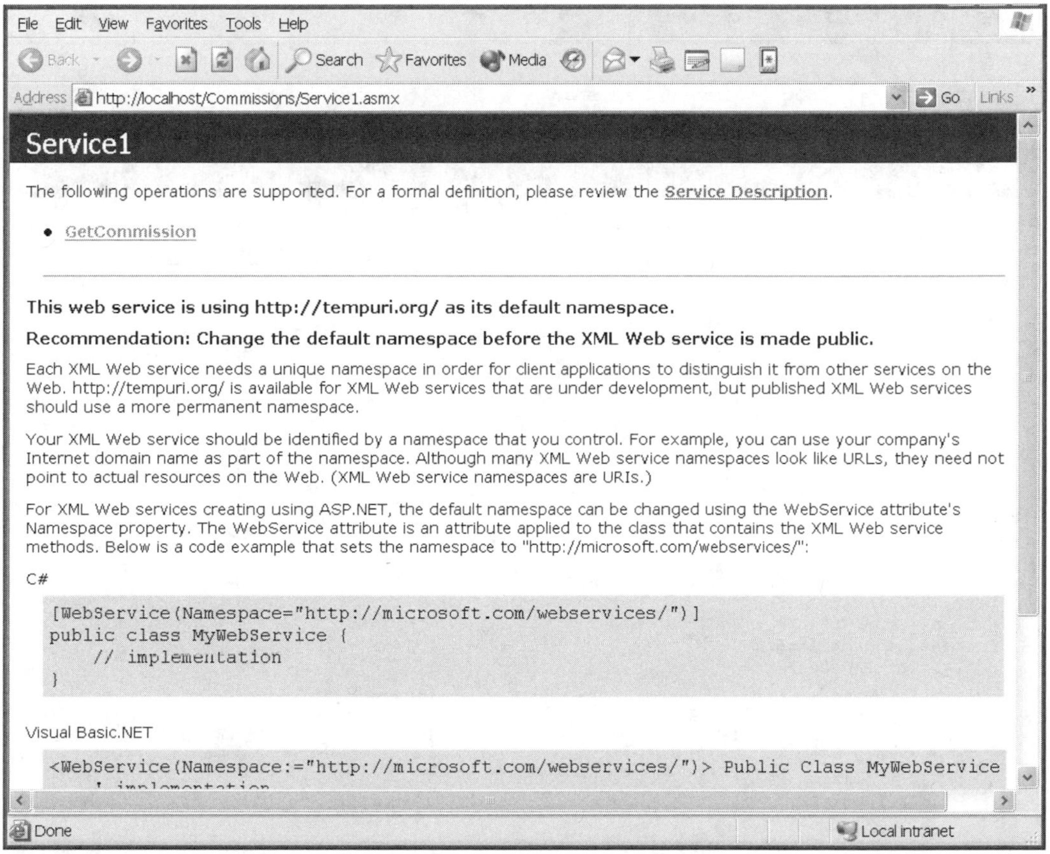

Figure 13.4 A test page returned by the Web Service when you navigate to the `.asmx` file.

vide you with an insight into how XML Web Services move data around the Internet.

Testing Web Services without the Integrated Debugger

Suppose you aren't the originator of a Web Service. You will still want to perform testing on the Web Service even if you don't have access to the source code. This kind of testing is referred to as *black-box testing* (testing from the outside without information about the implementation details of the code).

This second form of testing is accomplished by navigating to the URL that is hosting the Web Service, specifically navigating to the `.asmx` page.

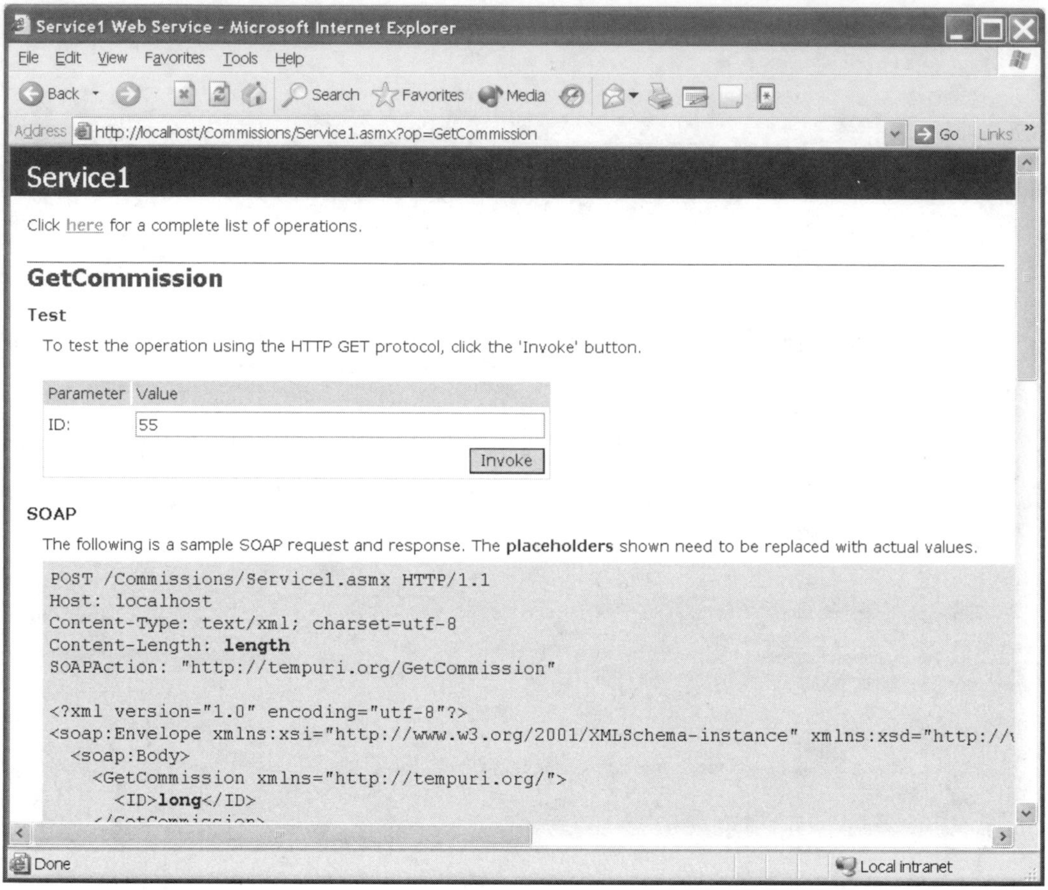

Figure 13.5 A page for entering input parameter values for Web methods.

Once you're there, the Web Service DLL will return the same kind of test page shown in the previous subsection. When you have the test page, you can select specific Web methods, enter input values for the parameters, and invoke the Web method. By examining the XML return values you can determine whether the Web Service is providing the correct result.

Testing Web Services with the Build and Browse Menu

As another testing alternative, you can click on the `.asmx` page in the Solution Explorer in Visual Studio .NET and select Build and Browse from the

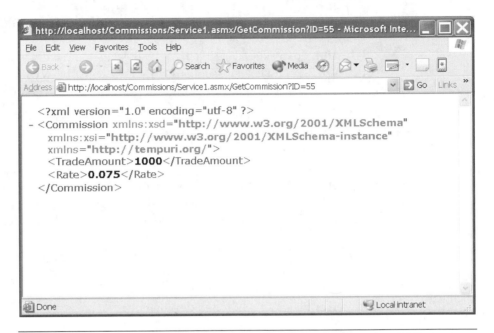

Figure 13.6 The results of invoking a Web method, displayed as XML text.

right-click context menu. The test Web page will be displayed in the browser built into Visual Studio .NET. From this point testing is identical to the previous two processes. Using the Build and Browse menu does not allow you to interact with the integrated debugger; you are performing a black-box test.

After you have tested the Web Services you have implemented, you are ready to deploy those services.

Deploying Web Services

Web Services are ASP.NET applications that run on the Web. The application is represented by a DLL—the Web Service—and the `.asmx` file that plays the role of the base URL for consumer applications. The following summarized steps describe what you need to do to deploy a Web Service.

1. Create a Web application directory from the Web server root.
2. Copy the `.asmx` file to the Web application directory you created.
3. Add a `.disco` file to support discovery (optional).

4. Add a `Web.config` file if you need configuration information other than the default behavior.
5. Create a `\bin` subfolder in your Web application directory and copy to it the Web Service DLL and supporting DLLs (except for .NET DLLs).

Much of what you can do with ASP.NET Web Forms applications you can do with Web Services applications. (As you will see in this chapter, this applies to security too.) As a benefit you can deploy a Web Service using the Project|Copy Project menu item in Visual Studio .NET. To copy a Web Service application, select the Web Service project from the Solution Explorer and select Project|Copy Project. This step displays the Copy Project dialog (Figure 13.7). Click OK to accept the default values of the Copy Project dialog.

It will be helpful to understand the technical steps for deploying Web Services in case you find yourself in the position of deploying a Web Service without Visual Studio .NET. This information will be especially helpful if you have to troubleshoot a botched deployment.

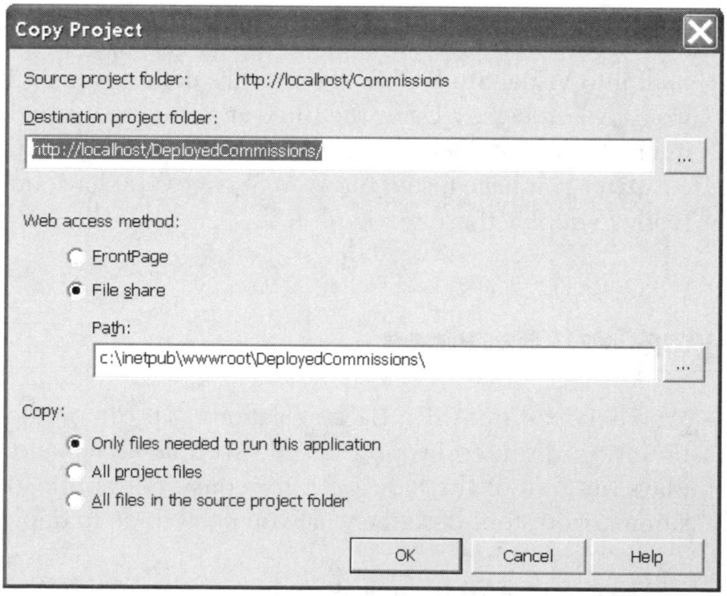

Figure 13.7 The Copy Project dialog, used to deploy ASP.NET Web Forms and Web Services applications.

Creating a Web Application Directory

The steps in this section describe how to create a Web application directory for the Internet Information Server (IIS).

The easiest way to create an application directory is to select the Web site in the Microsoft Management Console with IIS. Follow the numbered steps below to create the Web application directory. (Note: These instructions are for Windows 2000. You will have to make slight adjustments for other versions of Windows, but the steps are very similar.)

1. Select Start|Control Panel to open the Control Panel.
2. Double-click the Administrative Tools applet to the open the Administrative Tools folder.
3. Double-click on the Internet Services Manager applet to open the Microsoft Management Console with the IIS snap-in.
4. Navigate to the Web site in the IIS snap-in (Figure 13.8).
5. Right-click on the Web site to open the context menu and select the New|Virtual Directory menu item.

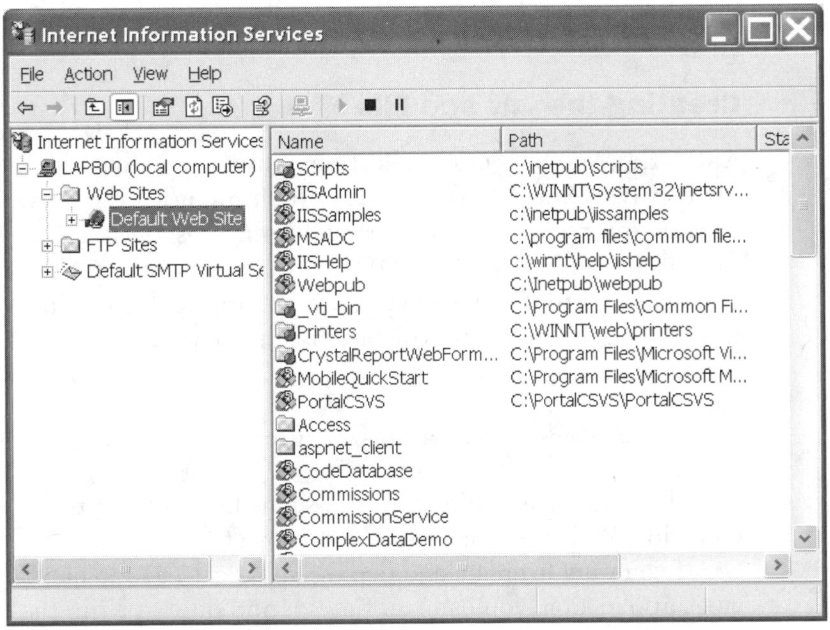

Figure 13.8 Selecting the Web site for the new application directory.

6. Complete the Virtual Directory Creation Wizard, providing a name for your application directory, a physical path, and directory permissions. The default options will suffice.

After completing the last step, you have a Web application directory that is recognized by the Web server. It is worth noting that the physical file folder does not have to reside in the Web server's root folder. The Web-sharing mechanism takes care of mapping a shared name to a physical file path.

Copying Essential Files

For your Web Service to run you will need to copy the `.asmx` file to the Web application directory. Additionally, you will need to add a `bin` directory to the Web application directory and copy the DLL application to the `bin` folder. For our example application the DLL is named `commissions.dll`. When you are finished with the basic necessary configuration, you will have files and folders that approximate the following structure:

```
C:\inetpub\wwwroot\commissions
C:\inetpub\wwwroot\commissions\service1.asmx
C:\inetpub\wwwroot\commissions\bin
C:\inetpub\wwwroot\commissions\bin\commissions.dll
```

Creating the `.disco` File

ASP.NET Web Services applications support dynamic discovery. If you enter the Web Service base URL (which includes the `.asmx` file) and the `?disco` query, the Web Service will return discovery information. This information can be used by UDDI (as demonstrated by the Add Web Reference dialog) to discover Web Service applications. For example, if we wanted the discovery information for the `commissions.dll`, we could enter the following command.

```
http://localhost/commissions/service1.asmx?disco
```

This command will return the same DISCO text that is created when you add a Web reference to a client project.

If you want to create and deploy a physical `.disco` file for your Web Services application, you can run the `?disco` query or run the command-line `disco.exe` utility. You can save the output from the `disco.exe` utility to a

.disco file. Modify the host name in the .disco file and copy that file to the Web application directory you made for your Web Service. Listing 13.5 shows the .disco file created when I imported the Commissions Web Service. This file can be changed and deployed with the Web Service.

Listing 13.5 The .disco File for the Commissions Web Service

```
<?xml version="1.0" encoding="utf-8"?>
<discovery xmlns:xsd="http://www.w3.org/2001/XMLSchema"
xmlns:xsi="http://www.w3.org/2001/XMLSchema-instance"
xmlns="http://schemas.xmlsoap.org/disco/">
  <contractRef ref="http://localhost/Commissions/
Service1.asmx?wsdl"
  docRef="http://localhost/Commissions/Service1.asmx"
  xmlns="http://schemas.xmlsoap.org/disco/scl/" />
  <soap address="http://localhost/Commissions/Service1.asmx"
  xmlns:q1="http://tempuri.org/" binding="q1:Service1Soap"
  xmlns="http://schemas.xmlsoap.org/disco/soap/" />
</discovery>
```

The discovery document was created by the **disco.exe** utility. You could write it from scratch if you are a glutton for punishment, but there is no reason to do so. Modify the .dicso file shown in Listing 13.5. Change the text set in bold to the name of the host server, and copy the .disco file to the Web application folder. In our example, the Web Service file is named **service1.asmx**, and we would name this file **service1.disco** and place it in the **C:\inetpub\wwwroot\commissions** folder.

Adding a **Web.config** File

As with every ASP.NET application, you can use the **Web.config** file to configure such options as whether or not debugging is enabled, the authentication and authorization information, and how the session is managed. For example, the default behavior is to use Windows authentication. However, this is suitable only for intranet applications. If you are deploying your Web Service for the Internet, you will likely want some kind of authentication. This topic is related to security, so I will defer further discussion of the **Web.config** file for the next section.

In the meantime, if you want to deploy a `Web.config` file, you can copy the one created by default with your Web Service to the Web application directory you created earlier in the chapter.

Understanding XML Web Services and Security

XML Web Services are part of ASP.NET. As such they use the same security model that ASP.NET uses. This means you can pick from Windows basic authentication, Windows basic authentication with secure sockets, Windows digest, Windows client certificates, Forms, and custom security in SOAP headers.

By default the `Web.config` file is configured to run the Web Service using Windows basic authentication, which is suitable for intranet Web Services or Web Services such as you are likely to use for application integration within the same enterprise. The reason for this basic kind of default authentication is so that you don't have to struggle with security while you are learning Web Service basics. Now that you have the fundamentals out of the way, you need to know how to apply security to Web Services. In this section I will demonstrate basic Windows authentication. (Refer to Chapter 18 for more on general security.)

Exploring the Default `Web.config` File

The default `Web.config` file created with each Web Service is shown in Listing 13.6. The parts we are interested in vis-à-vis security are highlighted in bold.

Listing 13.6 The Default `Web.config` File

```
1:  <?xml version="1.0" encoding="utf-8" ?>
2:  <configuration>
3:
4:    <system.web>
5:
6:      <!--  DYNAMIC DEBUG COMPILATION
7:        Set compilation debug="true" to insert
8:        debugging symbols (.pdb information)
9:        into the compiled page. Because this
10:       creates a larger file that executes
```

```
11:      more slowly, you should set this value to
12:      true only when debugging and to
13:      false at all other times. For more information,
14:      refer to the documentation about
15:      debugging ASP.NET files.
16:      -->
17:      <compilation defaultLanguage="vb" debug="true" />
18:
19:      <!--  CUSTOM ERROR MESSAGES
20:        Set customErrors mode="On" or "RemoteOnly"
21:        to enable custom error messages, "Off" to disable.
22:        Add <error> tags for each of the errors you want to handle.
23:      -->
24:      <customErrors mode="RemoteOnly" />
25:
26:      <!--  AUTHENTICATION
27:        This section sets the authentication policies of
28:        the application. Possible modes are "Windows",
29:        "Forms", "Passport", and "None"
30:      -->
31:      <authentication mode="Windows" />
32:
33:
34:      <!--  AUTHORIZATION
35:        This section sets the authorization policies of
36:        the application. You can allow or deny access
37:        to application resources by user or role. Wildcards:
38:        "*" means everyone, "?" means anonymous
39:        (unauthenticated) users.
40:      -->
41:      <authorization>
42:        <allow users="*" /> <!-- Allow all users -->
43:
44:        <!--  <allow users="[comma separated list of users]"
45:                     roles="[comma separated list of roles]"/>
46:              <deny users="[comma separated list of users]"
47:                     roles="[comma separated list of roles]"/>
48:        -->
49:      </authorization>
50:
51:      <!--  APPLICATION-LEVEL TRACE LOGGING
52:        Application-level tracing enables trace log output
53:        for every page within an application.
54:        Set trace enabled="true" to enable application trace
```

```
55:      logging.  If pageOutput="true", the
56:      trace information will be displayed at the bottom of
57:      each page.  Otherwise, you can view the
58:      application trace log by browsing the "trace.axd"
59:      page from your Web application
60:      root.
61:    -->
62:    <trace enabled="false" requestLimit="10" pageOutput="false"
63:    traceMode="SortByTime" localOnly="true" />
64:
65:
66:    <!--  SESSION STATE SETTINGS
67:      By default ASP.NET uses cookies to identify which
68:      requests belong to a particular session.
69:      If cookies are not available, a session can be
70:      tracked by adding a session identifier to the URL.
71:      To disable cookies, set sessionState cookieless="true".
72:    -->
73:    <sessionState
74:      mode="InProc"
75:      stateConnectionString="tcpip=127.0.0.1:42424"
76:      sqlConnectionString=
77:      "data source=127.0.0.1;user id=sa;password="
78:      cookieless="false"
79:      timeout="20"
80:    />
81:    <!--  GLOBALIZATION
82:      This section sets the globalization settings of
83:      the application. -->
84:    <globalization requestEncoding="utf-8" responseEncoding="utf-8" />
85:
86:  </system.web>
87:
88: </configuration>
```

Regarding security, the parts of the Web.config file we are concerned with are the authentication (lines 26 through 31) and authorization (lines 34 through 49) sections. If you examine the file, you can determine that the default authentication mode is Windows basic (line 31) and all users are allowed access (line 42). To change the security settings, we will have to change the Web.config file. Then clients will have to authenticate in coordination with the security model we select.

Using Windows Authentication at the File or Directory Level

You can use Windows authentication with Web Services. Windows authentication will work fine in all Windows intranet solutions. If a user attempts to run a Web Service and the current user name and password are not authorized, a Windows user name and password dialog (Figure 13.9) will be displayed, prompting the user for a new user name and password. If the user name and password entered cannot be authenticated, an Error 401 Not Authorized page will be displayed (Figure 13.10).

To define allowed users you can create several user names and assign them to a common new role, or you can define individual allowed user names. The first step is to add the user names and roles to the Windows file system, giving either the individual users or the roles access to the deployed Web Services files. As the name—Windows authentication—suggests, you are adding these users and roles to the access control list (ACL, pronounced *ackle*). After the users are added to the ACL for the Web Services files, you need to modify the `Web.config` file, adding the allowed and denied users to the authentication portion of the file. I will break down each piece of the process in the subsections that follow.

Figure 13.9 The Windows XP user name and password dialog displayed for Windows authentication.

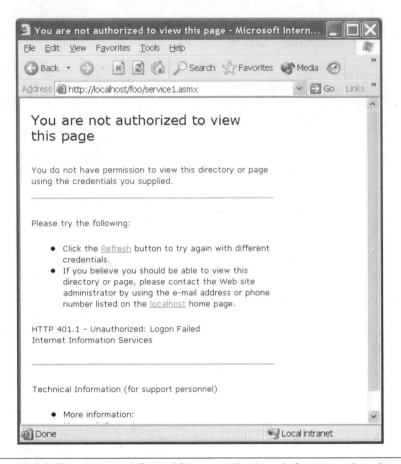

Figure 13.10 The standard Error 401 page displayed, for example, when a user unsuccessfully attempts to authenticate.

Adding Users or Roles to the Access Control List

We will use a specific scenario for the Commissions Web Service. We want only users in the broker_dealer group to be able to access the Web Service, so we will create a broker_dealer group and add users to that group. Only users in this group will be authenticated. For our purposes we will assume that the Web Service is deployed in a folder named `MyCommissions` on the IIS server.

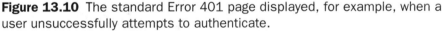

NOTE: The description and figures in this subsection for deploying a Web Service and configuring the Web Service for Windows authentication are particular to Windows XP. The process for configuring Windows 2000 is very similar.

To prepare the deployed Web Service and configure users for Windows authentication, follow the numbered steps, using the figures as a pictorial guide.

1. Open the Computer Management console by selecting Manage from the right-click menu for MyComputer (on your desktop). Select the Local Users and Groups section (Figure 13.11).
2. Select the Groups item and pick New Group from the context menu.
3. In the New Group dialog, enter the Group name broker_dealer and click Create (Figure 13.12). Close the New Group dialog.
4. In the Computer Management dialog (Figure 13.11), Local Users and Groups, select the Users item and pick New User from the context menu (Figure 13.13).
5. Using Figure 13.13 as a guide, create a couple of users by entering a user name, a full name, and a password. Click the Create button when each user's information is ready.
6. After you have created the new users and closed the New User dialog, select the users in the Computer Management dialog. Double-click to the user properties (Figure 13.14), change to the Member Of tab, and make the users members of the broker_dealer group.

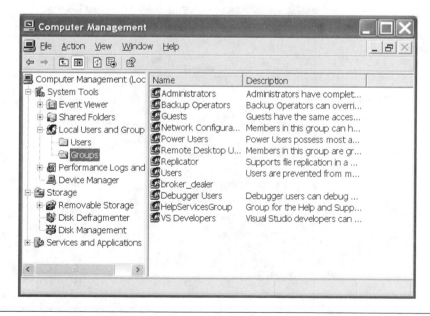

Figure 13.11 The Computer Management console is a central location for managing users, groups, services, and other facets of your system.

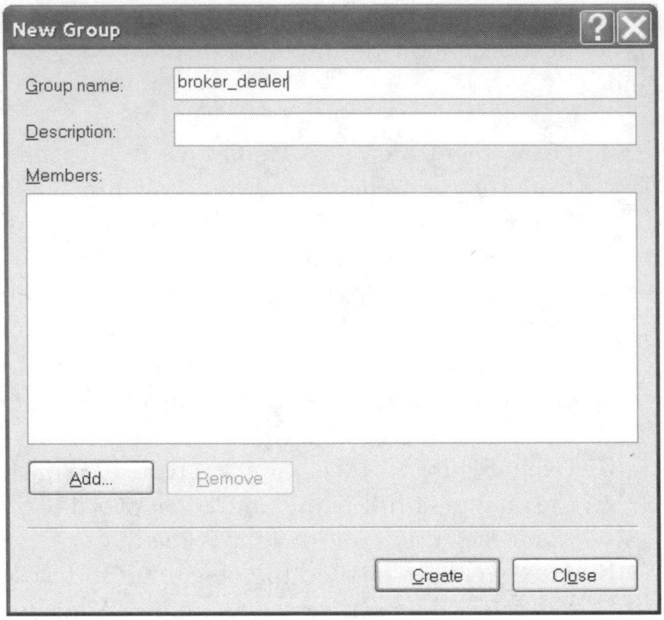

Figure 13.12 Define the broker_dealer group in the New Group dialog.

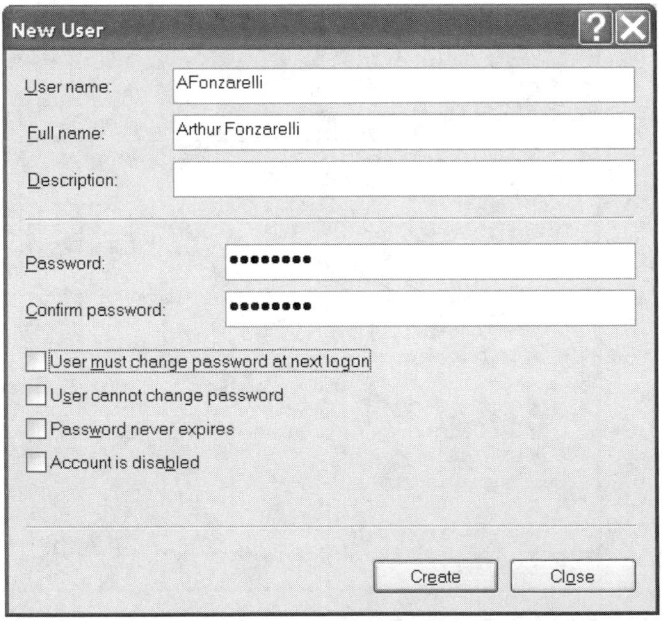

Figure 13.13 Create new users in the New User dialog.

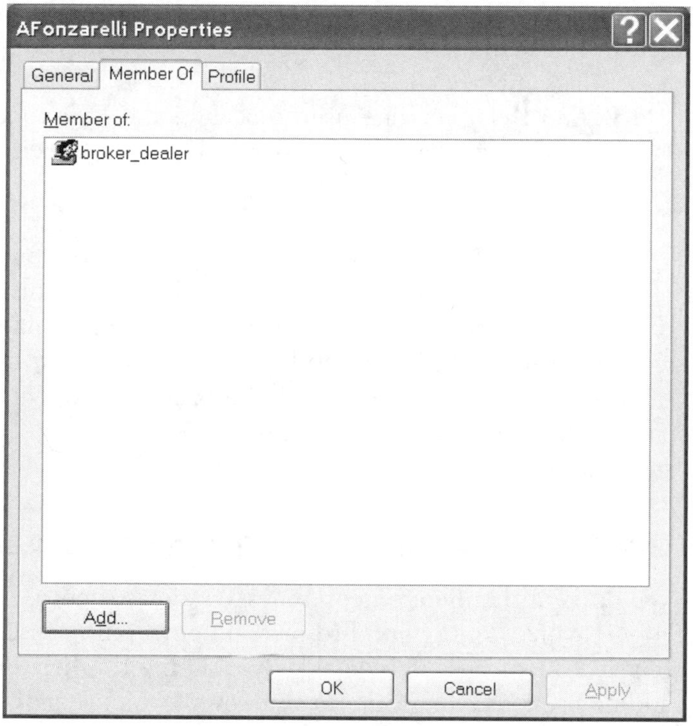

Figure 13.14 Modify the Member Of list, making the users members of the broker_dealer group.

7. Deploy the Web Service by making a new folder. Copy the `.asmx` file and the project's `Web.config` file to the deployment folder. Add a `bin` directory and place `Commissions.dll` in the `bin` folder.

8. Return to the Computer Management console and select Services and Applications, Internet Information Services.

9. Click Default Web Site and select New|Virtual Directory from the context menu.

10. Using the Virtual Directory Creation Wizard, name the virtual directory MyCommissions and set the physical file path to the directory created in step 7. Use the defaults for everything else.

11. After you have deployed the Web Service and created the Web application directory, open Windows Explorer. (We need to set directory and file permissions.)

12. Navigate to the physical directory for MyCommissions, and select Properties from the context menu.

13. In the MyCommissions Properties dialog, select the Security tab.
14. Click Add and add the broker_dealer group to group or user names lists (Figure 13.15).
15. Add the Everyone user, too. Give the Everyone user Full Control and the broker_Dealer group Read and Execute permissions (Figure 13.16).

After step 15 we are ready to modify the `Web.config` file. The Everyone account has access to the physical file folder. This allows us to modify the contents when we have physical access to the machine. For example, we'll need this access to modify the `Web.config` file. However, users browsing to our Web Service will be coming across an HTTP connection. They will be authorized based on the Windows users and groups and the settings in the `Web.config` file.

Modifying the `Web.config` File's Authorization Section

Windows authentication combines Windows security and ASP.NET security. It won't do any good to provide permission in a `Web.config` file if physical file access is blocked. By defining the broker_dealer group and adding users to that group (in Windows), we have sufficiently prepared the file system. Now we will modify the `Web.config` file.

Continuing our scenario, we want to allow only broker_dealer members to access the Commissions Web Service. By default the authentication mode is set to Windows. This is what we want. All we need to modify is the

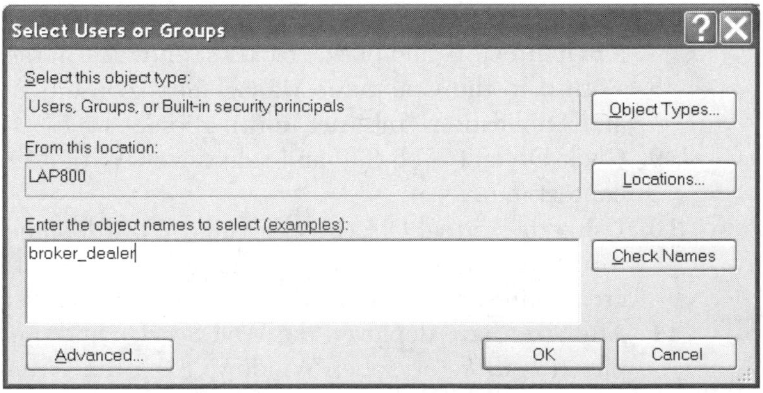

Figure 13.15 Add the broker_dealer group to the list of authorized groups and users.

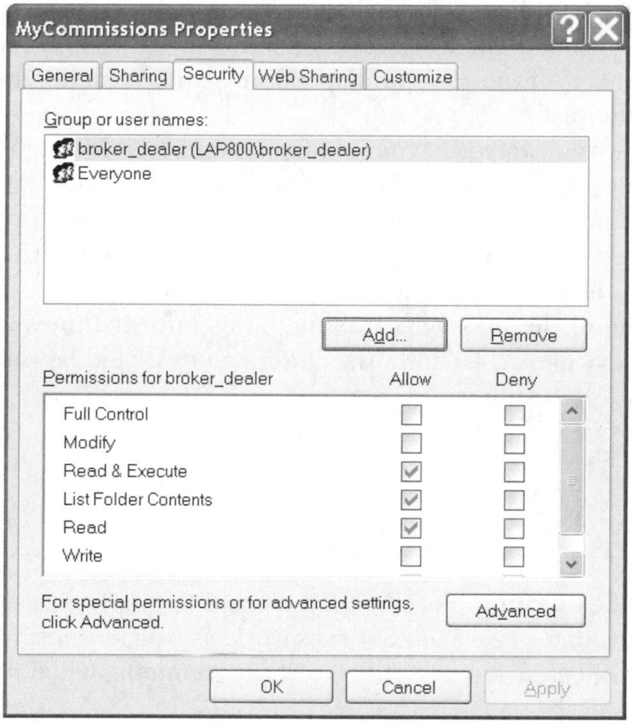

Figure 13.16 We will need Read and Execute permissions to run the Web Service.

authorization section. Based on an excerpt from Listing 13.6 (without the comments), Listing 13.7 contains the authentication and authorization sections of the `Web.config` file, updated for MyCommissions.

Listing 13.7 The Updated Authentication and Authorization Sections

```
<authentication mode="Windows" />
<authorization>
  <allow roles="lap800\broker_dealer" />
  <deny users="*" />
</authorization>
```

The `Web.config` file is read from top to bottom. The authorization section is read until an `allow` or `deny` section satisfies a request. Hence, if a user is authenticated and authorized by an `allow` section, no more processing occurs. The `allow` section in Listing 13.7 allows access by anyone in the broker_dealer group of lap800 (my laptop's name) and denies access by all other users.

You can verify your configuration by navigating to the Web Service using your browser. A user name and password dialog appears. If you enter one of the users defined as a member of the broker_dealer group and the password is correct, you should be able to browse to the Web Service page. (Remember to use the domain name. For example, lap800\AFonzarelli was one of the members I defined; this information would be entered as the user's name.) Unauthorized user names should be presented with the Error 401 Not Authorized page.

Summary

When writing this chapter I elected to emphasize the tools and technologies that make Web Services work, as well as one way to secure XML Web Services. The rest really is just programming when it comes to simple Web Services.

In this chapter you learned about WSDL, UDDI, proxy classes, the `Web-Service` and `WebMethod` attributes, as well as how to deploy and secure a Web Service using Windows authentication. You also learned about `.disco` files and the role of the `Web.config` file in Web Services. You are now well prepared for Chapter 14.

Chapter 14 will demonstrate advanced subjects related to Web Services. I will show you more examples of Web Services and tell you some things you are unlikely to find anywhere else. The next chapter will show you how to modify the proxy class to return fat objects, how to return ADO.NET `DataSet` objects and strongly typed collections, and how to invoke Web Services asynchronously. The strategies will let you maximize Web Services and offer optimal performance to customers who use your Web Services.

CHAPTER 14

Advanced
Web Services

Brevity does not mean inconsequence.

—*Jackson Wayfare*

Introduction

Chapter 13 prepared you to do anything possible with Web Services. If there is some fundamental thing that you do not completely grasp, you know enough about Web Services to track down any minute detail. We are ready to discuss advanced concepts.

This chapter shows you everything about Web Services that has been invented so far. In this chapter you will learn how to write Web Services that return simple and complex data types and how to modify the WSDL proxy files that describe complex types returned by Web Services. You will learn about returning an ADO.NET `DataSet` object from a Web Service and about the mechanism that makes it possible to do so, XML. By the time you are finished reading you will have mastered invoking Web Services synchronously and asynchronously (which is not possible without multithreading), and you will know how to block, poll, and wait for asynchronous Web method calls to return. Finally, I will demonstrate a way—in addition to using Windows Authentication—to secure your Web Services. In short, by the time you have finished this chapter you will be well equipped to make XML Web Services an integral part of your development arsenal.

I will begin the chapter with a synchronous Web Service that returns simple data and end the chapter with asynchronous Web Services. As a result I believe that when you are finished reading the chapter you will feel comfortable speaking competently with gurus about XML Web Services.

Returning Simple Data from Web Services

Chapter 13 demonstrated the technologies that support Web Services and how to implement a very basic Web Service, the Commissions Web Service. I will pick up from there and show you how to create a Web Service that returns simple data in a practicable way.

Prime numbers—numbers divisible only by themselves or by the number 1—are useful in a tremendous variety of mathematics equations as well as encryption. (Unbreakable encryption relies on huge numbers that are the product of two very large primes. The idea is that by the time any known algorithm can factor the product, the data is no longer relevant.) The Web Service in Listing 14.1 demonstrates how to determine whether a number is prime by using a 2,000-year-old technique devised by Eratosthenes, referred to as *the Sieve of Eratosthenes*.

You can look up Eratosthenes on the Internet for factual details and biographical information, but I will paraphrase the basic mathematics and theory here for brevity. The Sieve of Eratosthenes works on the premise of the product of primes. The basic idea is that all positive nonprime integers other than 0 and 1 are the products of prime numbers. Eratosthenes further resolved that when trying to determine whether a number is prime, it is necessary to check as possible divisors only those numbers less than or equal to the square root of the candidate number. This makes sense simply because if a candidate number has divisors (other than 1 and itself), one of the divisors will be less than or equal to the square root and the other will be greater than or equal to the square root (or the divisor will be the integer square root). Consider the number 7. The square root of 7 is less than 3 because 3^2 is 9. Thus if 7 had prime divisors (other than 7), the set of divisors would be the integer square root of 7 or one divisor less than 3 and a divisor greater than 3. Since all we need is one divisor (other than 1 or the number itself) to demonstrate that a number is not prime, we would only need to find a divisor less than or equal to the square root of 7.

Eratosthenes resolved that if one knew all the prime numbers preceding any possible prime, the unknown number could be evaluated by checking to see whether any known primes less than the square root were divisors. The basic sieve works by beginning with a known prime (2) and calculating all of the numbers greater than 2 in succession, using all the preceding discovered primes as possible divisors for each number in succession. The algorithm is pretty simple. In the next subsection I will demonstrate my implementation of the Sieve of Eratosthenes as a Web method, and following that subsection I will discuss a simple strategy for implementing Web Services.

Implementing the Sieve of Eratosthenes

The basic strategy I employ for all programming is to solve the problem regardless of the way in which I intend a particular consumer to use the solution. Essentially, even though I know I will be presenting a solution as a Web method, I solve the general problem first and then expose the solution for consumers as a Web method.

As a good general strategy, always solve a problem in the general sense as methods and a class, if applicable. For example, one method alone does not yield a very good class, but one method might be the first method in a math library. Here is the promised Listing 14.1, demonstrating my recollected interpretation of the Sieve of Eratosthenes. The listing is followed by a brief summarization.

Listing 14.1 A General Solution for Determining Whether a Positive Integer Is Prime

```
1:  Public Class PrimeLibrary
2:    Private FPrimes As ArrayList
3:
4:    Public Sub New(ByVal Max As Long)
5:      FPrimes = New ArrayList()
6:      Seed()
7:      Initialize(Max)
8:    End Sub
9:
10:   Public Function IsPrime(ByVal Number As Long) As Boolean
11:     Return FPrimes.IndexOf(Number) > -1
12:   End Function
13:
14:   Public ReadOnly Property Primes() As ArrayList
15:   Get
16:     Return FPrimes
17:   End Get
18:   End Property
19:
20:   Private Sub Seed()
21:     FPrimes.Add(2L)
22:   End Sub
23:
24:   Private Sub Initialize(ByVal Max As Long)
25:     If (Max < 3) Then Return
```

```
26:       Dim I As Long
27:       For I = 3 To Max
28:         If (Test(I)) Then FPrimes.Add(I)
29:       Next
30:     End Sub
31:
32:     Private Function Test(ByVal NumberToTest As Long) As Boolean
33:       Dim Prime As Long
34:       For Each Prime In FPrimes
35:         If (NumberToTest Mod Prime = 0) Then Return False
36:         If (Prime >= Math.Sqrt(NumberToTest)) Then Return True
37:       Next
38:
39:       Return True
40:     End Function
41:
42: End Class
```

The general solution is comprised of a class with several methods. The constructor initializes an array to store the list of primes. The `IsPrime` function and the `Primes` property represent the public interface to the `PrimeLibrary` class. The solution works by seeding the `ArrayList` object with the first known prime, 2, and then calculating all the primes from 3 to the last number we want to test. The number we want to test is represented by the `Max` argument.

Now that we have a solution that can be used by any application, I can play the role of class consumer and produce the Web Service. The Web Service can expose as much of the class as I'd like, but in this case we will simply expose the `IsPrime` function. This way we can conceal the complexity of creating the `PrimeLibrary` class and simply create a façade that provides the result.

Implementing the IsPrime Web Service

Visual Studio .NET supports the concept of the solution. Solutions can contain several projects and produce one or more assemblies. `PrimeLibrary.sln` contains `PrimeLibrary.vbproj`, a `TestPrimeLibrary.vbproj` console application (for scaffolding the general solution before building the Web Service), and the Web Service itself.

Chapter 13 described how project templates in the New Project dialog can create all the basic source code for an ASP.NET Web Service by using the template code. Because the template exists, we only have to worry about implementing our Web methods. Listing 14.2 contains the implementation of `PrimeWebService.vbproj`.

NOTE: You can create your own project templates. To create a new item or project template, copy an existing template that is close to the new template you want to create. Modify the existing template files to contain the code your template will add, create a Wizard Launching file (`.vsz`), and add an entry to a `.VSDir` file. For more information, look in the VS .NET help documentation.

Listing 14.2 A Web Service That Uses the `PrimeLibrary` Class

```
1:  Imports System.Web.Services
2:  Imports Library = PrimeLibrary.PrimeLibrary
3:
4:
5:  <WebService(Namespace:="http://tempuri.org/")> _
6:  Public Class Service1
7:    Inherits System.Web.Services.WebService
8:
9:    [ Web Services Designer generated code ]
10:   <WebMethod()> Public Function IsPrime( _
11:     ByVal Max As Long) As Boolean
12:
13:     Dim Instance As Library = New Library(Max)
14:     Return Instance.IsPrime(Max)
15:
16: End Function
17:
18: End Class
```

This Web Service is about as straightforward as it can be. `PrimeWeb-Service.vbproj` implements one Web Service using the default name `Service1`. I added a reference to `PrimeLibrary.vbproj`, which in turn gives me access to the `PrimeLibrary` class and the general solution for the prime test. In line 2 I used the aliasing technique that lets us substitute a local namespace alias for a long namespace and class reference. It just happens that my namespace and class are both named `PrimeLibrary`. Using the aliasing technique in line 2, I shortened the whole thing to just `Library`.

The single Web method is implemented in lines 10 through 16. The Web-Method attribute indicates that IsPrime will be callable from clients across a network. The two statements simply create an instance of the PrimeLibrary class using the alias and return the result of PrimeLibrary.IsPrime. Figure 14.1 shows the IsPrime Web Service accessible from the .asmx-generated test page.

This kind of Web Service supports the idea of Web Services as a way to return simple data. You will probably more often want to return complex data types. Complex data can be returned in the form of typed collections, instances of a class, or DataSet objects. The next section demonstrates how to return complex data from a Web Service.

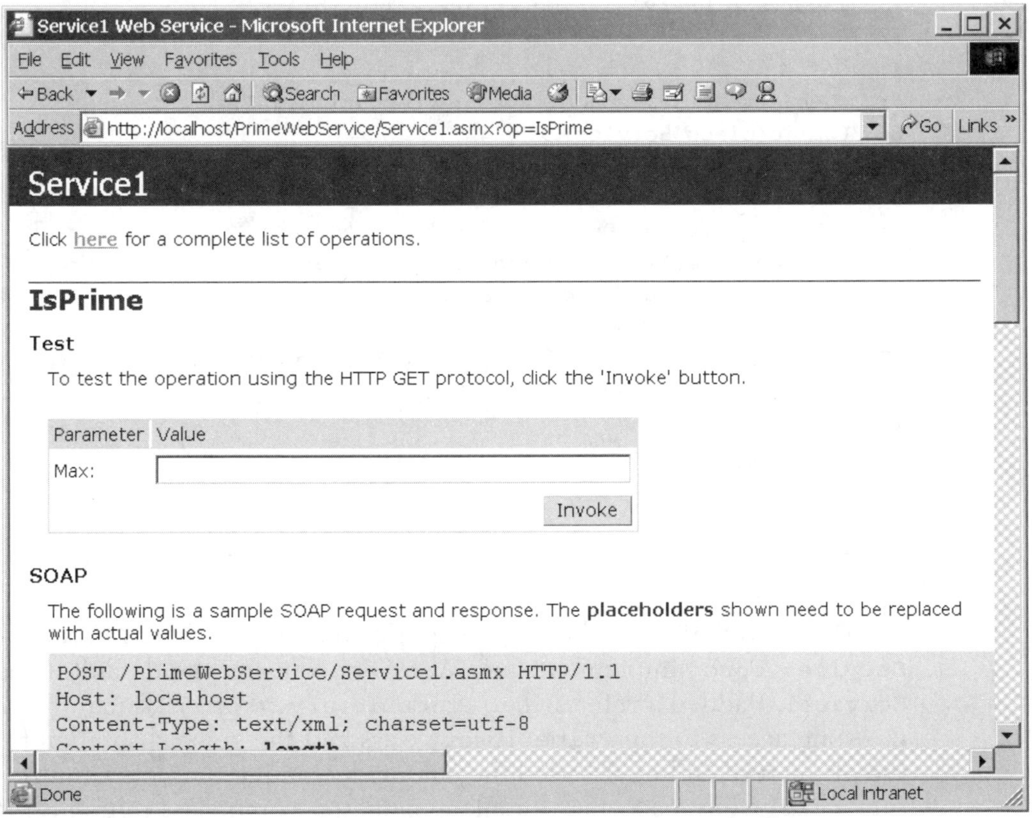

Figure 14.1 Access the IsPrime Web Service by browsing to the .asmx page.

Returning Complex Data from a Web Service

Simple data can be returned by using the HTTP protocol. Complex data (instances of structures or classes) uses the SOAP protocol. It is worth knowing when various protocols come into play. SOAP used to mean *Simple Object Access Protocol*; but now SOAP is just SOAP. However, the old expansion of the acronym describes nicely what SOAP does for us. SOAP makes it possible to transport an object across a network by using the self-describing nature of XML to include the description of the data along with the data.

Writing Web Services that return complex data types requires no special effort; however, you need to be aware of some additional things that happen with the related technologies. Thus I will show you a class and a Web Service that returns data representative of data that might be returned from a clearing corporation like the National Securities Clearing Corporation (if it were using Web Services) and the resulting impacts and opportunities for the Web Service consumers.

Implementing a Complex Type

Complex data in this context refers to structures or classes. You can define a class or structure and return it from a Web Service in much the same manner as you would return a class or structure from any DLL. The class I defined for this example (Listing 14.3) represents information that might be returned by a commissions clearing Web Service.

Listing 14.3 The CommissionsData Class

```
Public Class CommissionsData
  Private FSystemCode As String
  Private FRecordType As String
  Private FClearingSettlingFirmNumber As String
  Private FFundProcessingDate As DateTime
  Private FCommissionType As String
  Private FDebitCreditIndicator As String
  Private FDebitReasonCode As String
  Private FSettlementIndicator As String
  Private FRecordDate As DateTime
```

```
Public Property SystemCode() As String
Get
  Return FSystemCode
End Get
Set(ByVal Value As String)
  FSystemCode = Value
End Set
End Property

Public Property RecordType() As String
Get
  Return FRecordType
End Get
Set(ByVal Value As String)
  FRecordType = Value
End Set
End Property

Public Property ClearingSettlingFirmNumber() As String
Get
  Return FClearingSettlingFirmNumber
End Get
Set(ByVal Value As String)
  FClearingSettlingFirmNumber = Value
End Set
End Property

Public Property FundProcessingDate() As DateTime
Get
  Return FFundProcessingDate
End Get
Set(ByVal Value As DateTime)
  FFundProcessingDate = Value
End Set
End Property

Public Property CommissionType() As String
Get
  Return FCommissionType
End Get
Set(ByVal Value As String)
  FCommissionType = Value
End Set
End Property
```

```
Public Property DebitCreditIndicator() As String
Get
  Return FDebitCreditIndicator
End Get
Set(ByVal Value As String)
  FDebitCreditIndicator = Value
End Set
End Property

Public Property DebitReasonCode() As String
Get
  Return FDebitReasonCode
End Get
Set(ByVal Value As String)
  FDebitReasonCode = Value
End Set
End Property

Public Property SettlementIndicator() As String
Get
  Return FSettlementIndicator
End Get
Set(ByVal Value As String)
  FSettlementIndicator = Value
End Set
End Property

Public Property RecordDate() As DateTime
Get
  Return FRecordDate
End Get
Set(ByVal Value As DateTime)
  FRecordDate = Value
End Set
End Property

End Class
```

There isn't anything especially noteworthy about the `CommissionsData` class; it is comprised of fields and properties. I used the `F` prefix convention for fields and dropped the `F` prefix for properties. (Not even Microsoft is promoting the Hungarian notation anymore.)

Note that the class contains only fields and properties. We could implement methods and events for this class. However, there would be no impact on how we would implement the Web Service.

Implementing a Web Service

The CommissionsData class represents a complex type that we want to return from a Web Service. For our illustration it doesn't matter whether or not we have any data assigned to the members of CommissionsData. If we returned an instance of CommissionsData, that data would be returned along with the definition of the type when we invoked the Web method. Listing 14.4 demonstrates a simple Web method that returns a CommissionsData object.

Listing 14.4 A Web Method That Returns a CommissionsData Object

```
Imports System.Web.Services

<WebService(Namespace:="http://tempuri.org/")> _
Public Class Service1
  Inherits System.Web.Services.WebService

  [ Web Services Designer generated code ]
  <WebMethod()> _
  Public Function GetData() As CommissionsData.CommissionsData
    Return New CommissionsData.CommissionsData()
  End Function

End Class
```

If you compare the Web Services in Listings 14.2 and 14.4, you will note that there are fundamentally no differences in the mechanics of implementing the Web Services. All the differences occur when the WSDL utility generates the proxy class and when we use the Web Service that returns a complex type.

Referencing a Web Service

When you add a Web reference to a project consuming a Web Service (see Chapter 13), WSDL generates several files. These files help bridge the gap between your Web Service and the client that consumes the Web Service. If you click on the namespace created by WSDL and then click the Show All Files toolbar button, the `Reference.vb` proxy file will be displayed in the Solution Explorer (Figure 14.2). You can also select the `Reference.vb` file from Windows Explorer by navigating to it and opening that file.

Exploring the Proxy Class

When you have added a Web reference to the Commissions Web Service, a proxy class is added to your project. (You can open the proxy class for the Commissions Web Service and follow along as we explore.) Listing 13.3 in the previous chapter shows an entire proxy file, and of course you can create a Web Service, reference it, and examine that proxy file too. For now we are interested only in the treatment of our `CommissionsData` class by the WSDL utility. Listing 14.5 shows just the generated `CommissionsData` proxy file.

Figure 14.2 Click the Show All Files button to show the `Reference.vb` proxy file generated by the WSDL utility.

Listing 14.5 The CommissionsData Proxy File Generated by WSDL

```
<System.Xml.Serialization.XmlTypeAttribute( _
[Namespace]:="http://tempuri.org/")> _
  Public Class CommissionsData

    '<remarks/>
    Public RecordDate As Date

    '<remarks/>
    Public SystemCode As String

    '<remarks/>
    Public SettlementIndicator As String

    '<remarks/>
    Public RecordType As String

    '<remarks/>
    Public ClearingSettlingFirmNumber As String

    '<remarks/>
    Public FundProcessingDate As Date

    '<remarks/>
    Public CommissionType As String

    '<remarks/>
    Public DebitCreditIndicator As String

    '<remarks/>
    Public DebitReasonCode As String
  End Class
End Namespace
```

Note that the generated proxy class contains only fields—no properties, methods, or events (or anything else, for that matter). I refer to this as *flattening* the complex type. All our properties become public fields in the proxy class. If you think about this for a minute, it makes sense.

If Web Services returned *fat objects*—with methods, events, properties, and other code—Web Services would have to return all the assemblies and related assemblies across the wire. This means that Web Services would have to download and install binary files. For complex Web Services you might be referring to half of the CLR. Clearly, sending the CLR across the Web for each Web method invocation would not be a good thing. Even worse is that you might be dragging third-party code onto your workstation or server. (You don't know where that code has been.) Instead Web Services return a sanitary proxy class capable of containing data. So, in a way we are back to data-only data types, but just for Web Services. (Later in this chapter I will show you how to return fat objects from Web Services.)

Implementing the Web Service Consumer

The mechanism behind the WSDL tool is (probably) the CodeDOM. The CodeDOM contains classes that can generate very complex code. Thus far we know that almost everything about returning complex types in a Web Service is no more challenging than returning a simple type. The big difference is that the Web Service has the real class and the consumer gets a fields-only replica.

Clearly, you will not be able to invoke operations on the proxy class returned by the Web Service, but you can use the data. Listing 14.6 demonstrates a simple use of the proxy `CommissionsData` class: I use the fields information to generate a simple user input form. (This is for fun as much as for the hope that you'll find it a useful application for Reflection.)

Listing 14.6 Using Reflection to Generate a Simple User Interface

```
1:  Imports Service = CommissionsDataApp.localhost.Service1
2:  Imports System.Reflection
3:
4:  Public Class Form1
5:     Inherits System.Windows.Forms.Form
6:
7:  [ Windows Form Designer generated code ]
8:
9:     Private Sub Form1_Load(ByVal sender As System.Object, _
10:       ByVal e As System.EventArgs) Handles MyBase.Load
11:
12:      Dim Service As Service = New Service()
13:
14:      GenerateForm(Service.GetData().GetType())
15:
```

```
16:     End Sub
17:
18:     Private Sub GenerateForm(ByVal Type As Type)
19:
20:       Dim Info As FieldInfo
21:       Dim Y As Integer = 0
22:       Dim Label As Label
23:       Dim TextBox As TextBox
24:
25:       For Each Info In Type.GetFields()
26:
27:         Label = New Label()
28:         Label.Text = Info.Name
29:         Label.Location = New Point(10, Y)
30:         Label.AutoSize = True
31:         Controls.Add(Label)
32:
33:         TextBox = New TextBox()
34:         TextBox.Location = New Point(20 + Label.Width, Y)
35:         Controls.Add(TextBox)
36:         Y += 25
37:
38:       Next
39:
40:     End Sub
41: End Class
```

The code in Listing 14.6 is direct. I used the aliasing trick to shorten the namespace reference in line 1. I imported the `System.Reflection` namespace, which contains the `FieldInfo` class used to reflect the `CommissionsData` proxy class in lines 20 and 25. When the form loads (lines 12 and 14), I create an instance of the service and a simple user interface (Figure 14.3).

A practical application might be a form generator. For a commercial application we might employ the CodeDOM and generate actual code, supporting programmer customization. More likely, though, you will be using the data returned by the Web Service.

Downloading binary assemblies with executable code would not be secure. However, what if you download code that you know is reliable? For example, Microsoft supports returning `DataSet` objects from a Web Service, and these include methods too. Because the `DataSet` class contains

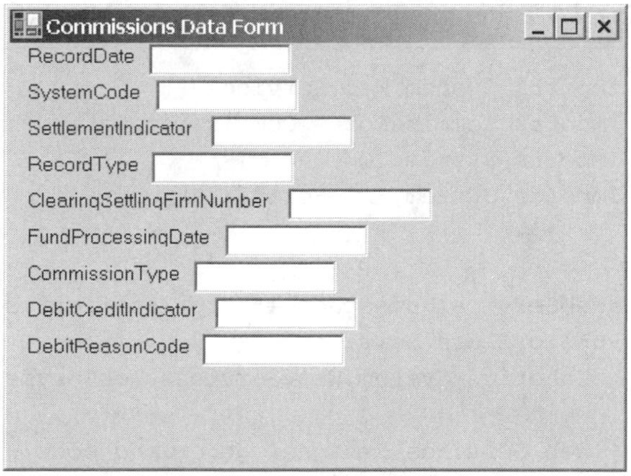

Figure 14.3 A user interface dynamically generated by using Reflection.

known code from Microsoft and it is assumed that you have the CLR on the machine using the DataSet Web Service, it seems reasonable to support fat DataSet objects from Web Services. Let's take a look at how that works.

Writing Web Services That Use DataSet Objects

When you define a Web Service to return a DataSet, you actually get a DataSet and not a proxy DataSet. You would agree that a DataSet is a powerful object. The listing in the subsection below demonstrates a Web Service that returns the CommissionsData object as a DataSet, which in a database application you might find more useful than a user-defined object. (And, as my smart friend Eric Cotter said, just think of a DataSet as a convenient way to store data, meaning that you can use a DataSet even with no database, as I will demonstrate next.)

Serializing an Object to an XML DataSet

Listing 14.7 provides a revised version of the GetData method from Listing 14.4. This version returns a complex type, an ADO.NET DataSet. The code also shows how to serialize objects into an XML DataSet.

Listing 14.7 Returning a DataSet from an XML Web Service

```
1:  Imports System.Web.Services
2:  Imports Commission = CommissionsData.CommissionsData
3:  Imports System.IO
4:  Imports System.Xml.Serialization
5:
6:
7:  <WebService(Namespace:="http://tempuri.org/")> _
8:  Public Class Service1
9:    Inherits System.Web.Services.WebService
10:
11: [ Web Services Designer generated code ]
12:
13:   <WebMethod()> _
14:   Public Function GetData() As DataSet
15:     Dim Data As Commission = New Commission()
16:     Data.SystemCode = "F"
17:     Data.RecordType = "30"
18:     Data.ClearingSettlingFirmNumber = "0"
19:     Data.FundProcessingDate = DateTime.Now
20:     Data.CommissionType = "01"
21:     Data.DebitCreditIndicator = "1"
22:     Data.DebitReasonCode = "1"
23:     Data.SettlementIndicator = "1"
24:     Data.RecordDate = DateTime.Now
25:
26:     Dim Serializer As XmlSerializer = _
27:       New XmlSerializer(Data.GetType())
28:     Dim Stream As Stream = New MemoryStream()
29:     Serializer.Serialize(Stream, Data)
30:     Stream.Position = 0
31:
32:     Dim DataSet As DataSet = New DataSet()
33:     DataSet.ReadXml(Stream)
34:
35:     Return DataSet
36:   End Function
37:
38: End Class
```

Let's take a moment to explore the code in Listing 14.7. If you have been skipping around in this book, this is a good place to see how a great framework comes together. In this one code example you will find streams, XML, ADO.NET `DataSet` objects, XML Web Services, serialization, and Reflection.

NOTE: You may have been programming in other languages, including VB6, prior to VB .NET. However, if you have previously programmed only in VB6, some parts of Listing 14.7 might surprise you. This listing demonstrates some of the capabilities that have been available in other languages like C++ and Delphi's Object Pascal, illustrating why some programmers have a bit of contempt for VB6. VB .NET provides us with the best of both worlds: a powerfully expressive yet easy-to-use language.

The Web method `GetData` serializes an object into an XML `DataSet`. The implication is that you can turn ordinary objects into `DataSet` objects with some very basic code. The `Imports` statements in lines 3 and 4 import the namespaces for streams (`System.IO`) and an `XmlSerializer` object (`System.Xml.Serialization`). The code in lines 15 through 24 simply provide some data for the serialization process to bite into. The real action begins in line 26.

Lines 26 and 27 declare an `XmlSerializer` object. We provide the type information of the kind of object we want to serialize. This can include classes, `DataSet` objects, or just about anything marked with the `SerializableAttribute`. Line 28 creates a new `MemoryStream` object. Polymorphism supports assigning a `MemoryStream` object (child class) to a `Stream` object (parent class). We could substitute `FileStream` for `MemoryStream` in line 28, and the same code would serialize the object to an XML file. (Try it as an exercise.) Line 29 serializes the instance of the `CommissionsData` object declared in line 15 into the `MemoryStream` object. Line 30 resets the stream position to the start position, and lines 32 and 33 create a `DataSet` object and read the XML from the `MemoryStream` object (lines 32 and 33, respectively).

When the code is finished, the `DataSet` contains an unnamed `DataTable` with one row. The columns are the `CommissionsData` property names, and each row of data contains the property values. In this example there is only one row of data. At this point—line 35—the `DataSet` can be returned from the Web method. (What you don't see is that XML serialization is used to get the `DataSet` across the wire as XML text.)

Looking at the Proxy Class for Web Methods That Return a `DataSet`

We can generate the `Reference.vb` proxy class by using the Add Web Reference dialog or the `wsdl.exe` utility. If you just want to generate the proxy class (shown in Listing 14.8), open the Visual Studio .NET Command Prompt (Figure 14.4). The Visual Studio .NET Command Prompt adds environment variables, making it easier to run command-line programs that ship with .NET like `wsdl.exe`. To generate the proxy class using `wsdl.exe`, follow these steps.

1. After opening a command prompt by using the Visual Studio .NET Command Prompt menu item (Figure 14.4), change directories to the folder to which you want the output proxy file to be written.
2. Enter `wsdl http://host/service.asmx /language:VB`, where *host* is the name of the computer hosting the Web Service (on your PC, this is `localhost`) and *service.asmx* is the name of the actual `.asmx` file containing the Web Service. The switch will write the proxy file in the same directory in Visual Basic .NET.

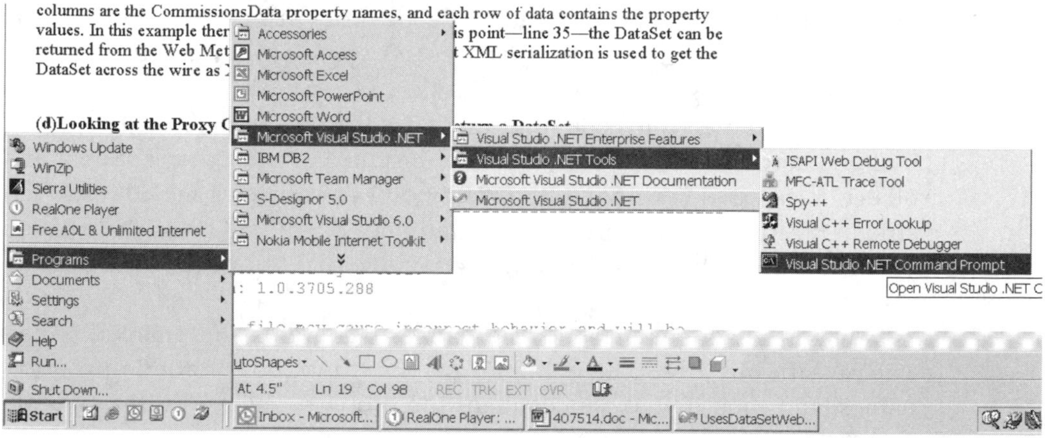

Figure 14.4 Open the Visual Studio .NET Command Prompt to run console utilities like `wsdl.exe`.

By default the proxy file is written in C# and the output filename will be the same name as the `.asmx` file but with a `.vb` extension. For example, if your `.asmx` file is named `Service1.asmx`, your WSDL-generated proxy file will be named `Service1.vb`. Listing 14.8 shows the source code for a proxy file that has a Web method that returns a `DataSet`.

Listing 14.8 A Proxy File That Has a Web Method That Returns a `DataSet`

```
'------------------------------------------------------------------'
<autogenerated>
'    This code was generated by a tool.
'    Runtime Version: 1.0.3705.288
'
'    Changes to this file may cause incorrect behavior
'    and will be lost if the code is regenerated.
' </autogenerated>
'------------------------------------------------------------------
Option Strict Off
Option Explicit On

Imports System
Imports System.ComponentModel
Imports System.Diagnostics
Imports System.Web.Services
Imports System.Web.Services.Protocols
Imports System.Xml.Serialization


'This source code was auto-generated by
'Microsoft.VSDesigner, Version 1.0.3705.288.
'
Namespace localhost

  '<remarks/>
  <System.Diagnostics.DebuggerStepThroughAttribute(), _
  System.ComponentModel.DesignerCategoryAttribute("code"), _
    System.Web.Services.WebServiceBindingAttribute( _
    Name:="Service1Soap", [Namespace]:="http://tempuri.org/")> _
  Public Class Service1
    Inherits System.Web.Services.Protocols.SoapHttpClientProtocol

    '<remarks/>
    Public Sub New()
```

```
    MyBase.New
    Me.Url = "http://localhost/" + _
            "CommissionsDataSetWebService/Service1.asmx"
End Sub

'<remarks/>
<System.Web.Services.Protocols.SoapDocumentMethodAttribute( _
    "http://tempuri.org/GetData",
    RequestNamespace:="http://tempuri.org/",
    ResponseNamespace:="http://tempuri.org/",
    Use:=System.Web.Services.Description.SoapBindingUse.Literal,
    ParameterStyle:=System.Web.Services.Protocols. _
    SoapParameterStyle.Wrapped)> _
Public Function GetData() As System.Data.DataSet
    Dim results() As Object = Me.Invoke("GetData", New Object(-1) {})
    Return CType(results(0),System.Data.DataSet)
End Function

'<remarks/>
Public Function BeginGetData( _
    ByVal callback As System.AsyncCallback, _
    ByVal asyncState As Object) As System.IAsyncResult

    Return Me.BeginInvoke("GetData",
        New Object(-1) {}, callback, asyncState)
End Function

'<remarks/>
Public Function EndGetData( _
    ByVal asyncResult As System.IAsyncResult) As System.Data.DataSet

    Dim results() As Object = Me.EndInvoke(asyncResult)
    Return CType(results(0),System.Data.DataSet)
    End Function
    End Class
End Namespace
```

As we have seen already, there is a lot of metadata associated with Web Services. We can ignore that information for the purposes of our discussion and simply focus on the lines of text set in bold.

Recall that when we returned a complex data type, we got a proxy class for the custom data type (see Listing 14.4). In Listing 14.8 you will note that no such proxy class is defined for the `System.Data.DataSet` object returned by the Web Service. Instead when the proxy class is generated, it is known that you have the .NET Framework installed (how else did you get the `wsdl.exe` utility?), and the return type is cast to the real type, the `System.Data.DataSet` class. As a result, what we get from Web Services that return XML `DataSet` objects is a fat `DataSet` with methods and everything else.

Modifying the Proxy Class to Return Fat Objects

By default Web Services return dehydrated classes. I call these classes *dehydrated* because when you return a complex type from a Web Service, you get a fields-only class. However, if you want a reconstituted object from a Web Service, you can get one with a bit of chicanery.

Assume for a moment that you are building Web Services to bridge applications internally or for select customers. These customers will have your library. If this is the case, you can modify the WSDL-generated proxy class by removing the generated proxy class and referencing your `.dll` assembly that contains the actual object. Voilà! You have created reconstituted, or fat, objects.

If you like your milk whole instead of powdered and real objects instead of flat versions of those objects, follow these steps.

1. Generate the proxy class for a Web Service that returns a complex type.
2. Edit the file containing the proxy code by removing the flat, fields-only proxy class that represents the complex type.
3. Add a reference to the assembly that contains the actual complex type code and definition of your Web Service client.
4. Add an `Imports` statement to the proxy class indicating the namespace of the real class.

When you are finished, your client application will think it is getting an actual object back from the Web Service.

As an alternative, suppose you have a Web Service that returns a complex type, but you do not have the original assemblies defining the real types instead of the generated types. Never fear—you can roll your own! That's right. Create a new assembly that has public properties with getters and setters that match the fields in the generated proxy class. Add the code you are interested in associating with the type returned from the Web Service, then modify the proxy file to refer to the custom type. Again, you have real objects instead of dehydrated ones.

Clearly, you don't have to do any of these things. You can take whatever the WSDL tool and the Web Service gives, but that wouldn't be very advanced. We are the masters of our domain, and the code bends to our will.

Returning a Strongly Typed Collection

The difficulty in building good object-oriented systems based on relational databases is the orthogonality between a relational database and an object-oriented structure. Databases are generally made of tables with rows and columns, and relationships are inferred from key columns. The closest analogy between a single object and a database is the row. The problem is that databases tend toward normalization, resulting in many pieces of what might comprise a single object existing in more than one table. The bending and contorting between rows of normalized data to objects, back and forth, is what makes it difficult to build object-oriented systems on top of relational databases.

On the one hand, you have the lightning speed of multi-row updates, deletions, insertions, and selections that are the hallmark of a relational database; on the other hand, how do you reconcile this with behaviors? Where is there room for a behavior in a `DataTable` or `DataRow`? A hybrid has appeared recently. This hybrid treats a `DataSet` as the base class for an object. The difficulty here is that you may have multiple rows of data and there is no concept of a single object; rather, the rows represent a collection of data with no closely related behaviors. The behaviors exist in the `DataSet`, the collection. (Attempts to solve this dilemma have led to object-oriented databases, like POET, but these databases don't seem to be catching on.)

There are many ways to build software, of course. You can compose the system from the perspective of the database, the graphical user interface, or a centralized solution captured in objects. The latter more consistently leads to reliable software but is not always easiest to implement. Perhaps until the dichotomy between relational databases and object-oriented systems is solved the best thing to do is assess the way you elect to build a particular application based on the complexity. (Very complex systems strongly lend themselves to object-oriented practices, even if the simplicity of persisting data to a relational database suffers.) While you are deciding what to do, let's look at another tool to add to your solution arsenal: returning serialized typed collections from XML Web Services.

Reviewing Strongly Typed Collections

Recall (from Chapter 5) that we can define typed collections by inheriting from the `System.Collections.ReadOnlyCollectionBase` class. (We can also define a writable typed collection by inheriting from the `System.Collections.CollectionBase` class.). A typed collection is a special class devised to collect a specific kind of object. Unlike an array, collections are capable of dynamically growing to accommodate more elements. Typed collections contain a known type. By combining the ease of use of an array of types with the dynamic growth capabilities of an array list, you end up with a typed collection. One additional benefit is that typed collections can be serialized. This makes them ideal for persisting as XML in any form, including returning them from XML Web Services.

Defining a typed collection is straightforward. Define a class that inherits from `ReadOnlyCollectionBase` or `CollectionBase` and implement a couple of methods and a default indexer. The indexer allows you to treat a typed collection like an array; the underlying collection and subsequent typecast allow you to treat the typed collection as a dynamically growing array of a specific type. Listing 14.9 demonstrates the rudiments of a typed collection of `CommissionsData` objects.

Listing 14.9 Implementing a Strongly Typed Collection with a Twist

```
1:  Imports System.Collections
2:  Imports CommissionsData.CommissionsData
3:
4:
5:  Public Class Commission
6:     Inherits CommissionsData.CommissionsData
7:
8:     Public Overrides Function ToString() As String
9:       Const mask As String = "Record Type: {0}{1}"
10:      Return String.Format(mask, SystemCode, RecordType)
11:    End Function
12:
13: End Class
14:
15: Public Class CommissionsDataList
16:    Inherits CollectionBase
```

```
17:
18:    Default Public Property Item( _
19:       ByVal Index As Integer) As Commission
20:    Get
21:       Return CType(List(Index), Commission)
22:    End Get
23:    Set(ByVal Value As Commission)
24:       List(Index) = Value
25:    End Set
26:    End Property
27:
28:    Public Function Add( _
29:       ByVal Value As Commission) As Integer
30:
31:       Return List.Add(Value)
32:
33:    End Function
34:
35: End Class
```

Two elements appear in Listing 14.9. Lines 15 through 35 implement the typed collection. I will return to that in a minute, preferring to proceed in a more orderly fashion from the beginning of the listing.

Line 1 imports the `System.Collections` namespace. The `CollectionBase` class I am inheriting from comes from that namespace. Line 2 imports the collected type. I generally don't name classes the same name as my namespace since it lends to confusion; however, in this instance I elected to leave it since it opens the door for another discussion, demonstrated by the `Commission` class beginning in line 5.

Line 5 introduces a new class. Instead of modifying an existing class that I know other code depends on (see the earlier discussions using `CommissionsData`), I took an intermediate step and introduced a new class that inherits from `CommissionsData`. The new class (lines 5 through 13) has a better name, `Commission`, and new behavior. The `Commission` class overrides the `ToString` method, providing clients with an alternate behavior. There is one additional modest benefit: if my client doesn't refer to behaviors defined in `CommissionsData` directly—recall that it is defined in a different assembly than the one in Listing 14.9—my client will not have to reference both assemblies. However, if, for instance I refer to `CommissionsData.RecordType` directly, I will need to reference the `CommissionsData.dll` too.

These are pragmatic matters that you should be aware of since they will aid in your mastery of Visual Basic .NET.

As mentioned, lines 15 through 35 implement the typed collection. It is easy to implement, with just two basic members, but it is deceptively powerful. I implemented an `Add` method (lines 28 through 33) to allow me to add `Commission` objects to the collection, and I implemented a default indexer (lines 18 through 26). The default indexer allows me to treat the typed collection, syntactically, as an array. Listing 14.10 demonstrates code that shows you the typed collection's `Add` method and the array- and collection-like capabilities.

Listing 14.10 Using Typed Collections Like Smart, Dynamically Sizing Arrays

```
1:   Imports TypedCollectionDemo
2:
3:   Module Module1
4:
5:     Sub Main()
6:
7:       Dim List As CommissionsDataList = New CommissionsDataList()
8:
9:       ' Adds a specific type, supported by the Add method
10:      List.Add(New Commission())
11:      List.Add(New Commission())
12:
13:      ' Uses IEnumerable implemented by CollectionBase
14:      Dim Item As Commission
15:      For Each Item In List
16:        Console.WriteLine(Item.ToString())
17:      Next
18:
19:      ' Treats CommissionsDataList like an array,
20:      ' supported by the indexer
21:      Dim I As Integer
22:      For I = 0 To List.Count - 1
23:        Console.WriteLine(List(I).ToString())
24:      Next
25:
26:      Console.ReadLine()
27:
28:    End Sub
29:
30: End Module
```

Lines 10 and 11 demonstrate the `Add` method in action. Notice that we are passing a specific, homogeneous type to the `Add` method. Lines 14 through 17 demonstrate using the `IEnumerable` interface inherited from `CollectionBase`. Interestingly, if you download a copy of Rotor (the source code for the CLR) from *http://www.microsoft.com*, you will see that `IEnumerable` lies at the heart of serialization. Lines 21 through 24 show the same typed collection being indexed as if it were an array. If you step through this code, you will see the default indexer property getter being invoked in line 23.

That's all there is to implementing a basic typed collection. You will want to exercise a modicum of care when returning a typed collection from a Web Service because the Web Service serialization mechanisms seem to be a bit more demanding. Read on.

Serializing a Strongly Typed Collection

XML is a portable standard for transmitting data, especially data that is describing an object and its state. If you want to save the state of an object to XML, you can use code very similar to that shown in Listing 14.7. All you need to serialize a typed collection to an XML stream is an `XmlSerializer` object and a stream. Listing 14.11 demonstrates serializing a typed collection using a `FileStream` object. The output target is a text file containing XML.

Listing 14.11 Serializing a Typed Collection to an XML Stream

```
Dim Serializer As XmlSerializer = _
  New XmlSerializer(List.GetType())

Dim Stream As FileStream = _
  New FileStream("..\list.xml", FileMode.CreateNew)

Serializer.Serialize(Stream, List)
Stream.Close()
```

The serializer accepts a `Type` object of the types we want to serialize. Then the whole list is serialized to the created `FileStream` object. The stream represents a file in this instance. At the end of the code, we need to close the `FileStream` object.

We can serialize typed collections (and other things) to XML because of the use of Reflection, the `SerializableAttribute`, and the `IEnumerable` interface. Both `ReadOnlyCollectionBase` and `CollectionBase` are adorned with the `SerializableAttribute` and implement the `IEnumerable` interface. The `SerializableAttribute` indicates that instances of a class can be serialized. Implementing `IEnumerable` means that the contractee will implement a method, `GetEnumerator`. `GetEnumerator` returns an object that implements `IEnumerator`, allowing all the elements in the collection to be enumerated.

All the public fields properties of a class are serialized if that class is marked with the `SerializableAttribute` unless you implement the `ISerializable` interface. When you want to take control of the serialization process—perhaps you want to serialize a conceptual value—you can implement the `ISerializable` interface. `ISerializable` defines an explicit method, `GetObjectData`, and an implied constructor for deserialization. Listing 14.12 demonstrates a revision to the `Commission` class that shows how to implement `ISerializable`. (It is worth noting that some forms of serialization use the `ISerializable` methods, but `XmlSerializer` does not.)

Listing 14.12 Implementing the `ISerializable` Interface

```
Public Class Commission
  Inherits CommissionsData.CommissionsData
  Implements ISerializable

  Private FTransmittedDate As DateTime

  Public ReadOnly Property TransmittedDate() As DateTime
  Get
    Return FTransmittedDate
  End Get
  End Property

  Public Sub New()

  End Sub

  Protected Sub New(ByVal Info As SerializationInfo, _
```

```vb
    ByVal context As StreamingContext)

    SystemCode = Info.GetString("SystemCode")
    RecordType = Info.GetString("RecordType")
    ClearingSettlingFirmNumber = _
      Info.GetDateTime("ClearingSettlingFirmNumber")
    FundProcessingDate = Info.GetDateTime("FundProcessingDate")
    CommissionType = Info.GetString("CommissionType")
    DebitCreditIndicator = Info.GetString("DebitCreditIndicator")
    DebitReasonCode = Info.GetString("DebitReasonCode")
    SettlementIndicator = Info.GetString("SettlementIndicator")
    RecordDate = Info.GetDateTime("RecordDate")
    FTransmittedDate = Info.GetDateTime("TransmittedDate")
  End Sub

  Public Sub GetObjectData(ByVal Info As SerializationInfo, _
    ByVal context As StreamingContext) _
    Implements ISerializable.GetObjectData

    Info.AddValue("SystemCode", SystemCode)
    Info.AddValue("RecordType", RecordType)
    Info.AddValue("ClearingSettlingFirmNumber", _
      ClearingSettlingFirmNumber)
    Info.AddValue("FundProcessingDate", FundProcessingDate)
    Info.AddValue("CommissionType", CommissionType)
    Info.AddValue("DebitCreditIndicator", DebitCreditIndicator)
    Info.AddValue("DebitReasonCode", DebitReasonCode)
    Info.AddValue("SettlementIndicator", SettlementIndicator)
    Info.AddValue("RecordDate", RecordDate)
    If (FTransmittedDate = DateTime.MinValue) Then
      FTransmittedDate = DateTime.Now
    End If
    Info.AddValue("TransmittedDate", FTransmittedDate)

  End Sub

  Public Overrides Function ToString() As String
    Const mask As String = "Record Type: {0}{1}"
    Return String.Format(mask, SystemCode, RecordType)
  End Function

End Class
```

The field playing the role of the conceptual business value is `Transmit-tedDate`, which was added in the `Commission` class. The uninitialized value for a `DateTime` variable is equivalent to `DateTime.MinValue`. In `GetObjectData` if `TransmittedDate` is uninitialized, the current date and time are serialized to the stream.

The basic idea is that you implement `GetObjectData` to serialize the object when `Serialize` is called. When deserialization is needed, it is implied that you are creating a new object. The Visual Studio .NET help documentation is misleading because it doesn't show the constructor—the symmetric operation to `GetObjectData`—to deserialize the object.

As I mentioned, `XmlSerializer` won't use this code, so you don't need it if your intention is to return the typed collection from a Web Service. However, a `BinaryFormatter` will use the `ISerializable` code. (You can read more about `BinaryFormatter` in the VS .NET help documentation.)

Returning a Collection from a Web Service

Implementing the typed collection is the hardest part of returning typed collections from an XML Web Service. Keep in mind that you will get a flattened version of the collection—but you won't even get that if you don't include the `ICollection.Add` method in your typed collection.

Outside of a Web Service, the `Add` method implemented by `CollectionBase` suffices. However, when you return a typed collection from a Web Service, .NET seems to be more particular. Suppose, for instance, that you forgot the `Add` method. When you build and browse the Web Service, you will get an `InvalidOperationException` (Figure 14.5) indicating that you did not implement the `ICollection.Add` interface method. So be savvy when creating Web Services—implement the `ICollection.Add` method.

When you declare the variable that will receive the data from the Web Service that returns a typed collection, it is important to note that the data type you declare will not be the collections typed. Instead you will declare a variable that is a `System.Array` of the collected type. For our example, the client would declare an array of `Commission` objects to receive the value from `GetCommissionsList`. This subtlety is illustrated in the next section in Listing 14.13.

Refer to `TypedCollection.vbproj` for the source code that returns an instance of `CommissionsDataList`. You can use the build and browse method described in Chapter 13 to see how the data in the typed collection is serialized and returned from the Web Service.

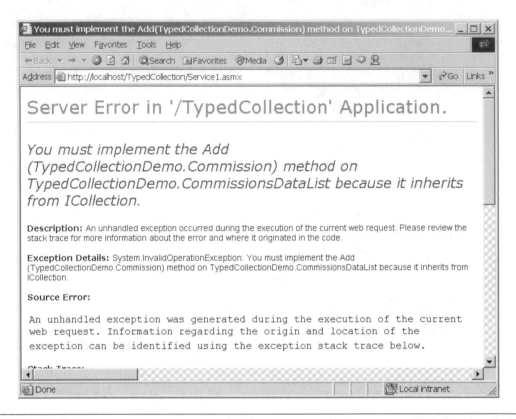

Figure 14.5 An InvalidOperationException occurs when you run a Web Service that returns a typed collection without the ICollection.Add method.

Invoking Web Services Asynchronously

One of the benefits of the multithreading model in Visual Basic .NET is the asynchronous invocation capabilities built on top of the threading model. (Refer to Chapter 6 for more information.) Asynchronous behavior is an integral part of .NET, and this capability is extended to XML Web Services. Following the basic concept of asynchronous behavior from Chapter 6, you can use exactly the same technique to invoke a Web Service asynchronously.

The WSDL utility always adds the asynchronous Begin*name* and End-*name* methods in the proxy class for each Web method (where *name* is the name of the Web method). Thus, if you want to invoke a Web method asynchronously, all you need to do is define a callback method, pass this method to the Begin*name* asynchronous proxy for the Web method, and block, or call End*name* when the Web Service returns. This is precisely how you invoke any method asynchronously in .NET.

To keep the discussion focused we will use the GetCommissionsList Web method referred to in the last section. The wsdl.exe utility generates the BeginGetCommissionsList and EndGetCommissionsList proxy methods for us. All we need to do is call BeginGetCommissionsList and choose a method for blocking or simply responding when the data is ready. (Chapter 6 demonstrated how to poll IAsyncResult, use WaitHandle, and retrieve the results with EndInvoke.) Listing 14.13 invokes GetCommissionsList asynchronously, retrieving the data when the callback method is called and safely binding the result to a Windows Forms control.

Listing 14.13 Invoking a Web Method Asynchronously

```
1:   Imports Service = AsynchWebServiceCall.localhost.Service1
2:   Imports Commission = AsynchWebServiceCall.localhost.Commission
3:
4:   Public Class Form1
5:     Inherits System.Windows.Forms.Form
6:
7:   [ Windows Form Designer generated code ]
8:     Private Sub Form1_Load(ByVal sender As Object, _
9:       ByVal e As System.EventArgs) Handles MyBase.Load
10:
11:      DoAsynchronousCall()
12:    End Sub
13:
14:    Private Instance As Service = New Service()
15:    Private Sub DoAsynchronousCall()
16:      Instance.BeginGetCommissionsList( _
17:        AddressOf AsynchCallback, Nothing)
18:    End Sub
19:
20:    Private Sub AsynchCallback(ByVal Result As IAsyncResult)
21:      Dim List() As Commission = _
22:        Instance.EndGetCommissionsList(Result)
23:      If (DataGrid1.InvokeRequired) Then
24:        Invoke(New Binder(AddressOf BindData), New Object() {List})
25:      End If
26:    End Sub
```

```
27:
28:    Private Delegate Sub Binder(ByVal List() As Commission)
29:    Private Sub BindData(ByVal List() As Commission)
30:      DataGrid1.DataSource = List
31:    End Sub
32:
33: End Class
```

Lines 1 and 2 shorten up the declaration of the Web Service and the type returned by the Web Service. (I will get back to this concept in a moment.) The `Form1_Load` event handler simply calls a method that gets things started. The real work begins in `DoAsynchronousCall` (lines 15 through 18).

Invoking the Web Method Asynchronously

In line 14 I created an instance of the Web Service proxy class. For our purposes this is fundamentally the same as creating an instance of the Web Service itself (the proxy class actually takes care of that for us). `DoAsynchronousCall` uses the Web Service proxy instance to call the asynchronous `Begin` method in lines 16 and 17. I passed the address of a callback method that matches the signature of an `AsyncCallback` delegate; no additional information is passed, as indicated by the second argument, `Nothing`. When the data is ready, the code inherited by the proxy class calls the `AsynchCallback` delegate. Lines 21 and 22 invoke the asynchronous `End` method, obtaining the results from the list.

Line 21 might be a bit confusing, so let's explore that further. Recall that we defined the `GetCommissionsList` Web method to return a `CommissionsDataList` object. Well, clients won't know anything about the typed collection. Instead clients will get an array of the collected type. Hence, we declare the return type as an array of `Commission` objects. You do have the option of implementing or using the typed collection itself if you have access to the original assembly (as we do in this case); however, when you are using third-party Web Services, you will probably not have the supporting assemblies.

Marshaling Data onto the Windows Forms Thread

Finally, `InvokeRequired` is checked in line 23, and `Invoke` is called in line 24. `InvokeRequired` is superfluous; it is really there just as a reminder. The proxy class will invoke the callback on a different thread than the one the Windows Forms controls are on. Since Windows Forms controls are not thread-safe, we need to marshal the data onto the same thread as the one containing the controls. This is the purpose of the `Invoke` method. We use a custom `System.Delegate` (I named it `Binder`) to define the method we are calling (`BindData`) and call that method by passing the delegate and an array of parameters to the `Control.Invoke` method. `BindData` is defined in the form, as shown in Listing 14.13 (lines 29 through 31), so we'll use the form's `Invoke` method to get the array of `Commission` objects onto the same thread as the one the data grid is on. Unfortunately, if you miss this last bit of code, your Windows Forms application will likely be unstable and may even crash.

Summary

Chapter 14 is a pinnacle chapter because many of the skills you have learned in earlier chapters all come together with Web Services. You know how to implement Web Services that return simple and complex data. You know how use ADO.NET with Web Services. You know how to create custom types and return proxy types or the original types. You can competently invoke and safely manage asynchronous Web Services, and you understand the important role the .NET Framework plays in implementing Web Services. Reflection and the CodeDOM support implementing the proxy classes that make Web Services easier to use. Attributes facilitate marshaling data across the wire, and delegates and the multithreading model support asynchronous Web Services.

Taken individually the technologies supporting XML Web Services are not brand new. However, Microsoft has made these technologies practical and easier to use. By implementing Web Services on top of open standards, Microsoft has hedged its bet, embracing the best technologies of the industry.

CHAPTER 15

Building ASP.NET Web Applications

*For it is the soloecisme of power, to thinke to command
the end, and yet not to endure the meane.*

—*Sir Francis Bacon*

Introduction

One of the roles of the author of an advanced book is to make a reasonable guess about the things readers do know and to patch in the gaps where readers might be struggling. I have been fortunate enough to have spent a couple of years now working on .NET projects, so I can borrow from that experience in making my guesses.

In this chapter I try to avoid the glaringly obvious and instead talk about things that presented problems to me or to others whom I have worked with or heard from. As a result this chapter presents a strategy for building ASP.NET Web pages in such a way as to be able to create them simply, consistently, and reliably.

I spent the last couple of years working on a system comprised of five applications. Half of the team members were seasoned programmers and Web application developers. The other half were mainframe developers. The techniques I use in this chapter come from three sources: solutions to the problems the mainframers had learning ASP.NET, solutions to the problems the experienced developers had making the adjustment, and best practices proposed by Microsoft's IBuySpy portal.

Designing the Screen Layout

The Form Designer for ASP.NET is a vast improvement over Visual Interdev. My friend Mark Davis said he'd rather create Web pages in Notepad than Visual Interdev. I wouldn't go that far, but I really like the Form Designer in ASP.NET. Ultimately it should be as easy to design an ASP.NET Web page as it is to design a Windows form. We are not quite there yet, though. One of the difficulties some new ASP.NET users have is controlling the position of controls on a Web page. In addition to managing the position of controls, there are several other techniques you can employ to make designing Web pages easier. Let's talk about some of them here.

Managing Control Position with Tables

With the Form Designer in ASP.NET you can use the HTML Flow Layout panel or the Grid Layout panel to help you manage the position of controls. An even easier technique is to use an HTML table, define the rows and columns, and place controls in the cells described by the rows and columns. By using this technique, the controls are constrained by the table position. The HTML table approach works well on a large variety and versions of browsers.

If you like to write HTML, you can write HTML text to describe the table. If you prefer a visual approach, you can use the Web Form Designer to describe the rows and columns. Figure 15.1 shows the header user control for the Software Conceptions Web site (*http://www.softconcepts.com*). In design mode it doesn't look like much, but that implies it was easy to implement. Figure 15.2 shows the same control partially completed with the var-

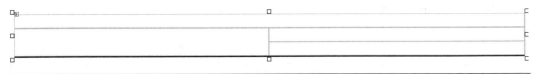

Figure 15.1 An HTML table used to control the layout of a page.

Figure 15.2 The rendered table with some nested user controls and a style sheet.

ious pieces filled in and a style sheet applied. The HTML text to create the table shown in Figure 15.1 is provided in Listing 15.1, followed by a description for creating the table visually rather than by writing the HTML.

Listing 15.1 The HTML That Describes the Table Shown in Figure 15.1

```
1:   <TABLE id="Table1"
2:     cellSpacing="0" cellPadding="0"
3:     width="100%" border="0" class="HeaderContent"
4:     style="BORDER-BOTTOM: black thin solid" runat="server">
5:     <TR>
6:       <TD colSpan="3" height="10" id="LinksContent"></TD>
7:     </TR>
8:     <TR>
9:       <TD rowSpan="2" id="LogoContent"
10:        vAlign="top" align="left"></TD>
11:      <TD colSpan="2" id="MarketingContent"
12:        vAlign="top" align="right"></TD>
13:    </TR>
14:    <TR>
15:      <TD height="100%" vAlign="bottom"
16:        align="left" colSpan="2"></TD>
17:    </TR>
18: </TABLE>
```

The basic tag is the <TABLE></TABLE> tag. The rows are defined first with each <TR></TR> tag pair, and individual cells are defined with the <TD></TD> tag. If you count the <TR> tags you can quickly ascertain that there are three rows. Fortunately you can manage all of this visually too.

When you add an HTML table to a user control or Web page, it will be added with three rows and columns by default. By selecting the context menu for the table you can visually insert and delete columns and rows by selecting menu items from the Insert and Delete context menus (Figure 15.3). When you have created the basic number of columns and rows, you can modify the basic layout to indicate that cells should span one or more rows or columns. This is accomplished by modifying the HTML table's rowSpan and colSpan properties. The properties, also referred to as *attributes*, are shown in Listing 15.1. You can modify these properties by selecting a cell and opening the Properties window. Find the alphabetically ordered property and modify its value.

	View HT<u>M</u>L Source
✂	Cu<u>t</u>
📋	<u>C</u>opy
📋	<u>P</u>aste
	Past<u>e</u> as HTML
✕	<u>D</u>elete
	Build <u>S</u>tyle...
	<u>I</u>nsert ▸
	De<u>l</u>ete ▸
	<u>M</u>erge Cells
	Run As Ser<u>v</u>er Control
🔍	View in <u>B</u>rowser
	View Client <u>S</u>cript
	View <u>C</u>ode
	Synchroni<u>z</u>e Document Outline
📋	P<u>r</u>operties

Figure 15.3 An HTML table's context menu, from which you can insert and delete columns and rows.

The table in Figure 15.1 is comprised of three rows and three columns. The first row has a `colSpan` of 2. The second row, first cell, has a `rowSpan` of 2. The second row, second cell, and third row, second cell, both have a `rowSpan` and a `colSpan` of 1. The result is that there is a large area for the logo in the lower-left corner, a whole row for navigation, and two separate regions for the marketing logo and the sublinks (depicted as a black region in Figure 15.2) on the lower-right corner of the header.

By using HTML tables to constrain the basic layout, all you have to do is place the user controls or individual controls into data cells—the table does the rest. This is significantly easier than using the Flow Layout or Grid Layout panels. If the table has the basic compartments you want, your page will look correct. The next piece of this visual puzzle is to use style sheets (or XML) to define colors, fonts, and so on to ensure uniformity and ease of maintenance.

Using Cascading Style Sheets for Consistency

When you encounter a Web page that contains dozens or hundreds of attributes applied in the HTML, you know that it is challenging to ensure that all the attributes have the values they are supposed to have. A great way to ensure this—rather than setting the attributes in the Properties window or putting the attributes directly in the HTML—is to use a cascading style sheet. Cascading style sheets end with a `.css` extension. You can add a link to them in your Web site and apply named styles to the `Class` and `Css-Class` attributes of controls and pages. Doing so ensures that all elements that use the same style are rendered the same way.

You can add a style block directly to the page, or you can add the same styles to an external text file and associate the external style sheet with each Web page. If you add the style to the page, use the `<style>` tag. If you create an external style sheet, the style tags are identical, but the external style sheet does not use the `<style>` tag. I prefer the external style sheet; however, you can define an external style sheet and a local style block to override the global styles for specific aspects of your page.

Defining a Local Style Block

Local style blocks are added to the `<head>` section of an HTML document. Listing 15.2 shows a single class for the `default.aspx` page at *http://www.softconcepts.com*.

Listing 15.2 A Local Style Block for a `.aspx` Page

```
1:   <HEAD>
2:     <title>Software Conceptions, Inc</title>
3:       <meta content="Microsoft Visual Studio 7.0" name="GENERATOR">
4:       <meta content="C#" name="CODE_LANGUAGE">
5:       <meta content="JavaScript" name="vs_defaultClientScript">
6:       <meta content="http://schemas.microsoft.com/intellisense/
                        ie5" name="vs_targetSchema">
7:       <style type="text/css">
8:         .VerticalLinks{
9:           background-color: Black;
10:          font-family: Verdana, Helvetica, sans-serif;
11:          font-size: 13px;
12:          font-weight: bold;
13:          color: gainsboro;
14:          text-decoration: none;
15:        }
16:      </style>
17: </HEAD>
```

Line 7 starts the local style block, and line 16 ends the block. The only style class in the block is the `VerticalLinks` class. An element that uses this style will have a black background; use Verdana, Helvetica, and sans-serif bold fonts; and be 13 pixels high. The font color will be gainsboro (a grayish-white color), and there will be no text decoration (for example, underlining).

You can experiment with various attributes to create different styles. A good way to come up with ideas is to look at sites you like and see what their creators did.

Defining an External Style Sheet File

If you define a local style block, it will override an external style sheet. I prefer to use the external style sheet for a couple of reasons. The first is that it is easier to manage the styles in one place rather than looking at every page for that page's style. A second reason is that Intellisense will display a list of available styles in an external style sheet. You don't have to remember all the attribute names; nor do you have to remember all the possible values for those attributes. Intellisense will display the attribute names (Figure 15.4) and possible values. Finally, you can use the Document Outline window to

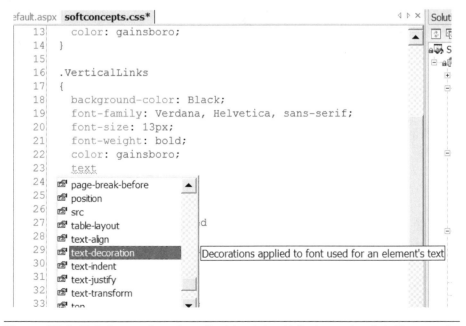

Figure 15.4 Pick from a list of applicable style attributes using Intellisense, in an external cascading style sheet.

quickly and easily manage and navigate the styles in your external style sheet (Figure 15.5).

TIP: To invoke the Intellisense list of attributes, in the style sheet begin typing the name of an attribute or press Ctrl+Enter. As you type, Intellisense will zero in on the specific attribute.

Using Document Outlines

Document outlines are available for a variety of views. By selecting View|Other Windows|Document Outline you can open the Document Outline view for a style sheet (Figure 15.5) when an external style sheet is selected. If you have an HTML view of a Web page selected, the document outline will be an outlined version of the HTML in that page. As with the style sheet, you can use the document outline to navigate and manage whatever view the outline is associated with.

Let's get back to style sheets. In an external style sheet, the document outline contains Elements, Classes, Element IDs, and @ Blocks folders. The Elements folder refers to HTML elements, like body, head, line breaks (`<br>` tags), and divisions (`<div>` tags). The Classes folder refers to user-defined style classes. The Element IDs folder contains styles for specifically identified elements. The @ Blocks folder contains styles for @ directives. For example, you can declare an @ `Page` block and set the page margins, orientation, and dimensions.

Figure 15.5 Use the Document Outline view to manage the external style sheet.

Enter the styles as text directly into the style sheet document itself, or use the context menu in the style outline to build styles visually. I will show you examples of both of these methods next.

Writing a Style Block in an External Style Sheet

Styles are comprised of a selector and a declaration. For example, if we wanted to define a body element style indicating the margins for the body of our document, we could manually enter a style rule for the body element. The selector would be `body` and the four declarations would be `margin-top`, `margin-bottom`, `margin-left`, and `margin-right`. Listing 15.3 shows the body element style for the `default.aspx` page of the Software Conceptions site. Figure 15.6 shows the header on that page before the style was applied, and Figure 15.7 shows the header after the style was applied.

Listing 15.3 The Body Element Style for the `softconcepts.css` External Style Sheet

```
body
{
  margin-top: 0;
  margin-bottom: 0;
  margin-left: 0;
  margin-right: 0;
}
```

Figure 15.6 The header as it would appear on the page with the default settings for body margins.

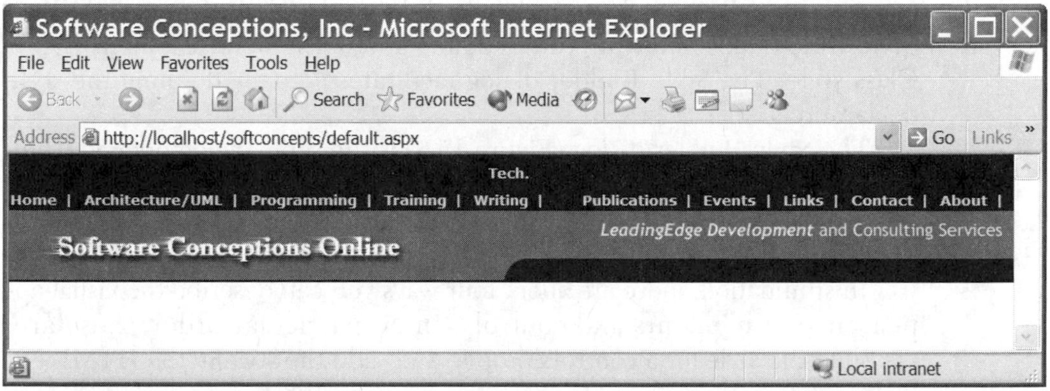

Figure 15.7 The header as it would appear with body margins set to 0.

The body element in Listing 15.3 sets all the margins to 0. Thus the content will occupy all the space on the visible page with no discernible margin.

The `.css` file is a text file. You can modify the elements, classes, identified elements, and @ blocks by simply typing them in the correct format. The basic format is to type the selector and the opening and closing brackets (`{}`); then within those brackets add the declarations in the following syntax: *declarationname: value;* (filling in the appropriate declaration name and value as desired). For example, Listing 15.4 defines an element identified as `#Red`. I dubbed it so because it applies the `Red` color.

Listing 15.4 Defining an Identified Element

```
#Red
{
  color: Red;
}
```

The id element can be applied by specifying an element's identifier. For example, `<hr id="Red">` would result in this specific horizontal rule being rendered as a red line.

Visually Building External Style Sheet Styles

As with many aspects of modern software development, you can build styles visually too. By clicking on the `.css` document in the editor or the style outline, you can select Build Style or Add Style Rule. Add Style Rule opens the Add Style Rule dialog, allowing you to define a new Element, Element ID, or Class style. The Style Builder dialog facilitates actually defining the style declarations.

The Style Builder dialog (Figure 15.8) is the same dialog opened when you click the elliptical button next to the style property of a control. In the former instance the style is added as text to the external style sheet. In the latter instance the style is added to the style property of the control.

In summation, there are about four ways you can describe the visual appearance of elements and controls. In no particular order, these are: (1) build the style for a control's property, (2) add the style in the HTML editor for the control, (3) write a local style block for the page, and (4) define an external style sheet. The results are approximately the same except that style cascading rule precedence applies.

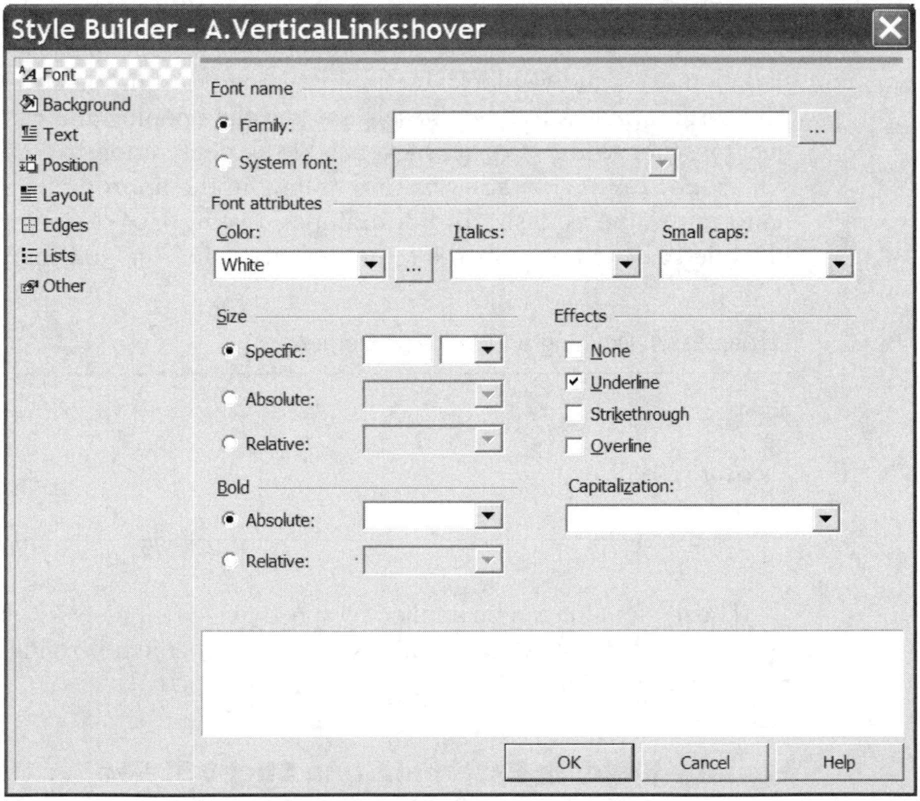

Figure 15.8 The Style Builder dialog.

Understanding the Cascading Application of Styles

External style sheets represent general or global styles. In the absence of any other style, the general styles in the style sheet apply. The next level are the styles defined in a local style block. The local style block styles override the general styles if both the external, general style and the local style define the same element or class styles. For instance, if I define a `.Vertical-Links` class in the external style sheet and one in a local style block, the local style block wins. Taking precedence over the local style block is the inline style. The easiest way to define an inline style is to use the Style Builder dialog invoked by clicking the ellipse for a particular control's style property.

This order of precedence (inline over local over general) of the application of style rules is what *cascading* in *cascading style sheet* refers to. Besides experimenting with various style declarations, you also need to know how to associate an external style sheet with a page.

Linking an External Style Sheet to a Page

External cascading style sheets are associated with a page by using the `<LINK>` tag in the header block of the page. The `<LINK>` tag for the `default.aspx` page of the Software Conceptions site follows.

```
<LINK href="softconcepts.css" type="text/css" rel="stylesheet">
```

The `rel` attribute describes the relationship to the linked document. The `type` attribute indicates the kind of document we are linking to (a text, cascading style sheet in the example), and the `href` attribute refers to the URL of the linked document.

You can type these values in the HTML editor directly, or if you are like me and often tend to forget cryptic attributes like `rel`, you can use the Document Styles window. To open the Document Styles dialog and associate an external style sheet visually, open the page in Design view and select Format|Document Styles from the menu. This will open the Document Styles window, allowing you to associate the external style sheet by clicking the Add Style Link button (Figure 15.9).

Applying Styles to a Control

Once you've defined the styles, the element styles are associated automatically. However, class styles need to be associated with a specific control's `Class` or `CssClass` property. These properties are string properties. You

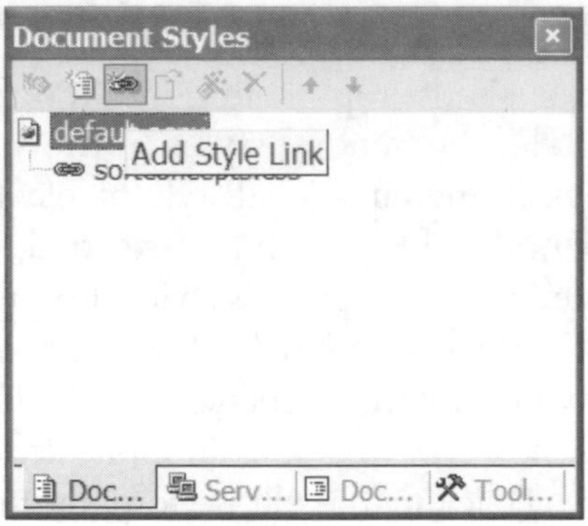

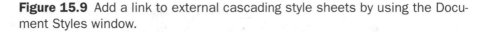

Figure 15.9 Add a link to external cascading style sheets by using the Document Styles window.

only need to associate the style sheet with the page (see the preceding subsection) and type the name of the style class in the `Class` or `CssClass` property, whichever the control has. (With HTML controls the property is named `Class`; Web controls use a property named `CssClass`.)

TIP: From the context menu select View In Browser to see the effects of your style sheet changes.

After you have associated the class name with a control, the effect will show up when you run the application and display the page. By default, styles defined in external style sheets are not rendered at design time. That's why you will see very generic-looking Web pages at design time (see Figure 15.1 or the IBuySpy portal's design-time Web pages).

Modifying Attributes Programmatically

You can programmatically set the values of attributes as key and value pairs. You can usually refer to a server control's property directly. However, if you are using a dynamically created HTML control, such as controls in a `Data-List`, you may not know the specific control name or have a reference to it. Even in this latter instance you can modify control attributes with code.

To demonstrate how control attributes are set programmatically I have provided two statements that perform identical operations on a control that runs on the server. The first uses the `HtmlTable.BgColor` property

(Listing 15.5), and the second sets the property through the `Attributes` collection (Listing 15.6).

Listing 15.5 Setting a Property of a Control Running on the Server

```
If ( ColorInfo Is Nothing = False ) Then
   Table1.BgColor = ColorInfo.HeaderBackColor
End If
```

Listing 15.6 Setting the Same Attribute by Using the `Attributes` Collection

```
If ( ColorInfo Is Nothing = False )
   Table1.Attributes.Add("bgcolor", ColorInfo.HeaderBackColor)
End If
```

The table in Listing 15.5 is a `System.Web.UI.htmlControls` HTML table; however, because I set the `runat` attribute to `server` I can refer to the control in the code-behind file. Listing 15.6 demonstrates how to set the attribute again by referring to the control but using the `Attributes` collection. The result is the same.

When you have a reference to the control, referring to the control properties directly is easiest. However, if you discover that an attribute is not exposed as a property, you can add the attribute by using the `Attributes` collection as demonstrated.

Creating the Presentation with User Controls

Most likely the best piece of advice you can get is to create your ASP.NET user interfaces with user controls. Referred to as *control compositing*, you can design a user control precisely as you would a Web page. The only difference is that user controls can be reorganized and reused on one or many Web pages. An excellent example of this technique is the very dynamic IBuySpy portal application available for download from Microsoft at *http://www.asp.net*. The portal refers to its user controls as *portal modules*. Each module shares a common base class, and the portal can be updated after the portal application has been deployed with an administrative login.

TIP: You can download and use any or all of the IBuySpy portal code without cost, as many companies are doing.

    I have used a similar technique with great success on a couple of projects and am employing this device as a reimplementation of *http://www.softconcepts.com* in ASP.NET after eight years as an HTML-based Web site. Some of the examples I will show you next demonstrate the compositing technique recommended by Microsoft and promoted as a good object-oriented approach in general.

Creating a Basic User Control Layout

Earlier I demonstrated how you can use an HTML table to manage the layout of a Web page. This technique is not entirely new; it's more in the category of "an oldie but a goody." I first used the technique when I realized in the mid-1990s that not every Web browser supported frames, but I wanted the compartmentalization of frames. More recently we used HTML tables on a project because some developers weren't happy with the control they had over layout, finding screen creation a bit tedious. Because user controls are essentially designable like Web pages we can employ the same HTML table technique to manage layout of user controls.

NOTE: Any recommended approach represents one of many ways to accomplish a given task. Here I'm promoting compositing through user controls as a best practice. As with any rules, experience dictates that sometimes you have to deviate from known best practices. That's how new best practices evolve. If you have found useful another way of implementing Web pages, feel free to send me an e-mail and a sample at *pkimmel@softconcepts.com*.

    The header control in Figure 15.7 is comprised of several user controls. I like to think of layering controls and compositing like hammered steel. Individually each control is easy to build; together they create a strong and resilient end result. The links across the top form the first part of the header control. Since this is a complete concept by itself, I created the links as a separate user control, a table with one data cell (Listing 15.7).

Listing 15.7 Defining the Table for the `Links` User Control

```
<%@ Control Language="c#" AutoEventWireup="false" Codebe-
hind="Links.ascx.cs" Inherits="softconcepts.Controls.Links" Tar-
getSchema="http://schemas.microsoft.com/intellisense/ie5"
enableViewState="False"%>
<TABLE>
  <TR>
    <TD>
    </TD>
  </TR>
</TABLE>
```

The first statement is the @ `Control` directive. Importantly, this directive associates the code-behind module with the visual part of the control. The table can be easily created by dropping an HTML table onto a new user control. The end result looks like a box on a user control.

The control directive information is coded for us if we use the designer to add the HTML table. We only need to modify this data if we code it manually or want to change something.

Creating Navigation Links

The next step is creating the actual navigation links. I could hard-code each link as individual cells with hyperlinks, but that would not be especially dynamic, and there is an easier way. By using an ASP.NET `DataList` control for the navigation links, I can reuse the `Links` control and dynamically change the content by binding a data source to the `DataList`.

To create links similar to those shown in Figure 15.7, follow these steps.

1. Drop an ASP.NET `DataList` control from the Web Forms tab of the Toolbox into the single data cell of the table defined in the last subsection.
2. Select the `DataList` on the user control and change the `RepeatDirection` property (in the Properties window) to `Horizontal`.
3. Right-click the `DataList` to display the context menu and select Edit Templates|Item Templates.

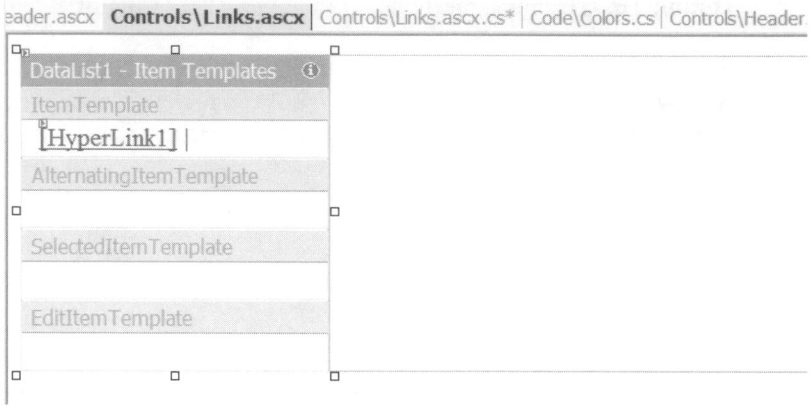

Figure 15.10 Defining the template in the template editor.

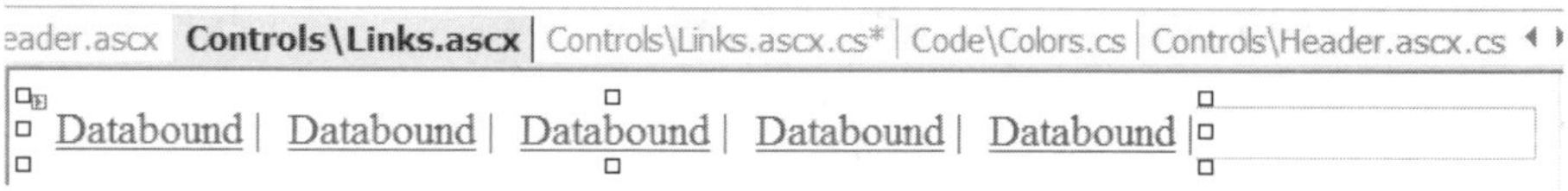

Figure 15.11 The finished design-time result after step 5.

4. In the ItemTemplate part of the template editor (Figure 15.10), add a space, an ASP.NET `HyperLink` control, and the pipe (|) character. (You are defining the template. Every link will repeat this pattern.)
5. Right-click and select End Template Editing from the context menu for the template editor. (Figure 15.11 shows the result to this point.)
6. The actual `ToolTip` property, the `NavigateUrl` property, and the display text are derived from a `DataSource` object. To complete this final part we need to modify the HTML directly and use a `Data-Binder` object (Listing 15.8).

Listing 15.8 Creating a Dynamic Runtime View for the `DataList` Links

```
1:  <%@ Control Language="vb" AutoEventWireup="false"
2:  Codebehind="Links.ascx.vb" Inherits="softconcepts.Controls.Links"
3:  TargetSchema=http://schemas.microsoft.com/intellisense/ie5
4:  enableViewState="False"%>
5:    <TABLE id="Table1" cellSpacing="0" cellPadding="0"
```

```
6:            width="100%" border="0">
7:            <TR>
8:            <TD class="HeaderLinks" noWrap>
9:              <asp:datalist id="DataList1"
10:               RepeatDirection="Horizontal" runat="server">
11:               <ItemStyle Wrap="False"></ItemStyle>
12:               <ItemTemplate>
13:                  
14:                 <asp:HyperLink id=HyperLink1
15:                   runat="server"
16:                   ToolTip='<%# DataBinder.Eval(Container.DataItem,
17:                   "Description") %>'
18:                   NavigateUrl='<%# DataBinder.Eval(Container.DataItem,
19:                   "Url") + "?LinkID=" +
20:                   DataBinder.Eval(Container.DataItem, "ID") %>'
21:                   CssClass="HeaderLinks">
22:                   <%# DataBinder.Eval(Container.DataItem, "Name") %>
23:                 </asp:HyperLink> 
24:                 <span class="HeaderLinks">|</span>
25:               </ItemTemplate>
26:             </asp:datalist>
27:         </TD>
28:         </TR>
29:     </TABLE>
```

The new information is comprised of the attributes on the `<TABLE>` and cell `<TD>` tags and the code between the `<TD></TD>` tags. (You can see this by comparing Listing 15.8 to Listing 15.7.)

I used the style `HeaderLinks` wherever styles were used. This style comes from the **softconcepts.css** style sheet we discussed earlier in the chapter. Most of the remaining modifications are contained in the `<ItemTemplate>` tag. This tag was added when I followed the numbered steps above.

Block script (`<%# %>`) blocks were used to bind the `ToolTip` property, the `NavigateUrl` property, and the display text values for the `HyperLink` control. For example, `ToolTip` is dynamically derived in lines 16 and 17 by using a script block and the `DataBinder` class's shared method `Eval`. The `DataBinder` class plays an intermediary role between a control that can be bound to data and the data itself.

```
ToolTip='<%# DataBinder.Eval(Container.DataItem, "Description") %>'
```

Understood in the simplest sense, the preceding excerpt means that HyperLink.ToolTip equals some derived value. DataBinder.Eval needs an object. The object is generically represented by the containing object's DataItem property. The fragment is understood to mean that there will be a hyperlink for each object in the data source, and that object will have a property named Description. Thus you should anticipate that the Data-List control is bound to a DataSource object containing objects that have a Description property. The same approach is used for the NavigateUrl property, displayed text, and LinkID. To satisfy the DataBinder.Eval statements used, we would need a data source that contains objects with Description, ID, Name, and URL properties.

TIP: You can add a third parameter to DataBinder.Eval that provides a string formatting rule.

Listing 15.9 provides an example of implementing the Links class as a strongly typed collection.

Listing 15.9 Implementing the Links Class as a Strongly Typed Collection

```
Public Class Links
  Inherits System.Collections.ReadOnlyCollectionBase

  Public Sub New()
  End Sub

  Public Shared Function HeaderLinks() As Links
    Dim Links As Links = New Links()
    Links.Add(New Link("Softconcepts home page", _
      "Home", 1, "default.aspx"))
    Links.Add(New Link("About softconcepts", _
      "About", "2", "About.aspx"))
    Return Links
  End Function

  Default Public ReadOnly Property Item( _
    ByVal Index As Long) As Link
  Get
    Return CType(Innerlist(Index), Link)
  End Get
  End Property
```

```
      Public Function Add(ByVal Value As Link) As Long
         Return InnerList.Add(Value)
      End Function

   End Class

   Public Class Link
      Private FDescription As String
      Private FID As String
      Private FName As String
      Private FUrl As String

      Public Sub New(ByVal Description As String, _
         ByVal Name As String, ByVal ID As String, ByVal Url As String)

         Me.FDescription = Description
         Me.FName = Name
         Me.FID = ID
         Me.FUrl = Url
      End Sub

      Public ReadOnly Property Description() As String
      Get
         Return FDescription
      End Get
      End Property

      Public ReadOnly Property ID() As String
      Get
         Return FID
      End Get
      End Property

      Public ReadOnly Property Name() As String
      Get
         Return FName
      End Get
      End Property

      Public ReadOnly Property Url() As String
      Get
         Return FUrl
      End Get
      End Property
   End Class
```

Listing 15.9 implements a strongly typed collection named `Links`. `Links` contains instances of the `Link` class, also defined in Listing 15.9. (For more information on strongly typed collections, refer to Chapter 14, which demonstrates and describes typed collections as return types for Web Services.) I could have implemented the links as a table in a database. Either way the code that consumes the link information is the same.

As you can see in the listing—in the shared function `HeaderLinks`—I implemented a factory method that creates an instance of the header links. There are only two links in the shared method. We just need to define the complete complement of `Link` objects and bind the return result to the `DataList` control. The `DataBinder` code in Listing 15.8 does the rest. The easiest way to bind a `Link` object to the data list is demonstrated in the `Page_Load` event handler for the `Links.ascx` user control (Listing 15.10). You can bind any object that implements `IEnumerable`, as does `System.Collections.ReadOnlyCollectionBase` (from which the `Links` class inherits).

Listing 15.10 Binding the `Links` Object

```
Private Sub Page_Load(ByVal sender As System.Object, _
  ByVal e As System.EventArgs) Handles MyBase.Load

  DataList1.DataSource = Links.HeaderLinks
  DataList1.DataBind()
End Sub
```

Adding a User Control to a Page

Adding the `Links.ascx` user control to a page is the easiest part of this whole process. All you have to do is drag the control from the Solution Explorer onto the page or another user control. In keeping with our concept of compositing, I actually implemented a `Links` user control and a `Header` user control. I wanted to reuse the `Links` control in another context, too: hyperlinks at the bottom of the page. Figure 15.12 shows the `Header` control as a work in-progress with the `Links.ascx` user control in place.

Loading User Controls Dynamically

By creating user controls you have a lot of flexibility in how you orchestrate your user interface. You also have a lot of flexibility in when you orchestrate your user interface. A good friend of mine, Geoff Caylor, demonstrated this by using the CodeDOM and dynamically loaded controls.

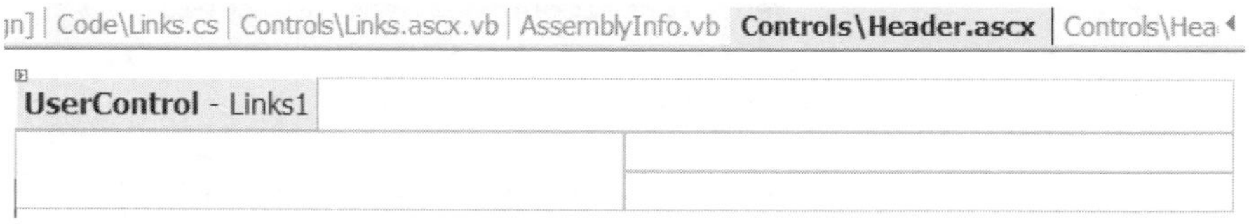

Figure 15.12 The `Links.ascx` user control as part of the composite `Header` user control.

The basic idea was to use the CodeDOM to generate some basic template classes that knew how to work with this particular dynamic page generator. Then, based on some state information in the application, these controls were loaded into a page at runtime. (A similar technique is used to make the IBuySpy portal application dynamic and flexible even after it has been deployed.) All we need to make this work is the `LoadControl` method, a control or user control, and somewhere to load the control into. The upcoming listing demonstrates how to load the `Links.ascx` user control into the `Header.ascx` user control at runtime instead of design time. But first we must do some preparation work.

Suppose we want to load the `Links.ascx` control into the top data cell of the HTML table at runtime. We need an object to refer to. By default, HTML controls don't have a reference in the code-behind file. However, if you make them server controls, you can refer to them in the code-behind file. This is actually very easy to do—follow these steps.

1. Click on the top cell of the table in the `Header` control.
2. In the Properties window, change the `(id)` property to `LinksPane`.
3. Right-click on the data cell in the designer and select Run As Server Control (Figure 15.13).

The last step adds a protected field named `LinksPane` in the code-behind file, and you will be able to refer to the HTML table cell with code at runtime. Listing 15.11 shows the code for dynamically loading the `Links.ascx` control into the `Header` control's `LinksPane` HTML table cell.

Listing 15.11 Loading `Links.ascx` at Runtime

```
1:  Public MustInherit Class Header
2:    Inherits System.Web.UI.UserControl
3:    Protected WithEvents LinksPane As _
```

```
 4:        System.Web.UI.HtmlControls.HtmlTableCell
 5:
 6:     [ Web Form Designer generated code ]
 7:
 8:     Private Sub Page_Load(ByVal sender As System.Object, _
 9:        ByVal e As System.EventArgs) Handles MyBase.Load
10:
11:        LinksPane.Controls.Add(LoadControl("Links.ascx"))
12:
13:     End Sub
14:
15: End Class
```

TIP: It might be a bit easier to follow Listing 15.11 if we declared a temporary variable for the `LoadControl` statement and then added that control to the `LinksPane.Controls` collection. However, as a general rule we want to avoid declaring unnecessary variables that add to the clutter and confusion of the code. New programmers may struggle a bit more with consolidated code.

The `System.Web.UI.HtmlControls.HtmlTableCell` control can be referred to in the code-behind file if we indicate that it is a server control. Line 11 loads the `Links.ascx` control and adds it to the `LinksPane.Controls` collection. The result is that the control appears in the header as if we had added it at design time. The benefit is that we could load something else if we desired, affording us a tremendous amount of flexibility.

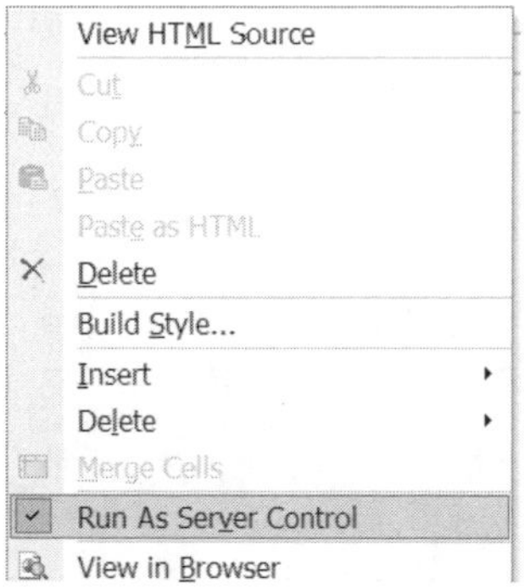

Figure 15.13 Select Run As Server Control to interact with HTML controls in the code-behind file.

You could borrow the concept of loading controls dynamically and generate an entire Web page at runtime. The pragmatics of doing this in a production application need some examination, but Listing 15.12 shows some code that creates a test page for the `Links` class defined in Listing 15.9. The test page can be used to ensure that the `Links` and `Link` classes are working correctly. Figure 15.14 shows the results of running the code in Listing 15.12.

Listing 15.12 Creating a Test Page for the `Links` Class

```
1:   Public Class TestPage
2:        Inherits System.Web.UI.Page
3:
4:   [ Web Form Designer generated code ]
5:
6:     Private Sub Page_Load(ByVal sender As System.Object, _
7:        ByVal e As System.EventArgs) Handles MyBase.Load
8:
9:        Dim DataGrid As DataGrid = New DataGrid()
10:        Controls.Add(DataGrid)
11:        DataGrid.Attributes.Add("width", "100%")
12:        DataGrid.DataSource = Links.HeaderLinks
13:        DataGrid.DataBind()
14:
15:
16:     End Sub
17:
18: End Class
```

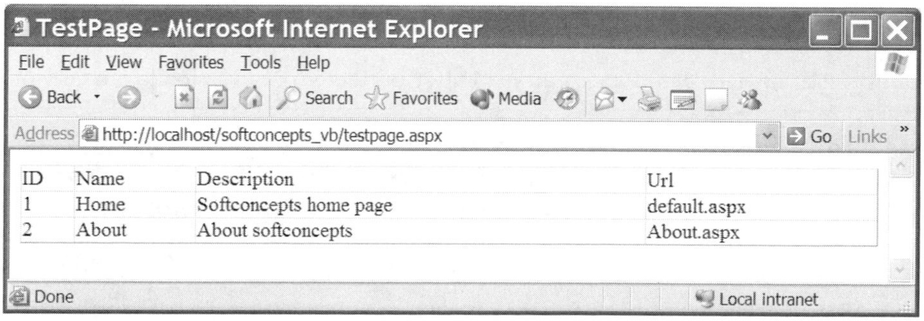

Figure 15.14 A dynamically created and bound `DataGrid` control.

The `DataGrid` control is created in line 9. There is nothing to prevent us from using the same technique to create individual controls like text boxes and labels or using `LoadControl` if we want to use user controls. The `DataGrid` control is added to the form's `Controls` collection. An attribute is set dynamically, to show an example of this technique in context. Finally, the `DataGrid` control's `DataSource` is provided, and the `DataBind` method is called. If we had added the `DataGrid` control at design time, we would have needed only the code in lines 12 and 13.

I like to use generated forms when I want to quickly test new objects. A generated form plays the role of scaffold, permitting me to focus on the object representing the business rules—in this case, `Links`—without spending a lot of time on a user interface for testing.

Converting a Web Page into a User Control

In the simplest sense a user control is a Web page. You design user controls like Web pages. You load user controls by referring to the filename, and they contain the same kinds of things as Web pages. User controls contain other controls and are associated with code-behind files. As a matter of fact, if you create or have a page that you want to convert to a control, you can do so by stripping just a few of the tags out of the HTML and making modest modifications to the code-behind file. As an example, let's make a copy of the `TestPage.aspx` page and convert it to a user control. Follow the steps below. (The related listings are interspersed among the steps.)

1. Copy the `TestPage.aspx` page to the Controls folder.
2. Rename the file from `TestPage.aspx` to `TestControl.ascx`. (`.ascx` is the extension convention for user control files.)
3. The HTML for the page will look like the text in Listing 15.13. Delete all the text set in bold in the listing below.

Listing 15.13 The `TestPage.aspx` HTML Code before Conversion to a User Control

```
<%@ Page Language="vb" AutoEventWireup="false"
Codebehind="TestPage.aspx.vb" Inherits="softconcepts_vb.TestPage"%>
<!DOCTYPE HTML PUBLIC "-//W3C//DTD HTML 4.0 Transitional//EN">
<HTML>
  <HEAD>
    <title>TestPage</title>
    <meta name="GENERATOR" content="Microsoft Visual Studio.NET 7.0">
    <meta name="CODE_LANGUAGE" content="Visual Basic 7.0">
```

```
    <meta name="vs_defaultClientScript" content="JavaScript">
    <meta name="vs_targetSchema"
      content="http://schemas.microsoft.com/intellisense/ie5">
  </HEAD>
  <body MS_POSITIONING="GridLayout">
    <form id="Form1" method="post" runat="server">
    </form>
  </body>
</HTML>
```

4. Replace the @ Page directive with the @ Control directive.
5. Change the Codebehind attribute to refer to TestControl.ascx. vb (be sure to change the original .aspx to .ascx).
6. Change the Inherits attribute to refer to softconcepts_vb.Test-Control (to reflect the new class name we'll use for the control). Listing 15.14 shows the final result for the HTML. (Note that the TargetSchema code is added automatically.)

Listing 15.14 The Converted Web Page Code, Now a User Control

```
<%@ Control Language="vb" AutoEventWireup="false"
Codebehind="TestControl.ascx.vb" Inherits="softconcepts_vb.TestControl"
TargetSchema="http://schemas.microsoft.com/intellisense/ie5" %>
```

7. In the TestControl.ascx.vb file, add the MustInherit modifier to the class declaration and change the Inherits statement to indicate that the control inherits from System.Web.UI.UserControl. Listing 15.15 shows the final result for the code-behind file.

Listing 15.15 The Converted Code-Behind File, Now a User Control

```
1:  Public MustInherit Class TestControl
2:      Inherits System.Web.UI.UserControl
3:
4:      [ Web Form Designer generated code ]
5:
6:      Private Sub Page_Load(ByVal sender As System.Object, _
7:          ByVal e As System.EventArgs) Handles MyBase.Load
8:
```

```
 9:        Dim DataGrid As DataGrid = New DataGrid()
10:        Controls.Add(DataGrid)
11:        DataGrid.Attributes.Add("width", "100%")
12:        DataGrid.DataSource = Links.HeaderLinks
13:        DataGrid.DataBind()
14:
15:    End Sub
16:
17: End Class
```

Note that the only real revisions to the class were to the `Class` header and the `Inherits` clause. A `UserControl` class is defined as abstract; this is the meaning of the `MustInherit` modifier. The class now inherits from `System.Web.UI.UserControl` instead of `System.Web.UI.Page`. That's all you need to do.

If you want to convert a user control to a Web page, you can perform the same steps in reverse, or you could simply place the user control on a Web page. My guess is that more often than not you will want to convert a page into a control to promote reusability and to facilitate composite pages. ASP.NET applications that employ control compositing are likely to have as many, if not more, user controls than pages.

Handling Application-Level Events

Files with a `.asax` extension are not served by Web browsers. However, each Web application is created with a `Global.asax` file. This file is used to warehouse application and session events. For example, each time a request is made to your Web application, the `Application_BeginRequest` event is fired. You can use this event as an opportunity to perform some preliminary tasks before the rest of the application code runs.

Listing 15.16 provides a listing for the `Global.asax` file, demonstrating how the color scheme for the Web site can be placed in the `HttpContext` object. The `HttpContext` object, instantiated as `Context`, is unique to each HTTP request. Here I am placing an instance of `ColorInfo` into the `Context` collection. The `ColorInfo` class could be defined to read the color scheme from a database, which means that if you change the database, you change the colors of the Web site.

Listing 15.16 Adding the ColorInfo Class to HttpContext When a Request Is Made

```
1:   Imports System.Web
2:   Imports System.Web.SessionState
3:
4:   Public Class Global
5:       Inherits System.Web.HttpApplication
6:
7:   [ Component Designer generated code ]
8:
9:       Sub Application_Start(ByVal sender As Object, _
10:        ByVal e As EventArgs)
11:          ' Fires when the application is started
12:       End Sub
13:
14:      Sub Session_Start(ByVal sender As Object, ByVal e As EventArgs)
15:
16:      End Sub
17:
18:      Sub Application_BeginRequest(ByVal sender As Object, _
19:        ByVal e As EventArgs)
20:        Context.Items("ColorInfo") = New ColorInfo(LinkID)
21:      End Sub
22:
23:      Private ReadOnly Property LinkID()
24:      Get
25:        If (Request.QueryString("LinkID") Is Nothing = False) Then
26:          Return Convert.ToInt64(Request.QueryString("LinkID"))
27:        Else
28:          Return 1
29:        End If
30:      End Get
31:      End Property
32:
33:      Sub Application_AuthenticateRequest(ByVal sender As Object, _
34:        ByVal e As EventArgs)
35:          ' Fires upon attempting to authenticate the user
36:      End Sub
37:
38:      Sub Application_Error(ByVal sender As Object, _
39:        ByVal e As EventArgs)
40:          ' Fires when an error occurs
41:      End Sub
42:
```

```
43:      Sub Session_End(ByVal sender As Object, _
44:        ByVal e As EventArgs)
45:        ' Fires when the session ends
46:      End Sub
47:
48:      Sub Application_End(ByVal sender As Object, _
49:        ByVal e As EventArgs)
50:        ' Fires when the application ends
51:      End Sub
52:
53: End Class
```

As the Web application evolves, I have found a need to read the color scheme information. By reading it in `Global.asax`'s `Application_BeginRequest` event handler (lines 18 through 21) and stuffing it into the `Context` property, I have to read the color information from the database only once. Subsequent references to `ColorInfo` will be in memory, read from the `Context` property.

If you want to know the order or timing of the `Global` events, you can look up this information in the help documentation or use a `System.Diagnostics.Debug.WriteLine` statement in each event handler. The order of events is an easy detail to forget.

Caching Objects

Caching is an important part of Web application development. Use caching fully and correctly and your application will yield optimal performance and reliability. Ignore caching and your application will pale in comparison with those of your competitors. If you are providing an online service, like shipping, your customers are likely to notice the effects of the lack of caching and choose another provider next time. (Personally, I prefer vendors that have responsive online services, and I avoid those that don't.) Reliability and responsiveness is a facet of customer service, and we have learned that service wins and keeps customers.

There are several facets to caching in ASP.NET. When we talk about caching, we might be referring to the `HttpApplicationState`, `HttpSessionState`, or `Cache` classes. Session state might be managed with either an in-process state server or one of two out-of-process state servers: SQL

Server and `aspnet_state.exe`. We might be referring to cookies and the view state. We might also be referring to page or partial page caching. We'll explore some of these facets in the following subsections.

Using the `HttpApplicationState` Class

Application state is used to share information across multiple requests and sessions. This cache is accessible via an `HttpContext` or `Page` object. The property is named `Application` and is defined as an `HttpApplication-State` object, which inherits from `NameObjectCollectionBase`. With all `NameObjectCollectionBase` classes, you index the collection with a unique name and stuff an object (any data) into that index location. You can store simple objects (like integers or arrays of strings) as well as complex objects (like collections and `DataSets`). What you put in the application cache depends on what you want to share across the application.

For example, on the Software Conceptions Web site (*http://www.soft-concepts.com*) we list all the books I have authored or coauthored. This information does not vary depending on the session. Various offerings are shown on different pages through the site. To make the data easy to manage I can store images, hyperlinks, and descriptions in a database; load the data into a collection of books; and store it in the application session. The list of books can be more correctly retrieved from the Application session cache.

There are several pieces to this solution. The first piece is the strongly typed collection of `Book` objects, named `Books`. The second piece demonstrates how to put the `Books` collection in the application cache. Assuming we paid for an expensive database read—instead of the in-memory typed collection—we would get a performance improvement, reading the database only one time for all users. The third piece is a user control that describes how one book should be displayed. The fourth piece is a bit trickier; I am actually using a user control inside of a `DataList`. The result is that the `DataList` manages repeating the user control for us. (I will go over this code carefully.) Finally, the user control containing the `DataList` is added to the `default.aspx` page.

Implementing the `Books` Collection

You already know how to implement a strongly typed collection (from Chapter 14 and earlier in this chapter). The `Books` class is a strongly typed collection of `Book` objects, containing information you might find useful to display any product in a Web page. Listing 15.17 contains the implementation of the `Books` and `Book` classes. Of course, in a production application you could just as easily read this information from a database or XML file. Everything else we will do in this section works equally well, whether you use an XML file, a `DataSet` object, or a strongly typed collection.

Listing 15.17 The Books Collection and the Book Class

```
Public Class Books
  Inherits System.Collections.ReadOnlyCollectionBase

  Public Shared Function MostRecentThree() As Books
    MostRecentThree = New Books()
    MostRecentThree.Add( _
      New Book("Visual Basic .NET Power Coding", _
               "Paul Kimmel", New DateTime(2003, 1, 1), _
               "Addison-Wesley", _
               "http://www.aw.com/catalog/" + _
               "academic/product/1,4096,0672324075,00.html", _
               ""))

    MostRecentThree.Add( _
      New Book(".NET Mobile Application Development", _
               "Paul Kimmel", New DateTime(2003, 1, 1), _
               "Wiley", _
               "http://www.wiley.com/cda/product/0,,0764548506,00.html", _
               "~/Books/Images/Wireless.jpg"))

    MostRecentThree.Add( _
      New Book("Advanced C# Programming", _
               "Paul Kimmel", New DateTime(2002, 8, 15), _
               "McGraw-Hill/Osborne", _
               "http://shop.osborne.com/" + _
               "cgi-bin/osborne/0072224177.html", _
               "~/Books/Images/csharp_dev_guide.jpg"))

  End Function

  Default Public ReadOnly Property Item( _
    ByVal Index As Integer) As Book
  Get
    Return CType(InnerList(Index), Book)
  End Get
  End Property
```

```
      Public Function Add(ByVal Item As Book) As Integer
         Return InnerList.Add(Item)
      End Function

End Class

Public Class Book

   Private FTitle As String
   Private FAuthor As String
   Private FPublicationDate As DateTime
   Private FPublisher As String
   Private FUrl As String
   Private FBookCoverLink As String

   Public Sub New(ByVal Title As String, _
      ByVal Author As String, _
      ByVal PublicationDate As DateTime, _
      ByVal Publisher As String, _
      ByVal Url As String, _
      ByVal BookCoverLink As String)

      Me.FTitle = Title
      Me.FAuthor = Author
      Me.FPublicationDate = PublicationDate
      Me.FPublisher = Publisher
      Me.FUrl = Url
      Me.FBookCoverLink = BookCoverLink

   End Sub


   Public ReadOnly Property Title() As String
   Get
      Return FTitle
   End Get
   End Property

   Public ReadOnly Property Author() As String
   Get
      Return FAuthor
   End Get
   End Property
```

```
Public ReadOnly Property PublicationDate() As DateTime
Get
   Return FPublicationDate
End Get
End Property

Public ReadOnly Property Publisher() As String
Get
   Return FPublisher
End Get
End Property

Public ReadOnly Property Url() As String
Get
   Return FUrl
End Get
End Property

Public ReadOnly Property BookCoverLink() As String
Get
   Return FBookCoverLink
End Get
End Property

End Class
```

I presented all the code in Listing 15.17 for completeness. This is the kind of code you might find in a business object layer. The only code likely to confuse you is the `MostRecentThree` method.

`MostRecentThree` is a shared method. Shared methods that create instances of classes are referred to as *factory methods*. This factory method initializes an instance of the containing class, `Books`. Clearly we could initialize the class from a data repository. In the listing I am using hard-coded values. I don't need to remind you not to do that in a production application. The part that might seem odd is the old usage of the function name as the return value—`MostRecentThree`. I prefer not to use temporary variables. However, here I do need a `Books` variable. In Visual Basic .NET, like VB6, we have a convenient temporary variable, the function name. This is a technique I employ sometimes. As you know, if you do declare a temporary variable, you can return it by assigning it to the function name—the old way—or use the `Return` keyword followed by the temporary variable.

Adding the Books Object to the Application Cache

I haven't found any notable limitations when it comes to adding data to the application cache. However, I must mention that I don't usually put a lot of data in the application cache. The application cache—represented by the Application property—can be used to store data shared between sessions and contexts in your application. That is, the data is effectively global. I generally put read-only data in the application cache.

Listing 15.18, the Global.asax file, demonstrates how I use the application cache to store the MostRecentThree books. As a result the code reads the Books collection from the cache for all users at once, rather than recreating the object for each user. The impact is minimal in this specific instance because the Books objects all reside in memory. The performance would improve markedly if we were reading a lot of data from a database.

Listing 15.18 Storing the Books Collection in the Application Cache

```
1:   Imports System.Web
2:   Imports System.Web.SessionState
3:
4:   Public Class Global
5:      Inherits System.Web.HttpApplication
6:
7:   [ Component Designer generated code ]
8:      Sub Application_Start(ByVal sender As Object, _
9:        ByVal e As EventArgs)
10:       Application("MostRecentThree") = Books.MostRecentThree
11:      End Sub
12:
13:    [+]Sub Session_Start(ByVal sender As Object, _
14:       ByVal e As EventArgs)
15:    Sub Application_BeginRequest(ByVal sender As Object, _
16:       ByVal e As EventArgs)
17:       Context.Items("ColorInfo") = New ColorInfo(LinkID)
18:    End Sub
19:
20:    Private ReadOnly Property LinkID()
21:    Get
22:      If (Request.QueryString("LinkID") Is Nothing = False) Then
23:        Return Convert.ToInt64(Request.QueryString("LinkID"))
24:      Else
25:        Return 1
26:      End If
```

```
27:    End Get
28:    End Property
29:
30:    [+]Sub Application_AuthenticateRequest(ByVal sender As Object, _
31:      ByVal e As EventArgs)
32:
33:    [+]Sub Application_Error(ByVal sender As Object, _
34:      ByVal e As EventArgs)
35:    [+]Sub Session_End(ByVal sender As Object, ByVal e As EventArgs)
36:    [+]Sub Application_End(ByVal sender As Object, _
37:      ByVal e As EventArgs)
38:    End Class
```

The [+] marker represents code outlining. I collapsed the empty methods we are not discussing. Note that Application_BeginRequest and the LinkID property were modified earlier in the chapter (see Listing 15.16 and its discussion), and I left them in place rather than collapsing them to illustrate how even the Global.asax file will take on mass as a project develops.

Lines 8 through 11 show Application_Start; the new code (compared with Listing 15.15) appears set in bold. When the application begins I stuff the Books collection returned by the factory method Books.MostRecentThree into the application cache. Now all users will have equal access and the performance hit will be divided by the number of users. A reasonable person might shout, "Hey, that's way too easy!" That reasonable person would be right. This is precisely how frameworks help us. The framework should do the work. Underneath the covers is a lot of code, but Microsoft wrote that for us.

This is my opportunity to pitch you. You want your code to converge and synthesize to the point where fundamental operations in your application are very simple. If you discover methods with dozens of lines, you are likely looking at hack code. Sometimes, especially while prototyping, it is okay to hack a bit. However, when the solution is understood, it is time to take out your patterns and refactoring books and synthesize the hacked code to a tidy class that is easy to use.

NOTE: Patterns are the study of recurring software solutions. Pick up a copy of *Design Patterns* by Erich Gamma et al. [1995] to learn more. Refactoring is the study of factoring code to make it better. Better may be smaller, faster, simpler, more reusable, or convergent. Pick up a copy of *Refactoring: Improving the Design of Existing Code* by Martin Fowler [2000] for more on refactoring.

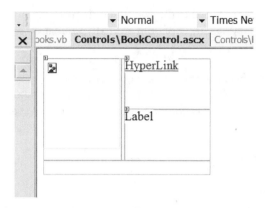

Figure 15.15 The BookControl design, based on a table.

Defining the BookControl

The BookControl is a user control in the solution that describes the layout of a single Book listing. The visual presentation is basically a table with three data cells and some spacer cells (Figure 15.15) that displays a graphic of the cover of the book and some details about the book. We already explored how to use an HTML table to constrain layout. The interesting piece of information comes in the next section. For now, I will show you the HTML for the BookControl (Listing 15.19) and the code-behind file (Listing 15.20).

Listing 15.19 The BookControl.ascx File as HTML

```
<%@ Control Language="vb"
AutoEventWireup="false"
Codebehind="BookControl.ascx.vb"
Inherits="softconcepts_vb.BookControl"
TargetSchema="http://schemas.microsoft.com/intellisense/ie5" %>
<TABLE id="Table1" cellSpacing="0"
cellPadding="0" width="262"
border="0" style="WIDTH: 262px; HEIGHT: 180px">
  <TR>
    <TD rowSpan="2" vAlign="top" align="left" width="120">
      <asp:Image id="Image1" runat="server"
      Height="140px" Width="120px"></asp:Image></TD>
    <TD width="5" rowSpan="2"></TD>
    <TD vAlign="top" align="left">
```

```
      <asp:HyperLink id="HyperLink1" runat="server"
      CssClass="BookContent">HyperLink</asp:HyperLink></TD>
  </TR>
  <TR>
    <TD vAlign="top" align="left">
      <asp:Label id="Label1" runat="server"
      CssClass="BookContent">Label</asp:Label></TD>
  </TR>
  <TR>
    <TD colSpan="3" height="10"></TD>
  </TR>
</TABLE>
```

(I will never get over how ugly HTML is.) You can determine from the @ directive that this is a control associated with the code behind the Book-Control.ascx.vb file. You can also pick up tidbits about the layout, the controls in the table, and the class. I used the BookContent class from the softconcepts.css style sheet. The table itself contains an ASP.NET image, hyperlink, and label. We will bind data to these in the code-behind file (Listing 15.20).

Listing 15.20 The Code-Behind File for BookControl.ascx.vb

```
Public MustInherit Class BookControl
  Inherits System.Web.UI.UserControl
  Protected WithEvents Image1 As System.Web.UI.WebControls.Image
  Protected WithEvents HyperLink1 As _
    System.Web.UI.WebControls.HyperLink
  Protected WithEvents Label1 As System.Web.UI.WebControls.Label
  Private FData As Book

[ Web Form Designer generated code ]

  Private Sub Page_Load(ByVal sender As System.Object, _
    ByVal e As System.EventArgs) Handles MyBase.Load
        'Put user code to initialize the page here
  End Sub

  Public Property Data() As Object
  Get
    Return FData
```

```
    End Get
    Set(ByVal Value As Object)
      SetData(Value)
    End Set
  End Property

  Private Sub SetData(ByVal value As Object)
    FData = CType(value, Book)
    Image1.ImageUrl = FData.BookCoverLink
    Image1.AlternateText = FData.Title
    Label1.Text = FData.Title
    HyperLink1.Text = FData.Title
    HyperLink1.NavigateUrl = FData.Url
    HyperLink1.Target = "_blank"
  End Sub
End Class
```

Taken alone the code is very straightforward. Consuming code needs to pass an instance of a `Book` object to the `Data` property. All the necessary attributes of the controls are set from this one object. So far so good. The next subsection demonstrates how to bind controls to methods via properties, providing exceptional flexibility and control.

Defining the `BookControlList`

Assigning one instance of an object to a control or a user control is not too difficult, but what if you want to repeat a complex object? Assigning an object to a `DataGrid` or `DataList` control is not difficult either, but what if you don't want the basic row and column presentation of a `DataGrid` or `DataList`? You could certainly guess at the number of times a user control is repeated and manually add that number of user controls to a page. Or you could go one step further; you could dynamically load a user control based on the number of elements, which would be a clever solution. Yet the best solution is to let a control like `DataList` figure all of that out for you.

You can take an object as complex as a user control. Plop it into the ItemTemplate of a `DataList` control and automatically create and populate as many user controls as there are rows in the data source. Perhaps best of all, the data source can still be any suitable data source, like a typed collection, an XML file, or a `DataSet` object. This is precisely what we did with the `BookControl`.

NOTE: If you have this all figured out, keep reading. I will work diligently to tickle your techie-bone before we are done.

To display a list of `Books` objects I created a new user control called `BookListControl`. `BookListControl` is initialized with a collection of books. The visual presentation is an HTML table with a `DataList` control. The ItemTemplate for the `DataList` is the `BookControl` we created in the preceding section. This part is easy to create. Getting the data to each dynamically created `BookControl` is the trick. To create the `BookListControl` follow these steps.

1. Create a new user control.
2. Drag an HTML table onto the user control.
3. Define the HTML table to have only one row and one cell.
4. Switch to the Web Forms tab of the Toolbox and drag a `DataList` into the single cell of the HTML control.
5. Right-click on the `DataList` to display the context menu and select Edit Templates|Item Template (see Figure 15.10 for a view of the DataList editor).
6. Drag an instance of the user control into the ItemTemplate area of the DataList template editor. (In our example this is the `BookControl.ascx` user control.) The result should look like Figure 15.16.
7. Right-click on the DataList template editor and select End Template Editing.

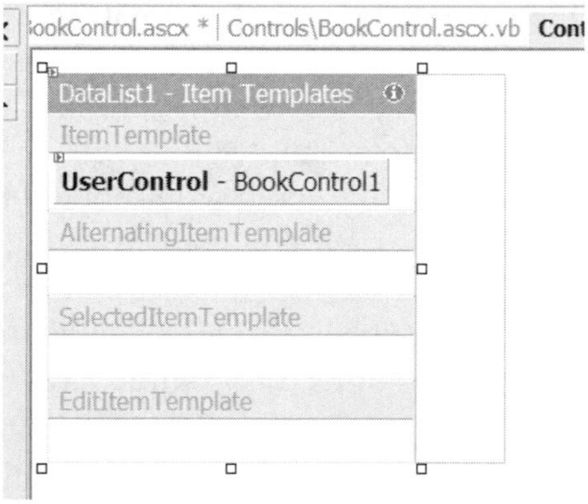

Figure 15.16 A `DataList` with the `BookControl` user control as the ItemTemplate.

Listing 15.21 contains the code-behind file for `BookListControl`. Listing 15.22 contains the HTML for `BookListControl` and the key to repeating user controls automatically.

Listing 15.21 The Code-Behind File for `BookListControl.ascx`

```
Public MustInherit Class BookListControl
    Inherits System.Web.UI.UserControl
    Protected WithEvents DataList1 As _
    System.Web.UI.WebControls.DataList

[ Web Form Designer generated code ]

    Private Sub Page_Load(ByVal sender As System.Object, _
    ByVal e As System.EventArgs) Handles MyBase.Load
      DataList1.DataSource = _
        CType(Application("MostRecentThree"), Books)

      DataList1.DataBind()
    End Sub

End Class
```

This code is very straightforward. The `MostRecentThree Books` object is retrieved, typecast to its original type, and assigned to the `DataList1.DataSource` property. To display the data we call `DataList1.DataBind`. Each `Book` object in `Books` gets to the user controls that are dynamically created in the HTML.

Here is Listing 15.22 with that promised key.

Listing 15.22 The HTML Implementation of `BookListControl`

```
<%@ Register TagPrefix="uc1"
TagName="BookControl"
Src="BookControl.ascx" %>
<%@ Control Language="vb"
AutoEventWireup="false"
Codebehind="BookListControl.ascx.vb"
Inherits="softconcepts_vb.BookListControl"
TargetSchema="http://schemas.microsoft.com/intellisense/ie5" %>
```

```
<TABLE id="Table1"
cellSpacing="0" cellPadding="0" width="300" border="0">
  <TR>
    <TD>
      <asp:DataList id="DataList1" runat="server">
        <ItemTemplate>
          <uc1:BookControl id=BookControl1
          runat="server" Data="<%# Container.DataItem %>">
          </uc1:BookControl>
        </ItemTemplate>
      </asp:DataList></TD>
  </TR>
</TABLE>
```

By now you are familiar with all of this code except perhaps the attribute set in bold. Each item in the ItemTemplate is a `BookControl` object. `BookControl` has a public property `Data` (see Listing 15.20). For each object on the data source, controls in the ItemTemplate are dynamically created. Each of these controls is a `BookControl` object. Each object, represented by `Container.DataItem`, is assigned to the `BookControl.Data` property. The private `SetData` method propagates all the data to the individual controls on the template user control. As a result there is an instance of `BookControl` for each object in the collection, and that `BookControl`'s `Data` property is set in the script block shown in the listing.

Viewing the Finished Result

Finally we are ready to use the control in a page. Fortunately for us and every subsequent consumer, the `BookListControl` is ready to go as is. All we have to do is place it on a page and it renders correctly. Figure 15.17 shows the `BookListControl` rendered with a modicum of styles and layout information applied. Ideally if you read the most recent books from a database, all you would have to do is update the database to update the Web site.

Perhaps the best benefit of using user controls is that we can nest, layer, composite, and repeat them to an almost unlimited degree of complexity. There is no reason why you can't use nested controls with several layers of related controls and even `DataLists` of `DataLists` for very complex layouts. The code, on the other hand, is relatively easy to write.

Figure 15.17 The BookListControl at runtime.

Using the `HttpSessionState` Class

The `HttpSessionState` class is a key and value repository accessible from an `HttpContext` object, Web page, or user control. The session cache works just like the application cache: provide a key as an index and read or assign a value to the `Session` property. The difference is in how and why you use one over the other. Use the application cache when you want to share something at the application level, among all users. Use the session cache when you want to store data pertinent to one session. For example, you might use the session cache to track a user's shopping cart. As is true with the application cache, you can stick just about anything in the session cache.

There are three ways to store session state in ASP.NET. The simplest and default means of storing `Session` objects is the built-in in-process session server. A second way to store session state is to use the out-of-process `aspnet_state.exe` state server. A third way is to configure and use SQL Server. Each state-managing modality has advantages and disadvantages.

The subsections that follow discuss the various session state servers you can use and provide examples, demonstrating how to store information in the session. (Each example could be used with any of the session servers; I simply offer three distinct examples.)

Configuring In-Process State Servers

Each session is associated with a session ID. By default the session ID is stored in a cookie on the client computer. If the client doesn't support cookies, the session ID can be embedded in the URL. For example, cookieless sessions are needed when using the session cache for wireless devices like cell phones. Wireless devices don't support cookies.

For each kind of session server, a unique session ID exists. This is true whether the device supports cookies or not. The default session server is the in-process session server built into the `aspnet_wp.exe` worker process application. The in-process session server is fast, easy to use, and configured by default. Listing 15.23 supposes that we want to pass information entered on one page to the next page in the sequence. This represents tracking a process that might span several pages, like a customer order. The code can be found in `SessionDemo.sln`.

Listing 15.23 Adding Simple Text to the `Session` Property

```
Private Sub Button1_Click(ByVal sender As System.Object, _
  ByVal e As System.EventArgs) Handles Button1.Click

  Session("Text") = TextBox1.Text
  Server.Transfer("Next.aspx")

End Sub
```

The code relies on a `TextBox` control and a `Button` control. When the button is clicked, the text is read from the text box and stored in the session cache through the `Session` property. The text will be unique to each session. Then, the efficient `Server.Transfer` method is called, transferring immediately to the page named `Next.aspx`. We can read the property from the session with code similar to the fragment shown in Listing 15.24.

Listing 15.24 Reading the `Session` Value from Another Location in the Application

```
Private Sub Page_Load(ByVal sender As System.Object, _
  ByVal e As System.EventArgs) Handles MyBase.Load

  Response.Write("You entered " + Session("Text"))

End Sub
```

The in-process session cache is configured by default in the `Web.config` file. Listing 15.25 shows the excerpt from the `Web.config` file, followed by a brief summary.

Listing 15.25 Managing Session State Servers

```
<sessionState
  mode="InProc"
  stateConnectionString="tcpip=127.0.0.1:42424"
  sqlConnectionString="data source=127.0.0.1;user id=sa;password="
  cookieless="false"
  timeout="20"
/>
```

The `<sessionState>` tag's `mode` attribute can be one of four values: `Off`, `InProc`, `StateServer`, or `SQLServer`. `Off` indicates that session state is disabled. `InProc` indicates that the in-process session state server should be used. (This is the default.) `StateServer` indicates that the `aspnet_state.exe` server application will be used, and `SQLServer` indicates that SQL Server will be used to manage state.

TIP: The `mode` attribute values are expressed as strings and are case-sensitive.

Caching the `stateConnectionString` indicates the IP address and port of the machine running the `aspnet_state.exe` server. To store state information on a separate machine, use that machine's IP address. By default the localhost address `127.0.0.1` and port `42424` are used. The `sql-ConnectionString` attribute is used if the mode is `SQLServer`. By default cookies are used to store the session ID, and the session cache data expires in 20 minutes. If you change the `cookieless` attribute to `true` and run the sample program, you will see the session ID embedded in the URL. When we talk about the other two state servers, we will be modifying values in the `Web.config` file's `<sessionState>` tag to indicate that we want to use one of the other servers. Figure 15.18 shows the session ID for my session embedded in the URL (highlighted) in the Address bar.

Configuring the Out-of-Process State Server

The out-of-process state server is a bit slower but it will tolerate both IIS and `aspnet_wp` (worker process) restarts. The `aspnet_state.exe` server is suitable if slower performance is acceptable to ensure that state information is maintained even if IIS or the worker process has to be restarted. You can configure the out-of-process state server to run by changing the `mode` attribute to `StateServer`. You need to change the `stateConnectionString` attribute only if you want to store state on a computer other than the one the Web application is running on.

You will also need to start the `aspnet_state.exe` state server. You can quickly start the state server by opening the Visual Studio .NET Command Prompt and typing `net start aspnet_state.exe`, or you can modify the services settings and reconfigure the `aspnet_state.exe` service to start automatically (Figure 15.19) when your computer boots up. (If you plan to

Figure 15.18 Cookieless session state management permits you to use session state with devices that don't support cookies or have cookies disabled.

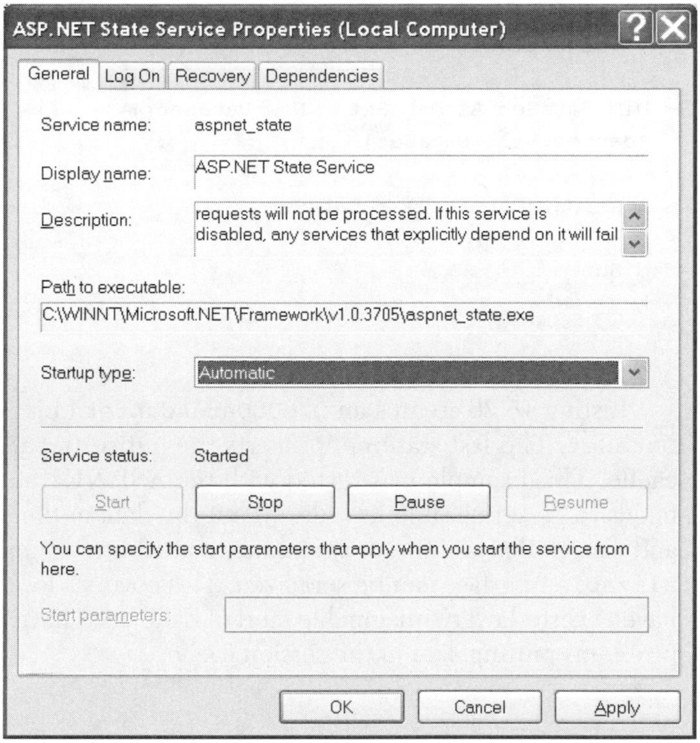

Figure 15.19 Configure the `aspnet_state.exe` state server to run automatically from the ASP.NET State Service Properties dialog.

use the out-of-process state server, you will want the service to start automatically.) Listing 15.26 demonstrates how you can place an entire `DataSet` into the session cache.

Listing 15.26 Storing a `DataSet` in the Session Cache

```
Private Sub Page_Load(ByVal sender As System.Object, _
  ByVal e As System.EventArgs) Handles MyBase.Load

  Const ConnectionString As String = _
    "Provider=Microsoft.Jet.OLEDB.4.0;" + _
    "Data Source=C:\Program Files\Microsoft " + _
    "Visual Studio\VB98\NWIND.MDB;Persist Security Info=False"

  Dim Adapter As OleDbDataAdapter = _
```

```
    New OleDbDataAdapter("SELECT * FROM ORDERS", _
    ConnectionString)

  Dim DataSet As DataSet = New DataSet()
  Adapter.Fill(DataSet)

  Session("DataSet") = DataSet

End Sub
```

Listing 15.26 creates an `OleDbDataAdapter` object and uses it to fill a `DataSet`. The last statement inserts the entire `DataSet` into the session cache. This example was tested with the ASP.NET state server. The data needs to be serializable in order to put the data in the session. Simple data and classes that use the `Serializable` attribute or implement the `ISerializable` interface can be serialized. This covers a lot of ground in .NET. I haven't tested every imaginable kind of data, yet I have not had any specific problems putting data in the session cache.

Configuring SQL Server for Session Management

SQL Server offers the greatest scalability for storing session information. In addition to sustaining session information between IIS and `aspnet_wp.exe` worker process restarts, SQL Server is intended to be used in multiprocessor or multicomputer Web farms. The mechanics of using the session cache are the same whether you are using the in-process session cache or SQL Server. However, you will first have to configure the SQL Server instance as a repository for the session cache and modify the `Web.config` file.

To configure SQL Server as the session state repository you need to run the `C:\winnt\Microsoft .NET Framework\`*`version`*`\InstallSqlState.sql` script. (This is the default directory, where *version* represents the version of the .NET Framework you are using.) You can run this query with Microsoft's SQL Server Query Analyzer (which works fine) or with `isqlw.exe` (which also works fine). The `InstallSqlState.sql` script will add a new database, ASPState, to your SQL Server instance. ASPState contains stored procedures for managing session state. Actual session data will be written as temporary entries in the tempdb database in the ASPStateTempApplications and ASPStateTempSession tables.

TIP: Run `UninstallSqlState.sql` to remove the ASPState SQL Server database and disable SQL Server state management.

Finally, you will need to change the `mode` attribute to `SQLServer` and ensure that the `sqlConnectionString` attribute is correct. If you are testing SQL Server state management on your workstation, the default value shown in Listing 15.25 will work.

After you have configured the SQL Server ASPState table you can re-run `SessionDemo.sln` (the code in Listing 15.26) to test the SQL Server session state configuration. You will notice a marked slowdown in page response, and you should see rows in the two tempdb tables mentioned a moment ago.

Following the instructions presented in these subsections is a very straightforward process to configure any of the three session state servers.

Using the Cache Class

One instance of the `Cache` class is created for each application domain. The Cache class is accessible through an `HttpContext` instance or `Page` property and exists to facilitate application performance. Unlike the session cache, the `Cache` property is not associated with a particular session, but it is useful for storing objects that require large amounts of server memory. Data is placed in the `Cache` class just like data is placed in the session or application caches and exists for the lifetime of the application.

The `Cache` class allows you to set expiration policies and create external dependencies, expiring or refreshing `Cache` data based on some external occurrence, like changes to a data file. For more information on using the `Cache` property and `Cache Dependency` objects, read the help documentation for the `Cache` and `CacheDependency` classes and refer to the example in the Using Dynamic Interfaces with XML section later in this chapter.

Using Cookies

Cookies are represented as instances of `HttpCookieCollections` that contain instances of `HttpCookies`. These classes represent small bits of textual information stored on each client machine. Suitable for cookie usage are things like the user name of a specific user relative to a Web site. Thus, for example, if you store a user's name on the machine, your application can look for that specific cookie to reidentify the user the next time he or she returns to your Web site.

Cookies are stored as text on a PC, so anyone who has access to your PC can search for cookie files, but only the originating host can read a cookie it stored on your PC. Unfortunately, due to security concerns and worries about applications sniffing for data in cookies, some users disable cookies. As a result, heavy reliance on cookies or storing sensitive information in a cookie is not a recommended practice.

A practical example of cookie use is how .NET uses a cookie to store the session ID for each session by default. However, even .NET does not rely on the universal availability of cookies and allows session IDs to be passed embedded in the URL when cookieless session state management is in use, as it will be for some mobile devices like wireless phones. In the fragment example below, I am creating an instance of `HttpCookie` keyed by the string `"Data"` and storing the value of the current date and time as a string in the cookie.

```
Response.Cookies.Add( _
  New HttpCookie("Data", DateTime.Now.ToString()))
```

At a later time in the program's execution I can retrieve this cookie from the `Response.Cookies` collection by indexing the `Response.Cookies` collection with the key `"Data"`. The example represents a suitable amount of data to store as a cookie, in part because there is a practical limit of 4K that can be stored as a cookie. Due to this size limitation and the fact that some users disable or delete cookie files from their machines, as mentioned above, I don't recommend relying heavily on cookies in your applications.

Enabling and Using the View State

Web Forms controls have a property named `EnableViewState`. If you rely on the default value of `True`, the states of Web controls are stored in encrypted text fields along with a page when the page is submitted to the server. The view state is used to reestablish the values of these controls when the page returns from the server.

As a benefit the view state information prevents you from needing to cache and reestablish control values for a page, but encrypting, decrypting, storing, and retrieving view state information takes CPU cycles. As a result, you should leave view state enabled (`EnableViewState=True`) only if you are actually using the view state. If you are assigning the value of a control from an object each time the page is rendered, disable view state for a performance boost. Listing 15.27 provides an excerpt from the rendered HTML for the `WebForm1.aspx` page, showing in bold the encrypted view state for the controls on this page.

Listing 15.27 An Excerpt from the HTML for a Page with an Encrypted View State

```
</HEAD>
  <body MS_POSITIONING="GridLayout">
    <form name="Form1" method="post" action="WebForm1.aspx"
id="Form1">
<input type="hidden" name="__VIEWSTATE"
value="dDwtMTkzOTEyMTQxNzs7Pgsi7Iwyvsw49Yof3poXc4Ka9N+a" />
```

You can enable or disable the view state for the page in the Properties window or in the HTML view by setting the `enableViewState` attribute to `True` to enable it and `False` to disable it. You can set the view state of individual controls by modifying their `EnableViewState` properties or manage all the controls and the page view state through the page's `EnableView-State` property.

Caching a Web Page

If you have a page that contains static content, such as an error page or a page that is not bound to any dynamic data, you can cache the page. Cached pages are rendered once and placed in a cache. Subsequent requests to the page are served by the cached page rather than running the code and recreating a new page for each request. This can boost your application's performance too.

You can indicate that a page is to be cached with the @ `OutputCache` directive in the HTML view, referred to as *declarative caching*, or you can cache a page programmatically in the code-behind file, referred to as *imperative caching*. With declarative caching you get caching statically as described by the @ `OutputCache` directive. With imperative caching you can change the cache policy at runtime based on some dynamic criteria.

To use declarative page caching add the @ `OutputCache` directive to the HTML at the top of the text where you will also find the @ `Page` directive. At a minimum you will need to provide values for the `Duration` and `VaryBy-Param` attributes. `Duration` indicates how long the page will be cached and is expressed in seconds. `VaryByParam` must be `None` at a minimum, or you can supply a parameter name. In this context *parameter* refers to a query parameter passed in an HTTP GET or POST. Here is an example of the basic OutputCache directive that will cache a page for 10 seconds.

```
<%@ outputCache Duration="10" VaryByParam="None" %>
```

You can experiment with CachingDemo.sln. For example, if you change the VaryByParam attribute to cust_id, then when the value of cust_id changed in the GET or POST a new version of the page would be rendered. Users requesting any version of the page with the same parameter value would get the same rendered page unless the cache had expired. You can also choose to set the VaryByHeader and VaryByCustom attributes. VaryByHeader will cache multiple versions of a page based on the HTTP Header information associated with a request. VaryByCustom will cache multiple versions of a page based on the browser type or a custom string value that you must provide.

Caching a Partial Web Page

You can apply the same strategy for caching partial Web pages that you use for caching Web pages. You can use the @ OutputCache directive to cache a user control. This is referred to as *partial page caching*. You can use partial page caching if you have a user control with data that doesn't change very often. The only limitation is that if you employ partial page caching, you cannot programmatically refer to the user control in the code-behind file because any particular rendering of the control may be a cached version.

TIP: You can indicate that a user control should be cached by using the @ OutputCache directive in the HTML or by applying the PartialCaching attribute to the class declaration for the user control.

If data for a user control is the same for all users unless some condition changes and everyone gets the reflected change, use partial page caching to enhance the performance of your application.

Using Dynamic Interfaces with XML

You can separate data by format by using an XML document to provide the data and an XSLT document to describe the layout. (Recall that XML is *eXtended Markup Language* and XSLT is *XML Style Transform*. XSLT is like a cascading style sheet for XML.) Combined with caching and caching dependencies, you can provide users with a custom view of the data separated from the data, needing to render a new page only if some external dependency changes. For example, you could provide users with an order status view, updating the rendered page only when the order status has been updated.

We'll look at each part of XML data, XSL Transform documents, and caching dependencies in the subsections that follow, bringing it all together at the end.

Using XML Data

Using XML data and XSL Transform documents is pretty easy in .NET because there is an `Xml` control on the Web Forms tab of the Toolbox. The `Xml` control has `DocumentSource` and `TransformSource` properties that provide you with a way to indicate the XML source of the data and the file containing the XSL Transform document you want to use to describe the data. As a benefit, you can change the source of the data or the source of the transform and have the new data or presentation offered to your users. This occurs independently of the other file.

Suppose for the sake of demonstration that you are tasked with providing a daily order report for your boss. Your boss prefers to review the report at the end of the day on the train home from Manhattan to Scarsdale. Your boss doesn't want to carry paper, nor does she want to have to try to figure out the data on her cell phone. Finally, every couple of months she wants the report presented in a new format. You decide that this is a perfect scenario for implementing a simple XML export you can e-mail to your boss before she undocks her PC for the evening.

NOTE: You don't need an elaborate scenario to justify using XML and XSLT. It is a good strategy to separate data from format, just as you would do with a Web page and a cascading style sheet. I was just having a bit of fun.

You probably wouldn't create the XML document by hand, but you could do so with a simple text editor like Notepad. We will assume you implemented some automated export process, saving the data to XML. Listing 15.28 contains the text for the XML document followed by a brief description of its contents and nature.

Listing 15.28 A Well-Formed XML Document Containing Only
Self-Describing Data

```xml
<?xml version="1.0" encoding="utf-8" ?>
<orders xmlns:HTML="http://www.softconcepts.com/">
  <product id="Instant Cup Noodles">
    <units>105</units>
    <revenue>10000</revenue>
  </product>
  <product id="Coffee Beans">
    <units>100000</units>
    <revenue>1000000</revenue>
  </product>
  <product id="Staples">
    <units>25000</units>
    <revenue>10000</revenue>
  </product>
</orders>
```

Extensibility (the *X* in *XML*) is a fancy way of saying that the document describes its contents. The first statement indicates that this document uses XML encoding. The second statement describes the contents of the document and an XML namespace. This document contains orders and is unique to other orders not in the `http://www.softconcepts.com` namespace. The `orders` document describes volume and gross revenue by product. Each `product` tag represents a unique instance of a product with `units` and `revenue` properties.

By itself the data would be hard to read and perhaps daunting to an average reader. To alleviate this problem we can associate the XML document with an XSLT document, formatting the data in a presentable way.

Implementing an XSL Transform Document

XSLT documents don't add content to XML; rather, XSLT documents transform how the data is presented. XSLT documents are similar in nature to cascading style sheet documents in that they describe how things appear, but XSLT documents support the addition of selection and sorting criteria. As a result you can describe how the data is formatted and ordered as well as which data is actually displayed. For example, the XSLT document could exclude data even though the data was contained in the XML document.

For our purposes we want to select and display all the data. Listing 15.29 contains the text from the `Orders.xslt` document that is part of `Cached-Demo.sln`. The XSLT simply describes the view of the document as an HTML table and dynamically selects and creates the HTML rows for the document.

Listing 15.29 An XSLT Document That Dynamically Creates an HTML Table

```
1:   <xsl:stylesheet version="1.0"
2:    xmlns:xsl="http://www.w3.org/1999/XSL/Transform">
3:    <xsl:template match="/">
4:       <table width="100%" border="1">
5:         <tr>
6:            <th>Product</th>
7:            <th>Units</th>
8:            <th>Revenue</th>
9:         </tr>
10:
11:        <xsl:for-each select='orders/product'>
12:          <tr>
13:            <td>
14:               <xsl:value-of select='@id' />
15:            </td>
16:            <td>
17:               <xsl:value-of select='units' />
18:            </td>
19:            <td>
20:               <xsl:value-of select='revenue' />
21:            </td>
22:          </tr>
23:        </xsl:for-each>
24:      </table>
25:    </xsl:template>
26: </xsl:stylesheet>
```

XSLT documents can become quite elaborate. Listing 15.29 describes an HTML table and creates table rows and cells based on the number of product elements in the associated XML document.

Lines 1 and 2 describe the content of this document as an XSL style sheet. Lines 3 and 25 are the opening and matching closing `<xsl:template>` tags. The `match` attribute indicates the nodes that this template applies to. (You can look up the `xsl:template` element in the help documentation for complete information.) Lines 4 and 24 define an HTML table. The data will be displayed and organized in an HTML table. Lines 5 through 9 define a single, static, header row for the table. The header will always be displayed with the constant data.

The `<xsl:for-each>` tag works like a `for` loop in Visual Basic. Line 11 is understood to mean "repeat the HTML between lines 11 and 23 for each product in the XML document." Hence, we need to provide a template for only a single row and, regardless of the number of rows, we will get the correct HTML table description. Lines 14, 17, and 20 demonstrate how to obtain the value of a single product for each iteration of the `for-each` statement. We had three products in the `Orders.xml` document, so we will get three rows in the HTML table. Figure 15.20 shows the result.

NOTE: XML and XSLT are big subjects. You will be well served to acquire a couple of separate books on XML and XSLT.

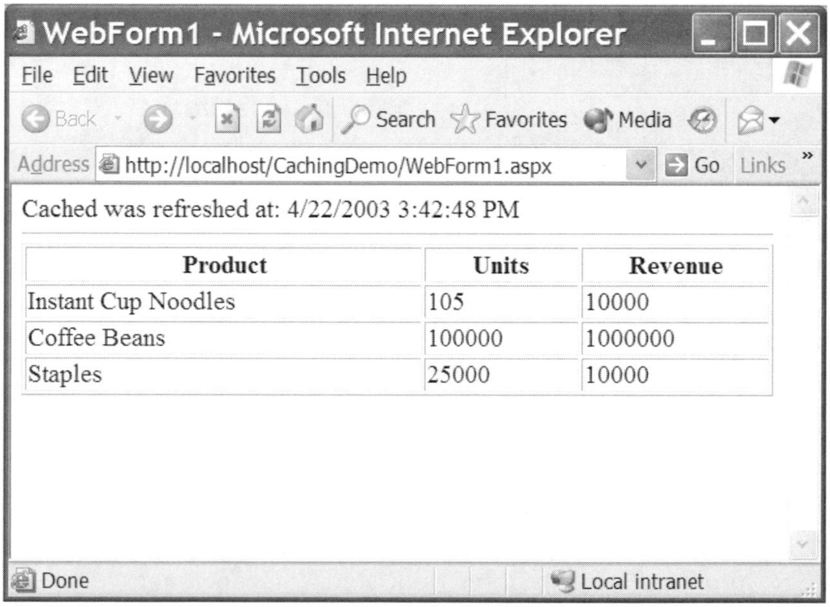

Figure 15.20 The dynamically created and formatted HTML table as described by the XML and XSLT documents.

To create the view shown in Figure 15.20, drop an `Xml` control on a Web page (or user control) from the Web Forms tab of the Toolbox. Assign the `Xml.DocumentSource` property to the `Orders.xml` file and the `Xml.TransformSource` to the `Orders.xslt` document. (If you are using your own data and transform files, substitute your files for the equivalent `Orders` files.)

Defining a Caching Dependency for an XSL-Formatted XML Document

So far so good. We have an XML document and a transform that describes the presentation of the document. Choosing a more elaborate presentation is a matter of experimentation. At this point we want to figure out how to reduce the number of times the XML and XSLT have to be read from the disk. By caching the XML and XSLT documents in the cache we can optimize our application. If we create a cache dependency, we can ensure that users get relevant data if the file data happens to change. The code for caching the XML document and transform source is identical, so I will demonstrate how to dynamically load, cache, and create a dependency on `Orders.xml`. (You can use the same technique for the XSLT file too.) Listing 15.30 demonstrates how to dynamically load the XML document and create a cache dependency so we can avoid reloading the data file unless it has changed.

Listing 15.30 Dynamically Loading an XML Document and Creating a Cache Dependency

```
1:   Imports System.IO
2:   Imports System.Xml
3:
4:   Public Class WebForm1
5:       Inherits System.Web.UI.Page
6:       Protected WithEvents Xml1 As System.Web.UI.WebControls.Xml
7:       Protected WithEvents Label1 As System.Web.UI.WebControls.Label
8:
9:   [ Web Form Designer generated code ]
10:
11:   Private Sub Page_Load(ByVal sender As System.Object, _
12:     ByVal e As System.EventArgs) Handles MyBase.Load
13:
14:     Label1.Text = String.Format("Cached was refreshed at: {0}", _
15:       DateTime.Now)
```

```
16:
17:     If (Cache("Orders") Is Nothing) Then
18:       Dim Document As XmlDocument = New XmlDocument()
19:       If (File.Exists(Server.MapPath("~/Data/Orders.xml"))) Then
20:         Document.Load(Server.MapPath("~/Data/Orders.xml"))
21:         Context.Cache.Insert("Orders", Document, _
22:           New Caching.CacheDependency( _
23:           Server.MapPath("~/Data/Orders.xml")))
24:       End If
25:     End If
26:
27:     Xml1.Document = CType(Cache("Orders"), XmlDocument)
28:
29:
30:   End Sub
31:
32: End Class
```

The `Page_Load` event checks to determine whether the cache contains a value at the `"Orders"` key (line 17). If no such value exists, we create a new instance of an `XmlDocument` object (line 18). We verify that the physical XML file exists, load it into the `XmlDocument` object, and insert the `Xml-Document` object into the cache (lines 19 through 23.) The argument represented by the `New Caching.CacheDependency` object creates a dependency on the physical XML file. If the physical file is modified, the cache will be flushed.

Combining the `@ OutputCache` directive with the cache means that the page will be cached for the duration expressed and then rerendered when `OutputCache` expires. However, unless the XML file has been modified, the actual XML document will not be reloaded.

Securing a Web Application with Forms Authentication

For varying kinds of risk you need varying kinds of security. For an intranet application it may be suitable to use Windows authentication (see Chapter 13 for more information), but for Internet applications you may want to use a more aggressive approach. For example, you may elect to have users log in using forms authentication and further restrict access based on assigned roles for those users. The first step is to authenticate the user. I will demonstrate forms authentication here. (For a good example of forms authentication and roles-based security, refer to the IBuySpy portal code available for download from Microsoft at *http://www.asp.net.com*.)

Forms authentication is just what it sounds like. You are going to provide a login form for the user to enter a user name and password; authenticate that user, and allow access if the person provides valid credentials. There are a few pieces to this puzzle. The first two occur in the `Web.config` file. We need to modify the `Web.config` file for the application that requires authentication; specifically we need to modify the `<authentication>` and `<authorization>` tags. Additionally, we will need to provide some sort of login form. Finally, we need to set an authorization cookie if the user is authenticated. Listing 15.31 shows the `Web.config` modifications.

Listing 15.31 Modifying the `Web.config` File for Forms Authentication

```
<authentication mode="Forms">
  <forms name=".ASPXAUTH"
    loginUrl="Login.aspx"
    protection="All">
    timeout="20"
  </forms>
</authentication>

<authorization>
  <deny users="?" />
</authorization>
```

The authentication mode is set to `Forms`. (The default is Windows integrated.) When we change authentication to `Forms` we need to include a nested `<forms>` tag, which specifies the cookie name, a login URL , a `protection` attribute that describes how the cookie is stored, and an expiration attribute, `timeout`. In Listing 15.31 we have indicated that the user should be redirected to a page named `Login.aspx` for authentication. The protection value `All` means that the authentication cookie is validated and encrypted, and the authentication cookie will expire after 20 minutes.

The authorization section is very simply set to deny all unauthenticated users. (The wildcard `?` means unauthenticated users.) With these settings all users will be redirected to the `Login.aspx` page for authentication. (The `Login.aspx` page is included in `CachingDemo.sln`.)

As mentioned above, if the user is authenticated, we need to set an authorization cookie. Listing 15.32 shows some very basic code for that.

Listing 15.32 Setting an Authentication Cookie for Authorized Users

```
Private Sub Button1_Click(ByVal sender As System.Object, _
  ByVal e As System.EventArgs) Handles Button1.Click

  ' Authenticate here!
  FormsAuthentication.SetAuthCookie(TextBox1.Text, True)
  Response.Redirect(Request.ApplicationPath + "/WebForm1.aspx")

End Sub
```

The `Button1_Click` code is from the `Login.aspx` page. The code simply authenticates everyone. In a production application you would read the user name and password from some repository. If the supplied user name and password were valid, you would call `FormsAuthentication.SetAuthCookie` and redirect the user to the requested path.

In the listing the second argument to `SetAuthCookie` indicates that the authorization cookie is persisted, which means the user will still be authenticated after the browser closes and until the cookie expires. Pass `False` if you want the cookie to reside in-memory and expire when the user closes the browser. Finally, in the `Redirect` statement I had to add the name of the page because I didn't use one of the default pages for my instance of IIS. Had the page been named `default.aspx`, I could return the user to the originally requested page with `Response.Redirect(Request.ApplicationPath)`.

This section covers basic forms authentication. To go beyond that, you will need to create an instance of a class that implements `IPrincipal`, add a string list of roles, and assign this principal object to the `Context.User` property. The string roles can be used to verify the roles of an authenticated user.

There are many levels of security. Necessity will dictate how much more exploration you will need to apply to your specific application. For more on another kind of security, code access security, refer to Chapter 18. For everything you ever wanted to know about .NET security, pick up a copy of *.NET Framework Security* by Brian LaMacchia et al. [2002].

Summary

Programming for the Web is a rich experience. In this chapter we covered a potpourri of topics on building Web applications. For example, an excellent strategy for designing user interfaces is to constrain the layout of controls with an HTML table and employ user control compositing to get the most of control reuse. Style sheets can provide you with a centralized way to manage the visual appearance relative to colors, fonts, and much more.

You also learned you can combine composite controls with session, application, page, and partial page caching to tune your Web application. We finished up with a discussion of XML, XSLT style sheets, and forms authentication. These are all topics you will need to master to build solid Web applications. The next chapter demonstrates how to add data to your Web applications by using ADO.NET.

CHAPTER 16

Combining ADO.NET and ASP.NET

The one who adapts his policy to the times prospers, and likewise that the one whose policy clashes with the demands of the times does not.

—The Prince, *Niccolò Machiavelli*

Introduction

ASP.NET and ADO.NET pack a powerful combined punch. However, speaking from experience, a basic Hello, World!–style application will not help you build real data-aware Web applications. I can tell you that building data-aware Web applications with ASP.NET and ADO.NET is vastly superior to building them with plain-vanilla ASP and ADO. Instead of trying to capture the essence of ASP.NET and ADO.NET programming in the introduction, let's just get started. I will show you some of the cool and useful tasks you can accomplish.

Connecting to a Database

Connecting to a data source is the same whether you are connecting on behalf of a Windows application or a Web application. Where Web applications are concerned, how you use the data will differ. Before we get started I do want to take a minute to show you how you can externalize the connection string. This step will allow you to modify a connection string and even change providers—if you program with interfaces—without recompiling your application.

In this section I will demonstrate how to define your database connection string in a Web application's Web.config file. I will also show you how to read those externalized settings, define a generic Database class by using ADO.NET interfaces, and how to write test code.

Defining the Connection String in the `Web.config` File

The idea of software code convergence is that any specific code occurs only one time in your application. The task of maintaining an application grows in complexity if there are several instances of the same code. This applies to connection string information and connections too. You can provide one externalized connection string that your entire application can use by defining a connection string as a key on the `<appSettings>` tag of the `Web.config` file. Listing 16.1 shows you how to define this tag, which makes application settings accessible to all programmers.

Listing 16.1 Externalizing a Connection String

```
<?xml version="1.0" encoding="utf-8" ?>
<configuration>

<appSettings>
  <add key="ConnectionString"
    value="Provider=Microsoft.Jet.OLEDB.4.0;Password=;User
    ID=Admin;Data Source=C:\Program Files\Microsoft Office\
    Office10\Samples\Northwind.mdb;" />
</appSettings>
```

Listing 16.1 is an excerpt from my `Web.config` file for `Connection-Demo.sln`. I added the text set in bold. There is more to a `Web.config` file than appears in this listing; I chose not to reproduce those parts unrelated to the current discussion.

The first statement indicates that the `Web.config` file is an XML file. The `<appSettings>` tag can have a combination of `<add>`, `<remove>`, and `<clear>` tags. The `<add>` tag works like a hard-coded dictionary of key and value pairs. The `key` attribute refers to the entry, and the `value` attribute defines the value. Together they form key-value pairs. (Due to the limitations of page size, we have to wrap the `value` attribute in Listing 16.1. In your `.config` file the `value` attribute should be set as all one line.)

This demonstration uses the Northwind sample database. You might store this database in a different physical location than the one I entered in the `value` attribute. When experimenting with this code, make sure the `value` attribute you enter reflects the location of the `Northwind.mdb` database on your PC.

Reading Configuration Settings

I want to take a moment to add a bit of an editorial. Some pundits have said Microsoft has had some difficulty in describing and selling .NET to business. As technologists you and I understand what .NET is: it is the framework. Unfortunately "It's the framework" is not a catchy sales pitch like the one used in Microsoft's "Start Me Up" commercials for Windows 95. Catchy or not, the real benefit is that the framework is coherent, cohesive, consistent, and convergent. It has approachable object-oriented code that takes the tedium out of programming and slogging through the chaotic API, giving developers an opportunity to be hyperproductive. (Now if I could just come up with a great slogan.)

One of the tedious tasks we don't have to do, thanks to .NET, is write our own externalized settings code or read `.ini` files. Although this isn't rocket science, the cumulative effect of tedious tasks leads to increased time-to-market. The `System.Configuration.ConfigurationSettings` class contains a shared `AppSettings` property. `AppSettings` contains an overloaded indexer that permits you to read configuration settings in the `<appSettings>` tag using an integer or string index. Thus we can read our connection string (from Listing 16.1) by indexing `System.Configuration.ConfigurationSettings.AppSettings["ConnectionString"]`.

You can shorten the `AppSettings` statement by adding a statement for the `System.Configuration` namespace. It is also important to note that the `AppSettings` property is a shared instance of `NameValueCollection`, which is defined in the `System.Collections.Specialized` namespace and is not case-sensitive. Hence, you could index the connection string using any case, but this is a bad habit to develop.

Defining a `Database` Class by Using Interfaces

The next thing we can do to promote consistency and convergence is to implement a basic `Database` class. We can use this class as a convenient, single place to request things like connections and connection strings. This is a better alternative to permitting each developer to repeat the steps for reading connection strings for `ConfigurationSettings`, creating connection objects, or implementing testing code, like NUnit. Additionally, I like the centralized approach to database access because it provides a convenient place to implement a strategy. For example, we could elect to use ADO.NET interfaces, which would help us write applications that support multiple database vendors. We might also elect to add code access security to this centralized database access point, or, as my colleagues and I did on a project in Oregon, we could begin the project with literal SQL and switch to stored procedures after we got rolling.

NOTE: NUnit is an interface-based testing approach for .NET. The basic concept is that you implement a specific interface for your classes. Then an NUnit tool can invoke operations on your classes through these interfaces, automating testing and test results. Several of these NUnit testing tools are available as free downloads. (Check out *http://www.nunit.org* for an excellent implementation of NUnit.)

Listing 16.2 demonstrates a `Database` class stub that centralizes my connection information. I can interact with this `Database` class very simply, which frees me from the task of retrieving connection strings and creating connection objects (so far). I also used ADO.NET interfaces. I will talk about these more in a minute.

Listing 16.2 A Simple `Database` Class for Centralizing Data Access

```
Public Class Database

  Public Shared ReadOnly Property ConnectionString()
  Get
    Return ConfigurationSettings.AppSettings("ConnectionString")
  End Get
  End Property

  Public Shared Function GetConnection() As IDbConnection
    Return New OleDbConnection(ConnectionString)
  End Function

End Class
```

As it exists in Listing 16.2, my `Database` class contains a public, shared `ConnectionString` property and a shared `GetConnection` method. Very simple code, but it is code I will have to write only one time. Notice that I used the `IDbConnection` interface as my return type rather than an `OleDb-Connection` object. Both OleDb and SqlClient classes implement generic interfaces. The benefit is that I can use an interface-based strategy and support more than one category of provider with the same code. This is helpful if we are switching between a production database and a workstation database, and it is also helpful if I am writing a product like StarTeam. StarTeam is a debug tracking, source management, and intrateam communication extravaganza. When you install it, you can switch between Microsoft Access and Microsoft SQL Server as your back-end database. If you wanted to support a client-electable back-end database—with a bit more work and SQL scripts for each vendor supported—you could allow the customer to choose the database provider. You could support this with the same body of code if you wrote your implementation with interfaces. This approach in general is referred to as the *abstract factory pattern*. (Read *Design Patterns: Elements of Reusable Object-Oriented Software* by Erich Gamma et al. [1995] for more information on patterns.)

Writing Test Code as You Go

The next thing I like to do is write self-testable code for unit testing. For example, if I want to make sure my connection string is correct and I can connect to the database, I will implement a simple test method. I can use such a test method in a console application, making it easy to test. That is, I don't need a whole application to test just my connection. I added the code in Listing 16.3 to my `Database` class from Listing 16.2.

Listing 16.3 A Scaffold for Unit Testing a `Connection` Class

```
<Conditional("DEBUG")> _
Public Shared Sub TestConnection()
  Dim Connection As IDbConnection = GetConnection()
  Try
    Connection.Open()
    Debug.WriteLine(Connection.State.ToString())
  Finally
    Connection.Close()
  End Try

End Sub
```

TestConnection declares an IDbConnection object and invokes Get-Connection. Because TestConnection is in the Database class we don't need to use the class name when invoking GetConnection. In TestConnection I request an instance of a connection using the interface. The connection is opened in the Try part of a Try . . . Finally block. The connection state is written to the Output window, and finally the connection is closed. If everything is working correctly, I will see the word "Open" in the Output window.

Using the ConditionalAttribute

I prefer to write test code as I go instead of coming back later and trying to figure out my code, but I don't want to drag the test code around when I deploy my application. It is likely that you will have a better understanding of your code when you write it the first time than you are likely to have at a later date. It is also easier to turn test code off and on than it is to write it from scratch after things are going wrong.

Notice that I used the ConditionalAttribute—<Conditional()>—on the first line of Listing 16.3. The ConditionalAttribute accepts a string. If the preprocessor token is defined, calls to code that uses the ConditionalAttribute are output by the compiler. If the preprocessor token is not defined, calls to conditional code are not output to the assembly. Figure 16.1 shows the IL code when the DEBUG token is defined, and Figure 16.2 shows the IL code when we configure the same code for release. (The Release configuration undefines the DEBUG token.)

```
WebForm1::Page_Load : void(object,class [mscorlib]System.EventArgs)          _ □ ×
.method private hidebysig instance void  Page_Load(object sender,
                                          class [mscorlib]System.EventArgs e) ci
{
  // Code size       16 (0x10)
  .maxstack  1
  IL_0000:  call       void ConnectDemo.Database::TestConnection()
  IL_0005:  call       class [System.Data]System.Data.IDbConnection ConnectDemo.Database:
  IL_000a:  callvirt   instance void [System.Data]System.Data.IDbConnection::Open()
  IL_000f:  ret
} // end of method WebForm1::Page_Load
```

Figure 16.1 The IL code when the DEBUG token is defined, showing the call to Database.TestConnection.

```
WebForm1::Page_Load : void(object,class [mscorlib]System.EventArgs)                        _ □ x
.method private hidebysig instance void  Page_Load(object sender,
                                          class [mscorlib]System.EventArgs e) cil managed
{
  // Code size       11 (0xb)
  .maxstack  1
  IL_0000:  call       class [System.Data]System.Data.IDbConnection ConnectDemo.Database::GetConnection()
  IL_0005:  callvirt   instance void [System.Data]System.Data.IDbConnection::Open()
  IL_000a:  ret
} // end of method WebForm1::Page_Load
```

Figure 16.2 The IL code after undefining the `DEBUG` preprocessor symbol by changing the configuration to `Release` mode.

Use the `ConditionalAttribute` anytime you have code that is for testing purposes only. This is a nice improvement over simply wrapping that code in preprocessor `#IF` conditional statements.

Using the `DataView` Class

The `DataView` class is a convenient class for presenting a subset of a data table, for filtering, sorting, searching, editing, and browsing data in Windows Forms and Web Forms applications. The easiest way to obtain a data view is to request the default view from a data table. The basic steps are to connect to a data source, fill a data set or data table, and request the default view. Listing 16.4 demonstrates how to obtain a data view and display the data in a data grid. (Refer to Chapters 11 and 12 for more information on updating data, including updating a database by using a data view.)

Listing 16.4 Binding the Default Data View to a Data Grid

```
Private Sub Page_Load(ByVal sender As System.Object, _
  ByVal e As System.EventArgs) Handles MyBase.Load

  Dim Adapter As IDbDataAdapter = _
    New OleDbDataAdapter("SELECT * FROM CUSTOMERS", _
    Database.GetConnection())

    Dim DataSet As DataSet = New DataSet("CUSTOMERS")
    Adapter.Fill(DataSet)
```

```
DataGrid1.DataSource = DataSet.Tables(0).DefaultView
DataGrid1.DataBind()

End Sub
```

Listing 16.4 declares an `IDbDataAdapter` interface and initializes it to an `OleDbDataAdapter` object by using a literal SQL statement and the `Database.GetConnection` shared method. (I am reusing the `Database` class from Listing 16.2.) Next, a `DataSet` object is created. `DataSet`, `DataTable`, and `DataView` objects are provider-neutral, so there is no need to use an interface here. After the `DataSet` object is created I use the `Adapter` instance to fill the `DataSet` object. The final two statements request the first `DataTable` object from the `DataSet` object's `Tables` collection and the `DefaultView` object from the `DataTable` object, then bind the `DataView` object. The result (Figure 16.3) is precisely the same in this instance as if we had assigned the `DataSource` property directly to the table.

We achieve a different view by sorting or filtering the view, or by creating a custom data view and adding those columns we are interested in showing

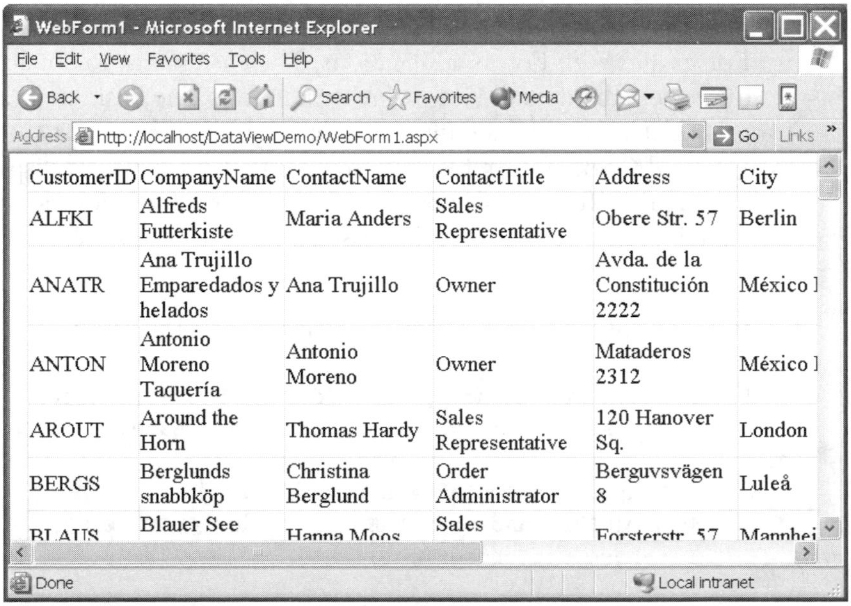

Figure 16.3 The default data view of all the Northwind customers.

the user. For example, suppose we want to show the user only the contact information, sorted by company. We can request all the data and switch to a contacts-only view without rehitting the database. (Refer to the section Caching Objects in Chapter 15 for more information.) Additionally, I will move the general code for requesting an `Adapter` instance to the `Database` class. Listing 16.5 contains the revised and additional code.

Listing 16.5 Creating a Customized Data View

```
1:   Imports System.Data
2:   Imports System.Data.OleDb
3:
4:   Public Class WebForm1
5:     Inherits System.Web.UI.Page
6:     Protected WithEvents Label1 As System.Web.UI.WebControls.Label
7:     Protected WithEvents DataGrid1 As _
8:       System.Web.UI.WebControls.DataGrid
9:
10:    [ Web Form Designer generated code ]
11:
12:    Private Sub Page_Load(ByVal sender As System.Object, _
13:      ByVal e As System.EventArgs) Handles MyBase.Load
14:
15:      Dim View As DataView = Contacts
16:      DataGrid1.DataSource = View
17:      Label1.Text = String.Format("Count: {0}", View.Count)
18:      DataGrid1.DataBind()
19:
20:    End Sub
21:
22:    Private Function GetAllCustomers() As DataView
23:
24:      ' Verbose code
25:      Dim Adapter As IDbDataAdapter = _
26:        New OleDbDataAdapter("SELECT * FROM CUSTOMERS", _
27:        Database.GetConnection())
28:
29:      Dim DataSet As DataSet = New DataSet("CUSTOMERS")
30:        Adapter.Fill(DataSet)
31:
32:      Return DataSet.Tables(0).DefaultView
33:
34:    End Function
```

```
35:
36:
37:    Private ReadOnly Property Contacts() As DataView
38:    Get
39:      Dim Table As DataTable
40:      Table = Customers.Tables(0).Copy()
41:      Table.Columns.Remove("CustomerID")
42:      Table.Columns.Remove("Address")
43:      Table.Columns.Remove("City")
44:      Table.Columns.Remove("Region")
45:      Table.Columns.Remove("PostalCode")
46:      Contacts = New DataView(Table)
47:
48:      Contacts = New DataView(Table, "", _
49:         "Country", DataViewRowState.CurrentRows)
50:    End Get
51:    End Property
52:
53:    Private ReadOnly Property Customers() As DataSet
54:    Get
55:      Customers = New DataSet("CUSTOMERS")
56:      Database.GetAdapter("SELECT * FROM CUSTOMERS"). _
57:      Fill(Customers)
58:    End Get
59:    End Property
60:
61: End Class
```

The code represents a single Web form with an HTML table, a data grid, and a label Web control. The data view is bound to the grid (as demonstrated in Listing 16.4). GetAllCustomers represents the code from Listing 16.4. The ReadOnly property Customers (lines 53 through 59) represents a simplified version of GetAllCustomers. I basically took the code in lines 25 through 27 and added a GetAdapter method to the Database class discussed earlier in the chapter. The interesting new code is in lines 37 through 51.

The ReadOnly property Contacts obtains all customers and then creates the custom data view by dropping columns we are not interested in viewing. The new data table is declared in line 39 and initialized in line 30. Lines 41 through 45 remove the columns we don't want, and line 46 creates the data view from our new, customized data table.

Lines 48 through 50 demonstrate how to filter, sort, and indicate the rows we want. The first argument to the `DataView` constructor indicates the table from which we should create the view. The next argument is a filter. For example, we could have written `"Country='Liberia'"` to only get Liberian contacts. The third argument indicates that we should sort by country, and the last argument indicates that we want all current rows in the table. I used an empty string for the filter, so the result returns all rows in the `Customers` table (Figure 16.4).

We could have created the same view by writing an SQL statement that returned only the columns we wanted and had an `ORDER BY` clause. (Try it as an exercise if you want.) However, in our implementation we have all of the customers' information and we can create various views without having to go back to the database (assuming we cache or serialize the data set). Our choice can provide dramatic improvements in the responsiveness of our application by eliminating extra reads from the database.

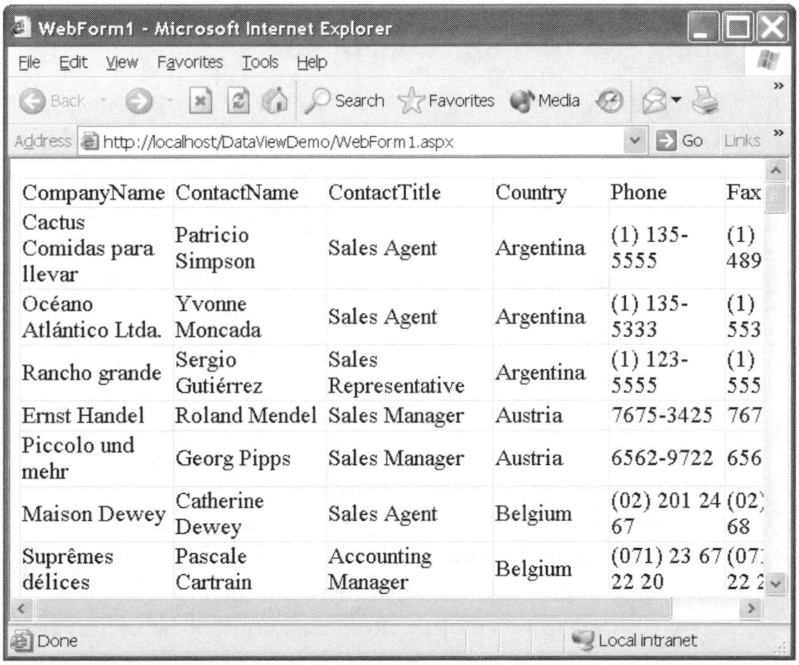
WebForm1 - Microsoft Internet Explorer
File Edit View Favorites Tools Help
Back Search Favorites Media
Address http://localhost/DataViewDemo/WebForm1.aspx Go Links
CompanyName ContactName ContactTitle Country Phone Fax
Cactus Comidas para llevar | Patricio Simpson | Sales Agent | Argentina | (1) 135-5555 | (1) 489
Océano Atlántico Ltda. | Yvonne Moncada | Sales Agent | Argentina | (1) 135-5333 | (1) 553
Rancho grande | Sergio Gutiérrez | Sales Representative | Argentina | (1) 123-5555 | (1) 555
Ernst Handel | Roland Mendel | Sales Manager | Austria | 7675-3425 | 767
Piccolo und mehr | Georg Pipps | Sales Manager | Austria | 6562-9722 | 656
Maison Dewey | Catherine Dewey | Sales Agent | Belgium | (02) 201 24 67 | (02) 68
Suprêmes délices | Pascale Cartrain | Accounting Manager | Belgium | (071) 23 67 22 20 | (07 22 2
Done
Local intranet

Figure 16.4 The custom `Contacts` data view created from Listing 16.5.

Binding Data to Single-Value Web Controls

Web controls are divided into two logical categories: single-value controls and multi-value controls. Controls like the TextBox, LinkButton, and Image controls are single-value controls. Those like the DataList, DataGrid, and Repeater controls are multi-value controls. In the next section we'll talk about multi-value controls; in this section we'll look at how we can get data into single-value controls, specifically the TextBox control.

Single-value controls do not have a DataSource property like multi-value controls do. The easiest way to get data into a single-value control is to assign the data value to the appropriate property. For example, you can assign data values to a TextBox.Text property. This is easy to do.

You can also define a data binding by using the DataBindings dialog or by entering a script block in the HTML editor. When you have defined the data binding, you can update all controls by calling the containing control's DataBind method. For example, Page.DataBind will bind both single-value and multi-value controls for a Web page (also referred to as a *Web form*).

Using the DataBindings Dialog

The DataBindings dialog is selected from the Properties window on a per-control basis. Click the control for which you want to define a data binding and press F4 to focus the Properties window (Figure 16.5). The first item in the list of properties—if the properties are sorted, rather than grouped—invokes the DataBindings editor (Figure 16.6).

To define a data binding for a control, select the property whose value you want to bind, and select the custom binding expression group, as shown in Figure 16.6. For single-value controls you are precisely defining where the data for that control comes from. For the example shown in the figure I defined a binding for the TextBoxCompany.Text property. It is natural to want to read the company name from some repository. The binding I defined is Contacts(CurrentIndex)("CompanyName"). This refers to an indexable object named Contacts and a variable I have to manage named CurrentIndex; the object return is indexable by a string. A DataView control is one example of a control that fits this description. An indexed DataView control returns a DataRowView control, which in turn is indexable by the string name of a column. Combined, row and column, a single field value is returned, which is exactly what we need for a TextBox control's Text property.

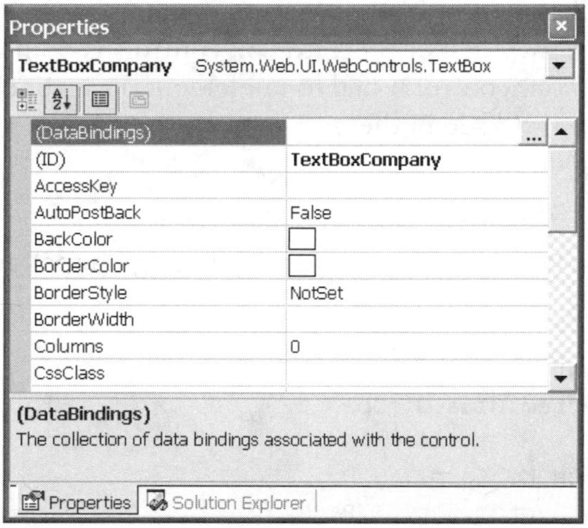

Figure 16.5 The Properties window for a `TextBox` control, from which you can access the DataBindings editor.

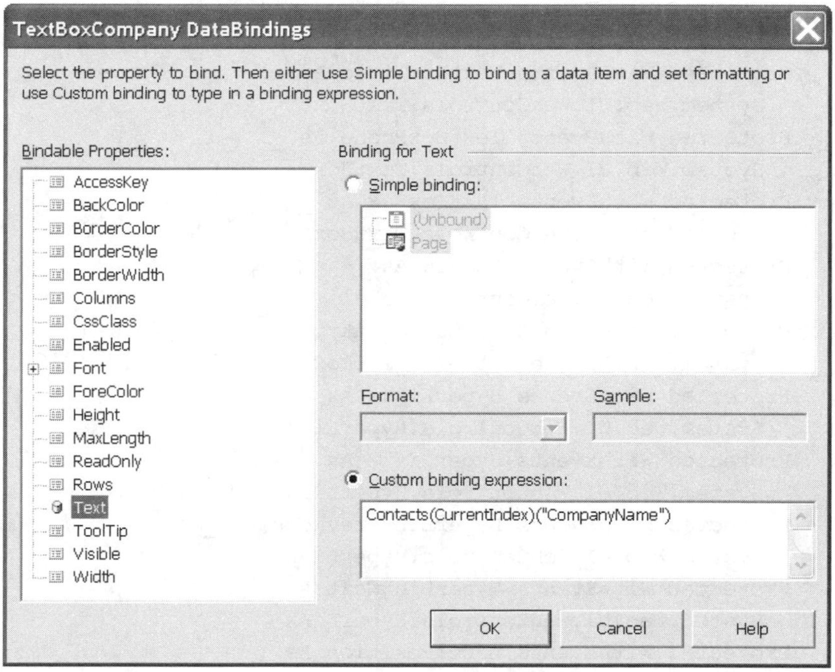

Figure 16.6 The DataBindings editor for a `TextBox` control.

The code in Listing 16.6 implements a single-row view of a `Contacts` data view. Each of the `TextBox` controls is bound to a suitable field in the `DataView` control. I had to implement navigation, tracking a current index. (As you will see in the next section, we can use a `DataList` or similar control to do this for us.)

Listing 16.6 Displaying a Single Row and Managing Navigation without Rehitting the Data Source

```
1:   Imports System.Data
2:   Imports System.Data.OleDb
3:
4:   Public Class WebForm1
5:     Inherits System.Web.UI.Page
6:     Protected WithEvents Label1 As System.Web.UI.WebControls.Label
7:     Protected WithEvents Label2 As System.Web.UI.WebControls.Label
8:     Protected WithEvents Label3 As System.Web.UI.WebControls.Label
9:     Protected WithEvents Label4 As System.Web.UI.WebControls.Label
10:    Protected WithEvents TextBoxCompany As _
11:      System.Web.UI.WebControls.TextBox
12:    Protected WithEvents TextBoxContact As _
13:      System.Web.UI.WebControls.TextBox
14:    Protected WithEvents TextBoxTitle As _
15:      System.Web.UI.WebControls.TextBox
16:    Protected WithEvents TextBoxPhone As _
17:      System.Web.UI.WebControls.TextBox
18:    Protected WithEvents TextBoxFax As _
19:      System.Web.UI.WebControls.TextBox
20:    Protected WithEvents Label6 As _
21:      System.Web.UI.WebControls.Label
22:    Protected WithEvents TextBoxCountry As _
23:      System.Web.UI.WebControls.TextBox
24:    Protected WithEvents HyperLink1 As _
25:      System.Web.UI.WebControls.HyperLink
26:    Protected WithEvents HyperLink2 As _
27:      System.Web.UI.WebControls.HyperLink
28:    Protected WithEvents HyperLinkPrevious As _
29:      System.Web.UI.WebControls.HyperLink
30:    Protected WithEvents HyperLinkNext As _
31:      System.Web.UI.WebControls.HyperLink
32:    Protected WithEvents LabelPosition As _
33:      System.Web.UI.WebControls.Label
34:    Protected WithEvents Label5 As _
```

```
35:      System.Web.UI.WebControls.Label
36:
37: [ Web Form Designer generated code ]
38:
39:   Private Sub Page_Load(ByVal sender As System.Object, _
40:     ByVal e As System.EventArgs) Handles MyBase.Load
41:
42:     CheckCommand()
43:     UpdatePositionLabel()
44:     Page.DataBind()
45:
46:   End Sub
47:
48:   Private Sub UpdatePositionLabel()
49:     LabelPosition.Text = String.Format("{0} of {1}", _
50:     CurrentIndex + 1, Contacts.Count)
51:   End Sub
52:
53:   Private Sub CheckCommand()
54:     If (Request.QueryString("CurrentIndex") Is Nothing = False) Then
55:       Try
56:         CurrentIndex = CType(Request.QueryString("CurrentIndex"), _
57:           Integer) - 1
58:       Catch
59:       End Try
60:     End If
61:   End Sub
62:
63:   Private Function GetMax() As Integer
64:     Return Contacts.Count
65:   End Function
66:
67:   Protected ReadOnly Property Contacts() As DataView
68:   Get
69:     If (Session("Contacts") Is Nothing) Then
70:       Session("Contacts") = GetContacts()
71:     End If
72:
73:     Return CType(Session("Contacts"), DataView)
74:   End Get
75:   End Property
76:
77:   Protected Property CurrentIndex() As Integer
78:   Get
```

```
79:      If (Session("CurrentIndex") Is Nothing) Then
80:        Session("CurrentIndex") = 0
81:      End If
82:
83:      Return CType(Session("CurrentIndex"), Integer)
84:
85:    End Get
86:    Set(ByVal Value As Integer)
87:      If (Value >= GetMax()) Then
88:        Session("CurrentIndex") = GetMax() - 1
89:      ElseIf (Value < 0) Then
90:        Session("CurrentIndex") = 0
91:      Else
92:        Session("CurrentIndex") = Value
93:      End If
94:    End Set
95:    End Property
96:
97:    Private Function GetContacts() As DataView
98:
99:      Const SQL As String = _
100:       "SELECT CompanyName, ContactName, " + _
101:       "ContactTitle, Country, Phone, " + _
102:       "Fax FROM CUSTOMERS ORDER BY Country"
103:
104:      Dim Adapter As IDataAdapter = _
105:        Database.GetAdapter(SQL)
106:
107:      Dim DataSet As DataSet = New DataSet("Contacts")
108:      Database.GetAdapter(SQL).Fill(DataSet)
109:      Return DataSet.Tables(0).DefaultView
110:
111:    End Function
112:
113: End Class
```

The result of the code is shown in Figure 16.7. Each `TextBox` control in the application uses a similar `Text` property–binding statement as the one shown in Figure 16.6. The only information that changes is the indexing column name. The solution itself is broken up into a handful of methods and properties: a `Page_Load` event handler, an `UpdatePositionLabel` method, a `CheckCommand` method, a `GetMax` Function, a `Contacts` property, a `Cur-`

Figure 16.7 Viewing the contact information from a single row of the Northwind database.

rentIndex property, and a GetContacts function. I will quickly review each of these.

Page_Load (lines 39 through 46) invokes CheckCommand, updates the record indicator, and calls Page.DataBind. Examining the code from bottom to top of this event handler, DataBind gets the data onto the Web page. UpdatePositionLabel displays the value index of total records shown in Figure 16.7 as 1 of 91. The CheckCommand subroutine examines the HttpRequest object's QueryString property to determine whether a new CurrentIndex has been passed to the page. I subtracted 1 from the CurrentIndex passed because internally the DataView control is zero-based, but I chose to show a one-based index (see Figure 16.7). If the passed CurrentIndex is invalid, it is silently ignored in the Try . . . Catch block in lines 55 through 59. QueryString values are passed as URL-encoded queries. For example, http://localhost/BindControls-Demo/WebForm1.aspx?CurrentIndex=3 is an example of a URI-encoded query string.

GetMax (lines 63 through 65) simply returns the number of contacts, which we will discuss next. The Contacts property is a lazy-instance, session-cached value. The lazy-instance idiom simply means I create the object on first use, not before. Combined with the session cache, the Contacts property checks to see whether an object referred to by the key "Contacts" is in the session cache (line 69). If the cache has expired or, as is the case on the first call, no object has been stuffed in the cache yet, I call Get-Contacts (line 70) to initialize the session cache. Finally, the value in the session cache is converted to the DataView object we know it is.

GetContacts uses code from earlier in the chapter to initialize a new DataSet object, from which we retrieve a DataView object. Lines 97 through 111 demonstrate how we can get the right data in the Default-View object by refining the SQL text. The SQL text in lines 99 through 102 selects on the contact columns. (Recall that Database is the class we defined earlier in the chapter.)

The final piece is the CurrentIndex property in lines 77 through 95. Again I used the session cache and the lazy-instance technique, placing CurrentIndex in the cache upon first request. The basic setter logic is that if the cache exceeds the maximum number of contacts in the DataView object, CurrentIndex is the maximum value. The same kind of logic is used for the low index. If a new CurrentIndex value is within range, we simply place it in the cache. Both Contacts and CurrentIndex in the data binding text are retrieved from the Contacts and CurrentIndex properties.

Defining a Data Binding in the HTML Editor

When I define data binding I usually do it in the HTML editor. Whether to use the HTML editor or the DataBinding dialog is simply a matter of preference. The actual result is identical. The code fragment below shows the result of the data binding statement for the TextBoxCompany.Text property from the HTML perspective.

```
  <asp:textbox id=TextBoxCompany runat="server"
Text='<%# Contacts(CurrentIndex)("CompanyName") %>'>
```

The <asp:textbox> tag represents how an ASP.NET TextBox control is rendered in HTML. (You can add a TextBox control by typing the text in the HTML editor directly, too.) The part we are interested in is the Text attribute (also referred to as the *Text property* in object-oriented programming terms.) Text='<%# Contacts(CurrentIndex)("Company-Name") %>' represents an inline script block assignment to the Text property. Think of the code between <%# and %> as a fragment of runnable code. This code performs precisely the same job as TextBoxCompany.Text = Contacts(CurrentIndex).Contacts("Company") would in the code-behind file.

An intuitive question might be, "Why would I use script blocks over code-behind files?" The answer is that you can use either, as long as you can use either. I am not trying to be glib here; it just seems that sometimes it's more convenient to use script blocks and other times code-behind files. As a programmer who started programming before the Web, I prefer code to script. In our example we could have used either code-behind files or script blocks to get the data in the TextBox controls.

Binding Data to Multi-Value Web Controls

Binding data to a DataGrid, DataList, or Repeater control is easiest of all. All you have to do is have an object that implements IEnumerable, assign this object to the DataSource property of the prospective control, and invoke DataBind on that control. The ease with which you can get data into these controls in no way mitigates their utility. You can perform mundane tasks, like simply binding a DataView object, or create elaborate, complex interfaces with a bit of clever invention. (Read the Using a DataList Control to Repeat Composite Controls section later in this chapter for more information.)

Refer to Listing 16.4 for a quick example of getting a DataView object into a DataGrid control. Listing 16.7 demonstrates how we can use a DataGrid control and specific bound columns as an alternate way to refine the view of data. Listing 16.7 uses the lazy Contacts instance from Listing 16.6 but specifies bound columns instead of auto-generating columns. In the example I bound only the contact name and phone number from the Contacts data view. Figure 16.8 shows the results.

Listing 16.7 Binding Specific Data to a DataGrid Control

```
Private Sub Page_Load(ByVal sender As System.Object, _
  ByVal e As System.EventArgs) Handles MyBase.Load

  ' Binds the Contacts data view to the DataList control
  DataGrid1.DataSource = Contacts
  DataGrid1.DataBind()

End Sub
```

The code in Listing 16.7 relies on the previously mentioned lazy instance of the Contacts data view from the Contacts property, the GetContacts method, and the Database class. It is important to understand that the code in Listing 16.7 demonstrates how we would bind any data source to a DataGrid control.

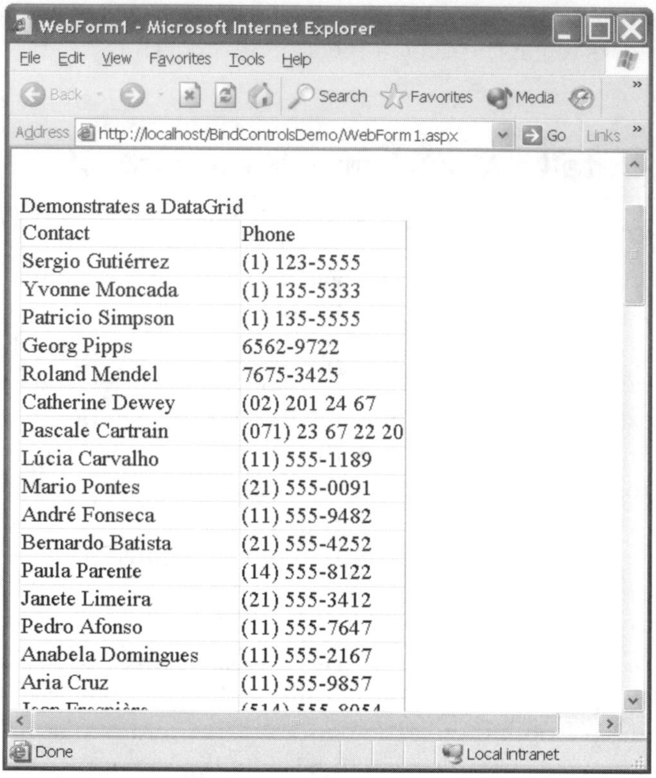

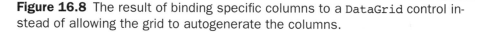

Figure 16.8 The result of binding specific columns to a `DataGrid` control instead of allowing the grid to autogenerate the columns.

Here are the steps for limiting the bound columns for the `DataGrid` control, as shown in Figure 16.8.

1. Select the `DataGrid` control.
2. Open the Properties window and change the `DataGrid` control's `AutoGenerate Columns` property to `False`.
3. Right-click the `DataGrid` control and select Property Builder from the context menu or select Property Builder from the Properties window when the `DataGrid` control is selected.
4. Select Bound Column from the Available columns list (Figure 16.9) and add two Bound Columns to the Selected columns list.
5. Select the first Bound Column and change the Header text to Contact and the Data Field to ContactName. Figure 16.9 shows these settings.

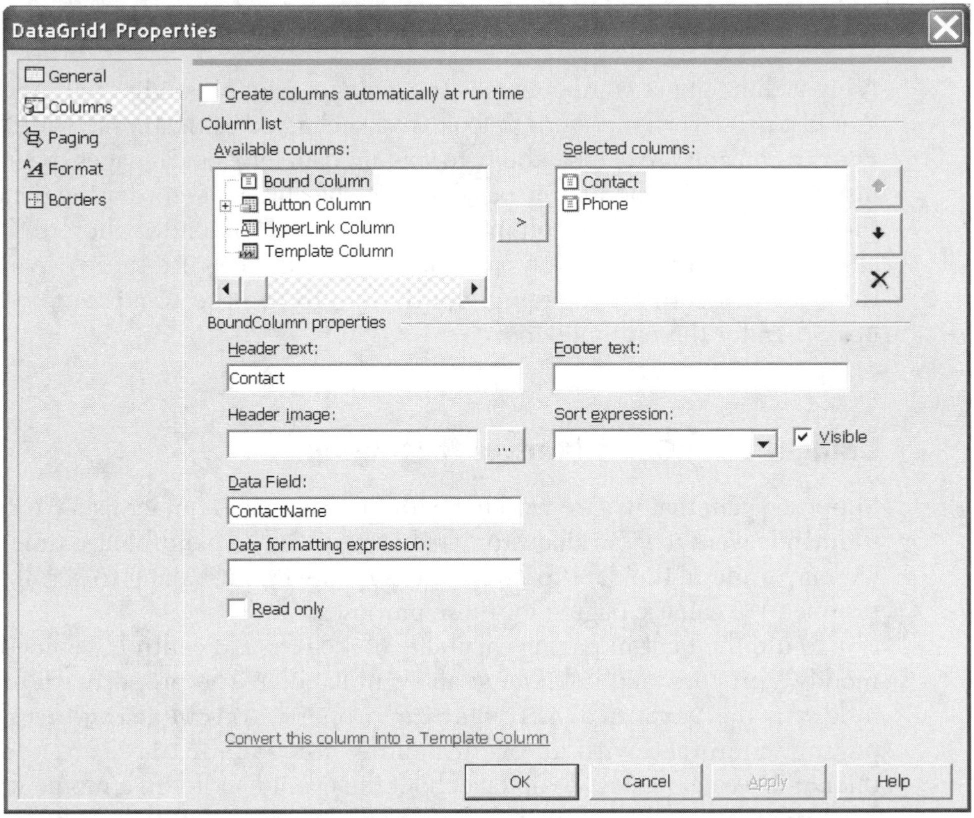

Figure 16.9 Defining bound columns in the `DataGrid` control's Properties dialog.

6. Select the second Bound Column and set the Header text to Phone and the Data Field to Phone.
7. Click OK to save your changes.

If you add the code from Listing 16.7 to the `Page_Load` event in Listing 16.6, you can run the application and see the results as shown in Figure 16.8.

Using the `DataGrid` control in the manner prescribed is pretty basic. In the next section we'll look at how the `DataGrid` control supports paging and sorting. The section after that will demonstrate how we can use a variation of the technique described in this section to repeat complex user controls, resulting in professional and elaborate-looking user interfaces.

Paging and Sorting with `DataGrid` Controls

A great thing about components is that you get a lot of goodies with them. You just need to know where to look. Two such goodies that come with `DataGrid` controls are (1) the ability to split up data into logical pages (paging) instead of a single, monolithic page, and (2) the ability to reorder the data in the `DataGrid` control by column (sorting). When you know where to find all the pieces, it is a relatively straightforward matter to use these capabilities. We will start with paging, continuing to use the `BindControls-Demo.sln` for this example, too.

Using a `DataGrid` Control for Paging

Suppose again that we are working with the customer contact list. We may ultimately want to view all customers but need only a handful at a time, or we may want all the data to fit on one screen without having to scroll the browser. We can use paging for these purposes.

To use the built-in paging capability of a `DataGrid` control, we need to modify a property and implement an event handler. The property we must modify is the `DataGrid.AllowPaging` property. `AllowPaging` turns on paging; combined with an event handler for `DataGrid.PageIndex-Changed`, we get paging. I will talk about the event handler in a moment.

For additional paging customizations we can change the default `Data-Grid.PageSize` from 10 to some other number. `PageSize` determines the maximum number of rows displayed on each page. We can also change the `DataGrid.PagerStyle.Mode` property from the default `NextPrev`, which gives pager controls < and > (less than and greater than), to `NumericPages`, which gives numbered links—up to 10—and adds ellipses on each end if there are more than 10 pages of data. (I prefer the number links because it seems easier to jump to a relative point in the list.)

Implementing the event handler is accomplished by switching to the Code Editor view, selecting the `DataGrid` control from the class name combobox, and choosing the `PageIndexChanged` event from the method name combobox. All we really have to do to support paging programmatically is to set `DataGrid.CurrentPageIndex` equal to `e.NewPageIndex` (where `e` is the event argument name for the `DataGridPageChangedEvent-Args` parameter), set the `DataGrid` control's `DataSource` property, and rebind the `DataGrid` control. Listing 16.8 shows an excerpt demonstrating this code.

Listing 16.8 Implementing an Event Handler for the DataGrid.PageIndexChanged Event

```
Private Sub DataGrid1_PageIndexChanged(ByVal source As Object, _
  ByVal e As System.Web.UI.WebControls.DataGridPageChangedEventArgs) _
  Handles DataGrid1.PageIndexChanged

  DataGrid1.CurrentPageIndex = e.NewPageIndex
  DataGrid1.DataSource = Contacts
  DataGrid1.DataBind()

End Sub
```

Figure 16.10 in the next subsection shows the combined effect of the paging and column sorting features as they appear applied to the grid.

Using a DataGrid Control for Sorting

Customers will more than likely want to reorganize data on an individual-user basis. You can give them this feature at a modest charge. (Sorry, a momentary lapse into mercenary contractor humor.) To implement sorting when the user clicks on a column header you need to set the DataGrid.AllowSorting property to True, implement an event handler for the SortCommand event, assign the DataView.Sort property to e.SortExpression, assign the Data-Grid.DataSource property, and rebind the DataGrid control. (This is assuming we are using the DataView object, as we are in this example.)

The DataView.Sort property might sound a little ominous, but this simply refers to the column name. The right-hand-side value e.SortExpression is an instance of the DataGridSortCommandEventArgs parameter passed to the SortCommmand event handler. Listing 16.9 gives the excerpt from BindControlsDemo.sln that shows the SortCommand event handler.

Listing 16.9 Implementing an Event Handler for the DataGrid.SortCommand Event

```
Private Sub DataGrid1_SortCommand(ByVal source As Object, _
  ByVal e As System.Web.UI.WebControls.DataGridSortCommandEventArgs) _
  Handles DataGrid1.SortCommand

  Contacts.Sort = e.SortExpression
```

```
DataGrid1.DataSource = Contacts
DataGrid1.DataBind()
```

End Sub

Things might go slightly and momentarily wrong if you set `AutoGenerateColumns` to `False` as we did earlier in the chapter. I mention it because this is the kind of thing that can frustrate anyone. Because we turned off the `DataGrid.AutoGenerateColumns` property, we need to return to the `DataGrid` control's Properties dialog (Figure 16.9) and indicate the column name as the sort expression. For example, we named our header for the contact name just Contact, but the sort expression needs to be `ContactName`. Just type this information in the Sort expression field in the Properties window. If we want to specify a sort order, we can add `DESC`—for descending—after the column name (or `ASC` for ascending). Thus the total value for the sort expression on the ContactName column is `ContactName DESC`. Repeat the process for each column for which you want to support sorting.

You will know that column sorting is supported because the column header will be rendered as a hyperlink (Figure 16.10).

Binding a `System.Array` Object to a `DataGrid` Control

Microsoft has made the base class libraries (BCLs) available for download. This source code for .NET is referred to as the *SSCLI* (shared source code library) or *Rotor*. I was poking around in the BCLs because I wanted to be

Demonstrates a DataGrid

Contact	Phone
Sergio Gutiérrez	(1) 123-5555
Yvonne Moncada	(1) 135-5333
Patricio Simpson	(1) 135-5555
Georg Pipps	6562-9722
Roland Mendel	7675-3425
Catherine Dewey	(02) 201 24 67
Pascale Cartrain	(071) 23 67 22 20
Lúcia Carvalho	(11) 555-1189
Mario Pontes	(21) 555-0091
André Fonseca	(11) 555-9482
1 2 3 4 5 6 7 8 9 10	

Figure 16.10 The combined effect of paging and sorting in a `DataGrid` control.

sure how serialization for binding worked. Tracing it to a single line of code, it appears that as long as an object implements `IEnumerable`, you are going to have a pretty good chance of binding to controls like `DataGrid` or serializing that class. It is worth mentioning that while it is helpful to understand how things work, it may be a mistake to write code that is completely dependent on that knowledge.

A simple and obvious candidate is any instance of `System.Array`; that is, an array of any type can be bound to a `DataGrid` control because `System.Array` implements `IEnumerable`. Generally, using a plain array of objects is weaker implementation then using a strongly typed collection or data set, but occasionally it may be convenient to use a simple array, or that may be all you have. (For example, you might have only an array of types if that is what a vendor returns in the code or in a Web Service.) Listing 16.10 demonstrates a custom type, `Contact`, and an array of `Contact` objects bound to a `DataGrid` control.

Listing 16.10 Binding an Array of `Contact` Objects to a `DataGrid` Control

```
1:  Public Class WebForm1
2:      Inherits System.Web.UI.Page
3:      Protected WithEvents DataGrid2 As _
4:         System.Web.UI.WebControls.DataGrid
5:      [ Web Form Designer generated code ]
6:
7:      Private Sub Page_Load(ByVal sender As System.Object, _
8:         ByVal e As System.EventArgs) Handles MyBase.Load
9:
10:        DataGrid2.DataSource = GetContactList()
11:        DataGrid2.DataBind()
12:
13:     End Sub
14:
15:     Private Sub DataGrid2_SortCommand(ByVal source As Object, _
16:        ByVal e As _
17:        System.Web.UI.WebControls.DataGridSortCommandEventArgs) _
18:        Handles DataGrid2.SortCommand
19:
20:        Dim List() As Contact = GetContactList()
21:        Array.Sort(List, New StringComparer(e.SortExpression))
22:
23:        DataGrid2.DataSource = List
24:        DataGrid2.DataBind()
```

```
25:    End Sub
26:
27:    Public Function GetContactList() As Contact()
28:      GetContactList = New Contact() { _
29:        New Contact("Mark Davis", "(503) 555-1212"), _
30:        New Contact("Robert Golieb", "(608) 555-1212"), _
31:        New Contact("Paul Kimmel", "(517) 555-1212"), _
32:        New Contact("Alex Kimmel", "Unlisted")}
33:
34:    End Function
35: End Class
36:
37: Public Class Contact
38:
39:    Private FName As String
40:    Private FPhone As String
41:
42:    Public Sub New(ByVal Name As String, ByVal Phone As String)
43:      Me.FName = Name
44:      Me.FPhone = Phone
45:    End Sub
46:
47:    Public Property Name() As String
48:    Get
49:      Return FName
50:    End Get
51:    Set(ByVal Value As String)
52:      FName = Value
53:    End Set
54:    End Property
55:
56:    Public Property Phone() As String
57:    Get
58:      Return FPhone
59:    End Get
60:    Set(ByVal Value As String)
61:      FPhone = Value
62:    End Set
63:    End Property
64: End Class
```

The `Contact` class in lines 37 to 64 is trivial. It is worth pointing out that if you bind to a `DataGrid` control, it will use Reflection to autogenerate the columns, and it will only reflect properties. Thus, if you deviate from convention by using public fields instead of properties, the `DataGrid` control will not be able to generate columns for you.

The abbreviated `WebForm1` class is implemented in lines 1 through 35. A factory method exists for the array, `GetContactList`, in lines 27 through 34. (This simulates getting, creating, or having an array of `Contact` objects.) The `Page_Load` event uses this method to obtain the array, assign it to the `DataGrid.DataSource` property (line 10), and call `DataGrid.DataBind`.

Lines 15 through 25 implement the `SortCommand` event handler for this `DataGrid` control. Instead of assigning the `DataView.Sort` property to the `e.SortExpression` value we need to implement custom sorting behavior. In our example I resolved to use the inherent `System.Array.Sort` method and define a class that implements `IComparer`. The next section elaborates on `IComparer`.

Implementing `IComparer` to Support Sorting a `System.Array` Object

The C++ programming language and some others like SmallTalk support templates, also referred to as *generics*. Templates represent an idiom that supports separating type from algorithm. That is, we can write an algorithm and supply the type at runtime, changing the type as we go. Thus, instead of writing a sort, for example, for integers, strings, `Contact` objects, and whatever else comes along, we can write one sort and supply any type. Visual Basic .NET does not support templates (nor does C#) in part because they can be challenging to use. However, we can accomplish some of the same goals with interfaces.

The point is to be able to separate an algorithm from a type. In this instance we have a sort algorithm in `System.Array`, but arrays cannot know in advance how to compare every object, especially those that haven't been created yet. Instead the `Sort` method in `System.Array` relies on the objects to be sorted to supply their own `Compare` method via the `IComparer` interface. In other words, you provide an instance of an object that implements `IComparer` and this object will know how to compare the objects. As a result the sort algorithm can be genericized except for anywhere that a comparison needs to be made. When such a comparison is needed, the code relies on you to do it. The net effect is that we all get a flawless, prewritten sort algorithm and all we have to do is provide the comparator.

Line 21 from Listing 16.10 demonstrates how to call the shared `System.Array.Sort` method and passes an externally defined comparator to that method. The `StringComparer` class (Listing 16.11) implements the

`System.Collections.IComparer` interface and will be used at the point in the `Sort` method where a comparison needs to be made. (If you open the `Array.cs` file in Rotor, you can see where the comparator is used to initialize an internal class named `SorterGenericArray`, which in turn uses a quick sort algorithm to sort the array.)

Listing 16.11 Implementing `IComparer` to Sort an Array of Any Kind of Object

```
1:  Public Class StringComparer
2:     Implements IComparer
3:
4:     Private FProperty As String
5:
6:     Public Sub New(ByVal Value As String)
7:        FProperty = Value
8:     End Sub
9:
10:    Public Function Compare( _
11:      ByVal x As Object, ByVal y As Object) As Integer _
12:      Implements System.Collections.IComparer.Compare
13:
14:      Return GetString(x).CompareTo( _
15:        GetString(y))
16:
17:    End Function
18:
19:    Private Function GetString(ByVal o As Object) As String
20:       Return o.GetType().GetProperty(FProperty). _
21:         GetValue(o, Nothing)
22:    End Function
23:
24: End Class
```

First, it is worth pointing out that I could have implemented `ICom-parer` in the `Contact` class. However, my solution simulates that case where you may not have access to the source type, in this case, `Contact`. Additionally, my solution is so generic that I can reuse it for any class that has string properties.

I certainly could have written the comparator to know about the `Contact` class, but that isn't very advanced. Not only is it not advanced but also it would mean that I would have to write a comparator for other types. The solution here doesn't know anything about the `Contact` class. Instead I used Reflection to request a named property—provided as an argument to the constructor in line 6—and read and compared the same property in both objects, `x` and `y`. The constructor is told about the property to compare. The private method `GetString` uses Reflection to obtain the value of that string, and the `Compare` method, which satisfies our contract with `IComparer`, calls the `String.CompareTo` method. I want to return an integer indicating whether the comparison is less than, equal to, or greater than, and `String.CompareTo` does this.

When `StringComparer` is finished I can use it as a comparator for an array of any object's string properties. `StringComparer` is definitely "write once, use many times" code that shows the kind of power and flexibility available in Visual Basic .NET.

Using a `DataList` Control to Repeat Composite Controls

Early access to new technology is a nice benefit of writing computer books. Using .NET for several years now and having written well over 100,000 lines of production code, I have come to appreciate the simplicity and utility of controls like `DataList`. The `DataList` control is easy and powerful to use. However, if you are using it (or the `DataGrid` control) just to display data sets or simple arrays of data, you are missing out on a subtle power that is also readily available. I mentioned it earlier in the chapter. If you create composite controls from a user control, you can also use these composite controls as elements of a `DataList`, `Repeater`, or `DataGrid` control. That is, you can repeat complex user interfaces automatically by placing them inside of the `DataList` control. (For our purposes, understand that when I say `DataList`, I also mean `DataGrid` and `Repeater` too. You can use these techniques for `DataList`, `DataGrid`, and `Repeater` controls.)

Remember earlier that we elected to display one contact record at a time by using labels and text boxes? Well, we can also define the presentation by using labels and text boxes on a user control, placing the user control in a `DataList` control, and letting the `DataList` control repeat and manage paging for us.

Defining the Composite User Control

Our solution is comprised of three basic parts. We need a source of data. For this we'll use the `Contacts` data view we have been using all along. (All

Figure 16.11 The design-time results of Listing 16.12, shown with an exaggerated border and cell spacing and cell padding for clarity.

the code for this section is defined in `CompositeControlDemo.sln`.) We will need a user control defined to display one row of data in the `Contacts` data view, and we will need a Web page with a `DataList` control on it. The `DataList` control will be the recipient of the composite user control. Since we are reusing the `Contacts` data view from earlier in the chapter, we will start with the user control.

Implementing the User Control

We will use an HTML table with four rows and four columns to manage the layout of the `Contacts` composite control. Figure 16.11 shows that there is one control in each cell. The rhythm is a label followed by a text box for the data associated with that label. This is repeated a second time for each row. Because there are six fields in the `Contacts` data view, we will repeat this process for three rows. (Two columns by three rows yields the correct number of data elements in `Contacts`.) The last row has one cell that spans all four columns. I added a `<HR>` (horizontal rule) tag to that row to provide a visual cue to the user. The actual HTML to create this view is shown in Listing 16.12.

Listing 16.12 The HTML for the `Contacts` User Control

```
<%@ Control Language="vb" AutoEventWireup="false"
Codebehind="Contacts.ascx.vb" Inherits="CompositeControlDemo.Contacts"
TargetSchema="http://schemas.microsoft.com/intellisense/ie5" %>
<TABLE id="Table1" borderColor="black" cellSpacing="0"
cellPadding="2" width="100%" border="2">
  <TR>
    <TD align="right"><asp:label
    id="Label1" runat="server">Company Name:</asp:label></TD>
```

```
    <TD><asp:textbox
    id=TextBoxCompanyName runat="server"
    Text='<%# DataRow("CompanyName") %>'></asp:textbox></TD>
    <TD align="right"><asp:label
    id="Label2" runat="server">Country:</asp:label></TD>
    <TD><asp:textbox id=TextBoxCountry
    runat="server" Text='<%# DataRow("Country") %>'></asp:textbox></TD>
  </TR>
  <TR>
    <TD align="right"><asp:label
    id="Label3" runat="server">Title:</asp:label></TD>
    <TD><asp:textbox id=TextBoxTitle runat="server"
    Text='<%# DataRow("ContactTitle") %>'></asp:textbox></TD>
    <TD align="right"><asp:label id="Label4"
    runat="server">Name:</asp:label></TD>
    <TD><asp:textbox id=TextBoxName runat="server"
    Text='<%# DataRow("ContactName") %>'></asp:textbox></TD>
  </TR>
  <TR>
    <TD align="right"><asp:label id="Label5"
    runat="server">Phone:</asp:label></TD>
    <TD><asp:textbox id=TextBoxPhone runat="server"
    Text='<%# DataRow("Phone") %>'></asp:textbox></TD>
    <TD align="right">
      <asp:Label id="Label6" runat="server">Fax:</asp:Label> </TD>
    <TD>
      <asp:TextBox id="TextBoxFax" runat="server"
      Text='<%# DataRow("Fax") %>'>
      </asp:TextBox></TD>
  </TR>
  <TR>
    <TD align="right" colSpan="4">
      <HR width="100%" SIZE="1">
    </TD>
  </TR>
</TABLE>
```

Defining the Data Member

We won't be binding data to the user control. Instead we will be binding
data to a `DataList` control, and each time a row is created we will need to
send that row of data to the instance of the user control. This is a little
tricky, but by breaking it up into chunks I think you will see it isn't too hard.

For now all we need to do is acknowledge that the user control will be getting an instance of a `DataRowView` object—one row of data from the `Contacts` data view. We can add a public field to accept this value. I defined it in the code-behind file for the user control as follows:

```
Public DataRow As DataRowView
```

Defining the Binding Statements for the Controls

The final step for the user control is to get the data into the `TextBox.Text` property. We know that we can use a simple binding statement to accomplish this, and you already learned how to write binding statements earlier in the chapter. The data itself actually will come from the `DataRow` field we defined, so we can define the binding statements in the context of the `DataRow` field. The actual binding statements I used are set in bold in Listing 16.12. This is all we have to do to create the user control. Now we need to *use* the user control.

Defining the Web Page with the `DataList` Control

At this point the `DataList` control comes into play. We will add a `DataList` control to the default Web page from `CompositeControlDemo.sln`. The `DataList` control accepts the user control, and we'll bind the `Contacts` object to the `DataList` control. We'll use a binding statement to get each row of data from the `DataList` control into each instance of the user control. (Figure 16.12 shows the results at runtime.)

Follow these numbered steps to complete the example.

1. Add a `DataList` Web control to the page.
2. Set the `DataList` control's `Width` property to 100%.
3. Right-click on the `DataList` control and select Edit Template|Item Templates. (We will use the template editor to add our user control; we could accomplish the same thing by modifying the HTML directly. The template editor is easier to use.)
4. Drag the user control from the Solution Explorer to the ItemTemplate (Figure 16.13).
5. Since we added a `DataRow` property to the user control, we can define a binding statement for this field. (The binding statement is set in bold in Listing 16.13.)
6. Assign the `DataList.DataSource` property to the `Contacts` data view and call `DataList.DataBind`.

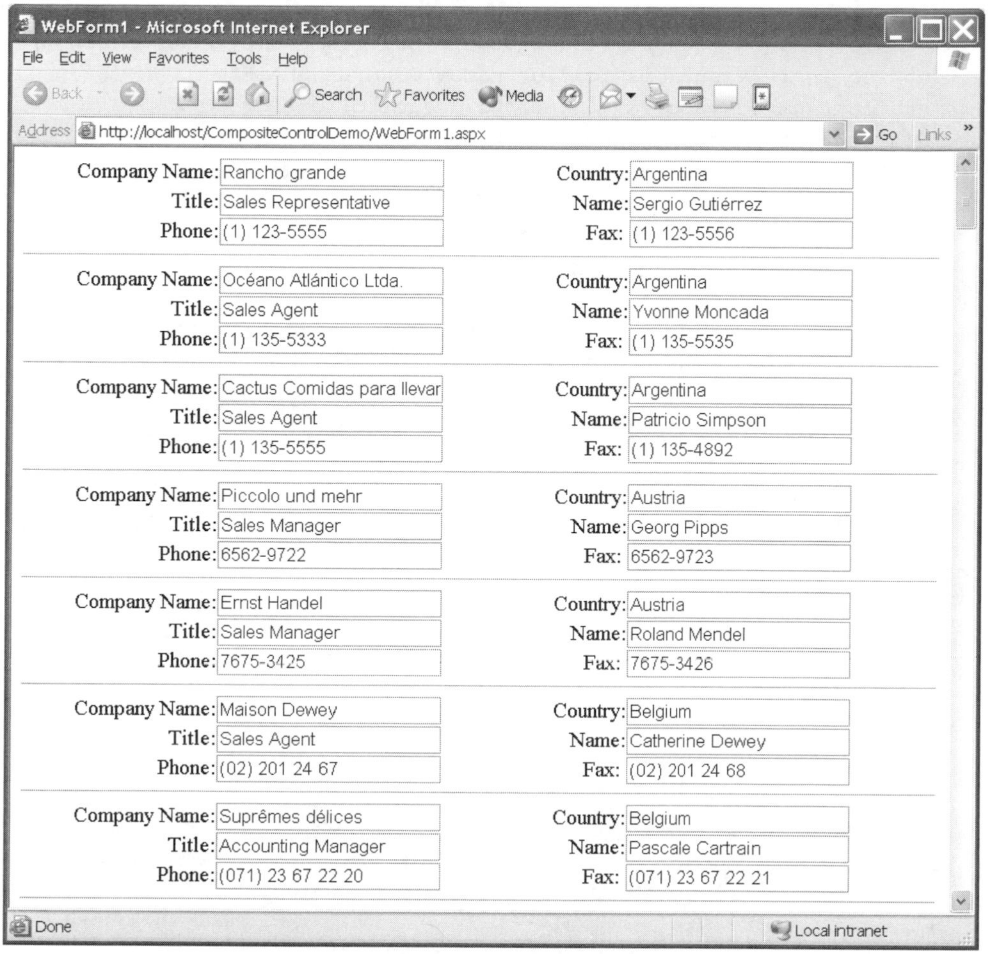

Figure 16.12 The `DataList` control automatically repeats the `Contacts` user control for us.

Listing 16.13 The HTML for the Web Page Demonstrating a Template Item

```
<%@ Register TagPrefix="uc1" TagName="Contacts" Src="Contacts.ascx" %>
<%@ Page Language="vb" AutoEventWireup="false"
Codebehind="WebForm1.aspx.vb"
Inherits="CompositeControlDemo.WebForm1"%>
<!DOCTYPE HTML PUBLIC "-//W3C//DTD HTML 4.0 Transitional//EN">
<HTML>
  <HEAD>
```

```
  <title>WebForm1</title>
  <meta content="Microsoft Visual Studio.NET 7.0" name="GENERATOR">
  <meta content="Visual Basic 7.0" name="CODE_LANGUAGE">
  <meta content="JavaScript" name="vs_defaultClientScript">
  <meta content="http://schemas.microsoft.com/intellisense/ie5"
  name="vs_targetSchema">
</HEAD>
<body MS_POSITIONING="GridLayout">
  <form id="Form1" method="post" runat="server">
    <asp:datalist id="DataList1"
    style="Z-INDEX: 101; LEFT: 8px; POSITION: absolute; TOP: 8px"
    runat="server" Width="100%">
      <ItemTemplate>
        <uc1:Contacts id=Contacts1 runat="server"
        DataRow="<%# Container.DataItem %>">
        </uc1:Contacts>
      </ItemTemplate>
    </asp:datalist></form>
  </body>
</HTML>
```

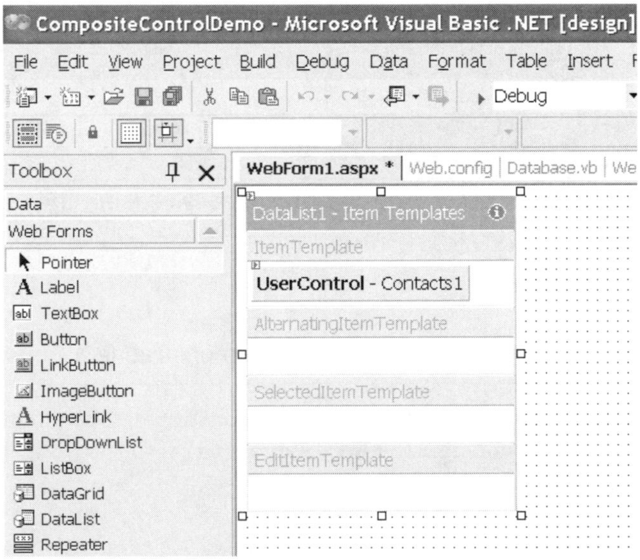

Figure 16.13 Adding controls to the ItemTemplate for a `DataList` control.

The user control is shown in bold font within the `<ItemTemplate>` tag. Understand the `DataRow` clause to be an assignment of the `Contacts.DataRow` user control.

There are several ways to get data into a user control used as a template. Using a binding statement is just one very direct way. Keep in mind that whether you accomplish this bit with a binding statement or in the code-behind file, all you are doing is assigning data to an object's property. It just isn't as clear in the HTML view.

I want to point out one more thing. If you recall, we put text boxes in the user control, and that control went into the ItemTemplate. If we wanted to make a clearer distinction between a browse view and an edit view, we could create two user controls, one with labels only and the other with text boxes. The labels-only version could be placed in the ItemTemplate, and the text-box version could be placed in the EditItemTemplate. This distinction would allow you to present a clearly editable version and a clearly read-only version.

To switch to edit mode you need to add a `LinkButton` object to the ItemTemplate, set the `LinkButton.CommandName` property to `Edit`, and implement a `DataList.EditCommand` event handler. In the `EditCommand` event handler, set the `DataList.EditItemIndex` argument to `e.Item.ItemIndex` (the event handler's argument index) and rebind the `DataList` control. This step will switch you to `EditItemTemplateControls`. To save your changes you will need a symmetric `Update LinkButton` object in the EditItemTemplate. When the user clicks the Update button, you will need to save your changes, set the `DataList.EditItemIndex` argument to `-1`, and rebind the `DataList` control.

I made a copy of `CompositeControlDemo.sln` (`CompositeControlDemo2.sln`) that demonstrates how to switch between a read-only view in the ItemTemplate to an edit view in the EditItemTemplate. I also added Cancel and Delete buttons to invoke the `Cancel` and `Delete` methods, respectively. Actually saving the modified changes was stubbed out for the example (and you can return to Chapters 11 and 12 for the update code). Figure 16.14 shows the revised example from `CompositeControlDemo2.sln`. Notice that the first row is in edit mode and is rendered with `TextBox` controls, while the rest of the page is rendered with labels.

TIP: If `Label` and `TextBox` controls are the only user controls you use in your code, you can create a version of just one control and use search and replace in the code-behind file and the HTML to replace all occurrences of `TextBox` with `Label` and vice versa.

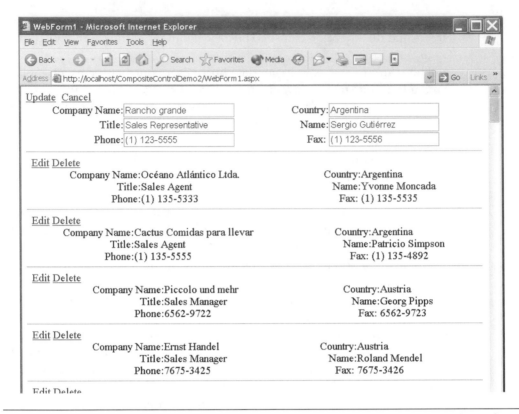

Figure 16.14 Two versions of a template control, one for editing (top row) and one for browsing (remaining rows).

Converting Bound Columns to Template Columns

You can manually define columns in a data grid if you prefer to design the columns rather than let them be autogenerated. Custom columns are defined by selecting from the available column types shown in Figure 16.9, adding those types to the selected columns list, and modifying the properties for the column. (We did this for the Contact Name and Phone columns in the `Contacts` data view earlier in the chapter.) When you do this you get basic text data in the grid cell. What I didn't mention is that you can convert a bound column to a template column by clicking on the link "Convert this column into a Template Column" (at the bottom of Figure 16.9). When you convert a column into a template column, you can add Web controls or composite user controls just as we did with the `DataList` control.

> **NOTE:** Of course, you can start with a template column if you know in advance that is what you want. Template Column is a type in the Available columns list in the DataGrid Properties dialog (Figure 16.9).

By combining bound columns and template columns with the rectilinear layout of the data grid you can create some advanced user interfaces. As is true with the `DataList` control, the `DataGrid` control will manage layout and repeating controls for you. For example, if we switch from `DataList` to `DataGrid` in `CompositeControlDemo.sln`, we can switch from returning and displaying all the contact information as a list to displaying it as a paged version of the same user interface—the `DataGrid` control will manage the paging for us. Figure 16.15 shows the results.

Recall all the work we did to manually implement paging by using the session cache and manually adding link buttons? Figure 16.15 shows that we can use a `DataGrid` control and a template column with a user control; the `DataGrid` control's inherent paging capability manages the paging for us. For ease of implementation and optimal performance we can combine the session cache to eliminate rehitting the database each time—and again the `DataGrid` control manages the paging for us.

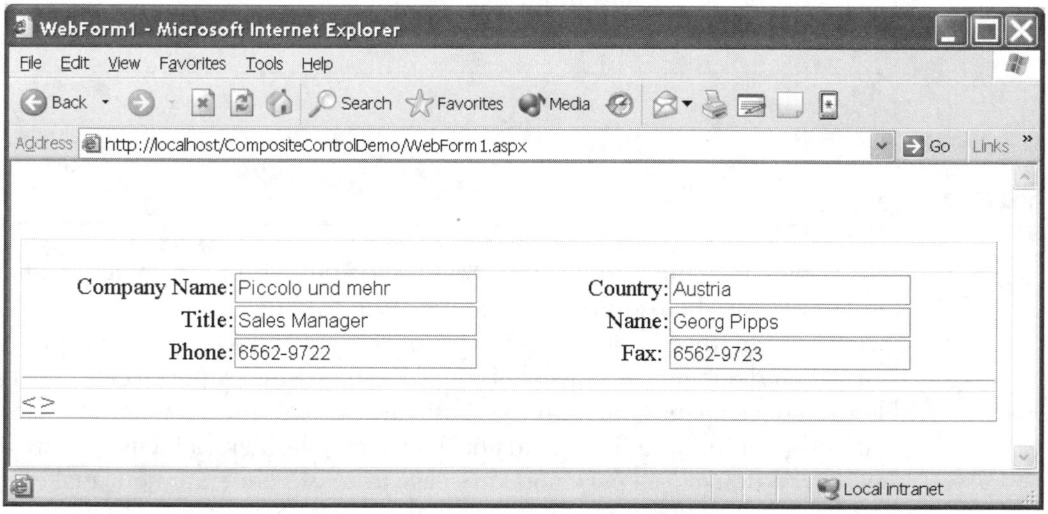

Figure 16.15 Using a `DataGrid` control to support paging through several instances of a user control used as a template. (The `PageSize` property is set to 1 in the example.)

To complete the visual effect, define styles for the grid regions and define header and footer templates. (Refer to Chapter 15 for more information.)

Managing Round-Trips to the Server

A Web page defines an `IsPostBack` property. You can poll the `IsPostBack` property to determine whether the page is being rendered as the result of a request or a user postback. For example, when we click the paging links for a `DataGrid` control, we are posting the page back, but the event handler is binding the `DataGrid` control. Hence we don't need to bind the `DataGrid` control in the `Page_Load` event a second time. You can use the `IsPostBack` property to eliminate the extra call to `DataBind`. Listing 16.14 demonstrates a `Page_Load` event that checks the `IsPostBack` property.

Listing 16.14 Using `IsPostBack` to Eliminate Extra Calls to `DataBind`

```
Private Sub Page_Load(ByVal sender As System.Object, _
   ByVal e As System.EventArgs) Handles MyBase.Load
   If (Not IsPostBack) Then
     DataGrid1.DataSource = New Contact()
     DataGrid1.DataBind()
   End If
End Sub
```

Summary

I was fortunate enough to have several discussions with Susan Warren and Rob Howard at Microsoft during many visits to the Redmond campus while working on another book. (Rob is a Wrox author and Microsoft Program Manager, and Susan is responsible for making the IBuySpy portal code available to all developers.) Early during these discussions Susan stated that composite user controls are the way to go. When you consider that a user control is as easy to design as a page and very easy to reuse, her statement makes a lot of sense.

Since those early discussions and after many hours of writing code for production and examples, I couldn't agree with her more. I have combined user controls with data grids and data lists with phenomenal success in terms of ease and time of implementation. This chapter described these fundamental techniques.

Define your user interfaces in chunks with composite user controls. By mixing and matching these user controls on pages or repeating them in other controls, you can create huge numbers of user interfaces in short order. Duplicating this basic strategy—using `DataList`, `DataGrid`, or `Repeater` controls of user controls—will allow you to create some very advanced and complex Web applications relatively easy. Perhaps as important, you can reorder the pages on the fly by loading the user controls dynamically. (Loading user controls dynamically was discussed in Chapter 15.) A great example of these strategies in practice is the IBuySpy portal code from Microsoft.

ADO.NET and ASP.NET are dance partners made for each other. Combining these two technologies provides you with superlative Web application development capabilities that significantly surpass historical ADO and ASP.

Debugging and Administration

Part IV explores the comprehensive diagnostics capabilities built into .NET and how to manage and employ code access security.

CHAPTER 17

Debugging .NET

An external enemy can be harmful to you today, but tomorrow could become very helpful, whereas the inner enemy is consistently destructive.

—His Holiness the Dalai Lama

Introduction

Several good books talk about debugging strategies. I could use this chapter to talk about such strategies in general, but then we couldn't explore the new debugging capabilities in Visual Basic .NET. So, given that choice, I'll discuss the latter. I recommend getting a book devoted to debugging if you don't already own one.

I will give you a piece of general advice: if you want bug-free code, don't write any bugs. This sounds a bit cheeky, but I have found that programmers who write singular, well-named, short methods end up with very few bugs.

A singular method is a method that does one thing. A well-named method uses a name that conveys exactly what the method does; such names usually rely heavily on verbs and nouns. A short method, as I use the term, has less than five lines of code. A good way to write code like this is to refactor, refactor, refactor. If you want to learn more about refactoring Visual Basic .NET, pick up my book *Sams Visual Basic .NET Unleashed* [Kimmel 2002b] or *Refactoring: Improving the Design of Existing Code* by Martin Fowler [2000].

There are many debugging features in .NET. Here I will cover as many of those capabilities as I can squeeze into one chapter.

Viewing Debug Windows

Knowing what your application is doing is the key to resolving problems efficiently. This has to do with the old adage that knowledge is power. Several

593

portholes allow you to peak into the viscera of your application as it cogitates. I will briefly review these here and leave the experimentation to you.

To provide you with a sufficient amount of code to debug I hacked together an object-oriented calculator. Listing 17.1 provides the code, which also appears in `DebugWindowsDemo.sln`. The calculator has nested classes, supports keyboard input, and uses classes for operands and polymorphic behavior for operators. For example, multiplication is represented as a `MultiplicationOperator` class. Because I hacked it together I am sure we will find some errors as we examine it. We will use the debugging capabilities of .NET to sleuth out as many bugs as we can in this chapter. (I'm sure you can find more. If you do find more bugs or contrive some nice revisions with refactoring, please let me know via e-mail at *pkimmel@softconcepts.com*.)

Listing 17.1 The Verbose Calculator Code for Debugging Practice

```
1:   Imports System.Text.RegularExpressions
2:
3:   Public Class Form1
4:       Inherits System.Windows.Forms.Form
5:
6:   [ Windows Form Designer generated code ]
7:
8:       Private Sub Number_Click(ByVal sender As System.Object, _
9:         ByVal e As System.EventArgs) Handles Button9.Click, _
10:        Button1.Click, Button2.Click, Button3.Click, _
11:        Button4.Click, Button5.Click, Button6.Click, _
12:        Button7.Click, Button8.Click, Button10.Click
13:
14:        Calculator.SendKey(CType(sender, Button).Tag.ToString())
15:
16:     End Sub
17:
18:      Private Sub ButtonExponent_Click(ByVal sender As System.Object, _
19:        ByVal e As System.EventArgs) Handles ButtonExponent.Click
20:        Calculator.Exponentiate()
21:     End Sub
22:
23:      Private Sub ButtonClearEntry_Click( _
24:        ByVal sender As System.Object, _
25:        ByVal e As System.EventArgs) Handles ButtonClearEntry.Click
26:        Calculator.ClearEntry()
27:     End Sub
```

```
28:
29:     Private Sub ButtonEquals_Click(ByVal sender As System.Object, _
30:       ByVal e As System.EventArgs) Handles ButtonEquals.Click
31:       Calculator.Summate()
32:     End Sub
33:
34:     Private Sub ButtonClear_Click(ByVal sender As System.Object, _
35:       ByVal e As System.EventArgs) Handles ButtonClear.Click
36:       Calculator.Clear()
37:     End Sub
38:
39:     Private Sub ButtonDivision_Click( _
40:       ByVal sender As System.Object, _
41:       ByVal e As System.EventArgs) Handles ButtonDivision.Click
42:       Calculator.Divide()
43:     End Sub
44:
45:     Private Sub ButtonAddition_Click( _
46:       ByVal sender As System.Object, _
47:       ByVal e As System.EventArgs) Handles ButtonAddition.Click
48:       Calculator.Add()
49:     End Sub
50:
51:     Private Sub ButtonMultiplication_Click(ByVal sender As _
52:       System.Object, ByVal e As System.EventArgs) _
53:       Handles ButtonMultiplication.Click
54:       Calculator.Multiply()
55:     End Sub
56:     Private Sub MenuItem5_Click(ByVal sender As System.Object, _
57:       ByVal e As System.EventArgs) Handles MenuItem5.Click
58:       Close()
59:     End Sub
60:
61:     Private Sub MenuItem6_Click(ByVal sender As System.Object, _
62:       ByVal e As System.EventArgs) Handles MenuItem6.Click
63:       Clipboard.SetDataObject(TextBox1.Text)
64:     End Sub
65:
66:     Private Sub MenuItem7_Click(ByVal sender As System.Object, _
67:       ByVal e As System.EventArgs) Handles MenuItem7.Click
68:        TextBox1.Text = CType(Clipboard.GetDataObject(). _
69:          GetData(GetType(String)), String)
70:     End Sub
71:
```

```
72:     Private WithEvents Calculator As Calculator
73:     Private Sub Form1_Load(ByVal sender As Object, _
74:       ByVal e As System.EventArgs) Handles MyBase.Load
75:       Calculator = New Calculator()
76:       AddHandler Calculator.OnSendKey, AddressOf SendKeyEvent
77:     End Sub
78:
79:     Private Sub SendKeyEvent(ByVal Sender As Object, _
80:       ByVal e As CalculatorEventArgs)
81:
82:       TextBox1.Text = e.Buffer
83:     End Sub
84:
85:     Private Sub Form1_KeyPress(ByVal sender As Object, _
86:       ByVal e As System.Windows.Forms.KeyPressEventArgs) _
87:       Handles MyBase.KeyPress
88:
89:       e.Handled = Calculator.SendKey(e.KeyChar().ToString())
90:     End Sub
91:
92:     Private Sub ButtonSubtraction_Click(ByVal sender As _
93:       System.Object, _
94:       ByVal e As System.EventArgs) Handles ButtonSubtraction.Click
95:       Calculator.Subtract()
96:     End Sub
97:
98:     Private Sub ButtonSign_Click(ByVal sender As System.Object, _
99:       ByVal e As System.EventArgs) Handles ButtonSign.Click
100:      Calculator.SendKey("±")
101:    End Sub
102:
103:    Private Sub ButtonDecimal_Click(ByVal sender As System.Object, _
104:      ByVal e As System.EventArgs) Handles ButtonDecimal.Click
105:      Calculator.SendKey(".")
106:    End Sub
107:
108: End Class
109:
110: Public Class CalculatorEventArgs
111:    Inherits EventArgs
112:    Public Buffer As String
113:    Public Sub New(ByVal NewBuffer As String)
114:      Buffer = NewBuffer
115:    End Sub
```

```
116: End Class
117:
118: Public Delegate Sub CalculatorEventHandler( _
119:   ByVal Sender As Object, ByVal e As CalculatorEventArgs)
120:
121:
122: Public Class Calculator
123:
124:   Private FLeftOperand As Operand
125:   Private FRightOperand As Operand
126:   Private FLastOperand As Operand
127:   Private FResult As Operand
128:   Private FOperator As Operator
129:   Private FBuffer As String = String.Empty
130:
131:   Public Event OnClear As EventHandler
132:   Public Event OnClearEntry As EventHandler
133:   Public Event OnAdd As EventHandler
134:   Public Event OnDivide As EventHandler
135:   Public Event OnExponentiate As EventHandler
136:   Public Event OnSubtract As EventHandler
137:   Public Event OnMultiply As EventHandler
138:   Public Event OnSummate As EventHandler
139:   Public Event OnSendKey As CalculatorEventHandler
140:
141:   Public Function SendKey(ByVal Key As String) As Boolean
142:
143:     Select Case Key
144:       Case "0", "1", "2", "3", "4", "5", "6", "7", "8", "9", "."
145:         If (FRightOperand Is Nothing = False) Then
146:           FRightOperand = Nothing
147:           FBuffer = String.Empty
148:         End If
149:
150:         If (IsNumeric(FBuffer + Key)) Then
151:           FBuffer += Key
152:           DoSendKey(FBuffer)
153:         Else
154:           FBuffer = "0."
155:           DoSendKey(FBuffer)
156:         End If
157:       Case "=", Chr(13)
158:         Summate()
159:       Case "+"
```

```
160:        Add()
161:     Case "-"
162:       Subtract()
163:     Case "*"
164:       Multiply()
165:     Case "/"
166:       Divide()
167:     Case "^"
168:       Exponentiate()
169:     Case "±"
170:       Multiply(-1)
171:     Case "C"
172:       Clear()
173:     Case "E"
174:       ClearEntry()
175:    End Select
176:   End Function
177:
178:   Private Sub DoSendKey(ByVal Value As String)
179:     RaiseEvent OnSendKey(Me, New CalculatorEventArgs(Value))
180:   End Sub
181:
182:   Private Sub ClearBuffer()
183:     FBuffer = String.Empty
184:     DoSendKey("0.")
185:   End Sub
186:
187:   Public Property LeftOperand() As Double
188:   Get
189:     Return FLeftOperand.Number
190:   End Get
191:   Set(ByVal Value As Double)
192:     FLeftOperand = New Operand(Value)
193:     FLastOperand = FLeftOperand
194:   End Set
195:   End Property
196:
197:   Public Property RightOperand() As Double
198:   Get
199:     Return FRightOperand.Number
200:   End Get
201:   Set(ByVal Value As Double)
202:     FRightOperand = New Operand(Value)
203:     FLastOperand = FRightOperand
```

```
204:    End Set
205:    End Property
206:
207:    Public ReadOnly Property Result() As Double
208:    Get
209:      Return FResult.Number
210:    End Get
211:    End Property
212:
213:    Public Sub ClearEntry()
214:      FLastOperand = Nothing
215:
216:      RaiseEvent OnClearEntry(Me, EventArgs.Empty)
217:    End Sub
218:
219:    Public Sub Clear()
220:      FLeftOperand = Nothing
221:      FRightOperand = Nothing
222:      FLastOperand = Nothing
223:      FOperator = Nothing
224:      ClearBuffer()
225:      RaiseEvent OnClear(Me, EventArgs.Empty)
226:    End Sub
227:
228:    Public Sub Add()
229:      If (Not ValidOperation(New AdditionOperator())) Then Return
230:      RaiseEvent OnAdd(Me, EventArgs.Empty)
231:    End Sub
232:
233:    Public Sub Subtract()
234:      If (Not ValidOperation(New SubtractionOperator())) Then Return
235:      RaiseEvent OnSubtract(Me, EventArgs.Empty)
236:    End Sub
237:
238:    Public Sub Divide()
239:      If (Not ValidOperation(New DivisionOperator())) Then Return
240:      RaiseEvent OnDivide(Me, EventArgs.Empty)
241:    End Sub
242:
243:    Public Sub Multiply()
244:      If (Not ValidOperation( _
245:        New MultiplicationOperator())) Then Return
246:      RaiseEvent OnMultiply(Me, EventArgs.Empty)
247:    End Sub
```

```
248:
249:    Public Sub Multiply(ByVal Value As Integer)
250:       If (IsNumeric(FBuffer)) Then
251:          FBuffer = (-1 * Convert.ToDecimal(FBuffer)).ToString()
252:          DoSendKey(FBuffer)
253:       End If
254:    End Sub
255:
256:    Public Sub Exponentiate()
257:       If ( Not ValidOperation( _
258:          New ExponentiationOperator())) Then
259:          Return
260:          RaiseEvent OnExponentiate(Me, EventArgs.Empty)
261:       End If
262:    End Sub
263:
264:    Private Function ValidOperation(ByVal Op As Operator)
265:       ' Case where we have a complete equation
266:       If (IsValid()) Then
267:          FLeftOperand = _
268:             FOperator.Perform(FLeftOperand, FRightOperand)
269:          If (TypeOf Op Is SummationOperator = False) Then
270:             FOperator = Op
271:             FBuffer = String.Empty
272:             FRightOperand = Nothing
273:          End If
274:          DoSendKey(FLeftOperand.Text)
275:          Return True
276:       ' Case where we have no operands
277:       ElseIf (FLeftOperand Is Nothing And IsNumeric(FBuffer)) Then
278:          FLeftOperand = New Operand(Convert.ToDecimal(FBuffer))
279:          FOperator = Op
280:          FBuffer = String.Empty
281:          Return True
282:       ' Case with a LeftOperand, no RightOperand, but one is ready
283:       ElseIf (FLeftOperand Is Nothing = False) Then
284:          If (IsNumeric(FBuffer)) Then
285:             FRightOperand = New Operand(Convert.ToDecimal(FBuffer))
286:             Return ValidOperation(Op)
287:          Else
288:             FOperator = Op
289:             FBuffer = String.Empty
290:             Return True
291:          End If
```

```
292:     Else
293:       Return False
294:     End If
295:   End Function
296:
297:   Public Sub Summate()
298:     If (Not ValidOperation(New SummationOperator())) Then Return
299:     RaiseEvent OnSummate(Me, EventArgs.Empty)
300:   End Sub
301:
302:   Private Function IsValid() As Boolean
303:     Return (FLeftOperand Is Nothing = False) And _
304:       (FRightOperand Is Nothing = False) And _
305:       (FOperator Is Nothing = False)
306:   End Function
307:
308:   Public Class Operand
309:     Private FNumber As Double
310:     Private FSet As Boolean
311:
312:     Public Sub New(ByVal Value As Double)
313:       Number = Value
314:     End Sub
315:
316:     Public Property Number() As Double
317:     Get
318:       Return FNumber
319:     End Get
320:     Set(ByVal Value As Double)
321:       FNumber = Value
322:       FSet = True
323:     End Set
324:     End Property
325:
326:     Public Overridable Property Text() As String
327:     Get
328:       Return FNumber.ToString()
329:     End Get
330:     Set(ByVal Value As String)
331:       FNumber = Convert.ToDecimal(Value)
332:     End Set
333:     End Property
334:
335:     Public ReadOnly Property IsSet() As Boolean
```

```
336:      Get
337:        Return FSet
338:      End Get
339:      End Property
340:
341:      Public Sub ChangeSign()
342:        FNumber *= -1
343:      End Sub
344:
345:      Public Sub Clear()
346:        FNumber = 0.0
347:        FSet = False
348:      End Sub
349:    End Class
350:
351:    Private MustInherit Class Operator
352:      Public Function Perform( _
353:        ByVal Left As Operand, ByVal Right As Operand) As Operand
354:        Return New Operand(GetResult(Left, Right))
355:      End Function
356:
357:      Protected MustOverride Function GetResult( _
358:        ByVal Left As Operand, ByVal Right As Operand) As Double
359:
360:      Public Overridable ReadOnly Property Sign() As String
361:      Get
362:        Return String.Empty
363:      End Get
364:      End Property
365:    End Class
366:
367:    Private Class MultiplicationOperator
368:      Inherits Operator
369:      Protected Overrides Function GetResult( _
370:        ByVal Left As Operand, ByVal Right As Operand) As Double
371:        Return Left.Number * Right.Number
372:      End Function
373:
374:      Public Overrides ReadOnly Property Sign() As String
375:      Get
376:        Return "*"
377:      End Get
378:      End Property
379:    End Class
```

```
380:
381:    Private Class DivisionOperator
382:      Inherits Operator
383:      Protected Overrides Function GetResult( _
384:        ByVal Left As Operand, ByVal Right As Operand) As Double
385:        Return Left.Number / Right.Number
386:      End Function
387:
388:      Public Overrides ReadOnly Property Sign() As String
389:      Get
390:        Return "/"
391:      End Get
392:      End Property
393:    End Class
394:
395:    Private Class MultiplicationOperand
396:      Inherits Operator
397:      Protected Overrides Function GetResult( _
398:        ByVal Left As Operand, ByVal Right As Operand) As Double
399:        Return Left.Number * Right.Number
400:      End Function
401:
402:      Public Overrides ReadOnly Property Sign() As String
403:      Get
404:        Return "*"
405:      End Get
406:      End Property
407:    End Class
408:
409:    Private Class SubtractionOperator
410:      Inherits Operator
411:      Protected Overrides Function GetResult( _
412:        ByVal Left As Operand, ByVal Right As Operand) As Double
413:        Return Left.Number - Right.Number
414:      End Function
415:
416:      Public Overrides ReadOnly Property Sign() As String
417:      Get
418:        Return "-"
419:      End Get
420:      End Property
421:    End Class
422:
423:    Private Class AdditionOperator
```

```
424:     Inherits Operator
425:     Protected Overrides Function GetResult( _
426:        ByVal Left As Operand, ByVal Right As Operand) As Double
427:        Return Left.Number + Right.Number
428:     End Function
429:
430:     Public Overrides ReadOnly Property Sign() As String
431:     Get
432:        Return "+"
433:     End Get
434:     End Property
435:   End Class
436:
437:   Private Class ExponentiationOperator
438:     Inherits Operator
439:     Protected Overrides Function GetResult( _
440:        ByVal Left As Operand, ByVal Right As Operand) As Double
441:        Return Left.Number ^ Right.Number
442:     End Function
443:
444:     Public Overrides ReadOnly Property Sign() As String
445:     Get
446:        Return "^"
447:     End Get
448:     End Property
449:   End Class
450:
451:   Private Class SummationOperator
452:     Inherits Operator
453:
454:     Protected Overrides Function GetResult( _
455:        ByVal Left As Operand, ByVal Right As Operand) As Double
456:        Return 0
457:     End Function
458:
459:     Public Overrides ReadOnly Property Sign() As String
460:     Get
461:        Return "="
462:     End Get
463:     End Property
464:   End Class
465:
466: End Class
```

I will elaborate on the code in Listing 17.1 as we proceed through the chapter. Normally I hate to put huge listings in a book. (Thick books are hard to carry around.) However, in this case I included everything (except the Windows Form Designer generated code) to illustrate the point that even moderately simple applications can yield huge numbers of lines of code that are extremely difficult to debug if the only tool you have is the ability to read the code. (I am working on a .NET project that will probably be a couple of hundred thousand lines when we are done.) Thus the more tools you can use to debug your code—and the simpler your code is—the more likely you will be able to resolve your problem in a timely manner.

Using the Locals and Autos Windows

Several windows let you examine your code as it runs. When your program is running in the IDE these windows are accessible through the Debug|Windows menu. Two such windows are the Locals and Autos windows. The Locals window shows all the variables defined within the current scope and context. The Autos window shows variables used in the previous and current statements. You can open either of these windows and modify values when your program is in break mode. Another helpful feature is that both the Locals window and the Autos window will show the return results of any functions within a particular function. If you think the return result of a function is causing your problems, you can modify the return result in either window and that new value will be returned from the function.

The most direct use of the Locals and Autos windows is to see what is going on with the currently relevant variables. If you use the Watch window (see the Using the Watch Window subsection below) to view contextually relevant values, you will have to add them to the Watch window, whereas contextually relevant variables are already in the Locals and Autos windows.

I used the Locals window to figure out why my ± button wasn't toggling the sign of the number in the calculator window. I wrote the original code as `Calculator.SendKey(241.ToString())`. I often get into trouble with things like ASCII key codes. Invoking `ToString` on a literal digit returns the string representation of that digit. Thus `241.ToString()` yields `241`. As a result I was sending the literal value `241` when what I wanted to send was the escaped code for ±. Since I couldn't recall how to get the special character into the editor, to get the job done quickly I had cheated and copied the special character from this Word document and pasted it as a string into my application. The Locals window showed me what was wrong—I had `241` instead of ± for the key value. Unfortunately the Locals window didn't tell me how to fix the problem.

NOTE: The escaped value 241 is the value for ± in DOS but not in Windows. The VB .NET code to use is `Chr(177)`. The `Chr` function converts a character code to a character, and 177 is the Windows code for the ± character.

Using the QuickWatch Window

The QuickWatch window is the debug window I use habitually. This window is hooked to Shift+F9 if your keyboard scheme is set to Visual Basic 6. (The default is Ctrl+Alt+Q, which is really confusing if people on the same project use different keyboard schemes and you begin typing on their keyboards.)

TIP: You can always access the QuickWatch window by selecting Debug|Quick-Watch.

Select a variable or expression in break mode and open the QuickWatch window. The expression and the evaluated name, value, and data type will be displayed in the window. You can enter new expressions or drill down into existing ones. Figure 17.1 shows the QuickWatch window for the `sender` argument of an event handler.

To simplify the calculator's code for the numeric keypad I used a trick that many programmers have used. I placed the value of the numeric button in the button's `Tag` property. The problem I encountered was that I kept getting 8 when I clicked the 9 button. I assumed correctly that I must have placed 8 in the 9 button's `Tag` property. The application was already running—otherwise I could have inspected `Tag` in the Properties window—so I added a breakpoint to line 14. By pressing the 9 button I forced the application to break and could quickly check the value of the `Tag` property.

Using QuickWatch is a good way to quickly verify (or not) an assumption about your application's state. There are some other ways too, but the QuickWatch window is the one I find most useful.

Using the Watch Window

The Watch window plays big brother to the QuickWatch window. The Watch window supports adding many expressions at a time, permitting you to observe the state of every value as your application runs. The items you add to the Watch window can be simple variables, complex objects, or expressions—including method calls—that yield a value. In this context all these things are referred to as *expressions*.

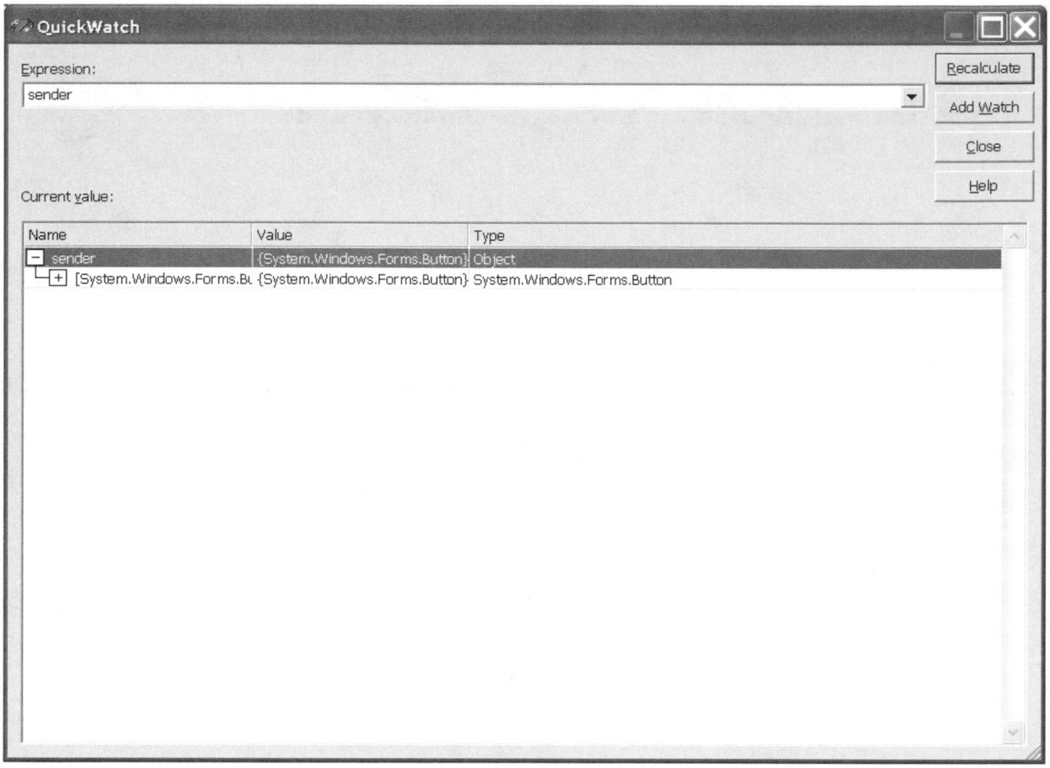

Figure 17.1 The QuickWatch window with the sender argument entered as the expression.

The Watch window is displayed at runtime from the Debug|Window|Watch menu item. You can add items to the Watch window by right-clicking on some code and selecting Add Watch or by typing the expression directly into the Watch window. The Watch window shown in Figure 17.2 contains an event argument, the value of the calculator's current LeftOperand, and a call to the shared regular expression Regex.IsMatch function. The last watch will let me know if there are any more instances of the Tag property with nonnumeric values. As you can tell from the last watch value, the expressions in the Watch window can be relatively complex. The Watch window will accept most expressions written in Visual Basic. Refer to the Visual Studio .NET help topic "Expressions in Visual Basic" for complete details.

Up to four Watch windows can be open at once, and you can add expressions to any one of them. I generally use only one Watch window at a time but perhaps slightly younger, more nimble minds can more easily focus on many tasks at a time.

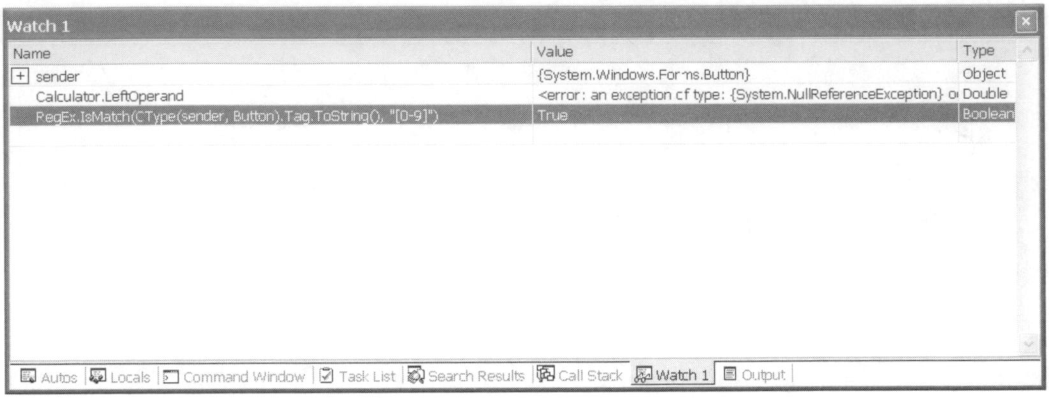

Figure 17.2 Adding expressions to the Watch window.

Using the Memory Window

The Memory window shows a memory dump. This kind of window was really quite helpful in assembly language, C, and C++ programming because we used a lot of pointers and addresses in those languages. I don't have occasion to use the Memory window too often in Visual Basic .NET, but it is there if you need it.

Using the Call Stack Window

The Call Stack window shows a stack of the recent method invocations that got you to the current point in your program. If you click on any line in the Call Stack window (Figure 17.3), the IDE will take you to that line of code. If the point in the stack is inside the CLR, you will be taken to a Disassembly window (see the related subsection below). The Disassembly window won't be that helpful even if you read assembly language because you can't modify the CLR. However, lines set in bold in the Call Stack window represent lines of source code you can edit.

The Call Stack window shows you the actual branch conditions taken by your application as it is running. This window is especially helpful for finding infinite loops because such an error will show up as a long list of calls to the same method.

You can insert breakpoints, run to a specific point in the Call Stack window, or show the Disassembly window all from the Call Stack window's context menu.

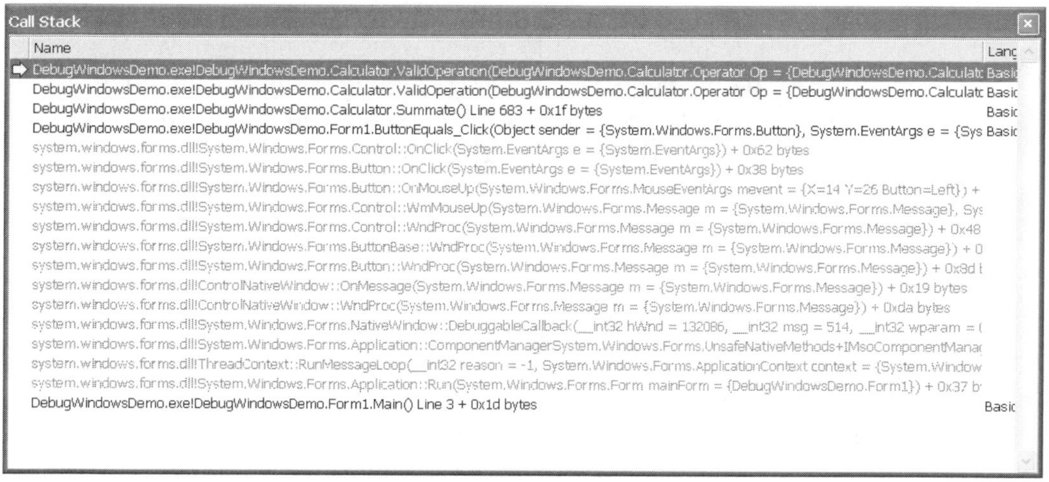

Figure 17.3 The Call Stack window showing the recursive nature of the calculator's `ValidOperation` method.

Using the Disassembly Window

Some languages like Object Pascal and C++ support integrating assembly language code. For example, Delphi's Object Pascal supports inline assembly interspersed with the Pascal code. However, Visual Basic .NET does not support mixing in assembly. Unless you are curious about what your Visual Basic code looks like as assembly or you want to see how many lines of assembly language a particular algorithm yields, you probably won't need this window much.

Using the Immediate/Command Mode Window

Probably all Visual Basic developers are familiar with the Immediate window. The Immediate window lets you enter VB .NET code directly in this window, and the IDE will execute the code. (Your application has to be running and in break mode for this to work.) What you may not be familiar with is the dual nature of the Immediate window in .NET.

When you select Debug|Window|Immediate, you get the Command window in Immediate mode. When you select View|Other Windows|Command Window, you get the Command window in Command mode. In reality they are the same window with different capabilities. Command mode is indicated by the presence of a > prompt. In Immediate mode that prompt is absent and the Command window caption reads "Command Window - Immediate". You can switch from Command mode to Immediate mode by typing the command `Immed`. You can switch from Immediate mode to Command mode by typing `>cmd` without the quotes.

So what can you do with this dual-mode window? I am glad you asked. In Immediate mode you can do many of the things you could do in VB6's Immediate window. For the most part you can run code, evaluate expressions, and print variable values. In Command mode, however, you can send commands to Visual Studio itself. For example, you can use Command mode to bypass the menus or send commands for menu items that don't appear in the menus.

The number of commands is huge. Fortunately when you begin typing a command an alphabetized drop-down list of commands appears. For example, if you type `File.AddNewItem` in the Command window, the Add New Item dialog will magically appear. Type just `g` for Go to resume your application after a breakpoint. If you type `alias`, you will see a list of shortcut aliases for longer commands, as is the case with `alias g` for `Debug.Start` (Figure 17.4). Another command that is not on the menu is `Tools.Shell`, aliased by `shell`. For example, `shell cmd` opens a DOS command prompt, and `shell devenv` opens another instance of Visual Studio .NET.

There are many interesting capabilities available directly from the Command window. If you need a break from programming, you may find some commands useful for the way you work. For example, the `Tools.LogCommandWindowOutput` command (`alias log`) allows you to send all input to and output from the Command window to an external text file. This might be

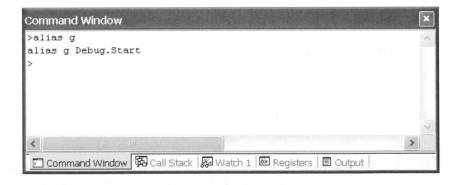

Figure 17.4 The `alias` command will list aliases, display the value of an alias (shown), or set new aliases.

useful when you need to go back and verify the things you have tried to solve a problem or to double-check the results of expressions you have previously examined. The syntax for `log` is `log filename [on|off] [/overwrite]`, where *filename* is the name and path of the log file, `on` and `off` indicate whether logging is on or not, and `overwrite` sets up an overwrite of an existing file with the same name. The complete list of commands is too extensive to cover here; refer to the "Visual Studio Commands" help topic for more details.

NOTE: VB6 supported expressions in the Immediate window at design time, whereas VB .NET does not. Another difference you might notice is that the Immediate window in Visual Studio .NET does not support Intellisense. In Visual Studio 6 the equivalent of Intellisense provided information about the objects and methods entered in the Immediate window.

Using the Output Window

The Output window (accessed by selecting View|Other Windows|Output) is used for a variety of purposes in the IDE. The most common uses are to show the build and compiler information and to display information from `Debug.Write` and `Debug.WriteLine` statements. The combobox at the top of the Output window can be used to select Output panes. There may be multiple panes to choose from depending on which tools in the IDE are using the Output window; by default you should see both Debug and Build choices in the panes combobox.

Managing Breakpoints

Breakpoints are the mainstay of application debugging. Press F9 on a line of code to toggle breakpoints on and off. Breakpoints are apparently one of the first things that programmers thought of when they created the operating system. Way back to MS-DOS and to this day, interrupt 3—a system–level function—is the debug, or breakpoint, interrupt. You can still insert an `int 3` instruction in an assembly language program (or even using the `debug.exe` application) and the program will break at that point. Fortunately, all we have to do is hit F9 and the mechanics are handled for us.

Adding a breakpoint to a line of code causes an application running in the IDE to stop at that line. The presence of a breakpoint is indicated by a small red circle in the margin of the Code Editor and a red background highlighting the line of code where the debugger will stop.

You can choose to set, enable, disable, edit, and delete a breakpoint. You can also manage breakpoints by using a conditional expression or hit count. Unfortunately, only Visual C++ seems to support data breakpoints. (A data breakpoint is a break set on a piece of data; when the data's value changes the debugger breaks.)

The Debug|Windows|Breakpoints window (Figure 17.5) is the easiest place to manage all the breakpoints in your application. For example, you can edit the breakpoint in line 491 (in the actual code, when the form generated portion is expanded) of the `Form1.vb` source file for the Calculator application by selecting Properties from the context menu. This opens the Properties window (Figure 17.6). You also have the option of right-clicking on the breakpoint line (highlighted in red) and selecting items from the context menu.

Two easy-to-implement and common modifications are (1) to break when a breakpoint has been hit a certain number of times, for example, near the end of a loop condition, and (2) to add an expression to the breakpoint, breaking when a condition is met at that point in your application. The default breakpoint—indicated when you press F9—is to always break without condition, as indicated in Figure 17.6. If you want to break on a condition, click the Condition button and indicate the condition. If you want to break after the breakpoint has been hit a certain number of times, click the Hit Count button and indicate the number of times. Figure 17.7 shows the Breakpoint Condition dialog, which indicates that the breakpoint should occur only when `ValidOperation(Op) = True`.

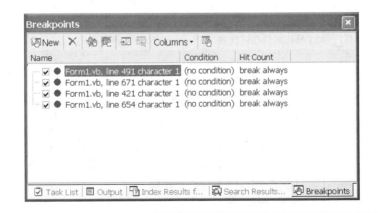

Figure 17.5 Use the Debug|Breakpoints window to manage all breakpoints in your application.

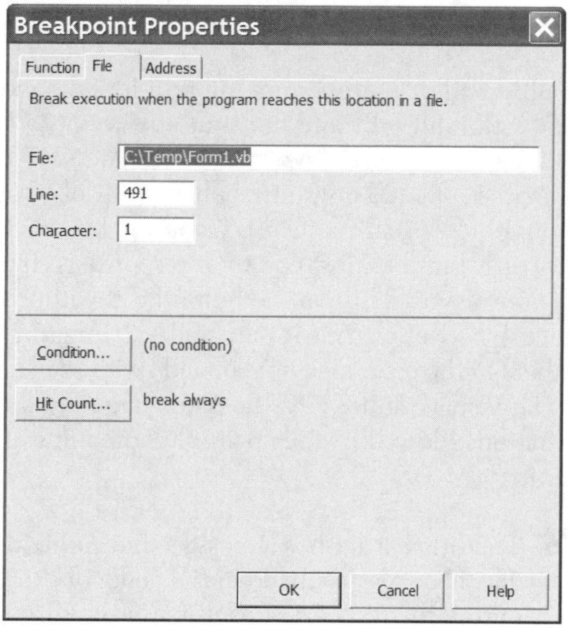

Breakpoint Properties

Function File | Address |

Break execution when the program reaches this location in a file.

File: C:\Temp\Form1.vb

Line: 491

Character: 1

Condition...   (no condition)

Hit Count...   break always

OK   Cancel   Help

Figure 17.6 Use the Breakpoint Properties window to fine-tune your breakpoints.

You will probably use a simple breakpoint most often, but if you discover an error that occurs only intermittently, it may be too tedious to break continuously. Under these circumstances conditional breakpoints help speed up debugging.

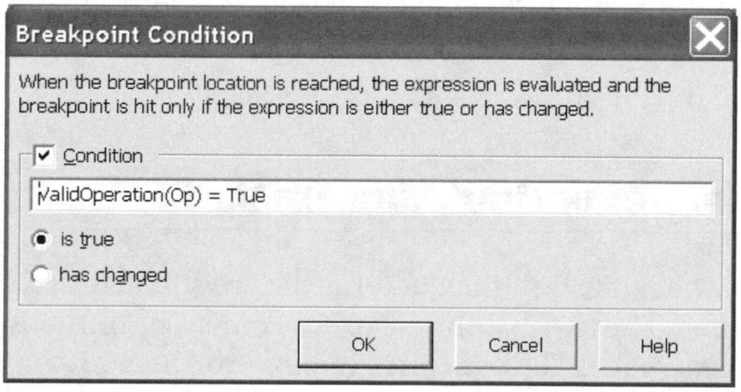

Breakpoint Condition

When the breakpoint location is reached, the expression is evaluated and the breakpoint is hit only if the expression is either true or has changed.

☑ Condition

ValidOperation(Op) = True

◉ is true
◯ has changed

OK   Cancel   Help

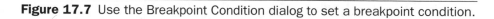

Figure 17.7 Use the Breakpoint Condition dialog to set a breakpoint condition.

Using Edit and Continue Behavior

Visual Basic .NET offers some support for edit and continue behavior; however, by default edit and continue behavior is disabled for Visual Basic .NET. This is one feature of Visual Studio .NET that is a bit misleading. If you enable edit and continue behavior (Tools|Options|Debugger|Edit and Continue) for Visual Basic .NET, you will be able to modify your code while debugging, but the most common response is that the changes are ignored until you restart. This can be helpful if it will prevent you from losing the changes you desire, but it may make debugging confusing since the line numbers in the code may not coincide with the references in the debug file.

The Visual Studio .NET help documentation under Edit and Continue, Limitations, describes four possible outcomes of using edit and continue behavior.

- The title bar flashes a message indicating the code is read-only.
- The changes are made in the code, but the debugger continues executing the old code, resulting in the discoordination between code and cursor positions during debugging.
- The changes are accepted, but the debugger stops and the code is rebuilt and restarted.
- The changes are made, but a dialog indicates that the changes cannot be made.

From the help files it is clear that edit and continue behavior is limited. The primary reason for this is that Visual Basic .NET is compiled instead of interpreted. It might be difficult to implement true edit and continue behavior in compiled code without recompiling. Fortunately, compiling even large applications does not take very long. In general, I use the edit and continue behavior to change code (rather than documenting changes to make later), but I usually have to restart shortly thereafter.

Debugging, Asserting, and Tracing

Debugging, asserting, and tracing are still mainstays of application debugging. These capabilities are tucked away in the `System.Diagnostics` namespace. The `System.Diagnostics.Debug.Write` and `System.Diagnostics.Debug.WriteLine` statements replace `Debug.Print` from Visual

Basic 6. The `Debug.Assert` shared method raises an exception if a condition fails. `Assert` is customarily used to ensure that application invariants—things that must be true about your application—remain true while your application runs. The `System.Diagnostics.Trace` class supports sending application trace information to a variety of locations.

NOTE: The `System.Diagnostics` namespace contains many more features than `Debug`, `Assert`, and `Trace`. However, these are old mainstays that every programmer needs to know.

Using the `Debug` Class

The `Debug` class is used primarily to send information to the Debug Output window while you are debugging your application in the IDE. There are also a couple of other capabilities like `Assert` (which we will talk about next) and a `Listeners` collection (see the Programming with Trace Listeners section later in the chapter). The `Listeners` collection allows you to define an Output window of your own. These Output windows are referred to as *listeners*.

`Debug.Write` and `Debug.WriteLine` are shared methods that facilitate keeping track of your application as it progresses without constantly breaking all the time. The benefit of using built-in capabilities like the `Debug` class is that Visual Studio .NET automatically manages the behavior in the design-time environment for you. For example, you can write `Debug.WriteLine` statements and leave them in place. When the DEBUG constant is defined and you are running your code in Visual Studio .NET, the `Debug` class will send information to the Output window. When you configure your application for release or run it outside the IDE, the `Debug` code is benign. The DEBUG (and TRACE) constants are defined in the Build Property Pages (Figure 17.8).

The `Debug` class is easy to use. Add a `Debug.WriteLine` statement and send any text you want displayed in the Output window to the `WriteLine` statement. For example, to use the `Debug` class in the Calculator application I could add a `WriteLine` statement after line 14 (in the originally blank line 15) in Listing 17.1. The following statement sends the value of the button's `Tag` property to the Output window. Figure 17.9 shows the results in the Output window after several buttons have been pressed.

```
Debug.WriteLine("Key:" + CType(sender, Button).Tag.ToString())
```

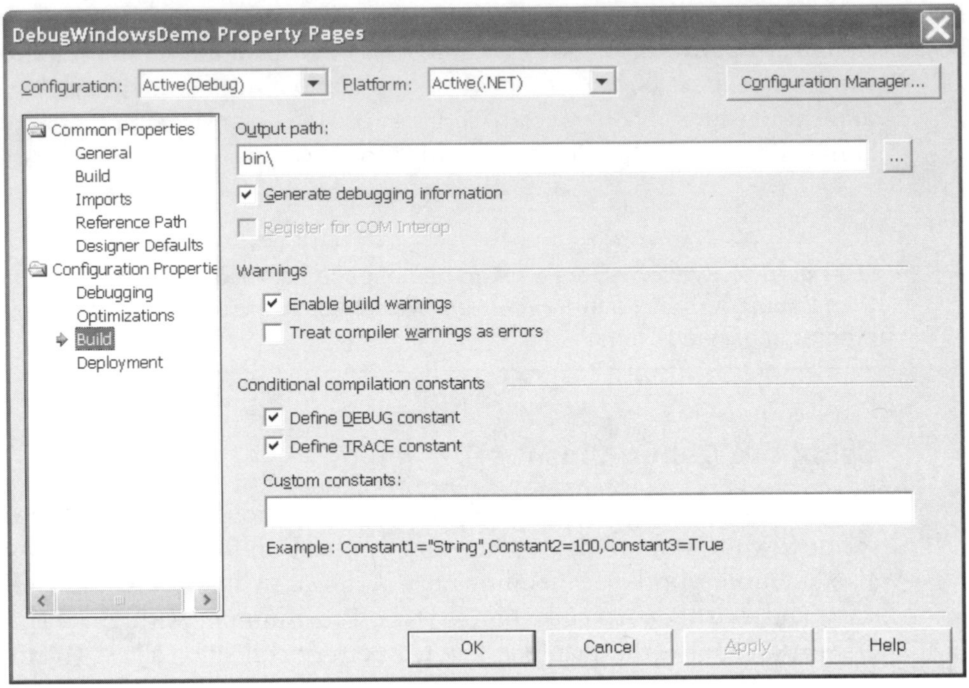

Figure 17.8 Use the Build Property Pages to manage conditional compiler constants like DEBUG and TRACE.

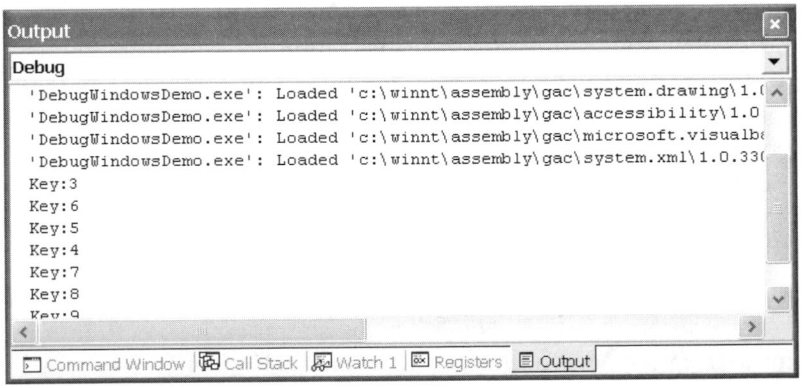

Figure 17.9 The Output window after pressing the 3, 6, 5, 4, 7, 8, and 9 buttons while the Debug.WriteLine statement is in place.

Using the `Debug.Assert` Method

A favorite quote of mine is from the book *No Bugs!* by Dave Thielen [1992]: "Assert the world!" If you understand what an assertion is, this makes sense to a certain degree.

The `Assert` method behaves precisely as the word *assert* suggests. *Assert* implies "to make sure," so applying computer-speak, *assert* means "to ensure that application invariants are true." To put it in a more colloquial vernacular, we use the `Assert` method to make sure that what we think about the state of the application is true, and if it is not, we want to know. `Assert` does this for us.

The `Assert` method in its simplest form accepts an expression and tells us when that expression evaluates to `False`. When told that our predetermined assumptions are false, we know that we have a logic error in the application. Thus, "Assert the world!" makes sense. For the Computer application, I could add an assertion to ensure that `Number_Click` gets only numbers between 0 and 9 inclusive. Listing 17.2 shows the revised `Number_Click` event handler with the assertion.

Listing 17.2 Adding an Assertion to a Method

```
Private Sub Number_Click(ByVal sender As System.Object, _
  ByVal e As System.EventArgs) Handles Button9.Click, _
  Button1.Click, Button2.Click, Button3.Click, _
  Button4.Click, Button5.Click, Button6.Click, _
  Button7.Click, Button8.Click, Button10.Click

  Calculator.SendKey(CType(sender, Button).Tag.ToString())
  Debug.WriteLine("Key:" + CType(sender, Button).Tag.ToString())
  Debug.Assert(CType(sender, Button).Tag >= 0 And CType(sender,
    Button).Tag <= 9)

End Sub
```

The meaning of the assertion is that the `Tag` value must be between 0 and 9 inclusive. If I accidentally assigned a nonnumeric button to this event or assigned a bad value to the `Tag` property, the `Assert` method would display an exception dialog with some options for continuing or stopping to resolve the problem.

If we want the Assertion Failed dialog (Figure 17.10) to contain additional, pointed information, we can add a text argument. For example, I could add the text `"Bad Number Key"` to the `Assert` method in Listing 17.2. This information would be displayed in the dialog, perhaps leading to a more pointed meaning of the stack trace.

With a modicum of creativity you can let your application do the hard work of debugging for you. A good strategy is to add calls to `Assert` as you are initially writing your methods. The first time you write a method you are likely to have greater insight about your perceived application's state than at any other time, other than when something goes wrong. However, if you use `Assert` at critical points, you will be able to quickly resolve inconsistencies between your assumptions and reality.

Using the `Trace` Class

The `Trace` class plays a cousin role to the `Debug` class. `Trace` is used to trace your code as it executes. There is a certain degree of overlap in the way that `Trace` and `Debug` are implemented in .NET because the relative

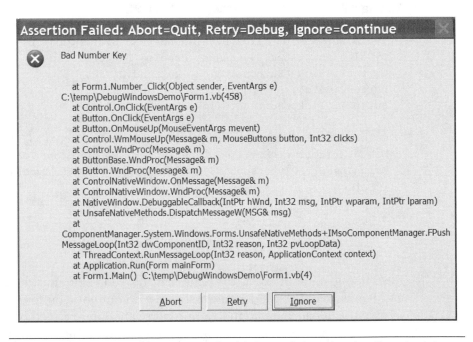

Figure 17.10 When an `Assert` method fails, a dialog showing the stack trace preceding the `Assert` statement is displayed by default.

capabilities are highly similar. To simplify the differences, think of De-bug.WriteLine statements and the Debug class as code meant for your use as a developer. Assume that the Trace.WriteLine method and the Trace class exist to help you diagnose a problem after your application has been deployed.

I use Trace to send information about the execution of my application to a log or some external resource, and I use the Debug.WriteLine and De-bug.Assert methods to provide me with an early warning about faulty assumptions. Note that this is a convention I follow out of habit based on older implementations of Assert and Trace rather than existing implementations of the Trace and Debug classes in .NET. Use Debug and Trace to your best advantage in .NET. Experimentation and circumstance will provide the best instruction.

Programming with Trace Listeners

Trace and Debug text has to go somewhere. We already know that by default Write and WriteLine information is displayed in the Output window. The Output window and other such recipients of Trace and Debug information are referred to as *trace listeners*.

It is clearly possible that some internal mechanism writes to the Output window directly, but this isn't exactly what happens. Both the Trace and Debug classes have a Listeners property that is a collection. Trace and Debug share the same underlying Listeners collection, so adding a listener to one class—for example, Trace.Listeners—effectively adds a listener to the other. There are four possible kinds of listeners: DefaultTraceListener (which is comprised of the Output window), TextWriterTraceListener, EventLogTraceListener, and any custom trace listener you define. A custom trace listener is any class that inherits from TraceListener and is added to a Listeners collection.

Every Listener collection already has the DefaultTraceListener added to it. A TextWriterTraceListener is literally an instance of the TextWriterTraceListener class initialized with any Stream class. The Stream class supports the mechanism for writing. Thus, to create a custom file-logging mechanism you can create an instance of the TextWriter-TraceListener and initialize it with a FileStream object; Trace and De-bug messages will be written to a file. The EventLogTraceListener directs Trace and Debug information to an event log, and a custom trace listener sends Trace and Debug information wherever you define it to go.

Let's go over a couple of examples that demonstrate how to use each kind of trace listener (except for the default `Trace` and `Debug` behavior supported by `DefaultTraceListener`, which doesn't need further explanation).

Creating a `FileStream` Trace Listener

It is reasonable to want to send information about the internal behavior of your application to some kind of external log file, so you can come back at a later date and time to diagnose your application. You can certainly create some custom mechanism as you may have done with VB6, or you can simply use `TextWriterTraceListener` and a `FileStream` object. (Think of a `FileStream` object as a representation of the data in a file in one continuously flowing rivulet, with a beginning and an end.)

For example, if we elect to log calculations made by the Calculator application to support an external auditor verifying the accuracy of the engine's calculations, we could log all the calculations and results and e-mail the file. Upon certification the calculator engine could be approved for use in calculating mortgage payments at a bank. (It could happen.) The steps we would need to take appear below.

1. Create a `FileStream` object.
2. Initialize `TextWriterTraceListener` with the `FileStream` object.
3. Add the listener to the `Trace.Listeners` collection.
4. Ensure we have some agreed-upon statements that trace the application's behavior, then let it rip.

Listing 17.3 shows code we might add to support sending calculation information to an external log file. To actually send messages to the log file all we need to do is include `Trace.WriteLine` messages as we normally would.

Listing 17.3 Initializing an Instance of `TextWriterTraceListener`

```
Public Sub New()
  Dim Stream As FileStream = _
    New FileStream("trace.log", FileMode.Create)
  Dim Listener As TextWriterTraceListener = _
    New TextWriterTraceListener(Stream)

  Trace.Listeners.Add(Listener)
  Trace.WriteLine("Calculator Constructor")
End Sub
```

The `FileStream` class requires the `System.IO` namespace, and `TextWriterTraceListener` comes to us from the `System.Diagnostics` namespace. The constructor in Listing 17.2 creates a new `FileStream` object, initializes a new trace listener with the `FileStream` object, and adds the `TextWriterTraceListener` instance to the `Trace.Listeners` collection.

Now if we add `Trace.WriteLine` (or `Trace.Write`) statements to our program, they will appear in the Output window and in a file named `trace.log`. For example, adding `Trace.WriteLine(Key)` to the `Calculator.SendKey` method included in Listing 17.1 will tell us about all the buttons and keys sent to the calculator. Listing 17.4 is a sample listing of the contents of the `trace.log` file after `Trace` statements were added to the Calculator application's `Constructor` method, `SendKey` method, and nested `Operand` constructor.

Listing 17.4 An Example of the `trace.log` File

```
Calculator Constructor
9
Key:9
New Operand: 9
8
Key:8
New Operand: 8
New Operand: 72
```

It is a good idea to call `Trace.Flush` before closing the application, especially when using a `FileStream` object. This ensures that all the trace data has been written to file. I usually add `Trace.Flush` to the form's `Closing` event. Because it is safe to call `Flush` on `Trace` whether or not we have created an additional listener, we don't have to worry about timing issues.

TIP: Normally we would want to hang on to a `FileStream` object and call its `Close` method. I double-checked Rotor and verified that `TextWriterTraceListener` does this for us when we use `FileStream` in conjunction with `TextWriterTraceListener`. If you use a `FileStream` object as a separate close, you will want to close the stream when you are finished using it. You can verify this information for yourself by checking out the `Dispose` method for the `TextWriterTraceListener` class in the Rotor file with the same name.

Using the `Trace` class and trace listeners for application logging means that you can effectively manage logging based on whether or not the `TRACE` constant is defined. To turn off tracing you don't have to remove all your important `Trace.WriteLine` statements; simply undefine the `TRACE` constant in the Build Property Pages (Figure 17.8).

Directing Trace Information to an Event Log

Instead of creating a custom log file format, why not use an existing format that comes with a known tool, the event log? Just as easily as we created the `TextWriterTraceListener` instance, we can create an `EventLogTrace-Listener` instance and use the Microsoft Management Console and snap-in to view our trace data as event log entries. Listing 17.5 shows an alternate constructor for the Calculator application that will send all our `Trace` statements to the event log. Note that I didn't change anything else about the sample code other than the revision to the constructor from Listing 17.3.

Listing 17.5 Using `EventLogTraceListener` to Send Data to the Event Log

```
Public Sub New()
  Dim Listener As EventLogTraceListener = _
    New EventLogTraceListener("Calculator")

  Trace.Listeners.Add(Listener)
  Trace.WriteLine("Calculator Constructor")
End Sub
```

The alternate constructor in Listing 17.5 creates an `EventLogTrace-Listener` instance. We need not modify any of our `Trace` statements; the results will now simply go to the event log in addition to anywhere else we may be sending `Trace` and `Debug` data. Figure 17.11 shows the event log version of one of the `Trace` statements output to the earlier `trace.log` text file (Listing 17.4).

You have to be circumspect when using the event log. If you send too much information to the event log, you are likely to fill it up and induce problems related to a full event log. (Refer to the Logging Application Events section later in this chapter for more information on using the event log.)

Creating a Custom Trace Listener

We need to define a new class that inherits from `TraceListener` to implement a custom trace listener. `TraceListener` requires that we provide an implementation for an overridable and overloadable version of a `Write` and `WriteLine` method. Inheriting from `TraceListener` and implementing `Write` and `WriteLine` is technically very easy. Deciding what to do with your custom trace listener is where the work is involved. How much effort you put into your listener is up to your imagination.

Listing 17.6 demonstrates a custom trace listener that dynamically creates a form with a text box; `Trace` information is sent to that form's `TextBox` control. As is the case with trace listeners in general, you do not have to change your `Trace` statements simply because you have added an additional trace listener to the `Listeners` collection.

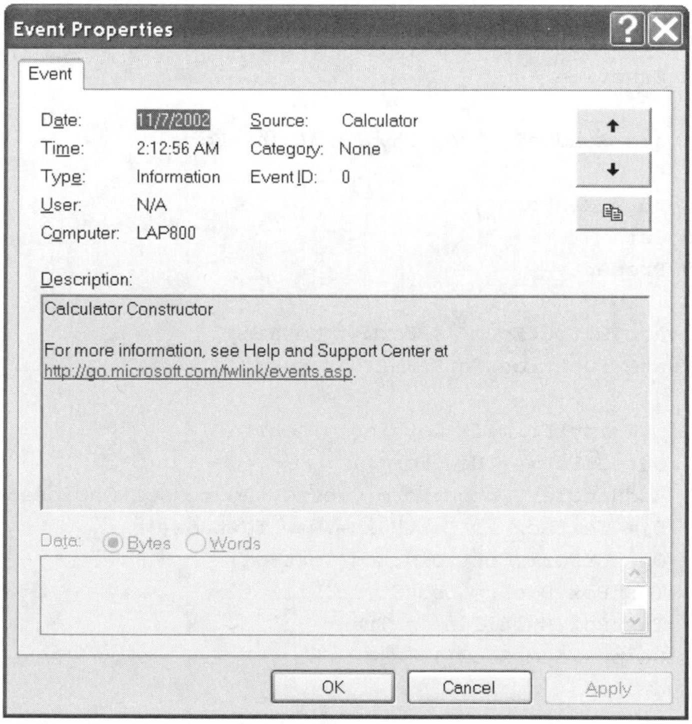

Figure 17.11 Trace information as it appears when written to the event log by using `EventLogTraceListener`.

Listing 17.6 Implementing a Custom Trace Listener

```
1:   Imports System.Diagnostics
2:   Imports System.Windows.Forms
3:
4:   Public Class MyListener
5:     Inherits TraceListener
6:
7:     Public Overloads Overrides Sub WriteLine(ByVal Message As String)
8:       Form.Controls(0).Text = Formatted(Message) + vbNewLine + _
9:         Form.Controls(0).Text + vbNewLine
10:    End Sub
11:
12:    Public Overloads Overrides Sub Write(ByVal Message As String)
13:      Form.Controls(0).Text = Formatted(Message) + _
14:        Form.Controls(0).Text
15:    End Sub
16:
17:    Private Function Formatted(ByVal Message As String) As String
18:      Return String.Format("{0}: {1}", DateTime.Now, Message)
19:    End Function
20:
21:    Private ReadOnly Property Form() As Form
22:    Get
23:      Return GetForm()
24:    End Get
25:    End Property
26:
27:    Private OutputForm As Form = Nothing
28:    Private Function GetForm() As Form
29:
30:      If (OutputForm Is Nothing) Then
31:        OutputForm = New Form()
32:        AddHandler OutputForm.Closed, AddressOf OnClosed
33:        Dim TextBox As TextBox = New TextBox()
34:        OutputForm.Controls.Add(TextBox)
35:        TextBox.Dock = DockStyle.Fill
36:        TextBox.Multiline = True
37:        OutputForm.Show()
38:      End If
39:
40:      Return OutputForm
41:    End Function
42:
```

```
43:    Private Sub OnClosed(ByVal sender As Object, _
44:       ByVal e As EventArgs)
45:
46:       OutputForm = Nothing
47:
48:    End Sub
49:
50: End Class
```

The requirements of inheriting the `TraceListener` class (line 5) are fulfilled by providing an implementation for `WriteLine` (lines 7 through 10) and an implementation for `Write` (lines 12 through 15). The rest of the code uses lazy instantiation—see `GetForm` in lines 28 through 41—to create a form with a text box as the actual recipient of the output text. (You can find the code for Listing 17.6 in the `MyListener.vb` source code file as part of the sample application for this chapter.)

TIP: Did you know that you can send `Trace` information to the console by initializing a `TextWriterTraceListener` instance with the standard output stream represented by `Console.Out`? Check out the `TraceListener.sln` file for a quick example.

Managing Debug Code with Boolean Switches

Most of us figured out at one time or another that we could use an external source—a text file, a `.ini` file, or the registry—to store external configuration information. Many clever programmers probably stumbled on this as a way to ultimately turn debug information on or off without rebuilding and redeploying an application. Well, now that you have mastered that trick, technology has evolved and we can accomplish the same thing more easily with an XML `.config` file and a class called `BooleanSwitch`. What you and I have been doing for years is finally part of the .NET Framework.

We shouldn't judge too harshly, though. For decades developers have been contriving idioms that solve problems and then become a standard part of programming. This is precisely how the Boolean switch evolved.

The `BooleanSwitch` class reads a `.config` file. If a value in the `.config` file indicates that the switch is enabled, the code wrapped within the

`BooleanSwitch` object runs; otherwise the code doesn't run. This is a convenient way to deploy code that contains self-diagnosing features and is probably a reasonable way to ship trialware. For example, make the switch a special Globally Unique Identifier. When the user registers the product, you send them the switch file that enables the trialware to run with all the features.

The basic mechanics of Boolean switches are first to define the entry in an `App.config` file (or `Web.config` for Web applications), then declare an instance of the switch in your code and wrap all conditional-run code inside a test determining whether or not the switch is on. To demonstrate in the next two subsections, let's use the `BooleanSwitch` class to manage the extra trace listener information in the Calculator application's constructor. If we enable the switch, the trace listener is created and used; otherwise, it is not.

Defining a Switch in an Application Configuration File

For Windows applications the `.config` file is identical to the application's name plus an additional `.config` extension. For example, the `Default-WindowsDemo.exe` application—the Calculator example—will look for an application configuration file in the same directory named `DefaultWindowsDemo.exe.config`. We can create a text file and add the XML directly to that file, but there is an easier way.

If we select the Application Configuration template from the Add New Item dialog, Visual Studio .NET will add an `App.config` file to the project's source code. When we compile the application, the `App.config` file will be output with the correct name—*application.ext*`.config`—in the correct location. All we have to do is add the switch information. Listing 17.7 shows the contents of the `.config` file with the Boolean switch defined.

Listing 17.7 The Contents of an `App.config` File for Managing a Boolean Switch

```xml
<?xml version="1.0" encoding="utf-8" ?>
<configuration>
  <system.diagnostics>
    <switches>
      <add name="UseListener" value="1" />
    </switches>
  </system.diagnostics>
</configuration>
```

The text set in bold represents the XML that I added. The remainder of the text was added automatically by the Application Configuration template. The `<system.diagnostics>` tag represents the XML namespace for the switch. The `<switches>` tag represents the section containing one or more switches, and the `<add>` tag names the switch and defines its state. For Boolean switches any nonzero value evaluates to an enabled switch; zero represents a disabled switch. You can also use `<remove>` and `<clear>` tags. The `<remove>` tag removes a named switch, and the `<clear>` tag clears switches defined higher in the configuration section. These might be switches that exist in the `App.config` file, literally preceding the `<clear>` tag, or in a `.config` file that has a larger scope (for example, the `machine.config` file).

Using a Boolean Switch in an Application

We need only one instance of the `System.Diagnostics.BooleanSwitch` class; all code in the same application can share that instance. After we initialize the shared `BooleanSwitch` object—to provide access to all interested code—we only need to check the `Enabled` property in a conditional statement to determine whether our switch is enabled. Listing 17.8 demonstrates a revision to the constructor from Listing 17.5, using the shared `BooleanSwitch` object to determine whether the `TraceListener` object should be created and added to the `Listeners` collection.

Listing 17.8 Using a Boolean Switch to Manage Debug Code after Compiling and Deploying

```
Private Shared Switch As BooleanSwitch _
  = New BooleanSwitch("UseListener", "Manage Trace Listeners")

Public Sub New()
  If (Not Switch.Enabled) Then Exit Sub

  Dim Listener As EventLogTraceListener = _
    New EventLogTraceListener("Calculator")
  Trace.Listeners.Add(Listener)
  Trace.WriteLine("Calculator Constructor")
End Sub
```

The `BooleanSwitch` object is defined as shared in the first statement. Notice that the first parameter matches the name of the switch from Listing 17.7.

(Case is not important for the switch name, but I try to match the case as well as the name.) The first statement in the constructor uses what I refer to as a *sentry*. The sentry works like a guard at a checkpoint who says, "The eagle soars" and lets you pass only if you respond, "Ever higher on a thermal." However, in this case the sentry allows admittance only if the `BooleanSwitch` object is enabled.

NOTE: It is interesting that the case of the switch's name need not match. But the `<system.diagnostics>` element must match exactly; that is, it must be in all lowercase or you will get a `ConfigurationException` at runtime.

You can use as many switches as you need or want. Simply define more switches in the `.config` file and instantiate a like number of `BooleanSwitch` objects in your code. Using Boolean switches is an excellent way to manage optional features, debug code, or some kind of diagnostics code after you build and deploy your application because all you need is a text editor to turn the switch—and by association the code—off or on. Note that you can use Boolean switches to manage Windows, console, and Web application code.

Logging Application Events

The event log is a single entity on a single computer. It is a reasonable candidate for a `Singleton` object, which is guaranteed to exist only once. (For example, `System.Console` is a `Singleton` object because there is only one console—think "command prompt"—on your PC.) However, instead of making a `Singleton` object out of the event log, Microsoft permits you to interact with the event log with predominantly shared methods. Additionally, you can create an instance of the `EventLog` class as you may want to do to send log information to a remote computer or a custom event log.

The event log is a repository for information tracking on a computer. Event information is broken into four general categories: the Application log, the System log, the Security log, and custom logs. The Application log contains user application information. The System log records things happening on the system in general. The Security log keeps track of information regarding the PC's security information. Finally, custom logs are any logs that you create (or an application creates on your behalf) for any use desired.

A good use of a custom event log is to log `Trace` and `Debug` information before you deploy your application. Using a custom log may be preferable to using the Application log to separate the entries made by your application from the general system noise introduced by other applications. There is another reason a custom log might be preferable for testing: writing a lot of entries may quickly exceed the capacity of the Application log, requiring you to clear the entries frequently. If you use the Application log, you may unwittingly delete other Application entries that you need to see in order to resolve some unrelated problem.

TIP: You can open the Event Viewer to view entries written to an event log from the Administrative Tools folder by selecting Start|Control Panel|Administrative Tools|Event Viewer or by typing `eventvwr.msc/s` at a command prompt.

Earlier I demonstrated how to use an `EventLogTraceListener` instance. By default `Trace` messages using `EventLogTraceListener` are written to the Application log. However, suppose we elect to use a custom log and want to send `Trace` and `Debug` information to that log? As an example, let's create a custom log for the Calculator application. We will start by looking at basic usage of the Event Log, then proceed to creating a custom log and associating it with our `EventLogTraceListener` instance.

Sending Information to the Event Log

The most challenging part about using the event log is to keep clear the distinctions between the machine name, log name, and log source. The machine name is the computer name. The period (`.`) refers to the local machine, or you can use an actual name like `LAP800`. The log name is literally a file with a `.evt` extension. For example, the Application log is the name of the `Application.evt` file used to store Application log entries. The tricky part is the source name. The source name must be distinct within a computer across all logs. For example, if we define the `Calculator` source in the Application log, we can have only one source named `Calculator` no matter how many logs we have.

NOTE: Log (`.evt`) files are stored on your hard drive, and log and source names are stored in the registry. `EventLog` registry entries are stored in `HKEY_LOCAL_MACHINE\SYSTEM\ControlSet001\Services\Eventlog`. Be sure to back up your registry before making any direct modifications.

To write to an event log you only need to invoke the shared method `EventLog.WriteEntry`. Pass the name of a unique source and some text, and the entry is written. For example, `System.Diagnostics.EventLog.WriteEntry("VB .NET", "Visual Basic is cool!")` will write the text "Visual Basic is cool!" to the Application log. Refer to the test application `EventLogDemo.sln` for some code to experiment with.

There are shared methods for determining whether an event log and source exist, and there are methods for creating and deleting logs and sources. Keep in mind that the source must be unique across all logs. The next subsection gives some examples of how to check for existing logs and sources and delete them if desired.

Defining a Custom Event Log

Suppose we elected to create a new log every time we ran the Calculator application. We could do this by checking for an existing source and deleting it if it existed, then checking for an existing log and deleting it if it existed. When we were sure that we had no preexisting custom log and source, we could then create new ones for the Calculator application to use. Listing 17.9 demonstrates interactions with the `EventLog` class that would support this specific behavior.

Listing 17.9 Recreating a Custom Log Each Time the Calculator Runs

```
Private Function GetLog() As EventLog
  Const Name As String = "Calculator"
  If (EventLog.SourceExists(Name)) Then
    Try
      EventLog.DeleteEventSource(Name)
    Catch
    End Try
  End If

  If (EventLog.Exists(Name)) Then
    EventLog.Delete(Name)
  End If

  Return New EventLog(Name, ".", Name)

End Function
```

The first step is to define a constant for the log and source names. The log and source names can be identical; we just can't have more than one log at a time with the same source registered. The next step is to ensure that no other log has this source defined. If the chosen source already exists, we want to delete it. (We have to be a bit circumspect here and make sure we don't delete the source for an important system application; such a maneuver might cause problems.) The second `If` block performs a similar operation, checking and deleting the custom `Calculator` log. You can check Event Viewer right before the `Return` statement near the end of Listing 17.9. You will see that there is no `Calculator` log immediately before the `Return` statement, and the `Calculator` log will appear after the `Return` statement executes. (You may need to refresh the Event Viewer or collapse and expand the list of logs before the new entry appears.)

Sending `Debug` and `Trace` Information to a Custom Event Log

When you have created the custom event log, you can use it as you would any other log, including simply writing entries to it. However, we decided to use our custom log as a trace listener. To send `Trace` and `Debug` information to the custom log we need to initialize the `EventLogTraceListener` constructor with the custom log. Simply pass the result of the `GetLog()` method as an argument to `EventLogTraceListener`—`New EventLogTraceListener(GetLog())`—to supplant the Application log with the custom log. Figure 17.12 shows the custom `Calculator` log with entries written by the Calculator sample program.

Using Performance Counters

Did you ever write a program that needed to check the available disk space, the free memory, or the status of a printer? When 640K was a lot of memory and hard disk drives had just started becoming popular, these kinds of checks were prevalent in software, at least software that didn't crash due to a lack of disk space or memory. These simple problems can occur, but in modern software we are just as likely to check TCP connections, threads, the status of IIS, Terminal Services, or the status of a service application.

Until recently programmers had to have some highly specialized knowledge of a lot of hardware and protocols to keep tabs on a wide variety of hardware and services. Fortunately, .NET captures all of this and more as *performance counters*. Performance counters converge the ability to measure an application's performance in the context of a computer and network

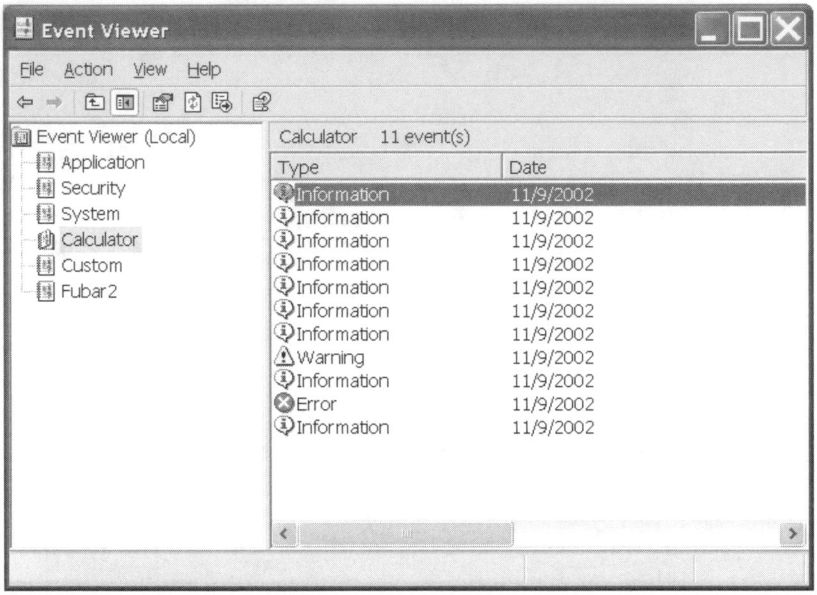

Figure 17.12 Log entries written when we invoke `Trace.WriteLine` and the `Calculator` log is used to initialize `EventLogTraceListener`.

into a common hierarchy of related interactions. If you examine the Server Explorer under the machine name, Performance Counters section, you will quickly see that it might be easier to figure out what can't be measured than what can be measured with a performance counter.

The key to using performance counters is to figure out what needs to be measured and then find the correct category of counter or counters. Finding the right counter is harder than using the counter because performance counters are components, and you can simply drag them onto your application to begin using them. For the most part everything else boils down to reading properties from the counter. You no longer have to know how to call some obscure API method to calculate available memory or disk-free space—just read the information from the appropriate performance counter.

The information available from each kind of counter is as varied as the counters are. `CategoryName` describes the category under which the counter is stored in the registry. `CounterName` describes what is being counted. `InstanceName` describes the instance of the counter if the same counter can be divided into different instances. For example, the percentage of time spent in the garbage collector (`% Time in GC`) is divided into two instances, the total time spent in the garbage collector (`_Global_`) and the amount of time Visual Studio .NET spends in the garbage collector (`devenv`). `MachineName` indicates the machine from which the counter is being read.

To demonstrate a performance counter we could express concern over using objects to represent operands and operators. (In our system this is not a real concern because we keep only two operands and one operator around at a time, but we might have valid concerns in a system with thousands or millions of instances of such objects.) We could use the `Available Mbytes` counter and display the amount of available physical memory in a status bar as our application is running. To include the `Available MBytes` performance counter I dragged the `Available MBytes` counter from the Memory category in the Server Explorer onto the main form for the Calculator application. I included a Timer to update the displayed value at one-second intervals. In the Timer's `Tick` event handler I wrote the value of the counter with some additional text explaining the scale of the counter. Listing 17.10 shows the event handler for the Timer and some extra code that displays the meaning of the counter as a tool tip in the status bar.

Listing 17.10 Displaying and Regularly Updating a Performance Counter Value in a Windows Application

```
Private Sub Form1_Load(ByVal sender As Object, _
  ByVal e As System.EventArgs) Handles MyBase.Load

  Calculator = New Calculator()
  AddHandler Calculator.OnSendKey, AddressOf SendKeyEvent

  ToolTip1.SetToolTip(StatusBar1, PerformanceCounter1.CounterHelp)

End Sub

Private Sub Timer1_Tick(ByVal sender As System.Object, _
  ByVal e As System.EventArgs) Handles Timer1.Tick

  StatusBar1.Text = PerformanceCounter1.RawValue & "M Bytes Available"

End Sub
```

Listing 17.10 comes from the completed Calculator example. (You can review the entire listing from 17.1—the `Timer1_Tick` event handler and use of the performance counter represents the revision—to regain context if you jumped to the middle of this chapter.) The `Load` event creates the `Calculator` object, adds an event handler, and sets the status bar's tool tip. In Visual Basic .NET tool tips are added by dragging a `ToolTip` control onto a form. This step dynamically binds a `ToolTip` property to `Controls`. You can literally set the dynamic `ToolTip` property in the Properties window or programmatically as shown in Listing 17.10.

The `Tick` event handler reads the current `RawValue` from the performance counter at regular intervals, adding some text to indicate what `RawValue` means, and assigns this information to the `StatusBar.Text` property. The net effect of using the tool tip, status bar, Timer, and performance counter in this way facilitates tracking memory usage as the application is running.

Using the `Process` Class

Less frequently now I venture back to VB6 to help someone or work on an existing application. Naturally I try to use some aspect of .NET and am quickly reminded of how much easier things have become in .NET. One such convenience is the `Process` class. The `Process` class facilitates spawning a new process. VB6 has the convenient `Shell` command, or we can use one of the API methods like `WinExec` for extended control, but comparatively the `Process` class seems tighter and more powerful.

Suppose we want to add a Tools menu to the Calculator application during debugging to facilitate examining the `Trace` information sent to the custom event log (refer to the earlier section Logging Application Events.) We could use the `Process` class to spawn an instance of the Event Viewer. This is much easier than remembering the forgettable `eventvwr.msc/s` command prompt trick. To demonstrate I added a Tools|View Event Log menu item to our chapter sample application. In the event handler for the menu's `Click` event I can invoke a named method, `ShowEventViewer`, that spawns the Event Viewer by using the `Process.Start` shared method. Listing 17.11 demonstrates how to start the external process.

Listing 17.11 Starting an External Application by Using the `Process.Start` Shared Method

```
Private Sub ShowEventViewer()
  Process.Start(Environment.SystemDirectory + "\eventvwr.msc", "/s")
End Sub
Private Sub MenuItem9_Click(ByVal sender As System.Object, _
```

```
    ByVal e As System.EventArgs) Handles MenuItem9.Click
    ShowEventViewer()

End Sub
```

The `Click` event for `MenuItem9` calls a named event. You could provide a more meaningful name for the menu, or as an alternative you could simply call a well-named method, which both facilitates comprehension and promotes reuse in a way a better menu item name won't.

The `ShowEventViewer` method calls the shared method `Process.Start`, passing the name of the process to start and arguments to that application. You could do something similar in VB6 with `Shell`; however, I find it especially convenient to be able to get the system directory—usually `C:\winnt\system32`—with the shared, read-only property `Environment.SystemDirectory`. All I have to do is concatenate the application (or file) to spawn. Clearly you could simply hard-code the `C:\winnt\system32\eventvwr.msc` path and filename and be right 95 percent of the time, but dynamically coding the path is better. And with VB .NET you don't have to remember which API to call to get environment variables or the system directory; this information is provided in a class. Very nice.

TIP: The `Environment` class is in the `System` namespace, and the `Process` class is defined in the `System.Diagnostics` namespace.

This kind of collective convenience promotes hyper-productivity. The .NET Framework is providing routine housekeeping for us so we can focus on solving new problems. (It would be great if we could simplify the keyboard in a like manner.)

Attaching to a Running Process

Occasionally you will need to start debugging a process that is already running. This has happened to me with ASP.NET applications. Every once in a while some inexplicable internal calamity will occur and I won't be able to start an ASP.NET application in debug mode. Instead of rebooting, which usually resolves the problem, I can start the application without debugging. (Start without Debugging is on the Debug menu immediately following the

Start menu.) After starting the application I can then successfully attach to the process and pick up debugging after the fact.

The key here is to know which process to attach to. If you are trying to debug a Windows application, you want to attach to the Windows process. If you are trying to debug an ASP.NET application, you can attach to the instance of Internet Explorer. After attaching, the debugger will stop on breakpoints and you can pick up debugging your application. Follow the numbered steps to attach to a running ASP.NET Web application and start debugging after the application is running.

1. Open Internet Explorer and browse to your Web application (or click Debug|Start without Debugging with the problematic project open).
2. Start VS .NET and open the project representing the Web site you are browsing.
3. Set any breakpoints in your code-behind file where you want the debugger to pick up.
4. Select Debug|Processes in VS .NET. From the Available Processes list select `aspnet_wp.exe` (ASP.NET Worker Process).
5. Click Attach and OK in the Attach to Processes dialog.
6. Close the Processes dialog.

When you perform an action that reaches a line of code with a breakpoint, the VS .NET debugger will break and the context will be switched to your code in VS .NET. (You can use the `AttachDebugger.sln` Web application to test attaching to a running process.)

TIP: A common cause of not being able to start with the debugger in ASP.NET applications is an error in the `Web.config` file. Double-check the `Web.config` file if the debugger won't start.

Attaching to a running process can be a useful trick when you are hot after a bug and can't start with debugging. Of course, you can restart VS .NET, restart IIS, or even reboot, but sometimes just getting the application started and debugging it will lead you to the problem that prevented starting with the debugger.

Debugging Windows Applications

Windows applications are the easiest to debug. You are working in the integrated environment, and Windows debugging tools are well developed. If you combine `Debug`, `Trace`, and `Assert` without breakpoints, you will find debugging Windows applications an almost enjoyable process.

Many of you have spent hundreds of hours debugging applications. Perhaps you have picked up books by Daniel Freedman and Gerald Weinberg [1990] or Dave Thielen [1992] for some advanced tips on debugging in general or worked as a tester when you were getting started. Thus I won't spend a lot of time talking to you about theory. (Besides, this isn't the best forum for that; a book on debugging would be better.)

I will tell you two secrets that work remarkably well for me, though, and you can make of them what you will. The first secret to minimizing bugs is to use objects. Even mediocre objects are better than structured code and global variables. The second secret, as I mentioned at the beginning of this chapter, is to keep your methods singular in nature and very short. A singular method is a method that does the one thing its name conveys, and a short method is short enough to comprehend at a glance. It is very hard to introduce bugs in short methods.

Debugging Web Applications

Debugging Web applications is easier in .NET because we are debugging Visual Basic .NET in the code-behind file, but it is still not easy. Debugging a Web application is harder than debugging a Windows application because we have several places to look for bugs. Pesky bugs can hide in the HTML, the code-behind file, some SQL stored procedure, or some script somewhere. Unfortunately, tools for debugging all these things are not as advanced as tools for debugging plain old VB code are.

Fortunately, there are some things you can do that may surprise you. You can set breakpoints in the HTML or ASP supporting a Web page or user control. You can use the same `System.Diagnostics` tools like `Trace`, `Debug`, and `Assert` that you can use in Windows applications, and you can step into stored procedures right in the Visual Studio .NET IDE, assuming you are using SQL Server. (Read Chapter 12 for more information on debugging stored procedures in VS .NET.) Script and SQL are probably the hardest things to debug because the integrated debugging tools for these two elements are as evolved as the integrated VB code debugger. To further mitigate this problem, try to eliminate or reduce your dependence on everything except code-behind. Of course, you won't be able to completely eliminate your dependence on SQL and script, but if you work from a reliable base of well-tested stored procedures and script, you can still constrain much of your debugging to new Visual Basic .NET code. Gratefully, the integrated debugger works just as well for Visual Basic .NET in Web applications as it does in Windows applications.

Debugging Multi-Language Programs

A very cool feature of .NET is the multi-language capability. I still hear discussions about which language is better, but I just don't think it matters that much any more. I don't know anyone (or any company) developing one application with language heterogeneity—for example, VB .NET and C#—in the same application, but you can do it. I have to be careful here because I haven't written an enterprise application that tests this presumption, but I have implemented Visual Basic .NET classes that inherit from C# classes and vice versa and traced through the source code in the debugger. Everything seemed to work fine. I have included a sample application in Listing 17.12 for you to play with; it is worth the "cool factor" alone.

TIP: A language must comply with the Common Language Specification to participate in cross-language interoperability.

Listing 17.12 A Multi-Language C# and Visual Basic .NET Demonstration

```
1:   // C# base class
2:   namespace TrafficControls
3:   {
4:     using System.Drawing;
5:     using System.Diagnostics;
6:
7:     public abstract class AbstractTrafficLight
8:     {
9:       public abstract void Draw(Graphics graphics);
10:
11:      public abstract class AbstractLamp
12:      {
13:        private Color color;
14:
15:        public AbstractLamp(Color color)
16:        { this.color = color; }
17:
```

```
18:        public Color Color
19:        {
20:          get{ return color; }
21:          set{ SetColor(value); }
22:        }
23:
24:        protected virtual void SetColor(Color value)
25:        {
26:          Debug.Assert(value == Color.Red
27:            || value == Color.Green
28:            || value == Color.Yellow);
29:          color = value;
30:        }
31:
32:        public abstract void Draw(Graphics graphics, _
33:          Rectangle r, bool isOn);
34:      }
35:    }
36: }
37: // Visual Basic .NET subclass
38: Imports System.Drawing
39: Imports System.Windows.Forms
40: Imports System.Drawing.Drawing2D
41:
42: Public Class TrafficLight
43:    Inherits TrafficControls.AbstractTrafficLight
44:
45:    Public Enum LightState
46:      Green
47:      Yellow
48:      Red
49:      Off
50:    End Enum
51:
52:    Private FState As LightState = State.Green
53:
54:    Public Property State() As LightState
55:    Get
56:      Return FState
57:    End Get
58:    Set(ByVal Value As LightState)
59:      FState = Value
60:    End Set
61:    End Property
```

```
62:
63:    Public Sub [Next]()
64:      FState = (FState + 1) Mod LightState.Off
65:      Debug.WriteLine(FState.ToString())
66:    End Sub
67:
68:    Private Lamps() As Lamp = New Lamp() _
69:      {New Lamp(Color.Green), New Lamp(Color.Yellow), _
70:       New Lamp(Color.Red)}
71:
72:    Public Overloads Overrides Sub Draw(ByVal g As Graphics)
73:
74:      g.FillRectangle(Brushes.Brown, New Rectangle(0, 0, 50, 160))
75:
76:      Dim I As Integer
77:      For I = 0 To Lamps.GetUpperBound(0)
78:        Lamps(I).Draw(g, New Rectangle(5, _
79:          ((2 - I) * 50) + 3, 40, 45), I = State)
80:      Next
81:      Next
82:    End Sub
83:
84:    Public Class Lamp
85:      Inherits TrafficControls.AbstractTrafficLight.AbstractLamp
86:
87:      Public Sub New(ByVal Color As Color)
88:        MyBase.New(Color)
89:      End Sub
90:
91:      Private Function GetBrush(ByVal isOn As Boolean) As Brush
92:        If (isOn) Then
93:          Return New SolidBrush(Color)
94:        Else
95:          Return New HatchBrush( _
96:            HatchStyle.DashedHorizontal, Color.Gray)
97:        End If
98:      End Function
99:
100:     Public Overloads Overrides Sub Draw(ByVal g As Graphics, _
101:       ByVal r As Rectangle, ByVal isOn As Boolean)
102:
103:       g.FillEllipse(GetBrush(isOn), r)
104:
105:     End Sub
```

```
106:
107:  End Class
108:
109: End Class
```

The 109 lines of sample code implement a rudimentary traffic signal with red, yellow, and green lamps. You can run `MultiLanguageDemo.sln` to see the lamp change colors at regular intervals. The code draws three colored circles inside a rectangle and is itself not very exciting. What *is* exciting is that these two files are in different assemblies (but in the same solution), and the VB .NET `TrafficLight` class inherits from the C# `AbstractTrafficLight` class. I made the code intentionally complex to test the multi-language capability and, in part, because I thought the solution made sense.

`AbstractTrafficLight` defines the concept of a traffic control comprised of illuminated (colored) lights. Because the light controls which lamps are on and which are off, I also implemented a nested `AbstractLamp` class. The VB .NET code mirrors the C# code by defining a `TrafficLight` class and a nested `Lamp` class. `TrafficLight` inherits from `AbstractTrafficLight`, and `Lamp` inherits from `AbstractLamp`. The code works perfectly, and debugging in and out of VB .NET and C# works flawlessly in Visual Studio .NET. I can easily use all the techniques we have discussed. (For example, line 65 demonstrates a `Debug.WriteLine` statement.)

Additional Topics

Reviewing the Debugging Object Model for Automation

Visual Studio .NET has a comprehensive extensibility model. This model includes macro capabilities as well as support for customizing Visual Studio .NET by programming against the Automation Model. The Automation Model includes objects for managing the integrated debugger and related concepts. The major objects in the EnvDTE supporting the Debugging Object Model are `Breakpoint`, `Debugger`, `Expression`, `Language`, `Process`, `Program`, `Stack Frame`, and `Thread`. You can read more about the Debugging Object Model by navigating to the `ms-help://MS.VSCC/MS.MSDNVS/vsdebugext/html/vxoriDebuggerObjectModel.htm` URL or searching for the Visual Studio Debugger Object Model in Visual Studio .NET help documentation.

Reviewing Available Debuggers

On no occasion so far have I found the integrated debugger lacking. However, you should be aware that other debuggers also ship with VS .NET, including the `Cordbg.exe` command-line debugger and the `DbgClr.exe` Windows debugger. `Cordbg.exe` is a text-based command-line debugger that was likely used to debug C# before VS .NET could do so, and `DbgClr.exe` probably had a similar role in testing Windows applications before VS .NET was ready.

`Cordbg.exe` is as cryptic as `debug.exe` (the old DOS-based debugger) but significantly more advanced. The command-line debugger would probably take quite a bit of practice to get used to; the `DbgClr.exe` Windows debugger looks and feels a bit like debugging in VS .NET. The VS .NET debugger contains substantial functionality and ease of use, but I suppose some could make an argument for using the command-line or Windows debugger just as some programmers make an argument for using *vi* (a common text-based UNIX editor still in use).

Summary

Debugging software is an expensive part of the maintenance process, which is itself a significant cost of software ownership. The more knowledgeable you are of the debugging process and the tools available that support debugging, the less time and effort you will spend finding and resolving bugs. Some well-known authors and developers have even suggested that testers should be at least as good at programming as the people who write the code themselves. I am inclined to agree that this would be a desirable state of affairs, but too often the only testing done is by the programmers. Thus we need to be well equipped to satisfy this unfortunate dual role.

In this chapter you learned that Visual Basic .NET has significant support for debugging and testing built into the Visual Studio .NET integrated debugger and classes in the `System.Diagnostics` namespace. A few of the capabilities are revamped mainstays, like `Debug`, `Trace`, and `Assert`. However, new capabilities like Boolean switches, the event log, trace listeners, and performance counters facilitate managing and discovering information about every aspect of your software before and after you deliver it.

CHAPTER 18

Code Access Security

Given enough eyeballs, all bugs are shallow.

—The Cathedral and the Bazaar, *Eric S. Raymond*

Introduction

More than a decade ago I used to write keyboard hooks. Placed on any DOS-based computer, a keyboard hook recorded every single keystroke, which made easy work of cracking e-mail accounts, logging into applications, and reading everything typed at that keyboard. For a month or two I played a few harmless pranks no worse than Fred and George Weasley of *Harry Potter* fame. In addition to being very successful I never came close to getting caught. (I also avoided pestering businesses; only fellow students and coworkers were fair game.) I quickly realized that this kind of tomfoolery could lead to serious trouble and that if I were able to manipulate operating systems and software so easily, I might be able to make a good living and avoid an unnecessary trip to the Lompoc or Danbury Federal Penitentiaries. Unfortunately there are hundreds, perhaps thousands of very intelligent people who either haven't grown up or have accepted a missionary zeal for hacking and mischief.

That's right. Some hackers are smart. They may even be some of the cleverest programmers around. Being a firm believer in a limited number of conspiracies, I wouldn't be surprised if a few of these clever hackers work in places that produce antivirus software or opposing forces operating systems, as well as in government agencies. This is big business, and we know that occasionally even agencies at the highest echelon participate in conspiracies. Ask Gordon Liddy.

For this reason security requires a holistic approach. Security is not Microsoft's problem alone. It is everyone's problem, and although the press would like to heap the blame squarely on the shoulders of Microsoft because such stories sell papers, many of the best hacks came from and probably do still come from the UNIX world. Did you ever write `while(1) fork();` and compile it with `gcc`, the UNIX command-line compiler? It will shut down an improperly configured UNIX network every time. If your company is relying on Microsoft to provide a foolproof, one-size-fits-all, whiz-bang security system, your company will suffer eventually, despite all the help Microsoft can provide.

Good security requires a combination of practices that include limited physical access to hardware; published and enforced policies relating to source code and data, especially if taken offsite; limited access to resources via VPNs, FTP, Telnet, and other dial-in connections; a separation of database servers and Web servers, placing a firewall between each physical server; careful management of Windows users and groups, especially administrative accounts; source code that checks for buffer overruns; application of the latest security patches and upgrades; and a hawkish diligence and proactive attitude toward security. In other words, if something must be protected, you need an expert—specifically a pedantic, super-paranoid expert capable of recommending, implementing, and enforcing security practices to the annoyance of all reasonable developers. You need the kind of person most developers will, ironically, find to be a bit of a nuisance. Security personnel are the police officers for your data. (And who doesn't find a police officer occasionally annoying, especially when you get pulled over because you failed to signal within a hundred feet of a turn and your birthday happens to coincide with Fat Tuesday and it is midnight? Personally, I love the police—but I digress.)

I don't profess to find security thrilling. I am one of those people who find the kind of security expert we need annoying because true security fanatics are zealots, and they often create speed bumps for productive programmers. Generally, I prefer a pragmatic approach to security, which is to apply what I believe to be a reasonable and sufficient amount of security tuning. As an architect I tend to rationalize trade-offs between cost of development and overkill, whereas a true security fanatic will likely find insufficiencies in any amount of security.

For our purposes here we will refine our discussion to some of the new features in .NET security, specifically *code access security*. Due to a limited amount of space I will assume that you have some knowledge of role-based security and management of Windows user accounts and groups. If you need a comprehensive presentation on security practices as a whole, I recommend *.NET Framework Security* by Brian LaMacchia et al. [2002].

What Is Code Access Security?

Code access security does not replace existing security; it is complementary. Code access security complements Windows security by describing the permissible behavior of code.

It is clear that Windows security describes what users and groups are permitted to do. If you are an administrator, any (unmanaged) code running while you are logged on can do anything that you can do as an administrator. The identified problem is that not all code originating from all locations can be equally trusted. If you write code on your disconnected, nonnetworked PC, you can trust it to do what you program it to do. The same is not true for code originating from someone else or, worse, somewhere else, like the Internet.

Code access security layers in permissions relative to what code is allowed to do, constrained by an administrable security policy and the origin, or zone, from whence the code originates. For example, by default, code originating from your machine has more privileges, and code originating from an intranet zone or Internet zone has fewer privileges.

Suppose, for example, you are logged in as an administrator. You, as an administrator, are permitted to modify or wipe out the registry. If you run some unmanaged code as an administrator, that code can wipe out the registry (or file system) too. Code access security works by setting a policy that dictates what code is permitted to do.

The relationship between code access security and Windows security is akin to the relationship between federal and state laws. Windows security represents federal laws, and code access security represents state laws. If the federal government outlawed the sale of alcohol, no state could make the sale of alcohol permissible. However, since the federal government currently permits the sale of alcohol, some states—or smaller groups within states, such as counties and cities—could prohibit or limit its sale. (I remember passing "Bernie's Last Chance" while driving south on Dixie Highway in Kentucky, then later encountering the same establishment as "Bernie's First Chance" while heading back north. Hazard County in Kentucky is a dry county, or at least it was when I lived there.) In other words, states can make laws that are more restrictive than federal laws but not less restrictive.

This is true relative to Windows security and code access security. If the Windows permissions provided to you limit the installation of software, for instance, then code access security cannot grant it. Windows wins. However, if Windows is silent on the issue of installing software—for example, with administrative privileges—then the code access security policy could still prevent software installation.

In short, the rule is that code access security can be more restrictive than Windows security but not less restrictive, and code access security applies these restrictions to code, not users, as long as that code is managed code. This raises the question: What is the difference between managed and unmanaged code?

Quite simply, managed code is .NET code, and unmanaged code is everything else. When you run a .NET executable assembly, a loader program loads the CLR into memory. All .NET code runs within the CLR. (Thus managed code is code run within the CLR.) Code access security and security policies are not applied to unmanaged code. Keep in mind, though, that managed code can run unmanaged code through COM Interop. Fortunately, the code access security policy allows you to specify whether or not managed code is permitted to run unmanaged code.

Naturally, then, code access security policy is very important for managed code that originates from very risky zones—the Internet and intranet—to low-risk zones like your disconnected PC. As a result, if you are building stand-alone applications that run on a single PC, especially one that is not connected, you can tolerate the relatively low risks of remaining a bit ignorant of code access security. However, the more connected you are, the more information you will need to acquire about security in general and code access security specifically.

Programming Defensively

Recall that I said that security is a holistic problem. It is not simply a matter of tuning Windows security and code access security; we need to consider how we write code too. Let me take a moment to address the "how" part of programming.

If a programmer writes classes with all public members, this code is at risk. The risk, again, is relative to the exposure to the outside world. For this reason, assigning moderately low-skilled object-oriented programmers to work on critical systems is like playing Russian roulette with a semiautomatic: every round is a loser. Additionally, if the DLLs that make up a system are downloaded to the client's PC, as is the case with smart clients (see Chapter 10) or various forms of .NET Remoting (see Chapter 8), the code can be reverse-engineered and explored. Worse, the code can be incorporated into new applications that subclass your types, bastardizing the original intent. For example, shadowing an existing behavior or overloading a polymorphic behavior can create a new behavior that easily supplants the original behavior. If new behavior, say, sends credit card numbers to folks who don't mind breaking a few laws, you have big problems. (And these are just a few ideas I came up with in a minute or two.)

To prevent a perversion of your code, it is critical that you understand where your code is going and how access to behaviors is provided. Here are a couple of good strategies you can use in any system to help reduce the risk and enhance the benefit of code access security, as well as the plethora of other security strategies available.

- Program with interfaces; use interfaces on client machines to prevent clients from having most of the actual code. If they don't have it, it will be harder to reverse-engineer.
- Use a façade that converges your framework to a few necessary, simple interactions. Fewer ingress points means less to protect.
- Make all data private, and permit access to fields only through properties. Code access security can be applied to classes and methods but not fields. (Properties are really methods.)
- Limit the number of public methods, and carefully evaluate behaviors that are protected and virtual. This prevents overloading intended behaviors with new undesirable behaviors.
- Avoid hiding secrets in your code. Embedded passwords, user names, account numbers, and the like will ultimately be discovered and shared.
- Make regular expressions a dietary staple. You can prevent buffer overruns, embedded special characters, and poor-quality or malicious data from entering your system with regular expressions. Give careful consideration to the idea of validating all input data against regular expressions (see Chapter 4). This is a powerful first line of defense.

TIP: Providing a façade for your business rules framework also means that your framework will be more easily used by other developers on your team since they will have fewer options to consider. For more on the façade pattern, refer to Erich Gamma et al. [1995], *Design Patterns*.

With few ingress points via your façade, a careful evaluation of Windows permissions, limited access to binaries, no embedded secrets, and input data carefully filtered with regular expressions, you are ready to take full advantage of code access security. Let's begin with a look at how to manage security policy.

Managing Security Policy

Levels of Security Policy

There are four levels of security policy: application domain, user, machine, and enterprise. The application domain security policy is subordinate to the user security policy, which is subordinate to the machine security policy, which in turn is subordinate to the enterprise security policy.

The Application Domain Security Policy

The application domain security policy is the result of an evaluation of security policy when an assembly is loaded by the CLR. Application domain policy is not configurable; rather, it is the security policy set applied to an assembly after each of the other three policies is evaluated.

The User Security Policy

The user security policy is the lowest level of configurable policy and is maintained for each user. Again, using the analogy of federal versus state laws, user policy can restrict but not expand machine-level policy.

The user security policy is literally maintained in `%USERPROFILE%\Application data\Microsoft\CLR Security Config\[version]\security.config` as XML, where `[version]` refers to a specific version of the CLR, for example, v1.0.3705. (Each version of the CLR has a security configuration file.) `%USERPROFILE%` is an environment variable. The value of an environment variable can be determined by typing `set variable` at a command prompt. For example, `set USERPROFILE` will typically display something like `C:\Documents and Settings\your_user_name`.

The Machine Security Policy

Whereas the user security policy sets the security policy for the user, the machine security policy sets the policy for the entire machine. The machine policy overrides the user policy.

The machine policy is literally maintained in `%WINDIR%\Microsoft.NET\Framework\[version]\Config\Security.config`. The environment variable `%WINDIR%` is usually `C:\WINNT`.

The Enterprise Security Policy

The enterprise security policy is the highest-level policy. The enterprise policy can be found in `%WINDIR%\Microsoft.NET\Framework\[version]\Config\enterprisesec.config`.

As the highest-level policy, if the enterprise policy defines a code access security permission, subordinate policies may not override it. When an App-Domain is created for one or more assemblies, the enterprise, machine, and user policies are combined to determine what the security policy is for a specific AppDomain.

Modifying Security Policy

Enterprise security policy is not automatically disseminated to individual machines. If the administrator wants to establish an enterprise policy different than the default, the policy modifications must be disseminated to the individual machines. However, before the default policy is changed the default policy should be evaluated and desired new outcomes should be established.

It is worth noting that modifying security policy can literally prevent Visual Studio .NET or .NET assemblies from loading and running. Consider making an incremental backup of each `.config` file before modifying it. This way if a specific policy change causes problems, just that change can be rolled back. Also, keep in mind that you can reset the policy to the default settings if you get stuck. Let's take a moment to talk about ways to modify the policy since there are several tools for doing so.

Modifying `Policy .config` Files

You can modify policy files by using any text editor, like `Notepad.exe`. However, you need to be very comfortable with XML configuration files and security policy management in general. This approach is not recommended but is available.

Modifying Policy by Using `caspol.exe`

.NET ships with a command-line utility for managing security policy, `caspol.exe`. To modify security policy using `caspol.exe`, open the Visual

Studio .NET Command Prompt, and run `caspol.exe`, passing the parameters that describe the new policy configuration information. This may be a good way to go if you need to automate policy settings as part of a custom configuration process. However, a better way to automate policy changes is to create a `.msi` Windows Installer package that modifies policy settings.

TIP: The Visual Studio .NET Command Prompt is a command prompt that sets environment settings that enable you to run .NET utilities by adding environment information that points to the directories containing these utilities.

You can get more information on `caspol.exe` from the Visual Studio .NET integrated help or by typing `caspol.exe /?` at the Visual Studio .NET Command Prompt. Table 18.1 contains a few commands that will provide you with quick information.

We haven't talked about things like code groups and permission sets specifically. We will in a few minutes. First let's wrap up the utilities available for setting security policy.

Modifying Policy with the Microsoft .NET Framework Wizards

If you want to quickly modify policy to trust a specific assembly, you can run a wizard. Using Windows XP, select Start|Control Panel|Administrative Tools|Microsoft .NET Framework Wizards|Trust an Assembly. (The steps are similar in other Windows operating systems.) This wizard will walk you through a step-by-step process that will permit you to trust an assembly for a particular user or the machine, modifying the appropriate policy `.config` file as a result. I provided a specific example that demonstrates this approach in Chapter 10. (Refer to that chapter's subsection titled Adjusting Security Policy for Application Assemblies if you need assistance with the Trust an Assembly wizard.)

Table 18.1 Helpful `caspol.exe` Commands

Command	Description
`caspol -l`	Lists code groups and permission sets
`caspol -lg`	Lists code groups only
`caspol -lp`	Lists permission sets only
`caspol -lf`	Lists fully trusted assemblies, like those that make up the .NET Framework
`caspol -ld`	Lists group names and descriptions

Modifying Policy with the .NET Framework Configuration Tool

Perhaps the easiest and most reliable way to manage security policy is by using the Microsoft .NET Framework Configuration tool. To open this tool select Start|Control Panel|Administrative Tools|Microsoft .NET Framework Configuration or type `mscorcfg.msc` at the Visual Studio .NET Command Prompt.

The Configuration tool is a Microsoft Management Console plug-in that offers a graphical way to modify every aspect of code access security policy. It provides a list of options relevant to a specific group or permission, as well as general operations that facilitate security management. To view a list of general security policy options expand the Runtime Security Policy node and right-click on that node (Figure 18.1). The New and Open menu items permit you to create a new security policy or adjust an existing policy, respectively. Reset All resets all policies to their original configuration values. Adjust Security runs the Security Adjustment wizard. The Evaluate Assembly item evaluates a specific assembly and tells you what the application domain policy will be for that assembly. (For example, select `System.Windows.Forms.dll` and the permissions granted will be unrestricted.) Trust Assembly runs the

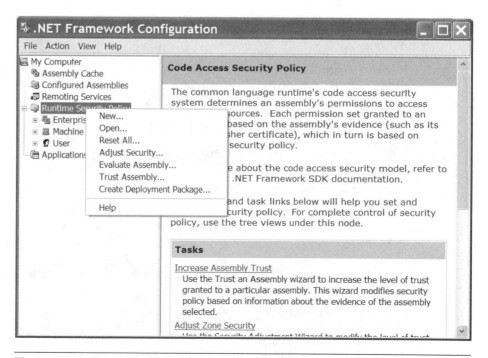

Figure 18.1 The Runtime Security Policy node of the Microsoft .NET Framework Configuration tool.

Trust an Assembly wizard, and Create Deployment Package exports policy settings to a Windows Installer package for deployment.

By expanding the Runtime Security Policy node you can quickly see that security policy is organized by enterprise, machine, and user policies. Expand any of these nodes in turn and you will see that each of the policy levels is further subdivided into code groups, permission sets, and policy assemblies. The code groups define criteria that code must meet to be part of a group. The criteria are determined by the assembly's evidence, which is comprised of assembly metadata including the application's installation directory, cryptographic hash, software publisher, host site, cryptographic strong name, URL, and zone, such as intranet zone. If an assembly meets the criteria for membership in a particular code group, the policy for that group is applied to the assembly. The permission sets contain grouped permissions by name. Policy assemblies are .NET assemblies that contain custom permissions or membership conditions and dependent assemblies that define the custom policy.

As suggested, it is preferable to ascertain whether or not existing policies are suitable for your assemblies before modifying policy settings. When you do begin to experiment with these settings, be sure to make backup copies of the `.config` files. Note that the most recent prior version of a policy file is stored with a `.config.old` extension. For example, if you modify the `enterprisesec.config` file with the Microsoft .NET Framework Configuration tool, the previous values will be stored in `enterprisesec.config.old`. It is also worth noting that changes are stored in the policy files as soon as you have modified the policy in the Configuration tool.

Creating a Windows Installer Package to Manage Security Policy

Suppose you have the responsibility of administering enterprise policy. You can fine-tune the enterprise policy section on a specific machine and create a `.msi` Windows Installer file to deploy that policy to other machines in the enterprise.

To create a deployment package for the enterprise policy follow these steps.

1. Click on the Runtime Security Policy node in the Microsoft .NET Framework Configuration tool.
2. Select the Create Deployment Package menu item.
3. In the Deployment Package wizard dialog, check the enterprise policy level and provide a path and filename ending in `.msi` for the deployment package.
4. Click Next and then click Finish.

After you complete the steps above, a Windows Installer file will be created at the specified location. Running this installer package will update the security policy for the level selected. In our example, the enterprise policy will be updated to coincide with the policy exported to the deployment package.

Permitting Downloaded Assemblies to Run

A practical problem you are likely to run into is an inability to run .NET assemblies downloaded from the Internet. Microsoft modified the default policy settings in .NET Service Pack 1 to prohibit code from the Internet to run directly.

For example, if you browse to *http://www.sellsbrothers.com/wahoo/wahoo.exe* to play the Tetris-like Wahoo! game, you will likely get a `PolicyException` dialog similar to that shown in Figure 18.2. (If you don't get an exception it may be because you have not installed .NET Service Pack 1, you ran the Windows Installer from that site while working through Chapter 10,

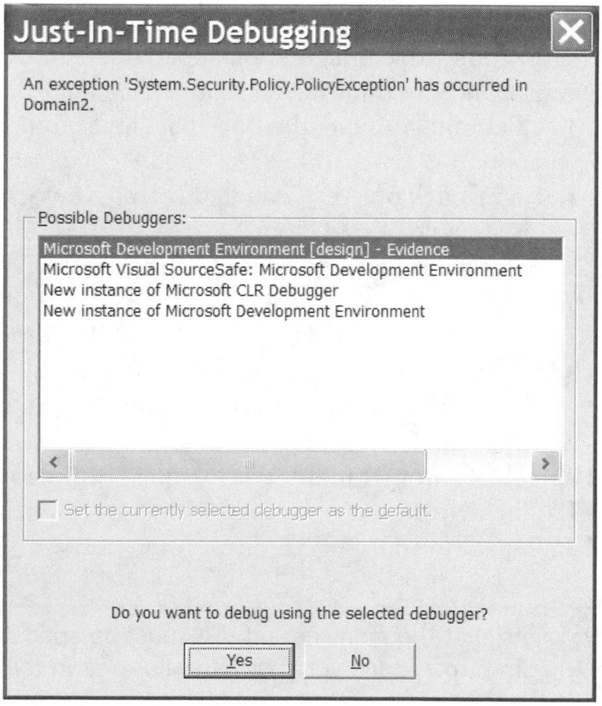

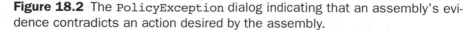

Figure 18.2 The `PolicyException` dialog indicating that an assembly's evidence contradicts an action desired by the assembly.

or your security policy was adjusted to be more lax.) The exception occurs because the `Wahoo.exe` evidence resulted in the code being placed in the Internet zone.

We could run the Windows Installer from the Wahoo! page to update the security policy. However, this won't help us understand how to configure security for ourselves. Instead we will modify the security policy manually to gain some experience.

Our object is to permit `wahoo.exe` to run. Of course, we could make security wide open by allowing applications in the Internet zone to run. However, remember that policy is accumulative. As a result, all the changes we make over time add up to make our systems more or less vulnerable. It is preferable to open the smallest gap necessary to achieve our specific purpose. In the case of the Wahoo! game this might mean that we permit only a single, specific version of `wahoo.exe` to run for a single user. To demonstrate a possible alternative, let's adjust the policy to allow assemblies from a specific URL to run. Follow the numbered steps to permit assemblies from *http://www.sellsbrothers.com/wahoo/* to execute for a specific user.

1. Click Start|Control Panel|Administrative Tools|Microsoft .NET Framework Configuration applet.
2. Expand the Runtime Security Policy node.
3. Click and expand the Machine node and then the Code Groups node.
4. Right click on All_Code and select New from the context menu to create a new code group.
5. Select Create a new code group and enter Wahoo in the node.
6. Click Next.
7. Select URL in the Choose the condition type drop-down list box.
8. In the URL field, enter http://www.sellsbrothers.com/Wahoo (see Figure 18.3) as the URL to which this code group applies.
9. Click Next.
10. Select Internet in the Use existing permission set drop-down list box.
11. Click Next.
12. Click Finish.

TIP: Note that the moniker and URL must be specific, which distinguishes ftp:// from http://, and you may use wildcards in the URL field.

After you have made the adjustments to the security policy above you should be able to navigate to the permitted *http://www.sellsbrothers.com/wa-*

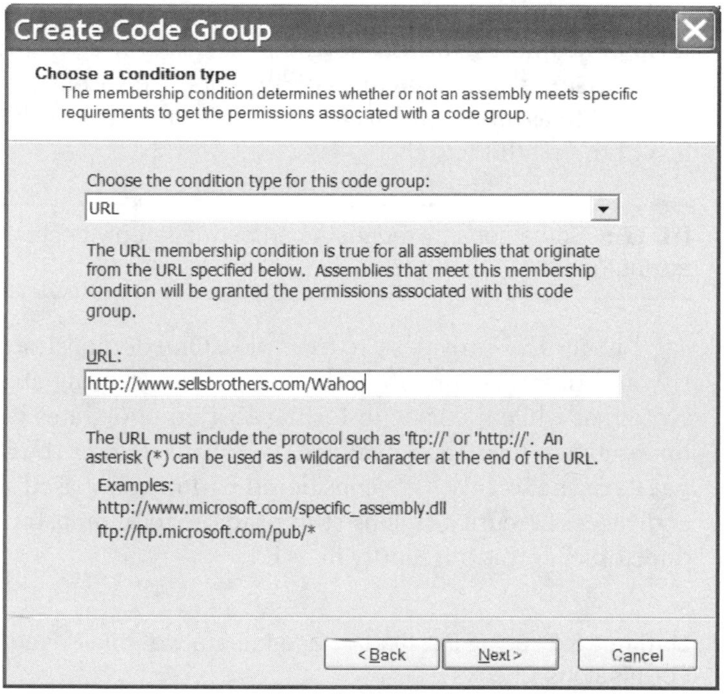

Figure 18.3 Using the Create Code Group dialog to permit assemblies from a particular URL to run.

hoo/wahoo.exe URL and run the Wahoo! game. (The Security permission set has now granted Enable Code Execution, permitting `wahoo.exe` to run.)

It would be impossible to cover all potential security configurations. Security tuning requires patient experimentation based on desired outcomes. When you find that you have made an error, you will need to modify the policy to tighten or loosen it as required.

Comparing Declarative and Imperative Security

Now that you understand how security policy is managed, even if you aren't the person doing the managing, it is important to understand how we make use of code access security in our code. Much of the CLR already interacts with security policy using declarative and imperative security requests. These requests are made in the form of attributes and code that instantiates a specific security-related class. When security requests are made in the form of attributes, this is referred to as *declarative security*. When security requests are made in the form of lines of code within a method body, this is referred to as *imperative security*. The results are roughly the same regardless of the method used.

NOTE: Some security requests can be made only declaratively, that is, as attributes.

Listing 18.1 provides two examples. One demonstrates declarative security and the other precisely the same request using an imperative syntax. Note that while the code in Listing 18.1 demonstrates both declarative and imperative syntax, the `PrincipalPermissionAttribute` and the `PrincipalPermission` class are considered part of role-based security rather than code access security. (I chose this example to demonstrate syntax and introduce other forms of security in .NET.)

Listing 18.1 Using Declarative and Imperative Role-Based Permissions Checks

```
1:   Imports System.Security.Permissions
2:   Imports System.Threading
3:   Imports System.Security.Principal
4:
5:   Public Class Form1
6:        Inherits System.Windows.Forms.Form
7:
8:   [ Windows Form Designer generated code ]
9:     Private Const user As String = "domain\user"
10:    Private Const role As String = Nothing
11:
12:    Private Sub Button1_Click(ByVal sender As System.Object, _
13:      ByVal e As System.EventArgs) Handles Button1.Click
14:
15:      Const mask As String = _
16:        "Current principal is: {0}"
17:
18:      Debug.WriteLine(String.Format(mask, _
19:        Thread.CurrentThread.CurrentPrincipal.Identity.Name))
20:
21:      DeclarativePermissionRequired()
22:
```

```
23:    End Sub
24:
25:    Private Sub Button2_Click(ByVal sender As System.Object, _
26:      ByVal e As System.EventArgs) Handles Button2.Click
27:
28:      Const mask As String = _
29:        "Current principal is: {0}"
30:
31:      Debug.WriteLine(String.Format(mask, _
32:        Thread.CurrentThread.CurrentPrincipal.Identity.Name))
33:
34:      ImperativePermissionRequired()
35:
36:    End Sub
37:
38:    <PrincipalPermission(SecurityAction.Demand, _
39:      Name:=user, role:=role)> _
40:    Public Sub DeclarativePermissionRequired()
41:
42:      MessageBox.Show("You have permission!")
43:
44:    End Sub
45:
46:    Public Sub ImperativePermissionRequired()
47:
48:      Dim Permission As _
49:        System.Security.Permissions. _
50:          PrincipalPermission = _
51:        New System.Security.Permissions. _
52:          PrincipalPermission(user, role)
53:
54:      Permission.Demand()
55:
56:      MessageBox.Show("You have permission!")
57:    End Sub
58:
59:    Private Sub Form1_Load(ByVal sender As System.Object, _
60:      ByVal e As System.EventArgs) Handles MyBase.Load
61:
62:      Thread.CurrentThread.CurrentPrincipal = _
63:        New WindowsPrincipal(WindowsIdentity.GetCurrent)
64:
65:    End Sub
66: End Class
```

The `WindowsPrincipal` class used in line 63 implements the `IPrincipal` interface. A principal object represents the user identity and roles under which the code is running. (This is part of roles-based security in .NET, but the example also demonstrates the declarative and imperative syntax.) The `Form.Load` event establishes the current Windows user as the current principal. This means that the code is running on behalf of the current user.

TIP: You can use the .NET utility `permview.exe`—as in `permview.exe` *myassembly.dll*—to view the declarative permissions used by an assembly.

Lines 12 through 23 write the identity of the current principal and call `DeclarativePermissionRequired`. The subroutine `DeclarativePermissionRequired` uses the `PrincipalPermissionAttribute`—a declarative demand—to demand that the identity of the person running this method must be the name of the supplied `user` and be in the role defined by the argument `role`. Because `role` is initialized to `Nothing` in line 10 we are only verifying that the user is the user defined by the `user` variable.

Lines 25 through 36 perform precisely the same task imperatively, that is, through statements inside the method. The real work occurs in `ImperativePermissionRequired`, which creates an instance of the `System.Security.Permissions.PrincipalPermission` class, initializing the class with `user` and `role`. Line 54 invokes the `Demand` method. If the current principal is not the one indicated by `user` and `role`, an exception is thrown. In fact, both the declarative and imperative forms of security throw the identical exception, as shown in Figure 18.4.

The only real difference between the two forms of usage—declarative and imperative security—of the `PrincipalPermission` class is when the permis-

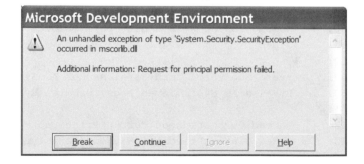

Figure 18.4 The `SecurityException` dialog that appears if the permission demand fails.

sion is evaluated. With the declarative example the procedure is not permitted to run at all, whereas the imperative example permits the code to run up to the point that the `PrincipalPermission.Demand` method is invoked.

NOTE: Security attributes are implemented in terms of the security classes with the same name. For example, `PrincipalPermissionAttribute` is implemented in terms of the `PrincipalPermission` class. Whether you use the attribute or use the class directly, you are running the same code, thus resulting in the same behavior.

The Advantages of Declarative Security

Declarative security offers a few distinct advantages over imperative security.

- While all security actions are codified as classes and attribute classes, every security action can be expressed declaratively. Some security actions like `LinkDemands` cannot be expressed imperatively.
- Declarative security actions can be evaluated without running code since attributes are stored as part of an assembly's metadata; imperative security actions are stored as IL. This implies that imperative security actions can be evaluated only when the code is running.
- Declarative security actions are checked immediately before a method is invoked, whereas imperative security actions may occur after a method has partially completed. The declarative security process prevents a method that will ultimately fail from wasting time.
- A declarative security action placed at the class level applies to every method in the class. You must repeat imperative security actions for each method individually.

In general, declarative security has more advantages, but imperative security offers some benefits of its own. Let's take a moment to look at these.

The Advantages of Imperative Security

Imperative security actions run as lines of code intermixed with your application's code. This offers a couple of distinct advantages.

- Because you write imperative security actions inside methods you can intersperse various security actions based on conditional logic. Declarative security yields an all-or-nothing approach to a security option.

■ You can pass dynamic arguments to imperative security actions. Declarative security actions require that you pass static values to these attributes as you write the declarative security code.

Both approaches offer benefits. It is worthwhile to evaluate whether to use declarative or imperative security in particular situations relative to the benefits each approach offers.

Using Code Access Security Demands

As you might imagine, there are security classes to express security for a wide variety of resources. An exhaustive list would require a considerable amount of space; I will leave this to the VS .NET help files. However, as an appetizer I'll mention that you can express security requests to determine whether operations like file I/O are permitted, whether common file dialogs can be shown, whether the registry can be written to—you can even check whether assemblies can be linked. You can begin your exploration by reading the Introduction to Code Access Security help documentation in the Visual Studio .NET IDE. To get you started I have included here some common security checks you might want to use in your code.

The examples in this section all use security demands. There are several other kinds of checks as well, which we will get to in a moment. Additionally, the examples demonstrate both declarative and imperative security. All the examples in this section are derived from the `System.Security.CodeAccessPermission` class. (You can check the IDE help documentation for examples of classes derived from the `CodeAccessPermission` class.)

What Is a Demand?

The notion of a demand in .NET seems a bit misleading. Dictionary.com defines *demand* as "to claim as just or due." To me this sounds as if a demand in .NET ought to mean that you are taking a permission from the operating system, as in, "My code demands that it be allowed to print." Perhaps the `Demand` method should instead be named *request* because when you demand a permission, the security policy might just say "No!"

Invoking `Demand` does mean that your code needs a permission, but it doesn't mean that it will get it. The security policy is like a good parent: sometimes a parent says no because something isn't good for the child. For example, code downloaded from the Internet might demand to be allowed to write to the %WINDIR% folder or the registry, but this might not be good for your PC, so the response is no. And it is the most preemptive no possible: an exception is thrown.

Security demands help enforce the contracts between various pieces of code. If your code needs to do something and isn't allowed to do it, you need to handle this problem. Generally, handling it means to catch the exception and tell the user. The code can electively do something else or bubble the command to the user. In turn, the user can ask for an amendment to the security policy, if the thing demanded is desirable, or let out a sigh of relief, realizing that a catastrophic mishap was handily avoided.

Demanding Printing Permission

The greater variety and number of projects a developer works on, the less often that developer will be surprised by requirements made by various applications. Printing is one of those things we often take for granted. In my home office network I print without a moment's hesitation. But what if you are writing software that is capable of printing medical records or a release from the county jail? Clearly you don't want code to be able to print someone's medical records or a jail release form without proper permissions. Under these circumstances a customer clearly would not tolerate a security policy that permitted any code to invoke the printing behavior; however, if you are writing the module that legitimately prints these kinds of things, printing is required. Listing 18.2 demonstrates how we can write code to demand (or indicate) that printing is required. Keep in mind that the policy may not permit it, although in our scenario the policy would need to be adjusted to allow the legitimate printing assembly to print.

Listing 18.2 Demanding Printing Permission

```
Imports System.Drawing.Printing
Private Sub PrintDemand()
  Try
    Dim Permission As PrintingPermission = _
      New PrintingPermission(PrintingPermissionLevel.AllPrinting)
    Permission.Demand()
    ' Print here
    MessageBox.Show("This code can print.")
```

```
    Catch
       MessageBox.Show("This code can't print!")
    End Try
End Sub
```

It is important to note that the default policy is defined to permit code that originates from your computer to be allowed to perform relatively unrestricted operations. This does not mean, however, that the default security policy where you work hasn't been amended. In addition, keep in mind that code originating from your computer could cause accidental errors, but generally code that originates outside your computer is riskier and likely to have significantly fewer permissions.

Demanding Registry Read Permission

The registry is organized similarly to the file system. When code needs to access the registry, you can demand registry permission, specifying the location in the registry that the code can write to or read from. Listing 18.3 demonstrates a demand to ensure that the code can read from anywhere in the registry. (To cause the demand to fail, create a policy for the DemandExamples.exe assembly that denies registry access.)

Listing 18.3 Demanding Registry Read Permission

```
1:  Private Sub ReadRegistry()
2:     Try
3:        Dim Permission As RegistryPermission = _
4:          New RegistryPermission(RegistryPermissionAccess.Read, "*")
5:
6:        Permission.Demand()
7:        MessageBox.Show( _
8:           "This code can read from anywhere in the registry")
9:     Catch
10:       MessageBox.Show(
11:          "This code can't read from anywhere in the registry.")
12:    End Try
13: End Sub
```

Suppose, for example, that you download a cool program from the Internet that keeps track of your favorite music playlists. It is unlikely that your company wants that vendor reading the registry to figure out if you are running a competitor's software. In fact, it is unlikely that you want to give the vendor any access to the registry unless it is perhaps to store configured playlists. By defining a policy that limits registry access, you could allow the vendor to store playlists but prevent it from poking around.

There are a dozen or more code access permission classes. Each has constructor arguments (if applicable) that refine how a particular instance of the permission fits in its context. You also have the option of creating custom security classes. Regardless of how you initialize the permission, relative to the Demand method, they all behave the same way: if the permission is supported by the policy based on the evidence supplied, the demand succeeds. Failure is exhibited by an exception.

Using Code Access Security Asserts

The code access security classes include several methods. In addition to the Demand method is the Assert method. .NET security checks to make sure that all callers in a method's call stack have permission to perform a desired operation. This prevents callers that do have permission to perform an operation from performing that operation on behalf of a caller that doesn't have permission. For example, if assembly A (which has permission to modify the registry) calls assembly B's registry modification method, assembly B must have permission to modify the registry too.

Walking the stack to make sure callers have permissions is how the .NET security framework behaves unless you invoke the Assert operation. Assert takes the responsibility for the permission on behalf of the callers. Repeating our scenario, then, if assembly A uses an Assert operation on registry modification, assembly A will be able to modify the registry on behalf of assembly B, even though assembly B doesn't have permission to modify the registry. However, if an assembly asserts a permission it hasn't been granted—that is, if a demand for that permission would fail—then the Assert operation fails too. Thus, for example, assembly A cannot assert registry modification permissions on behalf of assembly B if assembly A has not been granted those permissions itself.

Sandboxing Assemblies for Testing Purposes

By default, assemblies created on your computer will fall into the My_Computer zone, resulting in those assemblies having full trust. An assembly with no restrictions is difficult to test against security actions. To reconcile testing security actions for a likely deployment zone or specific security restrictions, we can *sandbox* the assembly into a zone with greater restrictions or a zone that implements a custom permission set.

To demonstrate the `Assert` security action, we will sandbox `AssertExample.exe` into the Internet_Zone. By default the Internet_Zone is the most restricted zone, and it excludes registry permissions. Follow the steps below to associate the policy for Internet assemblies with the `AssertExample.exe` assembly.

1. Start the Microsoft .NET Framework Configuration tool. (For example, type `mscorcfg.msc` at the Visual Studio .NET Command Prompt and press Enter.)
2. Expand the Runtime Security Policy|User|Code Groups|All_Code node.
3. Right-click on the All_Code node and select New from the context menu to create a new code group.
4. In the Create Code Group dialog, make sure Create a new code group is selected.
5. Enter a name—for instance, deny_registry_access—and description for the code group.
6. Click Next.
7. In the Choose the condition type drop-down list box, set the condition type to URL.
8. In the URL input field, enter the physical path and filename of the `AssertExample.exe` assembly. Use the URN convention, including the `file://` moniker (for example, `file://C:\temp\AssertExample\bin\AssertExample.exe`).
9. Click Next.
10. Make sure Use existing permission set is selected, and select the Internet permission set.
11. Click Next.
12. Click Finish.

After completing each step successfully, you should see a warning bubble (Figure 18.5) that indicates that `AssertExample.exe` is running in a

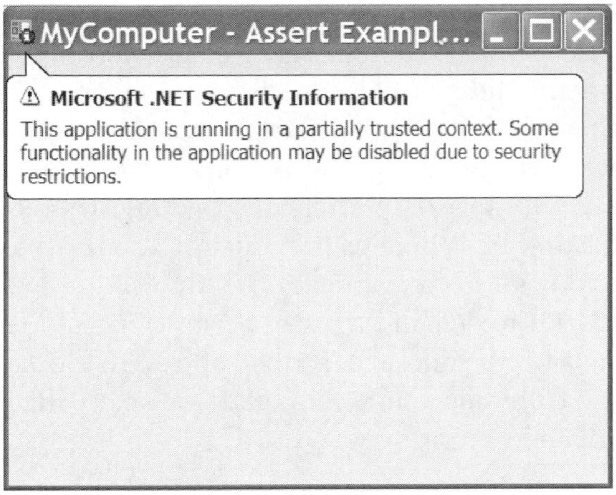

Figure 18.5 The message that appears when an assembly is running in a partially trusted context and security restrictions apply.

partially trusted context, which might disable some functionality. (You have seen this message before if you downloaded and ran the Wahoo! game in Chapter 10.)

Now we are ready to test the `Assert` security action. Suppose that every other assembly on the computer, except `AssertExample.exe`, is running with full trust. This means that `AssertExample.exe` will not be permitted to interact with the registry, for example, but other assemblies created on this computer will be able to do so. (Keep in mind that if the Internet permission set on your computer has been modified to permit registry access, you need to create or use a permission set that doesn't permit registry access for this example to work correctly.)

Demonstrating the Behavior of an `Assert` Action

If you downloaded an assembly from the Internet and this assembly attempted to interact with your computer's registry, a security exception would be raised. In the preceding subsection we sandboxed `AssertExample.exe` into the Internet_Zone to simulate this behavior. As a result, `AssertExample.exe` will throw a security exception when it tries to access the registry directly. A second class library project available for download, `AssertPermission.dll`, contains a method that accesses the registry. If `AsssertExample.exe` calls into `AssertPermission.dll`, which in turn attempts to access the registry, a security exception will be raised. The exception occurs because the CLR will perform a stack walk and determine that `AssertExample.exe` does not have registry permissions. However, as you will see in the example, if `AssertPermission.dll` uses an `Assert` operation on registry permissions, the stack walk won't get as far as checking the `AssertExample.exe` for registry permissions, and registry access will be permitted.

Listing 18.4 contains the code for `AssertExample.exe`. The example is a Windows Forms application with a single button. The `Button.Click` event tries to demand registry permissions and read from the registry. This call fails for the reason described above. In the same `Click` event handler, a second call is made into `AssertPermission.dll`. This call succeeds, again as explained above.

Listing 18.4 The Code for `AssertExample.exe`

```
1:   Imports System.Security.Permissions
2:   Imports System.Threading.Thread
3:   Imports System.Security.Principal
4:   Imports Microsoft.Win32
5:
6:
7:   Public Class Form1
8:       Inherits System.Windows.Forms.Form
9:
10:    [ Windows Form Designer generated code ]
11:
12:    Private Sub Button1_Click(ByVal sender As System.Object, _
13:      ByVal e As System.EventArgs) Handles Button1.Click
14:
15:      Try
16:        ReadRegistry()
17:      Catch
18:        MessageBox.Show("Code does not have registry read permission")
19:      End Try
20:
21:      Try
22:        AssertPermission.AssertsForme.ReadRegistry()
23:      Catch
24:        MessageBox.Show("Code does not have registry read permission")
25:      End Try
26:
```

```
27:     End Sub
28:
29:     Private Sub ReadRegistry()
30:       Dim Permission As RegistryPermission = _
31:         New RegistryPermission(RegistryPermissionAccess.Read, _
32:         "*")
33:
34:       Permission.Demand()
35:
36:       Dim Key As RegistryKey = _
37:         Registry.CurrentUser.OpenSubKey("Volatile Environment")
38:       Try
39:         MessageBox.Show(Key.GetValue("LOGONSERVER"))
40:       Finally
41:         Key.Close()
42:       End Try
43:     End Sub
44:
45: End Class
```

Lines 12 through 27 implement the `Button.Click` event handler. Lines 15 through 19 wrap the call to `AssertExample.exe`'s attempt to access the registry. Lines 21 through 25 wrap the call to `AssertPermission.dll`'s attempt to access the registry. The `Catch` block in lines 17 through 19 will run when `ReadRegistry` is called because `AssertExample.exe` does not have permission to access the registry. (In a real application we would allow this to fail if registry access were required and not permitted. Our example catches the exception to facilitate comparing the `Assert` behavior with the nonpermitted behavior.) Line 22 calls into `AssertPermission.dll`'s `AssertsForme.ReadRegistry` shared method, which we will cover in a moment.

`AssertExample.exe`'s `ReadRegistry` method creates a `RegistryPermission` object imperatively and demands read permission. The demand causes a security exception because `AssertExample.exe` has not been granted registry permission. Even if we removed the call to `Demand`, an exception would be raised when `OpenSubKey` is called in line 37.

Listing 18.5 shows the code for `AssertPermission.dll`, including the `AssertsForme` class. Note that since this code asserts registry permission, it also potentially opens a security hole.

Listing 18.5 The Code for `AssertPermission.dll`

```
1:  Imports System.Security.Permissions
2:  Imports Microsoft.Win32
3:
4:  Public Class AssertsForme
5:
6:    Public Shared Sub ReadRegistry()
7:      Dim Permission As RegistryPermission = _
8:        New RegistryPermission(PermissionState.Unrestricted)
9:
10:     Permission.Assert()
11:
12:     DoReadRegistry()
13:   End Sub
14:
15:   Private Shared Sub DoReadRegistry()
16:
17:     Dim Key As RegistryKey = _
18:       Registry.CurrentUser.OpenSubKey("Volatile Environment")
19:     Try
20:       MessageBox.Show(Key.GetValue("LOGONSERVER"))
21:     Finally
22:       Key.Close()
23:     End Try
24:   End Sub
25:
26: End Class
```

The private shared method `DoReadRegistry` performs the task identical to `ReadRegistry` in Listing 18.4; it simply reads an arbitrary value from the registry. The real action in Listing 18.5 occurs in the shared method `AssertsForme.ReadRegistry`.

`AssertsForme.ReadRegistry` (lines 6 through 13) is contained in an assembly created on a computer that has full trust. That is, this assembly can read from the registry. However, if `AssertExample.exe` calls this method, a security exception will still be thrown because the caller does not have registry permissions. This is true unless registry permissions are asserted in `AssertPermission.dll`. In Listing 18.5, lines 7 through 10 do in fact assert registry permission, so the call to `AssertPermission.Asserts-`

`Forme.ReadRegistry` in line 22 of Listing 18.4 succeeds. (Remove the `Permission.Assert` statement in line 10 of Listing 18.5 and you will get the expected security exception.)

Assume that we passed in the registry key and returned the read value in `AssertsForme.ReadRegistry` or that we passed in a key and a new value to write. From the example you can ascertain that a trusted assembly could take on the responsibility of yielding permissions to a less trusted assembly, resulting in an egregious security breach.

To avoid an embarrassing hole in security, use the `Assert` action sparingly and carefully. Rampant use will likely result in several holes in the security policy and some unhappy customers.

A Brief Review of Other Security Actions

There are many security actions. An exhaustive discussion would require a tome of its own. In fact, such a volume exists: *.NET Framework Security* by Brian LaMacchia et al. [2002]. Here is a brief explanation of security actions to help point you in the right direction when you have a specific need. (I excluded the `Demand` and `Assert` actions, which we have already covered.)

The `LinkDemand` Action

This security action applies to classes and methods. `LinkDemand` is evaluated when the assembly is JITted, and the immediate call must have the requested permission.

The `InheritanceDemand` Action

This security action applies to classes and methods. `InheritanceDemand`, evaluated at load time, requires that the subclass overriding and the inherited method have the requested permission.

The `Deny` Action

This security action applies to classes and methods. `Deny` is evaluated at runtime. It denies the specified permission to callers even if they have been granted the permission by the security policy. `Deny` is used to tighten security more than the policy does.

The `PermitOnly` Action

This security action applies to classes and methods. `PermitOnly` is evaluated at runtime and permits only the resources requested by the permission to be accessible even if the policy has granted access to additional resources.

The `RequestMinimum` Action

This security action applies only to assemblies. `RequestMinimum` is evaluated when the assembly policy is created, and it indicates the minimum permissions needed for the assembly to run. If the minimum permissions haven't been granted, the assembly will not load. For example, if we added the following attribute to the `assemblyInfo.vb` file for `AssertExample.exe`, the `AssertExample.exe` assembly would not event load.

```
<Assembly: Security.Permissions.RegistryPermission( _
    Security.Permissions.SecurityAction.RequestMinimum, All:="*")>
```

This assumes that we have altered the granted permissions for `AssertExample.exe`. Refer to the earlier subsection Sandboxing Assemblies for Testing Purposes for more information.

The `RequestOptional` Action

This security action applies only to assemblies. `RequestOptional` is evaluated at grant time and is used to request permissions that are optional. Use this action when you have a code workaround for a permission not granted. For instance, if a particular feature, such as logging events, isn't necessary for your application to run, you could request optional `EventLogPermission`.

The `RequestRefuse` Action

This security action applies only to assemblies. `RequestRefuse`, evaluated at grant time, is used to specify permissions that will not be granted by callers.

General Recommendations

Security pedants will tell you that there is never enough security; they sigh when they run out of ways to further tighten code. However, not all code requires the same attention to security detail. Here are some guidelines that will help you decide how much security tightening is required. Keep in mind that an adaptive strategy is best. In the rare instance when your best efforts have failed because some digital miscreant has stayed up all night trying to poke holes in your security, adaptability and responsiveness will serve you well. That is, be prepared to identify the security hole and plug it up.

As you begin to design your applications, consider these guidelines.

- The more connected the system is, the greater the risk. This doesn't mean that there aren't internal risks and that mistakes aren't made. Prepare for disconnected desktop applications that could cause un-intentional problems. Good testing will help eliminate some of these, but you may not get them all. A good security policy helps too.
- If the application is mission critical or the circumstances of failure are dire, hire an outside security expert. (Or consider hiring a full-time security administrator. Just make sure you pick someone who doesn't mind being unpopular.)
- Provide all employees with a written security policy that addresses things like telecommuting and securing access to data and source code.
- In general, allow security permission failures to be catastrophic. Let the application fail. This will send a clear signal that some code has attempted to violate the security policy.
- Use `Asserts` actions judiciously since they can cause holes in security.
- Tune security gradually, granting the minimal permissions necessary for the code to run, and keep a record of modifications to the security policy. This will allow you to roll back changes that don't work, as opposed to starting from scratch.
- Finally, I encourage you to not leave security to chance. Acquire as much knowledge as you can and share information as quickly as you can.

Security management is becoming as complex as the U.S. tax code. Unfortunately there doesn't seem to be a simple solution, and the world seems to produce a continual stream of mischief makers determined to poke holes in all security attempts. However, if you approach security holistically rather than blaming the entire problem on Microsoft, only the most determined and experienced troublemakers will find cracks.

Summary

A good friend of mine, Tony Cowan, said that the best way to secure a Web site is to run it from a CD-ROM. Clearly he meant "secure it from defacement" because even running a Web site from a CD-ROM will not prevent denial-of-service attacks.

Microsoft has shouldered a lot of the blame for security problems in Windows, but security breaches didn't start with Windows. Other operating systems like Linux have them too because both Linux and Windows can trace their ancestry to UNIX, and many of the security holes found today were discovered by exploiting holes in UNIX first. However, with code access security we have the mixed blessing of security that orthogonally complements role-based security, making .NET more secure but also more challenging to instrument correctly.

In this chapter I introduced you to how to administer security policy and how to make demands of that security policy. Time will tell whether the security challenges are so great that it is impossible to completely secure connected systems or to what degree code access security alleviates security holes. The best approach has always been to treat all aspects of security with care and to anticipate and adapt to security challenges.

Migrating Visual Basic 6 Applications to Visual Basic .NET

To paraphrase Thomas Jefferson: Microsoft has the splendid misery of innovating, which involves the daily risk of losing loyal customers.

—Paul Kimmel

Introduction

Microsoft has always demonstrated a continuing commitment to past and future customers. Sometimes this causes problems. For example, Microsoft had to drag bits of MS-DOS around for years while it patiently waited for customers to update to Windows. Perhaps no greater support has been shown to any other group than developers. After all, Microsoft is a software company that builds tools for software developers, targeting applications intended to run on its own operating systems. With this in mind I would like to offer you some perspective on the transition from VB6 to VB .NET.

One of the riskiest decisions Microsoft had to make regarding .NET was related to Visual Basic 6. Microsoft has a huge following in the VB6 arena—the largest after Microsoft Office. There are millions of us out there. However, Microsoft realized that innovations in software development methodology and technology mandated an overhaul for Visual Basic 6. When you get into Visual Basic .NET, you might never want to go back to VB6. I know I don't. However, in spite of the desperate need for an overhaul, which has now occurred, Microsoft has not abandoned VB6. We have options, and that's what I would like to talk about.

Before You Migrate

Two important questions must be asked and answered when it comes to migrations from VB6 to VB .NET: "Should I migrate my application to VB .NET?" and "If I do choose to migrate, what is the best practical way for me to do it?" The first question should be asked for every single application. The answers to these questions result in different desirable outcomes.

To Migrate or Not to Migrate

Before you we talk about how to migrate, let's talk about *whether* to migrate. If I had a VB6 application that worked fine and required no additional significant features, most likely I would not migrate it at all. However, if I did elect to migrate such applications, I would place this category way down on the priority list. Microsoft has not abandoned VB6 (the company hasn't even abandoned COM), so why migrate a perfectly good program? There is no reason to.

Unless some bizarre catastrophe occurs in the world, Microsoft will offer plenty of lead time—probably years—before VB6 is cast to the wayside.

So You Want to Migrate

Now you are telling me, "But I have to migrate." Your application is undergoing significant revisions, a manager has made a sweeping decision—say, for security's sake your company wants all managed code—or for some other reason you are in a position where you must migrate. If you must migrate, you still have choices.

You do not have to migrate your entire application. You have a couple of options here. First, of course, you can run the migration wizard, updating VB6 to VB .NET and manually fixing all the code that could not be automatically migrated. This is a valid option, and we will talk more about it in a moment. Second, you have the option of importing your VB6 libraries with COM Interop, leaving you to reproduce the presentation layer (graphical user interface) in VB .NET. Using COM Interop (see Chapter 7) is a great alternative to a complete migration. A third option is to implement application bridges using XML Web Services or .NET Remoting. This option should work very well, especially for VB6 applications that have OLE Automation interfaces. The fourth option, which is technologically sound but may be cost prohibitive, is to completely rewrite your VB6 applications in VB .NET, and there are compelling reasons to do so. (I offer the examples of what you can do with VB .NET, as described in this book, as my argument for a rewrite.)

Migrating just to learn VB .NET is not a good idea. The migration wizard produces verbose code that will not teach good object-oriented programming principles, nor will the migration wizard produce ideal object-oriented code. What the migration wizard will do is as much as necessary to allow your migrated code to compile, and it is highly unlikely that any but the most trivial applications will migrate completely and automatically.

If you are sitting on the fence and can't decide whether or not to migrate, you may want to run the migration wizard and examine the migration report. The report should tell you how much effort will be involved in migrating your VB6 applications, which you can in turn use to help you weigh the alternatives. (Refer to the upcoming section Migrating Visual Basic 6 Windows Applications for more details.)

Visual Basic 6 Features Not Supported in .NET

Before you migrate your VB6 application to VB .NET you should understand which VB6 features are not supported in VB .NET. If your VB6 application uses any of these unsupported features, one good strategy is to redesign them out of your application before you begin the migration process. Table A.1 contains a list of unsupported features in VB .NET.

The greater the number of unsupported elements, the greater the cost of migration will be. You will have to evaluate the cost and benefits of migration relative to the costs of choosing one of the previously mentioned choices, like a rewrite. As mentioned earlier, one good strategy is to run the migration wizard to determine the number of changes involved in a migration.

Migrating Visual Basic 6 Windows Applications

Because migrating a really trivial application would be misleading and a really long application would easily consume dozens, perhaps hundreds, of pages, I picked a sample application to migrate. The application consists of a separate client and server and is available with MSDN. (You will need to have MSDN for Visual Studio 6 installed, or you can acquire a copy of the source code from Microsoft to repeat the steps described here.)

Table A.1 VB6 Features Unsupported in VB .NET

Name	Comments
OLE Container Control	Leave it behind.
Dynamic Data Exchange (DDE)	Consider using the `SendMessage` API method.
DAO or RDO	Consider upgrading to ADO in VB6 or ADO.NET in VB .NET. (You can use regular ADO in .NET through COM Interop.)
VB5	Upgrade VB5 projects to VB6 and then migrate to .NET.
ActiveX DHTML page applications	These should not be upgraded, but they do interoperate with VB .NET since you can navigate between ActiveX DHTML pages and ASP.NET Web pages.
ActiveX documents	Leave these as VB6 code. You can navigate between ActiveX documents and ASP.NET Web pages.
Property pages	The Properties window is more powerful and extensible in VB .NET, alleviating the need for property pages. For an example of this extensibility, refer to the Using the `UITypeEditor` Class section in Chapter 9.
User controls	VB6 user controls can be used in VB .NET, but VB6 user control projects cannot be migrated.
Web classes	Web classes can interoperate but are not automatically migrated.
Visual Basic Add-Ins	Add-Ins need to be rewritten in VB .NET.
Games	You may need to rewrite graphics code in VB .NET with GDI+.
Graphics	Graphics methods like `Line` and `Circle` are not automatically upgraded; you must reimplement them in VB .NET with GDI+ classes.
Drag-and-drop functionality	Drag-and-drop functionality must be reimplemented in VB .NET.
Variants	Variant data types are converted to the new `Object` class; there may be some subtle differences between how a variant is evaluated and how an object is evaluated. Pay close attention to code that relies on variants.
Windows API	Many API calls will need to be revised; the .NET framework contains objects and methods that provide a lot of functionality that VB6 could access only through Windows API calls (for example, accessing the registry).

The two programs that comprise the application I elected to migrate were in my Visual Studio files in `C:\Program Files\Microsoft Visual Studio\MSDN98\98VSa\1033\SAMPLES\VB98\misc\booksale\Client\BOOK_CLI.VBP` and `C:\Program Files\Microsoft Visual Studio\MSDN98\98VSa\1033\SAMPLES\VB98\misc\booksale\Server\BOOK_SVR.VBP`. (These paths might vary depending on the exact version of MSDN you have installed. Search on the project names to find the files if necessary.) This is a modestly complex client and server application. The application contains many of the most common elements, including forms, classes, and modules. I will provide an overview of the process and some of the problems that have to be reconciled, but I will not provide the listing since it would require too many pages.

NOTE: The `booksale.vbg` group contains both the client and server application, but the migration wizard does not load automatically when you try to open a VB6 `.vbg` group (in fact, the .NET Open dialog won't allow you to open a `.vbg` file either). You must open and migrate each project individually.

Migrating the Sample Client Application

If you select File|Open|Project and select a VB6 project (a `.vbp`) file, the migration wizard will start automatically. I used all the default options in each of the five steps, and this part of the process is trivial. Figures A.1 through A.5 show you when you are in the right place and help you retrace my steps if you are so inclined.

NOTE: Someone e-mailed and asked about a way to automate the migration process since he had many applications to migrate. I imagine that you could tap into the EnvDTE and write a macro to migrate several projects at once. I intentionally did not explore that option here. I think each application is different and should be evaluated independently. Even if the migration process were automated, the bulk of the work is in reconciling the code that cannot be migrated.

When you are finished migrating, you should see an entire VB .NET solution (`.sln` file) with all the migrated files, references to COM Interop assemblies, and a file named `_UpgradeReport.htm`. The upgrade report is a good place to start. The `_UpgradeReport.htm` file (Figure A.6) provides you with a list of migrated files. Expand the list (Figure A.7) to see specific

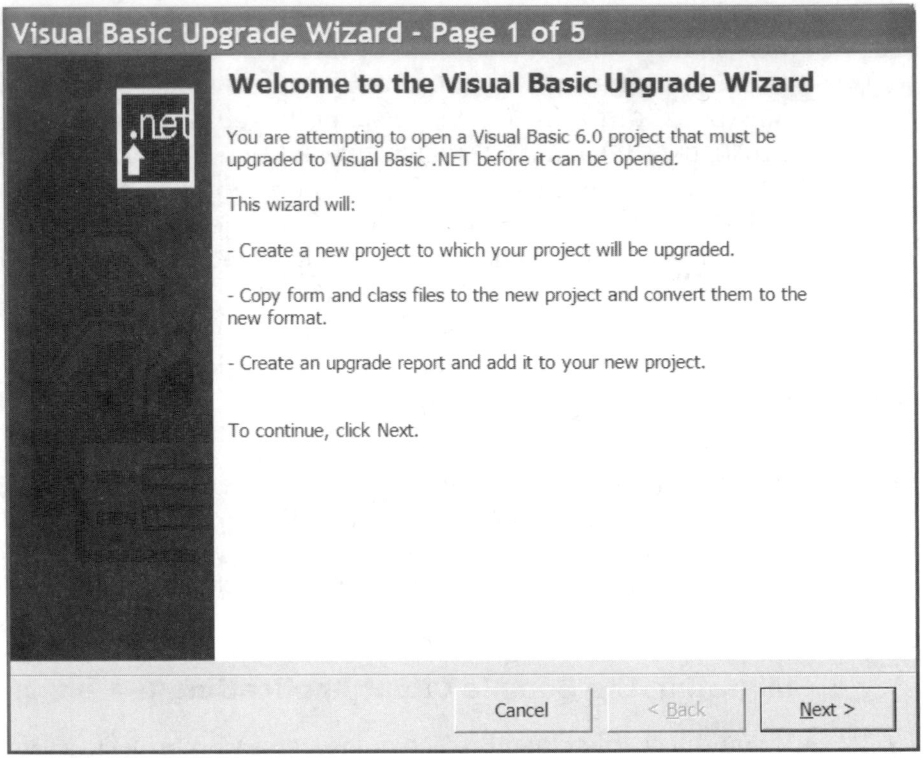

Figure A.1 This is the first step of the migration wizard, which you should see if you attempt to open a VB6 project.

problems with a hyperlink description. Click on the linked description to navigate to a specific help topic that will explain what the problem is and recommend a resolution.

TIP: You can select View|Show Tasks|All in Visual Studio .NET to see all the items added to the task list during migration.

A reasonable approach is to resolve all the items in the task list and get the code to compile. Then you will need to retest the application for logic errors. For example, calls to `IsObject` with a variant in VB6 are migrated to `IsObject` with an `Object` type in VB .NET, and the results are evaluated differently. Carefully retest your entire application.

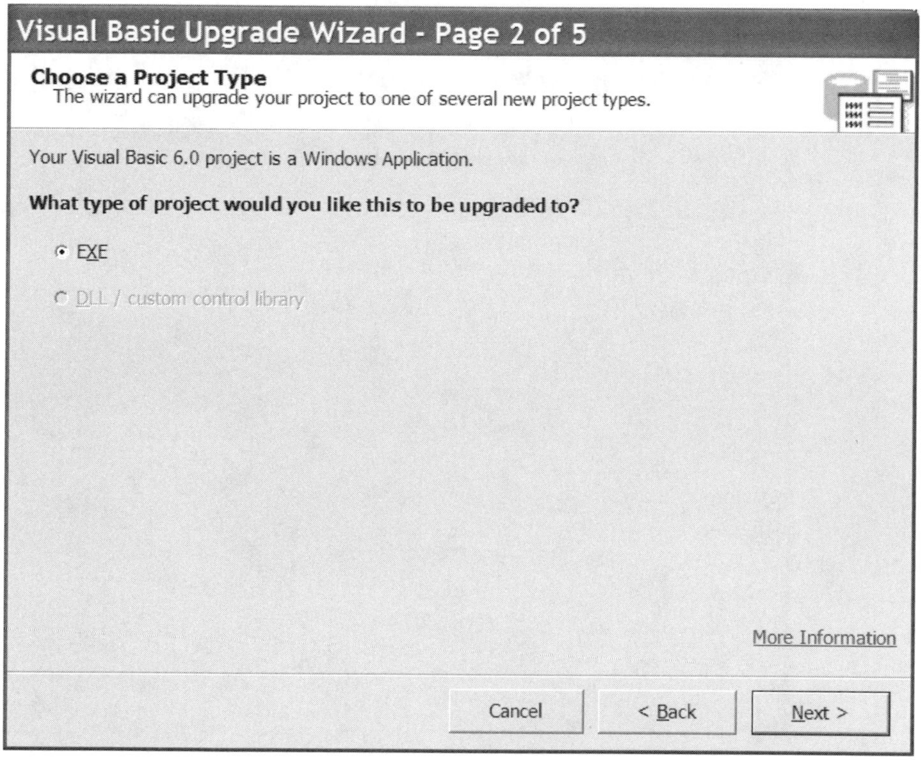

Figure A.2 This is the first step of the migration wizard, which you should see if you attempt to open a VB6 project.

Resolving Migration Errors

When I ran the migration wizard I had only four bonafide compile errors. Everything else was a warning. After fixing the errors and compiling I addressed the warnings to determine whether they were really errors waiting to happen and to figure out what could be done to resolve them. Professionally, I have a rule: I don't ship code with errors, warnings, or hints. Everything gets resolved 100 percent, one way or another.

To view compiler errors and resolve those first, select View|Show Tasks|Build Errors. This filters the task list to show you everything that is preventing your application from compiling.

The first error I tackled was "frmCogs is a type and cannot be used as an expression." By examining frmCogs we can determine that frmCogs has been migrated to a WinForms object; hence we must know how to rewrite

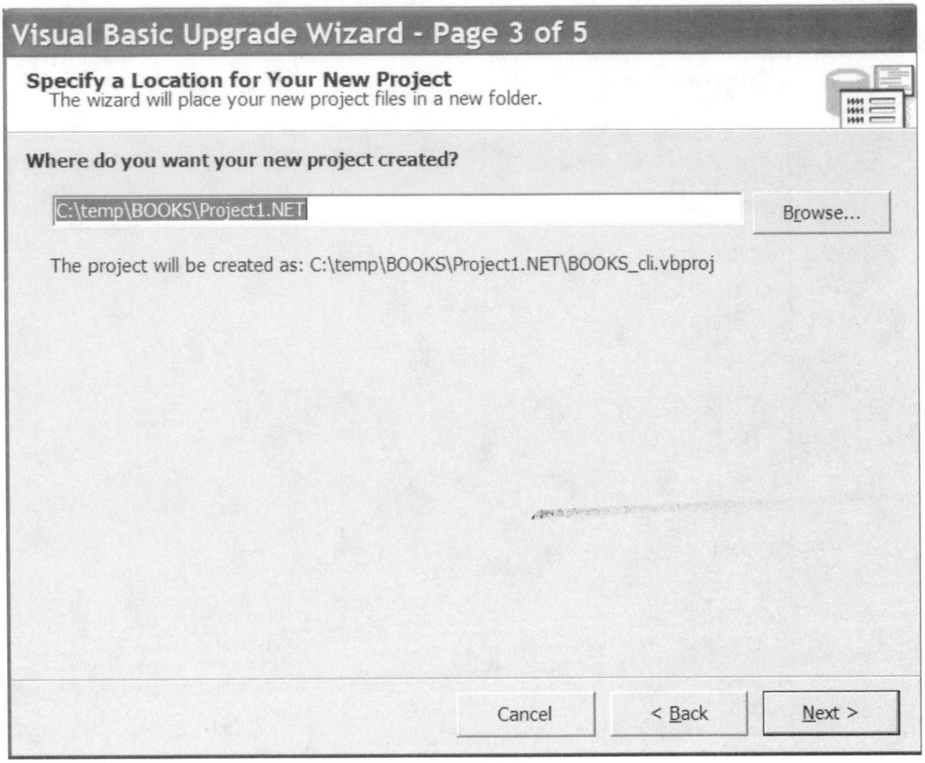

Visual Basic Upgrade Wizard - Page 3 of 5

Specify a Location for Your New Project
The wizard will place your new project files in a new folder.

Where do you want your new project created?

C:\temp\BOOKS\Project1.NET   Browse...

The project will be created as: C:\temp\BOOKS\Project1.NET\BOOKS_cli.vbproj

Cancel   < Back   Next >

Figure A.3 Navigate to the `.vbp` project you want to migrate.

this code in VB .NET. Listing A.1 contains the method in question, and Listing A.2 contains the revised code, which resolves the error.

Listing A.1 An Improper Way to Load a Windows Form

```
Private Sub cmdCogs_Click(ByVal eventSender As System.Object, _
  ByVal eventArgs As System.EventArgs) Handles cmdCogs.Click
  goStatusPanel.Text = "Determining Cost of Goods."
  'UPGRADE_ISSUE: Load statement is not supported. Click for more:
  'ms-help://MS.VSCC/commoner/redir/redirect.htm?key-
word="vbup1039"'
  Load(frmCogs)
  goStatusPanel.Text = ""

End Sub
```

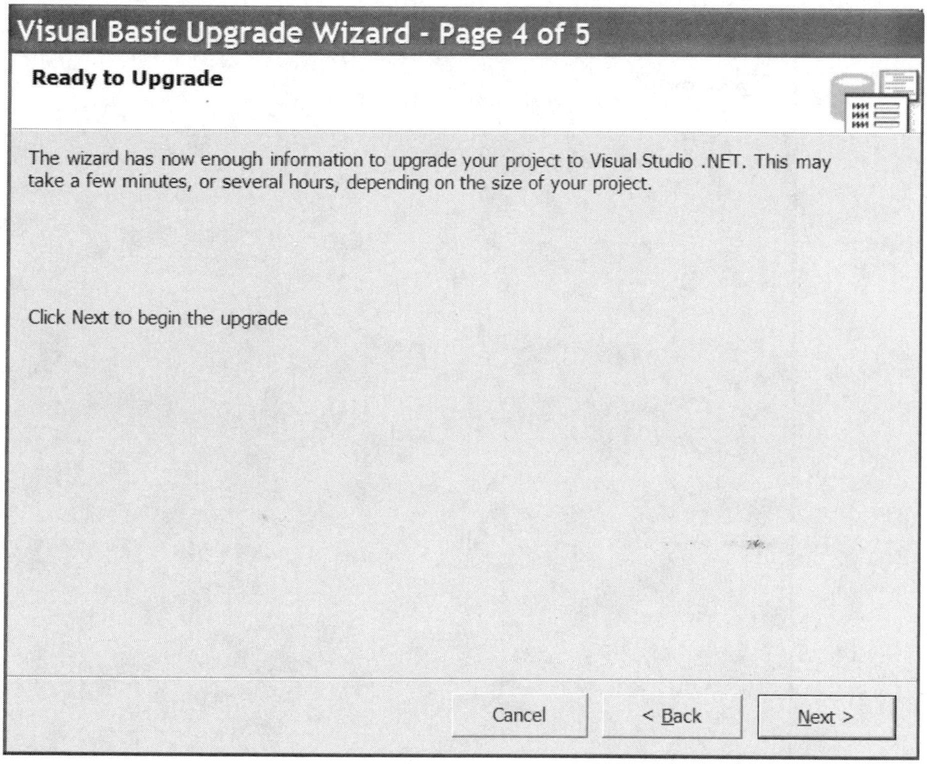

Figure A.4 The wizard begins the migration after you click Next on this screen.

Clicking on the hyperlink in the `_UpgradeReport.htm` file takes you to the VS .NET help topic `ms-help://MS.VSCC/MS.MSDNVS/vbcon/html/vbup1039.htm`. This help topic shows you VB6 code, what the VB .NET migrated code should look like, and a remedy. The problem I encountered, in short, is that the `Load` method isn't used to load forms in VB .NET. Forms are classes, and we use the new operator and invoke methods on forms just like any other class. Listing A.2 shows a revision that is correct and resolves the error.

TIP: You can click the hyperlink embedded in the `UPGRADE_ISSUE` remark to navigate to help documentation that will aid you in resolving the problem, too.

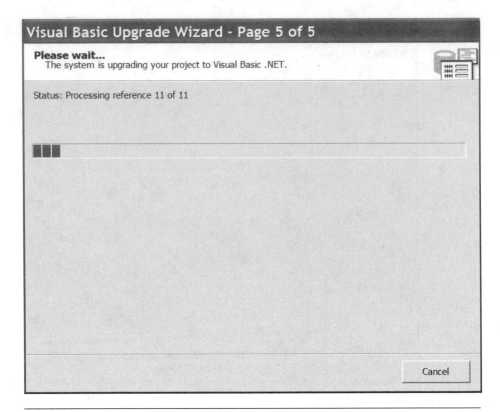

Figure A.5 The migration may take a few minutes, as suggested by the progress bar.

Listing A.2 Fixing the Load Error

```
Private Sub cmdCogs_Click(ByVal eventSender As System.Object, _
  ByVal eventArgs As System.EventArgs) Handles cmdCogs.Click
  goStatusPanel.Text = "Determining Cost of Goods."
  'UPGRADE_ISSUE: Load statement is not supported. Click for more:
  'ms-help://MS.VSCC/commoner/redir/redirect.htm?key-
word="vbup1039"'
  Dim form As frmCogs = New frmCogs()
  goStatusPanel.Text = ""

End Sub
```

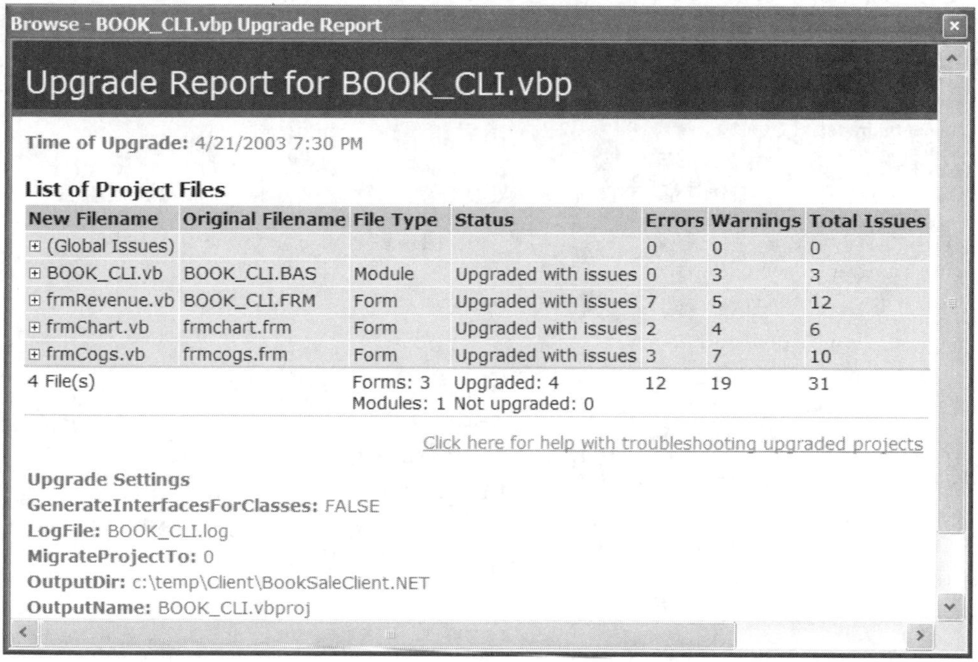

Browse - BOOK_CLI.vbp Upgrade Report

Upgrade Report for BOOK_CLI.vbp

Time of Upgrade: 4/21/2003 7:30 PM

List of Project Files

New Filename	Original Filename	File Type	Status	Errors	Warnings	Total Issues
⊞ (Global Issues)				0	0	0
⊞ BOOK_CLI.vb	BOOK_CLI.BAS	Module	Upgraded with issues	0	3	3
⊞ frmRevenue.vb	BOOK_CLI.FRM	Form	Upgraded with issues	7	5	12
⊞ frmChart.vb	frmchart.frm	Form	Upgraded with issues	2	4	6
⊞ frmCogs.vb	frmcogs.frm	Form	Upgraded with issues	3	7	10
4 File(s)		Forms: 3 Modules: 1	Upgraded: 4 Not upgraded: 0	12	19	31

Click here for help with troubleshooting upgraded projects

Upgrade Settings
GenerateInterfacesForClasses: FALSE
LogFile: BOOK_CLI.log
MigrateProjectTo: 0
OutputDir: c:\temp\Client\BookSaleClient.NET
OutputName: BOOK_CLI.vbproj

Figure A.6 The `_UpgradeReport.htm` file is the place to start after finishing the migration wizard.

Typically in .NET we create a form with the `New` operator and then call `Form.Show` or `Form.ShowDialog`. The migrated code actually contains the call to `Show` in the `Load` method, so we didn't need to do it here.

There was one more error like this plus two errors related to a mouse click event. In all, migrating `BOOK_CLI.VBP` took about five minutes, and resolving the basic errors took another five minutes. Thus after ten minutes the client application compiled and ran. In addition, because in VB .NET we can talk to VB6 servers, I was able to run both the client and the server by converting only the client. Figures A.8 and A.9 show the client and server running, respectively.

At this juncture we still clearly need to evaluate all the `UPGRADE_ISSUE` task items and resolve those. However, we have a choice, relative to the server. If the server is running, we can evaluate it as a separate application and decide whether or not to migrate it. It all depends on your needs, budget, time constraints, and priorities.

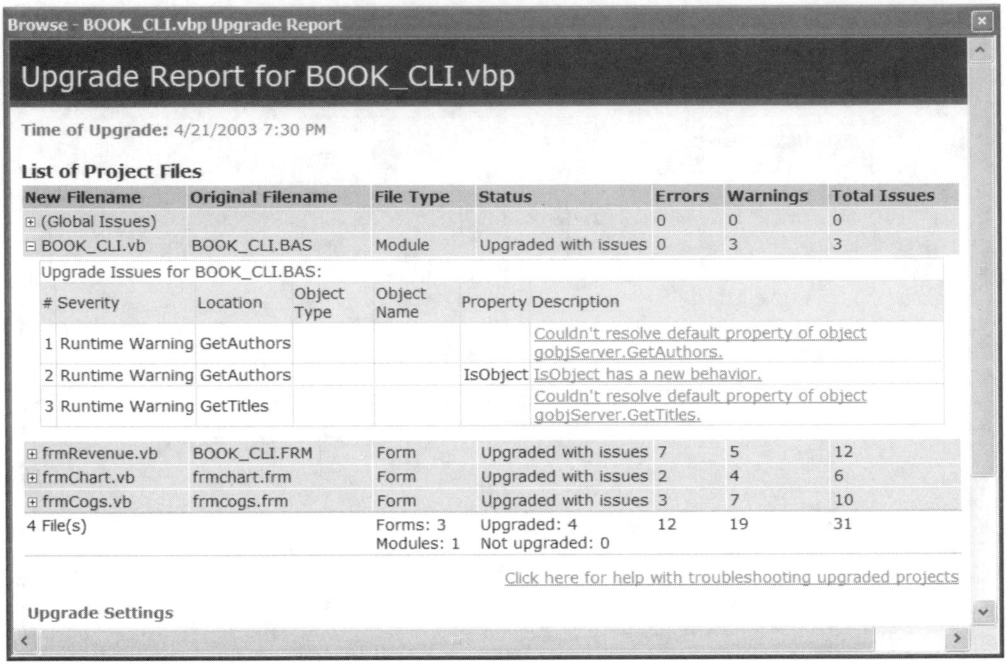

Figure A.7 Expand migrated files in the `_UpgradeReport.htm` file to navigate to the help link that documents the migration error and resolution.

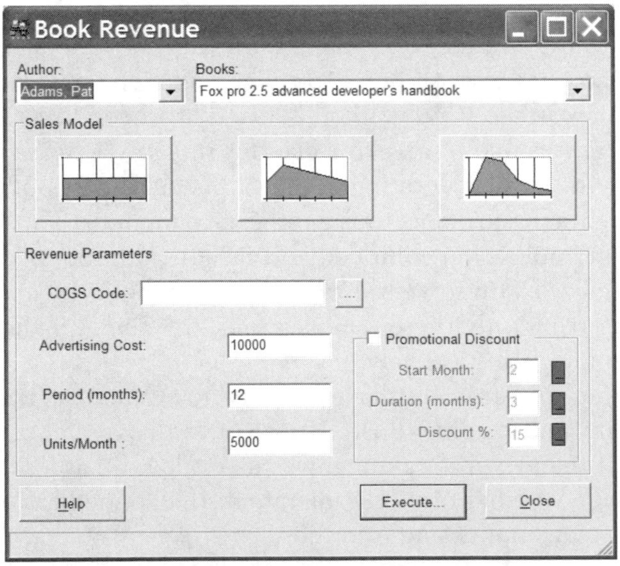

Figure A.8 The migrated client application running as a VB .NET assembly.

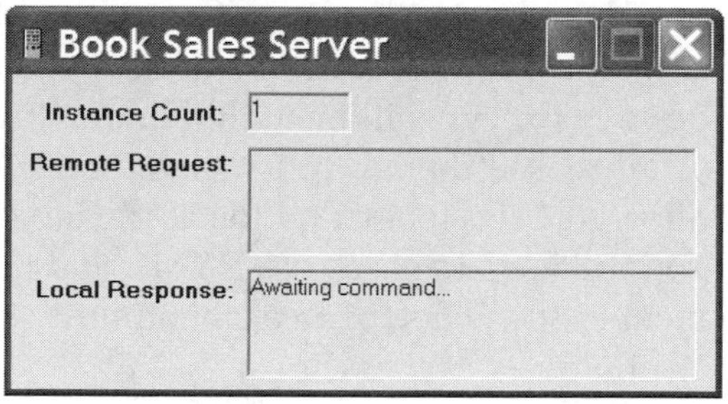

Figure A.9 The server application running as a VB6 executable, interacting with the .NET migrated client.

The number and variety of potential errors are too great to provide a comprehensive list of problems and resolutions. The best approach is to really understand the .NET Framework and in the meantime rely on the _UpgradeReport.htm file and the help documentation. Microsoft claims that the migration wizard will migrate about 95 percent of VB6 code, which should put you in pretty good shape.

Migrating Visual Basic 6 ASP Web Applications

As is true with VB6 Windows applications, you have options when it comes to migrating VB6 ASP Web applications to ASP.NET. The first thing to point out is that ASP and ASP.NET applications can coexist. Thus it is worthwhile to evaluate whether to migrate at all. Microsoft also recommends reading "Migrating Your ASP Applications to ASP.NET" and "Migrating to ASP.NET: Key Considerations" before you migrate. Both of these articles are available at *http://msdn.microsoft.com*.

To get you started, here's an overview of the steps that will help you migrate to ASP.NET.

1. Start Visual Studio .NET.
2. Open an existing ASP application or add an existing ASP application to the opened solution.
3. Select File|Add Existing Item and navigate to the ASP file.
4. Right-click on the .asp file in the Solution Explorer and change the extension to .aspx.
5. A dialog will appear suggesting that the name change will invalidate the file. Click Yes.

6. Visual Studio .NET will automatically add a code-behind file. For example, if your file is named `home.aspx`, a code-behind file named `code.aspx.vb` will be added and associated with the `.aspx` file. (You can see the newly associated code-behind file if you click the Show All Files toolbar button at the top of the Solution Explorer.)

7. You will need to check the HTML and make sure that a `<form>` element exists. The `<form>` element must contain the `runat="server"` attribute.

8. After step 7 you should be able to compile and run the ASP.NET application, browsing to the new page.

To keep it simple, if you change the names of your `.asp` files to `.aspx` files and open them in Visual Basic .NET, they will be treated as `.aspx` files. To make them more powerful you may want to migrate specific controls to Web server controls and add a code-behind file to the `.aspx.vb` file created by the IDE. However, simply renaming the extension will get you well under way.

Summary

The media likes to create villains. Despite all the bad press, Microsoft bends over backward to provide assistance to customers. Yes, without an MSDN subscription you have to pay a couple of hundred bucks per incident to get that help, but the company hangs in there, bringing in anyone who can get the job done. Considering the recent developments of corporate irresponsibility—I can't say this enough—Microsoft sets the standard for superlative customer service.

Even though it may come to pass that supporting COM through Interop may mean someone exploits the unmanaged aspects of VB6 and COM, Microsoft is paying attention. We have a bridge to the past because Microsoft hasn't abandoned us, even under harsh criticism (sometimes fair, sometimes undeserved). When I need assistance, there is no resistance, no excuses, and no hubris. I get what I need.

If you need to hang on to VB6 code for a while, you know you can, in one of several ways. You can choose not to port because Microsoft is still supporting VB6. You can use COM Interop to talk to your business rules and reimplement just the presentation layer. You can choose to bridge to VB6 applications with a wrapper, employing .NET Remoting or Web Services, or you can commingle VB6 clients and servers, as demonstrated in this appendix. Finally, the best choice of all is to rewrite the code in .NET.

I have been programming since 1978—ROM BASIC on a TRS 80—and picked it up professionally in the late 1980s. I am more excited than ever after all these years because things just keep getting cooler.

Bon soir!

Bibliography

Appleman, Dan. 2002. *Regular Expressions in .NET.* Berkeley, CA: Desaware.

Ashish, Jaiman. 2002. "COM Interoperability Part II: Using a .NET Component from COM." *C# Corner,* April. Available at *http://www.c-sharpcorner.com/Code/2002/April/COMInteropP2AJ.asp*.

Bulovic, Filip. 2002. "Calling Managed Code from Unmanaged." *C# Corner,* March. Available at *http://www.c-sharpcorner.com/Code/2002/Mar/CallingManagedCodeFromUnmanagedFB.asp*.

C, Aravind. 2001. "Understanding Classic COM Interoperability with .NET Applications." Posted on Codeproject.com, March. Available at *http://www.codeproject.com/dotnet/cominterop.asp*.

Fowler, Martin, Kent Beck, John Brant, et al. 1999. *Refactoring: Improving the Design of Existing Code.* Boston, MA: Addison-Wesley.

Freedman, Daniel P., and Gerald Weinberg. 1990. *Handbook of Walkthroughs, Inspections, and Technical Reviews: Evaluating Programs, Projects, and Products.* New York: Dorset House.

Freiburger, Paul, and Michael Swaine. 1984. *Fire in the Valley: The Making of the Personal Computer.* Berkeley, CA: McGraw-Hill/Osborne.

Gamma, Erich, Richard Helm, Ralph Johnson, and John Vlissides. 1995. *Design Patterns: Elements of Reusable Object-Oriented Software.* Reading, MA: Addison-Wesley.

Gough, John. 2002. *Compiling for the .NET Common Language Runtime (CLR).* Upper Saddle River, NJ: Prentice Hall.

Hollis, Billy. 2002. "Loading Classes on the Fly." *MSDN Magazine,* October. Available at *http://msdn.microsoft.com/library/default.asp?url=/library/en-us/dnadvnet/html/vbnet10082002.asp*.

———. 2001. "Death of the Browser?" *MSDN Magazine*: , October. Available at *http://msdn.microsoft.com/library/default.asp?url=/library/en-us/dnadvnet/html/vbnet10142001.asp*.

Kimmel, Paul. 2002a. *Advanced C# Programming.* Berkeley, CA: McGraw-Hill/Osborne.

———. 2002b. *Visual Basic .NET Unleashed.* Indianapolis, IN: Sams.

———. 2001. "Really Thin Client Programming in VB.NET." *VB Today,* November. Available at *http://www.codeguru.com/columns/VB/PK112001.html*.

LaMacchia, Brian, Sebastian Lange, Matthew Lyons, Rudi Martin, and Kevin T. Price. 2002. *.NET Framework Security.* Boston, MA: Addison-Wesley.

Mack, Donny, and Doug Seven. 2003. *Developing Custom Controls for ASP.NET.* Indianapolis, IN: Sams.

Microsoft Corporation. 2002a. "Upgrading Your Visual Basic 6.0 Applications to Visual Basic .NET." Available at *http://msdn.microsoft.com/vbasic/techinfo/articles/upgrade/vbupgrade.asp*.

———. 2002b. "Visual Basic .NET Upgrade Road Map." Available at *http://msdn.microsoft.com/vbasic/techinfo/articles/upgrade/roadmap.asp*.

Nathan, Adam. 2002. *.NET and COM: The Complete Interoperability Guide*. Indianapolis, IN: Sams.

Platt, David S. 2001. ".NET Interop: Get Ready for Microsoft .NET by Using Wrappers to Interact with COM-based Applications." *MSDN Magazine,* August. Available at *http://msdn.microsoft.com/msdnmag/issues/01/08/Interop/default.aspx*.

Rammer, Ingo. 2002. *Advanced .NET Remoting.* Berkeley, CA: Apress.

Sells, Chris. 2002a. "Increasing Permissions for Web-Deployed Windows Forms Applications." *MSDN Magazine,* November. Available at *http://msdn.microsoft.com/library/default.asp?url=/library/en-us/dnforms/html/winforms11122002.asp*.

———. 2002b. ".NET Zero Deployment: Security and Versioning Models in the Windows Forms Engine Help You Create and Deploy Smart Clients." *MSDN Magazine,* July. Available at *http://msdn.microsoft.com/msdnmag/issues/02/07/NetSmartClients/default.aspx*.

————. 2002c. "State Sanity Using Smart Clients." *MSDN Magazine,* May. Available at *http://msdn.microsoft.com/library/default.asp?url=/library/ en-us/dnforms/html/winforms05202002.asp*.

Tailor, Prashant. 2003. "COM Interoperability Part 1: Using COM Components in.NET Framework." *C# Corner,* January. Available at *http:// www.csharphelp.com/archives2/archive437.html*.

Thielen, Dave. 1992. *No Bugs! Delivering Error-Free Code in C and C++.* Reading, MA: Addison-Wesley.

Troelsen, Andrew. 2002. *COM and .NET Interoperability.* Berkeley, CA: Apress.

Index

Also of interest from Addison-Wesley

0-672-32343-5

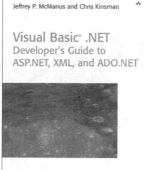

0-672-32131-9

0-672-32156-4

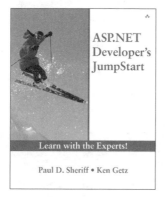

0-672-32357-5

0-672-32184-X

0-201-75866-0

0-201-76039-8

informIT